THIRD EDITION

Exploring ART

A GLOBAL, THEMATIC APPROACH

Margaret Lazzari
Gayle Garner Roski School of Fine Arts, University of Southern California

Dona Schlesier
Divine Word College

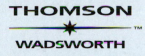
THOMSON
™
WADSWORTH

Australia • Canada • Mexico • Singapore • Spain
United Kingdom • United States

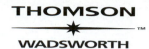

THOMSON

WADSWORTH

Exploring Art: A Global, Thematic Approach, Third Edition
Margaret Lazzari and Dona Schlesier

Publisher: Clark Baxter

Senior Development Editor: Sharon Adams Poore

Assistant Editor: Erikka Adams

Editorial Assistant: Nell Pepper

Development Project Manager: Julia Iannacchino

Executive Marketing Manager: Diane Wenckebach

Media Assistant: Sean O'Keefe

Marketing Assistant: Kathleen Tosiello

Marketing Communications Manager: Brian Chaffee

Senior Project Manager, Editorial Production: Kimberly Adams

Creative Director: Rob Hugel

Executive Art Director: Maria Epes

Print Buyer: Rebecca Cross

Permissions Editor: Joohee Lee

Production Service: Lachina Publishing Services

Text Designer: tani hasegawa

Photo Researcher: Lili Weiner

Copy Editor: Carolyn Crabtree

Cover Designer: tani hasegawa

Cover Image: **Cover.01** Courtesy: Mary Boone Gallery, New York. Photo © Zindman/Fremont. **Cover.02** © SCALA/Art Resource, NY. **Cover.03** © Réunion des Musées Nationaux/Art Resource, NY. **Cover.04** © Bildarchiv Preussischer Kulturbesitz/Art Resource, NY. **Cover.05** © Gianni Dagli Orti/Corbis. **Cover.06** © Erich Lessing/Art Resource, NY. **Cover.07** Courtesy of Gallery Koyanagi, Tokyo, and Deitch Projects, New York.

Cover Printer: Quebecor World - Dubuque

Compositor: Lachina Publishing Services

Printer: Quebecor World - Versailles

COPYRIGHT © 2008 Wadsworth, a part of The Thomson Corporation. Thomson, the Star logo, and Wadsworth are trademarks used herein under license.

ALL RIGHTS RESERVED. No part of this work covered by the copyright hereon may be reproduced or used in any form or by any means—graphic, electronic, or mechanical, including photocopying, recording, taping, Web distribution, information storage and retrieval systems, or in any other manner—without the written permission of the publisher.

Printed in the United States of America
2 3 4 5 6 7   11 10 09 08 07

Library of Congress Control Number: 2006933357
ISBN-13: 978-0-495-09487-6
ISBN-10: 0-495-09487-0

For more information about our products, contact us at:
Thomson Learning Academic Resource Center
1-800-423-0563
For permission to use material from this text or product, submit a request online at **http://www.thomsonrights.com**.
Any additional questions about permissions can be submitted by email to **thomsonrights@thomson.com**.

ExamView® and ExamView Pro® are registered trademarks of FSCreations, Inc. Windows is a registered trademark of the Microsoft Corporation used herein under license. Macintosh and Power Macintosh are registered trademarks of Apple Computer, Inc. Used herein under license.

© 2008 Thomson Learning, Inc. All Rights Reserved. Thomson Learning WebTutor™ is a trademark of Thomson Learning, Inc.

Thomson Higher Education
10 Davis Drive
Belmont, CA 94002-3098
USA

*To Michael and Julia Rose, with heartfelt thanks
for all the love, fun, and creativity in our lives.*
Margaret Lazzari

*For Douglas, Kimberly, Robert, Jackson Calder (Jake),
and Luca Peter Douglas, with gratitude and love
for the ongoing joy you give me.*
Dona Schlesier

Brief Contents

Contents

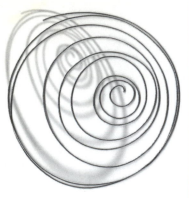

Preface

Art embodies human dreams, visions, and speculations. Art is creativity in physical form. It is visually rich, sometimes difficult, and often beautiful. Open this book and take a world tour.

Exploring Art: A Global, Thematic Approach examines essential art ideas and makes them concrete using examples from around the world. Western and non-Western art are almost equally represented, and contemporary art is covered well. There is a high percentage of artwork by women. In our thematic approach, we discuss art in context with religion, politics, social protest, family structure, sexuality, and entertainment. Rather than dry chronologies, our chapters present topics of deep interest to students as they see how contemporary and historical artworks make these ideas visible. Introductory chapters help define art, present the basic elements of art and architecture, and lay out the fundamental concepts in art criticism.

The third edition of *Exploring Art* builds on the strengths of the first and second editions, but also breaks exciting new ground.

NEW CONTENT

Chapter 3, *Media,* is completely new to this edition. It covers not only the actual material substances used to create an artwork, but also the disciplines of art making, such as painting or video. Traditional media has been used in drawing, painting, printmaking, sculpture and craft-making, both historically and in the present day. Non-traditional media appears in mixed media artwork, video and film, digital imaging, and performance. All are covered thoroughly in Chapter 3.

Chapter 16 is *Entertainment and Visual Culture.* A good portion of art today is intertwined with theater, sports, television, movies, tourist attractions, cartoons, and other forms of popular culture. Using visual culture as a framework, this chapter analyzes contemporary art and entertainment, and covers the range of images and visual objects produced in industrial and post-industrial nations, and the ways in which those images are disseminated, used, and received. Of course, some pre-industrial art was also allied with entertainment, and we look at examples of those as well.

Entertainment and Visual Culture "travels" from the sports areas of the ancient worlds to a modern Olympic stadium in Munich, to see how art and architecture frame our experience of sports. Examples of theater, dance, music, film, and comics come from around the world, and all overlap the visual arts.

Finally, a structure change: Chapter 2, *The Language of Art and Architecture,* contains material from two separate second edition chapters, *The Language of Art* and *The Language of Architecture.* We are delighted that this efficient combination of material allows us to present once again all the concepts that were covered in the second edition.

NEW ILLUSTRATIONS

This third edition of *Exploring Art* contains more than 130 new artworks, in addition to the 410-plus from the second edition. This is an exciting expanded array of teaching images! Included are stunning images of African sculpture, such as the *Royal Linguist Staff* and the *Ceremonial Mask Known as Mboom.* Photographs of African masquerades show such works within their ceremonial context. Three examples of mosques are added to existing coverage, as well as a Moslem prayer rug. Contemporary art is experiencing phenomenal growth in China now, and we include works by notable artists such as Cai Guo-Qiang and Huang Yong Ping. This is only the beginning!

In addition, we have illustrated the works of many prominent artists, or have added to their representation from the second edition. Among them are these historical artists:

Sandro Botticelli	Hannah Hoch	Olowe of Ise
Paul Cezanne	Eva Hesse	Meret Oppenheim
Edgar Degas	Paul Klee	Pablo Picasso
Marcel Duchamp	Willem de Kooning	José Guadalupe Posada
Théodore Géricault	Utagawa Kunisada	Mi Wanzhong

Recent artists are also well represented among the new offerings:

Kutlug Ataman	Marilyn Levine	Martin Puryear
Dale Chihuly	Takashi Murakami	Faith Ringgold
Christo/Jeanne-Claude	Bruce Nauman	Jaune Quick-to-See Smith
Gilbert and George	Shirin Neshat	Frank Stella
Andy Goldsworthy	Louise Nevelson	Andy Warhol
Tim Hawkinson	Claes Oldenburg	

GLOBAL COVERAGE AND THEMATIC APPROACH

The key ideas in *Exploring Art: A Global, Thematic Approach* are (1) understanding and appreciating the world's art and (2) examining art in the context of human needs and world cultures.

Art from around the world is fully integrated throughout this book. Each image adds to the evidence of the universal human impulse to create art. Students are enriched and challenged when studying art in the context of themes and ideas, rather than chronology or geography. And they see that these themes appear in every culture, across the ages. The themes *(Survival and Beyond, Religion, The State,* and *Self and Society)* show art to be a meaningful endeavor that deals with basic human concerns. By studying integrated global art traditions, the students can see the similarities that connect cultures as well as their differences.

HISTORICAL MATERIAL

Art and History in Context is a boxed feature that appears at the end of Chapters 7–16, which are the thematic chapters. Each one contains chronological summaries of world history and important developments in religion, culture, and technology. Each is accompanied by a map and timeline. In this edition, the historical material is better integrated with its accompanying chapter, with more cross-references between them. Students are made aware of the larger social, political, and cultural context that serves as a background to the art they are studying.

ACTIVE LEARNING

This book is structured around questions, to encourage readers to think critically about the artworks and ideas presented here. The book is divided into two parts, and each opens with questions: *What Is Art, Who Makes It, and What Do We Do With It?* and *Why Do We Make Art?* Once inside the chapters, each one opens with a list of questions for students to consider while reading, to help them critically evaluate the chapter's material.

At the end of each chapter, a short *Food for Thought* section asks students provocative questions about the unresolved debates and moral issues associated with art in our time and in the past. Some of the issues we ask students to ponder are: (1) the role of morality and censorship in the arts; (2) the effectiveness of social protest art that exists only in the gallery; (3) the status of "marginal" art forms such as graffiti and body art; and much more.

Connections are cross-references that appear throughout the book, relating works, artists, cultures, ideas, and themes. These lateral-thinking devices link ideas across chapters. For example, in Chapter 11, there is a discussion of African royal portraits from the twelfth century. The *Connection* prompts the reader to turn to other sections of the book to see more styles of African art, and to see the dress of contemporary African rulers.

We hope you enjoy the wealth of world art that is presented in this book.

ANCILLARY PACKAGE

FOR STUDENTS

ARTEXPERIENCE ONLINE

www.thomsonedu.com/login/

This resource includes many study aids for students including:

- *Foundations Interactive Modules*—Visual Elements, Principles of Design, Style, Form, and Content
- *In the Studio*—Video footage of studio classes (Drawing, Painting, Lithography, Wheelworking, Sculpture: Plastercasting, Architecture, Glassblowing)
- *Flashcards*—The fine art images in the text, maps, and illustrations
- *Timeline*—Looks at themes chronologically
- *Art and History in Context*—Expands upon the text feature with animated maps, commentary, and additional resources
- *Food for Thought*—Assistance in answering the end-of-chapter questions
- *Podcasts*—Compares works of art through dialog
- *Exploring Art Web Resources*—Glossary Term Flashcards, Critical Thinking Essay Questions, Internet Exercises, Study Guide, and Chapter Quizzes
- *Art Web Resources*—Art History Resources, Art History Careers, Art Links, Guide to Researching Art History, Tips on Becoming a Successful Student

SLIDEGUIDE

The *SlideGuide* allows students to take notes alongside representations of the art images shown in class. It features reproductions of the images from the book with full captions, page numbers, and space for note-taking.

FOR INSTRUCTORS

MULTIMEDIA MANAGER

Bring digital images into the classroom with this one-stop lecture and class presentation tool that makes it easy to assemble, edit, and present customized lectures for your course using Microsoft® PowerPoint®. The CD-ROM provides high-resolution images (maps, diagrams, and **fine art images** from the text) in PowerPoint presentation format, or in individual file formats compatible with other image-viewing software. A **new zoom feature** allows you to magnify selected portions of an image for more detailed display in class. You can also easily customize your classroom presentation by adding your own images. The *Multimedia Manager* also includes the Resource Integration Guide, an electronic Instructor's Manual and a Test Bank with multiple-choice, matching, short-answer, and essay questions in ExamView® computerized format. Also included are text-specific Microsoft PowerPoint slides created for use with JoinIn™ on Turning Point® software for classroom personal response systems ("clickers").

WEBTUTOR™ TOOLBOX FOR BLACKBOARD OR WEB CT

Preloaded with content and available via a free access code when packaged with this text, *Web Tutor ToolBox* pairs all the content of this text's Book Companion Website with sophisticated course management functionality. You can assign materials (including online quizzes) and have the results flow automatically to your grade book. *Web Tutor ToolBox* is ready to use as soon as you log on—or you can customize its preloaded content by uploading images and other resources, adding weblinks, or creating your own practice materials. Students only have access to student resources on the website. Instructors can enter an access code for password-protected Instructor Resources.

ACKNOWLEDGMENTS

We wish to thank once again the entire team at Wadsworth whose efforts and creativity help shape *Exploring Art.* Their insights and dedication were essential to realizing this third edition. Our Acquisitions Editor at the beginning of this revision cycle was John Swanson, whose advice was most helpful. The project is now being guided by our new Acquisitions Editor, Clark Baxter, and we look forward to a long working relationship with him. Sharon Adams Poore served once again as our Development Editor, and we could not be more delighted to work with someone as thoughtful and knowledgeable as she has been.

Of course, a book is nothing without its production staff, and we have been very fortunate to work with some outstanding people. Kim Adams has overseen the entire production phase as Production Project Manager. We have worked closely with our Project Manager, Sheila McGill of Lachina Publishing Services, and what a joy she has been throughout. Our Photo Researcher was Lili Weiner, whose research for new images was great, and who acquired all images and permissions. Thanks also to Carolyn Crabtree, whose copyediting raises the text to a high level of quality. We would also like to thank Erikka Adams, Assistant Editor; Nell Pepper, Editorial Assistant; Julie Yardley, Developmental Project Manager, and Diane Wenckebach, Executive Marketing Manager.

We relied tremendously on the feedback our reviewers gave us on the second edition. Their comments and advice guided us throughout our work, and we are very grateful to them. They include: Teresa Cotner, California State University–San Bernardino; Cat Crotchett, Western Michigan University; Margaret Doell, Adams State College; Kristin Fedders, University of Saint Francis; Raymond Gaddy, University of North Florida; Elizabeth Garber, University of Arizona; Heather Lynn Holian, University of North Carolina–Greensboro; Annette Lermack, Illinois State University; Denise Lugo, California State University–Northridge; Danielle Michaelis, University of San Diego; Laura Murphy, Adams State College; Micheline Nilsen, Indiana University, South Bend; Laura Parker, Los Angeles City College; Kaye Passmore, Rowan University; Denise Rogers, Miramar College; Susan Rule, Adams State College; Lori S. Sears, Radford University; Emilie Sizemore, Pepperdine University; Paul R. Solomon, Western Michigan University; Daniel Trutter, College of DuPage; Francine Tyler, Long Island University–Brooklyn; Diane Weintraub, Cuyamaca College; Carolyn J. Whitman, Central Piedmont Community College; and Paige Wideman, Northern Kentucky University.

We are grateful to our respective teaching institutions for their continued support. Dona thanks Divine Word College and its president, Fr. Michael Hutchins S.V.D, as well as the college's administration. For Margaret, her gratitude goes to the Roski School of Fine Arts of the University of Southern California and her ever-supportive mentor and friend, Dean Ruth Weisberg. We teach bright, caring students who come from all kinds of backgrounds, some from distant lands.

They continually motivate us to make each edition of this global, thematic art appreciation book better than the one before.

Thank you to our families and friends who have provided interesting perspectives, good advice, and moral support throughout. They are too many to name. We especially thank Dona's husband, Douglas Schlesier, and also Margaret's husband and daughter, Michael Dean and Julia Lazzari-Dean. Julia has grown up in the years that have passed since we started the first edition, and Dona has seen her two young grandsons through the beginnings of their lives. The wonder of these new lives continues to inspire us. And we thank each other, once again, for our mutual support and collaboration.

May there be peace and tolerance in our world.

Margaret Lazzari
Dona Schlesier

What Is Art, Who Makes It, and What Do We Do With It?

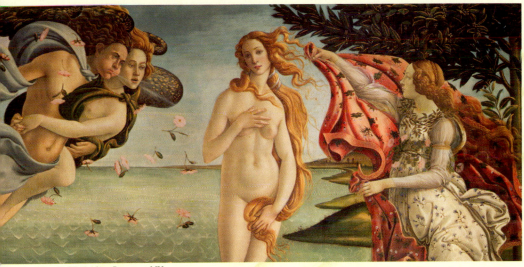

PART 1

© SCALA/Art Resource, NY

Art has a richness and an intelligence that illuminate our lives. The more we know about art, the more our existence is enhanced by it. For the next six chapters, discussion centers on the following areas:

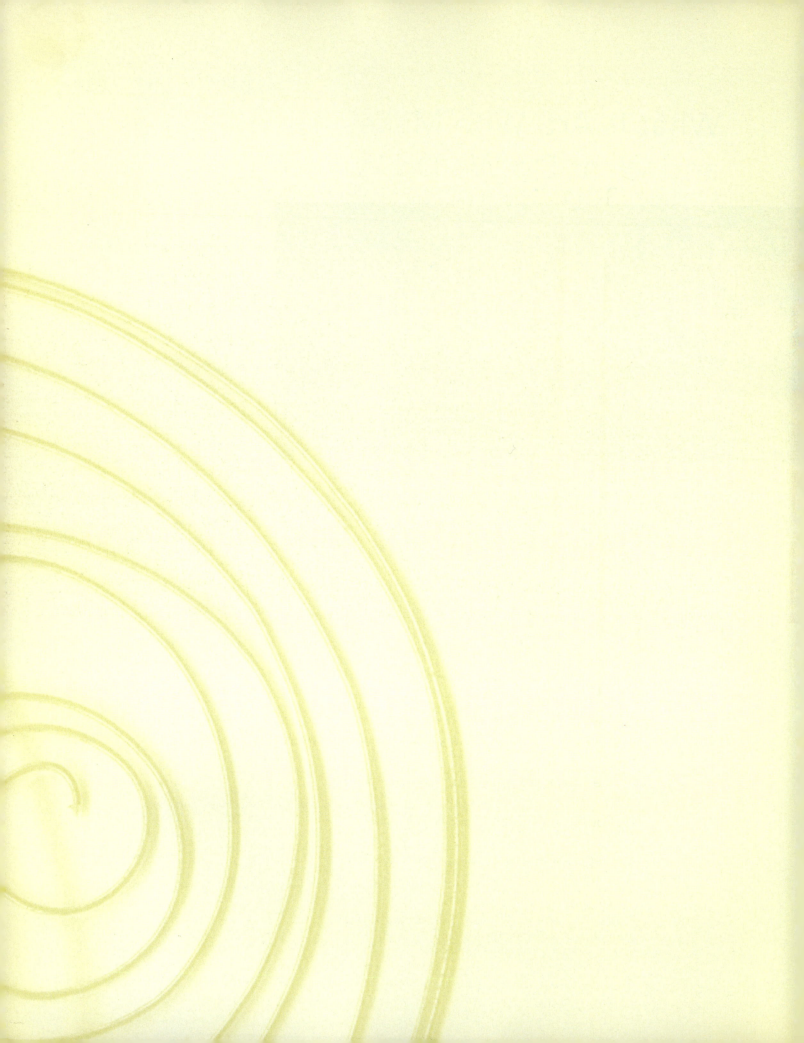

CHAPTER 1

A Human Phenomenon

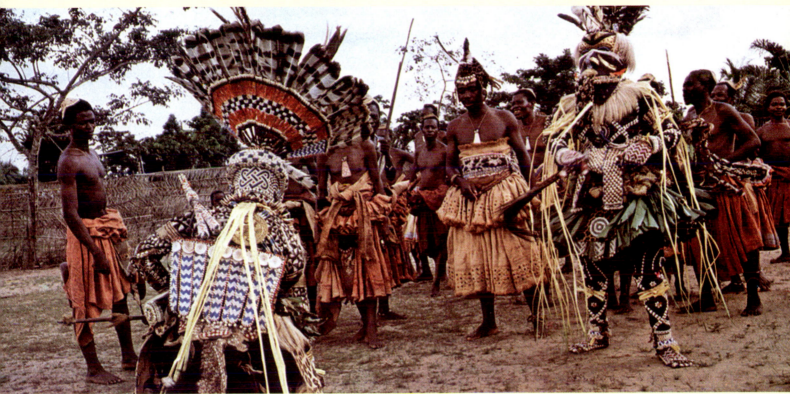

© Werner Forman/Art Resource, NY

INTRODUCTION

Art is strictly a human phenomenon. Some animals make tools, but they do not consider the aesthetics of their tools or attempt to carve beautiful handles for them. None except human beings makes art to better understand life or to communicate passions or ideas to others.

Consider the following questions:

- *What are some ways to approach a definition of art?*
- *What are the components of art making?*
- *What is creativity, and who is creative?*
- *How does culture influence artists and what we think about art?*
- *How do we categorize visual arts within cultures?*

TOWARD A DEFINITION OF ART

No definitions are universal, timeless, and absolute. All definitions are framed within larger systems of knowledge, and these systems shift and evolve.

Therefore, to answer the question "What is art?" we would have to ask: What is art *for whom*, and *when*? For the United States at the beginning of the twenty-first century, a good definition of art would be this: *Art is a primarily visual medium that is used to express ideas about our human experience and the world around us.* This definition holds true for many other cultures and periods, but not for all.

To get a better idea of what art is for a specific culture, we will center our inquiry on four major areas: function, visual form, content, and aesthetics.

FUNCTION

Art functions. At the time a work of art is made, it is intended to do a job within a culture, as in the following examples:

- Art assists us in rituals that promote our spiritual or physical well-being.
- Art reflects customs related to food, shelter, and human reproduction.
- Art communicates thoughts, ideas, and emotions.
- Art gives us pictures of deities, or helps us conceive what divinity might be.
- Art serves and/or commemorates the dead.
- Art glorifies the power of the state and its rulers.
- Art celebrates war and conquest, and sometimes peace.
- Art is a means for protesting political and social injustice.
- Art promotes cohesion within a social group.
- Art records the likenesses of individuals and the context in which the individuals exist.
- Art educates us about ourselves and the world around us.
- Art entertains.

Of course, music, dance, or literature does similar things, as do other fields of human endeavor. But one way to measure whether a work of art is "good" is to determine its intended function, and then see how well it succeeds.

Art also can function as an area for study. As cultural "documents," artworks can tell us volumes about existing and past cultures: how they were structured, what they valued, what was considered ideal, what roles men and women had, and so on.

Figure 1.1 is a sculpture from Nigeria, *Veranda Post: Female Caryatid and Equestrian Figure*, carved before 1938 by Olowe of Ise. This carved column supported a courtyard roof in a local king's palace among the Yoruba, a people in West Central Africa. The function of this sculpture was to visually reinforce the king's power. He holds a pistol and spear and is supported by female figures, called **caryatids,** below. Equestrian sculptures like this among the Yoruba are symbols of regional authority, for a ruler who can conquer with power and strength.

Figure 1.2 is another sculpture intended to assert authority. In the *Equestrian Statue of Marcus Aurelius,* from the Roman Empire around 175 CE, the emperor sits atop a spirited horse, and perhaps an enemy (now lost) cowered beneath the raised hoof. Among the Romans, this type of sculpture was the ultimate symbol of imperial dignity and power. The godlike Marcus Aurelius is oversized compared to the horse, and his lack of armor and outstretched hand may refer to the fact that he was a philosopher as well as emperor.

Both of these sculptures are now in museums, where their functions today are to educate the general public about another culture, to provide visual pleasure, and to entertain. Scholars also study these works, gleaning considerable information about the historical moments from which they come.

From Chapter 7 onward, we will study the functions of hundreds of artworks in greater depth.

VISUAL FORM

Art has a visual form, which includes:

- the materials from which the artwork is made
- its formal elements, such as line, shape, color, texture, mass, volume, space, and so on
- its overall composition (which is the arrangement of those formal elements), its size, its internal balance, and so on

Visual form is carefully considered and manipulated in an artwork, both to help it better fulfill its function and to enhance its visual appeal. Looking at the formal elements and composition of the *Veranda Post*, it is evident that horizontal elements are minimized, while verticality is emphasized, as seen in the stacked figures. Olowe

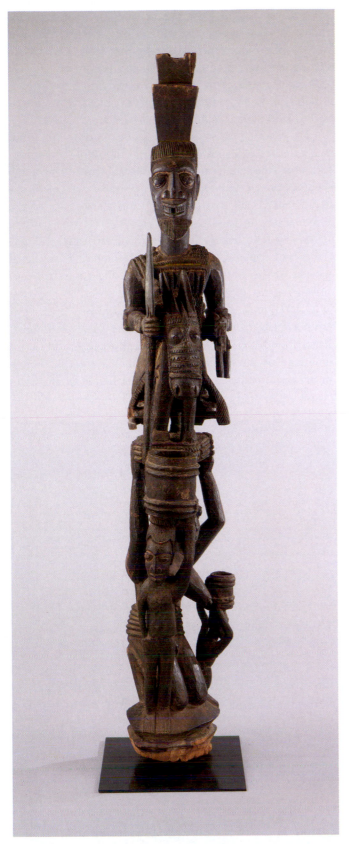

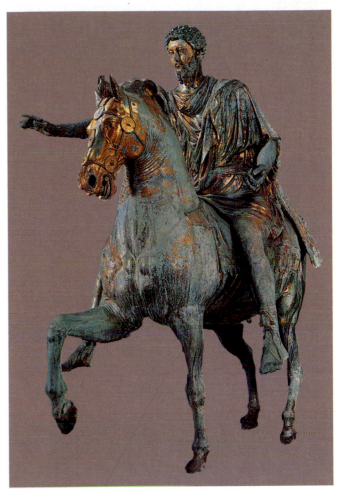

1.2   *Equestrian Statue of Marcus Aurelius*, Rome, c. 175 CE. Bronze, approx. 11' 6" high. Musei Capitolini, Rome.

1.1   OLOWE OF ISE. *Veranda Post: Female Caryatid and Equestrian Figure*, Yoruba, before 1938. Wood, pigment, 71" high. Metropolitan Museum of Art, New York.

of Ise, the most famous Yoruban master sculptor of his time, was known for his inventive visual forms, which he enhanced with deeply carved surface details. The rigid and dense figures above contrast with the more openly carved and diagonally arranged women below.

Materials are significant. The *Equestrian Statue of Marcus Aurelius* is hollow-cast bronze, a costly material sculpted using a difficult process. Because of the strength of bronze, this statue can be over eleven feet high, have amazing surface detail, and be supported on three horse legs. Bronze allowed the statue to survive for nearly 2,000 years, much of it outdoors. The very material of bronze is essential in this truly royal portrait.

The visual form is the physical embodiment of an idea. It allows the work to be seen or touched, and the idea to be communicated. The subtleties of visual form are what make nuances of meaning possible. Every work of art has visual form, which we will study throughout the book. In addition, visual form is discussed in depth in Chapter 2, The Language of Art and Architecture.

CONTENT

Art has content, which is the mass of ideas associated with an artwork and communicated through the following:

- the art's imagery
- its surroundings where it is used or displayed
- its symbolic meaning
- the customs, beliefs, and values of the culture that uses it
- the text incorporated with the work, or writings about the work

Content can both be immediately apparent and require considerable study. Just by looking at Sandro Botticelli's *Birth of Venus* (Fig. 1.3), from 1482, and Pablo Picasso's 1907 painting, *Les Demoiselles d'Avignon* (Fig. 1.4), you can see that both are paintings,

with multiple figures in the composition, and female nudity is at least part of the subject matter. *Venus* is painted in a more realistic, traditional style, yet is visually elegant and poetic. The blocky, simplified *Demoiselles* appears to be more modern and less interested in popular ideas of beauty. Both artworks seem balanced side to side, with a figure in the middle.

However, much content is not readily apparent, and a deeper study of the paintings' symbolic meanings and how they fit into their cultural framework can become quite complex. *The Birth of Venus* celebrates an ancient Greek myth and glorifies the beauty of the human body, in this case, female. When it was painted in 1482, it reflected the ideals of the early Italian Renaissance and was at odds with still-lingering medieval notions of the sinful body and Catholic Church prohibitions against pagan culture.

Les Demoiselles d'Avignon originally was to be a brothel scene of prostitutes with their male customers. Picasso made radical changes in progress, ending with an image of intertwined figures and space that began an art movement known as **Cubism.** Three of the faces

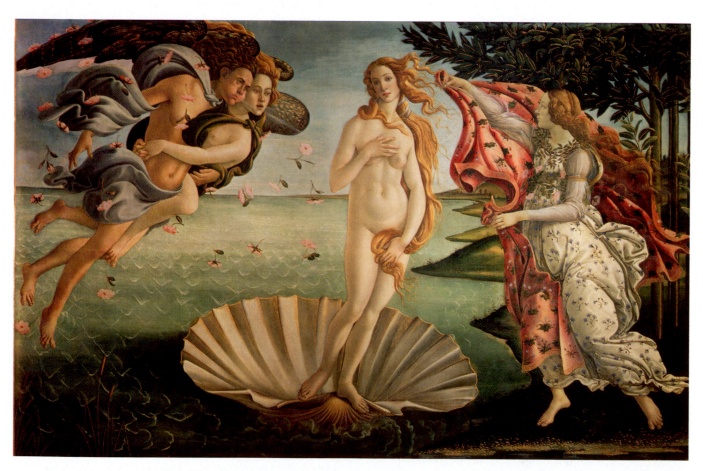

1.3   SANDRO BOTTICELLI. *The Birth of Venus,* Italy, c. 1482. Tempera on canvas, approx. 5' 8" × 9' 1". Galleria degli Uffizi, Florence.

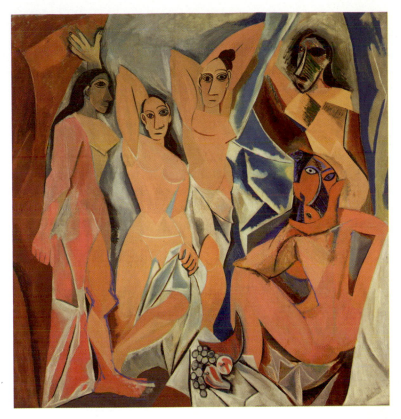

1.4   PABLO PICASSO. *Les Demoiselles d'Avignon*, Spain/France, 1907. Oil on canvas, 8' × 7' 8". The Museum of Modern Art, New York.

in the painting were influenced by African masks, like the *Ceremonial Mask known as a Mboom or Bwoom*, Kuba, Booshong culture of Central Zaire, from the nineteenth–twentieth centuries (Fig. 1.5). The painting reflects its cultural moment because African artworks like the *Mask* had been recently imported to Europe through colonial trade, and they dramatically influenced Western art. Also, Picasso's blending of figure and space echoes the theories of scientists like Albert Einstein on the fundamental nature of matter, energy, and space.

Likewise, the *Ceremonial Mask known as a Mboom or Bwoom* has its own obvious and hidden content. It is a decorated helmet mask, made of wood, beads, shells, and pieces of cloth. It was originally used in African **masquerades,** traditional celebrations that blended dance, art, song, and ritual. Masquerades are reenactments of creation events, spirit works, and ancestor stories. This mask represented the people over whom a king asserted his authority (see Fig. 1.10).

For more on how meaning is embodied in art, read Chapter 4, Deriving Meaning.

AESTHETICS

Art is an aesthetic experience. Aesthetics is the branch of philosophy that deals with art, its sources, its forms, and its effects on individuals and cultures. Writings on aesthetics date back to the ancient Greeks. Thinkers

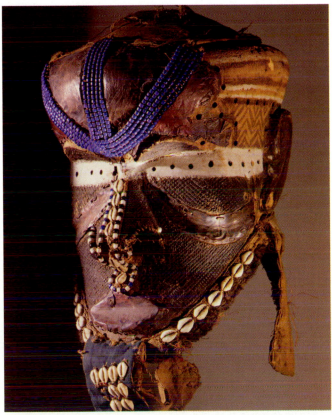

1.5   *Ceremonial Mask known as a Mboom or Bwoom*, 19th–20th centuries. Kuba, Central Zaire. Wood, beads, shells, cloth. Head-sized. Museum of Central Africa, Tervuren.

from India, Japan, China, and Western cultures have written for centuries about aesthetic issues. In several African, Oceanic, and Native American cultures, art practice demonstrated a clear aesthetic long before there was written material about it. You are thinking aesthetically when you read a book like this one.

Modern aesthetic theory in the West became a field of study in the eighteenth century, when many philosophers thought that art dealt with beauty, and that beauty could be universally defined for all times and places. Their standard of beauty was ancient Greek sculpture, which was enormously influential on eighteenth-century Western art and fashion. That universalist position is discredited now, because there is no worldwide agreement about what constitutes beauty. For example, an Italian from 1500, an African from 1900, and your next-door neighbor may have very different views of the aesthetic merits of *The Birth of Venus, Les Demoiselles d'Avignon,* and the *Ceremonial Mask.* In addition, philosophers today consider many qualities other than beauty as significant attributes of art.

CREATING ART

Perception, response, creativity, and expression are important components for creating art.

VISUAL PERCEPTION

Visual perception is the basis of artistic creation. It is the essential component as the artist makes the work, because in a sense the artist is the first viewer of the work. Vision is essential also for the broader audience perceiving most works.

The act of perceiving that is required for making or looking at art is focused and concentrated. Most of our everyday visual experience is disorganized and not memorable. With art, however, the artist carefully places colors and shapes, not simply to copy our everyday environment, much of which we ignore. Art is designed to be arresting, to engage our attention, to make us look and to be aware of our act of looking, and potentially to be enriched as a result. That gift of engaged vision, in contrast to our everyday inattentiveness, is one of the greatest benefits of art.

THE ARTIST'S RESPONSE TO THE WORLD

Although all artwork is based on visual perceptions, almost all artists' works are different from any others'.

Their work reflects their point of view, values, and individual experiences. They also learn from others.

Think of the thousands of flower pictures you have seen in your life, including paintings or photographs, on calendars, wallpaper, wrapping paper, linoleum, fabric, and so on. Each has its own visual form, content, and value. Every one of those representations of flowers was based on the visual perception of some artist or designer. All the artists used different means to achieve their results. For example, many artists choose to paint "from life," with their subject in front of them. Figure 1.6 is a delicate scroll painting entitled *Lotus Flowers and Ducks,* from thirteenth-century China. Generally, traditional Chinese paintings were not made directly from life, but from memory, because the Chinese

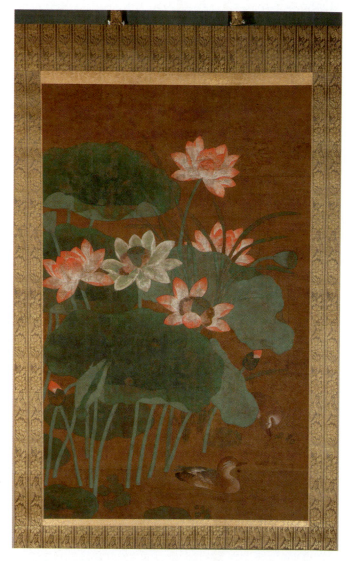

1.6 *Lotus Flowers and Ducks,* 13th century. Hanging scroll. Paint on silk, 50.4" × 30.7". China. Museum fuer Ostasiatische Kunst, Staatliche Museen zu Berlin, Berlin.

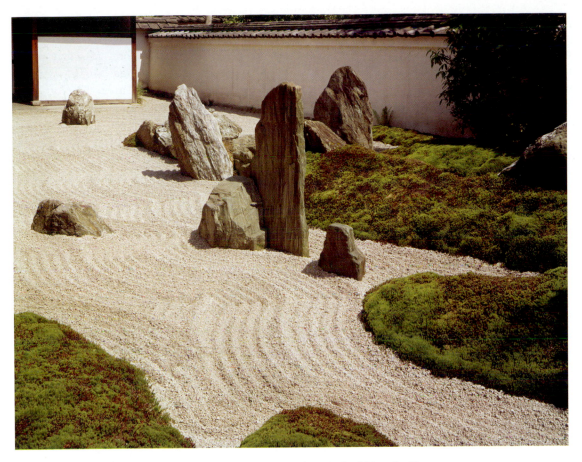

1.7   *Zen Stone Garden*, 1192–1333. Kamakura period. Daitokuji Temple, Kyoto.

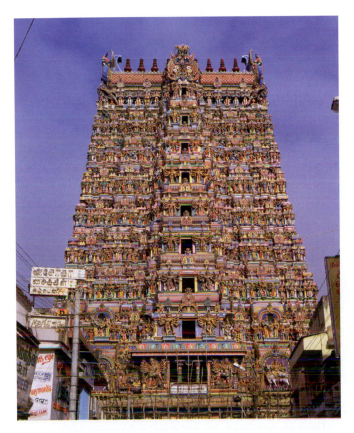

1.8   *Gopura, Sri Meenakshi Amman Temple*, 17th century. Madurai, Tamil Nadu, India.

believed memory and repeated experience allowed the artist to capture the broad essence of flowers rather than the specific details of one particular bloom.

Clearly, art reflects humankind's perceptions of and responses to all aspects of spiritual life and earthly life, from birth to death and the hereafter, and of everything in between. Figure 1.7 is *Zen Stone Garden* from 1185–1333, located at the Buddhist Daitokuji Temple and monastery complex in Kyoto, Japan. The *Zen Stone Garden* is a still, dry landscape meant to aid quiet meditation, which Buddhists believe is essential for spiritual growth. The white rocks can stand for the cosmic void, the emptiness of the mind, the flow of water, a journey, and so on, while the large, dark rocks represent material substances and worldly events. Figure 1.8 is a *Gopura* (or gateway) to the *Sri Meenakshi Amman Temple* at Madurai, India, a destination for thousands of pilgrims who attend the Hindu festivals there. This 150-foot-tall tower is covered with deities and attendants, so richly decorated and brightly painted that the surface almost seems to pulsate. This architecture embodies the Hindus' celebration of the divine force that animates the abundant life forms on earth.

Both the *Zen Stone Garden* and the *Gopura* seek to instill a sense of spiritual awareness, but how different each is. Yet each represents its creators' responses to the spiritual and natural worlds, as they experienced it.

ARTISTIC EXPRESSION AND CREATIVITY

Creativity allows us to originate something or to cause some object to come into being. What that means exactly can vary from culture to culture. In the United States today, creativity is often thought to have two essential ingredients. The first is innovation, or the making of something that is new. The second is self-expression, which refers to individual artists' own styles and personal concepts of the world, all of which are embedded in their unique works of art.

However, innovation and artistic self-expression are not always necessary ingredients in creating artwork. For some great art, the artists followed formulas or copied other works, because their culture valued the re-creation of old forms more than innovation. Also, some artists today devote their work to critiquing existing culture, rather than creating something new.

Jaune Quick-to-See Smith's *Genesis* (Fig. 1.9) contains aspects of innovation and self-expression, at the same time as she is re-creating old forms. On the expressive side, Smith has applied thick, gestural strokes of oil paint on top of a collaged layer of newspaper articles, photocopied images, and pieces of fabric. On the side of preserving old forms, in this case referring to Native American creation myths, she has incorporated native symbols, sculptures, and lines from stories, along with glorifying the buffalo, an animal with mythical standing. She has blended traditional native imagery and mythology into late-twentieth-century art styles. To Smith, all her works are inhabited landscapes, full of life, an essential native idea.

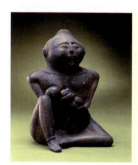

Connection *In the lower right corner of Genesis,* Jaune Quick-to-See Smith *has drawn an image of a 700-year-old Native American ceramic vessel called* Mother and Nursing Child *(see Fig. 8.29), showing the importance of re-creating and preserving old forms.*

As evident in the discussion of *Genesis*, creativity can be a complex mix of old and new. Although psy-

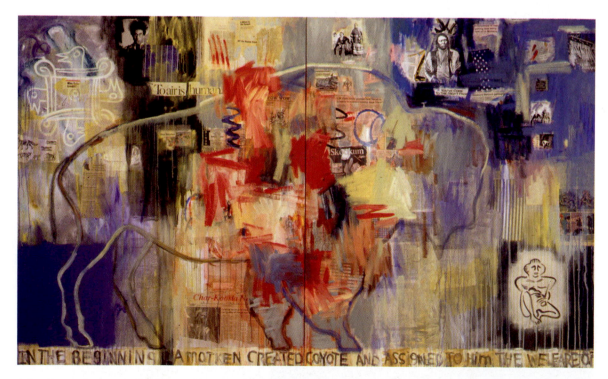

1.9   JAUNE QUICK-TO-SEE SMITH. *Genesis*, 1993. Oil, collage, mixed media on canvas, 5' × 8' 4". Museum of Art, Atlanta.

chologists have not fully identified the creative process in art making, some contemporary artists believe it begins with a formative stage, as an artist responds to a problem, a vivid experience, or a commission. This may be followed by periods of intense research or experimentation. The making of the artwork comes next, which may be quick or may take years. Picasso worked for two months in 1907 on *Les Demoiselles d'Avignon.* The making of *Gopura* from Madurai undoubtedly took much longer, even with the combined efforts of many craftsmen. In the case of **performance art,** often no art object is made, but the artist initiates some actions which are the art.

Once the work has been completed, or even while it is in process, artists critically assess their work. Other critiques come from peers, curators, writers, academics, and the audience. All this provides a certain degree of affirmation.

Who is creative? Artists and designers are, as well as mathematicians, scientists, health care professionals, social workers, teachers, parents, gardeners, and so on. Although we think of creativity as residing in the individual, it has a social dimension as well. With broad support, a person's artistic abilities can blossom. Negative social pressures can cause a person to squelch or divert creativity or to be embarrassed or ridiculed to the point of avoiding it. Creativity comes easily to children, but it must be nourished in adolescence, when peer pressure and self-criticism can cause us to stifle what is part of our natural human heritage.

CATEGORIES OF VISUAL ARTS

A few decades ago, a definition of art circulated in the United States, saying in effect that art is whatever the artist says is art. There is some truth in this, as artists often have taken the lead in defining new art forms long before society accepted them. However, when we view the long history of art, we see the greater truth to this definition: Art is whatever a society or a culture says is art. What does this mean? Basically, the definition of art is not universal and fixed in all its details, as we saw earlier. It fluctuates, because cultures are alive and changing.

Some peoples, both past and present, have no word that corresponds to ours for art. For example, masquerades in sub-Saharan Africa blur the boundaries between areas that Western cultures might consider very distinct, such as art, ritual, and social cohesion. In Figure 1.10, masqueraders are performing in the court

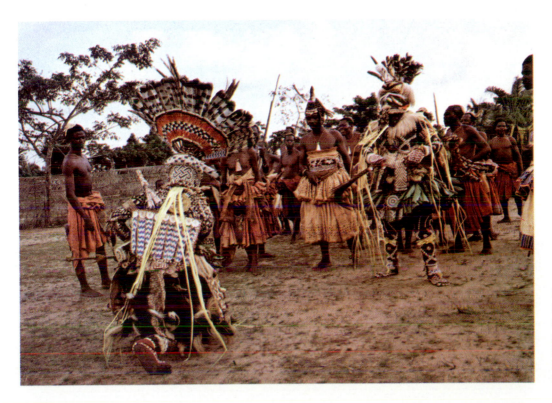

1.10 Mwashamboy (kneeling) and Bwoom (standing) maskers in a royal ceremony among the Kuba. Late 20th century. Democratic Republic of Congo.

of the Kuba king. Their masks and roles re-create archetypes that deal with the beginnings of the Kuba people, the rights of the king, and basic social values for young men. The standing performer to the right is wearing a mask similar to the *Mboom or Bwoom Mask* in Figure 1.5. Another example of different categories for art comes from the Japanese, who did not necessarily think of paintings as fine art until the late nineteenth century, when the concept of art history was exported from the West along with the idea of painting as fine art. The Japanese also value flower arranging and traditional puppetry as higher art forms than do Western cultures.

Connection *For more on Japanese Bunraku puppetry, see Fig. 16.17.*

In the United States today, we are inundated with images and visual objects. They surround us in galleries and museums and are everywhere in mass media and in stores. Some are considered art, and others are called popular culture. Crafts sometimes are distinguished from art. The following section includes some of the groupings we make today for visual objects.

FINE ART, POPULAR CULTURE, AND KITSCH

Fine art is a Western category of refined objects considered to be among the supreme cultural achievements of the human race. Fine art is believed to transcend average human works and may be produced by only the best artists with unique sensibilities. To be appreciated, fine art requires sensitivity on the part of its audience. One definition of fine art is simply that it is what is displayed in art museums.

Connection *For more on the development of museums in general, and art museums in particular, see Chapter 6, What Do We Do with Art?.*

The category of fine art has always been evolving. Prior to 1800 or so, regarding the visual arts as well as performing arts,

> "highbrow" and "lowbrow" . . . were both popular. Shakespeare appealed to lower class audiences; and the same can be said of most stage literature, of music (including grand opera), and of the visual arts. Norms now taken for granted did not exist; audiences were not demurely appreciative but highly demonstrative; there was an endless indiscriminate mixing of genres, of high art and kitsch. Relatively little was sacred. (Wallach 1998:14)

In the past, fine art tended to be media-defined: Its most traditional forms include painting, sculpture, and architecture. In the early and mid-nineteenth century, fine art was defined in Western industrialized nations solely in terms of classical art: Greek, Roman, and Italian Renaissance art, mostly sculpture. That Greek/ Roman-inspired model of fine art was so pervasive that when Théodore Géricault painted *The Raft of the Medusa* (Fig. 1.11), critics were horrified because it was too realistic, too much like life and not enough like "art." The painting, which shows starving survivors of a shipwreck just as they are being rescued, created huge sensations wherever it was displayed, and it caused political turmoil because it dramatized a shipwreck that was caused in part by its incompetent captain, who was a political appointee. Looking at the painting today, it may be hard to imagine that some thought it was not art.

Another major shift in the category of fine art occurred at the beginning of the twentieth century, when contemporary painting began to be favored, and successive waves of painters challenged existing conventions of art, leading to the development of the **avant-garde**. The paintings of Paul Cezanne, such as *Landscape at Aix, Mount Sainte-Victoire* (Fig. 1.12), from 1905, were critical in this development, as Cezanne broke conventions on how space and form were depicted. Later, the mid-twentieth-century critic Clement Greenberg defined avant-garde art, which he saw as detached from society, as "art for art's sake" and "pure poetry." "The avant-garde poet or artist tries in effect to imitate God by creating something valid solely on its own terms, in the way that nature itself is valid. . . . [A] work of art or literature cannot be reduced in whole or in part to anything not itself" (Greenberg 1939: 5–6).

In recent years, fine art as a category has expanded to include film, photography, prints, and, most recently, installation, performance, video, and computer art. In addition, definitions of fine art are in flux when Western people look at art from other cultures. In 1880, a work like the *Mboom or Bwoom Mask* would not have been displayed in art museums in the United States or Europe, but they are now.

Popular culture in Western nations consists of magazines, comics, television, tourist art, advertising, folk art, tattoos, customized cars, graffiti, video games, posters, websites, calendars, greeting cards, dolls, toys, movies (as opposed to film or cinema), and snapshots and commercial photography (as opposed to fine photography). Popular art is often perceived as being more accessible, inexpensive, entertaining, commercial, political, naive, colorful, or touristy than fine art.

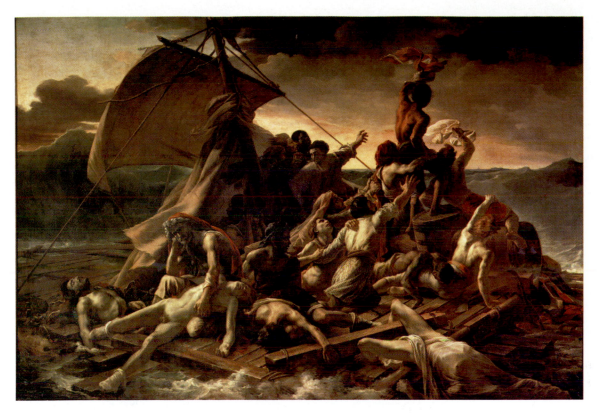

1.11   Théodore Géricault. *The Raft of the Medusa*, 1819. Oil on canvas, 16' 1" × 24' 1". Louvre, Paris.

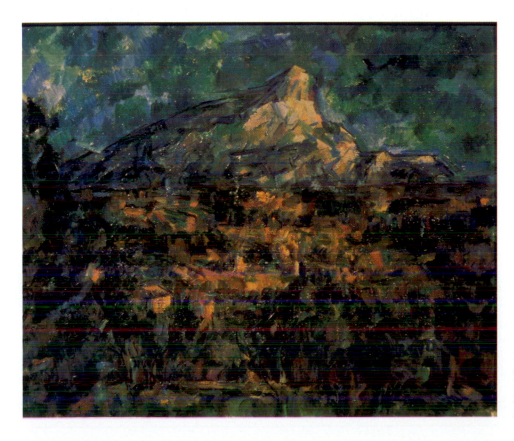

1.12   Paul Cezanne. *Landscape at Aix, Mount Sainte-Victoire*, 1905. Oil on canvas, 23½" × 28¼". Pushkin Museum of Fine Arts, Moscow.

Fine arts and popular culture can be seen as part of a continuum that contains much of the visual imagery that Western culture produces. Indeed, popular culture images and objects may share many attributes of high art. The work is often highly creative, innovative, and expressive. It shares the same attributes of function, visual form, and content. It reflects the values and structures of our social systems, political hierarchies, and religious beliefs. Popular culture is studied in many academic areas, including visual culture, art history, philosophy, and anthropology. It is often collected and may be displayed in museums. Art and popular culture often share the same images. Some objects from popular culture eventually "become" art, for example, popular prints like *Las bravisimas calaveras guatemaltecas de Mora y de Morales,* by Jose Guadalupe Posada (Fig. 1.13). This widely distributed print is like an editorial cartoon, with large, running skeletons (*calaveras*) that represent two assassins who brought death and chaos to Guatemala.

Some artists want to occupy the space between high art and popular culture. For example, *Tan Tan Bo,* 2001 (Fig. 1.14) is by the contemporary Japanese artist Takashi Murakami, who produces paintings, designer handbags, and installations of large-scale inflatable art, like enormous Mylar helium balloons. His work is a blend of U.S. and Japanese fine art, popular culture, and **animé** (contemporary Japanese animation), and always reflects a self-conscious consumerism. Murakami also sells multiple edition prints of works on paper and canvas through galleries and on artnet.com.

Webster's New World Dictionary defines **kitsch** as "art, writing, etc. of a pretentious but shallow kind, calculated to have popular appeal." Objects or images are kitsch if they display an emotional appeal that is

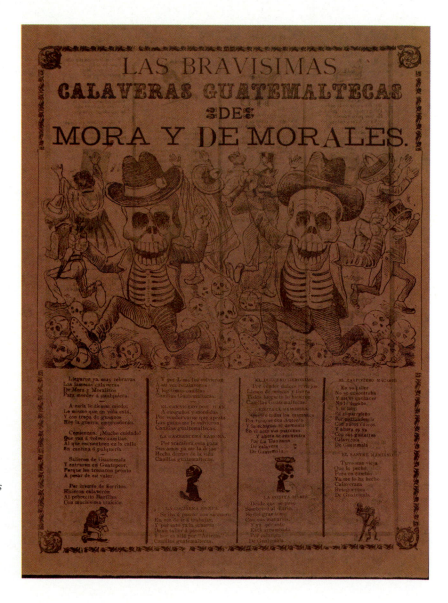

1.13 JOSE GUADALUPE POSADA. *Las bravisimas calaveras guatemaltecas de Mora y de Morales,* 1907. Pictorial broadside verse, full sheet, printed recto and verso, lavender paper; zinc etching. University of New Mexico Library.

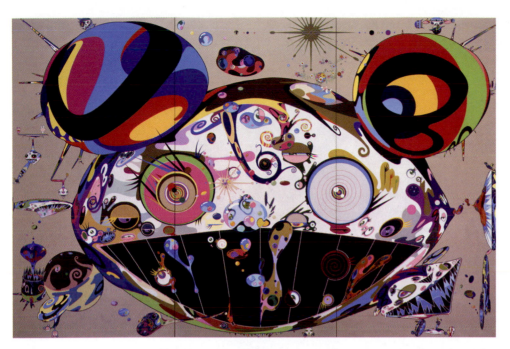

1.14   TAKASHI MURAKAMI. *Tan Tan Bo*, 2001. Acrylic on canvas mounted on board, 11' 9" × 18' 1" (3 panels). Tomio Koyama Gallery, Tokyo.

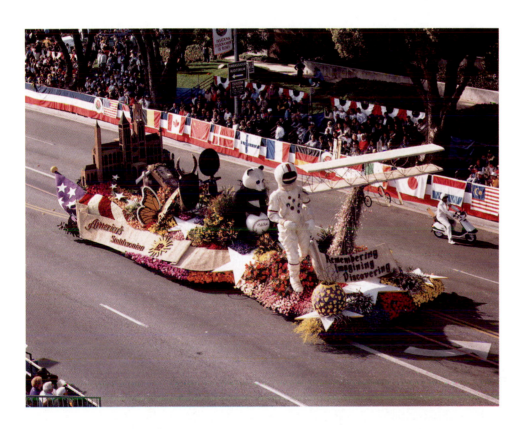

1.15   *The Smithsonian Institution's 150th Anniversary Float* in the 1996 Rose Parade in Pasadena, California.

generalized, superficial, and sentimental. Kitsch is the opposite of an original experience, a uniquely felt emotion, or a thoughtful, introspective moment, and is often used in advertising and in political propaganda. *The Smithsonian Institution's 150th Anniversary Float* in the Rose Parade (Fig. 1.15), with its collection of images from astronauts to the first airplane to pandas to butterflies to baseball, evokes a variety of kitsch emotions: Technology is wonderful! Come to the museum to see exotic things. Wild animals are cute! All of America loves the Smithsonian! A representation of the oldest building of the Smithsonian Institution rides at the back of the float. The building has been scaled down, its windows made proportionally larger, the most exotic features—its towers—emphasized. The building is much smaller in scale than the objects in front of it, to make the museum appear diminutive, cute, and fun. In this float, it does not appear to be a site of serious research.

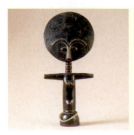

Connection *The Rose Parade float contains a translation of a small African Asante Akua'ba sculpture (see Fig. 8.8) into a six-foot-high maquette of seaweed and flowers.*

But, like all other categories of visual art, the idea of kitsch is evolving and changing. Critics such as Susan Sontag have reclaimed some kitsch as "camp," which means that objects and images of such extreme artifice (and often banality) have a perverse sophisticated and aesthetic appeal, and that they revealed "another kind of truth about the human situation" (Sontag 1966: 287). Other artists incorporate and transform kitsch in their work. The artist Tim Hawkinson, who is known for his inventive, humorous, or fantastic art, created a nearly 200-ton stone *BEAR* (Fig. 1.16), a cross between a teddy bear and Stonehenge. There is an interesting association between the surfaces of a soft, fuzzy childhood companion and the rounded, weathered surfaces of ancient stones.

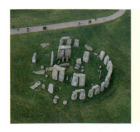

Connection *Stonehenge contains circles of ancient, enormous boulders, presumably set up for agricultural rituals, and is located in southern England. See Figure 9.24 on page 221.*

CRAFT

Craft refers to specific media, including ceramics, glass, jewelry, weaving, and woodworking. Craft usually involves making objects, rather than images or image manipulation, although craft may involve surface decoration. Often, craft objects have a utilitarian purpose or

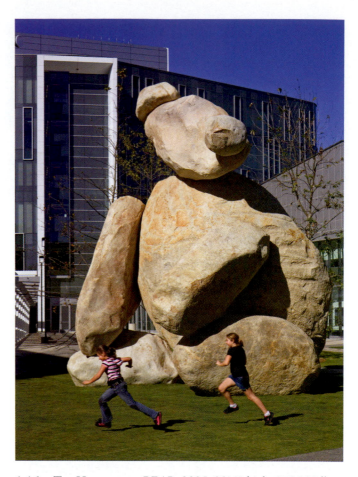

1.16   TIM HAWKINSON. *BEAR*, 2005. 23'6" high, 370,000 lbs., Stuart Collection, University of California, San Diego.

perhaps evolved from a utilitarian origin. In addition, however, they display aesthetic and/or conceptual dimensions that go beyond mundane use. Like the categories of fine art, popular culture, and kitsch, the art/craft distinction is culturally specific and in flux.

The *Gheordez Prayer Rug* (Fig. 1.17), from eighteenth-century Turkey, is a good example of an art object that might be categorized as craft or art. Like other woven objects, it is craft, but its aesthetic qualities and ritualistic uses carry it beyond utilitarian function. The intricate pattern echoes tile work in mosques, and the white niche in the center is like a **mihrab**, an architectural feature in a mosque that marks the direction of Mecca.

STYLISTIC CATEGORIES

Style is the manner of expression that is characteristic of art either made by an individual artist or from a his-

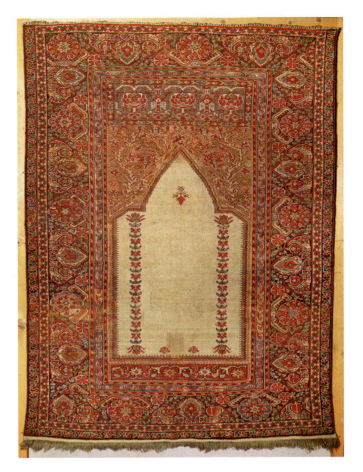

1.17 *Gheordez Prayer Rug*, 18th century. White mihrab (prayer niche) with two Turkish floral columns. Wool, height, 65³/₄", width, 48³/₄". Turkey. Museum fuer Angewandte Kunst, Vienna, Austria.

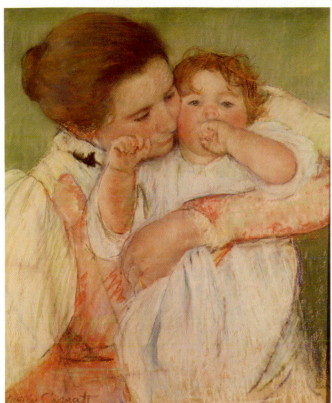

1.18 MARY CASSATT. *Mother and Child*, 1897. Pastel on paper, 21" × 17³/₄". Musée d'Orsay, Paris.

toric period or an entire civilization. So a rose might be a rose, but the styles of representation of it are not the same. Before looking at artists' or cultures' styles, it is helpful to have a basic vocabulary describing stylistic attributes.

STYLE VOCABULARY

Art that is **naturalistic** generally contains recognizable imagery that is depicted very much as seen in nature. Mary Cassatt's *Mother and Child* (Fig. 1.18), from 1897, is rendered in a naturalistic style. From repeated and long observation, Cassatt was able to capture the intense attachment a mother may feel toward her child. This work is also **representational**, as it contains entities from the world in recognizable form.

In **idealized** art, natural imagery is modified in a way that strives for perfection within the bounds of the

values and aesthetics of a particular culture. The *Veranda Post* (Fig. 1.1) and the *Equestrian Statue of Marcus Aurelius* (Fig. 1.2) are both rendered in idealized styles, yet are quite different because each culture had its own definition of "ideal." In African figurative sculpture, it is common to see oversized heads in idealized imagery (the figure is often divided into thirds: one third is the head, and the other two thirds are body and legs). Marcus Aurelius's large size and dignified gestures are ingredients for an idealized image.

Expressive or **expressionist** styles of art are those that communicate heightened emotions and often a sense of urgency or spontaneity. Expressive styles frequently appear bold and immediate, rather than carefully considered or refined. They often feature distorted or abstracted imagery and may appear asymmetrical or off balance. Textured surfaces and thick paint application signal an expressive style. Wassily Kandinsky's

Jüngster Tag (Fig. 1.19), from 1912, is an example of expressionist painting, as seen in the bold colors, strong contrasts from black to white, vigorous lines, and exploding, fragmented forms.

The term **classical** has several related meanings in reference to style. It can refer to art that is orderly, balanced, clear, and well proportioned vertically and horizontally, like *The Birth of Venus* (Fig. 1.3) seen earlier in this chapter. In this sense, classical is the opposite of expressive. "Classical" also describes a point in the evolution of styles: classical works represent the full development of a certain style, in contrast to its early formative stage or its late transformation into another style. When written with a capital C, Classical refers specifically to the art made in ancient Greece in the fifth century BCE. The *Equestrian Statue of Marcus Aurelius* (Fig. 1.2) is an example of a work influenced by Classical Greek art. The related term **classic** indicates a judgment of excellence, such as a classic work of art with widely recognized outstanding qualities.

Classic as in excellence applies to *Marcus Aurelius* as well as to the *Veranda Post* by Olowe of Ise (Fig. 1.1).

Surreal refers to art with a bizarre or fantastic arrangement of images or materials, as if tapping into the workings of the unconscious mind. Meret Oppenheim's *Object* (Fig. 1.20) is a fur-lined cup, which mixes and thus undermines the pleasures of two senses in a dreamlike way. The fur is sensual to touch, but miserable in the mouth, even though the cup should be delivering taste treats to the tongue. The title in French means *Luncheon in Fur,* which could refer to luxury or even sexuality, and yet humor is also a prominent part of the piece.

Nonobjective (nonrepresentational) art contains imagery that is completely generated by the artist. Frank Stella's *Abra III* (Fig. 1.21), 1968, focuses on the interrelation between colors and shapes, and nothing else beyond what a person sees while looking at the painting.

The term "abstract art" is often used to mean the same thing as "nonobjective," but there is an important distinction. **Abstracted** imagery may or may not be rec-

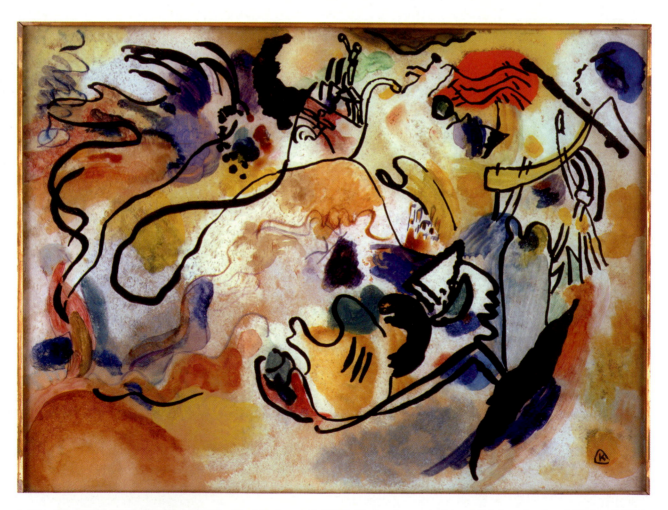

1.19 WASSILY KANDINSKY. *Jüngster Tag (Last Judgment),* 1912. Underglass painting with ink and color, 13¼" × 17½". Musée National d'Art Moderne, Centre Georges Pompidou, Paris.

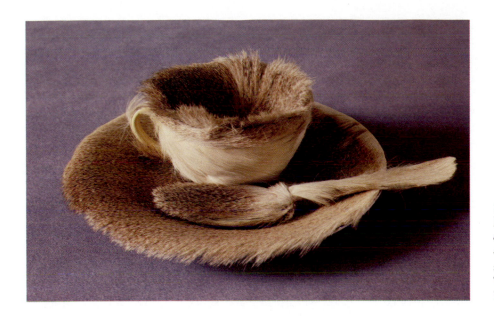

1.20   MERET OPPENHEIM. *Object (Le Dejeuner en fourrure),* 1936. Fur-covered cup, saucer, and spoon. Cup, 4³/₈" diameter; saucer, 9³/₈" diameter; spoon, 8" long; overall height, 2⁷/₈". The Museum of Modern Art, New York.

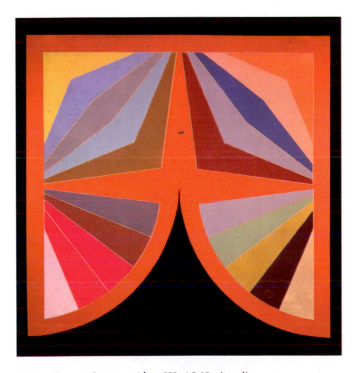

1.21   FRANK STELLA. *Abra III,* 1968. Acrylic on canvas, 10' × 10'. Collection of the artist. New York.

ognizable, but it has been derived from reality by distorting, enlarging, and/or dissecting objects or figures from nature. Pablo Picasso's *Les Demoiselles d'Avignon* (Fig. 1.4) is an example of abstracted imagery from earlier in this chapter, but it is still representational in the sense that the imagery is recognizable and taken from the world around us. Kandinsky's *Jüngster Tag* (Fig. 1.19) is more abstract than *Demoiselles*.

CULTURAL STYLES

A **cultural style** consists of recurring and distinctive features that we see in many works of art emanating from a particular place and era. Stylistic traits help us identify works from ancient Egypt, for example, and see them as distinct and coherent as a group. Stylistic differences make the art of ancient Egypt readily distinguishable from the art of, say, seventeenth-century France. Cultural styles reflect and express the cultures from which they come. Along with language, religion, and social customs, the styles of art and architecture form a culture's identity.

A few definitions are helpful here. **Culture** can mean the totality of ideas, customs, skills, and arts that belong to a people or group. This cultural totality is communicated or passed along to succeeding generations. A **culture** may also be a particular people or group, with their own ideas, customs, and arts. A **civilization** is a highly structured society, with a written language or a very developed system of communication, organized government, and advances in the arts and sciences. A country and a people with a high degree of social and cultural development can also be called a "civilization."

So, when referring to ancient Egypt, we may call it a civilization, as it was a structured society with government, written language, and the arts and sciences. We may also refer to Egyptian culture—that is, its collective ideas, customs, and beliefs, and the articles of art that it produced. Most important here is our ability to distinguish the Egyptian style of art, as one representation of its cultural identity.

Cultural styles are recognizable across a broad spectrum of art objects created by a people. These art objects share content and many formal qualities. For example, during the seventeenth-century reign of King Louis XIV of France, the court style, which was ornate and lavish, could be seen in everything from architecture to painting, furniture design, and clothing (see Fig. 5.5). Even hairstyles were affected. Men and women wore enormous, elaborate powdered wigs as they attended court events in fabulously decorated halls. Some hairstyles apparently even had jeweled model ships "floating" among the curls and waves. You can see broad cultural styles around you today. Do you notice certain shared qualities among some contemporary art, popular music, and the latest ads for clothing?

On the other hand, different cultural styles become apparent when studying a particular art form that appears in distant regions. For examples, Islamic mosques are built around the world to provide a place for Muslims to congregate and pray together while facing the holy city of Mecca. Those basic needs are translated into structures, but local solutions are different from each other, as we can see with the *Grand Mosque* at Djenne, in Mali, Africa (Fig. 1.22) and the *Badshahi Mosque* in Lahore, Pakistan (Fig. 1.23). Both are imposing, dramatic buildings with towers, yet each design is influenced by its cultural preferences and by locally available building materials.

Cultural styles are not static, but evolve due to many circumstances, such as changes in religion, historical events such as war, and contact with other cultures through trade or colonization. Prior to the twentieth century, European art since the 1400s emphasized the human form in a naturalistic, idealized, or Classical Greek–inspired manner, like *The Birth of Venus* (Fig. 1.3). We already saw that the art of Europe changed profoundly because of African influences, especially apparent in works like Picasso's *Les Demoiselles d'Avignon* (Fig. 1.4). Even looking only at the work of Picasso, his lifetime output is an amalgam of styles

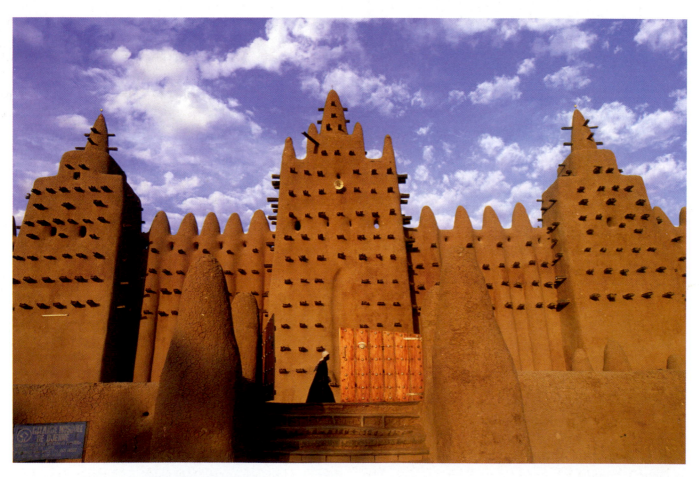

1.22 *Grand Mosque.* 1906–1907. Djenne, Mali.

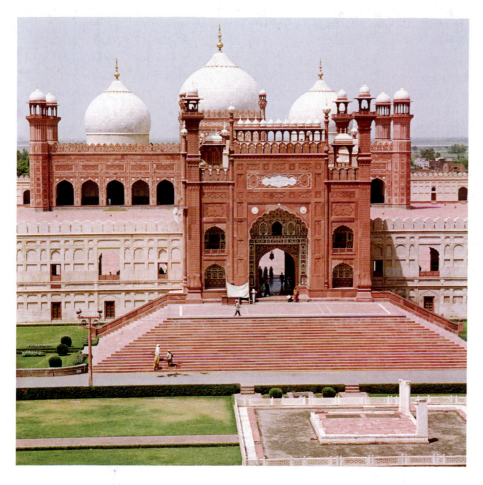

1.23 *Badshahi Mosque*, main entrance. 1672–1674. Lahore, Pakistan.

from Africa and Europe, with individual works in naturalistic, expressive, idealistic, or abstract styles.

ARTISTS' STYLES

Style can also refer to the distinguishing characteristics of one artist's work. Individual artists can develop unique, personal styles. In some cases, their names would be known even without the signature on their work. Artist Vincent van Gogh is famous for his expressive paintings rendered in thick paint with broad areas of strong colors. Using a palette knife, he applied his paint quickly, and frequently defined forms with bold lines around and through them. His unique style, readily distinguished from other European painters, can be seen clearly in his *Portrait of Mme. Ginoux (L'Arlesienne)* (Fig. 1.24) from 1889.

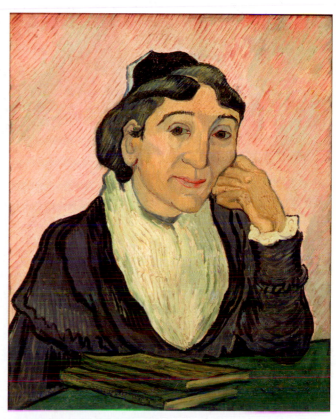

1.24 VINCENT VAN GOGH. *Portrait of Mme. Ginoux (L'Arlesienne)*, 1889. Oil on canvas. 23$\frac{1}{2}$" × 19$\frac{1}{2}$". Galleria Nazionale d'Arte Moderna, Rome.

Individual artists' styles are strongly influenced by their culture and environment. Even van Gogh's unique style shares attributes with other artists of his time, including Impressionists such as Claude Monet (see Fig. 15.11) and Post-Impressionists like Georges Seurat (see Fig. 14.28), Paul Cezanne (Fig. 1.12), or Paul Gauguin (Fig. 1.25). All these artists applied paint in a direct, bold manner. Most frequently they chose subject matter from everyday life. They usually painted in oil and used bright-colored, thick paint (called impasto), rather than thin washes of subdued color. Paul Gauguin and Vincent van Gogh were closely associated for a while, sharing lodgings and painting together, as evident in Gauguin's *Woman in a Coffeehouse, Madame Ginoux in the Cafe de la Gare in Arles* (Fig. 1.25). Not only did they occasionally share subject matter, they influenced each other's painting style as well as choice and use of color.

Some artists seek to develop their own styles and some do not. In twentieth-century U.S. and European art, innovation and unique personal style often were marks of artistic value. This has changed somewhat in the last few decades, as more artists in Europe and the United States have created work in collaborations or even incorporated copies of other images, so that a unique, individual style no longer necessarily denotes quality.

In some cultures, copying a venerable example is valued more than producing a new, unique object. For example, ancient Egyptian artists had a distinct style of rendering figures that was so well established and effective for their culture that very little change occurred in it over thousands of years. It was more important for the Egyptian artists to follow canons of representation than to invent new imagery or new ways to depict it. We see similar attitudes in some Chinese landscape

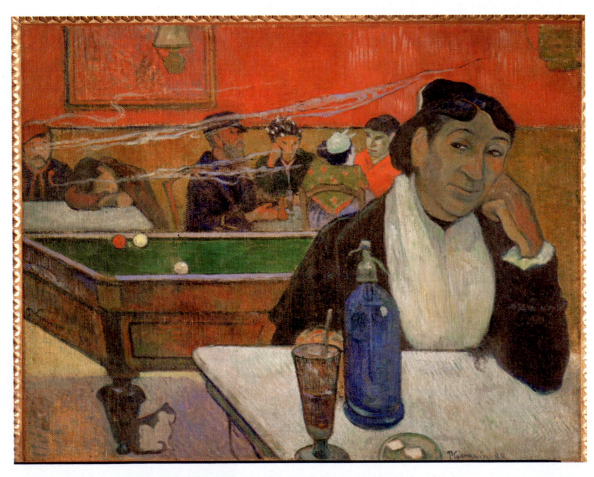

1.25   PAUL GAUGUIN. *Woman in a coffeehouse, Madame Ginoux in the Cafe de la Gare in Arles.* 1888. Oil on canvas, $28^3/4"$ × $36^1/4"$. Pushkin Museum of Fine Arts, Moscow.

paintings and in medieval Europe, where new religious manuscripts were carefully copied from old manuscripts. In the nineteenth and twentieth centuries, Native American artists from the Pacific Northwest also copied old forms that had meaning for their people, while investing new spirit and vigor in them. And Jaune Quick-to-See Smith's *Genesis* (Fig. 1.9) has Native American myths and old art forms featured in a contemporary painting.

Connection *Today, Native American sculptors of the Pacific Northwest continue to make works that share traits of traditional carvings like Arthur Shaughnessy's* Interior House Post *(Fig. 4.16, page 97).*

OTHER CATEGORIES

There are other ways to categorize art. Disciplines such as drawing, photography, or sculpture may be grouped as separate categories. Some cultures have art forms that do not translate directly into Western categories, such as Japan's ancient puppet theater (Fig. 16.17) or the masquerade in Africa (Fig. 1.10). We will see all these again in subsequent chapters.

Chronological categories follow a cultural style as it develops through the years, like "a history of Renaissance Art," or "a survey of art from the Middle Ages." A geographic approach studies the art from a particular area, usually also in chronological order. Western writers often take a geographic approach to art of other cultures, for example, "the art of Africa" or "the art of India."

Yet another approach is thematic, in which a group of fundamental ideas forms the basis for discussing art from many different cultures. This book is organized in that way, with each chapter from 7 through 16 looking at art associated with human survival, with political systems, with religion, and with our bodies, our culture, and our relation to nature and technology.

Other divisions are possible. Certainly all observers of art could create their own categories for grouping artworks, and these areas can vary according to preference. You are part of a living, growing culture, and the final word has not been written about it.

SYNOPSIS

No single definition of art absolutely applies for all times and places. Generally, however, art is a primarily visual medium that expresses ideas about our human experience and the world around us. Art engages our attention in a way that our everyday environment cannot. Various cultures have developed their own aesthetic systems that identify in detail what art is for them.

Creativity is the quality that allows us to originate something or to cause some object to come into being. In some cultures, creativity is tied to artistic expression and innovation, while in others, following precedents is essential.

Societies may group visual arts into various categories. In the United States today, groupings are made around fine art, popular culture, craft, or style. Other categories may be created, such as geographic boundaries, disciplines, or humanistic themes, as used in this book.

FOOD FOR THOUGHT

If art making is strictly a human phenomenon, then:

- *Could an evolutionary theory about humankind include the ability to make art?*
- *If all humans have the potential to be creative, can we all be artists?*

Categorizing art is also a human phenomenon! As we have seen, almost all studies of art are organized in one of three ways: chronologically, geographically, or thematically. Any of these three methods of study has its virtues and its pitfalls. Can you think of any particular advantages of each?

- *Does art include craft or popular culture?*

- *What is your definition of art?*

- *What is more important in your definition: (1) the artwork's meaning or (2) its aesthetic appeal?*

- *Is innovation and artistic expression essential in your definition?*

- *What is your family's definition of art? What about your friends'?*

Your Thomson Online Resources

 Go to **ArtExperience Online** for the Flashcards, Quiz, and Study Guide for this chapter.

CHAPTER 2

The Language of Art and Architecture

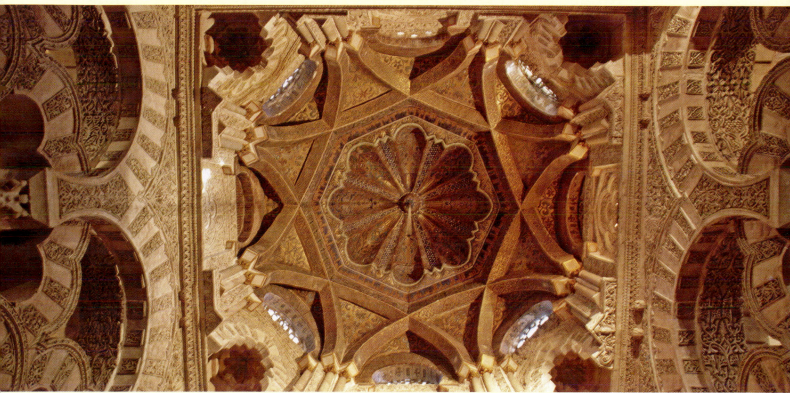

© Superstock

INTRODUCTION

We communicate ideas through languages: oral and written language, numbers, music, and, of course, art. For the language of art and architecture, the grammar consists of (1) the formal elements and (2) the principles by which those elements are composed or structured. Basic vocabulary terms are defined within the chapter and repeated in the Glossary.

Keep in mind the following questions:

- *What are the formal elements of the visual language of art?*
- *What is composition?*
- *Is composition different for painting? For architecture? For time-based arts?*
- *What are principles by which formal elements are composed?*
- *What structural systems do architects use for buildings?*
- *What principles organize building design?*
- *How do buildings relate to the natural environment?*

FORMAL ELEMENTS

Words are basic elements of oral and written languages. Likewise, the basic units of visual arts are the **formal elements:** line, light and value, color, texture and pattern, shape and volume, space, and time and motion. Some works also contain the elements of chance, improvisation, and spontaneity as well as engage senses other than sight.

LINE

Mathematically, a **line** is a moving point, having length and no width. In art, a line usually has both length and width, but length is the more important dimension.

Lines made with some material are **actual lines.** They physically exist and can be broad, thin, straight, jagged, and so on. **Implied lines** in an artwork do not physically exist, yet they seem quite real to viewers. For example, the dotted line has several individual, unconnected parts that can be grouped into a single "line." In Figure 2.1, some lines are actual lines, created by continuous stripes, while others are implied lines, created by aligning discrete dots that we perceive as lines. In fact, in the detail from a painting, we can see the image simultaneously as lines, dots, and areas. Lines come in great varieties, such as the bold, thick angular lines seen in *Shoki the Demon Queller,* c. 1849–1853 by Utagawa Kunisada (Fig. 2.2).

Lines have **direction:** horizontal, vertical, diagonal, curved, or meandering. A line's direction can describe spatial relationships in the world. Something is above something else; a path leads from left to right; an object starts at one location, and then moves to another. Horizontal lines may imply sleep, quiet, or inactivity, like the recumbent human body. Vertical lines may imply aspiration and yearning, as if defying gravity. Diagonal lines suggest movement, because they occur in the posture of running animals and blowing trees, while curving lines may suggest flowing movement. These are guidelines, not rules, because the overall context affects the understanding of specific lines. The upper body of *Shoki the Demon Queller* leans to the left, implying movement, as does the diagonal line of his sword. His robe's sweeping curves and jagged diagonal lines imply a furious energy.

Among groups of lines, repetition may suggest structure or order, as in parallel lines. Lines that collide or tangle may seem random, conflicting, or unbalanced. In Paul Klee's *They're Biting* (Fig. 2.3), from 1920, the meandering, interconnected lines are whimsical.

Lines can also express emotion. Some are precise and controlled, delicate or wavering, sweeping, broad or vigorous. Others are blunt, rough, or heavy, as if the result of a gouging, jabbing action. These expressive **gesture lines** not only depict the physical world but also express the artists' inner beings. Contrast the thick, angular lines of *Shoki* with the thin, playful lines of *They're Biting.*

An **outline** can show **shape,** which is a two-dimensional entity discussed more on page 37. **Contour lines** mark the outer edges of a three-dimensional object, allowing artists to eliminate internal detail but retain recognition of the object, as with the sailboat and buoy in *They're Biting.* **Cross-contours** are internal lines that delineate major areas within an object, like the belt around *Shoki*'s waist. Lines can also produce **tones,** or different areas of gray, as in the parallel lines of **hatching** or in layers to produce **crosshatching** that are visible in Albrecht Durer's *Artist drawing a model in foreshortening through a frame using a grid system* (Fig. 2.4).

Linear elements can exist in three dimensions. Any thin string, rope, wire, chain, stick, or rod used in a sculpture can function like a line. The length of the *Royal Linguist's Staff* from Ghana in the 1900s (Fig. 2.5) gives it an obvious linear quality. Advisors/translators who attend local rulers carry these staffs as signs of their position; the sculpture on top refers to local proverbs. In architecture, columns are linear elements, as are exposed beams or thick steel cables, as seen later in this chapter in Gunter Behnisch's and Otto Frei's *Olympic Stadium, Munich* (Fig. 2.43).

LIGHT AND VALUE

Light is the basis for vision, and thus necessary for art. **Light** is electromagnetic energy that, in certain wavelengths, stimulates the eyes and brain. The sun, moon, stars, lightning, and fire are natural light sources, while incandescent, fluorescent, neon, and laser lights are artificial. In art and architecture, light might be an actual element, as in Figure 2.6 showing Bruce Nauman's neon sculpture, *Human/Need/Desire,* 1983, here totally illuminated, but which actually alternates between "desire" and "need" to suggest the fluctuating motivations for human behavior. In buildings, the control of light is an essential design element, whether with skylights, windows, or artificial lights.

Most art does not emit or manipulate light itself, but reflects **ambient light,** which is the light all around us in our world. In two-dimensional art, artists use **value,** which is light and dark variation on a surface.

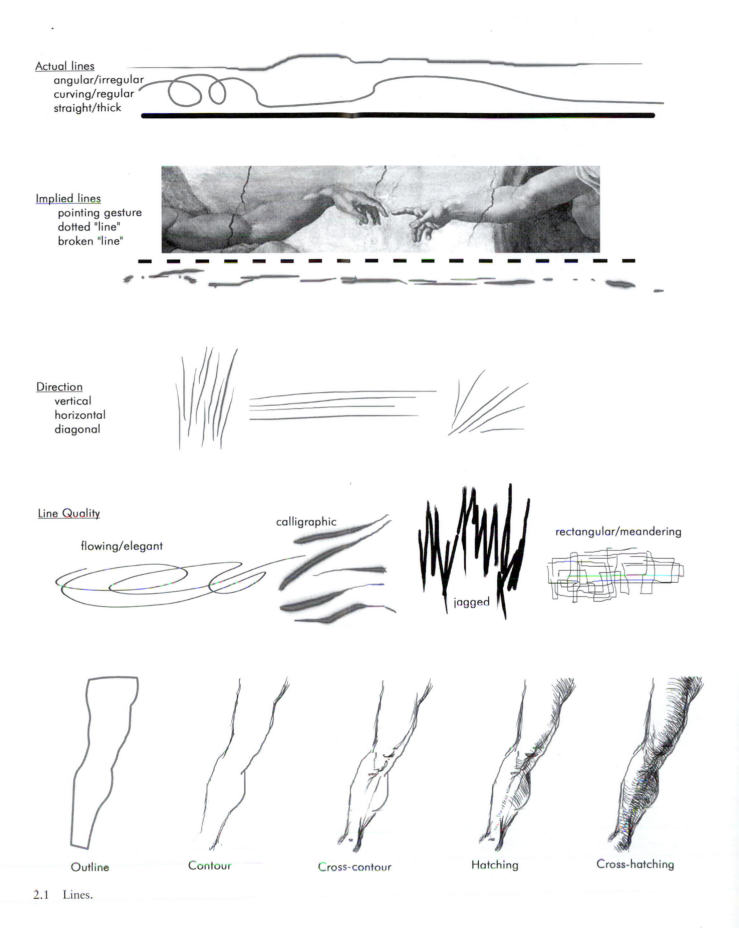

Actual lines
  angular/irregular
  curving/regular
  straight/thick

Implied lines
  pointing gesture
  dotted "line"
  broken "line"

Direction
  vertical
  horizontal
  diagonal

Line Quality

flowing/elegant

calligraphic

jagged

rectangular/meandering

Outline   Contour   Cross-contour   Hatching   Cross-hatching

2.1   Lines.

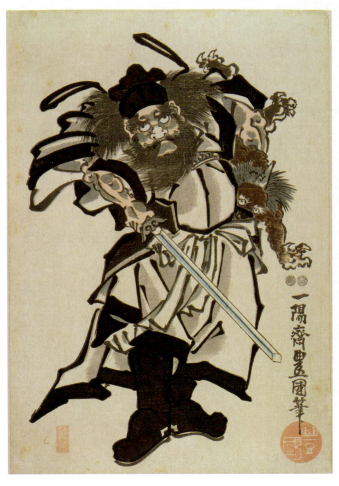

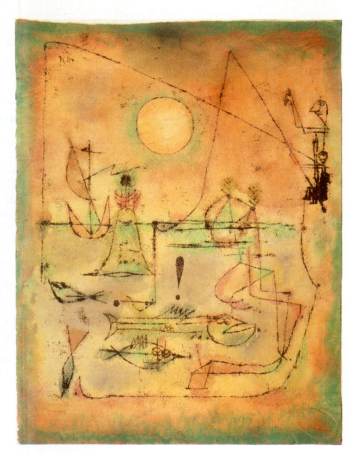

2.3 PAUL KLEE. *They're Biting*, 1920. Drawing and oil on paper, 12¼" × 9¼". Tate Gallery, London.

2.2 UTAGAWA KUNISADA. *Shoki the Demon Queller*, c.1849–1853. Woodblock print, 14 × 9½". Burrell Collection, Glasgow.

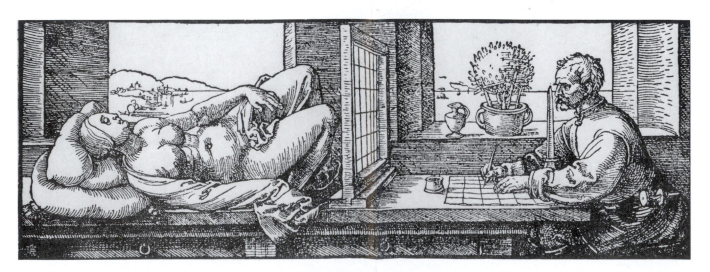

2.4 ALBRECHT DÜRER. *Artist drawing a model in foreshortening through a frame using a grid system* from "Unterweysung der Messung" (Treatise on Perspective). Woodcut.

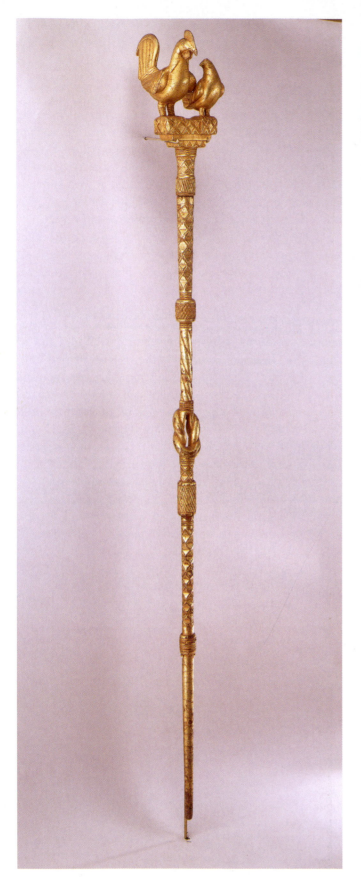

2.5 *Royal Linguist's Staff*. Akan Culture, 1900s. Asante Kingdom, Ghana. Wood, gold leaf, 65$\frac{1}{2}$" high.

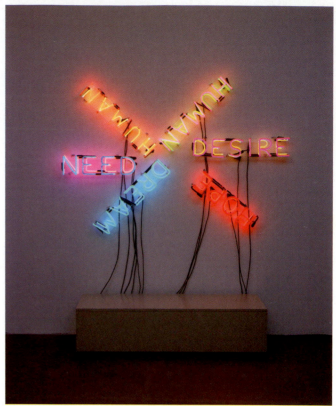

2.6 BRUCE NAUMAN. *Human/Need/Desire*, 1983. Neon tubing, transformer and wire, 7' 10$\frac{3}{8}$" × 70$\frac{1}{2}$" × 25$\frac{3}{4}$". The Museum of Modern Art, New York.

Value ranges from the extremes of white and black, with the continuum of gray tones in between, as in the **achromatic** value scale in Figure 2.7. Value can also be associated with color: red can still be red, but it can be lighter or darker, or different values of the color, as we see in the **chromatic** value scale in Figure 2.7. Artists can carefully manipulate gradations in values to create the appearance of natural light on objects. This is called **shading,** and it can be seen in the drawing of the ball in Figure 2.7. Renaissance Italians used the term **chiaroscuro** to describe these light-dark gradations that can depict objects in space. For example, in Rosso Fiorentino's *Recumbent Female Nude Figure Asleep*, 1530–1540 (Fig. 2.8), the value range of reddish-brown chalk, from dark to light, is clear.

A range of values can express emotion, too. Stark, high-contrast drawings may carry a strong emotional charge, like *Shoki the Demon Queller* (Fig. 2.2), while the more subdued tones in Fiorentino's drawing may lull.

Sculpture and architecture may have value difference simply because of the many angles at which light hits and reflects off their three-dimensional surfaces, as with Louise Nevelson's *Mirror Image I*, 1969 (Fig. 2.9),

A. Achromatic value scale

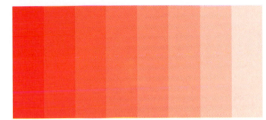

B. Chromatic value scale

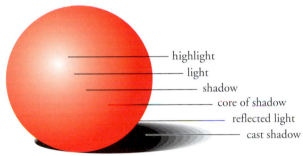

— highlight
— light
— shadow
— core of shadow
— reflected light
— cast shadow

C. Values creating the illusion of volume

2.7   Value Diagram.

with carved wooden forms inside stacked boxes, all painted black. Or their surfaces may be manipulated, like a painting's, for variety in value.

COLOR

Color is a wonderful phenomenon that people are lucky to enjoy. Color is visible in **refracted** light, when a prism breaks a light beam into a **spectrum** of color, or in a rainbow after a storm. Color is also visible in **reflected** light, when objects around us absorb some of the spectrum and bounce back the rest. Those rays that are reflected to our eyes are the color of the object.

The properties of color are hue, value, and intensity. **Hue** is the pure state of color in the spectrum and is that color's name, such as red, blue, yellow, green, purple, and orange. **Value** in color is lightness and darkness within a hue, as we already saw in Figure 2.7. When black is added to a hue, a **shade** of that color is created, while the addition of white results in a **tint** of that color. **Intensity** in color is the brightness and dullness of a hue. Synonyms for intensity are **chroma** and **saturation**. A high-intensity color is brilliant, vivid, and saturated, while a low-intensity color is faded or dull. We see high-intensity colors in the spectrum. Black and white have value but not intensity among their properties. **Neutral** colors are very low intensity colors such as cream, tan, or beige. In Thomas Gainsborough's *Mr. and Mrs. Andrews* (Fig. 2.10), the most saturated color is the blue satin dress, modified with tints and shades. In Mr. Andrews's neutral-color jacket, the variations

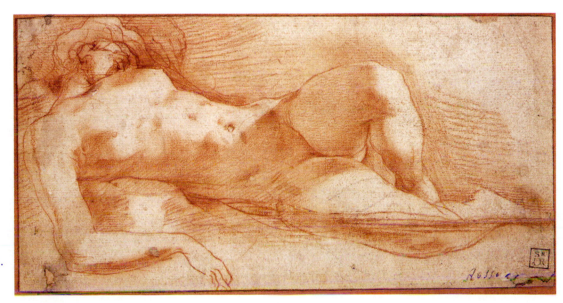

2.8   ROSSO FIORENTINO. *Recumbent Female Nude Figure Asleep,* 1530–1540. 5" × 9½". British Museum, London.

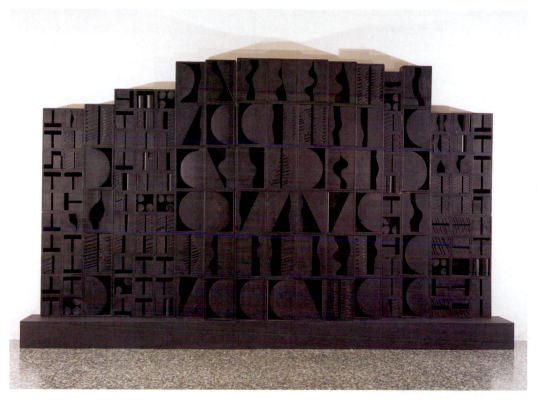

2.9   LOUISE NEVELSON. *Mirror Image I,* 1969. Painted wood. 117³/4" × 210¹/2" × 21". Collection of the Museum of Fine Arts, Houston.

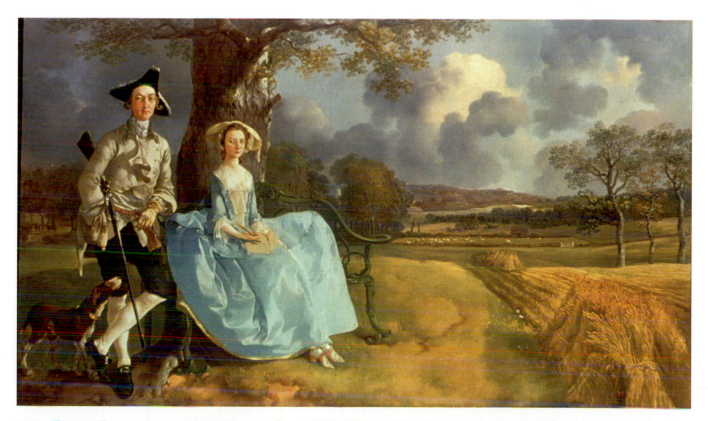

2.10   THOMAS GAINSBOROUGH. *Mr. and Mrs. Andrews.* 1750. 27¹/2" × 47". Oil on canvas. National Gallery, London.

are mostly value changes. Foreground greens are warm and intense compared to the cool, blue-gray greens in the distance. **Local colors** are the colors we normally find in the objects around us. In this painting, the blue dress, yellow hay, and gray-and-white clouds are all in local colors.

Artists mix colors through one of two systems: additive and subtractive (Fig. 2.11). The **additive color system** applies to light-emitting media. In additive color systems, absence of all light produces darkness (or black), and all light added together results in the brightest, whitest light at the center of Figure 2.11A. In

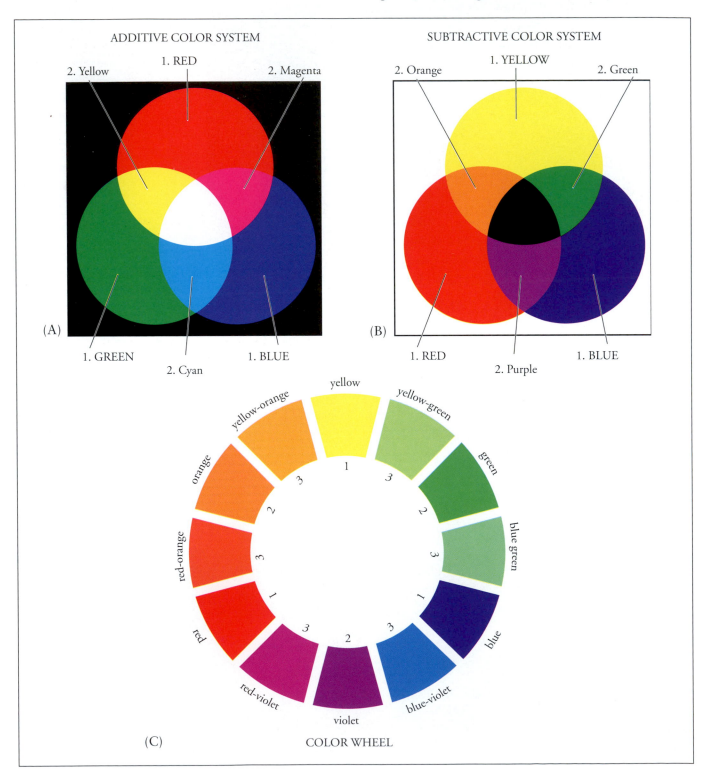

ADDITIVE COLOR SYSTEM

2. Yellow   1. RED   2. Magenta

(A)

1. GREEN   2. Cyan   1. BLUE

SUBTRACTIVE COLOR SYSTEM

2. Orange   1. YELLOW   2. Green

(B)

1. RED   2. Purple   1. BLUE

yellow
yellow-orange   yellow-green
orange   green
red-orange   blue green
red   blue
red-violet   blue-violet
violet

(C)   COLOR WHEEL

2.11   Diagram showing the Additive and Subtractive Color Systems, and the Color Wheel for mixing pigments.

our diagram, we see what happens as red, green, and blue lights are mixed. Theater lighting, performance art, light displays, and computer and video monitors use the additive color system.

In the **subtractive color system,** artists mix pigments to control the light that is reflected from them. **Pigments** are powdered substances ground into oil, acrylic polymer, or other binders to create paints. In the subtractive color system, white is a pigment that reflects almost the entire spectrum of light. Black absorbs almost all light, reflecting back very little. Our diagram shows the mixing of red, yellow, and blue. Mixing more and more pigments gives darker results, as the mixture increasingly absorbs the available light, as we see in the center of Figure 2.11B.

Primary colors combine to produce the largest number of new colors. Various art media have their distinct primary colors. For example, for light-emitting media, the primary colors are red, blue, and green, as we see on our additive color system diagram. **Secondary colors** result from mixing two primary colors. Again, in light-emitting media, the secondary colors are yellow, cyan, and magenta. For paints and pigments, the primary colors are red, yellow, and blue, while the secondary colors are orange, green, and purple. Mixing one primary color with one of its neighboring secondary colors produces **tertiary colors.** Blue-green is a tertiary color in paint. **Analogous colors** are those that are similar in appearance, especially those in which we can see related hues, such as yellow, yellow-orange, and orange. Analogous colors are next to each other on the color wheel. **Complementary colors** are opposites of each other and, when mixed, give a dull result. In paint, red and green are complementary colors. The color wheel again shows us this relationship. We can see the various colors on the **color wheel** in Figure 2.11C, which applies only to color mixing with paints and pigments.

Many color images we encounter in our lives are commercially printed, including the color images in this book. Commercial printers use semitransparent inks, with these primary colors: yellow, magenta (a bright pink), and cyan (a bright blue-green), plus black added for darkness and contrast. The secondary colors are blue, red, and green. You can easily see these primaries, and their resulting mixtures, if you use a strong magnifying glass while looking at a newspaper's color photograph. You encounter these same inks and the same CMYK (cyan, magenta, yellow, black; K = black) primaries in your home computer printer, and your printouts of color images are made from mixtures of these colors.

The chart in Figure 2.12 sums up the primary and secondary colors in various media, plus other color attributes.

Color perception is **relative,** meaning that we see colors differently depending upon their surroundings. Light-emitting media are much more dramatic in dim light, like watching television in the dark. In a very bright room, the television image is barely visible. Conversely, reflective media need a lot of light to be seen well. A spotlight on a painting makes its colors vivid, while a dim room makes them hard to see. Because

COLOR PROPERTIES IN VARIOUS MEDIA

	Paint	Light-Emitting Media (e.g., Computer Monitor)	Commercial Printing or Computer Printer
Color System	subtractive	additive	subtractive
Effects of Environmental Light Levels	more room light, the brighter the colors	less room light, the brighter the colors	more room light, the brighter the colors
Primary Colors	blue, red, yellow	red, green, blue	cyan, magenta, yellow, black (CMYK)
Secondary Colors	purple (blue + red) green (yellow + blue) orange (red + yellow)	yellow (red + green) cyan (green + blue) magenta (red + blue)	red (magenat + yellow) blue (cyan + magenta) green (yellow + cyan)
Complementaries	blue − orange red − green yellow − purple	red − cyan green − megenta blue − yellow	cyan − red magenta − green yellow − blue
Mixture of All Primaries	gray or dull neutral	white	black

2.12   Chart showing Color Properties in Various Media.

natural light is constantly changing, our visual perception is also, and so there is no single, fixed, permanent state that the painting "looks like."

We also experience **relativity of color perception** when we look at certain combinations of colors. In Figure 2.13, the colors in the center of the top row of squares appear to be different even though they are exactly the same, while the dull pink squares in the lower row appear to be the same, but are different. Eye fatigue also affects our color perception. Stare at the white dot in the center of the "flag" printed in Figure 2.13 for one minute. You will notice as the minute wears on that you have trouble seeing the colors, which

at first were so clear and bright. After the minute has passed, look at a white wall to see an afterimage of the flag, with colors shifted to red, white, and blue. Because of eye fatigue, your eyes see the complements, or opposites, of the printed colors.

Colors associated with the sun and fire, such as yellows, reds, and oranges, are considered **warm.** Colors associated with plant life, sky, and water, such as greens, blues, and purples, are **cool.** Warm and cool colors can affect an audience both physically and emotionally. Certain colors in the surroundings can actually influence your alertness, sense of well-being, and sense of inner peace.

The three small center squares above seem to be different shades of orange, but they are all the same.

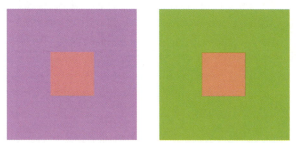

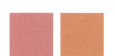

The two small pink squares above seem to be the same . . .   . . . but they are different.

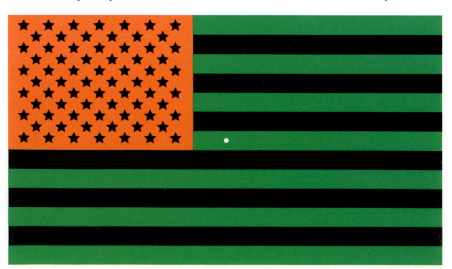

2.13 Diagram Showing the Additive and Subtractive Color Systems, and Relativity of Color Perception.

Stare at the white dot at the center of the flag for 30 seconds, then look at a white wall. It will appear to be red, white, and blue. Color perception shifts due to eye fatigue.

Colors can be symbolic and, thus, associated with ideas or events. The colors of a country's flag are tied to concepts of national identity and patriotism. Certain colors might mean a holiday or a celebration, such as red and green for Christmastime in Western cultures, or red for a wedding in Asian cultures. One color may be associated with different, and even contradictory, ideas. For example, you might think of blue in relation to the ethereal, to purity, or to depression. Yellow might mean cowardice, or it might mean youth, spring, and rebirth. Associations change from culture to culture (so the red for weddings in Asia becomes white in Western cultures).

TEXTURE AND PATTERN

Texture is a surface characteristic that is tactile or visual. **Tactile texture** consists of physical surface varia- tions that can be perceived by the sense of touch. Sculptures often have distinctive tactile textures, as in the *Lion Capital* from Sarnath, India (Fig. 2.14), c. 250 BCE. The gleaming smooth sandstone on the lion's legs contrasts with the rough texture of the lion's mane. Sometimes a medium has an inherent texture. For example, mosaic is a method of creating a picture out of small, colored glass or stone pieces, which are affixed to a surface, as seen in Figure 2.15, *Detail of Deesis Mosaic in Hagia Sophia*. Each mosaic piece reflects ambient light in a slightly different direction. A paint- ing may have a tactile texture when there are thick, textured brushstrokes. **Visual texture** is illusionary. In *Mr. and Mrs. Andrews* (Fig. 2.10), Gainsborough manip- ulated the paint to create the illusions of lustrous satin, bristly hay, and fluffy clouds, even though the painting surface is flat.

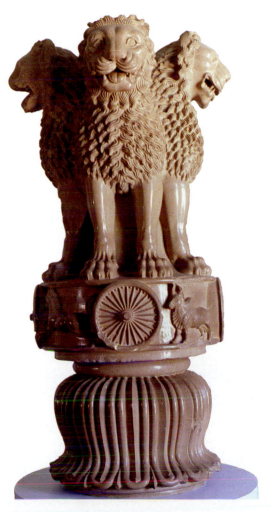

2.14 *Lion Capital* of column erected by Ashoka at Sarnath, India, c. 250 BCE. Polished sandstone, approx. 7' high. Archeological Museum, Sarnath.

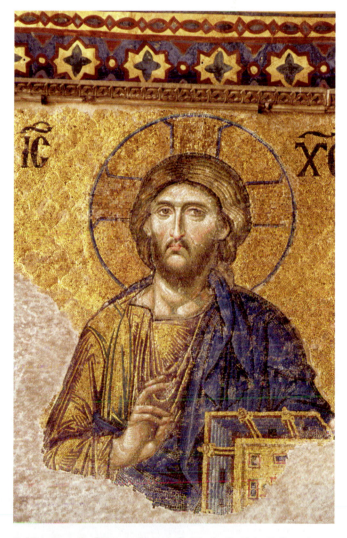

2.15 *Detail of Deesis Mosaic in Hagia Sophia*. Believed to be 1185–1204. Mosaic tile.

Texture can be simulated, abstracted, or invented. **Simulated** textures mimic reality, as in *Mr. and Mrs. Andrews.* Texture can be **abstracted** as well, meaning that it is based on some existing texture, but has been simplified and regularized. The mane on the *Lion Capital* is an abstracted texture. **Invented** textures are apparently products of human imagination.

Building materials often have unique textures. Just think of marble, stone, wood, concrete, cloth, glass, stucco, plaster, metal, brick, or glazed tile, each with a different visual appeal, each with its own texture.

Texture and pattern are related—if a pattern is reduced drastically in size, it is often perceived as a texture, and if a texture is greatly increased in size, it is likely to be perceived as a pattern. The lion's mane on the *Lion Capital* can be read as either texture or pattern. **Pattern** is a configuration with a repeated visual form (or forms). **Natural patterns** occur all around us, in leaves and flowers, in cloud and crystal formations, in wave patterns, and so on. In natural patterns, the repeated elements may resemble each other, but not be exactly alike. The intervals between elements also may vary. The tree branches and furrows in the field in *Mr. and Mrs. Andrews* (Fig. 2.10) simulate natural pat-

terns. **Geometric patterns** have regular elements spaced at regular intervals. They are common in math, interior design, and art. The Chilkat *Blanket* (Fig. 2.16) is covered with bold patterns abstracted from human and animal forms. The eyes overall were intended as a form of protection and power.

Pattern in art is often an organizing element, as with the *Blanket,* and the extensive use of pattern makes a striking visual impression. Some patterns are totally invented, some are geometric, some contain highly abstracted forms (like the *Blanket*), and some are inherent in the materials, like wood grain.

Architectural ornamentation is the embellishment of forms or surfaces beyond structural necessity. Ornamentation, however, frequently serves an important function. It may direct your eye to certain features of a building, like entrances. Pattern can also have symbolic value. In Islamic religious architecture, like the *Great Mosque of Cordoba* (Fig. 2.17), the amazing, rich patterns express the idea that all the wonder of creation originates in Allah (see also Chapter Opener image, page 25).

As **decoration,** pattern appears on wrapping paper, wallpaper, or fabric design. Pattern's function in these instances is to give visual pleasure. Yet pattern is also

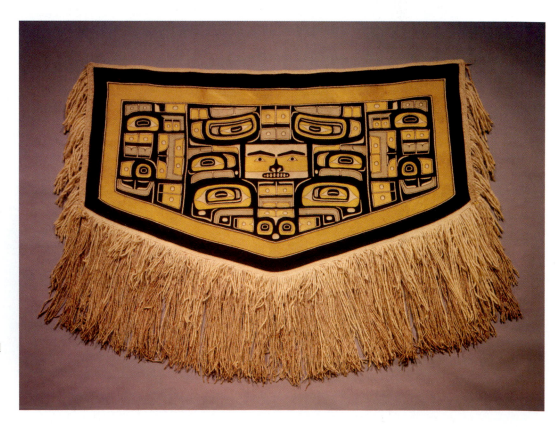

2.16 *Blanket.* Tlingit people. Chilkat style. Mountain goat wool and cedar bark, 31" × 71", excluding fringe. The Newark Museum, Newark, NJ.

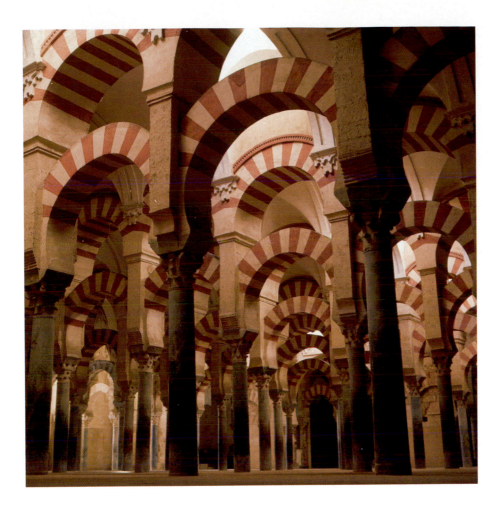

2.17 *Great Mosque of Cordoba*, interior, 786. Cordoba, Spain.

an important tool for thinking visually. Pattern helps organize ideas and concepts into visual **diagrams** that make relationships clear. Pattern is the basis of flowcharts, street maps, mechanical diagrams, and floor plans. We see patterns in the creative work of many artists, engineers, and scientists. Pattern is inherent in almost all structural systems in architecture, which is evident in the diagrams later in this chapter (pages 49–52).

SHAPE AND VOLUME

Shape is a two-dimensional visual entity. **Regular shapes** are **geometric**. We have names for many regular shapes, such as *circle, square, triangle, hexagon,* and *teardrop.* **Irregular shapes** are unique and have no simple, defining names. Instead, they are the color patches of a cat's fur, star clusters in space, or the outline of a human body. Irregular shapes are often **organic** or **biomorphic,** in that they resemble living beings. Outlines can define shapes, and so can areas of color or value changes. *They're Biting* (Fig. 2.3) contains many abstracted, biomorphic, outlined shapes.

Volume is a three-dimensional entity, in contrast to two-dimensional shape. Like shape, volumes can be regular or irregular, geometric or biomorphic. Shape and volume may simulate reality, may be abstracted from reality, or may be invented. Martin Puryear's *That Profile* (Fig. 2.18) is a regular volume but its name suggests that it is abstracted from a biomorphic form. Volumes may have more or less physical bulk, or **mass.** An open or wire-frame structure, like *That Profile,* can have a large volume but little mass. A more solid, blocklike piece has both mass and volume, as the *Lion Capital* (Fig. 2.14).

Shape and volume are key elements in architecture. Look at the buildings around you. What are their predominant shapes? What volumes do they enclose? How much mass do the structures have? What spaces surround them?

SPACE

In this section, we will look at three kinds of space in relation to art: (1) the space in two-dimensional artwork; (2) the space of sculpture and architecture,

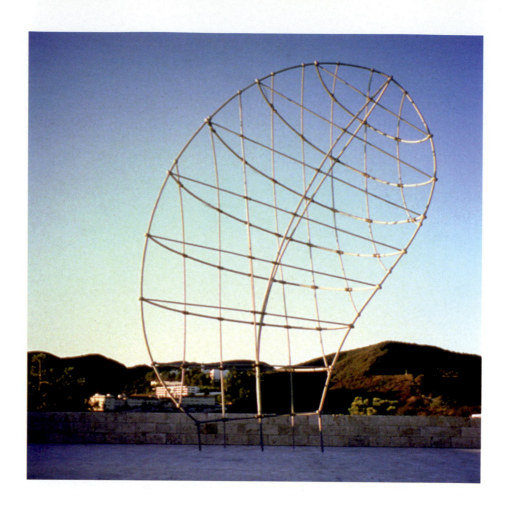

2.18 MARTIN PURYEAR. *That Profile,* 1997–1999. Stainless steel, bronze, 540" × 360" × 136". Getty Museum, Los Angeles.

which is both the area it occupies and the voids it contains; and (3) the space of performance art, installation, and inter-media work.

First, space in two-dimensional art: All two-dimensional art has is **planar space,** the height and width of the picture surface. In *They're Biting* (Fig. 2.3), the fish, boat, and fishermen are distributed across the height and width of the picture plane. Yet, artists can create the illusion of deep space on the flat surface of two-dimensional art. Overlapping imagery and placement on the page are two simple ways. Again, in *They're Biting,* the fish at the bottom of the picture seem closer than the boat and buoy near the top. And the boat and buoy themselves are pushed forward because they overlap the horizon, which then is moved back.

More complex illusions of space are created through **perspective,** a group of methods for creating the illusion of depth on a flat picture plane. **Atmospheric perspective** (or **aerial perspective**) refers to the light, bleached out, fuzzy handling of distant forms to make them seem far away. We have already seen two works that illustrate atmospheric perspective: (1) Durer's *Artist drawing a model* (Fig. 2.4), where foreground shapes

are bold and heavily shaded, versus the light, linear handling of the distant landscape; and (2) *Mr. and Mrs. Andrews* (Fig. 2.10), where the distant landscape is less colorful and less detailed.

Another kind of perspective is **linear perspective,** which operates on the theory that parallel lines appear to converge as they recede. They seem to meet on an imaginary line called the **horizon line,** or at eye level. The horizon line corresponds to the viewer's eye level in a picture, determining what the viewer perceives as "above" or "below."

The three types of linear perspective—one-, two-, and three-point—are shown in the diagram in Figure 2.19. In **one-point perspective,** the frontal plane of a volume is closest to the viewer, and all other planes appear to recede to a single vanishing point. In **two-point perspective,** a single edge (or line) of a volume is closest to the viewer, and all planes appear to recede to one of two vanishing points. In **three-point perspective,** only a single point of a volume is closest to the viewer, and all planes seem to recede to one of three vanishing points. Figure 2.4, *Artist drawing a model,* is a precise exercise in one-point perspective. Giovanni Battista

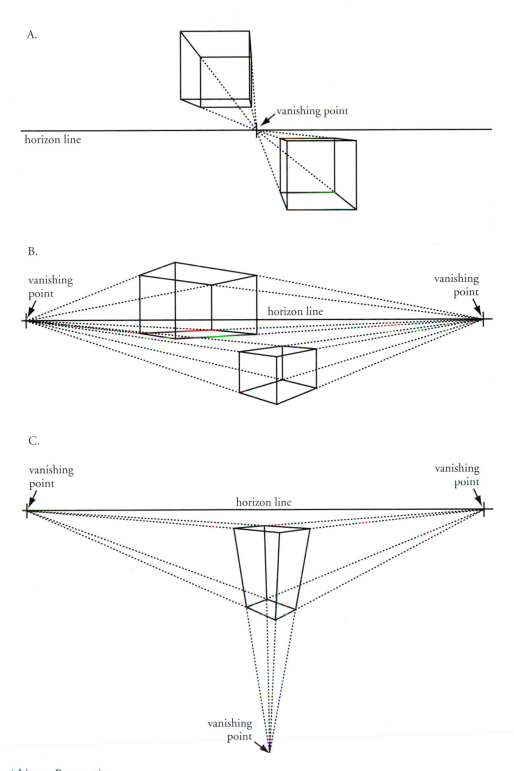

A.

vanishing point

horizon line

B.

vanishing
point

vanishing
point

horizon line

C.

vanishing
point

vanishing
point

horizon line

vanishing
point

2.19   Diagram of Linear Perspective.

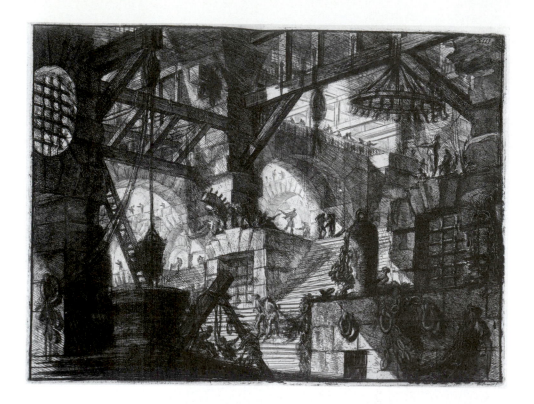

2.20 GIOVANNI BATTISTA PIRANESI. *Prisons, p. XIII.* c. 1760. Etching, 21½" × 16⅓". Giraudon /Art Resource, NY

Piranesi's *Prisons, p. XIII* (Fig. 2.20) is an example of two-point perspective. In this case, the eye level of the viewer is set very low, so that the architecture overwhelms and looms large.

Two other systems to show space in a picture are isometric perspective and oblique perspective. **Isometric perspective,** which is especially used in architectural drafting, renders planes on a diagonal that does not recede in space (Fig. 2.21A). The side planes are drawn at a thirty-degree angle to the left and right. In **oblique perspective,** a three-dimensional object is rendered with the front and back parallel (Fig. 2.21B). The side planes are drawn at a forty-five-degree angle from the front plane. Figure 2.22 is *Festivities,* a detail of a screen

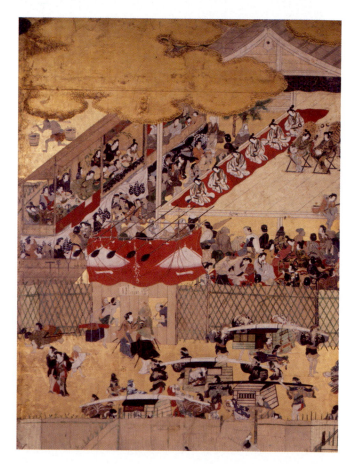

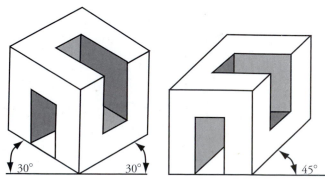

2.21 A. An example of an ISOMETRIC projection. B. An example of an OBLIQUE projection.

2.22 *Festivities,* detail of a screen depicting the popular festivities that took place at Shijo-gawa, Kyoto. Late Muromachi period, 16th century. Seikado Library, Tokyo.

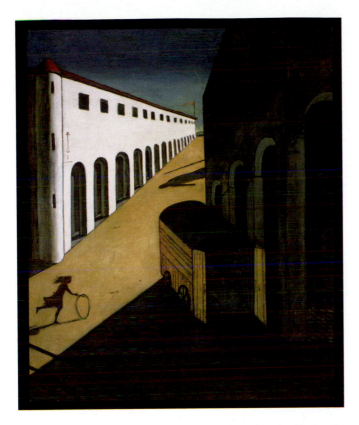

2.23   GIORGIO DE CHIRICO. *The Mystery and Melancholy of a Street*, 1914. Oil on canvas, 34 ¼" × 13½". Private collection.

empty space that the framework contains, and the back-drop of the sky and landscape that it activates. The voids and solids in Louise Nevelson's *Mirror Image I* (Fig. 2.9) create a rhythmic dance of dark shapes and even darker voids.

Finally, space in installation or performance art can be particularly significant, because such artwork may draw part of its meaning from its environment. Huang Yong Ping's installation, *Bat Project I (Shenzhen)*, 2001 (Fig. 2.24), is a replica of a U.S. spy plane that collided with a Chinese plane in April 2001 and had to land in China, which caused an international furor. Huang's reconstruction of the back half of the plane was to be exhibited as part of a major international exhibition amid skyscrapers in the city of Shenzhen. Before the installation was finished, the replica was removed without the artist's permission because officials feared that it might damage international relations between the

depicting popular festivities from the Muromachi period. Oblique perspective is used to depict the architecture and people behind the fence, under the cloud.

Artists may use **multipoint perspective** in an image, where they employ many different systems for various details all in the same drawing. They also may use amplified or distorted perspective to give their imagery dramatic emphasis. In *The Mystery and Melancholy of a Street*, 1914 (Fig. 2.23), Giorgio de Chirico used different horizon lines and vanishing points for the white building on the left and the dark structure to the right, to give a sense of the fractured space of a dream or a memory. He has also used extreme perspectival views, so that the white building seems to stretch far into space, while the other one leans down dramatically into the earth.

Now, let us turn to space in sculpture and architecture, which of course consists of the footprint occupied by the structure. But it also encompasses the voids and solids within each piece and immediately surrounding it. Look again at Martin Puryear's *That Profile* (Fig. 2.18), which is so memorable because of the large

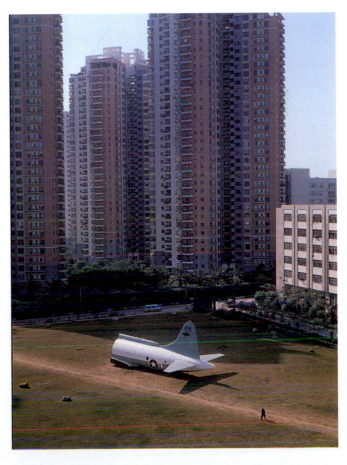

2.24   HUANG YONG PING. *Bat Project I (Shenzhen)*, 2001. Replica of an American spy plane from middle of body to tail. China.

United States, China, and France (a sponsor of the exhibition). It was later installed (again without the artist's knowledge) as a permanent feature in an amusement park. Thus, the impact of the same piece of art, which was too sensational for a major exhibition, was neutralized by the amusement park location.

TIME AND MOTION

A lot of art is static; it does not move. Yet time and motion can still be important elements. **Time** is the period that viewers study and absorb the message and formal qualities of an artwork. Motion can be implied, as in Marcel Duchamp's *Nude Descending a Staircase*

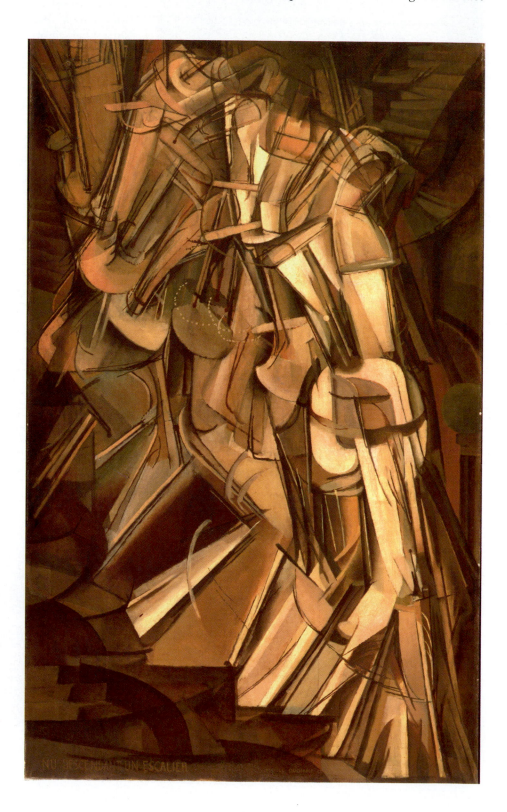

2.25 MARCEL DUCHAMP. *Nude Descending a Staircase (No. 2)*, 1912. Oil on canvas, 57⁷/₈" × 35¹/₈" (147 × 89.2 cm). The Louise and Walter Arensberg Collection, Philadelphia Museum of Art, Philadelphia.

(No. 2), from 1912 (Fig. 2.25). Factors that contribute to its illusion of motion are (1) the rhythmic repetition of abstracted forms in a walking pattern, and (2) the descending arrangement of elements from the upper left down to the lower right.

However, motion is integral to film/video, interactive digital art, kinetic sculpture, and performance. In these works, time and motion are related, as motion cannot exist without time, and motion marks the passage of time. Cai Guo-Qiang's *Black Rainbow: Explosion Project for Valencia, Spain,* 2005 (Fig. 2.26) is one of a series that occurs in cities such as Edinburgh and Beijing. These black rainbows were intended as omens of international unease, and although violence and explosive materials are frightening, they can also attract with their power and beauty. In a matter of mere min-

utes, the loud explosions are set off and black smoke appears in the sky, spreads into a rainbow-like arc, and then dissipates.

With architecture and large sculpture, we cannot grasp all their features in an instant, from a single point of view. These works unfold in time as we move through them or around them. For example, a traveler first sees the Ajanta Caves as doorways and porches carved into a curving hillside in west central India. This modest outside view does not prepare the viewer for the amazing *Ceiling of Cave 26* in a darkened, columned hall with a shrine to Buddha, all cut out of the living rock (Fig. 2.27). Yet even more unfolds in time and with the viewer's motion. To one side in Cave 26 is *Parinirvana* (Fig. 2.28), or a sculpture of the death of Buddha, behind a row of columns.

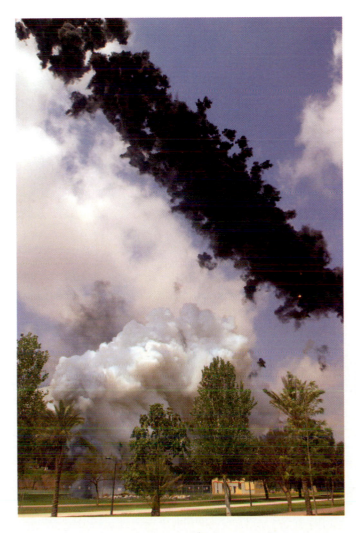

2.26　CAI GUO-QIANG. *Black Rainbow: Explosion Project for Valencia, Spain,* 2005.

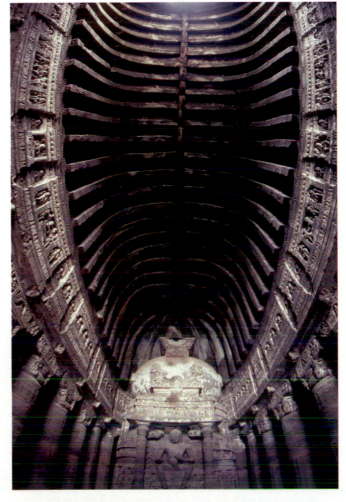

2.27　View of the *Ceiling of Cave 26,* one of the many caves at Ajanta dating back to 700 AD. Maharashtra, India. See Figure 2.28 for another view of the cave interior.

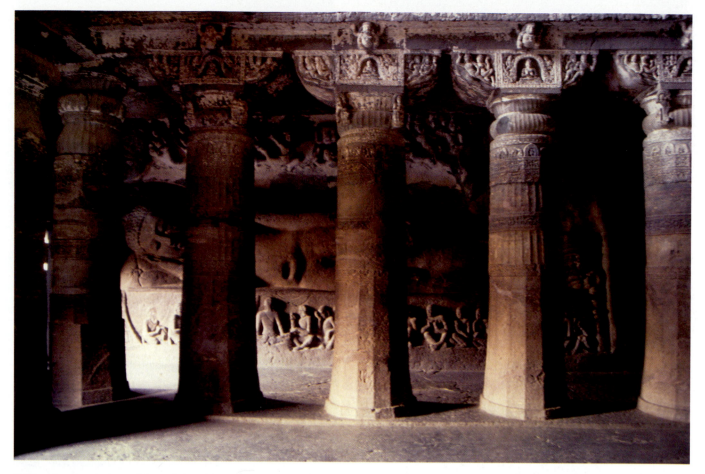

2.28   A second view of Cave 26 at Ajanta. *Parinirvana* between the columns. Cave 26 (chaitya hall). Late 5th century. Ajanta Caves, Maharashtra, India.

CHANCE/IMPROVISATION/ SPONTANEITY

Many artists purposely allow for chance, improvisation, or spontaneity, to add something unexpected in their work or to make it unique each time it is seen. Some aspects of chance are due to uncontrollable factors, such as atmospheric conditions at the moment that Cai Guo-Qiang's *Black Rainbows* explode into the sky. Other artists embrace chance and weave it into the very form of the work.

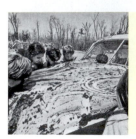

Connection *Allan Kaprow's Household (Fig. 16.21) was a Happening performed by several men and women, who worked from a simple premise but were free to improvise as the performance unfolded.*

ENGAGING ALL THE SENSES

Although we tend to think of art in visual terms, many artworks appeal to other senses as well. Cai Guo-Qiang's explosions are one obvious example. The *Ajanta Caves* stimulate sound, smell, temperature and visual sensations. Film, video, interactive digital art, and performance have sound components to accompany the visual.

African masquerades are art forms that incorporate art objects, singing, dancing, and community celebrations and rituals. The *Bwa Masqueraders* of Burkina Faso (Fig. 2.29) disguise their identities with masks and raffia costumes. Their performances bring spirits among the people, promote community well-being, and ensure good crops and other necessities. Masks are not considered static sculptures but are integral parts of the larger masquerade art form.

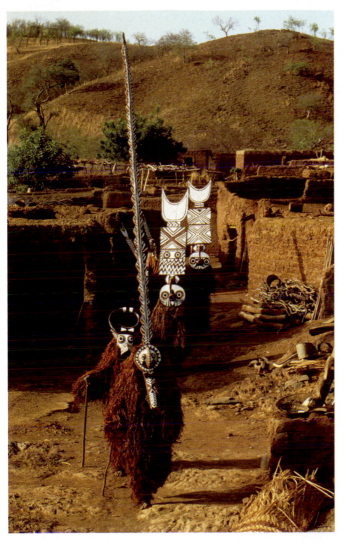

2.29 *Bwa Masqueraders.* Burkina Faso.

PRINCIPLES OF COMPOSITION

The arrangement of the formal elements in a work of art is called its **composition.** As artists compose a work, they employ the principles of composition: balance, rhythm, proportion and scale, emphasis, unity, and variety.

BALANCE

Balance in an artwork results from placing the elements so that their visual weights seem evenly distributed. *Weight* generally means the amount of attention an element commands from the viewer. For example, large shapes demand more attention than small; complex forms have greater visual weight than simple ones; and vivid colors are visually weightier than faded colors. In **symmetrical balance,** visual weight is distributed evenly throughout the composition. If an imaginary line is drawn vertically down the center of the work, one side would mirror the other, as in the Chilkat *Blanket* (Fig. 2.16). **Asymmetrical balance** is achieved by the careful distribution of uneven elements. In *The Mystery and Melancholy of a Street* (Fig. 2.23), the bright and dark areas are approximately balanced around a central vertical axis. **Radial balance** results when all the elements in the composition visually radiate outward from a central point. Radial balance is often an organizing principle in spiritually based art, featured in mandalas, church windows, temple plans, and mosque domes. The magnificent *Angkor Wat* temple in Cambodia is laid out in a modified radial plan (Fig. 2.30).

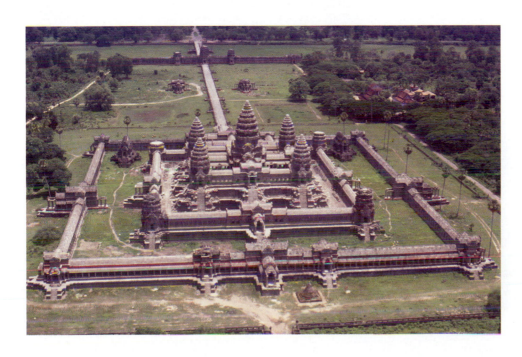

2.30 *Angkor Wat,* Central Temple Complex, c. 1113–1150 CE. Cambodia.

RHYTHM

In a composition, **rhythm** is the repetition of carefully placed elements separated by intervals. These recurrent visual "beats" move the viewer's eye through the composition in jerky, smooth, fast, or slow ways. Rhythm is related to pattern, but it affects the entire composition.

Regular rhythm is smooth and even, where some visual element is systematically repeated with a standard interval in between. Closely related is **alternating rhythm**, where different elements are repeatedly placed side by side, which produces a regular and anticipated sequence. In architecture, rhythm is often alternating solids and voids. **Eccentric rhythm** is irregular, but not so much so that the visual beats do not connect. In the bas-relief of the *Churning of the Ocean of Milk,* from Angkor Wat (Fig. 2.31), we see examples of regular rhythm (the heads), alternating rhythm (the legs), and eccentric rhythm (the dancing spirits overhead). The relief shows an eternal, cosmic struggle in which demons and gods churn the ocean for precious things that have been lost. The visual repetition is a fitting expression for this rhythmic physical struggle.

PROPORTION AND SCALE

Proportion refers to the size of one part in relation to another within a work of art, or the size of one part in relation to the whole. The small dancers at the top of *Churning of the Ocean of Milk* are proportionally much smaller than the larger figures below. For another example of proportion, return to the *Bwa Masqueraders* to see how large the masks are in relation to the dancers' bodies and, even within the masks, the size relationship between the face area and the elaborate forms above them.

Scale is the size of something in relation to what we assume to be "normal." Figure 2.32 shows a real scale shift upward with cars driving through *The Binocular Entrance to the Chiat Building* (sculpture by Claes Oldenburg and Coosje van Bruggen; architect, Frank O. Gehry).

Proportion and scale are expressive devices. The *Binocular Entrance* is meant to be dramatic, memorable, and humorous. The tall sculptural forms on the masks of the *Bwa Masqueraders* suggest their otherworldly power. **Hieratic scaling** is a device that points

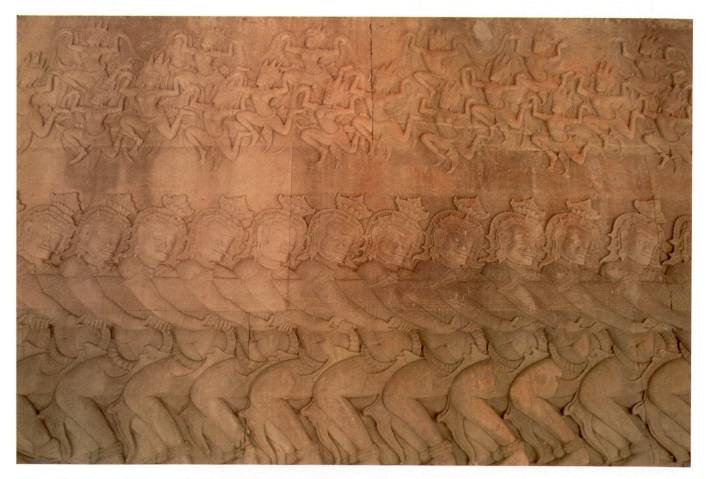

2.31 *Churning of the Ocean of Milk.* Bas-relief. Angkor Wat. Cambodia.

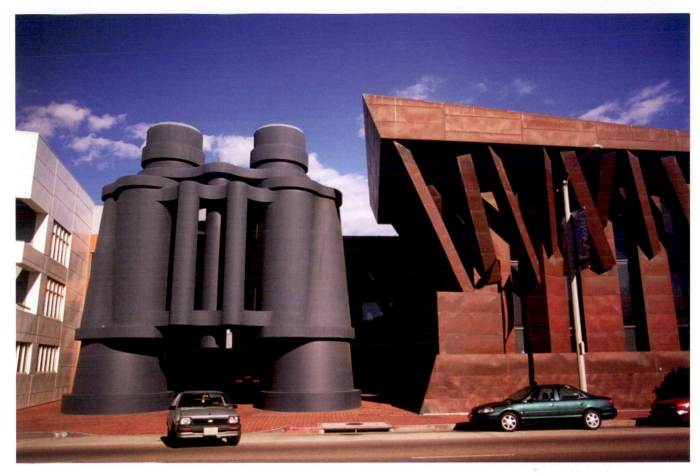

2.32   CLAES OLDENBURG, COOSJE VAN BRUGGEN, and FRANK O. GEHRY. *The Binocular Entrance to the Chiat Building,* 1985–1991. Venice, California.

to the highest-ranking person in the scene, as in *Parinirvana* (Fig. 2.28) where the reclining Buddha is enormous compared to all other figures around him. Scale in architecture is its overall size in relation to the human body, which also has expressive potential. Large-scale buildings dwarf and overwhelm people, while small buildings often seem comfortable to the individual.

In real life, most people see art in reproductions. But then scale can be very uncertain, with no way of knowing how large an artwork actually is. Reading the caption gives you some information, but you have to exert your imagination to really "see" the piece. This chapter contains several reproductions of paintings. Can you remember which was the largest: *Shoki the Demon Queller* (Fig. 2.2); *They're Biting* (Fig. 2.3); *Mr. and Mrs. Andrews* (Fig. 2.10); *Festivities* (Fig. 2.22); *Nude Descending a Staircase* (Fig. 2.25)?

EMPHASIS

Emphasis is the creation of one or more focal points in an artwork. When there are several focal points, lesser ones are called **accents**. In Figure 2.25, *Nude Descending a Staircase,* the lightest tones are the most emphasized. Emphasis in architecture means that one part of a building becomes a focal point. Architects often use ornamentation for emphasis. The *Binocular Entrance* is obviously the focal point on that building.

UNITY AND VARIETY

Unity is the quality of overall cohesion within an artwork. **Variety** is the element of difference within an artwork. They would seem on the surface to be mutually exclusive qualities, but, in fact, they coexist in all artworks, evoking in viewers a fascination that makes them keep coming back and keep looking. In *Nude Descending a Staircase,* unity is achieved with the brown palette, and also with the shapes, which are simplified geometric versions of the human body. Variety is introduced in the illusion of movement and the changes in lighting.

In architecture, unity is the quality that makes the disparate architectural parts coalesce, while variety adds opposing elements to buildings. It is interesting to see how architects use nature to create variety in their designs. House plants add variety to the interior, while planter beds and gardens relieve the austerity of the exterior. Within neighborhoods, rows of houses are juxtaposed with greenbelts and parks.

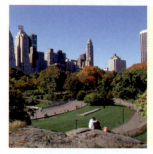

Connection *An extreme example of variety is the density of Manhattan relieved by the expansiveness of New York City's Central Park, designed by landscape architects Frederick Law Olmsted and Calvert Vaux (Fig. 16.6, page 436).*

STRUCTURAL SYSTEMS IN ARCHITECTURE

So far in this chapter, we have studied formal elements and principles of composition that apply to both art and architecture. Now we turn to structural systems, which apply to architecture only. Structural systems enable buildings to stand up and enclose space, using materials like brick, stone, wood, steel, and concrete.

Structural systems and materials strongly influence the design and visual appearance of buildings.

TRADITIONAL BUILDING METHODS

Load-Bearing Construction

Early architecture was made of shaped earth, bones, wood, or stacked stone. Builders used whatever materials were locally available. The igloo made of ice blocks is one example. Ancient houses in China were dug right out of the earth. In many places, people stacked material to create solid walls that were usually thicker at the bottom to provide stability. Early roofs were often lightweight, impermanent material like reeds or thatch, as in the sun-dried brick structures in the ancient Near East. This kind of architecture is called "load bearing" because all areas of the walls support the structure above them, and the walls have few openings.

An extreme example of a load-bearing structure is *El Castillo*, a Mayan pyramid and temple at Chichén Itzá, in Mexico (Fig. 2.33). The pyramid base is almost solid, with only a steep, claustrophobic tunnel inside that runs from the ground to the top. The small stone

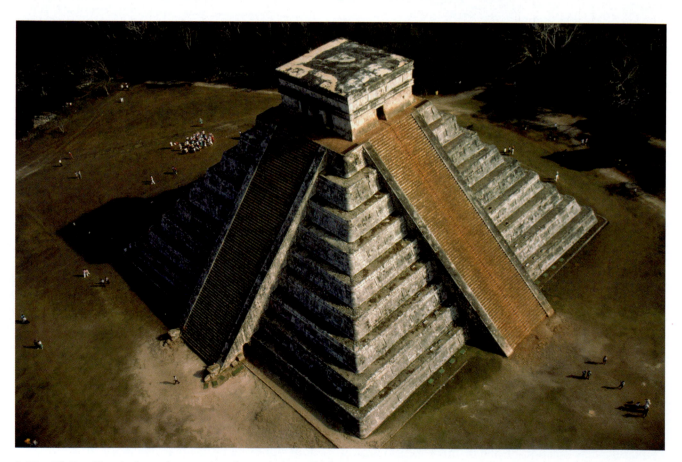

2.33 *El Castillo*, ninth–tenth centuries, elevated view. Chichén Itzá, Mexico.

structure on top has thick walls with small doorways, a necessity given the weight of the roof above.

However, since ancient times, people have made the aesthetic decision to have air and light in their buildings. The rest of this section looks at ways to open up structures and to make this possible.

Post-and-Lintel Construction

One ancient method of constructing walls, making openings, and supporting a roof is the **post-and-lintel system.** The basic module is two upright posts supporting a cross beam or lintel (Fig. 2.34). Posts can be either rectangular or cylindrical. Refined and decorated cylindrical posts are called **columns,** and a row of columns supporting lintels is called a **colonnade.** A grid of posts and lintels can support the roof of a large inte-

rior space (Fig. 2.34). This is **hypostyle** construction, marked by rooms filled with columns.

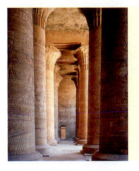

Connection *An example of a hypostyle hall is the* First Hypostyle Hall *at the Horus Temple at Edfu, Egypt (Fig. 9.32, page 229). The thick columns support a stone roof.*

Post-and-lintel structures are often rectilinear, with prominent vertical and horizontal lines, as evident in *The Temple of Athena Nike,* on the Acropolis in Athens, Greece (Fig. 2.35). The construction materials

BASIC POST-AND-LINTEL MODULE
Arrows indicate the downward distribution of weight

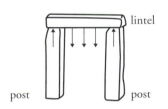

COLONNADE

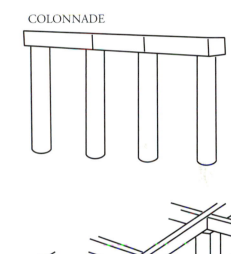

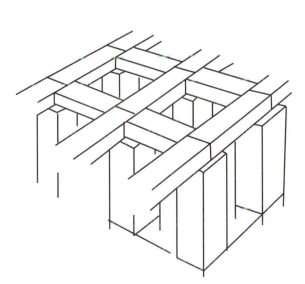

GRID OF POST-AND-LINTEL MODULES, IN STONE
Many interior posts are needed to support the stone lintels

2.34   Diagram Showing Post-and-Lintel Construction.

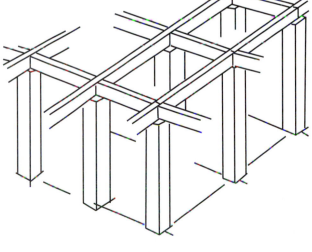

GRID OF POST-AND-LINTEL MODULES, WITH WOOD LINTELS
Fewer posts are needed, and longer lintels are possible

are important. Stone is durable, but heavy and brittle, so stone lintels need closely spaced supports. Wood, however, is light, flexible, and strong, and able to span great distances, so larger interior spaces can be opened up, and the posts can be thinned down. Of course, ancient wood buildings are long gone, while stone ones remain. The relative impermanence of wood and its ability to burn are its greatest drawbacks.

Important subcategories of post-and-lintel architecture are the Classical Greek and Roman architectural orders (Fig. 2.36). An order consists of a specifically designed column with a **base**, a **shaft**, a **capital**, and an **entablature**, all exhibiting standardized proportions and decorative ornamentation. The oldest is the **Doric Order**, originating in the Greek Archaic period (650–500 BCE). The simple design is geometric, heavy, and relatively without ornamentation. Its column has no base, and its capital is a simple cushion. The ancient Greeks considered the Doric Order to exhibit masculine qualities. The temple porch on the *Propylaea*, to the left in Fig-

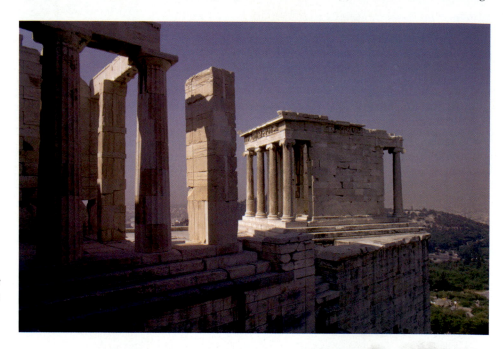

2.35 MNESICLES. The *Temple of Athena Nike* (right) and the corner of *Propylaea* (left), 437–432 BC. Athens.

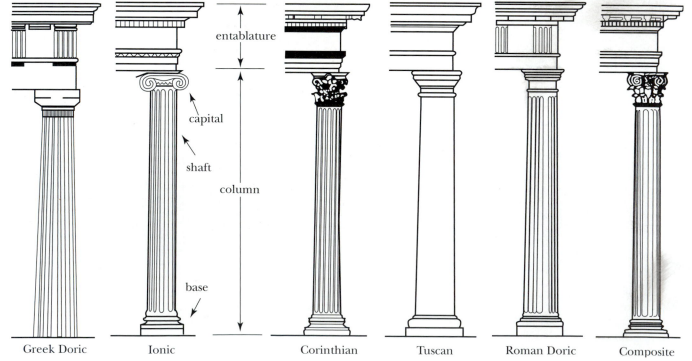

| Greek Doric | Ionic | | Corinthian | Tuscan | Roman Doric | Composite |

entablature

capital

shaft

column

base

2.36 Diagram of Greek and Roman Orders.

ure 2.35, is a Doric structure. The second order to appear was the **Ionic Order,** which is taller, more slender, and more decorative than the Doric, and was considered feminine. It has a stepped base and a scrolled, carved capital. It originated during the Greek Classical (Hellenic) period (500–323 BCE). *The Temple of Athena Nike* (Fig. 2.35 on the right) is Ionic. Later still was the **Corinthian Order,** which is the most complex and organic, with delicately carved acanthus leaves on its capital, dating from the Hellenistic period (323–100 BCE). Roman variations on those orders are Tuscan, Roman Doric, and Composite.

Wood Frame Construction

Wood frame architecture is very common in the East and the West. Wood frames have been used in the West especially for houses and small apartment buildings, and many feature load-bearing walls and trusses (see page 55).

The Chinese developed a distinctive wood frame architecture, based on the post-and-lintel model. This is the **complete frame system,** which contained these innovations: (1) totally non-load-bearing walls, (2) brackets, and (3) cantilevers. All the weight of the entire building was borne by large upright posts. Walls could be completely eliminated.

In the fifth century BCE, the Chinese developed **brackets,** which are clusters of interlocking pieces of wood shaped like inverted pyramids at the tops of upright posts, directly beneath the roof (Fig. 2.37). With brackets, fewer posts are needed, allowing for more spacious interiors. Two centuries later, the Chinese developed half-cylinder, overlapping roof tiles. Their considerable weight adds stability to the wood frame structure below, and they could be glazed different colors.

Beginning in the eighth century CE, Chinese architects first used the **cantilever,** a horizontal beam anchored to and projecting out from an upright post (Fig. 2.37). Cantilevers support deep roof eaves and balconies.

The roof design is often the most important and distinctive feature of significant historical Chinese

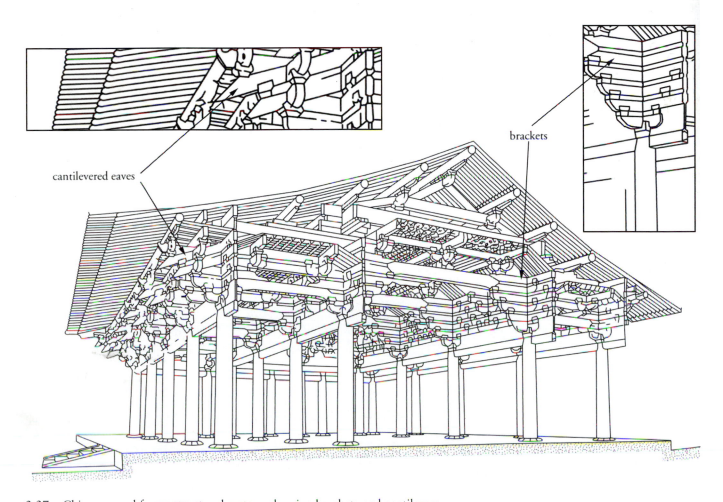

cantilevered eaves

brackets

2.37   Chinese wood frame structural system, showing brackets and cantilevers.

buildings. Supported by cantilevers, the roofs project away from the building, with shapes that incorporate very complex curves. Brackets are outlined and painted in bright colors.

Arches, Vaulting, and Domes

Stone would have limited use as a building material due to its weight and brittle nature were it not for the **arch** (Fig. 2.38), a structural innovation that dates back to ancient Egypt. The arch is made of wedge-shaped stones or **voussoirs** that are constructed from bottom to top, using a wooden scaffold for support. When the final **keystone** is placed in the center, the arch can support itself and the scaffolding can be removed. Arches can rest either on rectangular **piers** or on cylindrical columns, as we saw in the *Great Mosque of Cordoba* (Fig. 2.17).

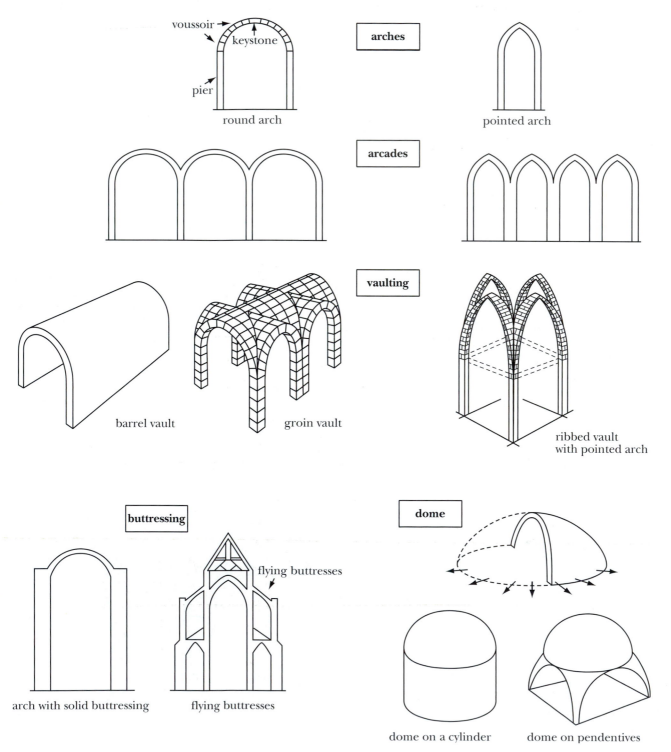

2.38   Diagram Showing Arches, Arcades, Vaulting, Buttressing, and Domes.

Arches can be either round or pointed (Fig. 2.38). With a round arch, the distance between the supports determines the height of the arch, because the arch is a semicircle. A pointed arch is actually a round arch with some of the center removed. Builders can make a pointed arch higher or lower, regardless of the distance between its supports. A straight row of arches placed side by side is called an **arcade.**

Unlike post-and-lintel structures in which the weight of the roof and lintel press down equally on all parts below, the weight of the arch is directed outward and then downward to the load-bearing columns or piers. There is no downward pressure over the void of the arch, and so higher and larger spaces can be spanned without need for additional support posts. Arches can be constructed of stone, brick, or concrete. Arches, however, do have to be supported from the outside to prevent lateral movement that would cause them to collapse. That support is called **buttressing** (Fig. 2.38), which is additional exterior masonry placed at key points to keep the arch stable. Buttresses can be solid

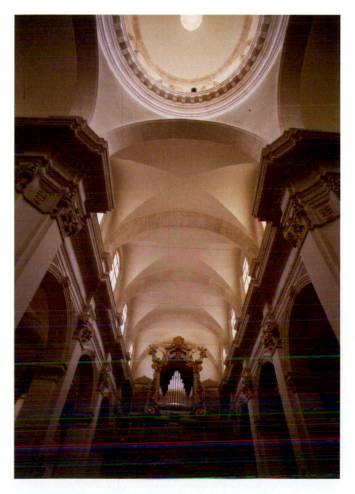

2.39 ANDREA BUFFALINI. *Cathedral of Dubrovnik: Nave Groin Vault.* Construction finished in 1713. Dubrovnik, Croatia.

masonry, or they may be opened up with their own internal arches, called **flying buttresses.**

Builders can expand and multiply the arch in a number of ways to create entire roofs made of stone. These stone roofs are called **vaults,** or **vaulting,** and are very durable and fireproof (Fig. 2.38).

A **barrel vault** is an arch extended in depth from front to back, forming a tunnel-like structure. Barrel vaults have the disadvantage of creating rather dark interiors, as there are no windows in the vault area (Fig. 2.38). **Groin vaults,** sometimes called **cross vaults,** are barrel vaults positioned at ninety-degree angles to cross or intersect one another. This innovation allowed light to enter vaulted spaces and gave variation to the interior space, as seen in the *Cathedral of Dubrovnik: Nave Groin Vault* (Fig. 2.39).

A **ribbed vault** (see Fig. 2.38) is a variation of the groin vaulting system in which arches diagonally cross over the groin vault, forming skeletal ribs. Pointing the arch in the ribbed vault creates a **gothic vault.** Used commonly in the Gothic era in Europe, this innovation allowed builders to eliminate large wall areas under arches and to fill the resulting space with gleaming stained glass.

A **dome** theoretically is an arch rotated on its vertical axis to form a hemispheric vault. Domes can rest on a circular drum, or they can be placed on **pendentives,** which are the triangular concave sections created when a dome is placed on arches. Domes may also be placed on a square or a polygonal base, in which case the spaces created between the dome and its base are called **squinches.** A dome is visible at the top of Figure 2.39, the *Cathedral of Dubrovnik.*

Vaulted or domed buildings are generally quite massive because of the material used to make them— stone, brick, or concrete. Vaults are very heavy structures and require thick supports. In many cases, architects disguise the massiveness of vaulted structures by placing buttresses on the exterior, out of sight of those enjoying the view of the interior. In the *Cathedral of Dubrovnik*, the plain, bright, airy vaults above contrast with the gray, heavy-looking arcade below.

RECENT METHODS AND MATERIALS

Modern buildings differ from older structures in many ways. New materials, especially steel and steel-reinforced concrete, have resulted in structures taller than anything ever built before the nineteenth century. Like the human body, many modern buildings feature an internal skeletal support system. The outer surface of the wall is like a skin stretched over the bones.

Our expectations of "basic" comforts have changed, too, so now buildings have a variety of operating systems, such as heating and cooling systems, electricity, plumbing, and telephone and computer wiring, as well as appliances, intercoms, and surveillance systems. Two hundred years ago, this was all unknown.

Steel Frame Construction

High-strength structural steel was developed in the late nineteenth century and, with the invention of the elevator, made very tall buildings possible for the first time. **Steel frame construction** essentially expands the post-and-lintel grid vertically as well as laterally, with steel (instead of wood or stone), which can function as a skeleton that will support multistoried buildings (Fig. 2.40). Floors are usually poured concrete with embedded metal reinforcing bars.

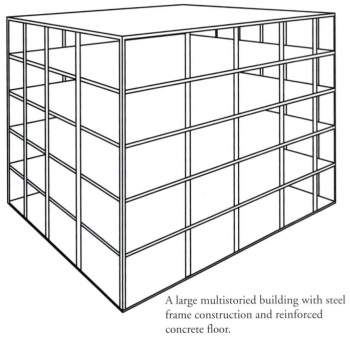

A large multistoried building with steel frame construction and reinforced concrete floor.

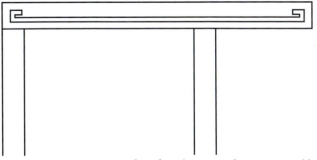

Diagram of reinforced concrete showing a metal bar embedded in concrete. This diagram shows a reinforced concrete floor with a cantilevered balcony.

2.40   Diagram of Steel Frame Construction and Reinforced Concrete.

At first, steel frame construction was disguised with stone facings so that buildings looked traditional, rugged, and durable. By 1900, however, the simple horizontal and vertical lines of steel frame construction were emphasized and apparent. Windows were opened up and big, reaching from framing member to framing member. Steel frame construction has been widely used ever since for all kinds of structures, but especially the high-rise office buildings that filled the downtowns of major cities all over the world from the mid- to late twentieth century, like the *Seagram Building at Night* (Fig. 2.41), designed by Ludwig Mies van der Rohe and completed in 1958. Called the **International Style,** these stripped-down, glass-covered, rectangular box buildings were enormously popular throughout the world. This image shows the Seagram Building nearing completion, and the appeal of the style is immediately apparent: the building is luminous and dramatic compared to the older structures around it. The skeletal structure is visible, and both horizontality and verticality are emphasized. International Style buildings generally had no ornamentation at all. Some critics have argued against the widespread, homogenizing use of the International Style in cities across the world, because many, many older structures were demolished, and they had given many civic centers their distinct character.

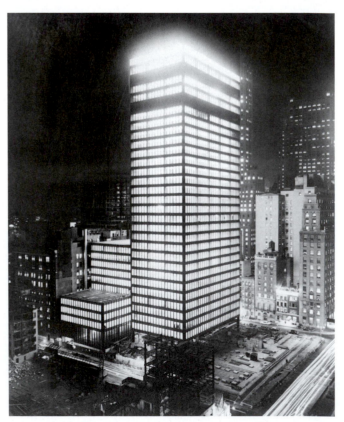

2.41   *Seagram Building at Night,* 1954–1958. New York City.

Reinforced Concrete

Another building innovation that resulted from the development of high-strength structural steel was **reinforced concrete,** also known as ferroconcrete. Concrete was used by the Romans, but it is brittle and cracks easily. Ferroconcrete—steel reinforcing bars embedded in wet concrete—gives the concrete tensile strength, while the concrete provides a durable surface. Reinforced concrete was used for the floors of skyscrapers from their early days.

Gradually, architects began using reinforced concrete as an external building material for the finished surfaces of buildings. Concrete can be poured over steel reinforcing rods or mesh that can be shaped into any form the architect wishes. It makes possible free-form architecture, which places no limitations on the shape and mass of a structure.

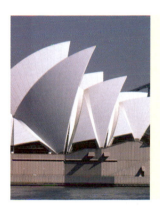

Connection *Three famous examples of reinforced concrete structures appear in this book: Le Corbusier's* Notre Dame du Haut *(Fig. 9.27, page 223), the* Solomon R. Guggenheim Museum *(Fig. 16.3, page 434) and the* Sydney Opera House *(thumbnail, and also Fig. 16.2, page 433).*

Truss and Geodesic Construction

Another skeletal structure, the **truss,** is based on a frame made of a series of triangles constructed in steel or wood (Fig. 2.42A). Trusses are very rigid because of the triangle and can be used to span great spaces or to support other structures. Steel trusses are common on railroad bridges, and wooden trusses can be found in the attics of most frame homes in the United States.

The geodesic dome (Fig. 2.42B) is a skeletal frame based on triangles that are grouped into very stable, strong polyhedrons, which are solid geometric figures having many faces and are found in nature. Geodesic domes can be very large, and they require no interior supports. Builders can easily assemble the skeletal frame from prefabricated modular parts. The framework can be sheathed in glass, plastic, plywood, or a variety of other materials.

The triangles of truss or geodesic structures may be left visible when buildings are finished. In these cases, the buildings have a pronounced geometric appearance. The linear network of the truss skeleton thus becomes an important visual feature.

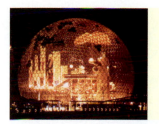

Connection *R. Buckminster Fuller's U.S. Pavilion (Fig. 7.33, page 163) was an enormous example of a geodesic dome.*

Suspension and Tensile Construction

Suspension and tensile construction consists of steel cables attached to vertical pylons or masts that can support structures like bridges, exhibition tents, or sport arenas. The *Olympic Stadium, Munich* (Fig 2.43), designed by Gunter Behnisch with Otto Frei, was part of a vast sports complex with peaked roofs that recall the mountains of the nearby Alps. Computers were used to assist in designing roof shapes and supports and in determining how the structure would react in weather conditions. Nothing before had been undertaken at this scale, with this type of construction. In this case, a cable net attached to vertical masts holds up the PVC-coated polyester roof. Otto Frei was a pioneer in lightweight design.

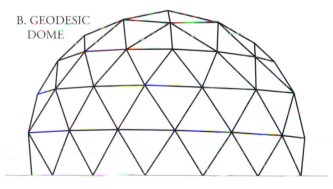

A. TRUSSES

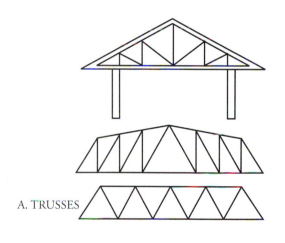

B. GEODESIC DOME

2.42   Truss (A) and Geodesic Dome (B) Structural Systems.

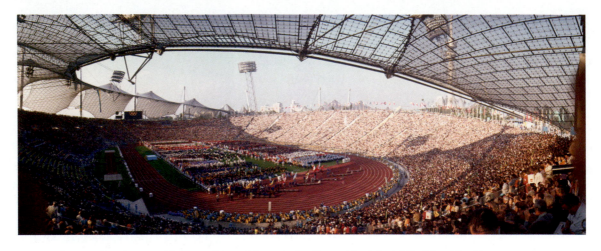

2.43   GUNTER BEHNISCH with OTTO FREI. *Olympic Stadium, Munich*, 1972. Munich, Germany.

SYNOPSIS

The elements of art are line, light and value, color, texture and pattern, shape and volume, space, time and motion, and chance, improvisation, and spontaneity. The principles of composition are balance, rhythm, proportion and scale, emphasis, unity, and variety. Some artworks engage senses other than just the visual.

Common structural systems in traditional buildings include load-bearing walls; post-and-lintel architecture; wood frame construction; and arches, vaulting, and domes. Recent innovations in materials or structural systems include steel frame buildings, reinforced concrete structures, truss and geodesic construction, and, finally, suspension and tensile construction.

FOOD FOR THOUGHT

You now have the necessary tools to formally analyze any artwork or building, which means identifying the important visual elements and determining how they have been combined. The following questions serve as guides:

- *What elements appear in this work: line, light and value, color, shape and volume, texture and pattern, space, time and motion, and chance, improvisation, and spontaneity?*

- *Which elements are dominant? Are the lesser elements important?*

- *How do the elements of the art piece work together, or do they not work together? What principles of composition are employed?*

- *Does the work evoke thoughts or emotions? If it does, what formal elements add to the effect?*

- *How do the media and materials contribute to the work?*

On a different topic, indigenous people around the world have produced all kinds of unique buildings, using locally available materials and responding to local conditions. Just a few examples are igloos of Alaska, native wood and thatch houses in Indonesia, and adobe homes in Peru. Now, indigenous housing styles are being replaced with more standard Western models, using nonrenewable imported materials, with higher energy costs associated with central air conditioning and heating. In addition, the uniformity of style has represented a cultural loss.

Increasingly, architects are being called upon to create buildings that are more energy efficient and responsive to the local conditions in which they are placed. Research some new developments in this field.

Your Thomson Online Resources

  Go to **ArtExperience Online** for the Flashcards, Quiz, and Study Guide for this chapter.

Media

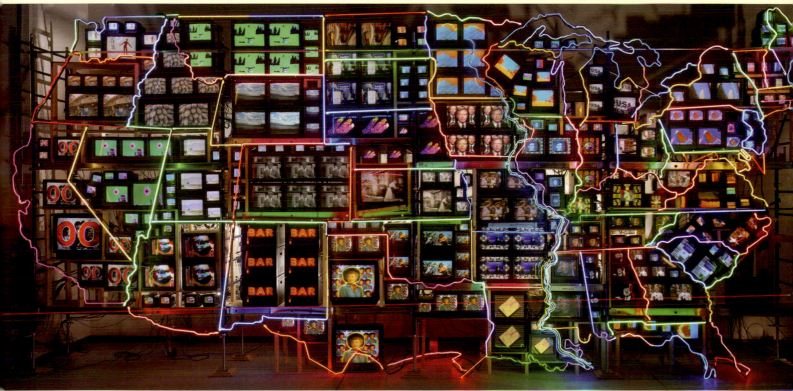

© Smithsonian American Art Museum, Washington, DC/Art Resource, NY.

In the previous chapter we studied the language of art and architecture, and how it can be composed into an artwork. Now we turn to the media artists have used to make artworks within various disciplines.

Since the earliest of times, traditional media have been used in drawing, painting, printmaking, sculpture, and craft-making. As knowledge and technology progressed, nontraditional media emerged for newly developed disciplines, including mixed media, video and film, digital imaging, and performance. **Media** *can be defined as the actual material substances used to create an artwork.* **Disciplines** *are the various branches of art making activity, like painting or video.*

Here are questions to consider regarding the use of media through the ages and across cultures:

- *What are the "disciplines" and "media" in art?*
- *What traditional and nontraditional media have been used by artists?*
- *How have new technologies influenced contemporary artists and their work?*

MEDIA IN TWO-DIMENSIONAL ART

DRAWING

Drawing not only is one of the oldest disciplines in the history of art making but also seems to be innate. The first marks a toddler makes are scribbles, which are primary to the act of drawing. We will look at various grounds along with dry and wet media that artists have used in drawing.

Supports and Grounds

The **support** in drawing, or in any other two-dimensional art, is the surface or material that underlies the artwork. Supports can range from natural surfaces such as a rock wall to many types of paper, parchment, or wood, or any surface that can hold wet or dry media or can be incised. An early example of a support used in drawing came from nature, as we see in Figure 3.1, *Royal Profile*. This image was drawn in paint on a fragment of limestone from the Ramesside period in Egypt, sixteenth–thirteenth centuries BCE. Although the rock surface is rough and unforgiving, the artist rendered a clear and precise profile with pristine contour lines.

Paper is a much more common support today, because it provides a flat surface that accepts a variety of media and styles of drawing, from fine controlled lines to vigorous bold marks. This chapter also contains examples of cardboard, canvas, clay, and even the human body being used as supports for drawing or for painting.

A **ground** can be the surface upon which a drawing is made, but grounds are generally liquid coatings applied to supports. For example, **gesso** is a white, paintlike substance that is brushed onto paper or canvas to serve as a ground for painting or silverpoint drawing (see Fig. 3.5).

Dry Media

Various forms of pencils, sanguine chalk, pastel, and silverpoint are examples of the range of dry media used in drawing.

One of the most common drawing tools is the **pencil**, a graphite rod in a wood or metal holder. The graphite comes in varying degrees of hardness, with the hardest creating thin, controlled lines. Pencil drawings range from quick sketches to incredibly detailed stud-

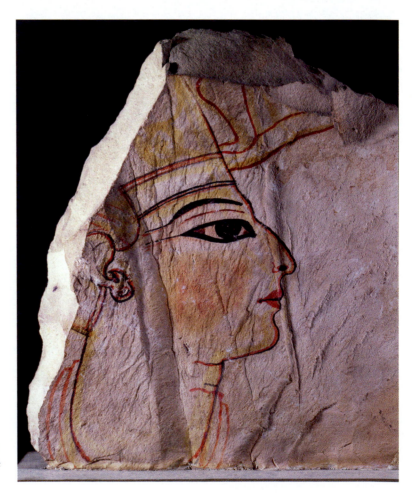

3.1   *Royal Profile*. Painted limestone. Egypt, Ramesside period. Louvre, Paris.

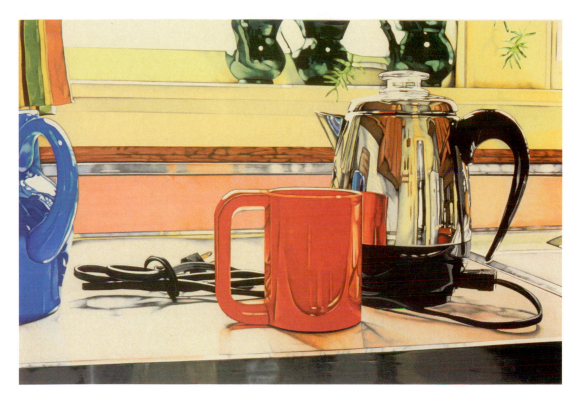

3.2   JEANETTE PASIN SLOAN. *Farberware Coffeepot no. VI*, 1976. Colored pencil on paperboard, 30" × 40". Smithsonian American Art Museum, Washington, DC. Photo by Smithsonian American Art Museum, Washington, DC.

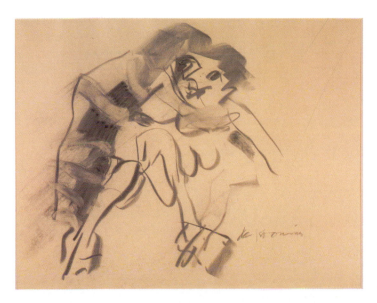

3.3   WILLEM DE KOONING. *Seated Woman*, 1966–1967. Charcoal on paper, 18¼" × 23¼". Collection of the Newark Museum, New Jersey.

ies. Colored pencils were used in Jeanette Pasin Sloan's *Farberware Coffeepot no. VI* (Fig. 3.2). The tight rendering and close values show no pencil marks, making the image look very much like a photograph rather than a pencil drawing.

Willem De Kooning's quick gesture sketch, *Seated Woman* (Fig. 3.3), was rendered in **charcoal**, a carbon stick created from burnt wood. De Kooning manipu-

lated and twisted the charcoal as he drew to create a range of lines, values, and tones to abstract the figure.

Chalk and **pastels** are colored materials held together by wax or glue and shaped into sticks. Sticks with more colored material and less wax produce soft smudgy lines, while those with more wax or glue render precise and controlled lines. Pastels and chalks can be used both precisely and expressively. Edgar Degas is a

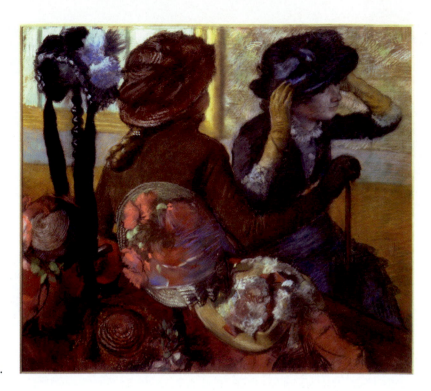

3.4   EDGAR DEGAS. *At the Milliner,* 1883. Pastel, 30" × 33¹/₂". Fundación Colección Thyssen-Bornemisza, Madrid.

master of pastel drawing, as seen in *At the Milliner* (Fig. 3.4), with expressive lines, colors, patterns, and textures.

A **silverpoint** drawing is produced by a thin stylus made of silver that leaves marks on a prepared support such as paper or wood coated with layers of gesso as a ground. (This stylus can vary in metals.) The metallic lines in a drawing will eventually tarnish and darken with age. This technique is seen in Albrecht Durer's *Open Book* (Fig. 3.5). He likely added pigment to the gesso to create a middle value ground to draw on. His

rendering in silverpoint defines the delicate lines and details of the book in the composition.

Wet Media

Ink, pen, and brush are also used in drawings. The combination of lines made by pen marks and washes applied by brush makes visually fluid imagery. This is seen in Mi Wanzhong's *Tree, Bamboo and Rock* (Fig. 3.6) with calligraphy by Chen Meng. Pen and brush each leave distinctive marks, with a wide range of effect resulting from

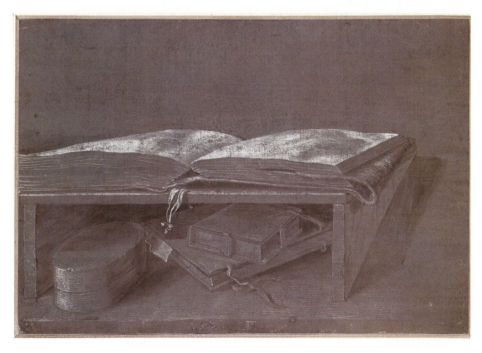

3.5   ALBRECHT DURER. *Open Book,* 1527. Silverpoint drawing. Graphische Sammlung Albertina, Vienna.

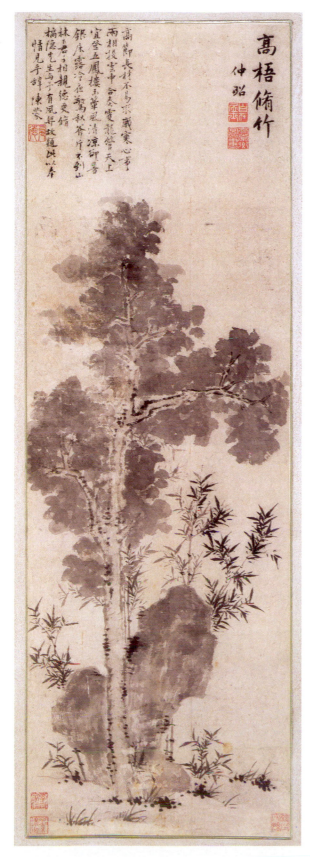

3.6　MI WANZHONG. *Tree, Bamboo and Rock*. Calligraphy by Chen Meng. Ink, 43⅓″ × 14¼″. Musée National des Arts Asiatiques-Guimet, Paris.

diluting the ink. Drawing and painting overlap in artworks done in ink; *Tree, Bamboo and Rock* could be classified as a drawing or as a monochromatic painting.

PRINTMAKING

Printmaking includes any medium that can produce multiple copies of an image or a design through a specific process. We will look at examples of relief, intaglio, lithography, and serigraphy printmaking. Monotype is a final category of printmaking, with unique qualities of its own.

Relief

In **relief** printing, areas not to be printed are cut away from the printing surface, so that the areas to be printed are left higher. Ink is applied to the higher areas, and the print surface is sent through a press or is hand rubbed to transfer the image to paper as shown in Figure 3.7A.

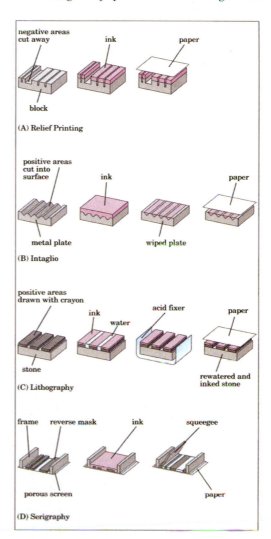

3.7　Printmaking Diagram, showing the processes used for (A) Relief, (B) Intaglio, (C) Lithography, and (D) Serigraphy.

Woodblock prints are examples of relief printmaking. The nineteenth-century print *The Printmaker's Workshop* (Fig. 3.8), from the School of Yokohama, began with an artist's drawing. It served as a guide for the cutter, who carved parts of that image on several wood blocks, using one block for each color printed. In our example, you can see the entire process of woodblock printmaking, including drawing the original design, cutting blocks, mixing colors, printing images, and drying the finished work on overhead lines.

Intaglio

Intaglio prints can have fine lines, a high level of detail, and rich dark tones. The word **intaglio** comes from the Italian verb meaning "to cut into." Artists cut into a flat surface, usually a metal plate, to make the image or design. Ink is applied to the cutaway area, and then paper and plate are put through a press to transfer the image to the paper (Fig. 3.7B). Several processes are used in making an intaglio print, including drypoint, engraving, etching, and aquatint.

To make a **drypoint** print, artists scratch a metal plate with a thin pointed tool called a burin, or a graver. The ink is then rubbed into the scratches, and then the plate and paper are put through the press. The results can resemble a pencil drawing.

Engraving entails cutting or incising lines into a laminated woodblock or a polished metal plate. The ink is rubbed into the recessed lines, and the block or plate is put through the press. An example of a wood engraving is *Escaped Adult Male Slave Hiding Out in the Woods, Huddling Next to Fire* (Fig. 3.9). Engraving produces thin precise lines that create both detail and rich values, as seen in this print.

In an **etching,** a metal plate is coated with a sticky protective ground, into which the artist scratches a design. The plate is then placed in an acid bath, which eats away or "etches" the exposed metal surface. The etched areas hold the ink during the printing. An example of an etching that was combined with drypoint and aquatint is seen in Pablo Picasso's *The Weeping Woman* (Fig. 3.10). In this work Picasso was able to achieve a variety of rich lines and values.

Aquatint is a process related to etching in which the metal plate is covered with a powder of acid-resistant resin. Heat is applied to the plate, which melts the resin and adheres it to the surface. The plate is also placed in an acid bath where the exposed areas are eaten away. The plate is then inked and printed in the same way as the other intaglio processes. With this technique, larger areas of flat tones and values can be created, whereas in the other printing processes these elements can only be achieved with linear hatching and crosshatching.

Lithography

Lithography starts with a drawing created with an oily crayon, pencil, or liquid on a limestone slab or a metal surface. Gum arabic, which is a water-based liquid, is applied to the surface. The oily marks resist it. The stone or plate is then inked with an oil-based ink, which adheres only to the greasy marks drawn on the surface (Fig. 3.7C). The plate or stone is then put through the press where the inked areas transfer to the paper. Figure 3.11 shows Wassily Kandinsky's cover of

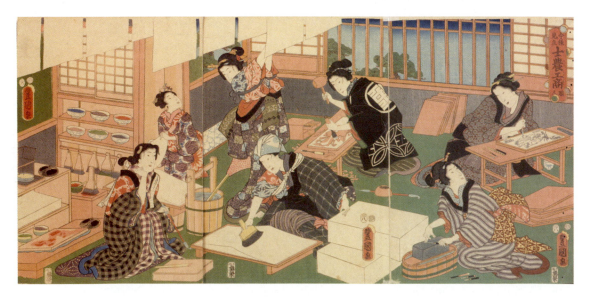

3.8 *The Printmaker's Workshop.* Color woodblock print. Japan, Edo period, School of Yokohama, 19th century. Musée National des Arts Asiatiques-Guimet, Paris. Photo by Thierry Ollivier.

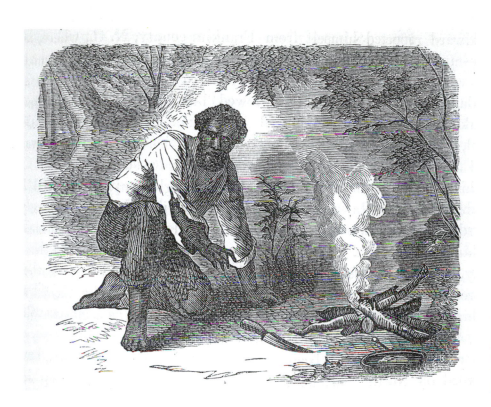

3.9   E.B. *Escaped Adult Male Slave Hiding Out in the Woods, Huddling Next to Fire*, 1872. Wood engraving. Photographs & Prints Division, Schomburg Center for Research in Black Culture, The New York Public Library, New York.

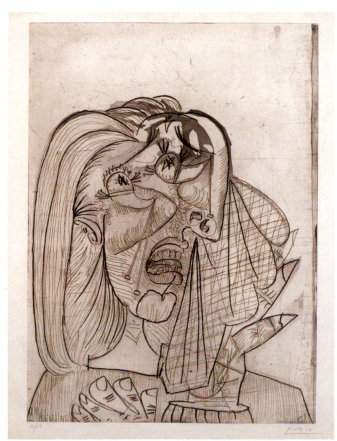

3.10   PABLO PICASSO. *The Weeping Woman (La Femme qui pleure)*, 1937. Etching, aquatint and drypoint; plate: 27^1/$_8$" × 19^1/$_2$"; sheet: 30^5/$_{16}$" × 22^5/$_{16}$", The Museum of Modern Art, New York.

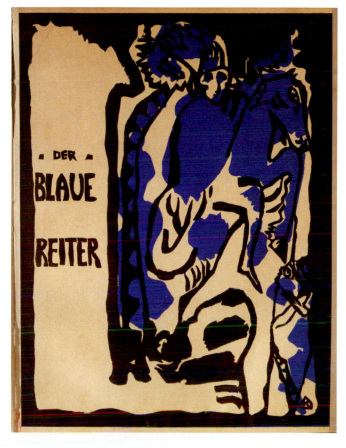

3.11   WASSILY KANDINSKY. Cover of the journal *Der Blaue Reiter*, 1912. Color lithograph, 11^3/$_4$" × 8^7/$_8$". Nationalgalerie, Staatliche Museen zu Berlin.

the journal *Der Blaue Reiter*. The abstract image of a blue horse and rider looks much like a painting. Lithography prints can have the visual qualities of drawings and paintings.

Serigraphy

Serigraphy, also called screen printing, is a process in which a stencil is attached to a piece of finely woven fabric stretched over a frame, which supports and gives strength to the stencil. Ink is then squeezed through the open areas of the stencil and deposited on the surface below (Fig. 3.7D).

Andy Warhol used multiple screen printing images of Marilyn Monroe in his *Marilyn Diptych* (Fig. 3.12). Repeating images in serigraphy is easy, and Warhol uses repetition to allude to mass production and commercialism.

Monotype

Unlike the previous printmaking processes we have just looked at, this process makes only one copy of an image, hence the name **monotype.** On a nonabsorbent surface, a drawing or painting is rendered in oil or a water-soluble paint. Paper is placed on top of the ren-

dering and hand rubbed or put through a press to make the transfer. In Paul Gauguin's *Two Marquesans* (Fig. 3.13), we see the original and only print that looks like a combination of both drawing and painting.

PAINTING

Painting media generally consist of two basic components: pigment and binder. **Pigments** are intense colors in powder form, derived from animals, plants, minerals, and synthetic chemicals. The **binder** is the substance into which the pigment is blended. The components are held together once the binder is dry. Binders can range from egg yolk to wax, glue, various oils, and acrylic liquid mediums, among others.

Although all paints contain colored material, there are some forms that use no binders. Sand painting is a traditional art form in Navajo rituals, used especially for healing. Different natural elements, such as colored sand, crushed stone, charcoal, and pollen, are carefully sprinkled on a clean, swept earthen floor. Artist priests chant and pray while they create their designs in sand. The sand paintings are then destroyed at the end of the ritual. Figure 3.14 shows a demonstration of a Navajo sand painting.

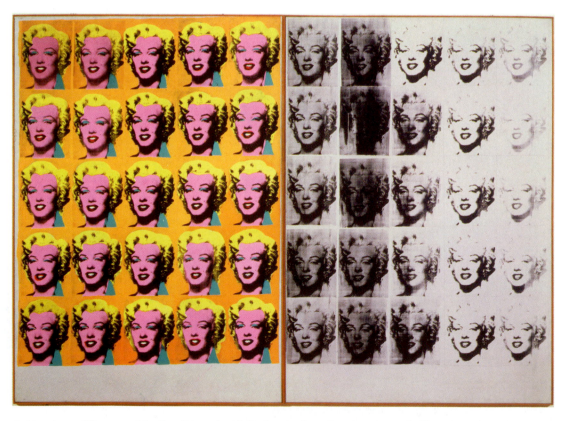

3.12 ANDY WARHOL. *Marilyn Diptych*, 1962. Synthetic polymer paint and silkscreen ink on canvas, 4'9" × 6'10". Tate Gallery, London.

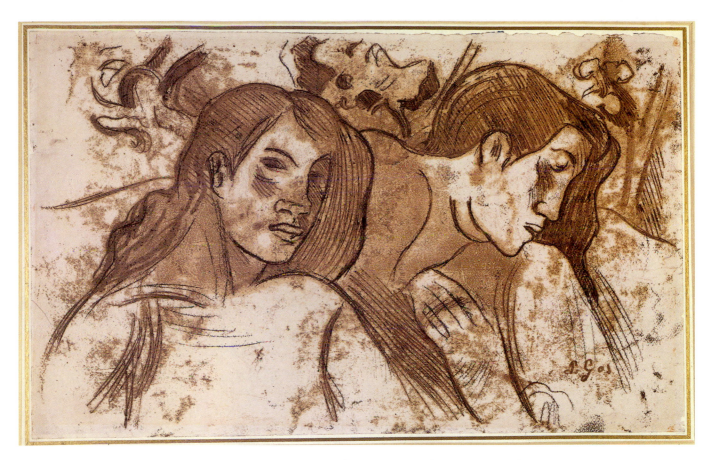

3.13   PAUL GAUGUIN. *Two Marquesans*, 1902. Monotype, 12^1/$_2$" × 20". British Museum, London.

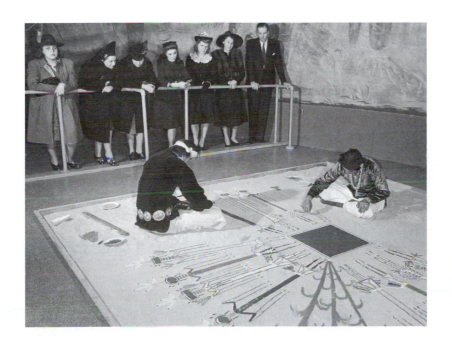

3.14   Navajo Indians executing a sand painting, March 26, 1941, during the exhibition "Indian Art of the United States." The Museum of Modern Art, New York. January 22, 1941 through April 27, 1941.

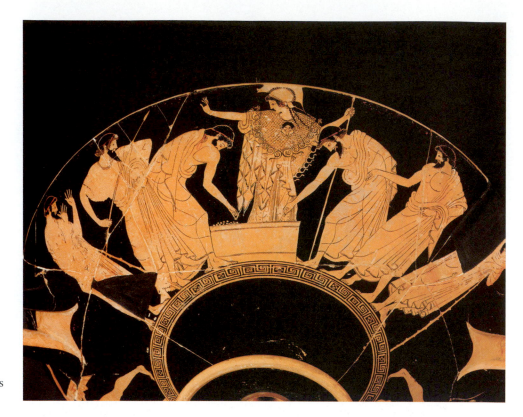

3.15   DOURIS. *Red Figure
Kylix,* 490 BCE. Slip on clay,
13" diameter. Kunsthistorisches
Museum, Vienna.

All kinds of things can be used as supports for paintings: stone, clay, plaster, wood panel, paper, fabric, and even found objects. The sand paintings we just discussed use the earth itself as the support. Some of the oldest surviving paintings were made on clay vessels, as in the *Red Figure Kylix* by the Greek painter Douris, from the fifth century BCE (Fig. 3.15). The **slip** (a liquid clay solution) acts as paint, which in this piece defined both the black background and the delicate black lines that add details to the figures. The support of unglazed red clay provides the mass for the figures depicted.

Many cultures in human history have used their bodies as surfaces to paint on. The Chinese opera performer in Figure 3.16 is painting his face in preparation for his character. His painted face, the text, costumes, music, and singing are all components of the genre.

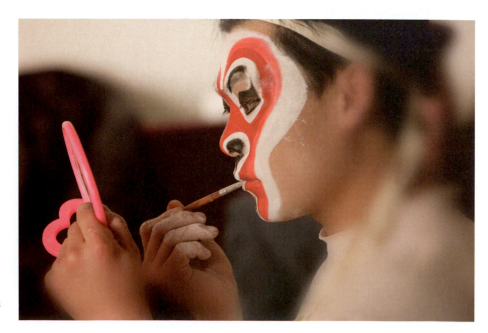

3.16   A Chinese opera
performer making up in
front of a mirror.

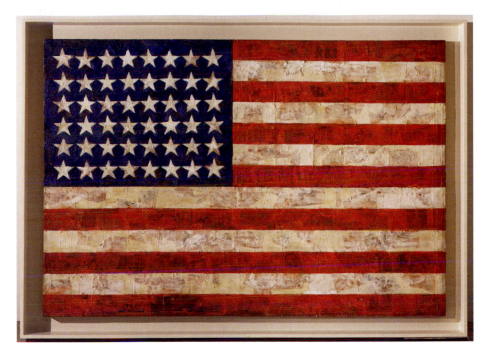

3.17 JASPER JOHNS. *Flag*, 1954–1955. Encaustic, oil, and collage on fabric mounted on plywood, 42$\frac{1}{4}$" × 60$\frac{5}{8}$". Gift of Philip Johnson in honor of Alfred H. Barr Jr. The Museum of Modern Art, New York.

Encaustic

Encaustic is one of the most ancient forms of painting media. Because pigments are mixed into hot beeswax, the medium can be manipulated in the composition until it cools. Some encaustic paintings thousands of years old retain their colors and lustrous surfaces. The medium is still used today. The top layer of Jasper Johns's *Flag* (Fig. 3.17) is translucent encaustic over a layer of newspaper scraps and photographs, allowing the viewer to see the imagery embedded in the flag.

Fresco

Fresco is often used for large murals. There are two kinds of fresco. In **buon fresco,** or true fresco, finely ground pigment suspended in water is applied to a wet plaster surface, which results in a very durable painting. The artist must work quickly and in small areas because of the fast-drying plaster. In **fresco secco,** paint is applied to a dry plaster wall. Buon fresco is remarkably durable, as evidenced by the *Glass Bowl with Fruit* (Fig. 3.18), a Roman painting from the first cen-

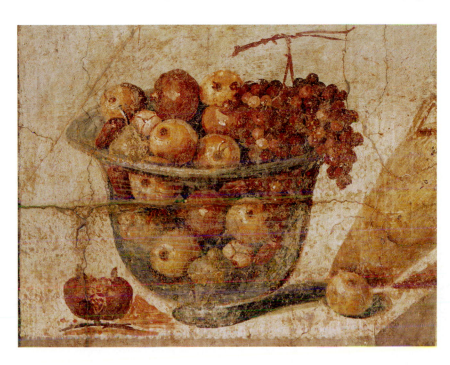

3.18 *Glass Bowl with Fruit.* Wallpainting, Roman, 1st century, found in the Mt. Vesuvius region, Italy. Museo Archeologico Nazionale, Naples, Italy.

tury CE that survived 2,000 years despite being buried by the eruption of Mount Vesuvius in 79 CE.

Tempera, Gouache, and Watercolor

Tempera, gouache, and watercolor are three waterbased paint media. Traditional **tempera** painting consists of pigments mixed with egg yolk, which is the binder. Egg tempera is a very strong, quick drying medium that is excellent for rendering sharp lines and details.

Today, commercially available tempera paints do not use egg, but other natural and synthetic binders and are common as children's art materials, as in Figure 3.19, Kimberly Bova's *A Farm Is a Place to Grow.* Modern tempera paintings resemble **gouache,** which is watercolor with Chinese white chalk added to create an opaque paint. Both gouache and tempera produce areas of flat, bright colors.

Watercolors are pigments suspended in a gum arabic binder, which is a natural water soluble glue. Watercolors are usually applied to paper in layers of thin stains without ever completely covering it.

Oil

Oil paint is made by blending powdered pigments with oil, usually linseed, and sometimes also turpentine. Oil paint is applied to a support, most often wood or canvas, and dries to a hard, durable, flexible film. Because oil paint is slow drying, artists can easily change their colors and details when working on the composition. When dry, oil paint can have intense colors with lustrous, glowing surfaces. These qualities are evident in Titian's *Venus of Urbino* (Fig. 3.20). Oil-based paints

are also used for body painting, like that of the Chinese opera performer in Figure 3.16.

Acrylic

Acrylic paint is made with pigment that has been ground with a synthetic polymer liquid binder that quickly dries into a flexible film. A twentieth-century invention, acrylics can be used thickly or thinned with water and can be applied to almost any support. David Hockney's *A Bigger Splash,* 1967 (Fig. 3.21), shows acrylic paint's versatility: some areas resemble oil painting, some look like flat latex wall paint, and others are thinned and fluidly applied to replicate splashing water.

Sprayed Paint

Thanks to current technology, paint can be sprayed in many ways. An **airbrush** is a small spray gun that is about the size of a pen. Compressed air is forced through the airbrush, which atomizes the liquid paint, allowing it to be sprayed onto a surface. An airbrush can render both large areas and fine details. Not only used for fine art, airbrushes also make their mark in illustration work, murals, signage, custom car finishes, and painting on the human body.

Spray paint is a commercial product in aerosol cans containing compressed air and quick-drying permanent paint, often used by graffiti artists (Fig. 3.22). Spray paint allows for broad areas of color and gradual transitions, but will not do fine detail work. As a result, most graffiti artists work on a large scale. For more thoughts on the positive and negative reactions to graffiti, turn to *Food for Thought* at the end of this chapter.

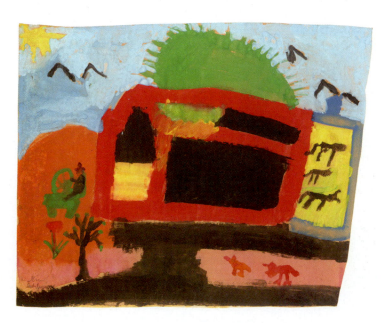

3.19 KIMBERLY BOVA. *A Farm Is a Place to Grow,* 1970. Tempera paint on paper, 18" × 24". Collection of Dona and Douglas Schlesier, USA.

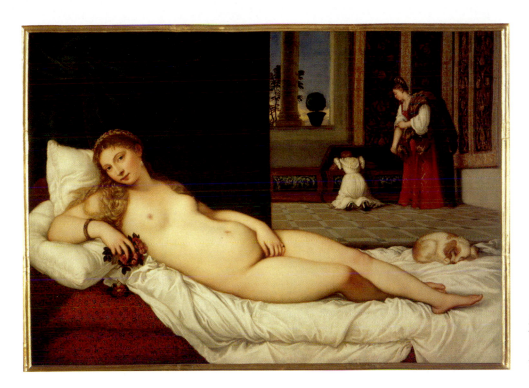

3.20 TITIAN (TIZIANO VECELLIO). *Venus of Urbino*, 1538. Oil on canvas, 4' × 5'6". Uffizi, Florence, Italy.

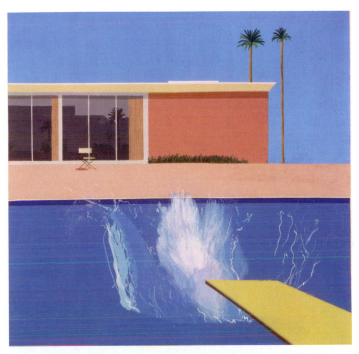

3.21 DAVID HOCKNEY. *A Bigger Splash*, 1967. Acrylic on canvas, 8' × 8'. Tate Gallery, London.

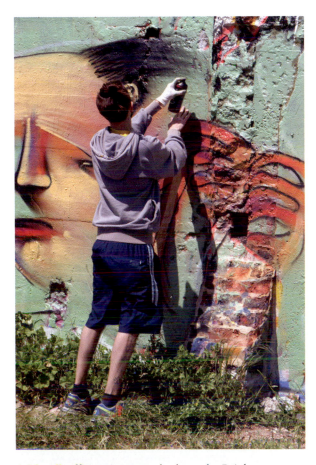

3.22 Graffiti artist at work along the Brighton seafront.

METHODS AND MEDIA IN THREE-DIMENSIONAL ART

Three-dimensional art ranges from traditional to new media, freestanding work, and relief sculpture. It can be site-specific and even kinetic. **Freestanding** sculptures are objects that are meant to be seen from all sides and could conceivably be placed in many different settings, like the *Monumental Heads* (Fig. 3.23), from the Easter Islands. A **relief** sculpture is meant to be seen only from the front, like the *Olmec Pectoral* (Fig. 3.24). An example of a **site-specific** sculpture is Richard Serra's 1981 *Tilted Arc* (Fig. 3.25). Made of steel, this sculpture was designed to be permanently installed in that spot to respond to its environment. If it were moved elsewhere, the artwork and its meaning would change.

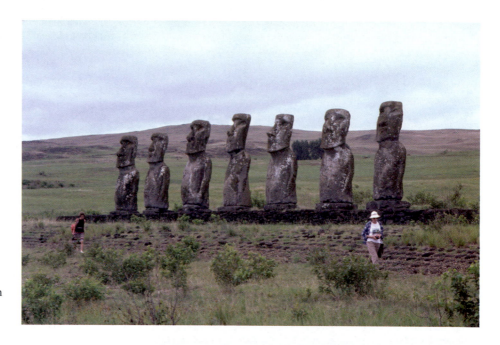

3.23 *Monumental Heads*, c. 15th century. Volcanic tufa. Easter Island (Rapa Nui), Polynesia.

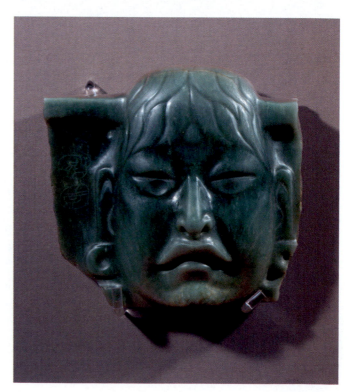

3.24 *Olmec Pectoral*, 900–400 BCE. Jade, 4" high. British Museum, London.

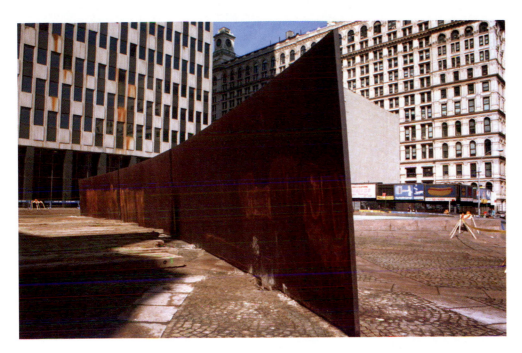

3.25 RICHARD SERRA. *Tilted Arc*, 1981. Raw steel, 120' long × 12' high.

However, Serra's sculpture received so much criticism that it was eventually destroyed (see Food for Thought, page 82). In **kinetic** works, movement is part of the piece, as in Alexander Calder's "mobiles." *Crinkly* (Fig. 3.26) from 1970, is made of metal, wire, and paint and is suspended so it moves randomly in the natural airflow.

Let us now look at media within specific sculptural disciplines.

CARVING

To make carved sculptures, artists cut away unwanted material from a large block of stone or wood or, more recently, synthetic products like Styrofoam. This is a subtracted process, because the material is taken away. Stone sculpting goes back to the Paleolithic era and appears across cultures. Wood was most likely carved by artists over the centuries, but did not have the durability of stone. We have just seen two examples of carving: in stone, the *Monumental Heads* (Fig. 3.23), and in jade, the *Olmec Pectoral* (Fig. 3.24).

MODELING

Sculptural forms are created by pushing and pulling a malleable substance, such as clay or wax. Often modeling is considered an **additive process,** because material is built up to create the final sculptural form. Clay is a

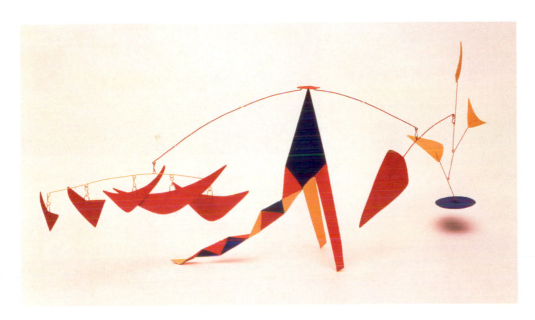

3.26 ALEXANDER CALDER. *Crinkly,* 1970. Sheet metal, wire, and paint, 28" × 65½" × 12". Private collection.

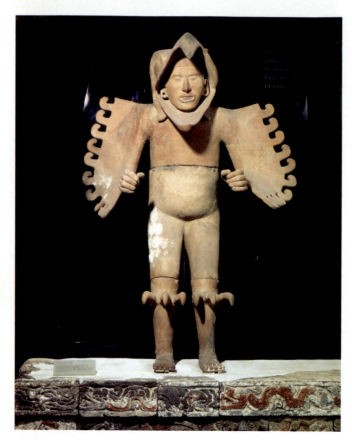

3.27 *Eagle Knight,* c. 15th century. Earthenware and plaster. 66⁷/₈" × 46¹/₂" × 21⁵/₈". Aztec, Museo Templo Mayor, Mexico.

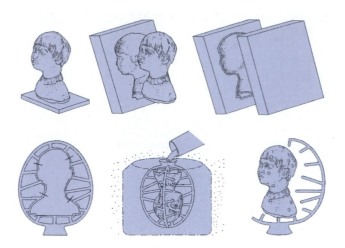

3.28 Cire Perdue, or Lost Wax, Casting Process.

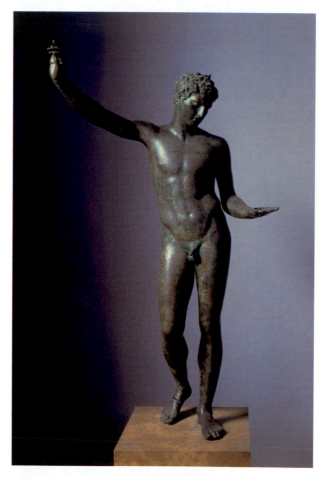

3.29 *The Marathon Boy,* 330 BCE. Bronze, 51" high. Greek, Hellenistic period. National Archaeological Museum, Athens.

common modeling material that, after firing, becomes hard and permanent. Figure 3.27 shows an Aztec *Eagle Knight* of earthenware clay and plaster, from Mexico.

Sometimes, a modeled sculpture is cast to become more permanent. A mold is made around the initial sculpture done in clay or wax, and then removed. A durable material such as plaster or molten metal is poured into the mold. Except for very small sculptures, all cast sculptures are created using the **cire perdue** process (**lost wax** casting method). This method produces hollow metal sculpture with thin walls. As illustrated in Figure 3.28, a thin layer of wax is suspended between an interior and exterior mold. The wax is then melted out of the mold and replaced with molten metal. The Classical Greek sculpture of *The Marathon Boy* (Fig. 3.29) is a cast bronze work, most likely made by using the lost wax method.

ASSEMBLING

Assembled works are made of various parts that are then put together. Almost any material can be assembled into sculptures, including wood, stone, metal, or plastic. Assembled art is often **mixed media,** which literally means mixing up the methods and their various media in a work. Mixed media works may contain traditional materials like stone or wood, but may also use manufactured goods, perishables, photographs, industrial fixtures, and the like.

Ready-mades, Assemblage, and Fabrication

Many non-Western cultures use natural objects in their sculpture, such as the shells and raffia seen in Figure 3.30, *Nimba, Goddess of Fertility*. When **found objects** or **ready-mades** (already existing objects) are incorporated into pieces, the resulting works are referred to as **assemblages.** Marcel Duchamp used ready-mades for his *Bicycle Wheel* (Fig. 3.31), assembling a wheel with a stool to create the sculpture. Robert Rauschenberg combined cloth, metal, leather, electric fixture, cable, oil paint, an automobile tire, and a wooden plank on the floor in his piece titled *First Landing Jump* (Fig. 3.32), from 1961. He coined the term **combines** for works that are both painting and sculpture. Sculptures can be **fabricated** using industrial and commercial processes, such as welding or neon lighting (see Fig. 3.38).

Installation

Installations are usually mixed media artworks designed for a specific interior or exterior space. In the Cornaro Chapel in the church of Santa Maria della Vittoria (Fig. 3.33), Gianlorenzo Bernini created a dramatic stage for

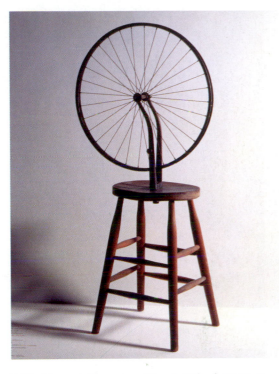

3.31 MARCEL DUCHAMP. *Bicycle Wheel*, 1963. Ready-made, found objects. Richard Hamilton Collection, Henley-on-Thames, UK.

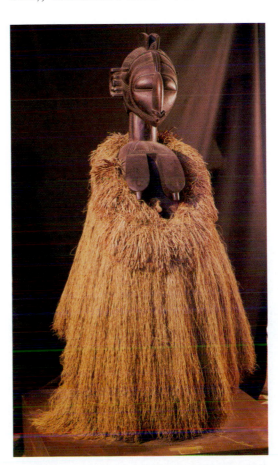

3.30 *Nimba, Goddess of Fertility.* Wood, shells, and raffia. Baga, Guinea. Musée du Quai Branly, Paris.

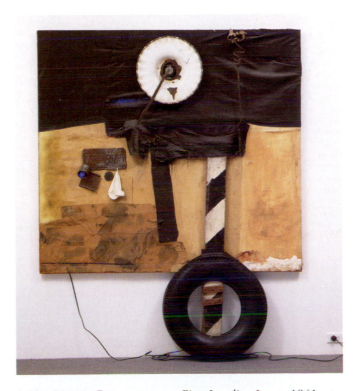

3.32 ROBERT RAUSCHENBERG. *First Landing Jump*, 1961. Combine painting: cloth, metal, leather, electric fixture, cable, and oil paint on composition board; overall, including automobile tire and wooden plank on floor, 7'5¹⁄₈" × 6' × 8⁷⁄₈". Gift of Philip Johnson. The Museum of Modern Art, New York.

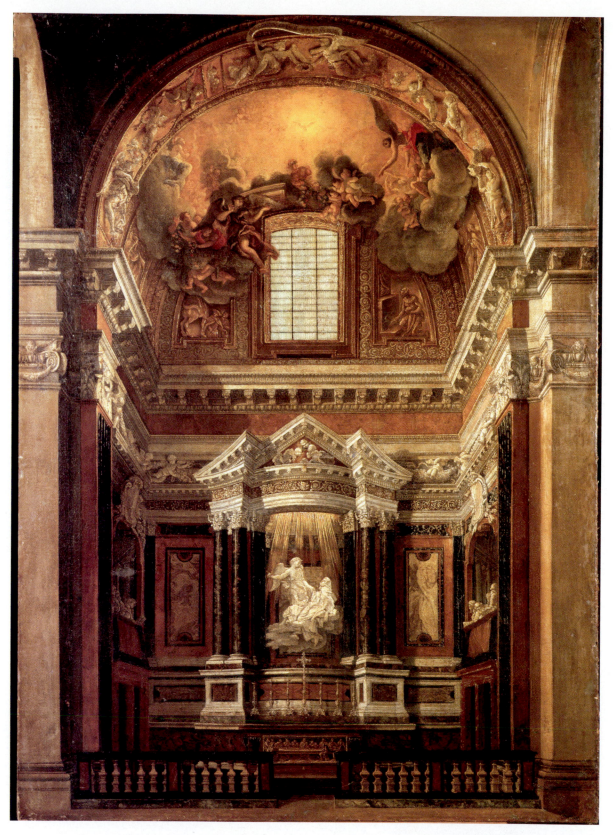

3.33　Gianlorenzo Bernini. Cornaro Chapel with the *Ecstasy of St. Teresa*, 1645–1652, in the Church of Santa Maria della Vittoria, Rome. Marble, stucco, paint, natural light; central figures are marble, 11'6" high. As illustrated by an anonymous 18th-century painting from the Italian School. The painting is located in the Staatliches Museum, Schwerin, Germany.

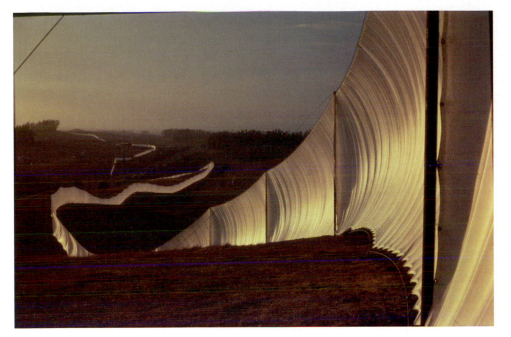

3.34 CHRISTO AND JEANNE-CLAUDE. *Running Fence, Sonoma and Marin Counties, California, 1972–76.* Height: 18 feet. Length: 24½ miles. 240,000 square yards of nylon fabric, steel poles, and steel cables. Photo: Jeanne-Claude. Copyright Christo 1976.

his sculpture, the *Ecstacy of St. Teresa.* The 11' 6" high sculpture of St. Teresa and an angel is the centerpiece of the chapel. The work represents the mystical, religious rapture of St. Teresa as she is pierced by the angel's arrow of divine love. The figures appear to float in midair and are lighted by heavenly rays. Bernini used the entire chapel space to amplify the ecstatic mood, blending architecture, sculpture, illusionistic painting, colored marble, bronze and natural light.

Creating exterior installations has been the life work of Christo and Jeanne-Claude. They install various materials in a specific site to enhance its natural beauty. In *Running Fence* (Fig. 3.34), fabric was stretched over the rolling countryside of Sonoma and Marin counties in California. The fabric fence visually emphasized the undulating contours of the land.

PERFORMANCE

Performance is a live-action event that is staged as an artwork. Several examples of performance art appear in Chapter 13, The Body, because performance art often requires the human body. Figure 3.35 shows Suzanne

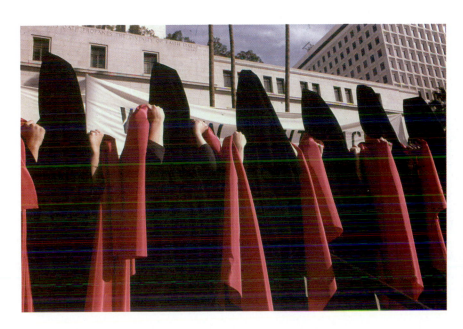

3.35 SUZANNE LACY AND LESLIE LABOWITZ. *In Mourning and in Rage.* Photo by Maria Karras.

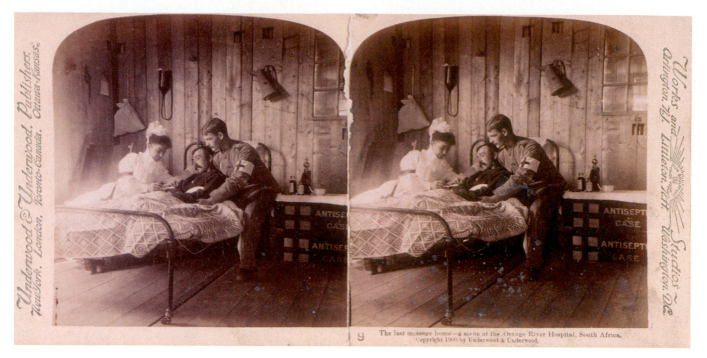

3.36 UNDERWOOD AND UNDERWOOD. *The Last Message Home*, c. 1900. Scene at the Orange River Hospital, South Africa. National Museum of Photography, Film & Television, Bradford, UK.

Lacy and Leslie Labowitz in a feminist performance piece called *In Mourning and in Rage*. In this protest performance, ten women dressed in black drove in a hearse to a Los Angeles city council meeting. They were expressing both their grief and outrage for the ten victims of the Hillside strangler and for the overall violence against women that is sensationalized in the news media.

TECHNOLOGY-BASED MEDIA

PHOTOGRAPHY, FILM, AND VIDEO

In **photography**, a light-sensitive surface such as film is exposed to light through a lens, which creates an image from the environment on that surface. Multiple copies can be made of that original image on other light-sensitive surfaces. Early examples of monochromatic photographic processes are daguerreotype, platinum prints, and silver prints.

The Last Message Home (Fig. 3.36), from 1900, is a stereoscopic image. When seen through a special viewer, the two images blend to create the illusion of one three-dimensional scene. *England* (Fig. 3.37), from 1980, is a large work by Gilbert and George that uses thirty individually framed black-and-white and color photos placed right next to each other to form a large wall installation.

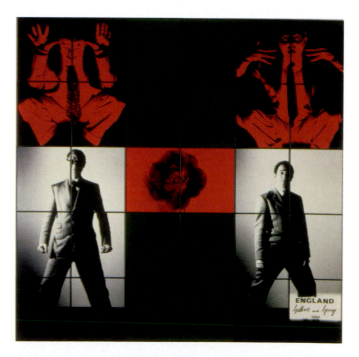

3.37 GILBERT AND GEORGE. *England*, 1980. Wall installation with 30 black-and-white and color photographs in black frames, 10' ×10'. Tate Gallery, London.

A film (or movie) is a sequence of still photographs shot in rapid succession on a strip of film. When projected onto a screen, the progression of the still images gives an illusion of movement.

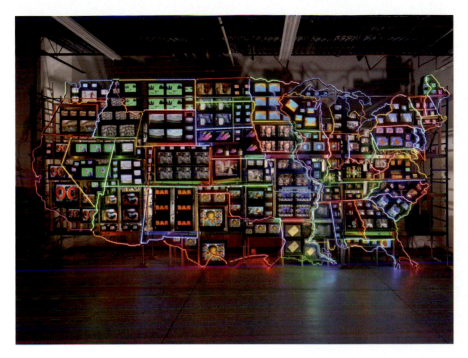

3.38 NAM JUNE PAIK. *Electronic Superhighway: Continental U.S., Alaska, Hawaii*, 1995. (Continental U.S. only.) 49-channel, closed-circuit video installation, neon, steel, and electronic components, 15' × 40' × 4'. Gift of the artist. Smithsonian American Art Museum, Washington, DC.

In video, both audio data and visual images are stored simultaneously on magnetic videotape and projected on television monitors. Video cameras first became accessible to the public and, thus, to artists in 1965. Video sound and image quality are generally considered to be lower than those of film.

DIGITAL MEDIA

Digital imaging involves the computer-based storage of still or moving images as digital information, with or without sound. In addition, all kinds of existing imagery can be scanned to become digital information. Digital images can be easily manipulated. Output from digital images can be printed on hard copy, displayed on computer monitors, or projected onto a screen. Figure 3.38 is a photo of Nam June Paik's *Electronic Superhighway: Continental U.S., Alaska, Hawaii*. This is an example of a forty-nine-channel, closed-circuit, digital video installation. Lorna Simpson combines black-and-white film (which has been digitized and now plays as a DVD) with an audio song in *Easy to Remember* (Fig. 3.39). The song is softly sung, which is intended to invoke memories of African American childhood.

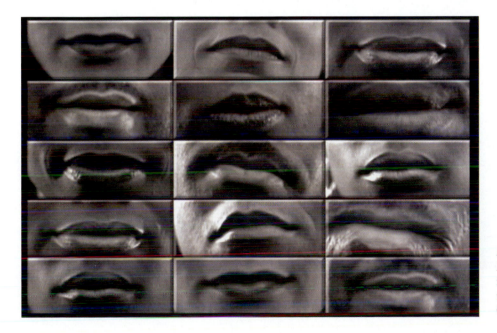

3.39 LORNA SIMPSON. *Easy to Remember*, 2001. Still from 16 mm film transferred to DVD, sound; 2$\frac{1}{2}$ minutes. Courtesy of the Sean Kelly Gallery, New York.

PHOTOMONTAGE AND COLLAGE

Photomontage is a composition of many photographs or of one photograph using many prints to create a new image. Hannah Hoch very effectively used this technique in her political satirical work titled *Cut with the Kitchen Knife Dada through the Lost Weimar Beer Belly Cultural Epoch of Germany* (Fig. 3.40). As a Berlin **Dadaist** artist, Hoch promoted the idea of absurdity in this work by using cutouts of photos and words from magazines to create a sense of chaos and instability.

Photomontage is related to **collage,** which can be made of practically anything that can be glued to a surface. Jasper Johns's *Flag* (Fig. 3.17) is a combination of encaustic paint, newspaper scraps, and photographs.

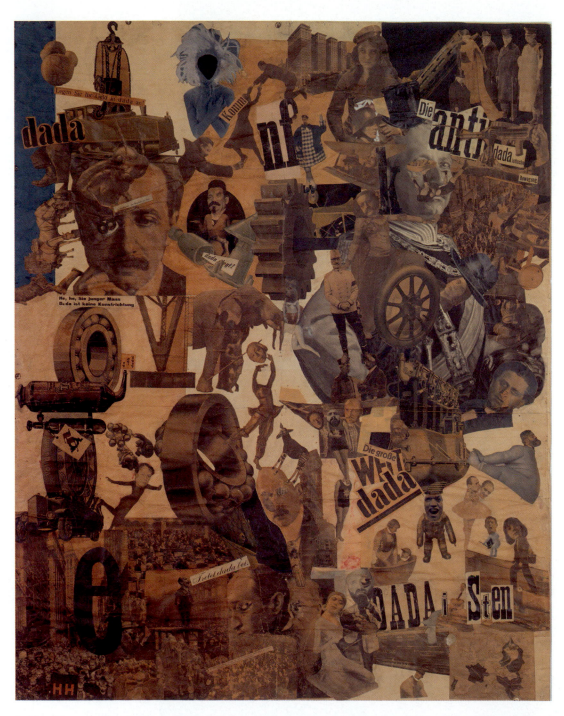

3.40   HANNAH HOCH. *Cut with the Kitchen Knife Dada through the Last Weimar Beer Belly Cultural Epoch of Germany,* 1919-1920. Photomontage, 3'9" × 2'11". Neue Nationalgalerie, Staatliche Museen, Berlin.

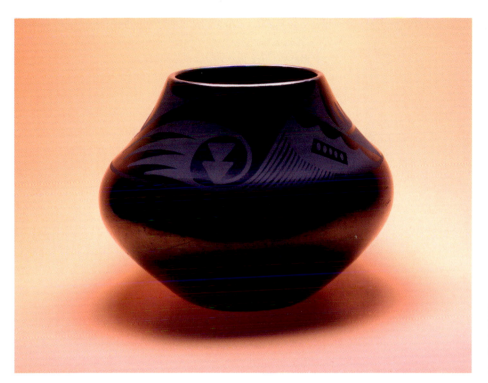

3.41 MARIA MARTINEZ. *Bowl*, Undated. Blackware, 6³/4" × 9¹/2". Gift of International Business Machines Corporation. Smithsonian American Art Museum, Washington, DC.

CRAFTS

In the art world, **crafts** are considered finely skilled handwork in various media, some of which include ceramics, glass, wood, metal, and fibers. The art made in these media can be either functional or nonfunctional and can be decorative in nature.

CERAMICS

Ceramic ware is a universal craft form found in almost every culture of humankind, from ancient eras to the present day. Functional pieces can be vessels, platters, cups, pitchers and the like. Ceramics can be hand molded or pinched into their forms, fashioned out of coils or slabs of clay, or thrown on a potter's wheel. Figure 3.41 shows a pinched black-on-black *Bowl* made by Maria Martinez, a Native American from the San Idelfonso Pueblo in New Mexico. She and her son perfected this technique and design, which blends both glossy and matte surfaces with decorative abstract symbols. This combination beautifully enhances the vessel's form. Marilyn Levine's *Golf Bag* (Fig. 3.42) shows her "fool the eye" ceramic sculpture, made of rolled and modeled clay slabs. A nonfunctional piece in the craft sense, the work makes the viewer want to touch it in order to believe it is actually made out of clay.

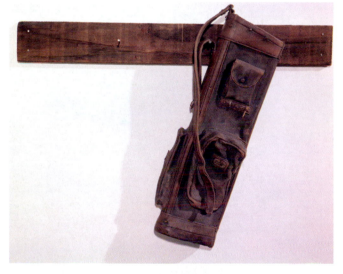

3.42 MARILYN LEVINE. *Golf Bag*, 1981. Ceramic, 34" × 10³/4". Private collection.

GLASS

Glass works have been found in several ancient cultures, and glass continues to be a medium used by artists. In medieval Europe, stained glass was perfected for the Gothic cathedral (see Fig. 9.37). The glass not only was beautiful but also functioned as a teaching tool for the illiterate. Stained glass is a medium still

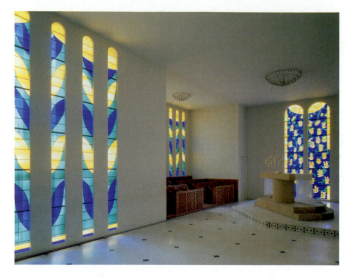

3.43 HENRI MATISSE. *Tree of Life,* 1950–1951. Stained glass. Chapel of the Rosary, Vence, France.

used by modern artists such as Henri Matisse, who designed the interior of the Chapel of the Rosary for the Sisters who cared for him while he was ill. His cut-paper designs were translated into stained glass, as seen in Figure 3.43, *Tree of Life.* Fine contemporary glass-

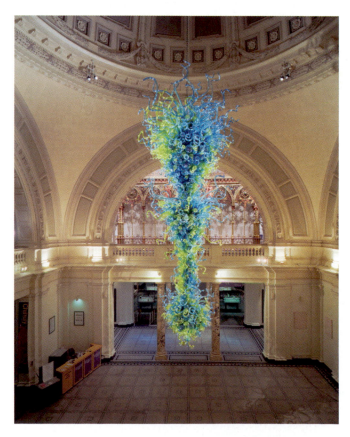

3.44 DALE CHIHULY. *Rotunda Chandelier,* 1999. Glass, 27' × 12' × 12'. Victoria and Albert Museum, London.

work has been created by Dale Chihuly. His extraordinary chandeliers are sculptures made of light and colored glass. The *Rotunda Chandelier* (Fig. 3.44) hangs in the Victoria and Albert Museum in London.

WOOD

Although wood has often been the medium of the sculptor, it is also the material used by the craft artist. Figure 3.45 shows a *Calabash* (feast bowl) carved in koa wood. These highly polished vessels were used and treasured by generations of Hawaiian monarchs. Many of these vessels represented the monarchs' genealogies and were designed to resemble a calabash or a gourd. Wood crafting also includes furniture, and art museums display many exquisite pieces from cultures around the world.

METALWORK AND JEWELRY

Like other craft media, metalwork has been around since ancient times. Over the years, metal has been poured into molds, beaten into forms, or hammered into shapes. Jewelry can be made of many materials; however, metals and gems have prevailed in many cultures. In Figure 3.46, we see a *Necklace and Pendant* from Tell Hariri, Syria, crafted with gold wire, lapis lazuli, and semiprecious stones. The image on the gold pendant is likely a goddess.

FIBER

Fiber is another medium that has been used by craft artists across cultures throughout human history. Using various fibers, woven work can range from baskets to cloth, carpets, quilts, and embroidery, among other

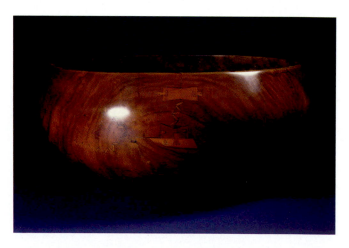

3.45 *Calabash* (feast bowl), c. 18th–20th centuries. Koa wood and other natural materials. Hawaii. © Private Collection/Bonhams, London.

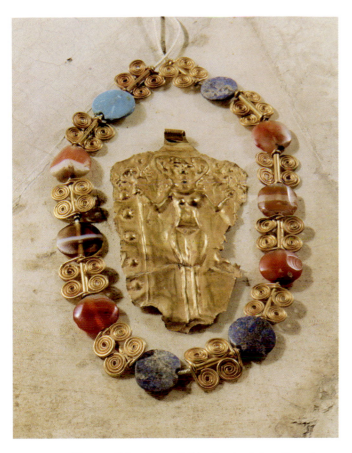

3.46 *Necklace and Pendant.* Gold wire, lapis lazuli, and other semiprecious stone. Late Middle Syrian period from tomb 125, Tell Hariri, Syria. National Museum, Aleppo.

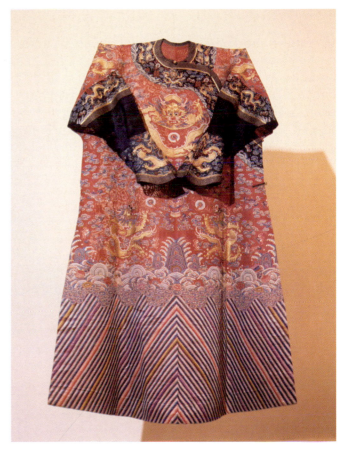

3.47 *Summer Robe.* Embroidered silk, China, 19th century. Private collection.

products. An exquisite example of embroidery can be seen in the *Summer Robe* (Fig. 3.47) from the Qing Dynasty. Intricate and complex designs including the imperial dragon have been closely stitched into the silk fabric. The robe belonged to a eunuch of the court of the Empress Dowager, who reigned in the nineteenth century.

Faith Ringgold used the craft of quilting as an art medium to express her views on African American culture in America. She did a series of quilts about her "tar beach," the tarred roof of the building she lived in as a child in New York City. The story told in her quilts became a famous children's book. In Figure 3.48, *The Bitter Nest, Part II: The Harlem Renaissance Party,* 1988, Ringgold creates a gathering of some of the luminaries of African American culture in the 1920s and 1930s.

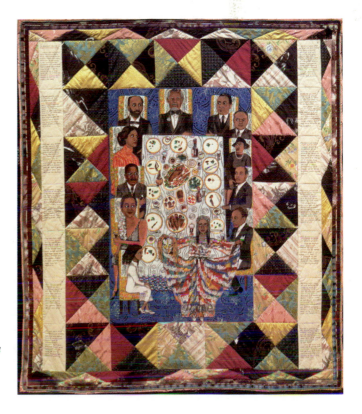

3.48 FAITH RINGGOLD. *The Bitter Nest, Part II: The Harlem Renaissance Party,* 1988. Acrylic on canvas with printed, dyed, and pieced fabric, 94" × 83". Smithsonian American Art Museum, Washington, DC.

SYNOPSIS

Various art media have been used by artists across the globe and throughout the ages. Media have ranged from simple and pure to complex and mixed. Media can also be materials that are natural, such as stone and clay, or synthetic, like acrylics and fiberglass. As technology has progressed, photography, film, recordings, videos, and digital imaging have become new media for artists. Traditional disciplines in art overlap with theater, with industry, with advertising, and more, resulting in new art forms and media. Today artists have the freedom to use any media they choose or create. Their choice can vary according to the idea or subject matter they wish to express in their work.

FOOD FOR THOUGHT

Richard Serra's sculpture, Tilted Arc (Fig. 3.25), was removed and destroyed eight years after it was created. The work was heavily criticized by those who worked nearby. Many objected to its enormous size, which forced them to walk around it when they wanted to cross the plaza. Part of Serra's intention, however, was to make people more aware of their surroundings as they walked past the sculpture. Some objected to the raw steel wall because its rust-like surface was often covered with graffiti and could not be completely cleaned. Others thought the sculpture might attract rats or terrorists.

Graffiti is a common sight in cities, and much of it is regularly cleaned off, painted over, or obliterated as quickly as it appears on bridges, subway trains, or warehouse walls. Many people perceive the spray-paint works as eyesores, signs of gang activity, or illegal damage to public and private property. Yet to many graffiti artists, their work is a way to make an individual mark on an uncaring city or is even a form of personal expression that should be respected (Fig. 3.22). They point out that people do not object when billboards and bus shelter ads appear without their approval. Recently, some art museums have commissioned graffiti art on walls near their institutions, and some graffiti artists ask permission before making a work.

- *Does art belong only in certain places?*
- *How does the medium influence the way we perceive art, and the value we may give to a particular piece?*
- *Should people have the right to determine what imagery is in public spaces around them, and how it looks?*
- *Does graffiti have merit?*

Your Thomson Online Resources

 Go to **ArtExperience Online** for the Flashcards, Quiz, and Study Guide for this chapter.

CHAPTER 4

Deriving Meaning

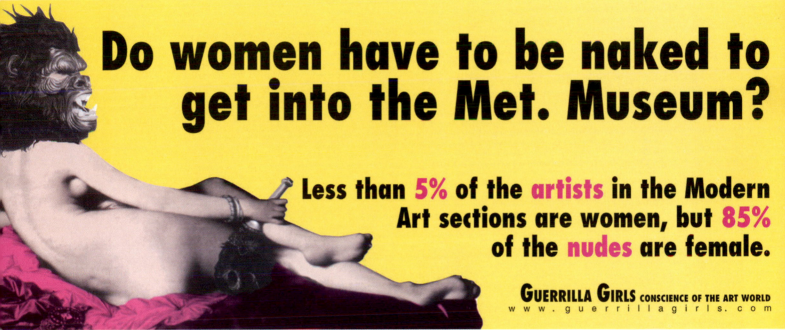

Do women have to be naked to get into the Met. Museum?

Less than **5%** of the **artists** in the Modern Art sections are women, but **85%** of the **nudes** are female.

GUERRILLA GIRLS CONSCIENCE OF THE ART WORLD
w w w . g u e r r i l l a g i r l s . c o m

Courtesy www.guerrillagirls.com

INTRODUCTION

Art and architecture have meaning. They are simultaneously expression and communication. Artists "shape" their work to visually express a complex set of ideas, and the audience receives that expression. Architects create usable spaces, but their structures are also significant beyond their functionality.

But how does that process work? Here are our questions for this chapter:

- How do artists or architects visually present ideas in their works?
- How does the audience understand the message?

This chapter focuses on four basic areas in regard to meaning: (1) formal analysis of artworks; (2) reading the content; (3) the influence of context; and (4) ways we encounter art.

FORMAL ANALYSIS

Chapter 2 presented the formal qualities of art and architecture, which are visual elements arranged into a composition, using the principles of composition. Beyond that, however, formal qualities add meaning to an artwork or architectural structure. **Formal analysis** is an integrated study of all the formal qualities of an art object that are apparent just by looking at the work, and the meaning that can be derived from them.

For example, a formal analysis of *Migrant Mother, Nipomo Valley*, 1936 (Fig. 4.1), shows that the photographer Dorothea Lange used formal elements to create a coherent composition with the woman's face as the focal point. Her face is near the center and is dramatically lit so that the strongest lights and darks are around it. The face and arm make a vertical axis leading to the face. Symmetry is an important organizing principle, with children like wings at the woman's sides. The space of the picture is shallow, with the woman and children on a large scale, almost entirely filling the available space.

Because the woman's face is formally most important, we take care to read her expression. Symmetry and verticality are often used for religious art. Here, they suggest that the woman and children share a strong, almost sacred, emotional tie. The textures are mostly rough and unkempt. Taking these formal elements together, we read the qualities of worry, fear, family devotion, and poverty in the picture.

The formal qualities of any other artwork could be similarly analyzed—for example, the *Palace Sculpture*, by Olowe of Ise, from Ikere, Nigeria, 1910–1914 (Fig. 4.2). Without knowing anything about the work,

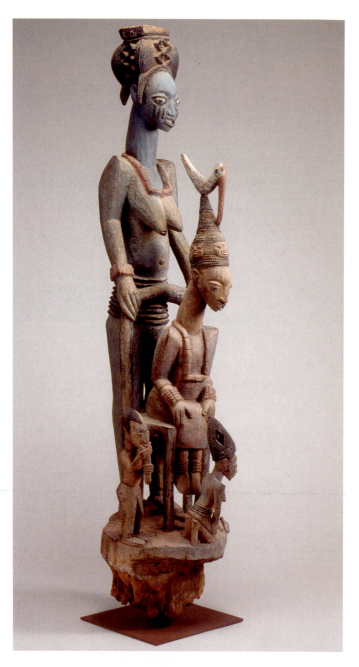

4.1 DOROTHEA LANGE. *Migrant Mother, Nipomo Valley*, 1936. Gelatin Silver Print, 1 negative: nitrate; 4" × 5". USA. From the Collections of the Library of Congress.

4.2 OLOWE OF ISE. *Palace Sculpture*, 1910–1914. Wood and pigment, 60⅞" × 13¼". Yoruba. Ikere, Nigeria. Photograph by Bob Hashimoto.

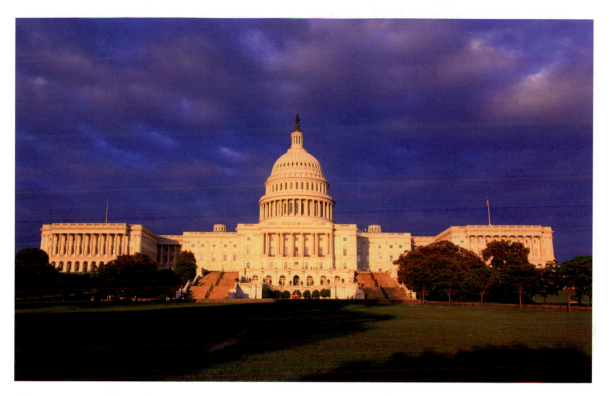

4.3   *U.S. Capitol Building,* begun 1793, exterior last renovated in 1960. Frequently redesigned, expanded, and restored under architects William Thornton, Stephen H. Hallet, George Hadfield, James Hoban, Benjamin Henry Latrobe, Charles Bulfinch, Thomas U. Walter, Edward Clark, and J. George Stewart. Terracing by Frederick Law Olmstead.

we can see that it is frontal and symmetrical, the most formal of all compositions. The smooth, simplified bodies contrast with textures on clothing and jewelry. There is a greater density of smaller shapes at the bottom, while the top forms are larger, surrounded by more empty space. Vertical forms dominate the composition, with several parallel diagonal lines. From our formal analysis, we know that the large figures represent important beings, because they are formally arranged and dominate the small, squatting figures below. The standing woman is most imposing, but she seems to play a supporting role to the smaller, seated figure.

Formal qualities add to an artwork because they are aesthetically satisfying. The arrangement of elements in the *Palace Sculpture* is balanced, hierarchical, and coherent. The thoughtful arrangement of gray tones and textures around the woman's arresting face in *Migrant Mother, Nipomo Valley* (Fig. 4.1) is memorable. Looking at art is a very different experience from looking at the general environment, which is visually disjointed and disorganized. The formal qualities of artworks make them satisfying visual experiences, adding considerably to the power of art.

Architecture can be formally analyzed, too. Consider, for example, *U.S. Capitol Building* in Washing-

ton, DC (Fig. 4.3), which is very large and symmetrical and with the dome as a centralized focal point. It sits high up, with many steps in front, so that people approach it with respect and awe. The formal elements make clear that this is an important building.

READING THE CONTENT

Content is an artwork's themes or messages. Some aspects of content may be obvious just by looking at an artwork. Others must be learned. Content is conveyed primarily in three ways: (1) through the artwork's subject matter; (2) through its symbolic or iconographic references that go beyond the subject matter; and (3) by studying the written materials and cultural background that explain the artwork's content.

SUBJECT MATTER

The most obvious factor in the content of an artwork is its **subject matter**. What is it about? With observation, we can grasp much of the subject matter of *Migrant Mother, Nipomo Valley* (Fig. 4.1). The image is not just tones and textures, but a woman whose body language tells us that she is the mother of the infant and two clinging children. The title adds more content to this image of fear and poverty: the woman is a migrant farmworker. From the date, we know that the photograph was taken during the Great Depression, a time of severe economic hardship in the United States.

The *Palace Sculpture* (Fig. 4.2) is a royal portrait of a king and queen of the palace at Ikere, which we may guess by observation. More can be learned from research. The king is ceremonially enthroned. Behind him is his senior wife, who is shown larger because the women were revered for their ability to procreate. Among the Yoruba people of Nigeria, the senior wife crowned the new king, bestowing upon him the procreative power of women and linking him to all previous kings. That power relationship is reflected in the positions of the figures.

All works of art have subject matter, even abstract works. In *Lucifer* (Fig. 4.4), painted by Jackson Pollock in 1947, the subject matter is paint itself and how it looks when dripped and splattered in layer upon layer on a very large canvas. Three kinds of paint were used—oil, aluminum paint, and enamel—each drying to a different sheen, with a different surface. Overall, *Lucifer* looks somewhat like a pattern, resembling a spread net.

As part of their subject matter, artworks also have **subtexts**, which are underlying themes or messages. The subtext in *Lucifer* is the energy of the artist himself, as he flung, dabbed, and poured the paint. This style of art is called **Abstract Expressionism**, with Pollock's works in a subcategory, tellingly entitled "Action Painting." Another subtext of this painting comes from its title, *Lucifer,* and the predominance of black paint in the topmost layer. The work seems to be alluding to the underworld as part of its subject matter.

ICONOGRAPHY

Artists can use metaphors or symbols to convey content. A visual **metaphor** is an image or element that is descriptive of something else. In *Lucifer,* splashes of paint are literally only splashes of paint. But they are also visual metaphors for artistic energy.

A **symbol** is an image or element that stands for or represents some other entity or concept. Symbols are culturally determined and must be taught. For example, in the United States today, a dove is a symbol of peace. But people from other cultures would not know by observation alone to connect "dove" and "peace."

Iconography, which literally means "image" (icono-) and "to write" (-graphy), is a system of symbols that allows artists to refer to complex ideas. For example, in the *Palace Sculpture*, the king's crown is topped by a bird, which is a Yoruba symbol for mothers and female reproductive power. We would not necessarily know that iconographic reference, but once we have learned it, its symbolic value adds a greater depth to our understanding of that sculpture. Other complex iconographic systems were associated with ancient Egypt, Byzantine art, medieval Europe, Buddhism, and Hinduism, to name only a few. In medieval Christian symbolism, the unicorn stood both for Jesus Christ and for a faithful husband in marriage. Mary, mother of Jesus, was often shown with flowers symbolizing purity or sorrow.

Figure 4.5 is *Yama,* from Tibet around the mid-seventeenth or early eighteenth century. Once we become

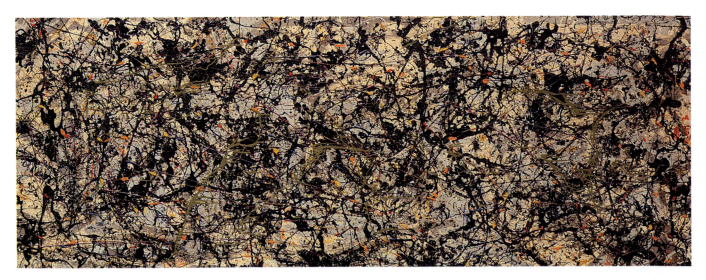

4.4 JACKSON POLLOCK. *Lucifer,* 1947. Oil, aluminum paint, and enamel on canvas, approx. 3'5" × 8'9". USA. Collection of Harry W. and Mary Margaret Anderson.

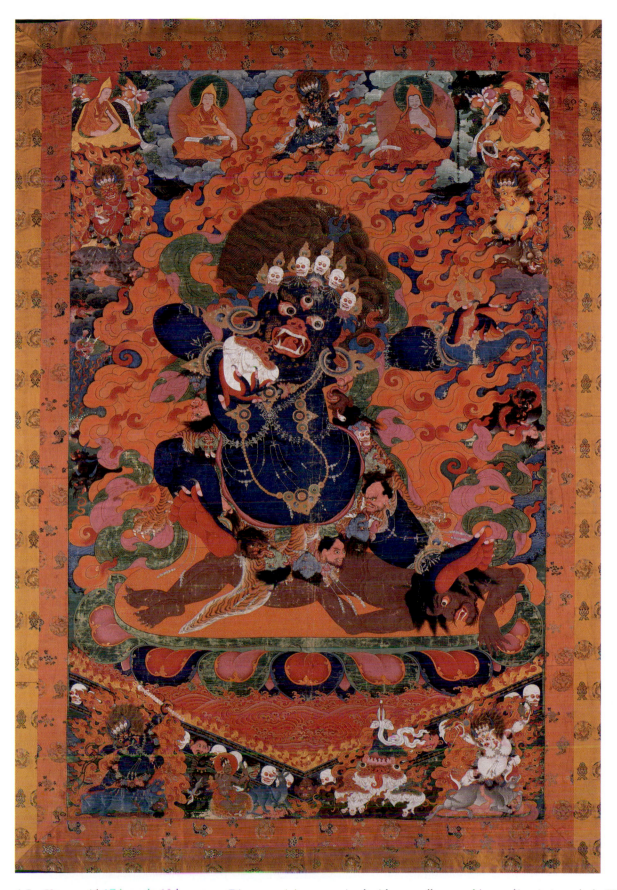

4.5 *Yama,* mid-17th–early 18th century. Distemper (pigments mixed with egg yolk, egg white, and/or size) on cloth, $72^3/8$" × $46^5/8$". Tibet. The Metropolitan Museum of Art, New York.

familiar with iconography, we would know that Yama is the Indian god of death, who later became the protector of the adherents of the Buddhist religion. Wearing a headdress of human skulls, Yama holds a thunderbolt chopper and skull, while standing on black lotus petals in a sea of blood. This fierce god fights against the inner demons like hatred and lust.

Iconography can be embedded in architecture. The *U.S. Capitol Building* (Fig. 4.3) reflects Greek and Roman architecture, to visually connect the government of the United States to the idea of democracy (Greece) and power (the Roman Empire). The building has two wings, instantly conveying the idea of the two houses of Congress and physically containing them. The central dome symbolizes unity.

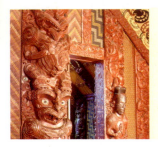

Connection The Maori Meeting House (Fig. 5.22 on page 113 and Fig. 11.15, page 289) contains political and religious iconography that is important to the native Maori people of New Zealand.

WRITINGS ABOUT ART

The writings of art professionals help us understand the full content of artworks. Art critics describe works of art and then evaluate their significance. Art historians are academics who primarily research art of the past and art of other cultures. Museum curators write catalog essays, wall labels, and educational material for museum exhibitions.

All these writings develop the content of artworks. Content is not fixed and permanent in artworks from the moment they are made. Rather, content is formed repeatedly, as people in subsequent periods reexamine and assess work. Writers from different periods can have different interpretations of the same works of art. The *Oath of the Horatii* (Fig. 4.6), painted by Jacques-Louis David in 1784, shows three young Roman men, standing together at the left, vowing to their father (in the center) that they will die if they do not return victorious from a duel against warriors representing a rival state. To the right, women grieve over the upcoming battle, as two women are related by blood and marriage to warriors on both sides of the conflict.

Here are excerpts from two twentieth-century writers discussing this painting. The first, John Canaday, writing in 1959, saw the painting as moral and revolutionary:

David invented a new style of painting . . . in order to express what amounted to a moral and philosophical revolution in art. . . . [T]he subject of "The Oath of the Horatii" is dedication and sacrifice. . . . [W]e have vigorous young males pledging their lives to the defense of their honor, their family and their country. The chaste matron and swooning girl express their grief with admirable reserve, submissive to the will of the dominant men. . . . Service to a moral and social ideal is glorified as a virtue as opposed to its parallel vice, the indulgence of personal yearnings. (Canaday 1959:11)

Another critic, Linda Nochlin, writing in 1988, asserted that this painting is based on widely held social assumptions about "[woman's] weakness and passivity, her sexual availability for men's needs, her defining domestic and nurturing function, her identity with the realm of nature, her existence as an object rather than a creator of art; the patent ridiculousness of her attempts to insert herself actively into the realm of history" (Nochlin 1988:2). Nochlin claimed that the painting not only reflected but actively reinforced social inferiority for women.

Each writer represents what the painting means to a certain group at a certain point in time. These messages may be contradictory. In fact, some of the greatest works of art have the capacity to convey conflicting, complex messages. They hold our attention longest, because they challenge us and because they are multilayered like life itself, with its compromises, conflicting claims, and profound (but sometimes very mixed) emotions. Meaning for a work of art develops over time. Why else would two twentieth-century writers still be occupied with a painting that is more than two hundred years old?

Most art professionals write from particular philosophical positions. The twentieth and early twenty-first centuries saw the rise of six major positions from which most write, and we will look very briefly at each now.

Formalist Criticism

The first philosophical position, from the mid-twentieth century, is **formalist criticism.** Formalist critics emphasized the importance of formal qualities in art. Formalism first appeared in England in the early twentieth century as a way to appreciate works of art from other cultures, in particular, the Japanese prints and African sculptures that were widely circulated in Europe. Although their subject matter and iconography were unknown to the European audience, it seemed possible to appreciate them from a formalist point of view.

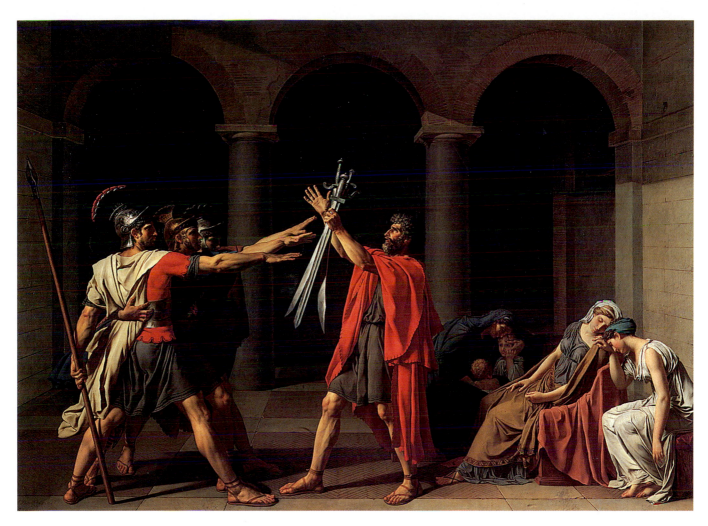

4.6 JACQUES-LOUIS DAVID. *Oath of the Horatii*, 1784. Oil on canvas, 10'10" × 14'. Louvre, Paris, France.

After World War II, formalist criticism came to be associated with Modern Art in the United States. The most famous formalist critic was Clement Greenberg, who promoted works such as Jackson Pollock's *Lucifer* (Fig. 4.4) because they were "self-critical," focusing on what was "unique to the nature of [their] medium," so that "art would be rendered 'pure'" (Greenberg 1961:13). *Lucifer* was "pure" painting because it was abstract and because it emphasized paint quality and the flatness of the painting surface. Formal qualities were most important, while representational elements, such as recognizable imagery, symbolism, or narrative, were considered detrimental distractions. Painting was the medium that most thoroughly represented the ideas of formalist critics in the late 1940s and 1950s.

By the mid-1970s, formalism was seen as too narrow a theory of art. It has been augmented by the five philosophical positions we will see next, which are associated with **Postmodern Art.**

Ideological Criticism

Ideological criticism, rooted in the writings of Karl Marx, deals with the political implications of art. All art, according to this position, supports some particular political agenda, cultural structure, or economic/class hierarchy. For example, *Lucifer* can be examined formally, as we have just seen. With ideological criticism, however, writers such as Serge Guilbaut argued that such art was amazingly successful for political reasons. After World War II, the United States was engaged in the cold war against Communist countries, and since the United States positioned itself as the land of democracy and freedom, the government helped to promote works like *Lucifer* that were about artistic freedom and individual expression.

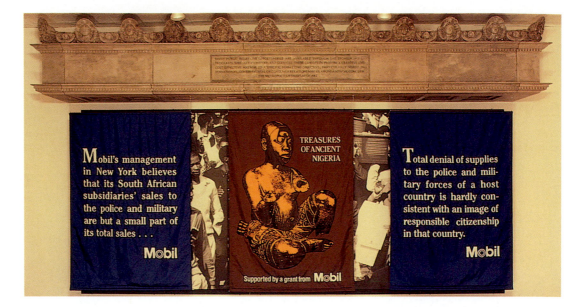

4.7 HANS HAACKE. *MetroMobiltan,* 1985. Fiberglass construction, three banners, photomural, 11'8" × 20' × 5'. Collection Centre Georges Pompidou, Paris.

Not all ideological criticism is written. Hans Haacke's 1985 piece, *MetroMobiltan* (Fig. 4.7), criticizes museums that encourage corporations to make donations for political purposes. In this case, Mobil Corporation had been supplying goods to the police who were oppressively enforcing apartheid, or forced racial segregation, in South Africa. In his artwork, Haacke "argued" that Mobil apparently hoped to improve its image with liberal protestors by sponsoring an exhibition of African Art at the Metropolitan Museum of Art in New York. *MetroMobiltan* showed that neither art nor art institutions were free from political entanglements, since museums depend on corporate sponsors to fund their exhibitions. *MetroMobiltan* contains architectural elements that resemble museum facades, banners with quotes from Mobil executives, and behind all, a stark black-and-white photomural showing a funeral procession for black South Africans shot by police.

Structuralist-Based Criticism

Structuralism is based on the premise that the study of art (or any other system of communication) cannot focus simply on the significance of any one artwork. The study of art must be the study of the structure of art, and individual artworks are only a part of that structure. Social and cultural structures also shape the meaning in art.

Structuralism was originally applied to the study of language, as was **semiotics,** which is the study of signs in verbal or written communication. These systems of communication represent ideas and are used to fabricate concepts about our world. However, the signs and structures of our languages have underlying biases and limitations. Language (or art) can convey concepts for which it has

words or symbols, but it limits knowledge because it cannot express ideas beyond its "vocabulary."

Deconstruction holds that there is a multiplicity of meanings to any text or image, and that these texts and images do not refer to any authentic, coherent world outside themselves. For example, deconstructionists hold that the Western view of the world is constructed, not real, and it serves a Western point of view. Such systems of knowledge limit any knowledge outside themselves, again because our ability to conceive and express ideas is limited by our systems of language and representation. Thus, from the inside, one perception of reality will come to seem universal and natural. Deconstructive artists and philosophers seek to "deconstruct" (or undermine and reveal) that constructed world by revealing its myths, clichés, and stereotypes.

A good illustration of these ideas is Cindy Sherman's *Untitled Film Still #35* (Fig. 4.8), a photograph from 1979. This work is one of many such "film stills" that together constitute Sherman's self-portraits. In them, she takes on feminine movie stereotypes, such as girl-next-door or vulnerable hitchhiker. She stages her work to look like film stills, which are themselves staged imagery. In her "self-portraits," there is no real Cindy Sherman. Her identity and behavior are copied. As the critic Douglas Crimp wrote,

> Sherman [as a person] is literally self-created in these works; her self is therefore understood as contingent upon the possibilities provided by the culture in which Sherman participates, not by some inner impulse. As such, her photographs reverse the terms of art and autobiography. They use art not to reveal the artist's true self, but to show the self as an imaginary construct. There is

no real Cindy Sherman in these photographs; there is only the guises she assumes. And she does not create these guises; she simply chooses them in a way that any of us do. (Crimp 1989, reprinted in Risatti 1990:138–39)

Structuralist-based artists and critics in the late twentieth century often focused on the medium of photography, which easily copies existing things and allows for multiple copies, as well as for the wide distribution of these copies. This fits with the Postmodern idea that there is no original, no "real," only copies. In contrast, Formalist critics placed great importance on the unique art object, which like paintings were seen as being original, one of a kind, and "handmade" by a gifted artist.

Psychoanalytic Criticism

Psychoanalytic criticism looks at art as the product of individuals who have been influenced and shaped by their pasts, their unconscious urges, and their social histories. Sigmund Freud wrote what was probably the first psychoanalytic examination of art when he looked at Leonardo da Vinci's work in light of Leonardo's presumed homosexuality and episodes from his early childhood. Psychoanalytic criticism seems appropriate to apply to work that deals with strong emotional content, intuition, dream imagery, or fantasy, such as the 1941 painting *The Beautiful Bird Revealing the Unknown to a Pair of Lovers* (Fig. 4.9). The work of Joan Miró seems based on hallucination, fantasy, or dream, and his imagery alludes to microscopic organisms or

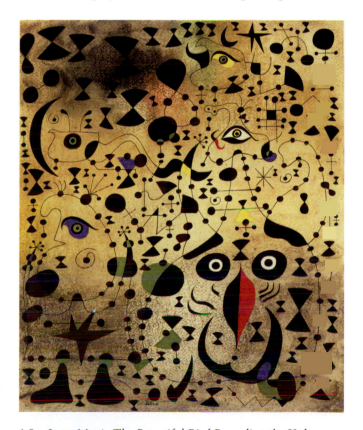

4.8 CINDY SHERMAN. *Untitled Film Still #35*, 1979. Gelatin Silver Print, 10" × 8". USA. Collection of Eli and Edythe Broad, Los Angeles.

4.9 JOAN MIRÓ. *The Beautiful Bird Revealing the Unknown to a Pair of Lovers*, 1941. Gouache and oil wash on paper, 18" × 15". The Museum of Modern Art, New York.

the star clusters in distant space. The artist developed a process of working that allowed him to switch between conscious and unconscious decisions as the image developed.

FEMINIST CRITICISM

Feminist criticism is another late-twentieth-century philosophical position that is concerned with the oppression of groups (especially women) in a given society along with the oppression of their belief systems. Feminism advocates equal social, political, and economic rights for all women and men. Feminist criticism borrows from the ideas and methodologies of ideological criticism, structuralist-based criticism, and psychoanalytic criticism. A specific area of feminist criticism deals with the representation of gender in art and how this representation can be used to support male-dominated social structures, as exemplified by Linda Nochlin's earlier quote in reference to *Oath of the Horatii*. Feminist critics seek to reveal these power relationships because they can be "invisible and can be exercised only with the complicity of those who fail to recognize either that they submit to it or that they exercise it" (Nochlin 1988:2).

The Guerrilla Girls' 1986 poster *Do Women Have to Be Naked . . .* (Fig. 4.10) is an example of an artwork functioning as feminist criticism. The poster protests the small number of female artists whose works were included in the collection of New York City's Metropolitan Museum of Art. In contrast, the museum contains many female nudes, almost all done by men for men. Feminists point out that while women make art, their work is marginalized by social and cultural struc-tures. In contrast, images of sexually available women are given the highest recognition in museums.

Gender issues are also explored in Chapter 14, Race, Gender, Clan, and Class.

Writings on Visual Culture

The most recently developed topic in critical writing is **visual culture,** a discipline that attempts to integrate and analyze the visual components of the whole of contemporary culture. To give you an idea of what that might encompass,

> you can buy a photograph of your house taken from an orbiting satellite or have your internal organs magnetically imaged. If that special moment didn't come out quite right in your photography, you can digitally manipulate it on your computer. At New York's Empire State Building, the queues are longer for the virtual reality New York Ride than for the lifts to the observation platforms. Alternatively, you could save yourself the trouble by catching the entire New York skyline, rendered in attractive pastel colors, at the New York, New York resort in Las Vegas. . . . Life in this alter-reality is sometimes more pleasant than the real thing, sometimes worse. . . . This is visual culture. It is not just part of your everyday life, it *is* your everyday life. (Mirzoeff 1998:3)

People in industrialized nations consume massive numbers of images every day, seeking information, meaning, or pleasure. To writers in visual culture, art is only part of this intense barrage of images and absolutely must be analyzed in relationship to film, advertisements, the Internet, television, and so on. People have become spectators rather than participants in their own lives, and the

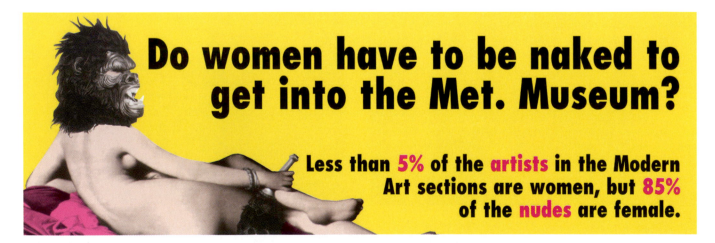

4.10   GUERRILLA GIRLS. *Do Women Have to Be Naked to Get into the Met. Museum?* 1986. Street Poster. USA.

writers examine how we receive and use this diverse imagery. Chapter 16 deals with visual culture in detail.

PERSONAL INTERPRETATION

Finally, in reference to meaning, let us look at how you, an individual, may produce your own meaning for a work of art. While you might formally analyze an artwork, consider its subject, or read about it, ultimately your response is based on your own ideas, personal tastes, experiences, and history. In addition, you may have an emotional response to the work. In the end, the work may mean something to you that it may not mean to everyone else. Also, that meaning often shifts as you age. A work of art may seem very different to you now than it did a few years ago.

THE INFLUENCE OF CONTEXT

Context consists of the interrelated social and political conditions that surround a work of art. Context includes a host of factors, such as historical events, economic trends, contemporary cultural developments, religious attitudes, other artworks of the time, and so on. It is important to consider how the context influenced artists while they were making their art, and how that helps us understand work as we look at it today.

Historical context and geographic location had an enormous influence on Rembrandt van Rijn as he worked on the large painting, *The Company of Captain Frans Banning Cocq* (Fig. 4.11), also popularly called *The Night Watch*. During Rembrandt's lifetime, almost all countries in Europe were ruled by powerful kings or nobles, and all large paintings were made for the palaces of royalty and nobility, or for majestic Catholic churches. Yet Rembrandt and other Dutch artists worked for middle-class clients in the Netherlands, a republic run by city-dwelling manufacturers and merchants made prosperous by trade. No king or saint is depicted, only Captain Cocq and his civil guardsmen, assembling for a parade. This large painting never would have been commissioned had Rembrandt lived under a seventeenth-century monarch. The painting hung in a banquet room in an Amsterdam militia hall, where years of candle and fire soot darkened its varnish, resulting in the mistaken notion that this is a night scene.

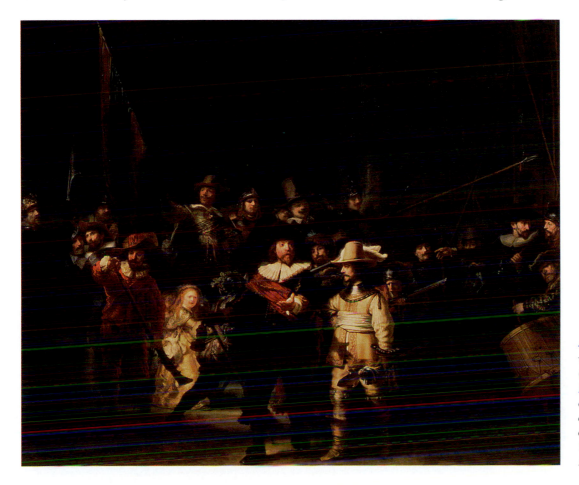

4.11 REMBRANDT VAN RIJN. *The Company of Captain Frans Banning Cocq*, or *The Night Watch*, c.1642. Oil on canvas, 11'11" × 14'4". Rijksmuseum, Amsterdam.

Of course, context is just as important in artwork produced today. In the 1990s, Shirin Neshat produced a series of photographs called *Women of Allah*, one of which is *Speechless* (Fig. 4.12). Neshat was born in Iran and immigrated to the United States as a teenager, just as Iran was being transformed into an Islamic state led by clerics. Her subject is Islamic women/femininity in a country where women's actions and rights are limited by religious law. In her photographs, women's hands or faces emerge from beneath veils, often framed by guns or flowers. On the photos, Neshat wrote religious quotes or poetry in Farsi, the language of Iran. Neshat's poignant photos are even more moving given the current international tensions.

In some cases, context may determine whether we see an object as a work of art at all. Brazilian artist Cildo Meireles's 1970 work, *Insertions into Ideological Circuits: Coca-Cola Project* (Fig. 4.13), appears at first to be ordinary Coca-Cola bottles. However, on Coke bottles that were used repeatedly (sold full, returned for a deposit, refilled, and then put out again on the market shelf), Meireles silk-screened extra words, including "Yankees, go home!" and "Projeto Coca-Cola." When the bottles were empty, the message was nearly invisible. When full, and in the hands of the Brazilians drinking the beverage, the message was readable. Meireles was protesting U.S. economic ventures that were detrimental to Brazil, that resulted in the clearing of rain forests and the uprooting and destruction of Brazilian indigenous populations. He was using an existing system of distribution to get other Brazilians to see his artwork.

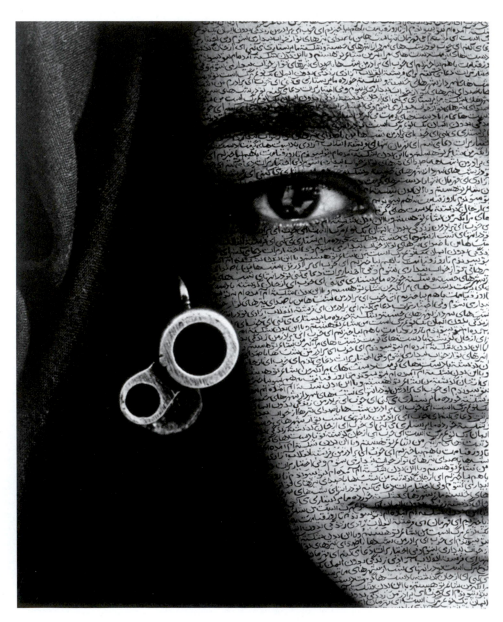

4.12 SHIRIN NESHAT. *Speechless*, 1996. Pen and ink over gelatin silver print, 49" × 36".

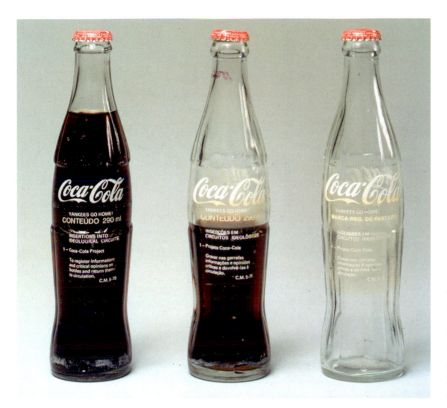

4.13 CILDO MEIRELES. *Insertions into Ideological Circuits: Coca-Cola Project*, 1970. Screen print on Coca-Cola bottles. Brazil. Courtesy of the artist and Galerie Lelong, New York. See also the text accompanying Figure 12.15.

WAYS WE ENCOUNTER ART

We encounter art in all kinds of ways—in newspapers, in museums, out on the street, at religious sites, in public parks, in government or corporate buildings, in schools, at festivals, in malls, and so on. The nature of our encounter adds meaning to the artwork.

Migrant Mother, Nipomo Valley was originally a news item. It first appeared as a grainy, low-resolution reproduction in a San Francisco newspaper just a few days after Lange took the picture. At the time, it affected people so much that they rushed donated food and supplies to the Nipomo Valley to feed the hungry workers. Today, we see *Migrant Mother, Nipomo Valley* as a high-quality reproduction in an art book or as a print in an art museum. To us, it is a work of art, not news. It refers to events in the past and is not a call to action.

So photographs change, based on how they are reproduced and where they are seen and what history they represent. If this is true for a photograph such as Lange's, then it is even more so for our experience of architecture, sculpture, large paintings, and performance art. Alexander Calder's *Bent Propeller* from 1970 (Fig. 4.14) was a large public sculpture that stood in the World Trade Center complex, and visitors before

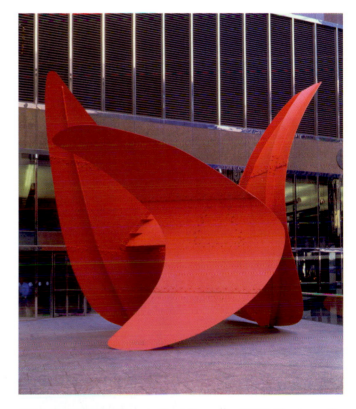

4.14 ALEXANDER CALDER. *Bent Propeller*, 1970. Sheet metal, bolts, and paint, 25' high. Destroyed on September 11, 2001, during the attack on the World Trade Center. World Trade Center, New York.

2001 appreciated it in relation to its location, which was one of the huge economic and trading hubs in the world. Now it exists only in photographs, and its meaning is forever altered by the events of September 11, 2001.

Photographs communicate only a fraction of the total experience of most artworks. The *Potala Palace* in Lhasa, Tibet (Fig. 4.15), begun in the seventeenth century, is an enormous structure high in the Himalaya mountains and the home of the Dalai Lama, the traditional spiritual and political leader of Tibet (the current Dalai Lama has lived in exile since the Chinese invaded in the 1950s). Looking at the photograph at your leisure, you can marvel at the palace as a whole, framed against majestic peaks and reflected in a nearby lake. Were you to actually approach and enter the palace, your experience would be quite different: physical exertion while climbing steep stairways, brisk mountain weather, partial glimpses of buildings rather than "the perfect shot," encounters with other pilgrims, tour buses at the base of the mountain, and so on.

Even when we look at the actual art and not at photographic reproductions, art changes as a result of where we encounter it. For example, we can go to the Seattle Art Museum to see the *Interior House Post* (Fig. 4.16), a traditional artwork from the Kwakiutl tribe of Native Americans from the Northwest Coast of Canada. The museum favors our experiencing art with our eyes. Most museums are very quiet and forbid touching anything. But the people for whom this house post was carved had a very different experience of it. It was one of four main supports in a large ceremonial house, first used in 1916 for a **potlatch,** an elaborate and sometimes raucous celebration lasting several days with feasting, performances, singing, masquerades, and storytelling. The ceremonial animals and figures carved on the house posts were integrated into these festivities. The potlatch was an experience for all the senses. Afterward, people lived every day with these large carvings in their houses. The house post was part of the very structure of their house and the fabric of their family lives. This is so different from our modern museum experience of the *Interior House Post*.

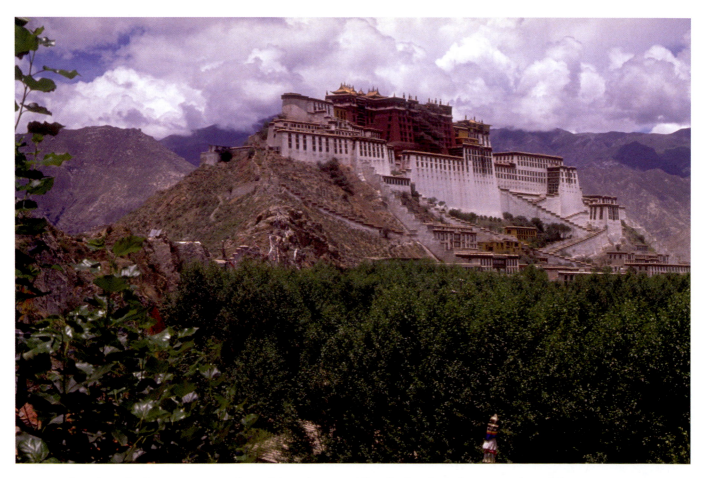

4.15 *Potala Palace*, the former summer palace of the Tibetan Buddhist leader, the Dalai Lama. Lhasa, Tibet.

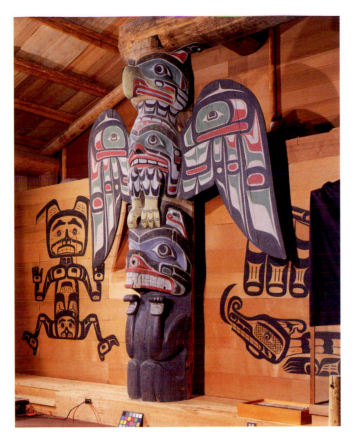

Connection *Turn to Figure 7.17, page 153, to read about a feast dish used at a potlatch celebration.*

Our discussion of the *Interior House Post* brings up another aspect of art and the ways we encounter it. Art is both mimetic and performative. It is **mimetic** because its appearance mimics or resembles something, or it represents an idea. Art is **performative** because it is used, and, in its use, it performs specific functions. The way we encounter the art greatly influences its mimetic or performative aspects.

The carvings on the *Interior House Post* are mimetic. They imitate the forms of bears and thunderbirds and are part of the native iconographies along the Northwest Coast. The carvings are also performative, obviously, for those who attended the potlatch in 1916. But how is the *Interior House Post* performative to the people who visit the Seattle Art Museum today? Rather than being something to live with or to celebrate with, the *Interior House Post* in the museum is an object to study or appreciate for its striking, bold formal qualities and for its references to Kwakiutl philosophy of the interrelatedness of animals and people.

4.16 ARTHUR SHAUGHNESSY. *Interior House Post*, c. 1907. Carved and painted red cedar, 180" × 132" × 34". Kwakiutl. Gilford Island, British Columbia, Canada. Seattle Art Museum. Gift of Mr. John H. Hauberg. See also the text accompanying Figure 14.14.

SYNOPSIS

Art communicates complex ideas and emotions through its formal qualities, its content, its context, and the ways in which we encounter it. Formal analysis is essential for appreciating most art. Regarding content, we saw six philosophical positions from which art has been analyzed for the past seventy years and even today: formalist criticism, ideological criticism, structuralist-based criticism, psychoanalytic criticism, feminist criticism, and visual culture. The meaning of art is not fixed, but changing and sometimes contradictory.

Every work of art was created within a historical, political, social, or religious context. Knowing about that context broadens and deepens our understanding of a work of art. How we encounter art affects what we think about it. All art is both mimetic and performative.

FOOD FOR THOUGHT

We have talked a lot about writing in relationship to art in this chapter. But what do artists think of writings about art? Georgia O'Keeffe frequently painted details of flowers, up close and large, as in Yellow Calla, 1926 (Fig. 4.17). In private letters, the artist wrote that her art came from her deep love of the colors and patterns, inspired by landscape and plant forms of nature. She wrote in one letter:

There has been no rain since I came out but today a little came—enough to wet the sage and moisten the top of the dry soil—and make the world smell very fresh and fine—I drove up the canyon four or five miles when the sun was low and I

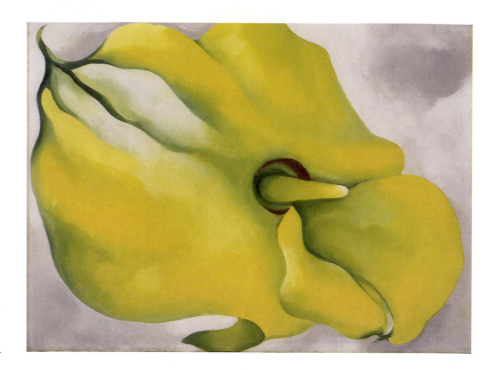

4.17 GEORGIA O'KEEFFE. *Yellow Calla*, 1926. Oil on canvas, 9" × 12³/₄". Smithsonian American Art Museum, Washington, DC.

wish I could send you a mariposa lily—and the smell of the damp sage—the odd dark and bright look that comes over my world in the low light after a little rain. (Cowart 1987:239)

Other writers have perceived a feminist content to O'Keeffe's work. In particular, they thought her flower imagery represented female sexuality in a positive way, a notion that O'Keeffe rejected. Nevertheless, feminist writer and artist Judy Chicago wrote:

[O'Keeffe] seemed to have made a considerable amount of work that was constructed around a center. . . .There also seemed to be an implied relationship between [her] own body and that centered image. . . . In her paintings, the flower suggests her own femininity, through which the mysteries of life could be revealed. (Chicago 1975:142)

Here are other examples. The artist Mark Rothko wrote frequently about art in general and his paintings in particular in the early part of his career, but ceased doing so after 1950 because "I simply cannot see myself proclaiming a series of nonsensical statements, making each vary from the other and which ultimately have no meaning whatsoever" (Clearwater 1984:67). Yet other artists have been very prolific writers, like Judy Chicago or Donald Judd, a leading artist of the 1960s and 1970s, whose articles and essays were widely published.

- *Does the written word add to the public's experience of art?*
- *Do writings bias or limit our experience of art?*
- *How important is the artist's intention versus the critical reception of the work? Which should be most important in interpreting a work?*

Connection *Judy Chicago led a group of women who produced* The Dinner Party *(Fig. 7.19, page 154). See also Figure 15.26, page 420, for more information about Mark Rothko's painting* Green, Red, Blue.

Your Thomson Online Resources

 Go to **ArtExperience Online** for the Flashcards, Quiz, and Study Guide for this chapter.

Who Makes Art?

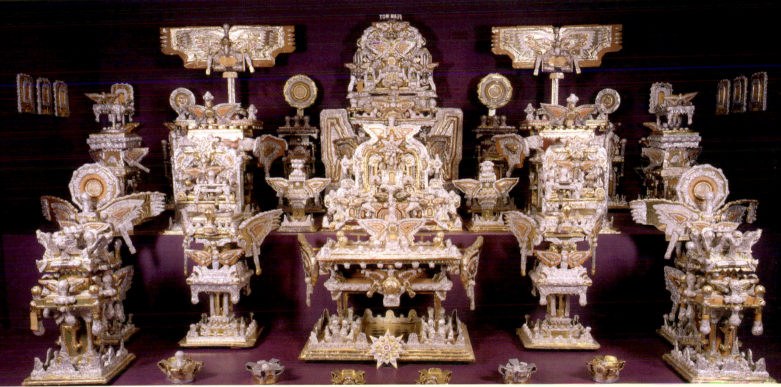

© The Bridgeman Art Library

INTRODUCTION

One might answer "Artists make art," in response to the title for this chapter. But a more thorough answer comes with researching a number of issues: Who conceives the idea? Who actually makes the object? Who supplies materials and training? Who provides support?

Consider the following:

- How is art an individual's endeavor, and how is it a social product?
- Who are artists? How are they educated?
- What social role do artists have, and what functions do they fulfill?
- Do artists work alone, in groups, or both?
- Who supports the making of art?

ART PRODUCTION AS A SOCIAL ACTIVITY

We may think that the process of art making consists of artists who apply their skills, work a while, and finally, there is the art! But many people contribute to this process:

- The culture develops a tradition of art making and an understanding of what art is. Artists operate within that framework.
- Teachers and manufacturers supply the materials and knowledge for making art.
- Others often support artists while they make art.
- Rulers, priests, teachers, shamans, masters, publishers, art critics, merchants, connoisseurs, gallery owners, and curators set standards for determining what art is within a culture.

In every respect, the pyramids of ancient Egypt were social products, even though they were the tombs of individual pharaohs. The first grand tomb ever, the *Stepped Pyramid of Djoser* (Fig. 5.1) was designed by Imhotep and dates from 2650 BCE. But Imhotep was influenced by earlier, smaller Egyptian tombs, and he was working within a culture that already had developed complex belief systems about the afterlife, tombs, and mortuary temples. Funds for the *Stepped Pyramid of Djoser* as well as later pyramids came from the Egyptian economy, supported by the general population. Thousands contributed to pyramid construction, including architects, engineers, priests, skilled workers, and laborers.

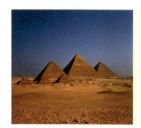

Connection The Stepped Pyramid of Djoser *predates the Great Pyramids of Giza (Fig. 10.2), and was a great influence upon the later pharaohs who had them constructed.*

Other art forms—film, architecture, or any work of large scale—obviously require the active participation of many to be realized. Even small-scale work,

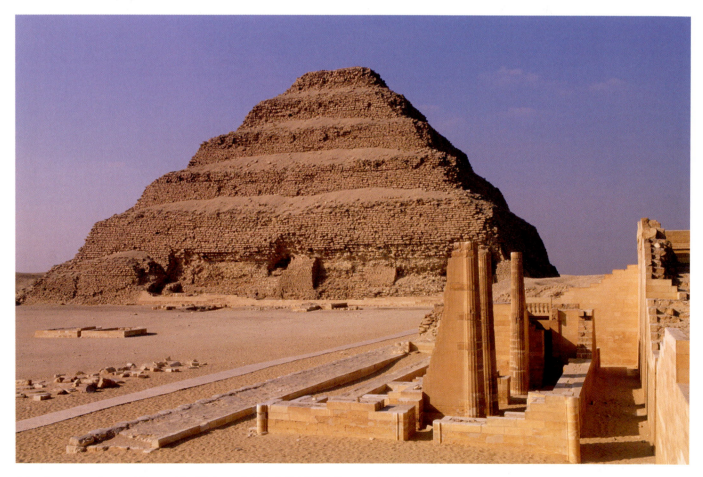

5.1 IMHOTEP. *Stepped Pyramid of Djoser*, 2650–2631 BCE. Saqqarah, Egypt.

such as a student's painting, requires input of teachers, past oil painters, and art critics to provide the necessary background of skills and ideas. The materials were developed by artists and scientists, and manufactured by art supply firms. The student probably has financial support, showing that parents, politicians, wealthy donors, and university administrators consider the study of oil painting to be important enough to pay for it.

ABOUT ARTISTS

The fact that art is a social production does not diminish the importance of artists. Artists are creative people with exceptional skills who take meaningful ideas and embody them in a visual form.

TRAINING OF ARTISTS

Artists need to learn their skills, and traditionally, many started as apprentices working directly with mature artists to learn materials, manual skills, and styles. Sometimes very skilled apprentices make part of the master's artwork, but the final product is owned by and credited to the master artist. Leonardo da Vinci was apprenticed for many years to the artist Andrea del Verrocchio and painted the face of the angel on the left in the *Baptism of Christ* (Fig. 5.2). The other angel's face was painted by the student Lorenzo de Credi. Throughout Africa, artists traditionally were trained by the apprentice method, learning the tools and methods as well as aesthetic standards, as in the *Shrine of Shango* (Fig. 5.3). Among the Yoruba artists in modern Africa, "the final sharp cutting is best done by the master" while apprentices do the "mechanical aspects of the work, and as their skill increases, more and more is entrusted to them" (Fr. Kevin Carroll, quoted in Willett 1993:236).

In medieval Europe, specialized societies called **guilds** preserved technical information for artists and regulated art making. They also protected artists' interests, as well as those of goldsmiths, stone workers, weavers, barrel makers, and bakers. Guilds contributed many craftsmen who worked on large medieval churches. Sometimes, the guild system created unusual groupings. For example, in medieval Florence, painters belonged to the guild of "Medici e Speziali" (physicians), and sculptors belonged to the "Fabbricanti" guild of builders or to the goldsmiths' guild, which included jewelers.

Art academies, or schools that provide systematized art instruction, are a more recent invention for the training of artists. An early example of academy-like

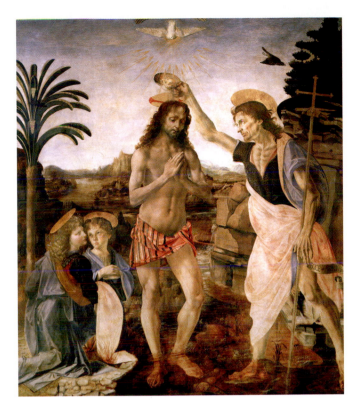

5.2   ANDREA DEL VERROCCHIO (1436–1488). *Baptism of Christ*, 1472–1475. Painted in collaboration with his pupils Leonardo da Vinci and Lorenzo di Credi. Wood, 69³/₄" × 59¹/₂". Uffizi, Florence.

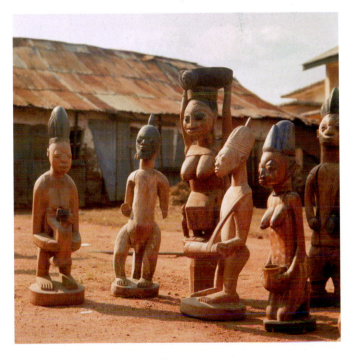

5.3   *Shrine of Shango*, the Yoruba god of thunder, furnished with figures of women devotees, 20th century. Oroko wood, average 30" high. Collection of Oba Laoye II, Temi of Ede, Nigeria.

training comes from thirteenth- to seventeenth-century Persia (Iran). The *kitab khana* were libraries and workshops sponsored by royalty that produced fine illuminated manuscripts executed by highly trained Islamic artists. Students were taught the fine arts of calligraphy and illumination, copied master works, and later collaborated with senior artists. The kitab khana eventually spread to India under the Mughal shahs, where this tradition of art training continued. *Scribe and Painter at Work*, from the *Hadiqat Al-Haqiqat* (The Garden of Truth) by Hakim Sana'i (Fig. 5.4), shows the palace-like conditions where the best artists worked.

Academies in Europe gradually replaced the guilds, beginning in the fifteenth century. Academies were usually supported by the state or by some powerful patron, ensuring an outstanding level of art production to increase the sponsor's own fame. Among their many functions, European academies generally (1) provide art training for students; (2) sponsor lectures in theory and established aesthetic standards; and (3) accept mature artists as members. For example, in 1648, France's King Louis XIV founded the powerful Royal Academy (Académie Royale de Peinture et de Sculpture). Through his ministers and the academy, the king controlled the decorative arts, architecture, painting, and landscape architecture for his enormous, lavish palace at Versailles and its surrounding gardens, as well as his other residences. Among mature artists, only those whose work conformed to certain standards received commissions. Nicolas René Jollain the Elder's *Portrait of Louis XIV holding the plan for the Royal House at Saint-Cyr* (Fig. 5.5) shows an absolute ruler dedicated to his own glory and majesty. Jollain's painting is a product of the Academy's influence.

Although art academies still exist in much-modified form, most artists in the United States today study in a college or university. Even within the university, however, the apprentice method persists in internships, where students receive college credit for working with art professionals.

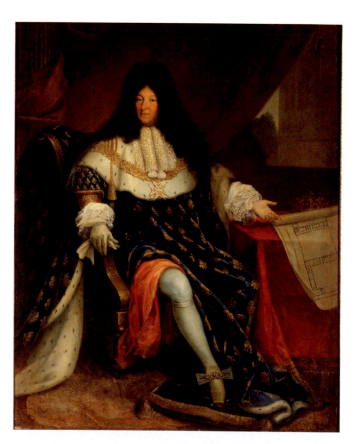

5.4 JAGANATH. *Scribe and Painter at Work,* from the *Hadiqat Al-Haqiqat* (The Garden of Truth) by Hakim Sana'i, 1599–1600. First Miniature, folio 15. Pen and ink on paper. Mughal.

5.5 NICOLAS RENE JOLLAIN THE ELDER. *Portrait of Louis XIV holding the plan for the Royal House at Saint-Cyr,* 1661–1715. Oil on canvas, 87" × 65". Chateaux de Versailles et de Trianon, Versailles.

Some artists are self-taught, meaning that they have received no formal art training. Some work in isolation. Often, their art is labeled as naive, outsider, or folk art, yet they may have vision and energy that rival all other artists. For fourteen years in Washington, D.C., James Hampton worked on *The Throne of the Third Heaven of the Nations Millennium General Assembly* (Fig. 5.6), from the time he left his day job as a janitor until the middle of the night. He dreamed of opening a storefront ministry after retirement. By the time he died, he had produced a heavenly vision with 180 pieces, made from inexpensive or cast-off materials.

THE CONTEXT FOR ART MAKING

Who makes the art object? Sometimes the artist, and sometimes others, as we will see.

Workshops

Workshops consist of apprentices and assistants who operate under the name of a master artist. Some might assist the artist, prepare art materials, excel at certain crafts, or handle the workshop's business affairs. The output from workshops can be prodigious. We have already discussed apprentices in workshop situations in Italy and in Africa (see page 101), as well as the kitab khana of Persia (see page 102). Many prominent European artists maintained workshops from the fifteenth through the nineteenth centuries.

Community Art Making

In community art making, large groups of people not normally considered artists contribute directly to the production of a work of art. Collectively they may realize big projects.

In medieval Europe, many small, growing cities built impressive cathedrals that were symbols of community pride. Armies of craftsmen worked on these structures, but equally importantly, the townspeople, from the wealthy to the poor, also contributed their labor and often substantially paid for the church. Abbot Haimon wrote an eyewitness account in a letter that describes the townspeople of Chartres dragging building materials and food to the construction site:

> Who has ever seen!—Who has ever heard tell, in times past, that powerful princes . . . nobles, men and women, have bent their proud and haughty necks to the harness of carts, and that, like beasts of burden, they have dragged to the abode of Christ these waggons, loaded

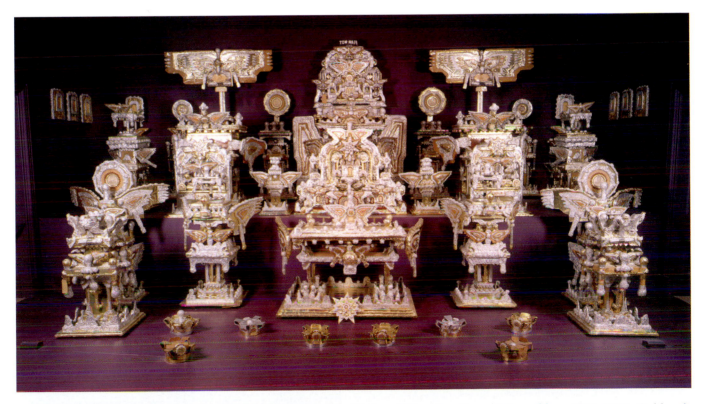

5.6   JAMES HAMPTON. *The Throne of the Third Heaven of the Nations Millennium General Assembly*, c. 1950–1964. Gold and silver aluminum foil, Kraft paper, and plastic over wood furniture, paperboard, and glass, 180 pieces in all; overall configuration: 10^1/$_2$" × 27' × 14^1/$_2$'. Smithsonian American Art Museum, Washington, DC.

with wines, grains, oil, stone, wood and all that is necessary for the wants of life, or for the construction of the church? (Holt 1947:45)

Sometimes, these contributions were memorialized in the stained glass or sculptures of these grand cathedrals. Figure 5.7 is a detail from Chartres Cathedral's window of St. Lubin, titled *A wine merchant transports a cask of wine.*

Among the Hindu-Balinese people on the South Pacific island of Bali, almost everyone makes art, either visual art, dance, or music, although certain people are recognized as teachers or people of superior ability. Art, religion, and social institutions are completely intertwined. The visual arts alone consist of stone temples with carved reliefs, wooden pagodas, wooden statues for smaller shrines, paintings, large decorated cremation towers used in funerals, items for personal adornment, masks for performances, textiles, sculptures made of baked dough, and food offerings for temples (see Fig. 9.13). Although simple offerings are made every day to deities, ancestors, and demons, Balinese women make large sculptures of fried, colored rice dough like the *Sarad offering* (Fig. 5.8) for temple festivals. Offerings like this exist but a short time and can be used only once, but the obvious care and skill that go into them indicate the significance of art in everyday life.

The *AIDS Memorial Quilt,* begun in 1989 (Fig. 5.9; another view is on page 266), provides us with another example of community art making. The *AIDS Memorial Quilt* is a composite of thousands of three-by-six-foot panels, each made by ordinary people to memorialize someone they lost to AIDS. It is a collection of individual remembrances, and each remembrance is an equal contribution to the fabric of the whole. The people who made the panels communicated their love and loss in ways that may be naive or may be sophisticated, but collectively are very moving. The quilt is an ongoing effort of the Names Project, begun by gay activist Cleve Jones in San Francisco in the 1980s. It is also used as a fund-raising tool for AIDS research.

Fabricators, Construction Assistants, Technicians, and Production Staff

A lot of artists hire others to make their artwork, either totally or partially. Printmakers may hire other printers to make their editions of prints, and sculptors may hire

fabricators to make part or all of their artworks. Filmmakers hire crews. Robert Smithson's *Spiral Jetty,* dated 1970 (Fig. 5.10), is a long spiral of rock that extends outward into the Great Salt Lake in Utah. Smithson required the assistance of an engineer to plan the work, and then hired a construction crew to make this piece about the human manipulation of the earth, energy potential, and the passage of time.

The Artist as Object Maker

In many cases, individual artists make their own artwork. Michelangelo Buonarroti did most of the painting on the colossal *Sistine Ceiling* because he was dissatisfied with the work that collaborators did. Vincent van Gogh painted all his own paintings, because, as he wrote to his brother Theo, he valued the act of creation more than life itself.

Eva Hesse made seventy sculptures during the few years of her life, even though she was very ill much of the time. She was driven to create work that seemed off balance and expressed life's absurdity and fundamental strangeness. Pieces lean against walls, spread across the floor, or hang from ceilings, often made from materials that seem fragile or barely there. *Repetition 19, III,*

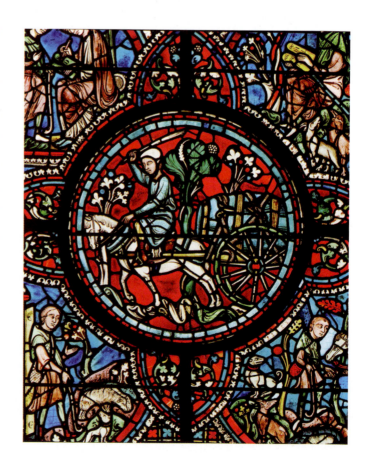

5.7 Detail of Gothic stained-glass window of St. Lubin, 1200–1210. North side of nave. Chartres, France.

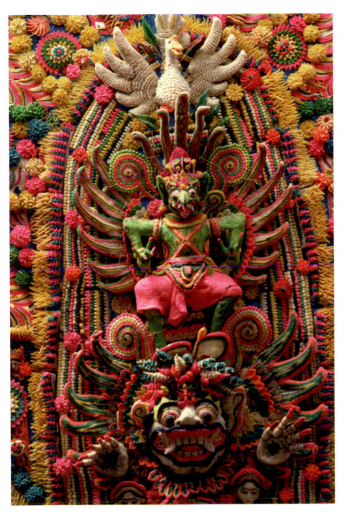

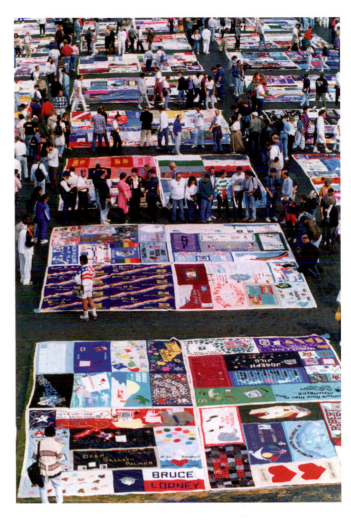

5.8   *Sarad offering* in Bali. Crafted of dyed rice dough, intricate sarad offerings are made during temple festivals by Balinese women. Photograph c. 1990. Bali, Indonesia.

5.9   Displaying the *AIDS Memorial Quilt,* October 11, 1992. Washington, DC.

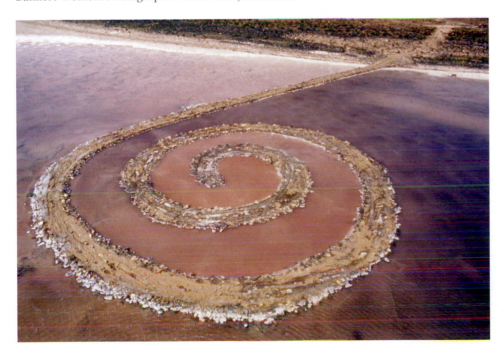

5.10   ROBERT SMITHSON. *Spiral Jetty,* 1970. Black rocks, salt crystals, earth, red water (algae), $3^1/2'$ high × 15' wide × 1,500' long. Great Salt Lake, Utah (often submerged). For more on this artwork, see the text accompanying Figure 15.18.

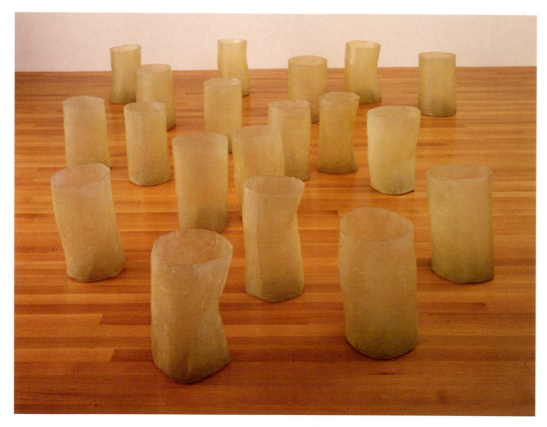

5.11   Eva Hesse. *Repetition 19, III,* 1968. Nineteen tubular fiberglass units, 19–20" high × 11–12 ²/₃" diameter . The Museum of Modern Art, New York.

from 1968 (Fig. 5.11) consists of irregular, almost organic-looking vessels of fiberglass that seem caught between growth and dissolution.

Collaborations

In many instances, art making is a collaborative activity among professionals of equal standing. The knowledge and skill of each collaborator are essential to the final art product. An example is traditional Japanese prints, like *Basket Ferry* (Fig. 5.12) by Ando or Utagawa Hiroshige, requiring the combined skills of many professionals all commissioned by a publisher. While the artist made an original drawing, a papermaker, engraver, and printer were required to bring the final print to fruition, as illustrated in Figure 3.8.

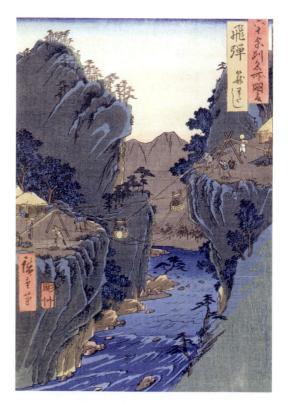

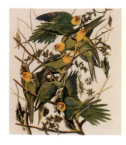

Connection *Another example of artistic collaboration is John James Audubon's Carolina Paroquet from Birds of America. The book required the combined efforts of Audubon, a naturalist, and a professional engraver. See Figure 15.22, page 417.*

5.12   Ando or Utagawa Hiroshige. *Basket Ferry,* 19th century. Woodblock print, 13¹/₂" × 9". Kagowatashi, Hida Province. Leeds Museums and Galleries (City Art Gallery), UK.

THE ROLE OF ARTISTS IN VARIOUS CULTURES

The artist's position in society reflects how that culture uses art, how it values art, and what it expects the artist to do.

ART MAKING BASED ON GENDER

In some cultures, men make certain art objects, while women make others. This usually reflects the different roles, rights, and responsibilities of males and females within their social groups. For example, Balinese women make most of their daily and festival offerings (Fig. 5.8). In contrast, the major architectural monuments and the sculpture of the ancient Greeks were all made by men. This reflects the realities of Greek society, where women were secluded in their homes and excluded from political and public life.

Among the Navajo people, men conduct rituals and, thus, make sand paintings, which are part of ritual ceremonies. During rituals, sand painters sprinkle natural pigments directly onto the earth (Fig. 5.13), creating symbols and sacred images to cure the sick, promote fertility, promote general well-being, or ensure successful hunting. Women produce other arts, primarily the weavings. This division reflects broader Navajo philosophy about the nature of men and women. For sand paintings to be effective, each must look like its traditional prototype, or the ceremony may not achieve its desired results. The Navajo view men as static in nature. Women, by contrast, are seen as dynamic, and they aspire to innovation in their weavings. Each work is new (Anderson 1990:98, 107).

Among the Sepik peoples of Papua New Guinea, art making is men's work, and combined rituals and art create male solidarity within a tribe and protect their power from women or other hostile men. The *Male Spirit Mask* (Fig. 5.14) is worn by men in initiation rituals for boys, and it represents a water- or tree-dwelling male ancestor spirit. Individual men, with the help of a master artist, produce paintings and carvings that become vehicles by which an older man can pass his spirit to a younger man. By these means, the men's

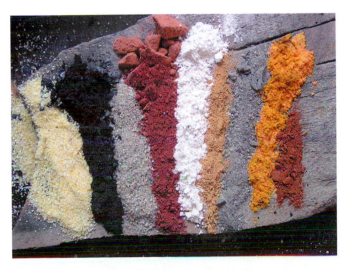

5.13   Natural pigments, similar to those used by the Navajo people to prepare ritual sand paintings. From left to right, the pigments are corn meal, pulverized charcoal, brown sand, red ochre, ground gypsum, yellow ochre, gray sand, pollen, and brown clay. Photo by Margaret Lazzari.

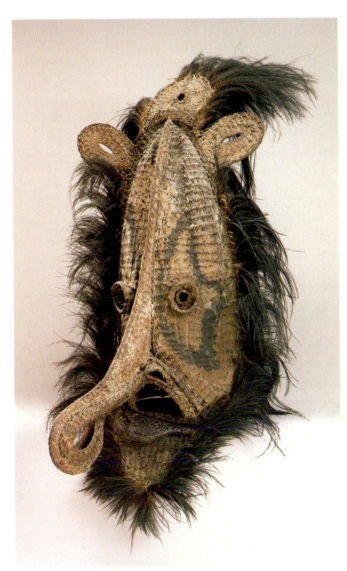

5.14   *Male Spirit Mask*, possibly by the Arambak culture, 20th century. Middle Sepik, Papua New Guinea. Cane, other plant fibers, cassoway feather, mud, and paint, 47" × 27" × 23$\frac{1}{2}$". Museum of Fine Arts, Houston, Texas.

collective power and knowledge are preserved within their group.

Connection Read more on Sepik rituals and artworks in Chapter 14, page 371.

THE ARTIST AS SKILLED WORKER

In some cultures, artists are anonymous skilled workers or laborers. For example, Medieval artists and craftsmen who built the large cathedrals were not famous "personalities," but were more like union members, people of skill who were part of a new, emerging middle class. In Communist China from the 1950s through the 1980s, artists were not to seek personal glory, but to work anonymously making art for the common good.

Among the Baule people of Western Africa (Ivory Coast), artists are skilled professionals, and the best earn prestige and high pay. However, the owner is associated with a sculpture, not the artist who made it, because the spiritual purposes of the work are more important than its appearance, and it is the owner of the piece who performs rituals and develops the artwork's spiritual cult. A well-made piece such as the *Baule Seated Female Figure* (Fig. 5.15) can be equally effective ritualistically regardless of the quality of work, and may indeed be less effective if its human maker is emphasized. Our example may represent a spirit wife, and so was hidden away in a personal shrine in the home, perhaps not seen even by other family members.

Connection See Chapter 13, page 347, for a related Baule sculpture.

THE ARTIST SCIENTIST

Science, art, and math are linked at many times throughout history. In many Islamic cultures, especially those of Persia and the Middle East, patterns in math, geometry, art, and architecture are seen as means of reconciling the apparent contradiction between unity and diversity, between one Creator and the variety of life forms. The endless pattern on the dome of the *Masjid-i-Shah*, or Royal Mosque of Isfahan, 1612–1637 (Fig. 5.16), expresses boundless variety, but there is unity in its underlying geometric grid, a metaphor for the infinite spirit of Allah. The three smaller diagrams to the right show how the pattern was developed through spirals superimposed on squares. Islamic philosophers from the tenth century saw the square as representing what was rigid and earthbound, like rocks and crystals,

whereas the circle represented heat, organic things, movement, and closeness to the Creator. The circular dome (= heaven) sits above the square structure below (= earth).

Connection More discussion of the Masjid-i-Shah is in Chapter 9 on pages 235–237.

One of the most famous of all Western artist-scientists was Leonardo da Vinci. Although he is well known for two paintings, the *Last Supper* and the *Mona Lisa*, he also filled many notebooks with his own observations on hydraulics, zoology, geology, optics, physics, botany, and anatomy, like the *Proportions of the Human Figure* (Fig. 5.17). In a letter to the Duke of

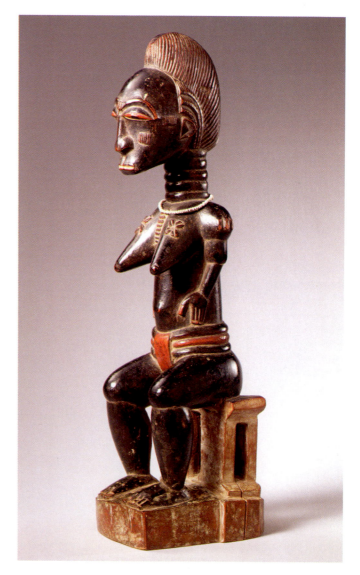

5.15   *Baule Seated Female Figure*. Wood. Private collection.

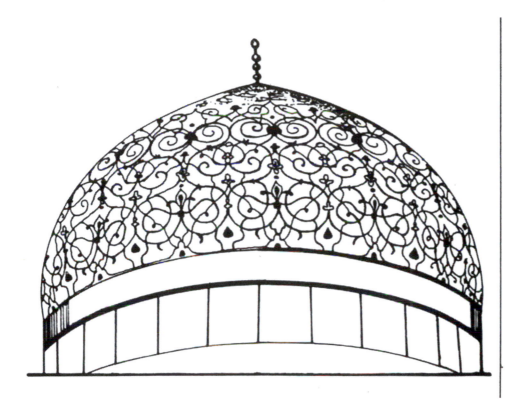

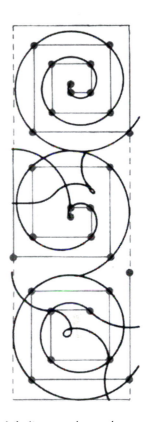

5.16   Diagram of the Dome of the *Masjid-i-Shah*, or Royal Mosque, 1612–1637. Isfahan, Iran. The left diagram shows the pattern design on the dome, while the three on the right show the interrelatedness of the square, spiral, circle, and the geometric basis of the patterns. Review the information on the Masjid-i-Shah mosque accompanying Figures 9.40 and 9.41.

Mantua asking for a position in his court, Leonardo outlined his many skills:

> I have a sort of extremely light and strong bridges, adapted to be most easily carried, and with them you may pursue, and at any time flee from the enemy. . . . And if the fight should be at sea I have kinds of many machines most efficient for offence and defence; and vessels which will resist the attack of the largest guns. . . . In case of need I will make big guns, mortars and light ordnance of fine and useful forms. . . . In times of peace I believe I can give perfect satisfaction . . . in architecture and the composition of buildings, public and private; and in guiding water from one place to another. . . . I can carry out sculpture in marble, bronze, or clay, and also I can do in painting whatever may be done, as well as any other, be he whom he may. (Holt 1947:169–70)

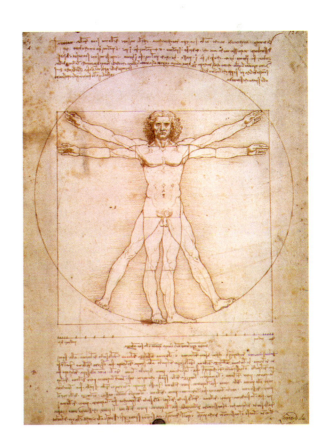

5.17   LEONARDO DA VINCI. *Proportions of the Human Figure (Vitruvian Man),* c. 1492. Pen and ink on paper, 13½" × 9⅔". Galleria dell' Accademia, Venice.

To Leonardo, observation was essential to understanding the mechanics and the beauty of the world and, thus, the foundation of both science and art. Careful observation was more important to Leonardo than the authority of religion or examples from antiquity.

THE ARTIST PRIEST

Art is often a vehicle for spirituality. The artist who makes spiritual art is sometimes also a holy person, priest, or shaman.

The sculpture *God Te Rongo and His Three Sons*, c. 1800–1900 (Fig. 5.18), is a representation of a deity from the Cook Islands in Polynesia and was used in religious rituals exclusively by the group's most important leaders. The sculptors who created ritual pieces such as *Te Rongo* were specialists called *Ta'unga*, a word that also means "priest." They trained for a long time as apprentices, not only to attain art skills but also to acquire the spiritual power inherent in their tools and materials.

During the early medieval period in Europe, one of the major art forms was illuminated manuscripts, which were handwritten and illustrated prayer books or Bibles. Monks in monasteries made them. In the early Renaissance, a monk who came to be called Fra Angelico painted several versions of the *Annunciation* (Fig. 5.19), when an angel appeared to Mary and she conceived Jesus. The sweetness, simplicity, and serenity of Fra Angelico's paintings led to his nickname.

Connection Calligraphic renderings of Quran verses set in stone adorn the Taj Mahal (Fig. 10.18). The calligraphy was designed by the artist Amanat Khan, who also selected many of the verses. Of all the craftsmen, builders, and architects who worked on the Taj Mahal, only Amanat Khan is known.

Among Native Americans there is a tie between some kinds of art making and ritual performances. As we have seen, the men who make Navajo sand paintings perform the sacred ceremonies at the same time. The Hopi and Zuni men who made kachina dolls like the *Buffalo Kachina* (Fig. 5.20) also performed important spiritual ceremonies to ensure the welfare of their community and good crops. There were several kinds of dolls, each related to a particular spirit, and this kachina was used in rituals to promote the seasonal return of animals. Performers themselves dressed in similar costumes while conducting each ritual.

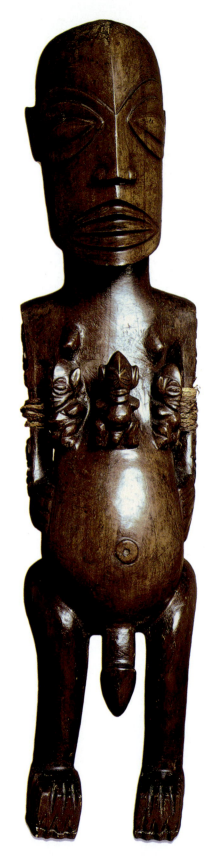

5.18 *God Te Rongo and His Three Sons*, c. 1800–1900. Wood, 27" high. Cook Islands, Polynesia. The British Museum, London. See also the text accompanying Figure 8.3.

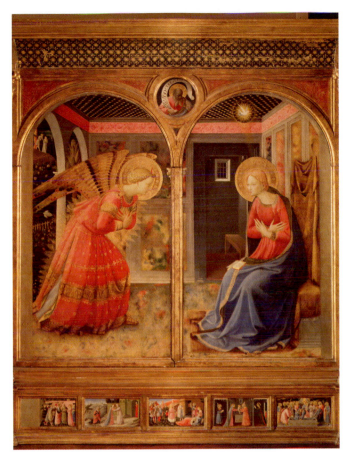

5.19 Fra Angelico. *Annunciation*, 1430s. Montecarlo Altarpiece, 76³/4" × 62¹/2". S. Maria delle Grazie, S. Giovanni Valdarno, Italy.

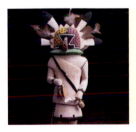

Connection *Another example of a kachina is the Ahola Kachina (Fig. 9.18, page 215), with symbols that represent north, south, east, and west as well as the heavens above and the nadir below.*

THE CREATIVE GENIUS

Some cultures believe that an artist is a creative genius, with almost transcendent abilities. Imhotep, the architect of the *Stepped Pyramid of Djoser* (Fig. 5.1), is the first artist recorded in history and he was associated with the concept of genius, not only because of the *Stepped Pyramid* but also because he was a priest, scribe, physician, and minister to the pharaoh. After his death, Imhotep was worshiped as one of the Egyptian gods.

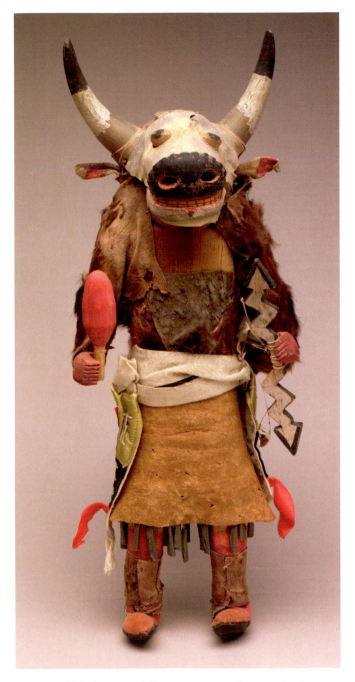

5.20 Buffalo kachina doll, c. 1915. Wood, paint, feathers, horns, leather, buffalo fur, rawhide, cotton, satin ribbon, tin, nails, and string, 17" × 6" × 5¹/2". Zuni Pueblo. Museum of Fine Arts, Houston, Texas.

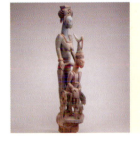

Connection *Some artists from the Yoruba culture in Africa were so great that they were referred to in heroic and grand terms. See the discussion of Olowe of Ise and his Palace Sculpture (Fig. 11.13, page 287).*

In Europe, the concept of the artist as a creative genius began to emerge during the Renaissance, around the fourteenth century, with the rise of humanism, which asserted an individual's worth and emphasized learning. Michelangelo, more than any other at this time, exemplified the notion of the artist as creative genius. During the Romantic era in Europe, roughly 1750 to 1850, the notion of the artist as creative genius expanded to include personal creativity, uniqueness, strong feeling, adventure, individuality, and imagination, as exemplified in artistic freedom and expressiveness. These attitudes developed at the same time as the rise of the bourgeoisie, who saw themselves as self-made, unique individuals.

A final variation of the idea of creative genius is the artist as the troubled, tragic, or alienated genius, like Vincent van Gogh. Although van Gogh was devoted to painting, his life was unhappy. In one of his later paintings, *Starry Night* (Fig. 5.21), the darkness, the agitated brushstrokes, and the turbulent sky suggest a troubled person. He committed suicide at age thirty-seven. The idea of the tragic, damaged, or alienated artist persists today and has become a hero type in industrialized nations.

RULERS AS ARTISTS

Rulers sometimes have been responsible for the creation of important artworks. Most often, they are patrons who oversee the work, as we will discuss later in this chapter. In some cases, they actually make the work.

Among the Maori of New Zealand, sculptors were usually chiefs or members of ruling families. This was especially true for carvings in meeting houses, which were so important that the activity was seen as fitting only for a leader. The meeting house reinforced clan identity. The clan gathered there for political and social events. Children were educated in clan history, using the carvings on the walls that represented their ancestors, like those on the entrance doorway of *Te Mana O Turanga* (Fig. 5.22), from 1883. Thus, the meeting house consolidated the group, just as effective leadership would.

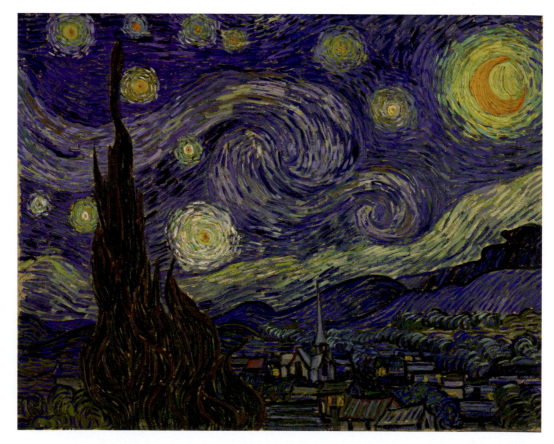

5.21   VINCENT VAN GOGH. *Starry Night*, 1889. Oil on canvas, approx. 2'5" × 3'1/4". Museum of Modern Art, New York. Acquired through the Lillie P. Bliss Bequest.

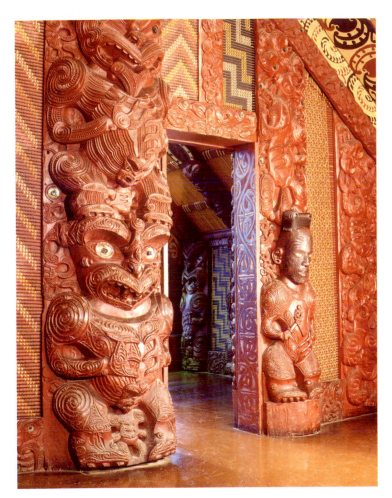

5.22 RAHARUHI RUKUPO AND OTHERS. Entrance doorway of a Maori meeting house called *Te Mana O Turanga*, opened 1883. Carved and painted wood. New Zealand. © Werner Forman / Art Resource, NY. See also Chapter 12 for more information on Maori meeting houses.

SUPPORT FOR ART MAKING

Art reflects the needs, ideas, and aspirations not only of the artist but also of those who support the artist.

PATRONAGE AND PRIVATE SUPPORT

Throughout history, private patrons have contributed to the support of artists. Often, these are persons of power or wealth, and some become known as champions of the arts. Many commission works either for their homes or as monuments for after they have died. The Medici were a famous and powerful family who produced four generations of rulers in Italy and were patrons to many fine artists during the Renaissance. They supported the young Michelangelo. One of the Medici, Cosimo, founded the Academy of Design in 1563. We saw a classic example of royal patronage with Louis XIV (Fig. 5.5), who commissioned works to further his own glory. Other rulers and leaders have done the same.

Religious groups also provide considerable funds for the creation of artworks that serve their beliefs, as evident in many of the images in Chapter 9, Deities and Places of Worship. The history of art is filled with religious works, but even today, a large number of artworks are commissioned for religious purposes, including those for the recently completed cathedral in Los Angeles.

The university in the United States today is a major patron of the arts. Many contemporary artists make their living as teachers in colleges and universities. These regularly paying teaching jobs in higher education mean that artist-teachers are not dependent upon sales of their art and can be free to experiment with new art forms.

But it is important to realize that ordinary people, both individually and in groups, support art that is important to them. Japanese woodblock prints like *Basket Ferry* (Fig. 5.12) were made for the merchant class. Much of Baule sculpture, like the *Seated Female Figure* (Fig. 5.15), is commissioned by ordinary individuals for their personal shrines. Among the Baule, all artwork is owned by individuals, who specify how they want it to look. The *AIDS Memorial Quilt* (Fig. 5.9) is funded by private donations. On Bali, ordinary people who hold demanding jobs often support other artists who create their daily or festival offerings (Fig. 5.8). And finally, artists often receive monetary and moral support from their family, like Vincent van Gogh, whose brother Theo took Vincent's paintings, sent him money, provided art supplies, and was his emotional anchor.

THE MARKET

Today, many artists create for the open market, working on speculation, which involves making art that they later try to sell, either directly or through agents. This is the opposite of working on commission, when artists make specific works for patrons.

The Fine Art Market

In the fine art market, artists make works to sell through commercial galleries. Dealers not only sell work but also promote the artist's career, for example, by arranging museum exhibitions. In exchange for these services, the sale price of an artwork is usually split 50/50 between artist and dealer. The fine art market is very competitive, with more artists wanting to display their work than there are galleries to accommodate them.

The fine art market also consists of auction houses, where art is resold. A few works of art have brought fabulous prices in auctions. For example, some van Gogh paintings have sold for tens of millions of dollars. Because auction houses resell art that was already in the hands of collectors or museums, artists are not directly benefited by auction house sales.

The Tourist Market

Traditional indigenous artworks sometimes are sold in the tourist market, on speculation. These artworks are made specifically for foreign collectors or tourists. The work that artists make for the tourist trade is high-quality, professional work. But it does not have the meaning or the spiritual dimension of the work they make for their own culture.

The tourist market may help local art production to survive. For example, in Papua New Guinea, the making of ritual art like the *Male Spirit Mask* (Fig. 5.14) and the making of tourist art are mutually dependent enterprises, each supporting and invigorating the other. On other, more remote islands, where there is little tourism and therefore little tourist trade, the visual arts are falling into a general decline (Lewis 1990:149–63).

TAX-SUPPORTED ART

Taxes have paid for a lot of art production in one of two ways: (1) artists receive government-sponsored stipends or grants; or (2) tax monies finance specific buildings, paintings, or sculptures. Almost all public monuments, government buildings, and palaces, including ancient Greek temples and Louis XIV's Versailles, were funded by tax revenues. All tax monies come ultimately from ordinary people and the agriculture and commerce they generate.

In Japan, taxes support traditional Japanese art forms. Traditional artists are designated as Living National Treasures (*Ningen Kokuho*) because they are Bearers of Important Intangible Cultural Assets. Ningen Kokuho include musicians, dramatists, and visual artists, such as masters of Bunraku puppetry (Fig. 5.23), a serious form of puppet theater, also discussed in Chapter 16 on page 443. Outstanding fine artists, such as painters and printmakers, may be honored by being appointed to the two-hundred-member Japan Art Academy.

European countries, such as the United Kingdom, France, and Austria, set aside tax monies to support artists and art making. For example, the Austrian government actively supports artists, in part because the fine art market is not very large in Austria, and subsidizes galleries. Tax support for art in the United States consists of Percent for the Arts Program funding, in which a small percentage of the cost of any public building goes to purchase art for that building. In many states, the Percent for the Arts Program covers any federal, state, county, or city building as well as private ventures that receive tax abatements in redevelopment zones. Percent for the Arts Program funding represents considerable income for some artists. These programs have also enriched the urban environment with murals, installations, or sculptures. Sometimes federal and local agencies combine their resources for major projects, like the *St. Louis Gateway Arch* (Fig. 5.24), designed by Eero Saarinen and Associates, and the Museum of Westward Expansion below it.

The process of making public art—getting approval for work and completing the projects—is governed by review committees. In some cases, a competition is held, with artists invited to submit written proposals for a work that is site-specific, addressing the history of that location or the needs and values of the people. Committees of artists, members of the public, and government representatives choose a winning proposal or oversee the completion of the work or both.

Connection *A few public art commissions go awry. See the discussion of Richard Serra's* Tilted Arc *in Chapter 3, page 71), or Robert Arneson's* Portrait of George *(Fig. 12.29, page 328).*

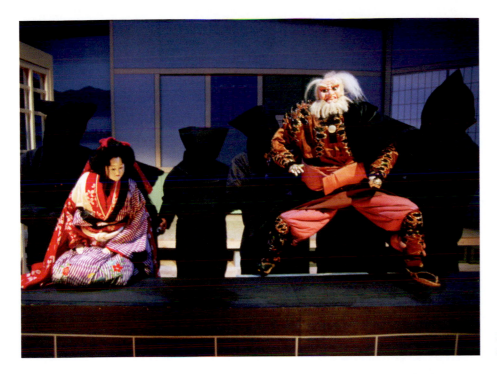

5.23   Bunraku performance on stage, c. twentieth century. Japan.

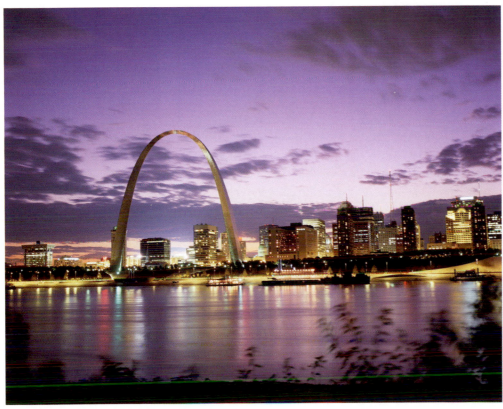

5.24   EERO SAARINEN AND ASSOCIATES. St. Louis Gateway Arch. Stainless steel exterior, 630' high. Constructed 1963–1965. St. Louis, Missouri.

SYNOPSIS

Artists make art, but they depend upon others to provide materials, support, training, technical expertise and cultural standards.

Artists fill many different roles within their cultures: worker, priest, ritualist, scientist, genius. They also may be ordinary people, or they may reflect their culture's gender divisions.

Private patrons, religious groups, universities, family members, the art market, and government tax revenues all support art making, enabling artists to do their work and sometimes greatly influencing how that art looks.

FOOD FOR THOUGHT

What do you think of the following?

■ *Creativity can be seen as the "job" of the artist in societies in which most other kinds of work no longer seem creative. Creativity can then seem to be cut off from "real" life and become superfluous, self-indulgent, or unnecessary. How do you perceive creativity in our society? In business? In the arts? In different kinds of jobs?*

■ *A popular Western myth portrays artists as completely asocial, isolated geniuses whose work is not recognized as important during their lifetimes. Do you think that the nonconformist (or even tragic) artist might fulfill an important role in a particular society?*

■ *When people from first-world nations buy the art of third-world countries, they often want something "authentic," meaning that the artwork conforms to traditional styles. Museum collections also favor traditional styles. But artists alive today are subject to influences from all over the world, through media, travel, and trade. Worldwide, contemporary art is often a mixture of foreign and indigenous influences. What is authentic art?*

■ *If a traditional, indigenous art object is made for the tourist market, is there any reason why it should be inherently more or less valuable than a work made for local cult use?*

■ *Artists have tailored their work to suit the market or the tastes of a particular patron. Leonardo da Vinci was willing to devote his time to whatever the Duke of Mantua dictated, including weapons building or painting. Artists making public art projects work with committees, politicians, and architects. How does this dovetail with their personal creative expression?*

■ *The public art process is reviewed by committees composed of politicians, the public, and artists. Can public art (or any art by committee) ever be controversial? Should it be? If taxes are used to support art making, should that art reflect the ideas of the population? If so, what percentage of the population?*

■ *Michelangelo's Creation of Adam (see Fig. 9.20) and Leonardo da Vinci's Mona Lisa have been (mis)used for commercial reasons, appearing on beach towels, in food commercials, in advertisements, and so on. Figure 5.25 is a souvenir pen from a traveling Vatican exhibition with a detail of Michelangelo's Creation of Adam. When you move the pen, Adam's hand floats toward God's through the liquid contained in the barrel. The message on the other side is "Keep in Touch." The sale of such souvenirs to tourists supports museums and traveling exhibitions. How does this relate to the tourist trade that we discussed earlier in relation to indigenous art? How do commercial art and fine art support each other? Do they invigorate each other?*

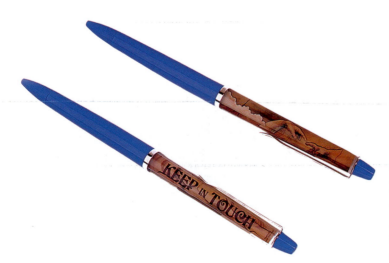

5.25   Souvenir pen from a traveling exhibition of angels from the Vatican. The right end of the barrel contains a detail from Michelangelo's *Creation of Adam*, suspended in liquid. On the reverse appear the words "Keep in Touch."

Your Thomson Online Resources

www   Go to **ArtExperience Online** for the Flashcards, Quiz, and Study Guide for this chapter.

What Do We Do with Art?

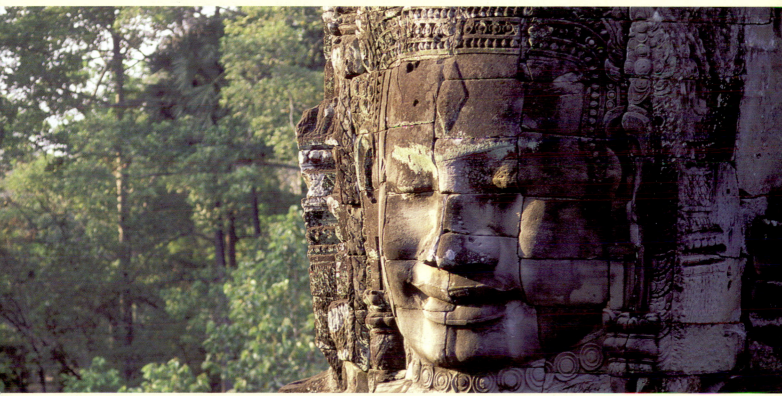

© Andy Goldsworthy. Courtesy of Galerie Lelong, New York

INTRODUCTION

A vast quantity of art treasures, from both the recent and distant past, is with us today. What do communities, nations, institutions, religious groups, armies, scholars, and others do with it?

- *How is art displayed or performed?*
- *Why do nations and cultural groups keep art, even beyond its original use?*
- *Who assembles art collections and why?*
- *What kinds of museums keep art, and how do they operate?*
- *For what reasons does art deteriorate?*
- *How can art be preserved or restored?*
- *Why do people purposefully destroy art?*
- *What academic disciplines study art?*

USING ART

People use art to add meaning and richness to their lives. Their use is either through performance or display, as we have seen in many previous examples. The *Equestrian Statue of Marcus Aurelius* (Fig. 1.2); the Chinese hanging scroll, *Lotus Flowers and Ducks* (Fig. 1.6); Vincent van Gogh's *Starry Night* (Fig. 5.21), and many more are artworks that are primarily displayed. Art used in performance includes the *Royal Linguist's Staff* (Fig. 2.5), Cai Guo-Qiang's *Black Rainbow: Explosion Project for Valencia* (Fig. 2.26), and, again, many others.

These categories of art use are not clear-cut, however, either historically or today. The Native Americans of the Northwest Coast carved masks, totem poles, and other items that were used in ceremonies and performances as well as for display, as can be seen in the historic photograph of *The Hamatsa Great Winter Ceremony* (Fig. 6.1). A contemporary example of art with both performance and display attributes is Kutlug Ataman's *Küba* (Fig. 6.2), from 2004, a forty-channel video installation played on a classroom-like arrangement of cheap televisions and mismatched furniture. Upon first entering the space, the viewer encounters a room full of murmuring. But on all sets are recordings of individuals telling their stories of hardship and survival in the Istanbul neighborhood called Küba, with its community of marginalized people existing outside of social traditions, and where Ataman lived intermittently for two years while developing this work. The poignant and life-affirming piece is both a totality in display and a performance that unwinds as the viewer stays with the piece.

KEEPING ART

Why do we hold on to art, often beyond its original use? What efforts are necessary to keep art for long spans of time? We will discuss art collections, both public and private, and the purposes and functions of museums, as well as art preservation and restoration.

WHY KEEP ART?

People keep art because it is pleasurable, aesthetic, and stimulating. Some find that art gives them a transcendent or spiritual experience. Governments keep it for political purposes and to increase commerce. All of these factors are aspects of the *Cathedral of St. Basil the Blessed* in Moscow (Fig. 6.3), built between 1555 and 1561. Aesthetically, *St. Basil* is fantastic—tall, brightly colored, elaborately patterned, with nine domes, one over each chapel inside. Its religious purpose was to represent a heavenly Jerusalem, a vision of paradise on earth. The very building of this church, though, is a reflection of secular power. Czar Ivan the Terrible commissioned it to celebrate his military victories over the Mongols.

In 1918, the Czarist government was overthrown and religions were discredited with the rise of the Com-

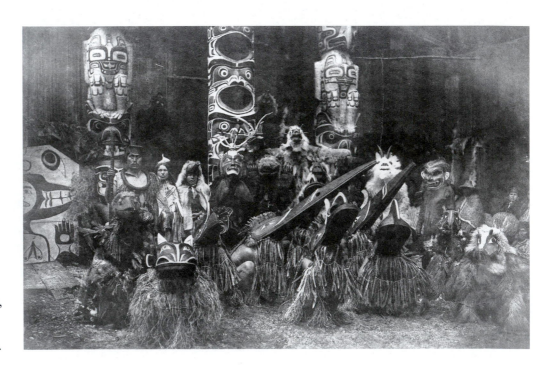

6.1 *The Hamatsa Great Winter Ceremony*, 1914. Costumed and masked dancers, house posts, inside the ceremonial house. Kwakiutl. Northwest Coast, British Columbia, Canada. American Museum of Natural History, New York.

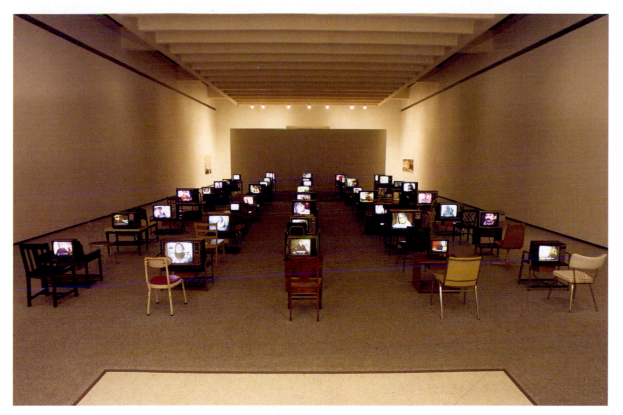

6.2 Kutlug Ataman. *Küba,* 2004. 40-channel video installation with tables and chairs; color, sound. Commissioned by 2004–2005 Carnegie International, Carnegie Museum of Art, Pittsburgh; Lehmann Maupin Gallery, New York; Thyssen-Bornemisza Art Contemporary (T-B A21), Vienna; and Theater der Welt, Stuttgart.

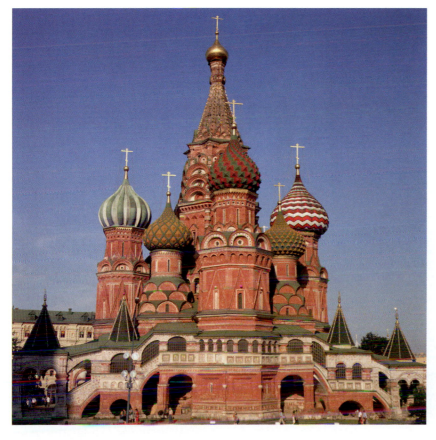

6.3 Exterior of the *Cathedral of St. Basil the Blessed,* 1555–1561. Moscow.

munist regime in Russia. *St. Basil* was closed, since it represented both the Czar and Christianity, and by 1930, there were at least two serious proposals to tear it down to make more room for political parades in Red Square, where it is located. Apparently because of the efforts of a few individuals (at least one went to prison over this), the church was spared.

Today, *St. Basil* is the symbol for old Russia and a popular tourist attraction—it is hard to believe that anyone in the Russian government today would propose its demolition. It has become part of the nation's pride, and, indeed, another political reason for keeping art is national glory. Almost every nation has distinctive artwork that it has claimed as particularly representative of itself. The Statue of Liberty, Mount Rushmore, and the Capitol Building (see Fig. 4.5) are all works of art associated with the United States. Greece is known for its ancient temples. Many countries maintain national landmarks, monuments, museums, and preservation sites.

Connection *Some governments even support traditional artists as part of their national glory. See Chapter 5, page 114, for information about Japan's Living National Treasures.*

So, politically, art can promote the glory of a nation, but it can promote subgroups within a nation as well. The photograph of *The Hamatsa Great Winter Ceremony* showed the historic artwork of the Northwest Coast people. Even today, however, their descendents carve totem poles and other traditional works to maintain their separate identity and cultural traditions, even though politically they have been absorbed into Canada. The eight *Totem Poles* (Fig. 6.4) in Stanley Park, Vancouver, are contemporary reinterpretations of native art forms and legends.

Another part of a nation's treasure is the art it seizes as booty, as a sign of domination over another people. The last Aztec ruler, Moctezuma, gave his magnificent *Headdress* (Fig. 6.5) to the invading Spanish as a desperate measure to avoid his own demise. The Spanish conqueror Hernando Cortés accepted as tribute or took as plunder hundreds of Aztec works of art and sent them to the Spanish king, Charles V. The German artist Albrecht Durer saw these objects in Brussels:

A sun entirely of gold, a whole fathom broad; likewise, a moon, entirely of silver, just as big; likewise sundry curiosities from their weapons, armor, and missiles; very odd clothing, bedding, and all sorts of strange articles for human use, all of which is fairer to see than marvels. These things were all so precious that they were valued at a hundred thousand guilders. But I have never seen in all my days that which so rejoiced my heart, as these things. For I saw among them amazing artistic objects, and I marveled over the subtle ingenuity of the men in these distant lands. (Miller 1986:202)

However, unlike Durer, most Spaniards valued the gold used in Aztec art more than they valued the artworks themselves. Among the objects Durer saw, every one made of gold or silver was melted down for its precious metal.

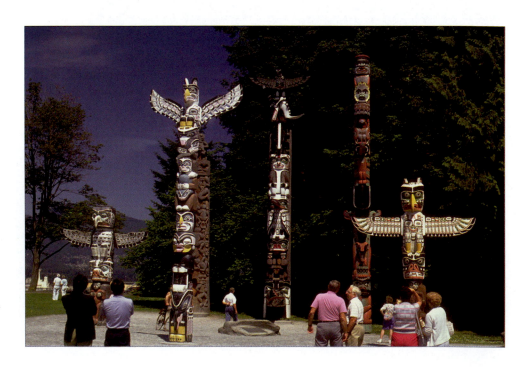

6.4 *Totem Poles* in Stanley Park, Vancouver, British Columbia. Poles date from the 1950s through the 1990s and were carved by various artists.

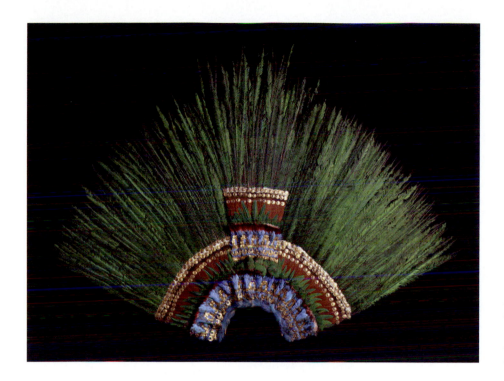

6.5 *Feathered Headdress of Moctezuma*, c. 1519. Quetzal and cotinga feathers, gold plaques. 45½" × 69". Aztec. Kunsthistorisches Museum. See also the text accompanying Fig. 11.32.

Sometimes nations take foreign art to augment their own cultural treasures. Egypt in particular has suffered from having its art treasures hauled off by foreign invaders, much to the detriment of Egypt itself. The ancient Romans took a large number of Egyptian artifacts to Rome, some of which were still around centuries later to reawaken interest in Egypt among Europeans. In 1798, French troops under Napoleon invaded and occupied Egypt, seizing a number of treasures that ended up in the Louvre Museum. The British did the same shortly afterward. The British also removed considerable amounts of art from Greece in the early nineteenth century, such as the *Herakles or Dionysus* (Fig. 6.6) from the Parthenon in Athens, as well as many other sculptures that are currently housed in the British Museum.

In World War II, the Nazis stole millions of works of art, and many are still missing or are in dispute. In

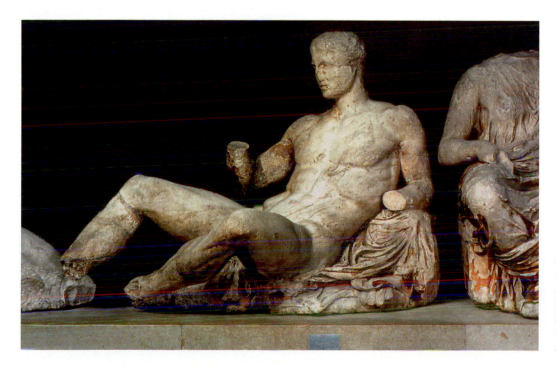

6.6 *Herakles or Dionysus*, c. 447–432 BCE, from the east pediment of the Parthenon, Acropolis. Athens, Greece. Marble, approx. 3'6". British Museum, London. See also the text accompanying Figures 9.29 and 9.30.

addition, after World War II, Russia seized art from 325 German museums; many of those artworks had been taken by the Nazis from Jewish collectors in the 1930s. Attempts to have the stolen art returned have caused international uproars. Even more recently, U.S. and British troops invaded Iraq in 2003, and before security was established, the treasures of some Iraqi museums were stolen.

Finally, nations keep art because art helps the economy and is good for business. Art attracts tourists. The presence of a major archeological, religious, or architectural site like *St. Basil* stimulates the entire economy, and thousands of local jobs are created as a result. Cities with major museums attract millions in tourist monies. In 1999, a traveling exhibit of van Gogh paintings from Amsterdam was reported to have been the most economically beneficial single event in the history of Los Angeles.

MUSEUMS AND PRIVATE COLLECTIONS

Much of the art in this book is part of art collections. An art collection is an accumulation of art objects that are publicly held or are owned by private individuals. Since ancient times, rulers, nobles, and priests have collected art and kept it in palaces or temples for aesthetic pleasure, for personal or ritual use, or for the display of power. In ancient Rome, art was displayed in baths, such as the *Baths of Caracalla* (see Fig. 16.5).

The term *museum* comes from the ancient Greek word *mouseion,* referring to an institution similar to a university. The word *museum* was resurrected in fifteenth-century Europe to refer not to buildings but to collections consisting of paintings, sculptures, coins, curios, and natural objects like ostrich eggs. The *Studiolo of Francesco I de' Medici* (Fig. 6.7), originally built between 1570 and 1572, is a chamber in Florence's Palazzo Vecchio, where Francesco I de' Medici, the Grand Duke of Tuscany, stored and experimented with his collection of rare and odd items. They were housed in twenty cabinets once located below the wall paintings, which were related thematically to the objects in the cabinets. Closely related to those eclectic collections are the many artworks, crafts, or exotic items that ordinary people display in their homes today.

In the eighteenth century, some industrialists, adventurers, and entrepreneurs joined the ranks of the nobility as private art collectors, accumulating works in vast numbers. Many of these large personal collections remained private, but some were donated or sold to public museums for personal gain, for personal fame, or for preservation for posterity. Many wealthy private collectors eventually became members of museums' boards of directors. By this time, *museum* came to mean the building in addition to the collection.

Museums became common in Europe in the nineteenth century. The intellectual climate behind collecting art was shaped both by the Enlightenment of the eighteenth century, which emphasized knowledge, reason, and cultural achievement, and by the Romantic movement of the early nineteenth century, with its fascination for the unknown, the sensual, and the exotic. Capitalism, with its emphasis on ownership, control, and possession, encouraged museum growth. Colonialism was another factor supporting the establishment of museums. It provided great wealth to Europeans, which made art collections possible, and the art of colonized countries filled European museums. Colonialism also spread the European-model museum to the rest of the world.

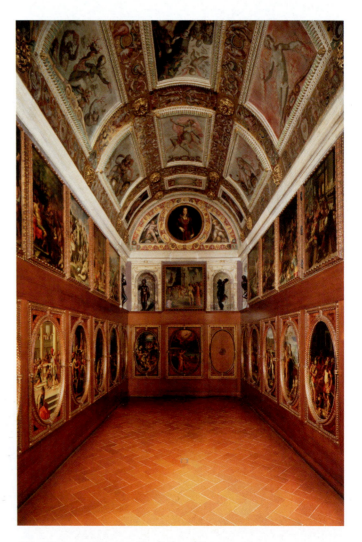

6.7 GIORGIO VASARI. *Studiolo of Francesco I de' Medici.* Studiolo, Palazzo Vecchio, Florence.

The next segments discuss four different kinds of museums that deal with art. Each type is unique in what it shows, how it functions, and how it is funded.

National Museums

The national museum is a large institution with collections in several areas, such as the British Museum in London, the Louvre in Paris, the Smithsonian Institution in Washington, D.C., or the Vatican Museum and Galleries. Many were founded in the eighteenth and nineteenth centuries, in the same atmosphere that led to the development of the encyclopedia. Because of their size, almost all museums are funded by national governments. Their holdings consist largely of donated or purchased private collections.

The British Museum (Fig. 6.8) was founded in 1753 for the "inspection and entertainment of the learned and the curious, for the general use and benefit of the public." Its first collections focused on ancient Greece and Rome and Renaissance Italy, cultures that Europeans then believed to have produced the highest achievements in art. The museum's Greco-Roman façade reflects that belief. More private collections were added, such as the Elgin Marbles, which are original sculptures from the Parthenon, including *Herakles or Dionysus* (Fig. 6.6).

Large museums in general benefited from conquest and colonization, which enabled the British Museum to accumulate large non-Western collections, notably Chinese porcelain and sculptures from India. Some countries have demanded the return of their lost art heritage. Greece, for example, wants the Parthenon sculptures returned. The British Museum has refused, claiming that it legally owns the works and that it saved them from damage and destruction.

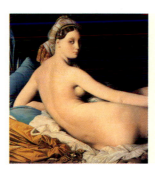

Connection *During the colonial era, the fascination of Europeans with "the exotic" was reflected not only in their art collections but also in the art of the day, such as* Grande Odalisque *(Fig. 8.18, page 186) by Ingres.*

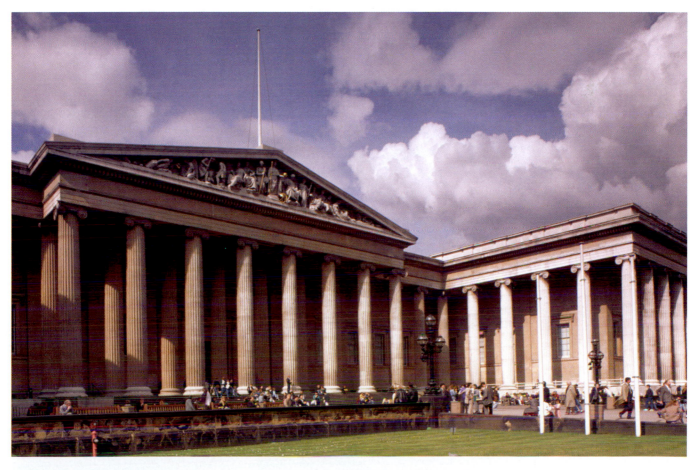

6.8 SIR ROBERT SIDNEY SMIRKE. *The British Museum*, 1823–1847. Portico, south façade. London.

Art Museums

Art museums are recent inventions. The first U.S. art museums, from the 1800s, featured plaster copies of famous classical sculptures in European collections. In the early twentieth century, art museums expanded to include painting, sculpture, printmaking, and decorative arts. Art museums may be private institutions, public museums supported by tax money, or university-run museums.

The art museum displays art to maximize its formal, aesthetic qualities. Historical, social, or political information is often not presented with the art. Museums of modern art are a subset of art museums. They are dedicated to the most current art, which is often unusual or challenging to the public. One example is the *Guggenheim Bilbao* (Fig. 6.9) in Northern Spain, designed by Frank O. Gehry and completed in 1997. Resembling a contemporary sculpture, the building emphasizes abstract flowing form and monumental scale.

All modern art museums are faced with an intrinsic problem: as time passes, their collection grows and then grows old. Gradually more of the museum's space, budget, time, and resources go to maintaining the collection, which severely curtails the museum's ability to acquire new works. Recently, a number of contemporary art centers have sprung up. They generally mount exhibits of current art, but maintain no permanent collections.

Regional Museums

Regional museums serve the interests of a specific locality and reflect that area's cultural history. For example, in China, the Museum of Qin Terra-cotta Soldiers and Horse Figures was established to house and preserve the clay figures and other grave goods from the tomb compound of the emperor Shi Huangdi (Fig. 6.10).

A great variety exists in regional museums' missions, their collections, and the programs they sponsor. Regional museums also tend to be more experimental than either the national museum or the art museum, because they serve local needs. For example, the Anthropological Museum at the University of Ibadan not only preserves the Yoruban culture in Nigeria, but also is a "vigorous meeting place . . . where new breakthroughs in political crafting as well as domestic and industrial crafts were invented." This model works better with "African peoples' traditions of visioning and thinking, and ways of praying, designing, planning, speaking and doing things; of organizing socio-politically and of exploiting the natural resources of their environmental setting" (Andah 1997:15–16).

Museums and New Technology

Recent technology has had a great influence on art, resulting in such new categories as computer-based art, interactive art, video, and, to some extent, film. These new technologies have produced two innovations in the concept of the museum: (1) the media museum, and (2) the virtual museum.

Like the art museum, the media museum exists primarily to display works of art; however, the artwork is all technology driven. One media museum, the *Center for Art and Media,* 1997 (Fig. 6.11), or ZKM (Zentrum für Kunst und Medientechnologie), sees itself as

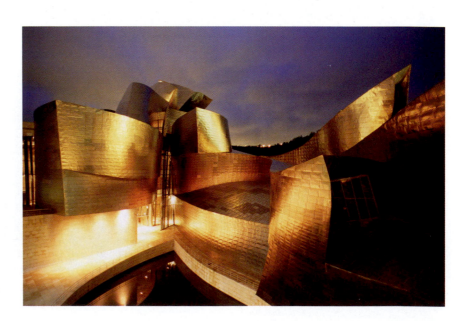

6.9   FRANK O. GEHRY. *Guggenheim Bilbao.* Bilbao, Spain.

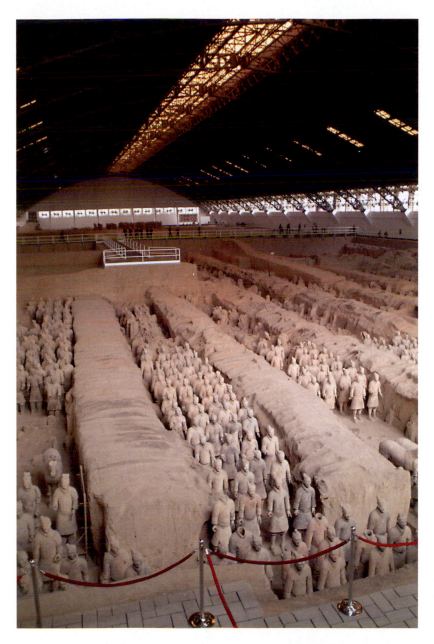

6.10   Army of the First Emperor of Qin in pits next to his burial mound, c. 210 BCE. Lintong, China, Qin Dynasty. Painted terracotta, average figure 5'10" high.

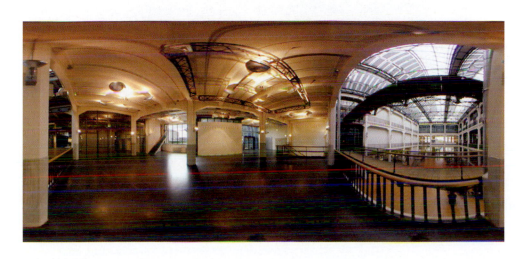

6.11   *Center for Art and Media*, opened 1997. View of foyer and some exhibition spaces (Musik Balkon). Karlsruhe, Germany. Redesigned by Architects Schweger and Partner.

resembling not only art museums but also radio and television archives, film museums, and science centers, such as the Exploratorium in San Francisco. In addition, amusement parks such as Disney World are influential because they have raised the public's exposure to and expectations of computer-based art (Schwarz 1997:26–33). Located in a renovated munitions factory, the Center resembles industrial spaces and shopping malls. The architecture is open, with no fixed walls, allowing for flexible configuration of smaller, dark projection rooms or soundproof spaces.

One special problem faced by media museums is that in addition to collecting art, they must store necessary hardware and software, which rapidly become obsolete. Even mounting an exhibit of current media-based artworks presents huge technological problems.

> But who is really prepared for the maintenance requirements of a Reality-Engine 2 or for correctly putting on head mounted displays or whole body suits? Who knows what strength a glass fibre cable must have, in order to transport an appropriate amount of image information to the work of art, or which LCD projector is powerful enough to provide the necessary image brightness for a work of art while maintaining a humane room brightness? Not to mention the almost insoluble problems caused by painfully competing soundtracks. There is still no model, no useful solution for how media art can be displayed appropriately and presented in a technically flawless way. (Schwarz 1997:13)

Virtual museums and galleries are available on the Internet. The websites of several contemporary art museums contain media art pieces made specifically for the Web, so what you are seeing is the original work itself. In other cases, the images shown are digital pictures of artwork, in which case the virtual museum really cannot replace the traditional museum nor the experience of looking at actual art objects.

PRESERVATION AND RESTORATION

Because art is valuable, enormous human effort and financial resources are devoted to preserving art from the ravages of time, the environment, industrial by-products, and even other human beings. Restoring works that are already damaged presents an entirely different set of problems, and we will look at them.

Preservation

Small art objects are the easiest to preserve, because they can be kept where humidity, temperature, and light are controlled and where no one can touch them. Then, art objects become enshrined or removed from everyday life. It becomes hard to remember that most works of art were made to be handled or used, and that few were ever designed specifically to be displayed in a museum.

For very famous works of art, the protective measures may become obstacles to seeing the work at all. For example, the curators of the Louvre Museum have surrounded Leonardo da Vinci's *Mona Lisa* (c. 1503–1506) with walls and bulletproof glass (Fig. 6.12). The lighting on the painting itself is very subdued to better preserve it. Large crowds congregate

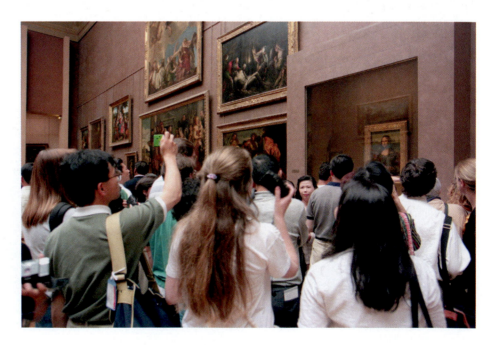

6.12 LEONARDO DA VINCI. *Mona Lisa*, c. 1503–1506, as it is currently displayed behind bulletproof glass. Oil on wood, 30¼" × 21". Italy. Louvre, Paris.

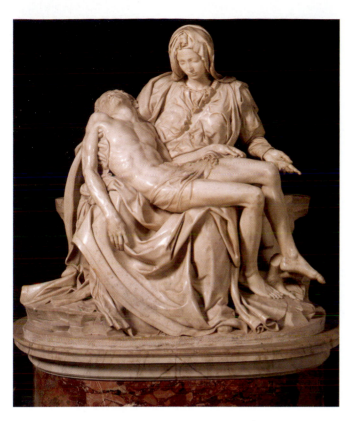

before it, even though it is now very difficult to see. The protective measures were considered necessary to deter vandals who might attack such famous works with knives, hammers, and so on, as happened to the *Pietà* by Michelangelo. In 1972 Laszlo Toth attacked the statue with a hammer, breaking off one arm and damaging Mary's face. Toth was committed to a mental institution, and the *Pietà* was later restored (Fig. 6.13).

If art does not fit into a climate-controlled building, preservation must counter (1) normal weather, which causes rust, fading, erosion, and cracks; (2) environmental pollution, such as smog and noise and vibrations; (3) wear and tear from tourists' feet, fingers, and breath; (4) damage by souvenir hunters, plunderers, adventurers, and vandals; and (5) damage from war.

Ancient paintings sealed in tombs or caves can deteriorate when exposed to air or humidity. Twenty-five years after their discovery, the caves at Lascaux, France (see Fig. 7.1), were closed to visitors because mold was destroying the images. In Spain, the *Hall of the Bison* (Fig. 6.14) likewise was closed to the public,

6.13   MICHELANGELO BUONARROTI. Pietà. 68½" high × 76¾" width at base. Vatican, Rome.

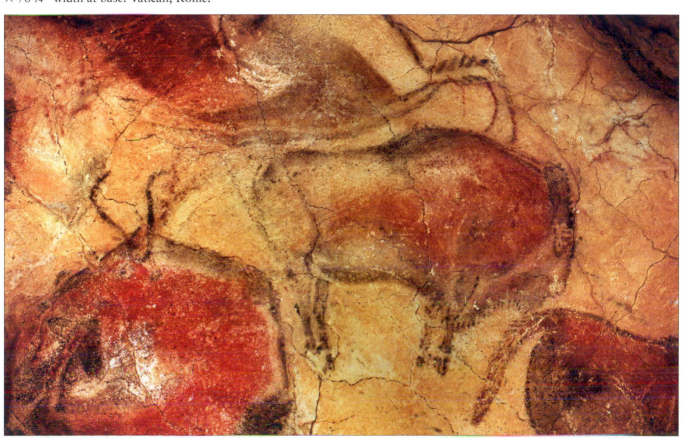

6.14   *Hall of the Bison.* Paleolithic cave painting, 15000–8000 BCE. Altamira Caves, Spain. Art Resource, NY.

and a replica of the cave was constructed nearby and opened in 2001. In 1994, more magnificent cave paintings were discovered at Chauvet, France. Only researchers are allowed inside, and even then only four weeks per year for a few hours a day, with little oxygen.

Exposure to regular weather erodes art, as can be seen on *Herakles or Dionysus* (Fig. 6.6), which was left in the open for centuries. Vibration from traffic is causing ancient ruins to crumble in Rome. Rain plus smog creates acidity that eats away stone. The threat is worldwide. In Mexico, air pollution is eating away at ancient Mayan temples in the Yucatán peninsula. In Athens, a thin layer of marble on ancient Greek temples is washed away with every downpour of acid rain. Many ancient Greek sculptures have been moved to climate-controlled buildings and have been replaced onsite with cast concrete copies.

New media—film, video, and computer art—present preservation problems. Old nitrate-based film stock gets gummy and brown and can spontaneously combust. Of all the U.S. films made before 1951, only half survive in any form. Old films on nitrate stock can be copied but that process takes an enormous amount of time and money and many have to be restored, as discussed on page 136. Film used in movies today fades in as few as five years. Videotape is also very fragile, and can be easily damaged. A lot of old television and video art has been lost. Another complication for video archiving is that old videotapes were created on equipment that is now obsolete. Even if you have intact videotape, you may have trouble finding equipment on which to play it.

Video and computer-based art is plagued by rapid obsolescence. Kutlug Ataman's *Küba* (Fig. 6.2) requires hardware that will be obsolete and replaced by newer technologies in a few years. Storage for digital files changes constantly. Compact discs are evolving; DVDs are replacing them, and something else will soon replace DVDs. Updating your storage media every few years is necessary to avoid losing older work. Even printed computer art suffers archiving problems, as many of the inks, binders, and other materials used in printing are impermanent.

Restoration

The goal of art restoration is to return damaged or deteriorating art to its original condition, as much as possible.

A massive effort is under way to restore the terracotta army surrounding the tomb of the first emperor of China, Shi Huangdi (Fig. 6.10). Each soldier was once brightly painted with mineral colors, which have almost entirely worn away. Weapons, iron farm tools, and silk, bone, linen, and jade objects were also buried with the soldiers. The clay horses of the charioteers had bronze and leather bridles and pulled now-disintegrated wooden chariots.

The restoration of Shi Huangdi's terra-cotta army presents two major problems. The first is the cost. Especially in poor countries, how much time, money, and energy should go to saving relics of the past? It will take decades to excavate and restore Shi Huangdi's twenty-square-mile funeral complex.

The second problem is how to "restore" artworks when no one knows their original appearance. Although this excavation is carefully preserving all archeological evidence, the restoration still involves guesswork. Even modern artworks are difficult to restore. For older movies, various copies have to be located and spliced together to replace deteriorated parts. *Gone with the Wind* (Fig. 6.15), made in 1939 but recently restored, had its color and soundtrack "enhanced" during restoration. Who is to say whether the "enhancement" really represents the original film version or merely reflects modern tastes for richer colors and fuller sound?

Questionable restoration practices continue to be used. Centuries-old temples in Southeast Asia, overgrown with tropical vegetation, have been scrubbed with modern detergents and sprayed with modern herbicides in efforts to clean off mold and fungus and to retard new plant growth. The enormous sculptures at Angkor Thom in Cambodia (Fig. 6.16), for example, have been subjected to this treatment. Yet no one knows if the stones and carvings may have suffered long-term damage from the application of strong chemicals. At Coba, an ancient Mayan site in Mexico, most of the pyramids and other monuments are still engulfed in tropical jungle growth. How will they be restored so that future researchers can actually study what was left and tourists will be provided a satisfying experience?

Cleaning painting is equally tricky. Michelangelo's *Sistine Ceiling* has been cleaned recently, removing layers of old varnish and candle soot that gave the painting a brown, somewhat darkened appearance. For years, scholars had written that Michelangelo avoided

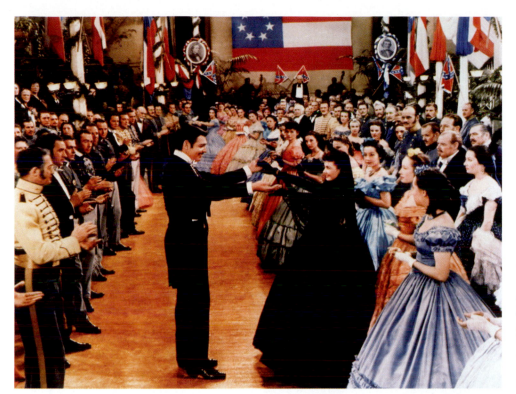

6.15 *Gone with the Wind*, 1939. MGM film starring Clark Gable as Rhett Butler and Vivian Leigh as Scarlett O'Hara. USA. Copyright Metro Goldwyn Mayer. See also the text accompanying Fig. 16.27.

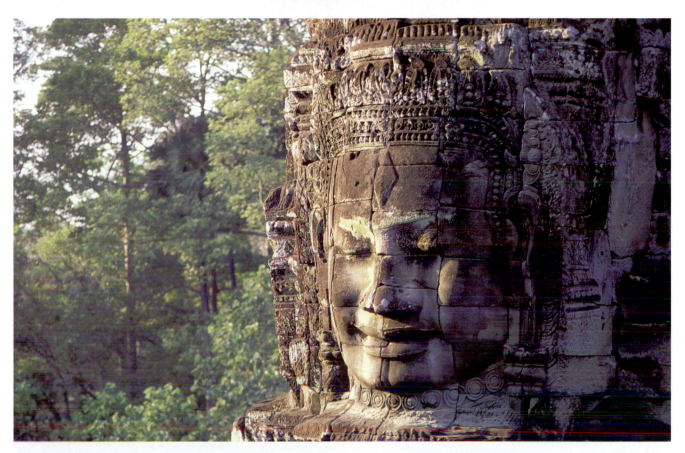

6.16 Buddha face carved in stone. Temple of Bayon, complex of Angkor Thom. Angkor, Cambodia.

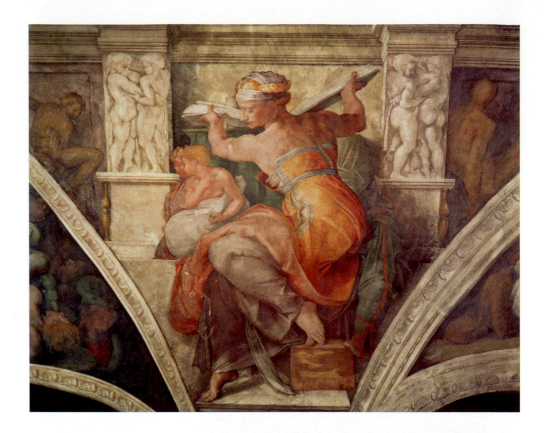

6.17 MICHELANGELO. *The Libyan Sibyl*. 1508–1512, Fresco. Detail of the *Sistine Ceiling*. Sistine Chapel, Vatican Palace (before restoration).

using bright colors and favored defining forms through shading, as can be seen in the pre-restoration detail of *The Libyan Sibyl* (Fig. 6.17). After cleaning, colors became vivid greens, blues, and oranges, as well as a rainbow of pastels. Cracks were filled or minimized. Many experts argued that the restorers went too far and removed Michelangelo's final layer of muted paint, and what we see now is the overly bright, hard-edged underpainting. Other scholars respond that the cleaning was well executed and requires a rethinking of Michelangelo's use of color (Fig. 6.18).

Sometimes restoration may present an artificially complete view of a work. Many famous but damaged paintings have been heavily repainted, and concrete replicas have replaced original statues. Do we still regard these works as "original" or "authentic"?

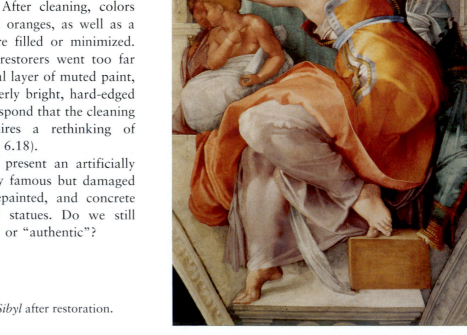

6.18 MICHELANGELO. *The Libyan Sibyl* after restoration. Sistine Chapel, Vatican Palace.

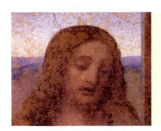

Connection *Very little of the original paint of Leonardo da Vinci's Last Supper (Fig. 7.16, page 152) remains today, due to deterioration and restoration. This detail is the Head of Christ.*

WHEN ART IS NOT SAVED

Sometimes art is purposefully destroyed in conflicts when one culture or religion seeks to obliterate another. In other instances, art is destroyed as it serves its purpose in rituals. And some artists simply choose not to make enduring art objects.

ART DESTROYED IN CONFLICTS

In national, religious, or regional conflicts, art is often destroyed as a sign of dominance, as a result of negligence, or as part of ethnic cleansing.

Iconoclasm is the destruction of sacred images. For example, during the seventh and eighth centuries, many Christian icons in southern Europe and Asia Minor were destroyed because some Christian factions considered devotion to religious images to be idolatry. Icono-

clasm continues today. For example, the former regime in Afghanistan, the Taliban, ordered the demolition of the large fourth-century *Bamiyan Stone Buddha* in 2001, because the Koran forbids religious images (Figs. 6.19 and 6.20).

Many monuments from ancient Rome were damaged or destroyed because medieval Europeans were indifferent to their artistic merit. Marble was stripped from Roman monuments and used on medieval churches. Bronze sculpture was melted and reused as decoration or functional items. Sometimes older monuments are destroyed to make way for newer construction, such as the older *Temple of Quetzalcoatl and Tlaloc* (Fig. 6.21) at Teotihuacán, a pre-Aztec city in central Mexico. The temple was once covered with 366 painted sculptures representing the days of the year; only a few remain at the bottom because they were buried when the Teothuacanos used that part of the old temple for the foundation of the new temple constructed on top.

Much Aztec, Mayan, and Incan art and architecture were destroyed by the sixteenth-century Spanish conquerors, as discussed in reference to Moctezuma's *Headdress* (Fig. 6.5). Spanish missionaries ordered the destruction of all idols and books to eradicate the native religion. This was a huge loss, as those native libraries contained not only religious books but also splendid artwork and the histories of many Mesoamerican

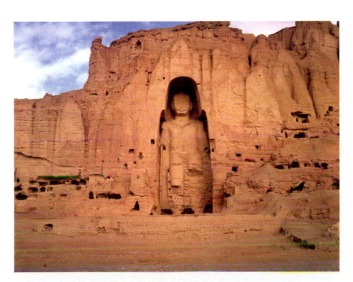

6.19   *Bamiyan Stone Buddha,* 4th or 5th century CE; demolished March 2001. 165' high. Bamiya, Afghanistan.

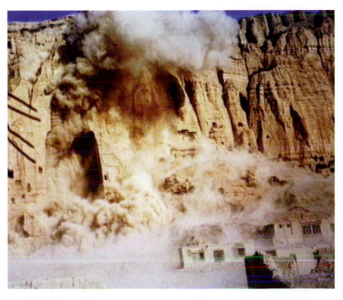

6.20   Destruction of the large Buddha in March 2001. Bamiya, Afghanistan.

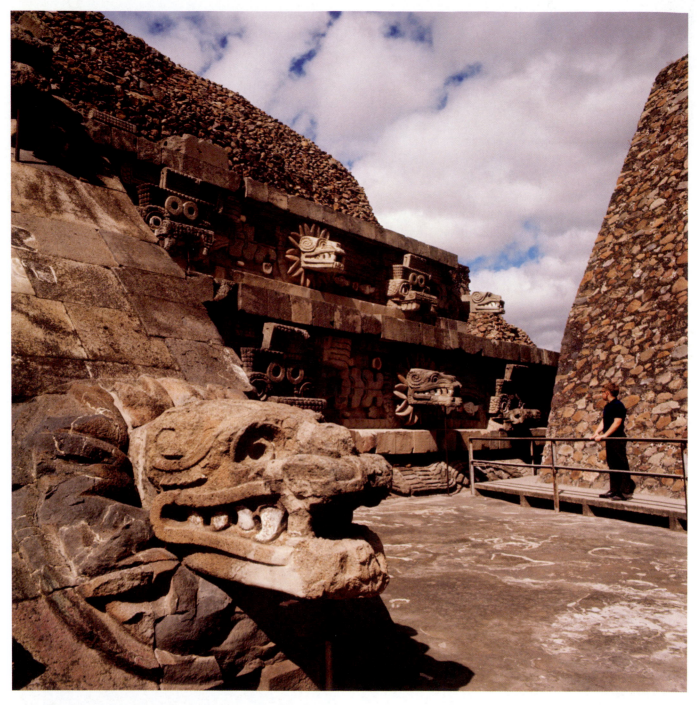

6.21 *Temple of Quetzalcoatl and Tlaloc,* Palace of Quetzalcoatl, Teotihuacán, Mexico.

civilizations. However, the missionaries also wrote about the culture they encountered, and to some extend preserved it.

Missionaries to other areas of the world have contributed to the destruction of native cultures. In the case of the *Figure of a Deity: A'a Rurutu* (Fig. 6.22), collected in 1820 and now in the British Museum, missionaries preserved the art object and sent it back to Europe, but without information on the meanings or the indigenous uses of this piece because it was not important to them.

Hundreds of years ago, invading Moslems in Northern India destroyed the Hindu temples they found there. During World War II, in an effort to wipe out Slavic cultures, German Nazis purposefully destroyed ancient Byzantine religious icons and many monu-

and may end up in museums across the world, as in Figure 6.23.

Navajo *Sand Paintings* are also destroyed to complete the ritual for which they are made. Navajo attitudes about beauty, art, and permanence are expressed in the following:

> A Navajo experiences beauty most poignantly in creating it and in expressing it, not in observing it or preserving it. The experience of beauty is dynamic; it flows to one and from one; it is not in things, but in relationships among things. Beauty is not to be preserved but to be continually renewed in oneself and expressed in one's daily life and activities. (Witherspoon 1977:178)

As is the case with the *Bis or Bisj Poles*, some museum curators, scholars, and tourists make efforts to preserve the art that the Navajos themselves do not keep (see Fig. 3.14). Sand paintings on glue-covered boards are now sometimes made for the tourist trade. And some museums have commissioned the making of "permanent" sand paintings within the museum.

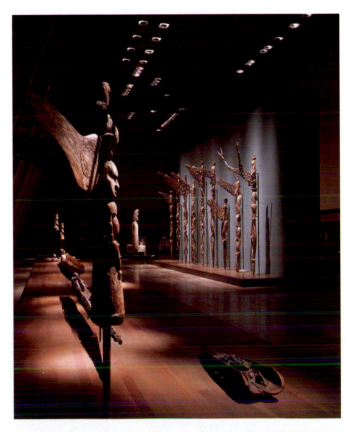

6.23 *Bis or Bisj Poles,* mid-20th century. New Guinea, Irian Jaya; Asmat people, Omandesep. The Michael C. Rockefeller Memorial Collection, Bequest of Nelson A. Rockefeller, 1979. Metropolitan Museum of Art, New York. See Fig. 14.16 to review the discussion of the rituals and meaning attached to the Bis or Bisj Poles by the Asmat people.

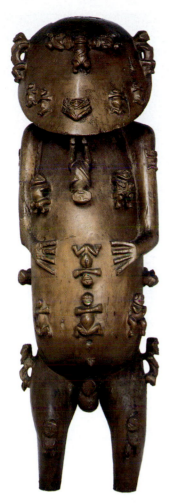

6.22 *Figure of a Deity: A'a Rurutu.* Wood, 44" high. Austral Islands, Polynesia, collected in 1820. The British Museum, London. See Fig. 8.4 to review ways that this sculpture and other artworks are intended to ensure human fertility.

ments during their occupation of western Russia. Art continues to be lost in conflicts in Afghanistan and Iraq.

ART USED DYNAMICALLY IN RITUALS

Art can be lost or destroyed as part of rituals or dramatic performances. The Asmat men of New Guinea made *Bis or Bisj Poles,* c. nineteenth to twentieth centuries, as part of rituals to promote male power, pass the spirits of the dead on to the living, and avenge the deaths of deceased clan members. Afterward, the poles were left to rot away among the sago palms, the Asmat's primary food source, to promote their fecundity. Thus, the deterioration of the art was an important part of rituals that redirected the human spirit after death. Nowadays, such poles are often preserved

NON-OBJECT ART

Some artists choose not to make permanent art objects. Andy Goldsworthy's *Dandelion Line* (Fig. 6.24) from 2000 was an outdoor installation with natural materials that rotted or blew away shortly after completion. Goldsworthy, however, does document his installations and sells those photographs through galleries. Another example comes from performance art, in which artists create an experience for people, rather than an object. Once the work is performed, it no longer exists in any material form, except for photographs that document the event. Other artists give their art away or sell it at minimal cost. This is especially true for artwork that can be easily copied or broadcast. The work of many Web artists is free to those who can log on.

STUDYING ART

The study of art is part of many academic disciplines, including art history, archeology, cultural anthropology, and some areas of psychology.

Art history is the historical study of visual arts and art objects. Art historians are able to study an unfamiliar art object and attribute it to a period, a style, and an artist, and determine whether a work is authentic or a copy. Early art historical writings focused on Western painting, sculpture, architecture, and prints, but now have expanded to include more media, a global perspective, and broad political, social, religious, and economic contexts. More now specialize in art of Africa, the Americas, Oceania, and Asia. Art historians also examine the workings of museums, the institutions that educate artists, the functioning of the gallery, and the role of the collector and critic.

Aesthetics is a branch of philosophy, primarily Western, that focuses on the beautiful—its understanding and appreciation—both "universally" and within specific cultural contexts. We discussed aesthetics in Chapter 1, page 7.

Art criticism consists of judgments about the value of art exhibits and events. The writings of art critics are circulated in newspapers and magazines and on radio, television, and video. Art criticism is also educational and encourages viewers to think for themselves. For more on art criticism, see Chapter 4, page 88.

Archeology is the scientific study of the physical remains of past human life and activity. It includes all things that are buried or thrown away, such as bones, stone tools, art objects, weapons, utensils, and other

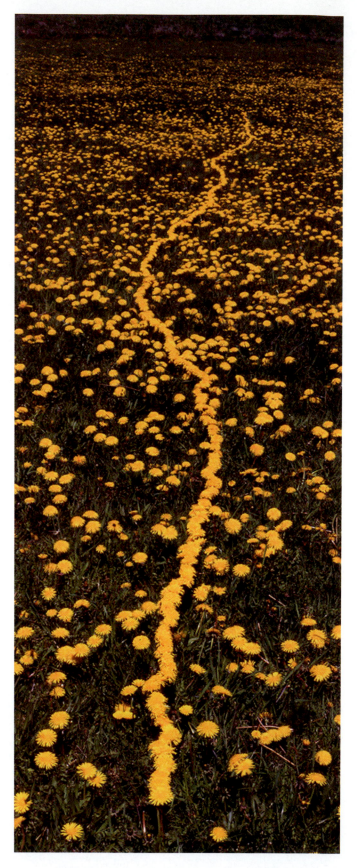

6.24 ANDY GOLDSWORTHY. *Dandelion Line*, 2000. Storm King Sculpture Park, New York.

functional objects. It also includes monuments and buildings. Archeologists conduct fieldwork in which they carefully excavate, classify, record, and date the artifacts they find. In the early 1800s, archeologists were less disciplined, often carelessly removing artwork to their own museums as well as causing damage to what was left. Today, excavations are controlled and conducted in cooperation with the host government.

Cultural anthropology is the study of humanity within cultures, including human behavior, social organization, and the creation and use of objects. For living cultures, the cultural anthropologist does fieldwork (that is, lives with the people) and collects data on human behavior and social organization. The visual arts are important because they reflect the social structure, religious beliefs, domestic practices, and aspirations of a people.

Art has also been used to study **human development.** Various theories of human growth and acquisition of cognitive and conceptual skills have been based on the study of ordinary drawings. The Swiss psychologist Jean Piaget developed theories on the formative stages of childhood, based in part on the study of children's drawings. Art therapy is an area of medical treatment that uses the patient's artwork to help diagnose and treat mental illnesses. Because art is another language, patients can provide information visually, when perhaps words cannot be uttered.

SYNOPSIS

Art is experienced through performance or display. People keep art because it is meaningful to them. Governments keep art for its sacred or aesthetic qualities, for national pride, for enriching their cultural treasure, and for a stronger economy.

Art is kept in private and public art collections. Museums vary in kind and in purpose and include large national museums, art museums, regional museums, and museums devoted to new technologies.

Art preservation and restoration bring economic, aesthetic, and technological challenges. Ancient buildings as well as yesterday's computer art are threatened by political events, environmental destruction, and technological changes.

Not all people are interested in preserving works of art. Invading armies often destroy the art of those they vanquish. Other people dynamically create, use, and then destroy their art as part of rituals or performances.

Various academic disciplines study art, including art history, art criticism, archeology, philosophy, cultural anthropology, and psychology.

FOOD FOR THOUGHT

In addition to everything else that happens to art, sometimes it is censored. Censorship is the prohibition of certain art for moral, political, or religious reasons. The German Nazis in the 1930s and 1940s practiced an extreme form of censorship by seizing or destroying art that varied from the official art style, which was idealized and naturalistic and promoted Nazi policies. Artists who deviated from this style could be banned or imprisoned.

In the United States today, questions of censorship come up in association with art making and art exhibitions. In 1990, the director of a Cincinnati museum was placed on trial for obscenity because his institution had hosted a large photographic exhibition that included seven images that many people thought were sexually offensive. The jury acquitted him. More often, censorship means withdrawing funding or other support for artists and museums if politicians find their art to be offensive. In 1999, the Brooklyn Museum drew the fire of then Mayor Rudolph Giuliani for an exhibit called "Sensation," which included the work of Chris Ofili (see Fig. 15.5).

■ *What is obscene? Who defines it? What is acceptable material for an adult versus an adolescent?*

- *Some people claim that their tax dollars should not support art that they find offensive. Is that position different from those who object to tax dollars being spent on a military project they think is wasteful, or medical research that they find unethical?*

- *Should all individuals decide for themselves what they can read, look at, or listen to? What happens if their choices conflict with community standards?*

- *Should art be uplifting? Should it be moral?*

- *Does location make a difference? Is it different if a questionable image appears in a museum, in a private gallery, on the Internet, or in an individual's home?*

This subject will continue to be controversial in the United States during your lifetime, and your vote and opinion on such issues will count.

Your Thomson Online Resources

 Go to **ArtExperience Online** for the Flashcards, Quiz, and Study Guide for this chapter.

PART 2

Why Do We Make Art?

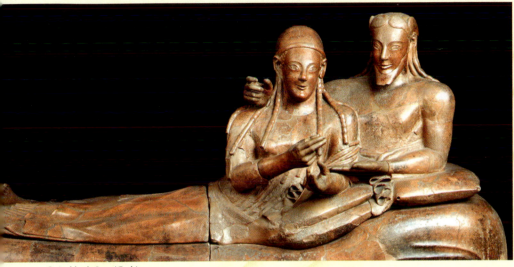

© Araldo de Luca/Corbis

Art fulfills basic human pleasures and needs. It is functional and aesthetic. In the next ten chapters, we group the discussion of why humans make art into four sections:

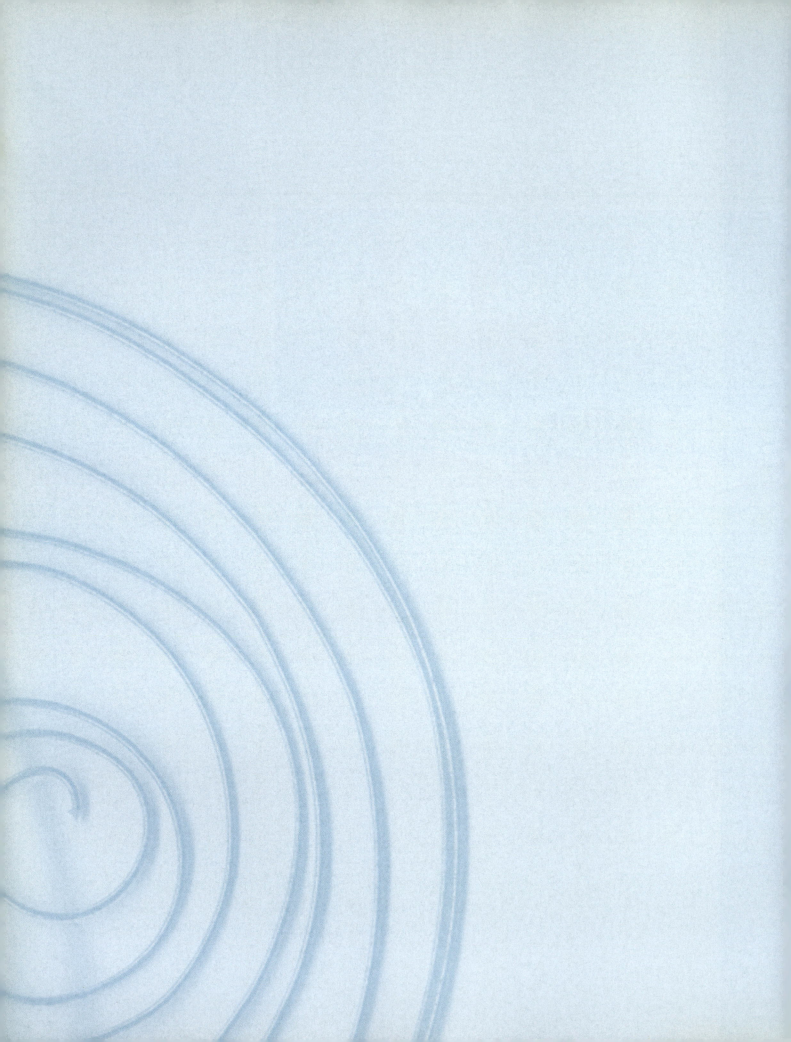

Survival and Beyond

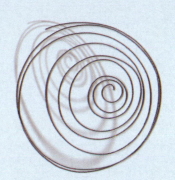

*Food, shelter, and reproduction are basic to human survival,
regardless of how civilized or sophisticated we might be in the
modern world. What role does art play in these?
The major topics in the next two chapters are:*

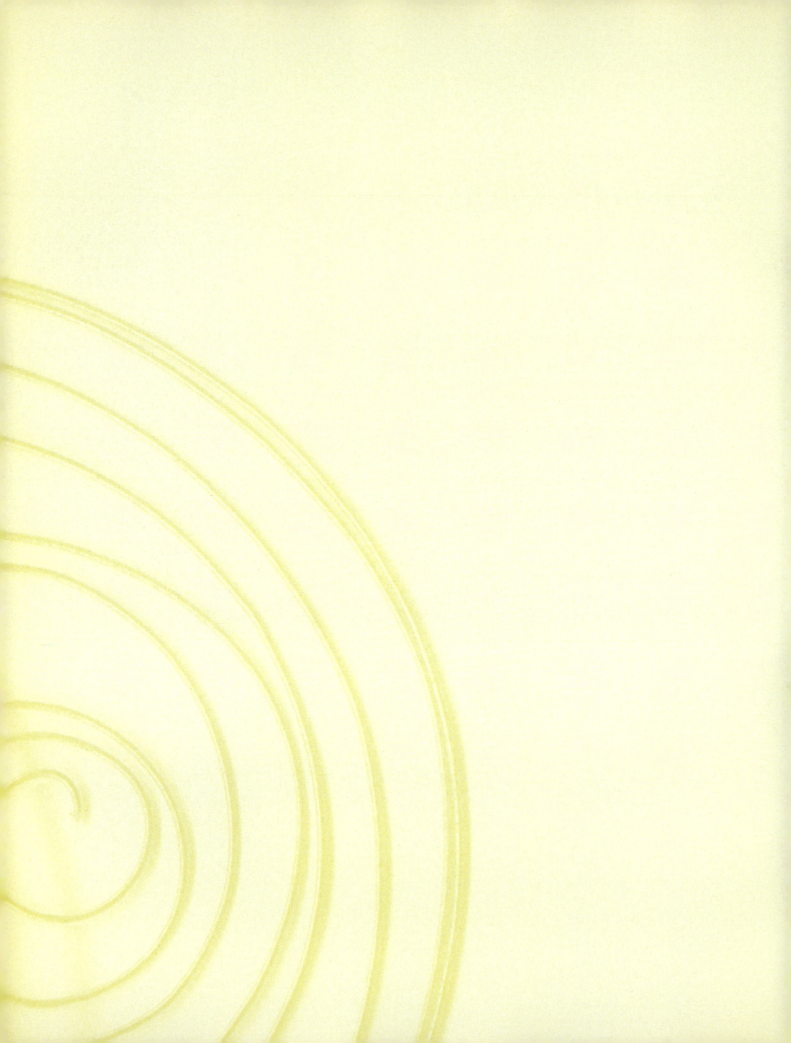

CHAPTER 7

Food and Shelter

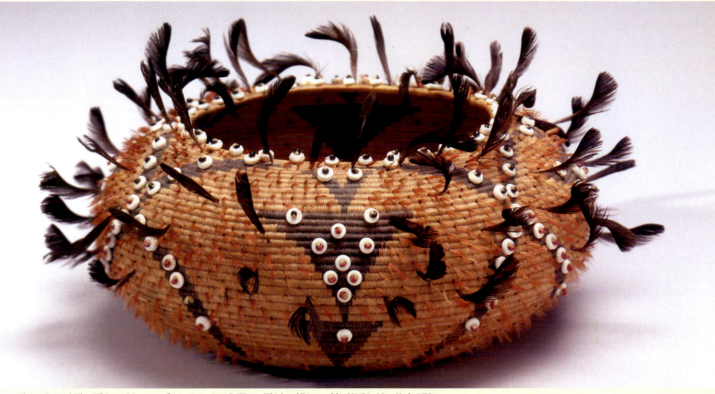

Photo © 2004 The Whitney Museum of American Art. © Wayne Thiebaud/Licensed by VAGA, New York, NY.

INTRODUCTION

Food is essential for life itself, and people need protection from extreme weather, human enemies, and animal threats. Yet our relationship to food and shelter goes beyond simple survival.

- *In what ways are food and ritual linked?*
- *How have artists glorified food in their artworks or enhanced our experience of it?*
- *How have artists depicted the act of eating and its significance?*
- *What shelter has been designed for group living or individual homes?*
- *What architecture has been developed for the commercial world?*

This chapter covers domestic and commercial architecture. For other coverage, see:

Chapter 9, Deities and Places of Worship: architecture used in religious rituals

Chapter 11, Power, Politics, and Glory: palaces and government buildings

Chapter 16, Entertainment and Visual Culture: theater and museum design

SECURING THE FOOD SUPPLY

Among hunters, gatherers, and early farmers, art and ritual are linked to accomplish tasks like bringing rain for crops. This is "sympathetic magic," and the artist/shaman could attain great status in society, and in some cultures still does.

Food, art, and ritual are likely linked in prehistoric cave drawings, like those at Lascaux in southern France, dated c. 15,000–10,000 BCE (Fig. 7.1), with huge woolly mammoths, horses, rhinos, aurochs (wild cattle), and reindeer. Their exact purpose is unknown, but some anthropologists propose that rituals could be performed on the animals' likenesses to ensure a successful hunt. Spears and arrows were painted in or perhaps actually thrown at the image of the prey, ritualistically killing it. Other scholars argue that the painted "arrows" are few and could be plant forms. They propose that these drawings were homage to earth and animal spirits. Either way, the current consensus is that these images had a ritual purpose linked to bounty in nature and the human food supply in the Paleolithic era.

The paintings, done from memory, were quite naturalistic, focusing on the animals' energy and movements and using the side view for easy recognition. Color came from naturally occurring materials, such as tar and charcoal for black, colored earth for yellow and brown, and rust for red. Dry pigment could be applied as powder or brushed on with animal fat. Given the crude materials and the rough stone walls, the drawings are especially amazing.

While Paleolithic humans were hunters and gatherer, Neolithic humans turned to farming and herding. Once again, this is reflected in art, as shown in the *African Rock Painting* on page 167.

In Australia up to the present day, we see the same phenomenon of linked food, art, and ritual. The "Ancestor Dreaming" of the Aboriginal people of Australia is a system of beliefs that accounted for the cosmos, from creation to death, and includes food gathering. Knowledge was passed by song, chants, dance, and painting. For paintings in the past, Aboriginal artists applied colored dirt on the ground and destroyed the work at the ritual's end. Since the 1970s, Aboriginal artists have been making their paintings with more permanent materials.

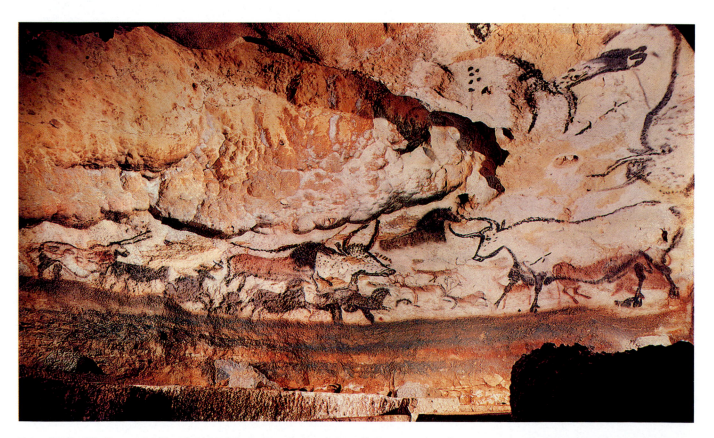

7.1   *Hall of Bulls*, c. 15,000–10,000 BCE. Cave painting, left wall, Lascaux, Dordogne, France. French Government Tourist Office. Photo Hans Hinz.

Witchetty Grub Dreaming, by Paddy Carroll Tjungurrayi, from 1980 (Fig. 7.2), is a kind of contour map with symbols, indicating the location of precious food and water in arid central Australia. The work is strongly patterned, with alternating lights and darks and curving and straight lines, all radiating from a circle in the center point showing the source of the ancestor grub. The small squiggled lines represent other grubs, an important food source, beneath the ground. Symmetry suggests the balance of the cosmos and the ancestors, providing sustenance for humans.

The Bamana people of Mali use masks, dance, and ritual to help ensure successful crops. The *Tyi Wara (or Chi Wara) Dance Headdresses,* from the late nineteenth or early twentieth century (Fig. 7.3), consist of male and female antelope masks, with the female bearing a baby antelope on her back. While the ground is being prepared for planting, young male dancers with masks and costumes perform the leaping movement of the antelope dance, a ritual that causes the return of the mythical antelope who first gave humans the knowledge

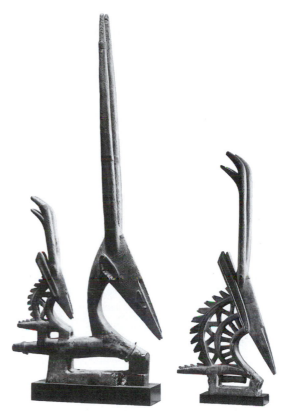

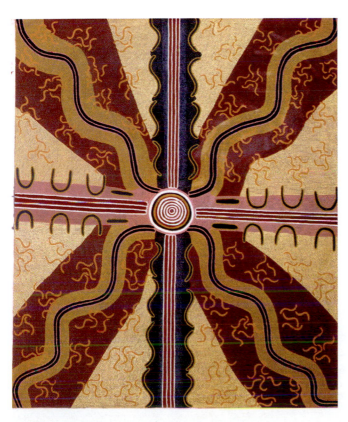

7.2 PADDY CARROLL TJUNGURRAYI. *Witchetty Grub Dreaming,* 1980. Paint on canvas. Australia, Aboriginal, from Papunya. Photo by Jennifer Steele. © Jennifer Steele/ Art Resource, NY.

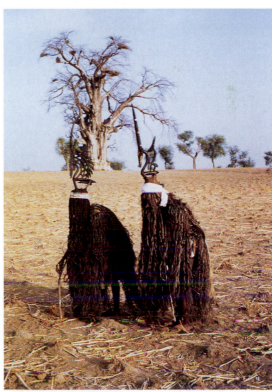

7.3 *Tyi Wara (or Chi Wara) Dance Headdresses,* late nineteenth or early twentieth century. Wood, brass tacks, string, cowrie shells, iron, quills; female: 38½" high; male: 31½" high. Bamana people, Mali, Africa. The lower image shows Tyi Wara dancers on a field. Photo by Pascal James Imperato.

of agriculture. Plant life (crops), animal life (antelope), and humankind (ancestors) are united in this ritual. Pattern and rhythm are important visual elements, with interwoven negative and positive shapes.

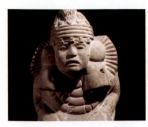

Connection *Many cultures have appealed to a deity spirit for food. One example, from Mesoamerica, is Xilonen, Goddess of Young Corn (Fig. 9.11, page 210).*

In most industrial societies today, few people hunt and process the meat they eat, or gather food, or farm. Instead of religion, technology and business ensure the food supply. British artist Sue Coe's *There Is No Escape*, from 1987 (Fig. 7.4), is unmistakably a harsh indictment of the contemporary meat industry. It is part of a large series entitled "Porkopolis," in which Coe shows living animals being transformed into packaged cuts of meat. Inside a slaughterhouse, Coe emphasizes the carnage and sympathizes with the pigs' fear, while the workers seem sadistic or subhuman. This emotional image is overall very dark, with a few lurid, glaring

lights, but Coe wants us to see it as fact and to tie it to the contemporary meat-heavy Western diet.

STORING AND SERVING FOOD

The following are examples of the many kinds of vessels created around the world to hold food. Each combines utility with aesthetics and meaning.

The ancient Chinese made bronze vessels for storing liquids, such as ritual wine. These vessels may have been placed beside a shrine of deceased ancestors to receive blessings for a successful crop or good health. Some are elaborately and densely patterned over their entire surface, with monster faces at key locations, such as the handles, perhaps to keep away evil. Balance and harmony are important, visually expressing ancient Chinese philosophy and values.

In our example (Fig. 7.5), we see a Zhou *Three-Legged Ting with Cover*, dated c. sixth century BCE. It has a simple shape with bands of patterns, supported by the three legs, or feet. Delicately incised abstract

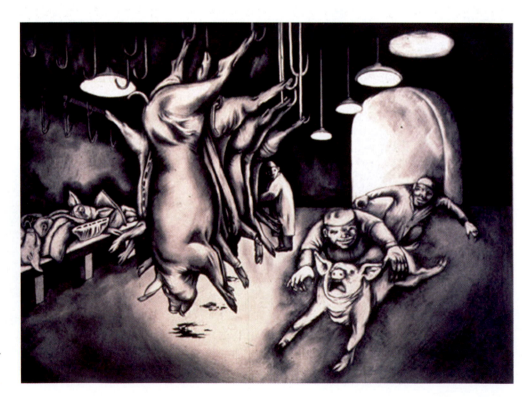

7.4 SUE COE. *There Is No Escape*, 1987. Watercolor and graphite on paper, 22" × 30". Britain. Courtesy Gil Michaels. © 1988 Sue Coe/Courtesy Galerie St. Etienne, New York.

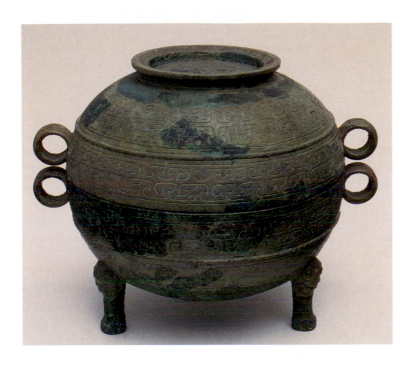

7.5 *Three-Legged Ting with Cover*, c. sixth century BCE. Cast bronze, 5¾" high. Zhou Dynasty, China. Ashmolean Museum, Oxford, UK.

lines complement its overall form. Circles are repeated, even on the ting's cover, decorated with a quatrefoil pattern and cleverly designed to be used as a serving bowl.

Water is essential, so various peoples have developed inventive systems for storing liquids, using clay, leather, wood, and straw. The ceramic Greek hydria, *Women at the Fountain House* (Fig. 7.6), dated 520–510 BCE, has a well-designed silhouette, with its body gracefully curving outward to the handles, which accentuate the widest part of the pot. From that point, the "shoulders" move inward dramatically, while the vessel's "neck" echoes but opposes the curves of the body. This is an example of black figure painting, in which a thin coating of black-firing clay covers the red clay of the vessel itself. Details are scratched in with a needle. Graceful women effortlessly collect water from the fountainhead, reiterating the purpose for the vessel itself. The scene is framed with floral and geometric designs.

Like water, salt is essential. At times it has been a form of wealth. The European nobility used elaborate saltcellars as a status symbol, while medieval Europeans used salt to distinguish the status of guests: prestigious people sat "above the salt," while people of lower rank sat below. The ivory *Saltcellar* from the sixteenth

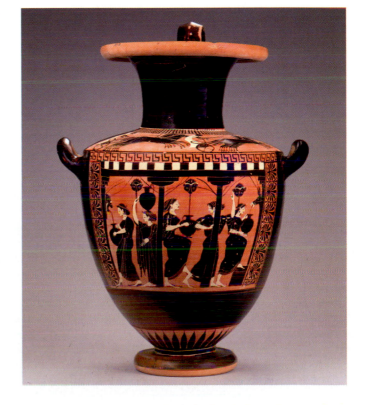

7.6 *Women at the Fountain House*, 520–510 BCE. Greek hydria. "AD" Painter. Ceramic, 20¾" high. Museum of Fine Arts, Boston, William Francis Warden Fund.

century (Fig. 7.7) was carved by African artists for export to Europe. The salt is held in the orb that is topped by an execution scene, showing a victim about to be sacrificed. Alligators serve as vertical supports below. The style reflects both African and Portuguese tastes, and both cultures valued the warmth and luster of ivory and used it for diplomatic gifts. The Portuguese likely drew the original design on paper, but African artists interpreted it, especially in the figure proportions, which echo African aesthetics with the large heads, simplified bodies, and short legs (see Chapter 13, The Body). The ivory has been worked very skillfully, with intricate patterning relieved by smooth areas, and with solid shapes punctuated by empty spaces.

Women of California and Pacific Northwest Coast tribes excelled at weaving baskets using willow and spruce twigs, pine needles, grapevines, and flax plants. The different colored materials in the basket wall resulted in geometric designs that were symbolic and often referred to nature, such as geese flying or sunlight breaking through stormy skies. These watertight baskets could be used for boiling acorns by placing hot rocks inside when they are filled with water. The *Basket* in Figure 7.8, dated 1890–1910, from the Pomo tribe, has been covered with feathers and shells over the basic woven design, adding layers of pattern. Mothers in California tribes made these special ceremonial gifts to mark significant moments in their daughters'

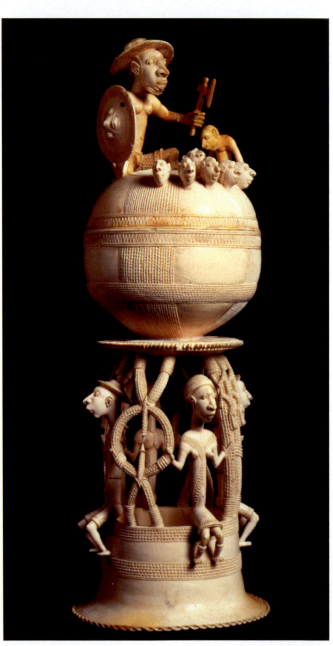

7.7 *Saltcellar*, sixteenth century. Ivory, 17" high. Afro-Portuguese, Sherbro Peninsula (Bulom), Sierra Leone. Museo Nazionale Preistorico Etnografico.

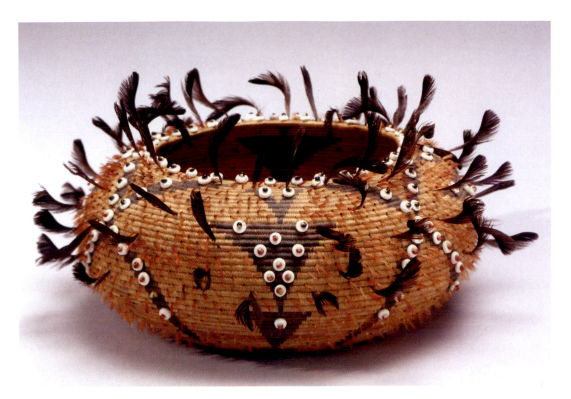

7.8 *Basket*, 1890–1910. Clamshell disks, red woodpecker feathers, quail topknots, tree materials, 7" diameter. USA, Pomo tribe. © Newark Museum/Art Resource, NY. Photo by Peter Furst.

lives, such as birth or puberty. Women treasured the baskets and were cremated with them at death. Though extremely delicate-looking, baskets such as this were used in everyday life and developed stains on the inside. The colored feathers represent the bravery and courage of the birds from which they came.

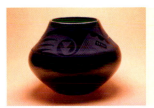

Connection Maria Martinez's black pots are examples of contemporary Native American vessels. See Fig. 3.41 on page 79.

In contrast to the decorative Pomo basket, the *Milk Storage Jar* (Fig. 7.9) from Kenya is elegant and simple. Made of carved wood, leather, and fiber, the vessel has a clean, curvilinear shape that both stores the staple and makes it portable. The subtle texture of the wood and leather is relieved by the braided

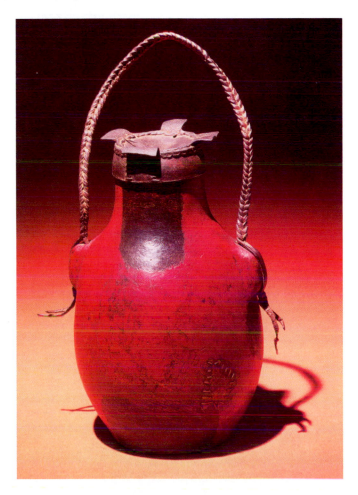

7.9 *Milk Storage Jar*, c. 1980. Carved wood, leather, and fiber, 11" high. Kenya, Africa. Ernie Wolf III Collection, Los Angeles. Photo by Frank J. Thomas, Los Angeles.

handle—a far cry from today's plastic butter and milk containers.

Andy Warhol's *Heinz 57 Tomato Ketchup* and *Del Monte Freestone Peach Halves*, dated 1964 (Fig. 7.10), are silk-screened wooden sculptures that look like mass-produced cardboard packing boxes for common grocery store items. In the United States, packaged foods are often more familiar than food in its natural condition, and Warhol is celebrating this commercialism, indicating that most people enjoy it and are comfortable with it. To him, the design of a ketchup box is art and, therefore, as meritorious and meaningful as any other work of art. Its formal qualities are bright colors, large type, simple graphics, and an organized layout. Yet there is a sense of irony to the work, because whatever is merely comfortable eventually becomes hollow and meaningless.

Connection *Can a utilitarian vessel be art, or not? Read the discussion in Chapter 1 on fine art, popular culture, and craft.*

Later in this chapter, we will study more vessels for serving food, specifically those used for ceremonial meals (see Figs. 7.17 and 7.18).

ART THAT GLORIFIES FOOD

In addition to sustaining us, food is beautiful. Various cultures depict food in ways that reflect their values, as we see in their landscapes, still life paintings, and other representations.

LANDSCAPE

Pieter Bruegel the Elder showed a vast Netherlands landscape in *The Harvesters,* dated 1565 (Fig. 7.11), filled with Earth's bounty of golden wheat. Taking a bird's-eye view, he filled the foreground with warm, broad fields, with cool seas in back. Bruegel integrated the peasants into this glorious landscape: they eat, sleep, and walk directly on the grain they harvest.

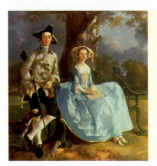

Connection *In contrast to Bruegel's peasants, European paintings of nobility often show the wealthy as much larger than the background and separate from the land, as in Gainsborough's Mr. and Mrs. Andrews (Fig. 2.10, page 31).*

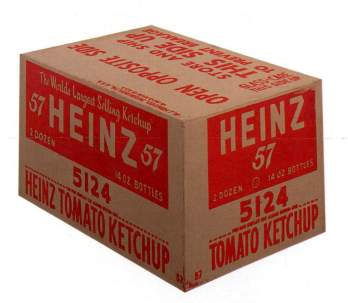

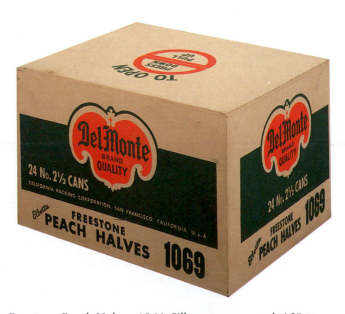

7.10 ANDY WARHOL. *Heinz 57 Tomato Ketchup* and *Del Monte Freestone Peach Halves*, 1964. Silk screen on wood, 15" × 12" × 9½". USA. Edith C. Blum Collection, Art Institute, Bard College. © 2004 Andy Warhol Foundation for the Visual Arts/Artists Rights Society (ARS), New York.

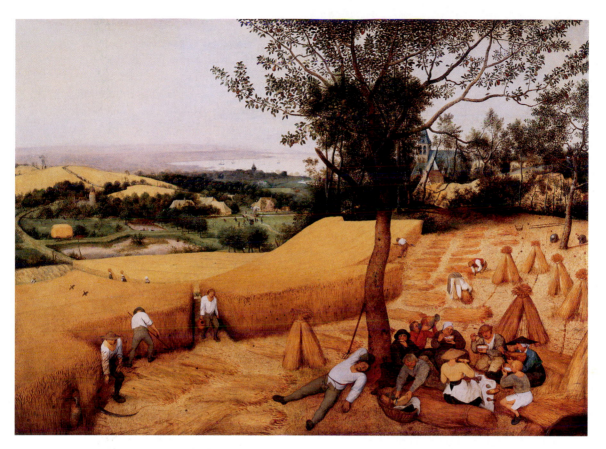

7.11   PIETER BRUEGEL THE ELDER. *The Harvesters*, 1565. Oil on panel, 46$^{1}/_{5}$" × 63$^{1}/_{4}$". Netherlands. The Metropolitan Museum of Art, Rogers Fund 1919 (19.164). Photograph © 1998 The Metropolitan Museum of Art.

STILL LIFE

Mu-Qi's *Six Persimmons*, dated c. 1269 (Fig. 7.12), reflects Zen Buddhism, which emphasized the importance of meditation and simplicity in life. This simple arrangement, with contrast between the plump fruits and the angular stems, and the spare richness of their color, is orderly yet irregular. Empty space is an important visual element. Many Zen masters chose to make ink paintings because of the form's spontaneity and simplicity, but the strokes must be practiced for years to make them confidently, without erasing or correction.

Seventeenth-century European still life paintings reflect a different set of cultural and religious beliefs. Lavish displays boast of wealth and abundance, in which food has become an aesthetic experience for refined taste. Paintings of food take on almost a fetish

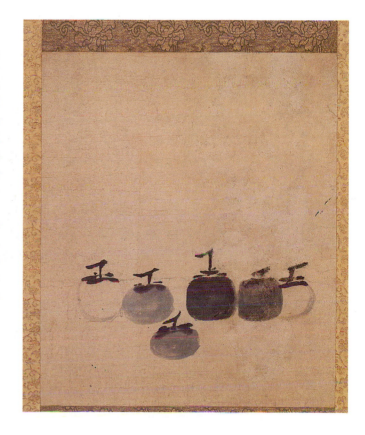

7.12   MU-QI. *Six Persimmons*, 13th century. Ink on paper, 14$^{1}/_{4}$" wide. Southern Song Dynasty, Dailoxu-ji, Kyoto. Photo: Shimizu Kohgeisha Co., Ltd. Permission Ryoko-in Management.

quality, detailed and lovingly painted, like Jan Davidsz de Heem's *A Table of Desserts,* dated 1640 (Fig. 7.13), with sumptuous fruits and sweets on silver platters, laid on velvet. The food is not shown as a person standing or sitting at a table would see it, but is elevated to eye level, centralized and formally arranged, surrounded by heavy draperies and musical instruments. Oil paint makes deep, rich colors and textures possible. Yet, moral themes were part of *A Table of Desserts.* The tipping trays and half-eaten, soon-to-spoil food alludes to the idea of "vanitas," that is, the impermanence of all earthly things and the inevitability of death.

In Europe and the United States in the early twentieth century, the still life became a vehicle for abstraction and experimentation with media. The early-twentieth-century focus was on innovation in art and invention in industry. Edward Weston's *Artichoke Halved,* 1930 (Fig. 7.14), reveals the complex design and grace of natural forms, but it also shows off the technical achievement of photography, with the capacity to zoom in close and instantly capture minutely detailed images. There was little interest in food as sustenance.

U.S. artist Wayne Thiebaud's 1963 painting *Pie Counter* (Fig. 7.15) deals with food as a visual display and as a popular icon, rather than as nutrition for the body. *Pie Counter* shows the plentifulness, standardization, and bright colors in contemporary mass-produced cafeteria food, so appealing to many. The thickly textured paint and bright colors are visually seductive, and very different from de Heem's style. Thiebaud also alludes to the fact that for many, the abundance of fattening food has become something to resist rather than

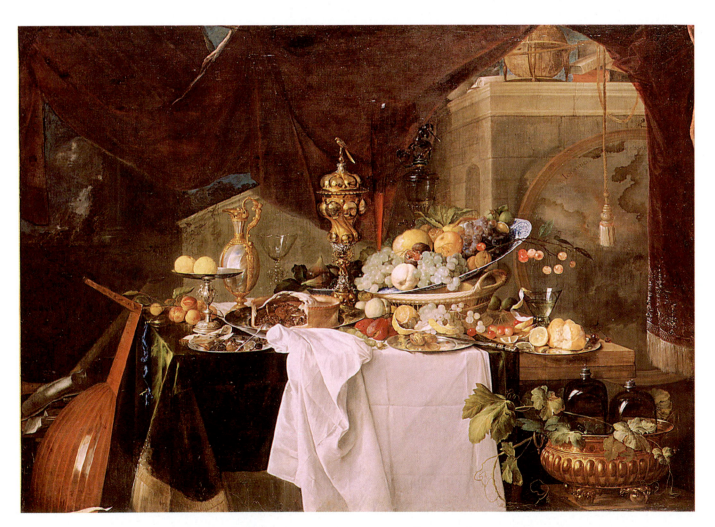

7.13   JAN DAVIDSZ DE HEEM. *A Table of Desserts,* 1640. Oil on canvas, 58^{7}/10" × 79^{9}/10". Netherlands. Louvre, Paris. © Réunion des Musées Nationaux/Art Resource, NY.

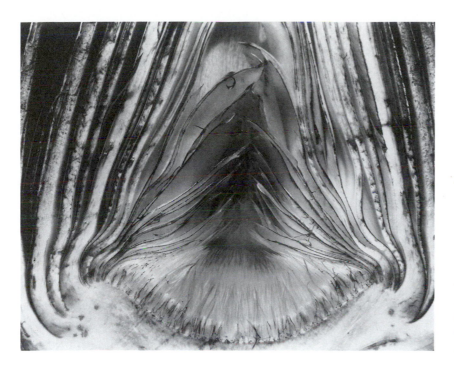

7.14 EDWARD WESTON. *Artichoke, Halved*, 1930. Photograph. USA. The Museum of Modern Art, New York. © Center for Creative Photography, Arizona Board of Regents.

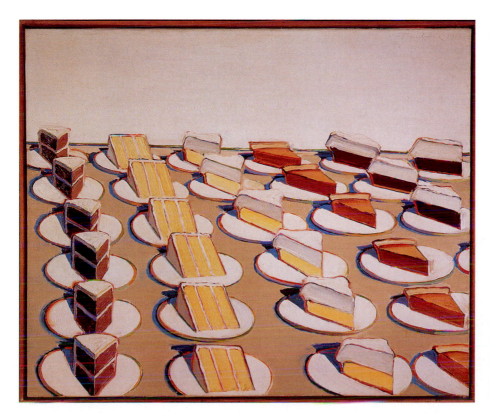

7.15 WAYNE THIEBAUD. *Pie Counter*, 1963. Oil on canvas, 30" × 36". USA. Photo © 2004 The Whitney Museum of American Art. © Wayne Thiebaud/Licensed by VAGA, New York, NY.

something to eat, while mass media advertising pushes it. Thiebaud's painting and Warhol's *Heinz 57 Tomato Ketchup* (Fig. 7.10) are of the same moment.

Connection Food can also be a symbol of honor. A ruler or warrior-priest of the Moche Civilization in Ancient Peru wore a **Peanut Necklace** of gold and silver (Fig. 10.11).

ART AND THE ACT OF EATING

We eat for nourishment, but how we eat is full of meaning, especially for ritual meals, religious celebrations, and formal holidays. Such meals are very structured, often with a ceremony for specially invited people who act as approving witnesses, signified by their partaking of the meal. Seating is often prearranged, as at weddings, and the food predetermined.

Italian artist Leonardo da Vinci's *Last Supper*, 1495–1498 (Fig. 7.16), depicts the ritual meal as a religious ceremony. The composition is very formal and symmetrical, with the most important figure, Jesus, at the center, framed by the distant doorway. His hands, arms, and head form a triangle. Six followers are on each side, in groups of three. The perspective lines in the ceiling and wall radiate from Jesus' head. All are on one side of a long table like a head table; this seating arrangement implies that a large crowd, not shown, is also present at the meal, of which we as viewers are part. Da Vinci's formula for depicting the *Last Supper* was so effective that this painting has become the standard.

The Native Americans of the Northwest Coast developed elaborate feasting and gift-giving rituals, called potlatches. The potlatch was the formal mechanism for establishing social order among the people. The most powerful people gave the most lavish feasts and gifts, and the guests acknowledged that superior status by eating the food and by accepting the gifts. Some traditional serving dishes were as long as twenty feet, and were prized possessions passed down through families. Stan Wamiss's *Halibut Feast Dish* (Fig. 7.17) is a contemporary serving dish for potlatches. Traditionally, carved animal forms were abstracted and rendered as geometric patterns, usually symmetrically

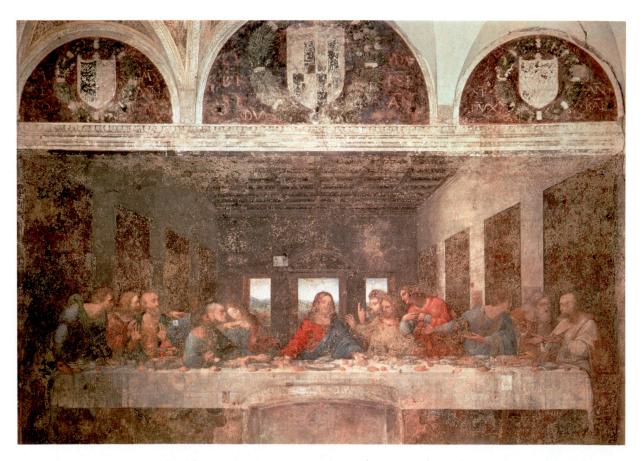

7.16 Leonardo da Vinci. *Last Supper*, 1495–1498. Experimental paint on plaster, 14'5" × 28'. Milan, Italy. Refectory of Santa Maria della Grazie. © Edimédia/CORBIS.

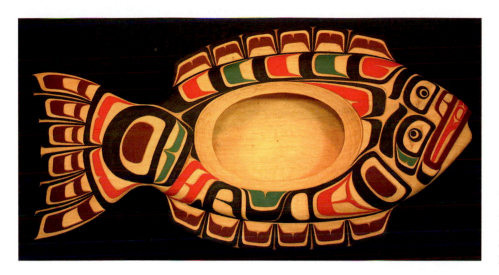

7.17 STAN WAMISS. *Halibut Feast Dish*, 2005. 25" long × 13" wide × 3½" deep. Yellow cedar or cypress. All detail has been carved and then painted.

around a vertical axis. Certain features, such as eyes, beaks, and claws, were emphasized, and black outlines establish the skeletal framework for the entire design. Contemporary pieces like this are brightly colored because the artists used commercially available paints instead of natural dyes and pigments.

In Japan, the tea ceremony is a formal, ritualized partaking of tea, influenced by Zen Buddhism, the philosophy behind *Six Persimmons* (Fig. 7.12). In Zen, personal meditation leading to enlightenment can include the most common of life's activities, including the making of tea. The host for a tea ceremony would carefully prepare the room, select vessels, and invite guests, guided by the idea that each gathering for a tea ceremony is a supremely intense and precious moment that can never be re-created. Tea bowls were unique, often "imperfect" in design, to convey the concepts of humility and of beauty embodied in humble things. The *Tea Bowl* (Fig. 7.18), from the seventeenth century, gracefully combines a series of opposites: smooth glazes and textured glazes, round and square shapes, horizontals and diagonals and verticals.

Some artwork references a ritual meal, although no food is shown. *The Dinner Party*, 1974–1979

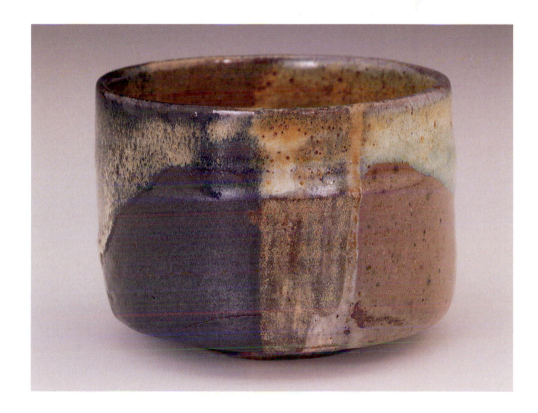

7.18 *Tea Bowl*, seventeenth century. Ceramic, Satsuma ware, 4²/₅" diameter at mouth. Japan. Courtesy of the Freer Gallery of Art #F1899.83.

(Fig. 7.19), is the setting for an imaginary, formal meal to celebrate significant women in Western culture. For five years, many artists collaborated to produce the "women's-work" ceramics, china painting, and needlework, under the direction of U.S. artist Judy Chicago. Thirty-nine place settings each contain a painted porcelain plate and stitched runner with symbols and text that honor a woman in Western history. The triangle is a female symbol and the symbol of the ancient goddess thought to have brought forth all of life unaided. Each side of the triangle has thirteen settings, the number of men painted in renditions of the *Last Supper*. (Chicago thought the *Last Supper* was an interesting interpretation of the Passover Meal, which, in the Jewish tradition, cannot be held unless a woman is present.) The number 13 is also the number in a witches' coven. The "Heritage Floor," beneath the table, is covered with triangular tiles inscribed with the names of 999 significant women. The *Dinner Party* project also produced much scholarship on important women who had not been previously well known.

Most meals are informal, everyday events and are not like the ritual meals we have just described. However, even the most casual reveal how people live and their social habits.

U.S. artist Duane Hanson's *Self-Portrait with Model*, 1979 (Fig. 7.20), presents the meal as a site for companionship. Yet there is more here. His life-size sculptures seem real at first. Hanson glorifies his subjects, but without idealizing them. The woman is very

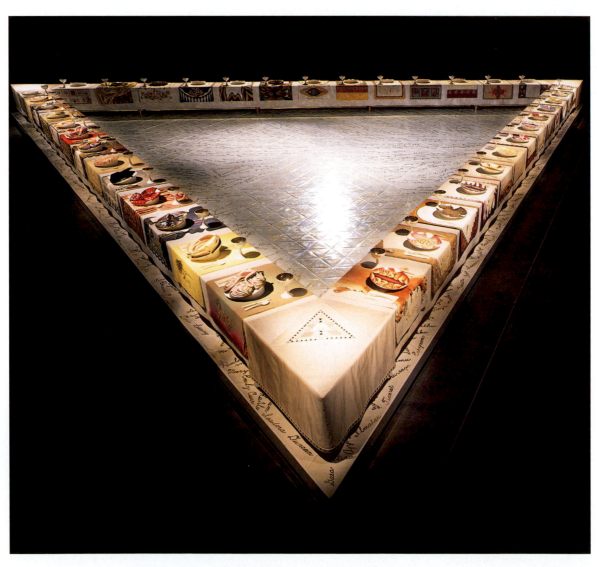

7.19   JUDY CHICAGO. *The Dinner Party*, 1974–1979. Painted porcelain and needlework, 48' × 42' × 36'. USA. Collection, "The Dinner Party" Trust. Photo © Donald Woodman. © 2004 Judy Chicago/Artists Rights Society (ARS), New York.

ordinary, and the artist is not an exalted genius, but part of the sculpture, "breaking bread" with the model. The simple props—furniture, napkin holder, and salt and pepper shakers—suggest a greasy-spoon diner.

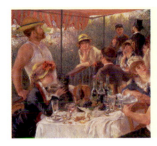

Connection *Another example of informal gatherings over meals is the* Luncheon of the Boating Party, *by Pierre August Renoir, in the Chapter 15 Art and History Box, on page 427).*

The last piece on the topic of eating is *Gnaw* (Fig. 7.21), dated 1992, by New York–based artist Janine Antoni, which began as a six-hundred-pound cube of chocolate and an equally large cube of lard. Throughout the run of the show, Antoni "sculpted" each block by biting and gnawing the edges. The chocolate was spat out and cast into the heart-shaped trays found inside candy boxes, turning the repulsive into sentimental prettiness. The lard she spat out was mixed with pigment and beeswax and cast into 130 lipsticks. The clean cubes of chocolate and lard became lumpy, gnawed masses, while the newly made trays and lipsticks were then shown in display cabinets, seen in the

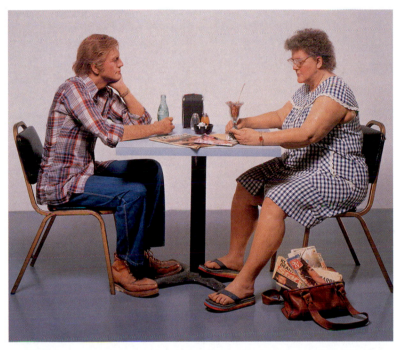

7.20 DUANE HANSON. *Self-Portrait with Model*, 1979. Painted polyester and mixed media, life-size. USA. Art © Estate of Duane Hanson/ Licensed by VAGA, New York, NY.

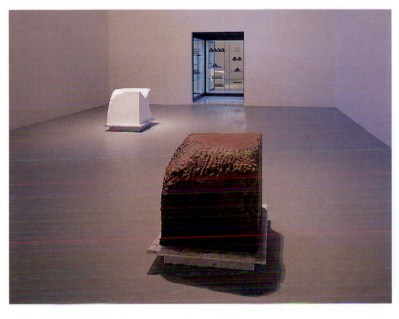

7.21 JANINE ANTONI. *Gnaw,* 1992. Three-part installation. Chocolate: 600 lbs. of chocolate gnawed by the artist; lard: 600 lbs. of lard gnawed by the artist; display: 130 lipsticks made with pigment, beeswax, and chewed lard removed from the lard cube; 27 heart-shaped packaging trays made from the chewed chocolate removed from the chocolate cube, dimensions variable. USA. Courtesy of the artist and Luhring Augustine.

background of Fig. 7.21. Replacing the traditional hammer and chisel with her mouth, Antoni transformed the act of eating into an artistic process. She was intimately relating to her creations—as babies put things into their mouths in order to know them, so, too, the artist consciously engaged in this experience. Using materials and objects that are socially defined as female fetishes, Antoni recast them in an art historical frame to raise questions about the position of women in art.

DOMESTIC ARCHITECTURE

Over the centuries, people have developed a wide range of houses, all serving the broad function of shelter, but done in amazingly different styles, due to the following factors:

- the need for protection from human foes, weather, animal predators, or insects
- historical necessity, as some event required people to change their housing styles
- the availability of materials
- aesthetic choice
- the desire to follow precedent, or to imitate a foreign style or a palace design
- symbolic importance; the structure or decoration of houses may reflect important social values or religious beliefs
- self-identity, as the house can be a reflection of its owner's beliefs or aspirations

GROUP LIVING

Human beings tended to cluster together in communities for fortification against danger and to increase their chances of survival. The earliest examples of domestic architecture feature group living, which was practiced as long ago as 25,000 BCE, with large huts accommodating several families. In cold, treeless areas of Russia and Ukraine, where the winter is harsh, early humans interlocked tusks and bones of the woolly mammoth for hut frames, creating much more ambitious structures than what was dictated by sheer necessity. Eight thousand years ago, ancient towns in Turkey featured clusters of connected houses, made of wood and mud brick. There were no streets or ground-level doors, as holes in the roofs served both as entry and as chimney vents.

Pueblo Bonito at Chaco Canyon (Fig. 7.22) was constructed by the Anasazi peoples in New Mexico, North America, around the eleventh century. The Anasazi are believed to be the ancestors of the Hopi, Zuni, Acoma, and the peoples of the Rio Grande. They were skilled farmers in a dry climate. *Pueblo Bonito* was a ceremonial fortress that may have been reserved for the Anasazi elite. It was built all in one piece over the rubble of previous construction, with precisely aligned walls and doors. The structure has smooth, sweeping lines, contrasting with the rough vertical cliffs behind it. The walls cover four acres, with five-story structures and approximately 660 rooms surrounding dual plazas to accommodate perhaps 1,000 residents. Various clans occupied certain sections of the pueblo. The round, underground structures are kivas, centers for ceremony and contemplation.

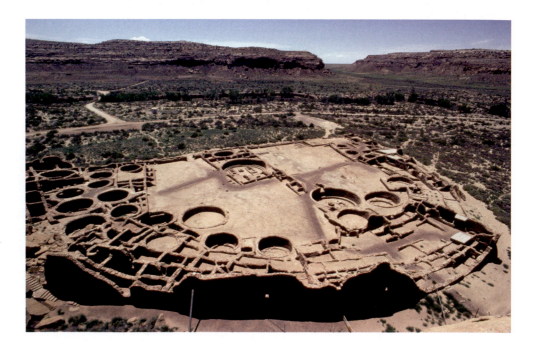

7.22 *Pueblo Bonito*, 11th century. Anasazi. New Mexico, USA. Photo by Paul Logsdon. © Dewitt Johnes/Corbis.

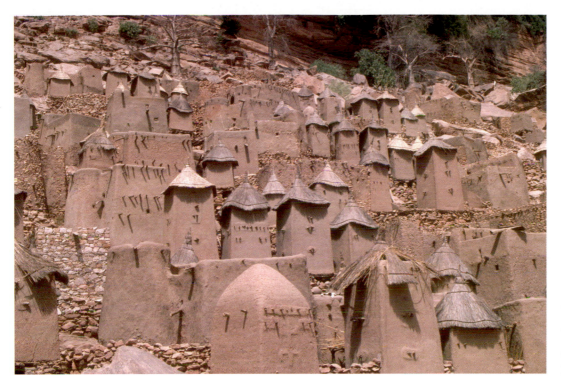

7.23 *Dogon Cliff Dwellings with Granaries*, Mali, Africa. © Wolfgang Kaehler/Corbis.

Group living occurs also in the villages of the Dogon people in Mali, Africa, dating from 1200 and currently in active use. Clinging to steep cliffs that extend for 125 miles, Dogon villages (Fig. 7.23) are dense collections of adobe houses, shrines, and granaries often irregular in shape and built on different levels to use all available space. Flat land is reserved for farming. Stone and mud walls make clusters for joint family households or compounds. The houses and granaries form an aesthetically pleasing pattern of vertical geometric shapes against the cliffs. Horizontal wooden beams project from the outer walls, providing footholds for maintenance as well as a pleasing pattern. Unused buildings deteriorate quickly and return to the earth.

In the late twentieth century, group living again became an attractive or even a necessary idea, given cost, congestion, and lack of community within large cities. In creating *Habitat* (Fig. 7.24), Israeli/Canadian architect Moshe Safdie was influenced by several features of pueblo architecture: (1) energy efficiency, due to compact design; (2) use of available natural resources; and (3) comfortable living for many in a relatively small space. As an alternative to single-family urban sprawl housing, as well as the impersonal high-rise apartment, Safdie created low-cost housing that minimized land use and provided privacy and individualized living within a group setting. The prefabricated units are building blocks that can be stacked and arranged in many unique configurations providing garden spaces on roofs. While

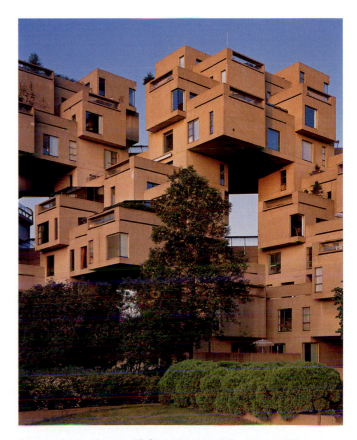

7.24 MOSHE SAFDIE. *Habitat.* Designed for Expo '67 in Montreal, Canada. Photo by Russell Thompson. The Arkansas Office, Inc.

pueblo influence is important, the structure is also the product of twentieth-century modernism with the emphasis on simple, unornamented, geometric shapes.

INDIVIDUAL HOMES

The designs of individual homes embody climate concerns, aesthetic preferences, and cultural choices.

In the first century CE, average Romans lived in cramped, unheated multistory apartment buildings with no sanitary facilities. In contrast, housing for the wealthy was spacious and beautiful, like the *House of the Vettii* (Fig. 7.25), excavated in the city of Pompeii. The exteriors were rather plain, but inside, individual rooms opened onto courtyard spaces that brought fresh air and light into the center of the house. Figure 7.25 shows the front atrium with a pool, called the "impluvium," for collecting rainwater, and behind it a Greek-style garden. Paintings and mosaics covered most walls and floors, and the garden was furnished with marble tables and fountains. The Roman house was organized symmetrically around an axis that ran from the entrance to the back of the house, aligning a succession of lovely views and providing illumination throughout the dwelling.

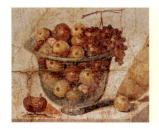

Connection *An example of wall painting for a wealthy Roman residence is the first century fresco* Glass Bowl with Fruit *(Fig. 3.18, page 67).*

The *Villa Rotonda* (Fig. 7.26) is a sixteenth-century Italian house influenced by Greek and Roman designs. The designer, Andrea Palladio, was the chief architect of the Venetian Republic and wrote books promoting symmetry and stability as controlling elements of architectural design. Centuries later, his writings influenced Thomas Jefferson's design of his home, Monticello. Palladio's villa has a centralized plan, with thirty-two rooms and four identical porches, united by the central, dome-covered rotunda. The harmonious geometric shapes represent Renaissance philosophical principles of orderliness and hierarchy. Steep flights of stairs lead up to the structure, very much like a Roman temple on a platform.

Traditional Chinese house design reflects different cultural values and different responses to the environment than the houses we have just seen. Houses for the wealthy were modeled after the palaces of the first emperor of China, Shi Huangdi (ruled 221–206 BCE). No houses from the Han era have survived, but

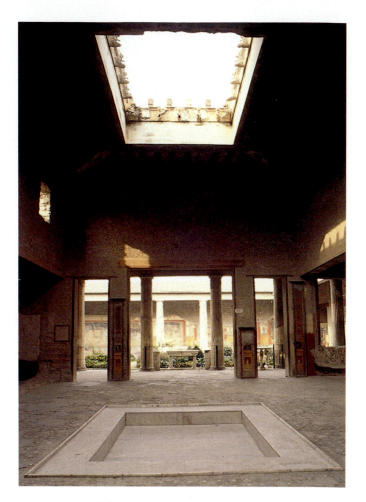

7.25 *House of the Vettii,* 62–79 CE. Atrium, reconstructed. Pompeii, Italy. Naples Archaeological Museum. Henri Stierlin.

ceramic models of them were buried in tombs. A wealthy person's home typically had several stories, each slightly smaller than the one below. Capping each level were wide eaves that were both functional and aesthetic, adding horizontal emphasis. Balconies encircled the house. Precious materials, such as gold and jade and bronze, were used for house ornamentation and accents. Inside, wall paintings would have illustrated Daoist fables and Confucian aphorisms with floral designs in brilliant colors. These features are evident on the relatively modest *Tomb Model of a House* (Fig. 7.27), dating between 25 and 220 CE. It may have served as a watchtower and probably had one or more courtyards, where chores were done. This timber frame house had non-load-bearing walls of compressed earth or mud that the wide eaves protected from rainfall. Elaborate brackets supported the roof.

In Indonesia, distinctive wooden houses were designed in response to the tropical climate, with heavy rainfall, thick vegetation, heat, and insects. The *Toba Batak House* (Fig. 7.28) has a very steep roof

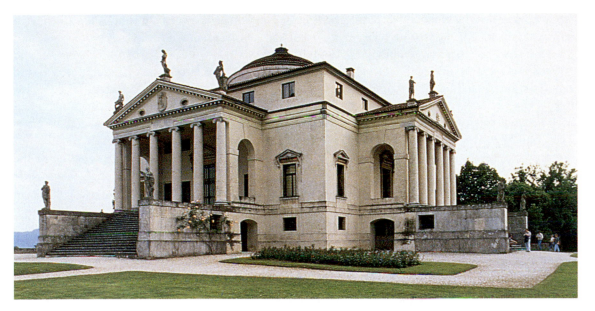

7.26 ANDREA PALLADIE. *Villa Rotonda*, 1552. Vicenza, Italy. © Scala/Art Resource, NY.

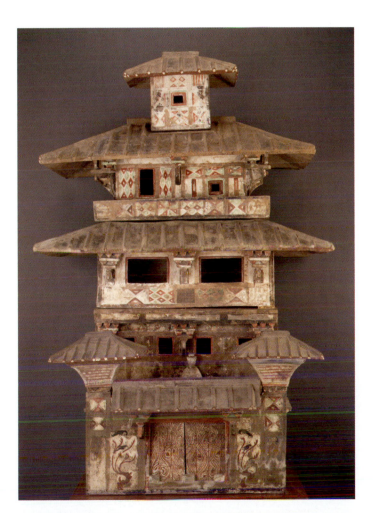

7.27 *Tomb Model of a House*, 25 – 220 CE. Ceramic, 52" × 33" × 27". Eastern Han Dynasty. China. The Nelson–Atkins Museum of Art, Kansas City, Missouri (Purchase: Nelson Trust) 33-521. Photo by Robert Newcombe.

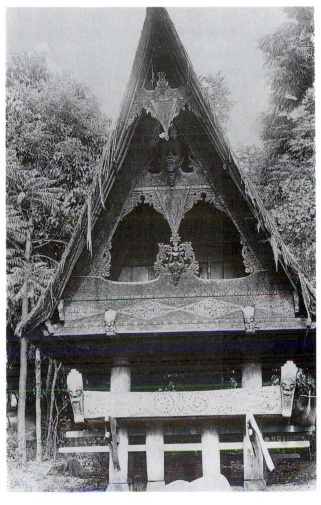

7.28 Decorated façade of *Toba Batak House*, c. 19th/20th centuries. Sumatra, Indonesia. Royal Tropical Institute, Amsterdam.

that quickly sheds rain to keep it from soaking the thatch. Overhanging eaves shield the generous windows. When seen from the side, the roofline is highest at each end and curves downward at the center. The second and third levels have small sleeping and storage areas, so most people spent the day outdoors. Stilts raise the house to catch breezes, to protect the sleeping people from mosquitoes, and to provide security. Sometimes animals were kept on the ground level. Stilts are made of thick, hardwood tree trunks, necessary to support the heavy thatched roof, and soft wood was used for non-load-bearing walls. The entire house is pegged together instead of nailed, and the stilts sit on rocks, so that the structure flexes during earthquakes.

The parts of the *Toba Batak House* have symbolic meaning, with the internal spaces seen as maternal or womb-like. The house is seen as a "transformer [that] tames the terrifying vastness of the universe and at the same time inflates human concerns with cosmic grandeur" (Richter 1994:57). The house echoes the human body, with stilts as legs, the roof as the head, and the trapdoor entrance as the navel. From a cosmic perspective, the three levels are like the upper, lower, and middle worlds of the Indonesian universe; from a social

perspective, the three levels of the house are likened to the social hierarchy separating slaves, commoners, and nobility (Dawson and Gillow 1994:14). This house, and others by this clan, is covered with painted patterns and guardian figures for fertility and protection.

Housing can also be shaped by historical necessity. For thousands of years, the Native Americans of Eastern and Central North America were stable populations who hunted and gathered food. With the coming of the Europeans, these peoples were displaced from their homelands and for a while lived on the Great Plains in movable houses, like the *Tipi*, c. 1880 (Fig. 7.29), originally a small tent used during hunting season. When later used as year-round housing, tipis were built as large as twenty-five feet high and were moved by horses. Animal skins, buffalo hide, or canvas covered the framework of slender poles. Adjustable flaps kept out wind or rain and ventilated smoke. Tipi covers and liners were often painted. Before the 1830s, the imagery consisted of stiff figures, while later ones often showed the tipi owner's personal adventures in nature or at war.

Fallingwater, 1936–1938 (Fig. 7.30), is arguably the most famous modern house in the United States. Frank Lloyd Wright designed it for the wealthy Kaufmann

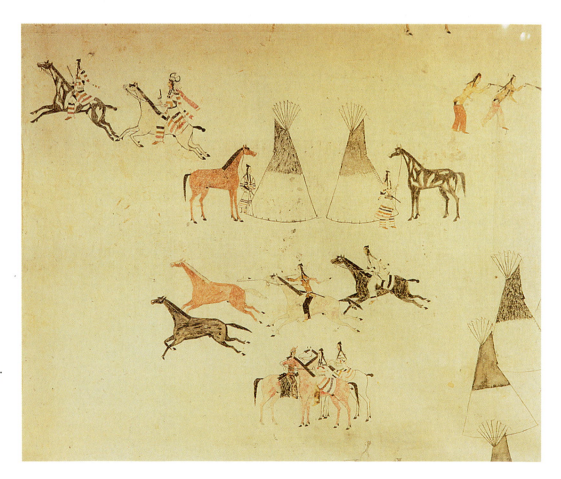

7.29 *Tipi* cover, c. 1880. Decorated with images of tipis and equestrian warrior figures. North American Sioux. © Werner Forman/Art Resource, NY.

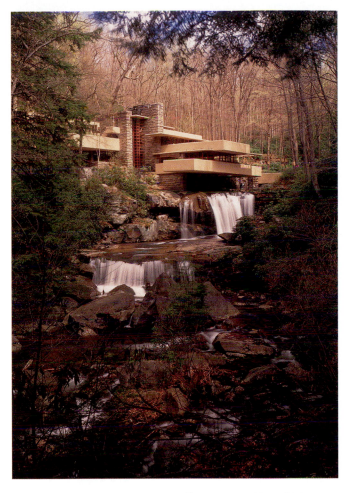

7.30   FRANK LLOYD WRIGHT. *Fallingwater*, 1936–1938. Kaufmann House, Connellsville vicinity, PA. ESTO © Scott Frances.

family from Pittsburgh as a weekend home in the woods to balance their urban lives. Wright believed that houses should be unified wholes that merge into their natural settings, using local materials. A large boulder is the base of the house's central fireplace, while stones for walls came from nearby quarries. Geometric blocks, some vertical but most horizontal, sit low to the ground. There is no decoration, except the contrasting textures of stone and concrete. The house is arranged to allow maximum sunlight inside. Long, rectilinear windows frame views of the surrounding trees.

Fallingwater shows much influence from Japanese and Chinese architecture, especially in its cantilevered porches. Also, like much of the traditional domestic architecture of Asia, the walls in *Fallingwater* are not load bearing, but act as privacy screens. Also from Japan was the idea of a flowing interior space, with few walls and large windows.

Connection *Another Wright building is the Solomon R. Guggenheim Museum (Fig. 16.3, page 434).*

COMMERCIAL ARCHITECTURE

Commercial architecture provides shelter for the needs of business and trade. Here are a few examples considered to be important milestones in art.

The *Markets of Trajan*, 100–112 (Fig. 7.31), is a multistoried complex that held administrative offices

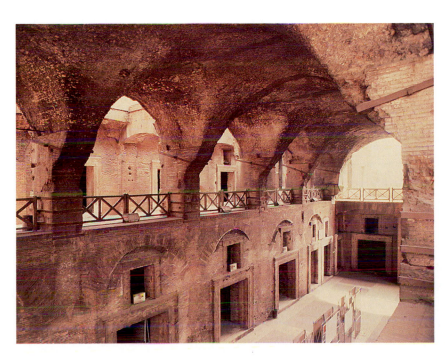

7.31   Interior of *Markets of Trajan*, CE 100–112. Rome. © Scala/Art Resource, NY.

and more than 150 shops. This large building on a very steep slope has a paved street cutting through at about mid level. Its design was likely influenced by the enclosed markets of the Middle East called "souks" or "bazaars," and it looks a lot like today's shopping malls. There were two levels of shops, called "taberna," each with a wide doorway and attic storage accessible through a window on top. Although drab today, the interior was once quite decorative and enlivened with vendors, shoppers, and wares of all kinds. A terrible fire destroyed large sections of Rome in 64 CE, so newer construction like the *Markets* used concrete because it was cheap, flexible, and fireproof and could be covered with beautiful veneers of brick, marble, stucco, gilding, or mural paintings. Concrete construction made large, well-lit, multistoried projects feasible. Walls are load bearing, yet the arches channel the tremendous weight of the roof to massive piers, allowing large windows to pierce the walls. This was a tremendous accomplishment architecturally. The massive, muscular Roman style of architecture would have been impossible with only wood construction.

Connection *Romans were known for their ambitious public buildings, such as the* **Baths of Caracalla** *(Fig. 16.5, page 435), the* **Colosseum** *(Fig. 16.9, page 438), and the* **Pantheon** *(Fig. 9.25, page 222).*

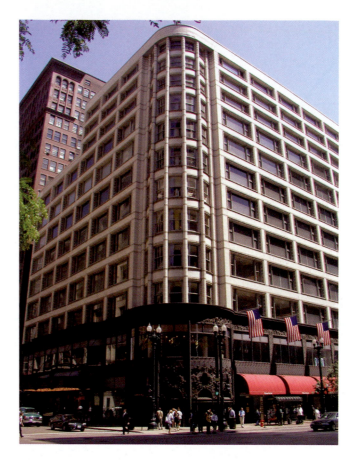

7.32 LOUIS H. SULLIVAN. *Carson Pirie Scott and Company,* 1904. Chicago, IL. Photo courtesy of Stephen A. Edwards.

Today, stores and businesses are often located in high-rise buildings. The *Carson Pirie Scott* building, dated 1904 (Fig. 7.32), was one of the first innovative tall buildings in the twentieth century. The architect, Louis Sullivan, believed that "form follows function," meaning that buildings should not be shaped according to preconceived ideas, but should be an outgrowth of their function and of the materials used. He exploited the new design possibilities of steel frame construction, coupled with the invention of the elevator. Although iron and steel had been used in the past, those buildings were often sheathed in stone or brick or were novelties like the Eiffel Tower. Like the human body, with the skeleton a rigid armature covered by muscles and skin, Sullivan's buildings were supported by the steel framework, with non-load-bearing walls stretched like skin over it. Height was emphasized more than horizontal elements.

On the ground floor, Sullivan introduced the large display windows that have become familiar fixtures in almost every retail store in the United States today. Sullivan saw these display windows as pictures, so he framed them with ornate cast ironwork with organic motifs referencing birth, flowering, decay, and rebirth. In contrast, the upper floors are plain with large horizontal windows that make evident the steel structure underneath. The curved corner provides vertical emphasis, with narrower, taller windows. The roof is de-emphasized, with no overhanging eaves or cornices. Rather, the building gives the impression that several more floors, similar in design, could be added right on top of the existing structure.

LATE-TWENTIETH-CENTURY PUBLIC STRUCTURES

R. Buckminster Fuller was an architectural engineer, inventor, designer, and mathematician with an interest in utopian design. He believed that well-guided technology would get maximum gain for minimum expenditure of energy, giving everyone more affordable shelter with more conveniences. His geodesic dome came to be a symbol for twentieth-century innovation and progress, while its emphasis on geometry and its use of the flexible metal framework made it continuous with the innovations of Sullivan's *Carson Pirie Scott* building. The domes are spherical networks of steel-frame tetrahedrons (a tetrahedron is a three-sided pyramid sitting on a triangular base). Depending upon the number of modules used, the domes could be flat or tall and could be made to any size. (Fuller even proposed a three-mile-wide dome to enclose midtown Manhattan in a climate-controlled environment.) Domes enclose the largest internal volume within the least amount of wall surface, thus saving on materials. The framework of inexpensive, modular, linear elements could be assembled in a short time and could resist both internal and external pressures. The dome could be covered with a variety of materials, such as glass, plastic, cloth, wood, or paper.

Fuller's design for the *U.S. Pavilion* at Montreal's Expo '67 (Fig. 7.33) was built along with Safdie's *Habitat*. The nearly spherical dome, 250 feet in diameter, created a dramatic silhouette and glowed at night like an otherworldly orb. Because the dome is self-supporting, the interior can be configured in any way desired. Although geodesic domes have been used as factories, greenhouses, mobile military living units, experimental biospheres, and research stations, they have yet to become popular for businesses or homes.

The rectangle continued to dominate architectural design for twentieth-century office buildings, which were often spare, rectangular shafts of steel and glass devoid of ornamentation that rose from street-level plazas. This was called the International Style because of its global prevalence in large cities.

Connection *One of the most influential architects of the International Style, Ludwig Mies van der Rohe, summarized this aesthetic with the phrase "less is more." The unadorned, simple, geometric style was seen as new, modern, heroic, and even utopian, as architects sought to transform urban centers with functional forms. See van der Rohe's* Seagram Building *(Fig. 2.41, page 54).*

However, within a few decades, there arose a resistance to the International Style, which some saw as sterile and oppressive. The rectangle is dissolved into triangles and diagonals with the *Bank of China*, dated

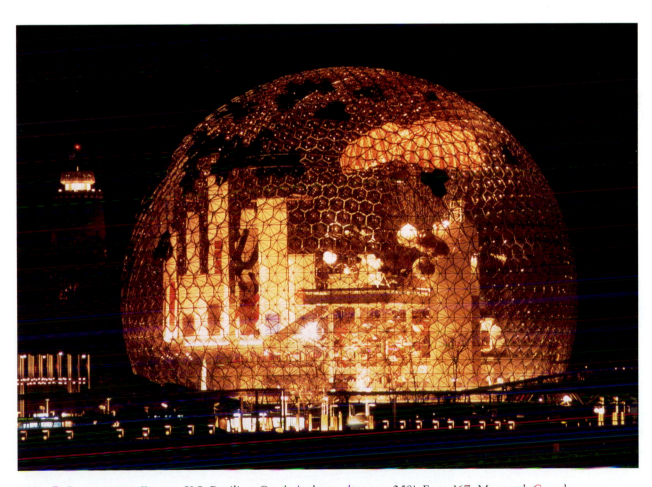

7.33   R. BUCKMINSTER FULLER. *U.S. Pavilion.* Geodesic dome, diameter 250'. Expo '67, Montreal, Canada.

1989 (Fig. 7.34), by the architectural firm of I. M. Pei and Partners. The base is subdivided into four equal triangular sections, and more triangles are created by the diagonal braces that stabilize the skeletal frame, a necessary addition because of earthquakes and high winds. Pei emphasized rather than hid the braces. The skeletal support for the building is innovative. At the corners are four massive columns. Beginning at the twenty-fifth floor, a fifth column at the center supports the load from the upper floors; that load is transmitted diagonally to the corner supports. The exterior of the *Bank of China* is gray anodized aluminum with reflective glass windows. The lower floors surround a twelve-story-high central atrium, while on top, dining and entertainment establishments boast spectacular views.

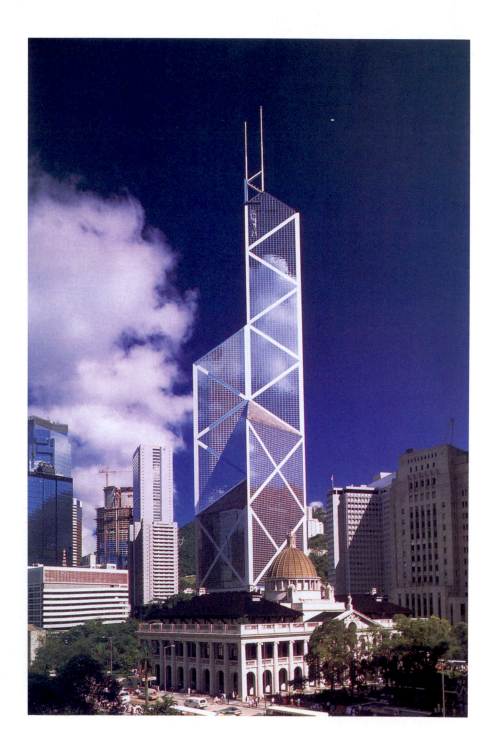

7.34 I. M. PEI AND PARTNERS. *Bank of China*, 1989. Hong Kong. Courtesy, Pei Cobb Freed & Partners.

Other reactions against the International Style were more radical, like the *Piazza d'Italia* (Fig. 7.35) in New Orleans by Charles Moore with U.I.G. and Perez Associates. Moore believed that cities had lost much of their unique character because of new skyscrapers that all looked alike. He favored maintaining distinctness and the "presence of the past" in any location. The **Postmodern** architectural style of *Piazza d'Italia* emphasizes visual complexity, individuality, colorfulness, and even fun. It is symbolically complicated as well, combining elements from the Roman Empire, the Italian Renaissance, and twentieth-century entertainment sites. To Postmodern architects, "less is a bore." A map of Sicily sits at the center of the plaza, connected to the larger map of Italy that joins the curved architectural fragments behind it. Like much of New Orleans, *Piazza d'Italia* suffered from the ravages of Hurricane Katrina in 2005.

Architecture continues to evolve past the Postmodern *Piazza d'Italia*. The past few years has seen the rise of **Deconstructivist** architecture, which rejects established conventions and seeks to shake the viewer's expectations. Deconstructivist buildings can be disorienting and irregular, and outside forms may give no clue to the space of their interiors. Many deconstructivist buildings resemble abstract sculptures more than traditional architecture.

Connection *Two examples of Deconstructivist architecture are Frank Gehry's* Guggenheim Bilbao *(Fig. 6.9, page 124) and his* Walt Disney Concert Hall *(Fig. 16.4, page 435).*

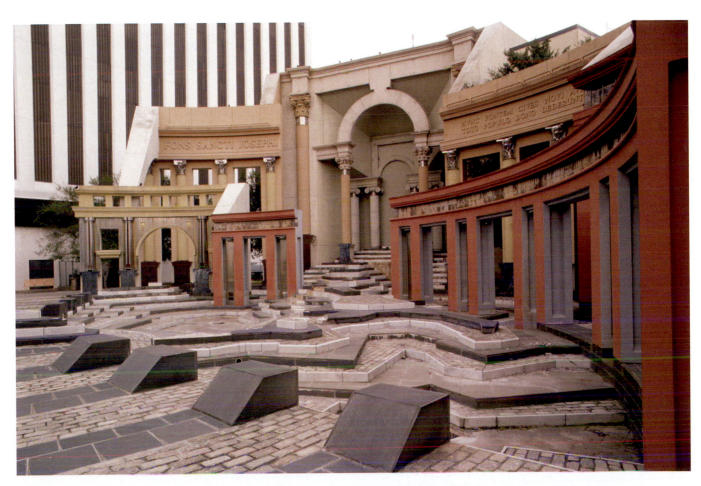

7.35   CHARLES MOORE WITH U.I.G. AND PEREZ ASSOCIATES. *Piazza d'Italia*, 1975–1980. New Orleans, USA. © Robert Holmes/Corbis.

Human life began in Africa, and then spread northward to Europe and Asia. Humans reached the Americas last, by crossing over the land bridge that likely existed long ago between Alaska and northeast Russia.

Food and shelter were immediate concerns for early humans. They hunted wild animals and gathered berries, seeds, fruits, and plants for food. They lived in small, nomadic bands, moving on to find new food sources as needed. They controlled fire for light and warmth, and made tools, first from stone and later from bone, including axes, spearheads, fishing sinkers, beads, harpoons, and even needles for sewing. This Paleolithic era, or Old Stone Age, saw the beginning of technology and art making as integral parts of human existence.

Paleolithic cultures first appeared as long ago as 25,000 BCE. As early as 10,000 BCE, some of these evolved into Middle Stone Age (Mesolithic) cultures, where humans continued to live by hunting and gathering but also experimented with farming. Around 8000 BCE, some groups advanced into the New Stone Age (Neolithic

era), with expanded agriculture and the beginnings of cities. But it is important to remember that some Stone Age cultures survived thousands of years, even into the twentieth century.

Stone Age cultures used art and ritual to secure and protect what was vital to them: food and shelter, as we saw in Chapter 7, as well as human procreation, to be discussed in Chapter 8. Animals were painted—in all likelihood for ritual purposes—in caves and rock shelters in Spain, Africa, and southern France (*Hall of Bulls*, Lascaux, Fig. 7.1; and *Hall of the Bison* from Altamira, Fig. 6.14). Small, life-like sculptures in bone or stone have been found much more broadly throughout Europe, Asia, and Africa. They represented animals or were fertility figures like the *Venus of Willendorf* in Figure 8.1. Often they were found near the hearth, reinforcing the connection between art, ritual, food, and procreation. Early humans lived together for protection, in huts, rock shelters, or structures built of mammoth bones covered with turf and skins. As cultures evolved, so did the imagery in their art, as in the *African Rock*

Map 1 The Spread of Homo Sapiens Sapiens (or wise, wise humans). Courtesy of Replogle Globes, Inc., Broadview, IL.

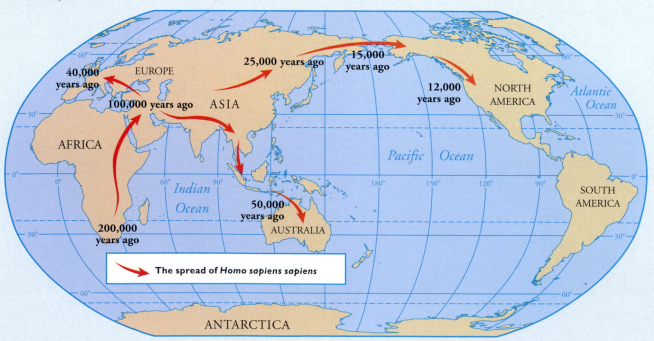

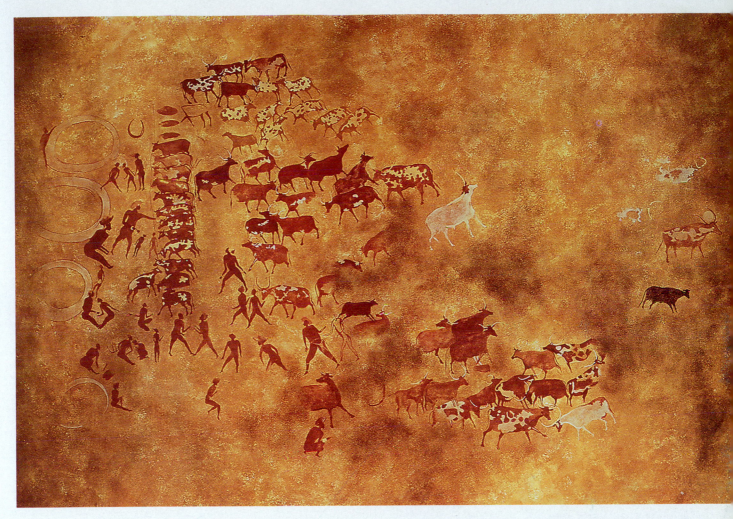

7.36 *African Rock Painting.* Illustrates herding activities in Neolithic Africa. Fresco from Tassili N'Aijer. Henri Lhote Collection, Musée de l'Homme, Paris. © Erich Lessing/Art Resource, NY.

Painting in this box, showing humans herding cattle as agriculture was first developed.

Thus the Stone Age people linked art and rituals to secure their food and shelter. In some cultures, this linking continued beyond the Stone Age, and even into the twentieth century. The *Three-Legged Ting with Cover* (Fig. 7.5) is an artwork used to receive the blessings of ancestors. *Tyi Wara Dance Headdresses* (Fig. 7.3) from twentieth-century Africa were integral in rituals for successful crops. The guardian figures at the corners of the early-twentieth-century *Toba Batak House* (Fig. 7.28) protected the house and its occupants. From Aboriginal Australia in 1980, *Witchetty Grub Dreaming* (Fig. 7.2) is both painting and ritual combined to assist in securing food in a desert environment.

Coming up in Chapter 8 are several works that continue the link between art, ritual, and survival, in this case, the continuation of human life through children. These artworks include the *Venus of Willendorf*, already mentioned, as well as other works dating from 3000 BCE through the twentieth century: the *Idol from Amorgos* (Fig. 8.2), the *God Te Rongo* (Fig. 8.3), the *Figure of a Deity: A'a Rurutu* (Fig. 8.4), *Potawatomi Male Figure* (Fig. 8.5), *Bamana Female Figure* (Fig. 8.6), *Initiation Rites of Dionysos* (Fig. 8.7) *Asante Fertility Figures from Ghana* (Fig. 8.8), two Moche pots (Figs. 8.13 and 8.28), and *Mother and Nursing Child* (Fig. 8.29).

Timeline

Event	Date	Artwork
Paleolithic Era		Hall of Bulls, Lascaux
	10,000	
Mesolithic Era		
Domestication of Sheep	8000	
Settlements in China and Chile		
Birth of Agriculture in Mesopotamia and Mexico		
	7000	
Neolithic Era		
Settlements in India		
Domestication of Cattle	6000	Catal Hüyük
Mesopotamia Civilizations		
Unification of Egypt		
Irrigated Farming in Andes	2000	
Shang Dynasty—China	1600	
Bronze Vessel Casting, China		
	1000	Three-Legged Ting with Cover
Greek Pottery	500	Women at the Fountain House
	200	
		House of the Vettii
Arch and Concrete in Roman Architecture	1 CE	Markets of Trajan
Moche, Peru	200	Tomb Model of a House
Middle Ages, Europe	500	
Use of Cantilever in Chinese Architecture	800	
	1000	
Anasazi Culture		Pueblo Bonito
Spread of Chinese Culture to Japan	1200	Mu-Qi: Six Persimmons
		Dogon Cliff Dwellings established
	1300	
Aztec Empire		
Renaissance		
Incan Empire	1400	

Event	Date	Artwork
Ming Dynasty—China		da Vinci: Last Supper
Mughal Dynasty—India		Saltcellar
		Bruegel the Elder: The Harvesters
		de Heem: A Table of Desserts
		Tea Bowl, Japan
		Palladio: Villa Rotunda
Colonial Era	1700	
Industrial Revolution	1800	
Rise in Urban Population		Basket, Pomo
Steel Frame		Tyi Wara (or Chi Wara) Dance Headdresses
		Tipi cover, Sioux
Architecture	1900	
		Toba Batak House
		Sullivan: Carson, Pirie, Scott Building
		Weston: Artichoke, Halved
	1939	
World War II		Wright: Fallingwater
	1960	
		Thiebaud: Pie Counter
		Warhol: Heinz 57 Tomato Ketchup
		Safdie: Habitat
		Fuller: U.S. Pavilion, Geodesic Dome
Food in Outer Space		
		Chicago: The Dinner Party
		Moore: Piazza d'Italia
		Hanson: Self-Portrait with Model
		Tjungurrayi: Witchetty Grub Dreaming
		Milk Storage Jar
		Coe: There Is No Escape
		Pei: Bank of China
	1990	Antoni: Gnaw
	2000	
World Population 6 Billion		
		Wamiss: Halibut Feast Dish

Many cultures have called upon art and ritual to guarantee the food supply. Some contemporary artists have looked critically at modern food production. To store and serve food, artists have designed a wide variety of vessels, often with shapes and decorations that are meaningful to those using them.

Artists have made paintings, sculptures, and photographs that glorify food and earth's bounty. These works also reveal broad social values and religious beliefs. The way food is eaten is significant. Ritual meals and feasts can be religious ceremonies or major social events with elaborate art objects. Paintings show us the significance of ritual meals as well as informal ones.

Shelter is essential for human life, but the design of shelter is not always limited to function. Cultures choose to develop group housing or individual homes in a wide range of styles, reflecting broad social values, climate constraints, and historical necessity. Commercial architecture has evolved from concrete to steel frame construction.

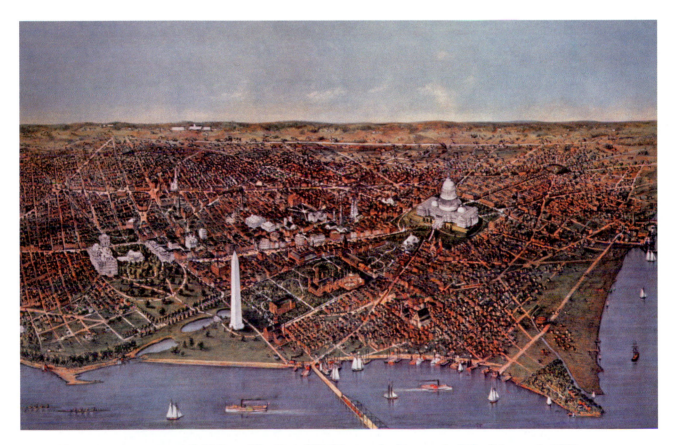

7.37   NATHANIEL CURRIER AND J. M. IVES. *The City of Washington, looking north*. Color lithograph, 1892.

FOOD FOR THOUGHT

In the early twentieth century, the Italian Futurists believed that humans were machines, and that in a machinelike way, people based their actions on what they ate. Futurists wrote cookbooks designed to shock and excite the senses, but not to fill the stomach, for they believed a full stomach was dulling. In one recipe, "Raw Meat Torn by Trumpet Blasts," the diner is to take mouthfuls of raw electrified beef, and to blow loud blasts on a trumpet in between those mouthfuls of beef.

- *What are your experiences of eating?*

- *What besides hunger is being satisfied?*

- *What food images have you seen today?*

In the United States today, housing construction uses a lot of wood. Yet hardwood forests are seriously depleted, and wood produced by tree farms is spongy and prone to warping. Some ecologists are raising alarms about deforestation. A few architects are considering building houses of rammed earth, pumice, or straw bales. Recycled steel studs, made from steel beams of demolished buildings, have been used in commercial buildings and are beginning to be used in residences. Steel is stronger than wood and is resistant to earthquakes and termites.

What are your ideas about the following questions?

- *How much can architects design housing with alternative materials, when construction workers are trained to use wood?*

- *Should urban planners and architects have utopian concerns as the basis of their work?*

- *Should ecological concerns be on the mind of the artist/architect?*

- *What kinds of grassroots support are needed for new ideas in architecture and urban planning to be successful? There are issues to consider not only with the types of shelter that are built today, but also with how they are arranged in an urban setting. In the nineteenth century, city planners often emphasized broad boulevards with monuments. Washington D.C. was laid out around streets that radiate from the U.S. Capitol Building, and spread out far and wide. See Figure 7.37. The major government buildings are aligned along Pennsylvania Avenue. What do you think of that plan today?*

Your Thomson Online Resources

 Go to **ArtExperience Online** for the Flashcards, Quiz, and Study Guide for this chapter.

Reproduction and Sexuality

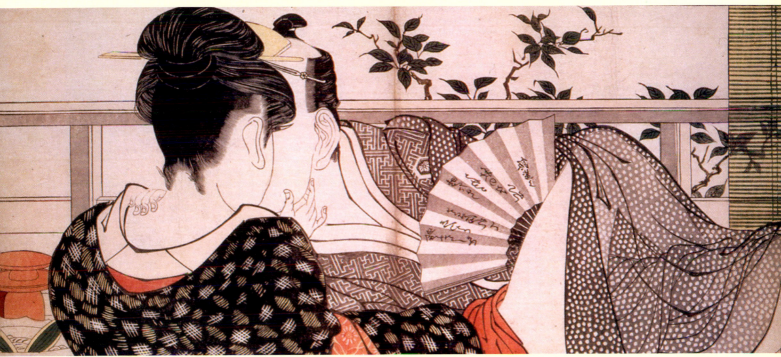

© Victoria & Albert Museum, London/Art Resource, NY.

INTRODUCTION

Through the ages, artists have created artworks that have aided, symbolized, and depicted human fertility, lovemaking, pregnancy, birth, and the newborn. In this chapter, we also will look at sexuality.

Some artworks in this chapter reinforce existing attitudes and ideas, while others use images to subvert them. In any case, the works are highly charged, powerful images that create or perpetuate ideas about reproduction, fertility, beauty, personal worth, and sexual desirability. Major topics are outlined in the following questions:

- *How are art, magic, and ritual intertwined to promote human fertility?*
- *What art was made to ensure human fertility?*
- *What primordial couples exist in various cultures?*
- *How do primordial couples relate to images of human couples in marriage?*
- *Why has art documented lovemaking for the sake of procreation?*
- *How has art depicted pregnancy and offspring?*
- *How does art show sexuality as a libidinal drive?*
- *How does art show sexuality as social choreography with predetermined roles?*

THE PROMISE
OF FERTILITY

As we have seen in the previous chapter, some art images and objects were created and used for the purpose of securing food. Cave paintings, elaborate masks, wood carvings, and ceramic sculptures helped the hunter-gatherer and farmer to ensure an abundant food supply. Likewise, art and art objects have functioned to ensure human reproduction, again with "sympathetic magic" invoked through art objects.

FERTILITY GODDESSES
AND GODS

Some of the earliest artifacts thought to relate to human fertility come from the Paleolithic and Neolithic periods of history. Some were small sculptures of female figures, depicted as abundantly fleshy and swollen, with their bellies, breasts, and thighs accentuated. They are called Fertility or Mother Goddesses, suggesting that they were part of a fertility ritual and cult.

The *Venus of Willendorf* (Fig. 8.1) is a well-rounded, abstracted female figure, only four inches high, carved from a found, egg-shaped piece of limestone. The ancient artist-carver may have believed that the power of fertility was already contained in the natural egg-shape of the stone even before it was carved. Its shape, along with the natural indentation that became the navel, may have been the reason the artist chose it. The figure was discovered near a hearth at an excavation site near the town of Willendorf, Austria, in 1908. The small, Paleolithic sculpture was considered part of the Gravettian culture dating approximately between 30,000 and 18,000 BCE. The name "Venus" was given arbitrarily to the female figurines by the archaeologists who found them.

Although sometimes labeled as a "fertility goddess," the figurine was likely more a charm or a fetish, used to invoke the magic of the art object and the stone itself. The bulbous forms were carved and painted, giving repetition and pattern to the piece, emphasizing femininity in the swelling forms. Even the head, perhaps covered with curls of hair or a headpiece of some sort, repeats the bulging, round bumps. Could this featureless head symbolize a budding bloom about to burst into flower? Clearly, the figure does not realistically represent someone, but rather represents the physical essence of fertility. She is small enough to hold in the palm of your hand, yet appears to be large, strong, and robust. With her hands resting on her breasts, she suggests stability in

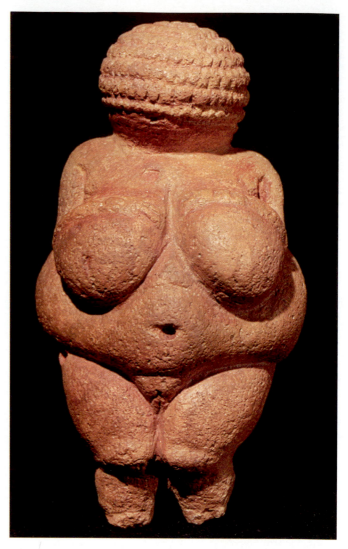

8.1 *Venus of Willendorf*, Austria, c. 25,000–20,000 BCE. Stone, 4" high. © Ali Meyer/Corbis.

addition to the power of fertility. People may have held the figurine for her power during childbirth or to ward off death or wish for good health. Whatever her function, she was likely a talisman for good fortune.

Thousands of years later, we see in the Cycladic Islands off mainland Greece a probable descendant of the mother goddesses. Figure 8.2 is called the *Idol from Amorgos,* from 2500–2300 BCE, and is thirty inches high. Other figures like this range from a few inches to life-size and were found buried with the dead. The marble was carved with obsidian blades and polished with emery. Traces of paint were found on some figures, indicating that the eyes and jewelry (necklaces and bracelets) were accentuated in color. With her oval or egg-shaped head tilted back and her toes pointed, the *Idol of Amorgos* is thought to be a reclining figure.

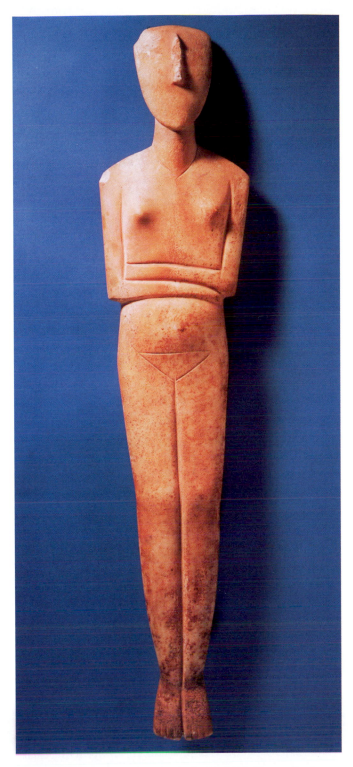

8.2 *Idol from Amorgos,* Cycladic Islands off mainland Greece, 2500–2300 BCE. Marble, 30" high. The Ashmolean Museum, Oxford.

Slender and delicate, this abstract nude seems to emphasize feminine youth, in contrast to *Venus* and the *Female Fertility Figure* on page 207. Because these figures were found in burials, their purpose may have been

to give new life to the dead, just as a young woman has the potential to give life. Sculpted very economically, the overall shapes are angular and wedge-shaped. However, the breasts, belly, and navel are subtly swelling on an otherwise stiff, plank-like body (these figures are sometimes called "plank idols"). Incised lines indicate the neck fold, arms, pubic area, legs, and toes, and connect the geometric and organic forms.

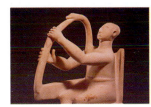

Connection The Harp Player *is a male version of the early Cycladic figures. Turn to page 441 and Figure 16.15 to read more about it.*

Much later, in the nineteenth century, male fertility pieces were produced by Oceanic cultures. Figure 8.3 shows the *God Te Rongo and His Three Sons* from

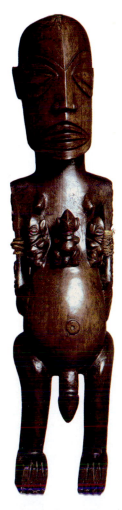

8.3 *God Te Rongo and His Three Sons,* Cook Islands, Polynesia, c. 1800–1900s. Wood, 27" high. The British Museum, London.

Rarotonga, part of the Cook Islands in Polynesia. Carved of wood, he is balancing three small, human figures on his belly. Four more figures, in the same style but in low relief, are carved on the arm and forearm. The figure is endowed with a large penis in comparison to the rest of the figure, visually giving emphasis to the virility of *Te Rongo*. The exact character of this god is not known, as the European missionaries who collected such artworks were not interested in preserving the indigenous religion.

As we take a closer look at *Te Rongo*, we can see the precise, contained style of sculpture that is typical of works carved from a single block of wood. Careful planning was required to keep the proportion of the head equal to one-fourth of the body height. In addition, incorporating the small figures must have been challenging to the artist. The chest, a bit sunken in order to make room for the smaller figures, exaggerates the belly and penis, again suggesting reproduction. The oval shape of the head and the delineation of the facial features are repeated in the smaller figures, which clearly seem like infant images of the large figure. The surface of the wood is smooth and polished, keeping focus more on the subject of the piece and less on its texture.

Male sculptures and art pieces such as *Te Rongo* were carved for religious rituals by specialists called *Ta'unga*, which is also the word for "priest." The specialist was trained through a long apprenticeship during which he acquired the skill to attain and control the *mana* (power) in the materials and tools he used. In some cultures, the art object was created for one ceremony and then discarded, whereas in others, the object was meant to endure and be passed down from one generation to the next. The more the object was used in religious ceremony, the more mana it gained. With this power, these art objects became symbols of prestige and rank, and with them, their owners displayed their place in the hierarchical order of the gods, priests, monarchs, chiefs, and people. Taboos were connected with these pieces in order to protect their status, restricting their use to those of power and rank. When passed down through many generations, the artifacts became more imbued with mana, due to their age and historical significance. They also became objects of sacred information, such as the family lineage.

Some sculptures were figures representing an ancestor. Eventually, through generations of veneration, the ancestor, who was first of a lineage, would be elevated to the realm of the gods. This may have happened with *Figure of a Deity: A'a Rurutu* (Fig. 8.4) from the Aus-

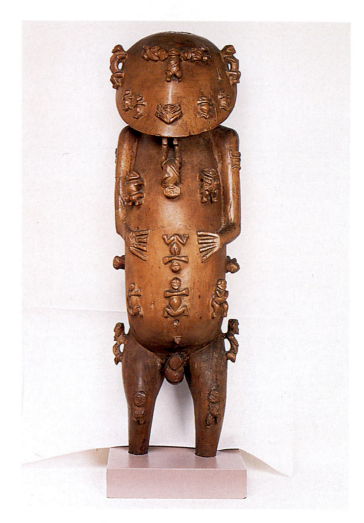

8.4   *Figure of a Deity: A'a Rurutu,* Austral Islands, collected in 1820. Wood, 44" high. The British Museum, London.

tral Islands in central Polynesia. These specific ancestor deities were known as *Tangaroa* figures and represented a creator in the act of creating human beings. Family lineage was critically important in Oceanic cultures, and thus this godlike creator may well have been connected to a family ancestor. The figure is carved from one block of wood. Like *Te Rongo*, this deity sculpture is rendered in a contained style, compact and stiff. However, his body is covered with crawling, infantlike figures. Even the facial features seem to be made up of the clinging little bodies. The back of the figure is hollowed out and contains additional small figures. We might be looking at the mythical creation of humankind in this figure, or the creation of a specific ancestral line.

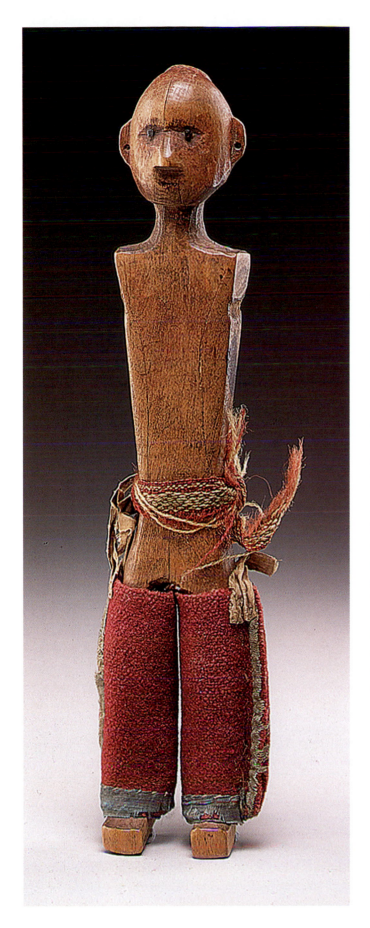

Connection *Goddesses dominated ancient rituals for thousands of years before gods came to prominence. For more on deities, read Chapter 9.*

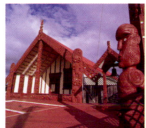

Connection *Ancestry is also important among the Maori of New Zealand, another Oceanic people. Read the discussion of the Maori meeting house associated with Figure 11.15, page 289.*

FERTILITY FIGURES

The next few examples are considered to be "fertility figures," probably created to aid human reproduction through the magic and power they contained

The Native American *Potawatomi Male Figure* (love doll) from Wisconsin, dated 1800–1860 (Fig. 8.5), is carved in wood and partly adorned in wool fabric. These figure-like carvings (note the lack of arms) were used as "medicine" to control human behaviors and health. This type of figure could be used as a love charm to cast a spell on someone whose attentions were desired. The spell could be dangerous, as those under the magic of this charm found themselves powerless and would be helpless against its strength. Ethnologist Alanson Skinner stated: "It is often that the captor tires of his or her conquest, and leaves the victim, who is still under the spell of such a charm. Such a person will become frantic, and even go crazy, following the user of the charm everywhere" (Skinner 1923:207). To have successful "medicine," the owners of the love dolls would have to be spiritually prepared and, through dreams or visions, be given special powers by the spirits.

8.5 *Potawatomi Male Figure* (love doll), Crandon, Wisconsin, 1800–1860. Wood and wool fabric, 9" high. Photo © The Detroit Institute of Arts. Cranbrook Institute of Science.

From the Bamana culture of Mali, Africa, the *Female Figure* (Fig. 8.6) is made of wood and brass. Such figures were associated with a female fertility cult and were stored in special houses created for them. On occasion, such figures were brought out for public display or for elaborate rituals to aid women having difficulties in conceiving and childbearing. This figure has sharp, angular planes and geometric forms. The head is also defined in angles, with the nose dominating the front of the face. The hair is arranged in an elegant, abstract coiffure. The shoulders and chest are fairly squared until the protrusion of the conical breasts. The elongated, erect torso has a slight swell at the navel down to where the abdomen connects to the short, bent legs. The entire figure is incised with geometric lines, some perhaps indicating body scarification. Interesting buttonlike forms vertically line her chest, ending below her breasts, again suggesting body ornamentation. Attention has been paid to the rich, shiny patina that causes finer details to show up well on the surface. The geometric forms are connected by lines, resulting in an aesthetically rich blend of the two- and three-dimensional elements in the piece.

RITUALS

Most of the fertility figures we have seen were likely used in connection with now-lost rituals. One ancient ritual has been preserved in a group of wall paintings (Fig. 8.7) from the middle of the first century, found in the Villa of Mysteries in Pompeii, Italy. Pompeii was buried in volcanic ash when Mt. Vesuvius violently erupted in 79 CE, which preserved the city and these mystical images for modern inquiry and appreciation. This cycle of paintings, which wrap around the four walls of a room, depicts a solemn ritual of the mystery cult of Dionysos that may have been associated with sexual intercourse and fertility. The exact meaning of these paintings is not known and is disputed among scholars. However, in the pictorial succession of events, we see a young female novice being prepared to join with Dionysos, the god of wine and fertility. The novice apparently is taking the role of Ariadne, his mythological mate, who is shown along with Dionysos and their accompanying entourage of mythological beings. Dionysos and the others appear to be witnessing the initiation. There is also an older woman who offers comfort to the frightened initiate, while nudes are dancing to the music played on a lute-like instrument. A priestess is ready to uncover and reveal the cult's draped sacred objects, which likely held the secrets of the mysteries of Dionysos and perhaps a concealed

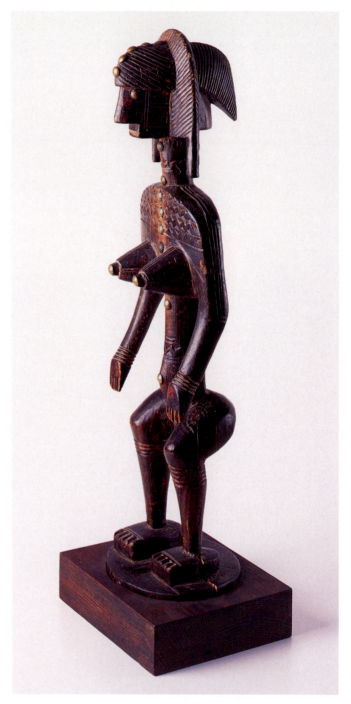

8.6 *Bamana Female Figure,* Mali, Africa, 1947. Wood and brass, 21" high. Photo courtesy Galerie Carrefore, Paris.

phallus. The event also includes a winged figure who is whipping the young initiate.

The rite takes place in an illusionist frieze, with the figures striking classic Greek poses against deep, rich, "Pompeian Red" panels. The paintings depict a shallow space, with evenly spaced columns that subdivide the running narrative into scenes. The nearly life-size figures, with convincing volume and anatomy, move

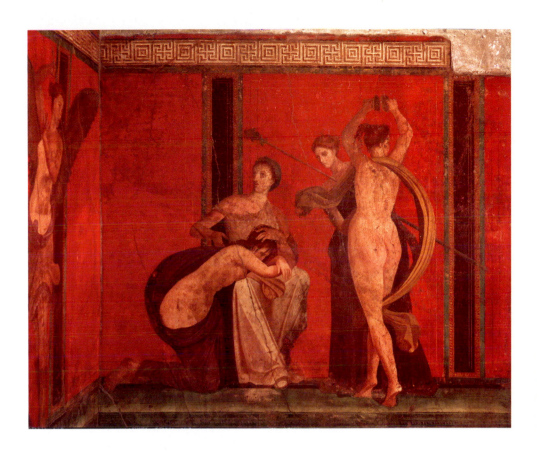

8.7 *Initiation Rites of Dionysos,* Villa of Mysteries, Pompeii, Italy, c. 50 CE. Fresco,. Detail. Frieze is approximately 5'4" high. © Scala/Art Resource, NY.

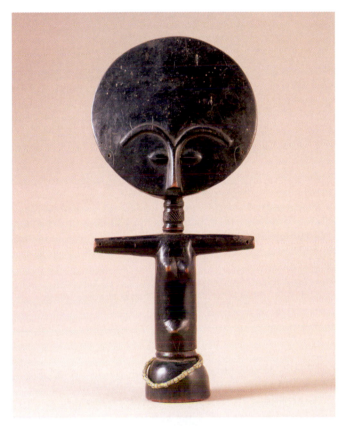

8.8 *Asante Akua'ba Doll,* Ghana, Africa, c. 20th century. Wood, 13" high. The British Museum, London.

and turn in that shallow space, which is a **trompe l'oeil** ledge. The frescoes in the Villa of Mysteries are excellent examples of Roman painting at that time. The artist paid special attention to the preparation of the walls. They were coated with several layers of plaster mixed with marble dust, beaten smooth with a trowel, and polished to a marble-like finish. The process contributed to the rich colors of the frescoes.

It is significant that this series of paintings was located in a villa, or private home, in the country. The cult of Dionysos was one of various cult religions that were practiced in Rome and were generally tolerated and even welcomed as long as they were confined to the home and did not upset the social and political order. In the case of the cult of Dionysos, the adherents were all women, who were housebound.

In contemporary Africa, there are sets of rituals and art dealing with fertility. The twentieth-century *Akua'ba* (Fig. 8.8) from the Asante (Ashanti) culture in Ghana is a fertility sculpture created solely for a ritual for women who are having difficulty in conceiving, and also to ensure a healthy and beautiful baby. *Akua* is the name of the first woman who used this ritual doll successfully and was able to conceive a baby. Consequently, *ba* (child) was added to the name *Akua;* hence, the dolls were called "Akua's child." *Akua'mma* is the plural form of the term. *Akua'mma* average about twelve to thirteen inches in height and are carved in wood.

To begin this ritual, a woman would consult a priest, who would advise her to have a doll carved. She would then adorn the doll in beads and care for it as an actual baby, carrying it wrapped on her back as mothers traditionally carry their babies. She would take care not to gaze upon any deformity in a human or *Akua'ba* doll, so her baby would not be born with these traits. Instead, she was to gaze upon the well-carved *Akua'ba* that expressed the Asante ideal of beauty. If the ritual was successful, the woman might place the doll in a shrine in order to recognize the power of the priest she confided in, or she might give it to her child for a toy.

In this figure, we see the interpretation of beauty reduced to uncomplicated forms. The *Akua'ba* head, neck, arms, and torso are rendered in a circular disk and a series of cylinders. The figures are always female. The canon of beauty is suggested as a round face with a small mouth, a high forehead, and a long neck and torso. The linear facial features are cleanly carved in the lower half of the smooth facial disk, which is supported by a stack of disklike forms that suggest necklaces. The breasts and navel are minimal forms, but clearly express the female gender.

ART DEPICTING PRIMORDIAL AND HUMAN COUPLES

Human couples have been depicted throughout the ages, some as primordial or first couple, the mother and father of humankind, and others as human couples representing the marriage ritual and its implications within cultural contexts. These depictions were rooted in creation myths of many religions. They also come from marriage rituals that frame procreation in many cultures.

Figure 8.9, from the Dogon culture of Africa, represents the *Primordial Couple* seated on an *imago mundi* (image of the world) stool. Art historians categorize its style as being part of the Sudanese Group, characterized by the use of simple tools and the lack of nonferrous metals. Like the Oceanic figures, the sculptures are usually carved from one block of wood using the subtractive method. Sometimes, naturally occurring

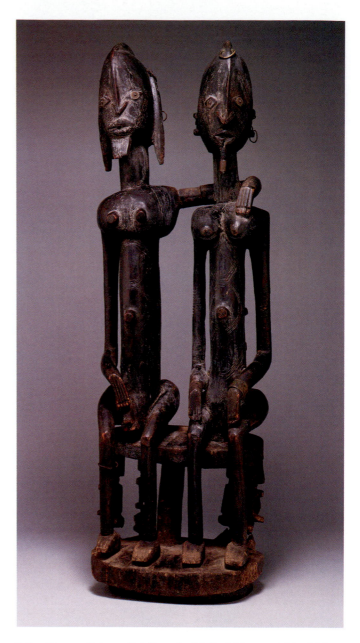

8.9 *Dogon Primordial Couple*, Mali, Africa, c. 19th–20th century. Wood, 29" high. Metropolitan Museum of Art, New York, Gift of Lester Wunderman, 1977 (1977.394.15). Photograph © 1993 The Metropolitan Museum of Art.

features in the wood block, such as a bend or a knot, are incorporated into the finished sculpture.

Seated in a frontal position, the *Primordial Couple* is stately and formal. They relate the harmony of the union of the first male and female, both of whom are equally exalted in the sculpture. The male unites the figures with his arm embracing the female at her neck and his hand resting on the upper part of her breast. His other hand is resting on his penis, symbolizing their sexual union. They wear jewelry that symbolizes

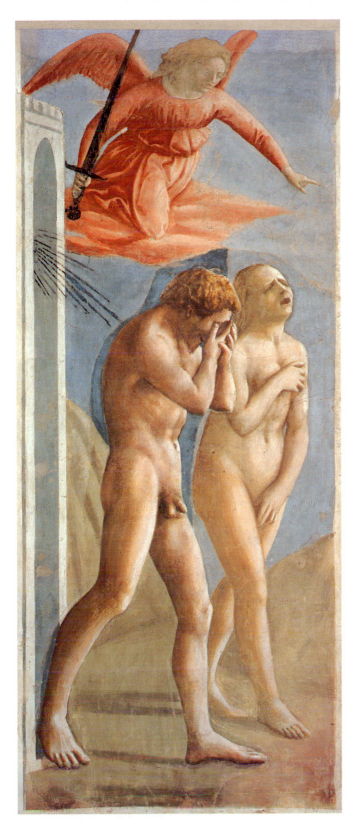

their sexual power. On their backs are carved representations of the roles they have in life. As hunter, warrior, and protector, he wears a quiver, while she has a child clinging to her. Other details in the sculpture suggest the couple's high position and perhaps their origin. She wears a mouth ornament called a "labret," and he wears a chin beard trimmed very much like the beards worn by Egyptian pharaohs.

The piece is vertically emphasized by the two elongated figures and their proportions and by the negative space we see throughout the figures. Visually there is a balance between the positive mass and the negative space in the sculpture. For the Dogon, a balanced design is a symbol for an ordered human culture (Roy 1985:31).

Another primordial couple is Adam and Eve, found in the Jewish, Christian, and Muslim religions and depicted widely in European art. In the Bible, Genesis 1:28, their creator commanded the couple to "be fruitful and multiply, fill the earth and conquer it." Later in Genesis, the Fall is described, and Adam and Eve are exiled from the Garden of Eden. It is this point in the story that a young Italian Early Renaissance artist named Masaccio painted in *The Expulsion from Paradise* (Fig. 8.10) on the wall of the Brancacci Chapel in the Church of Santa Maria del Carmine, in Florence, Italy, in 1427.

Masaccio has captured Adam and Eve's anguish in *The Expulsion*. One can almost hear Eve's cry and feel Adam's pain as they shamefully walk from the gate. Their movement is slow, every step more agonizing than the one before. Now God's commandment to "fill the earth" has become a painful burden. The artist paid particular attention to modeling the figures, using soft contrasts of values and color. Only essential details are included with Adam and Eve, specifically the gate to the Garden of Paradise and the angel with a sword barring their return.

In a Mesoamerican chronicle, the *Codex Mendoza*, we see a pictorial documentation of a wedding of a

8.10 MASACCIO. *The Expulsion from Paradise*, Italy, 1427. Fresco. 7' × 2'. Brancacci Chapel, Santa Maria del Carmine, Florence, Italy. Canali Photobank.

human couple. Figure 8.11, *Aztec Marriage Couple*, depicts a man and woman seated on a mat, literally tying the knot. Aztec marriage ceremonies took place in the groom's home in front of the hearth. The codex tells us that this man is about twenty years of age, while the woman is fourteen or fifteen. The groom's parents selected a bride, aided by a matchmaker and a soothsayer who studied the couple's birth signs in order to ensure their compatibility. The bride's family also investigated the groom to be assured of his good manners. The bride's parents gave the wedding banquet, which began at noon. The bride was covered with yellow powder and adorned in red feathers. When darkness arrived, the bride was carried on the matchmaker's back to the groom's home, where the formal vows were performed by tying together their wedding garments, as seen in the illustration. Afterward, the bride and groom prayed for four days, then were blessed by a priest and permitted to consummate their marriage (Townsend 1992:188).

The *Aztec Marriage Couple* has outlined flat shapes, filled with color. Clothing is depicted with simple flowing lines, which contrast with the angular pattern of the woven mat that surrounds the couple. The

drawing of their hair provides more pattern in the image. The Aztec religion acknowledged a primordial couple, and this human couple in our image is depicted in a similar way.

The *Wedding Portrait*, or *Giovanni Arnolfini and His Bride*, from 1434 (Fig. 8.12), by Flemish artist Jan van Eyck, shows Giovanni Arnolfini, an Italian businessman living in the Flemish city of Bruges, and his betrothed. More than just a double portrait, this is a wedding certificate, with both obvious and hidden symbolism. The couple is shown in their bedroom chamber rather than in church. They are joining in marriage in the place where it will be consummated, suggesting the hope for many children. Indeed, the woman holds her clothing in a way that indicates she may be already pregnant. Less obvious symbols also fill the bedroom. In the chandelier, there is one candle burning although it is daytime, representing divine presence. The couple has removed their shoes, showing they are on holy ground. In the frame of the mirror appear medallions that depict the passion of Christ. On the chest and windowsill are oranges, the golden apples of the Hesperides, representing the conquest of death. There is a dog at the feet of the couple, symbolizing fidelity.

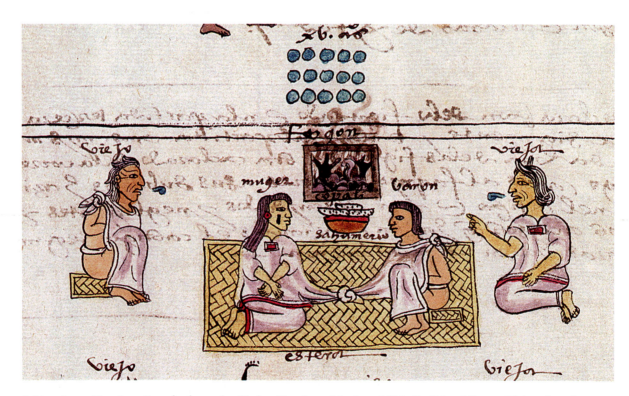

8.11 *Aztec Marriage Couple*, from the *Codex Mendoza*, Mexico, 1434. Bodleian Library, University of Oxford. Photo by Peter Furst.

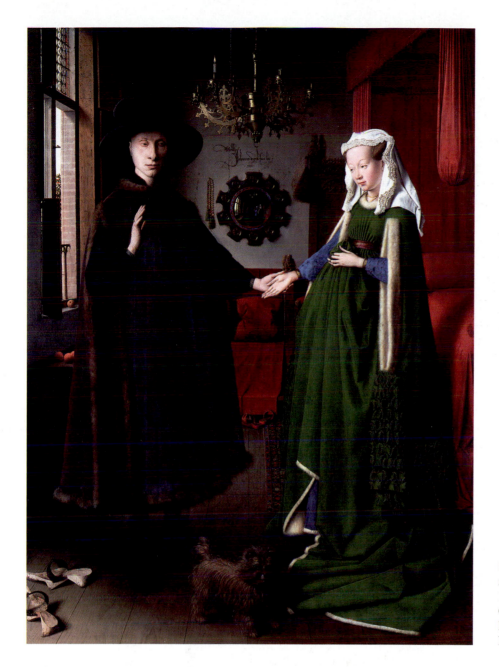

8.12 JAN VAN EYCK. *Wedding Portrait*, Flanders, Northern Europe, 1434. Oil on wood panel, 32" × 25". © National Gallery Collection; By kind permission of the Trustees of the National Gallery, London/Corbis.

Arnolfini himself raises his hand in a gesture of blessing. The prayer for fertility is also seen as the bed drapes are opened, and on the bedpost finial is a statuette of St. Margaret, the patron saint of childbirth. A whisk broom is also hanging on the post, suggesting setting up a household. To complete this document, van Eyck includes official witnesses, including himself. In this one-point perspective rendering, the vanishing point is located above the mirror where we see written in script, "Johannes de eyck fuit hic," which translates to "Jan van Eyck was here." And in the mirror, two figures appear, most likely the artist with a companion.

Van Eyck was a pioneer in oil painting, and this work is approximately contemporaneous with Masaccio's *Expulsion*.

Connections Compare Jan van Eyck's portrayal of a couple in his Wedding Portrait with that of Menkaure and His Wife, Fig. 11.1, page 276, from the Egyptian culture.

We have seen that married couples are associated with fertility. Fertility is also linked to the idea of rebirth and the afterlife, and so appears in some of the funerary art in Chapter 10.

ART ABOUT LOVE MAKING, SEXUALITY, AND GENDER

Lovemaking is essential in procreation. Sexuality is a libidinal urge that is gratifying, positive, and even energizing. But it is also surrounded with cultural strictures and power relations, as seen in culturally defined gender roles.

Our first example depicts the act of lovemaking as a matter of fact. The *Moche Pottery Depicting Sexual Intercourse* (Fig. 8.13) was probably created during the height of the culture around 1000–1250, in the desert coast of Peru. The Moche was a thriving, artistically active civilization that preceded and was brought down by the Incas. The Moche custom was to bury ceramic pots with the dead. These pots had naturalistic imagery that recorded a way of life and tribal customs, including lovemaking. The depictions of lovemaking were explicit and candid, and likely were made by the women of the culture, as they usually made the pottery. The figures are often lying on or under a blanket with a rolled pillow. Their faces exhibit no emotion. How-

ever, the variety of the sexual acts and the positions in which they are sculpted display a wide range of sexual pleasure and preference. Nothing was left to the imagination, as numerous sexual acts besides intercourse between a man and a woman appear. Such sculptures may have been designed as visual aids for sex education, illustrating not only human reproduction but perhaps birth control as well.

This buff clay and slip-decorated piece was made by pressing clay into a mold. We are looking down on the top of the pot, where we can see the stirrup handle and spout at the right, and the figures on the left. Thus, in addition to showing intercourse, the pot could certainly function very well as a vessel, probably to contain *chicha* (corn beer). The linked limbs of the figures create a circular shape that echoes the stirrup handle. The figures themselves are shown economically, with a minimum of detail.

One of the most beautiful works of art depicting lovers was done by the famous Japanese printmaker Kitagawa Utamaro, known as one of the best of the "Golden Age" wood block designers in Japan (1780–1810). Utamaro designed *A Pair of Lovers* (Fig. 8.14) as the frontispiece for *Poem of the Pillow*. The work is considered to be in the *ukiyo* or "floating world" category of subject matter, and this particular work is a *shunga* print, which provocatively depicts erotica. Chinese and Korean Buddhist missionaries brought the printmaking technique as well as the notion of the "floating world" to seventeenth-century Japan. Non-samurai classes translated the Buddhist concept of the transience of life into the notion of prizing life's fleeting moments of pleasure—in other words, eat, drink, and be merry. These images often centered on female beauty, the theater, and entertainment, and these prints were produced and collected much like movie star posters or baseball cards are today.

The shunga print (translated as "spring pictures") we are looking at now is just under ten by fifteen inches and is the cover of a book. Inside are more prints illustrating the poem, prints considered to be Utamaro's finest shunga works. Gently and intimately erotic, the print captures a private moment in the closeness of these lovers. The exquisite interplay of pattern and line of the kimonos with the figures gives emphasis to the intertwining of their bodies as they make love. Even their heads and hands are eroticized, with the closeness of their faces and the strokes of their fingertips. This is a visual poem of line, pattern, and color that compose this "floating world" image of these lovers' pleasure.

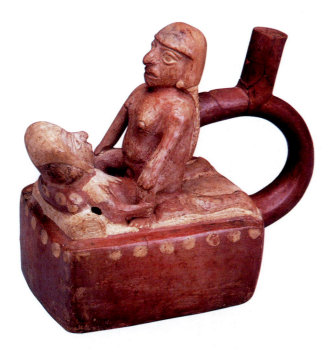

8.13 *Moche Pottery Depicting Sexual Intercourse*, Peru, c. 1000–1250. Ceramic. Museo Arqueologico Rafael Larco Herrera, Lima, Peru.

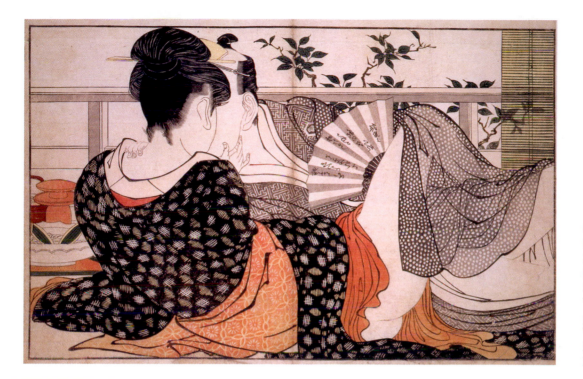

8.14 KITAGAWA UTAMARO. *A Pair of Lovers*, frontispiece from *Poem of the Pillow*, Japan, 1788. Wood block relief print, 9¾" × 14¾". Victoria and Albert Museum, London/Art Resource, NY.

Connection Komurasaki of the Tamaya Teahouse *(Fig. 14.31, page 393) is a ukiyo-e print depicting a courtesan.*

Jeff Koons, a contemporary artist in the United States, has approached acts of love through large paintings, small sculptures, and live performances, such as *Made in Heaven* (Fig. 8.15). The paintings and sculptures depict various erotic poses, while in the performances, he and his partner Cicciolina assume various sexual positions in front of viewers, which the artist frames in religious terms: "I went through moral conflict. I could not sleep for a long time in preparation of my new work. I had to go into the depths of my own sexuality, my own morality, to be able to remove fear, guilt and shame from myself. All of this has been removed for the viewer. So when the viewer sees it, they are in the realm of the Sacred Heart of Jesus" (Koons 1992:130). Our example, a billboard that publicized the performances, is heavily influenced by movie publicity posters and the covers of romance novels. In this work, Koons has blurred many boundaries, such as

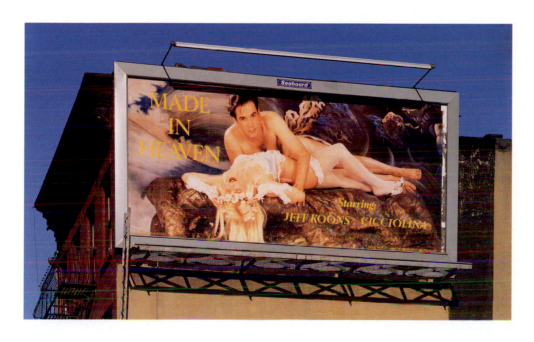

8.15 JEFF KOONS and partner Cicciolina. *Made in Heaven*, USA, c. 1995. Lithographic Billboard, 125" × 272". © Jeff Koons.

the division between fine art and popular culture, representation in art and performance that may seem like "real life," and, some would argue, good and bad taste.

Obviously, Koons's sculptures, paintings, and performances are controversial. Whether they are works of art or pornography can be argued. Likewise, categorizing the Moche pots or the Japanese shunga prints may be equally difficult, as they are erotic works that were created to stimulate and give pleasure to the viewer.

Images of ideal erotic sexuality were relatively common in India, both as sculptures from Hindu tem-

ples and in a number of miniature paintings from northern India from the seventeenth and eighteenth centuries. *Krishna and Radha in a Pavilion*, dated c. 1760 (Fig. 8.16), shows Radha, a shepherdess, and Krishna, one of the incarnations of the god Vishnu, in a scene of tender lovemaking. They sit beneath a golden pavilion, surrounded by rich weavings, delicate flowers, and ripe fruit, as the lightning of their passion flashes across the sky. Krishna is conventionally depicted as blue. Both Krishna and Radha are graceful, serene figures, bedecked in jewels, outlined with flowing lines,

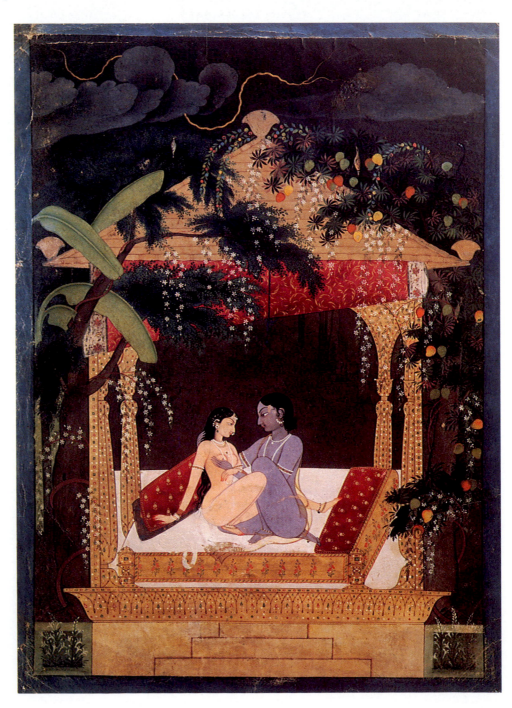

8.16 *Krishna and Radha in a Pavilion*, India, from Punjab, c. 1760. Opaque watercolor on paper, 11" × 7¼". National Museum, New Delhi.

and filled out with delicate details. They are placed in the center, and their forms are emphasized by the white bedding and dark background. The gold pavilion and red cloth frame them. Ornate patterns and textures add to the visual delight of the painting.

Krishna is a deity, and the scene is highly idealized and represents an uneven power relationship between the two characters. But the pleasure, affection, sweetness, and erotic energy Krishna shares with Radha were meant to be like the physical and spiritual union that all humans could experience through lovemaking. That union in lovemaking, by extension, was also like union with God. Such images as *Krishna and Radha in a Pavilion* were meant to be instructive, and the mythical sexual act was intended to be reincarnated regularly among living couples.

Men and women engaged in sexual union and masturbation appear in relief carvings on the *Kandarya Mahadeva* temple at Khajuraho, India (Fig. 8.17). Many of the carvings on the structure are openly erotic, with nude, sleek, full-bodied figures dancing, twisting, or writhing. Our example shows a scene with intertwined voluptuous bodies. The Hindu religion openly celebrates sexual love, as erotic coupling and self-pleasuring reflect the divine union with the Unbounded. To experience this carnal bliss is a virtue and a path that leads to redemption.

Connection *This sculpture is part of the extensive carvings on the exterior of the Kandarya Mahadeva temple, Figure 9.35 on page 232.*

THE FEMININE BODY AND THE GAZE

How does sexuality work in an image when only a single figure is depicted? The meaning of such images depends upon the subject of the picture, for whom it is made, and why.

The *Grande Odalisque* (Fig. 8.18) was painted by Jean-Auguste-Dominique Ingres in 1814. It is a long, horizontal painting of a nude woman seen from behind. She is an odalisque, a member of a Turkish harem. Blue, gold, and cream tones predominate in the painting. The curve of the upper body echoes the curve of the hanging blue drapery. Accents occur at the woman's face and at her hand, holding the peacock-feather fan. Her back is extremely long, creating a sensual flow that complements the curves of her legs, arms, breast, and buttocks. Outline is emphasized, and the soft, flawless skin is delicately shaded. The smooth flesh contrasts with the patterned and textured cloth, feathers, and beads that surround and adorn the woman. Her pose is sensually relaxed.

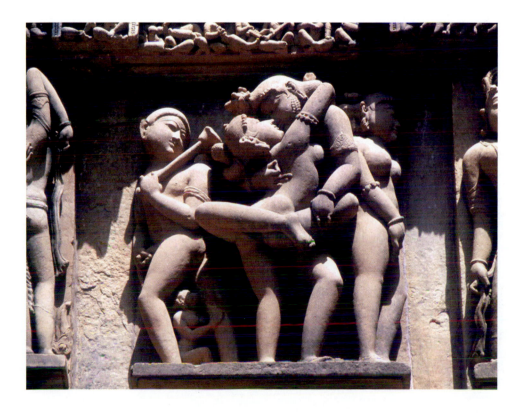

8.17 *Relief Carving from the Kandarya Mahadeva Temple,* Khajuraho, India, c. 1000. © 2003 Charles Walker/ TopFoto/Image Works.

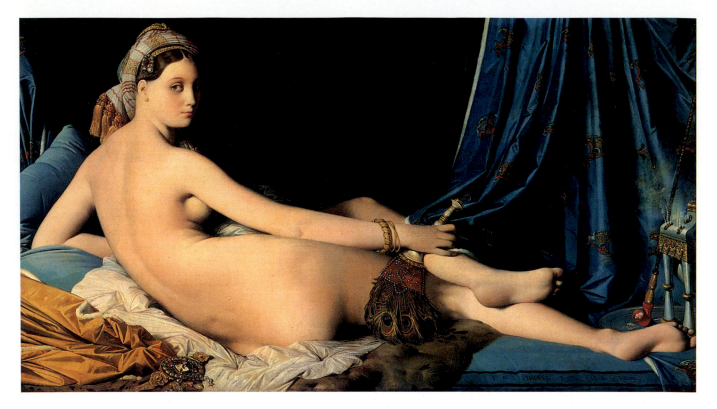

8.18 Jean-Auguste-Dominique Ingres. *Grande Odalisque*, France, 1814. Oil on canvas, 35" × 64". Louvre, Paris. © Scala/ Art Resource, NY.

Nineteenth-century female nudes in Europe and the United States were made for nineteenth-century men. They were the privileged audience for such pictures, as viewers whose gaze completed the sexual exchange implied in the painting. As critic Linda Nochlin wrote:

> As far as one knows, there simply exists no art, and certainly no high art, in the nineteenth century based on women's erotic need, wishes or fantasies. Whether the erotic object be breast or buttocks, shoes or corsets . . . , the imagery of sexual delight or provocation has always been created about women for men's enjoyment, by men. . . . Controlling both sex and art, and fantasies conditioned the world of erotic imagination. (Nochlin 1988:138–39)

The fact that only the female is present in a sexual scene is significant. Without a lover in the scene, the odalisque is sexually available for the viewer—presumably the European male—who gazes upon her and "consumes" without being seen or consumed himself. The viewer took the place of the imagined Turkish sultan, with many women at his disposal.

Edward Manet's *Olympia*, from 1863 (Fig. 8.19) is superficially similar to the *Grande Odalisque*. But

Olympia scandalized the public, in part because its sexuality and nudity were not of a distant place and time. The woman, Victorine Meurant, also known as Olympia, was a famous Paris courtesan. This image is similar to a well-known Italian Renaissance painting of a heavenly goddess, the *Venus of Urbino* by Titian (see Figure 3.20). In nineteenth-century Europe, the concepts of prostitute, courtesan, and goddess were conflated. Mythological paintings of goddesses were an acceptably distant way to present the nude woman for the pleasure of the male viewer. Nineteenth-century wealthy men euphemized their "companions" as embodiments of beauty, like goddesses. Manet's painting shattered those illusions. Olympia's unromantic expression made clear that sex and money would be exchanged in her associations with wealthy men. Her gaze identifies and implicates a viewer, whereas in the *Grande Odalisque* the nature of the viewer is less explicit. The wealthy were horrified that their sexual dalliances could be seen in that light. Manet's painting also reveals the social status accorded different races, with the African woman in the role of maid, the white woman as mistress.

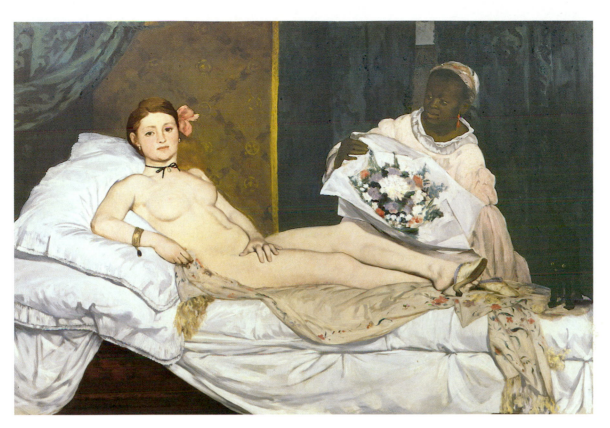

8.19   EDWARD MANET. *Olympia*, France, 1863. Oil on canvas, 51¼" × 74¾". Photo: Musées Nationaux. Musée d'Orsay, Paris. © Scala/Art Resource, NY.

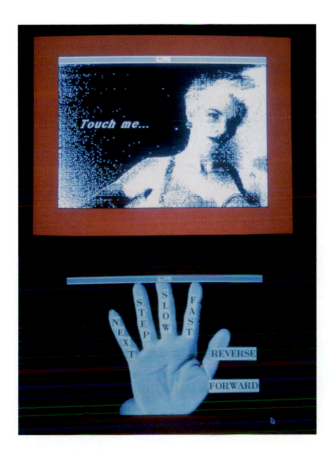

Although Manet's painting was attacked for its content, his defenders praised the work for its innovative paint quality. Manet painted thickly, directly on the white surface of the canvas ground, in a style called "alla prima" painting. His colors were flatter and brighter than the subdued tones of traditional academic painting. The body of Olympia is brightly lit. Light areas are separate from the dark, as distinct from most oil paintings since the Renaissance where midtones predominate. Manet's personal style of brushwork led to many of the painterly concerns of twentieth-century artists, such as gestural mark making, flatness versus illusion of depth, and experiments in applying paint.

In the computer-video installation *Deep Contact*, from 1990 (Fig. 8.20), the artist Lynn Hershman looks at the ways sexuality is delivered in our culture. At the beginning of the piece, the "guide" or hostess, Marion, dressed in sexually seductive clothing, knocks at the

8.20   LYNN HERSHMAN. *Deep Contact*, USA, 1990. Interactive computer-video installation at the Museum of Modern Art, San Francisco. Courtesy of the Artist.

windowlike surface of the touch screen and asks the viewer to touch her to begin the performance of the artwork. By touching different parts, the viewer can create interactive fictions, enter a paradise garden with various characters, or see video clips on reproductive technologies and women's bodies. Although the entire content of *Deep Contact* is not sexual, everything in the piece has been eroticized, including ideas about technology, self-awareness, and intimacy. The viewer of *Deep Contact* cannot be passive; if you do nothing, nothing happens. Thus, the viewer is dislodged from the position of anonymous, distant voyeur, and, at times, a nearby surveillance camera flashes the viewer's face on the screen in the midst of a performance.

Untitled (Your body is a battleground), dated 1989 (Fig. 8.21), summarizes both the shifting attitudes and the heated conflicts that surround women, sexuality, and reproduction. The artist, Barbara Kruger, took a political slogan from the 1960s and combined it with a photograph of a woman's face, split down the middle, positive image on one side and negative on the other. The woman looks like a model from a perfume or makeup ad in a fashion magazine. In fact, this image originally was part of a poster promoting an abortion rights rally. We viewers become part of the piece, as the staring woman makes us either identify with her or see her as opposite to ourselves. This poster alludes to other "battleground" body issues, such as race (black/white) or sexuality (homo/hetero).

To whom does "your" refer in Kruger's work—we the viewers or the staring woman? Kruger uses pronouns that are gender neutral, with no fixed subject, to imply that attitudes about sexuality (as well as race) are not fixed by nature. Kruger sees these categories as changing entities under social, political, and religious influence. Yet Kruger recognizes how harshly divided the rhetoric can be in these areas. The division down the middle, with black and white sides, indicates how polarized societies can be on these issues.

Connection Kruger's background is both in fine arts and in the mass media. For a period in the 1980s, she was chief designer for the popular fashion magazine Mademoiselle. Her artwork resembles the pasting of text over images, a design technique commonly found in magazines today. For more on the increasingly blurred relationships between fine art and the mass media, see the section Categories of Visual Arts in Chapter 1.

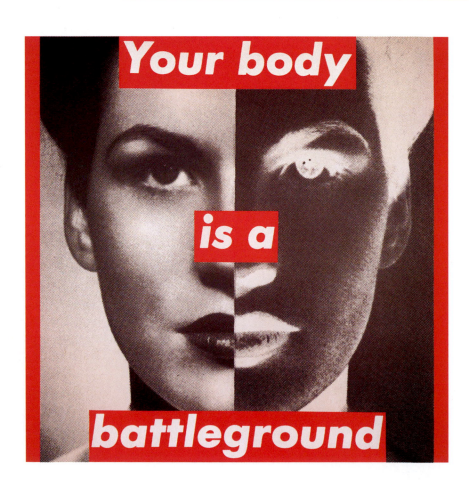

8.21 BARBARA KRUGER. *Untitled (Your body is a battleground)*, USA, 1989. Photographic silk screen on vinyl, 112" × 112". Eli Broad Family Foundation Collection, Los Angeles. Courtesy: Mary Boone Gallery, New York. Photo © Zindman/Fremont.

Catherine Opie's *Justin Bond*, 1993 (Fig. 8.22), is a photograph of a cross-dressing male whose attire and hair suggest both "good girl" and sexual potential. Opie's many photographs of homosexuals, transsexuals, and dominatrixes make apparent the complexities of gender roles and sexuality. She is interested in using photographs to catalog and archive the wide range of people and places around her. In addition, the existence of such photographs complicates the idea of the privileged male viewer. *Justin Bond* meets the viewer's gaze with directness and confidence, challenging any attempt by the viewer to see his behavior as pathological. The image is distinct because of the rich colors, near-symmetry, and mixed messages.

ABSTRACTED SEXUAL IMAGERY

Sexual imagery in art can be abstracted. Its forms may allude more or less to the human body, but humans themselves need not be represented.

Georgia O'Keeffe's *Grey Line with Lavender and Yellow,* dated 1923 (Fig. 8.23), is an enlarged flower image. The simple, near-symmetrical composition is suffused with subtle color gradations interrupted by occasional lines. O'Keeffe, throughout much of her life, painted natural objects that verged on abstraction, with simplified forms and heightened color that increased a sense of beauty and desirability. She used these forms to express emotions rather than copying nature slavishly. Many critics, artists, and viewers have associated her flower imagery with the female body, especially

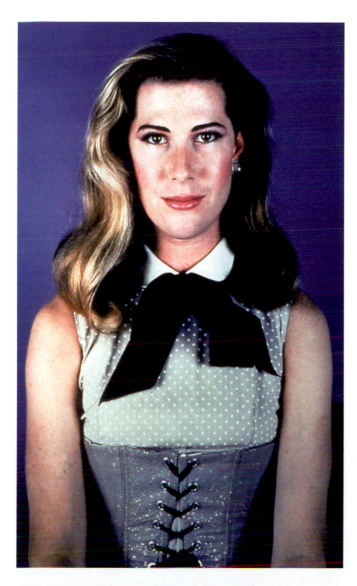

8.22 CATHERINE OPIE. *Justin Bond*, USA, 1993. Chromogenic print, edition of eight, 20" × 16". Courtesy of Gorney Bravin & Lee, New York, and Regen Projects, Los Angeles.

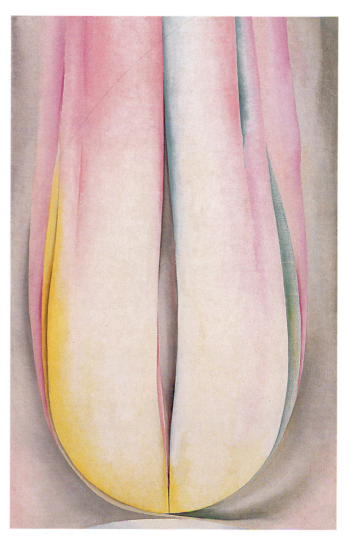

8.23 GEORGIA O'KEEFFE. *Grey Line with Lavender and Yellow,* USA, 1923. Oil on canvas, 48" × 30". The Metropolitan Museum of Art © 2004 The Georgia O'Keeffe Foundation/Artists Rights Society (ARS), New York.

female genitalia, as the structures of both can often be similar. Feminists have seen in her work a positive, female-based imagery that glorifies and beautifies female sexuality.

Connection *Throughout her life, Georgia O'Keeffe denied any feminist content in her artwork. How important is the artist's intention versus the critical response to the work? For more on this discussion, see the Food for Thought section of Chapter 4, pages 97–98.*

Figure 8.24, *Torso of a Young Man* (1924) by the twentieth-century Romanian sculptor Constantin Brancusi, abstracts male sexuality. Influenced by the philosophy of the eleventh-century monk Milarepa, Brancusi sought to understand the universality of all life. With this inspiration, along with the Romanian folk art of his youth and the influence of African tribal art that so strongly affected many European artists, he created works intended to capture the essence and universality of pure form, working in related themes such as creation, birth, life, and death. He would finish his pieces by hand to a precious perfection, leaving no visual signs of his handicraft, whether using marble, wood, or bronze. Some of his pieces look as if they have been machine tooled. As he developed an idea, his forms became more and more simplified. He is quoted as saying, "Simplicity is not an end in art, but one arrives at simplicity in spite of oneself, in approaching the real sense of things" (Janson 1995:817). *Torso of a Young Man* is eighteen inches tall, with three cylindrical forms of highly polished bronze placed on a base composed of several geometric forms. One sculpture seems to be resting on another, contrasting the cylindrical "torso" with rectangular volumes. The simplified torso becomes an obvious phallic symbol.

Louise Bourgeois's abstracted imagery is much more explicitly sexual than O'Keeffe's or Brancusi's. In *Blind Man's Bluff,* from 1984 (Fig. 8.25), the "body" is sexual, as the sculpture is like a large phallus covered with round, organic forms. The gender dualism of male as a discrete category versus the female is blurred. In its

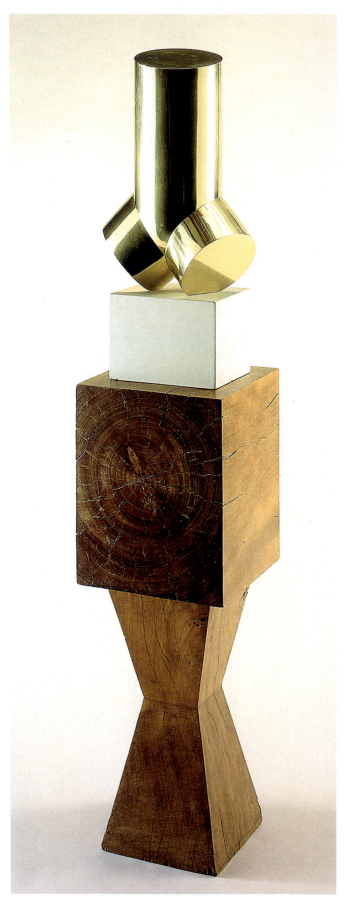

8.24   CONSTANTIN BRANCUSI. *Torso of a Young Man,* Romania, 1924. Polished brass, 18" high. Hirshhorn Museum, Smithsonian Institution, Washington, D.C. © Artists Rights Society (ARS), New York/ADAGP, Paris.

IMAGES OF PREGNANCY, CHILDBIRTH, AND PROGENY

Images of childbirth are seen in many cultures and have existed for ages. An interesting ceramic figurine depicting pregnancy is found in the Guatemalan Maya culture dated between 250 BCE and 100 CE (Fig. 8.26). She is known as a *Kidder Figure* and is about ten inches high. The seated female has a babylike body with a swollen belly suggesting she is pregnant. She emphasizes her enlarged abdomen by gently resting her hands on it. The expression on her face seems to be one of contentment and joyous anticipation of the expected event. The Mayans developed the figurines and identified them with fertility cults. They linked general procreation with female maternity and fertility, and related it to the earth. The small, infantile figures represent the bearers of human offspring as well as the mother of nature and the progenitor of plant life.

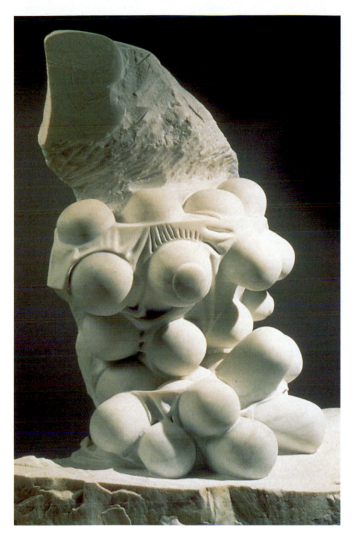

8.25   LOUISE BOURGEOIS. *Blind Man's Bluff*, USA, 1984. Marble, 36" × 35.5" × 25". Collection Cleveland Museum of Art. Courtesy Cheim & Read, New York. Photo by Allan Finkelman. Art © Louise Bourgeois/Licensed by VAGA, New York, NY.

appearance and name, *Blind Man's Bluff* invites touch. The marble at the center is polished to a silky finish, while the top and bottom are left roughly cut. The piece is fetishlike, suggesting a fixation on sexual body parts without necessarily any attachment to an individual as a whole. The plethora of organs has the quality of pleasure overload. Bourgeois's bulbous forms are ambiguous, as they are both breastlike and penislike, or they may represent the sensitive nerves in the tongue or in genital organs. With Bourgeois's work, multiple interpretations of the forms are often possible and always subjective. Bourgeois's work stands in contrast to the duality common in heterosexual imagery.

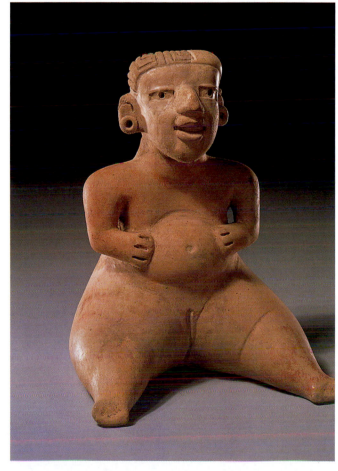

8.26   *Kidder Figure,* Maya, Guatemala, 250 BCE–100 CE. Ceramic vessel, 10" × 7¹/₂" × 6³/₄". © Justin Kerr.

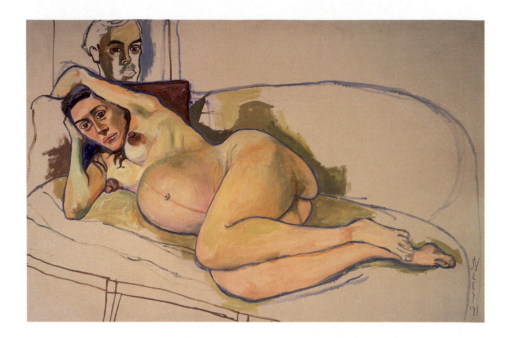

8.27 ALICE NEEL. *Pregnant Woman*, USA, 1971. Oil on canvas, 40" × 60". Courtesy of the Robert Miller Gallery, New York. © The Estate of Alice Neel.

In contrast, Alice Neel's 1971 painting *Pregnant Woman* (Fig. 8.27) shows us the physical effects of pregnancy on one woman's body and self. Her swollen belly and enlarged nipples contrast with her bony arm and ribs showing through the skin. Her pink, blood-flushed belly contrasts with the rest of her yellow flesh. Her facial expression seems wooden, passive, dazed, or fearful. The man's portrait behind her suggests that men can be both intimate and distant during pregnancy. His picture may also suggest possession or protection. Neel mostly painted portraits, often nude, creating a sense of drama with her unrelentingly direct images. She captured subtleties of expression, as well as subtle color shifts, like the difference between yellow and pink flesh.

We return to the Peruvian Moche culture for our next example, in which ceramic artists depict childbirth in as straightforward a manner as they depicted sexual intercourse. Figure 8.28, *Moche Pot Depicting a Woman Giving Birth Assisted by Midwives,* is another stirrup handle vessel with small figures connecting the handle with the body of the pot. The figures clearly illustrate the act of childbirth. The mother giving birth shows a bit of a grimace, while the faces of the midwives seem expressionless. The scene seems to be clinically illustrating an event rather than capturing the moment of physical and emotional anticipation or even pain. It records the Moche birthing position and technique and may have taught expectant mothers and students of midwifery. Again, as in our other Moche example, the figures sit on top of the pot, near the stirrup handle. The handle seems to function as the back support to the midwife who holds the laboring woman. The bod-

ies of those two women suggest a curving shape that turns down and concludes at the head of the midwife catching the emerging infant. Compositionally, the figures and the handle are well integrated.

Mother and child imagery is widespread across many cultures. We will look at two examples, but there are many more examples from which to choose. The first piece is a ceramic human effigy vessel featuring a *Mother and Nursing Child* (Fig. 8.29) from the Mississippian

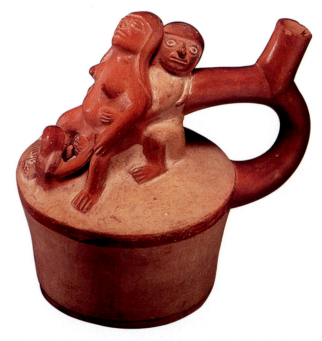

8.28 *Moche Pot Depicting a Woman Giving Birth Assisted by Midwives,* Peru, c. 1000–1250. Ceramic. Museo Arqueologico Rafael Larco Herrera, Lima, Peru.

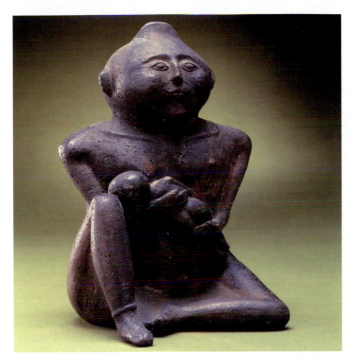

8.29 *Mother and Nursing Child*, Cahokia, IL, 1200–1400. Ceramic effigy vessel, Mississippian Period. St. Louis Science Center./Photo © 1985 Dirk Bakker, Detroit Institute of Arts.

period (1200–1400), in an agricultural civilization located near the confluence of the Mississippi and Illinois rivers around Cahokia, Illinois. The Mississippians built large, truncated pyramid mounds topped with temples. Their religion strove to predict and control nature, with much attention paid to death. The *Mother and Nursing Child* was buried in a tomb that likely belonged to a high-ranking person. Tombs contained a quantity of elaborate naturalistic and fanciful funeral pottery, mostly effigies that captured the spirit of the dead they honored. The *Mother and Nursing Child* expresses a graceful and serene image of a woman and her baby. A simple rendering, there is emphasis in the detail of the mother's face and in the nursing babe. Triangular shapes appear in the rest of the pose, as the mother's broad shoulders suggest an inverted triangle, and her folded legs suggest two other triangles. The simple, geometric form adds to the stability and calm of the figure. Representing a mother and her progeny in life, the effigy vessel may have insured her potential to bear children in the afterlife.

The mother and child is a familiar Christian icon, personified as Mary and Jesus. We will look at an example by the northern Renaissance Flemish painter Rogier van der Weyden. A student of Jan van Eyck (see Fig. 8.13), Rogier became the influential master painter of Brussels in 1436, and his work was often copied in the fifteenth century. Although he signed none of his work, his style is distinctive, with linear forms and brilliant

color. *Virgin and Child in a Niche* was painted in 1432–1433 and is only 7¼ inches by 4¾ inches (Fig. 8.30). Despite her size, Mary appears majestic in a delicately carved architectural space, crowned as the Queen of Heaven. Yet she nurses the newborn redeemer, holding him tenderly. Rogier's subject matter was Christian, with many paintings of the Virgin Mary. The Christian primordial couple, Adam and Eve (see Fig. 8.11), appear here as carvings on the niche. Adam, who has covered himself in shame, is about to be pushed off his pedestal by a hovering angel, expelling him from paradise. Eve holds the apple under the Tree of Knowledge, while the serpent looks down from the branches. In the center above, God the Father and a dove observe the scene, completing the Trinity. The gentle and loving gaze of Mary upon her baby is calm, yet ominous in its understanding of the fulfillment of Old Testament prophecies.

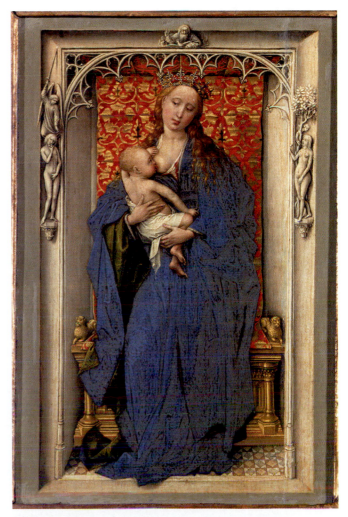

8.30 ROGIER VAN DER WEYDEN. *Virgin and Child in a Niche*. Flanders, Northern Europe, c. 1432–1433. Oil on panel, 7¼" × 4¾". Kunsthistorisches Museum, Vienna. © Erich Lessing/Art Resource, NY.

Fertility was an important concern during the New Stone Age (or Neolithic Era), which ended around 4000 BCE. Groups of people around the world began to depend increasingly on agriculture for their food in addition to hunting. They began making stone tools and continued domesticating animals. The city of Çatal Hüyük (8000–4000 BCE), located in present-day Turkey, was an early farming and trading settlement with several thousand people. They were among the first to produce pottery and make metal and obsidian objects. They connected their houses for greater protection and built many shrines. The *Female Fertility Figure* (see History Box illustration), found in a Çatal Hüyük grain bin, shows a powerful, enthroned woman with attending lions.

Throughout this period through about 2000 BCE, we see the emergence of civilizations around the world. The following factors influenced the growth of civilizations:

- Major rivers or bodies of water were necessary for civilizations to develop.

- Farming produced surplus food, which allowed for the development of cities and the division of labor within urban areas.

- Cities became political, economic, social, cultural, and religious centers.

- Trade became important among groups of people and between urban centers.

- Formal religions developed, often with many gods and with rulers as stewards of those gods.

- Political and social structures emerged, with hierarchical governments and sometimes bureaucracies. Society was organized around class systems, with priests, warriors, and the wealthy at the top.

- Writing developed in some areas.

- The military or warrior class emerged.

- Independent city-states were gradually merged into larger empires.

- Patriarchy became dominant in social organization.

Map 2 The Development of Agriculture. Courtesy of Replogle Globes, Inc., Broadview, IL.

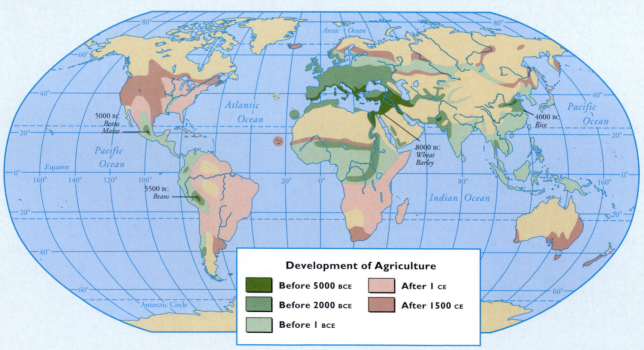

Development of Agriculture

Before 5000 BCE
Before 2000 BCE
Before 1 BCE
After 1 CE
After 1500 CE

In Mesopotamia, around 3000 BCE, a number of city-states arose along the Tigris and Euphrates rivers. They included Eridu, Ur, Uruk, Umma, and Lagash, and were located in an area called Sumer. Surrounded by walls, these cities had political and economic control over the surrounding states. Here, people first scratched cuneiform symbols and other forms of writing into wet clay tablets. Here also is the first evidence of use of the wheel. Around 2300 BCE, the ruler Sargon united several of these city-states into the Akkadian Empire.

Many agricultural communities developed along the Nile River in Egypt. Travel along the Nile was swift and relatively easy, and the upper and lower areas of Egypt were united around 3100 BCE. A series of Egyptian dynasties ruled the area for hundreds of years, and the surrounding desert kept the land relatively free from foreign invasion. The Egyptians developed hieroglyphic writing. The Old Kingdom lasted from 2686 BCE to 2125 BCE, while the Middle Kingdom (2100–1700 BCE) saw increased contact with the outside world, especially in Africa and the Middle East.

South of Egypt, around 3500 BCE, the Nubian civilization emerged. At first, Nubia was a trading partner with Egypt, but later came under Egyptian control.

Small centers of civilization emerged throughout the Americas. In 3000 BCE, skilled artisans around Lake Superior worked copper into jewelry and tools. Along the Supe River in Peru, the city of Caral flourished around 2600 BCE.

People began growing rice, bananas, sesame, wheat, barley, black pepper, and cotton along the Indus River Valley (present-day Pakistan) around 6000 BCE. In 2500 BCE, the great city of Mohenjo-Daro was established, with a population of 40,000. Many craft workers, sculptors, and potters lived in the city, which maintained a thriving trade in handcrafted and agricultural products.

In China along the Huang He (Yellow River) Valley, farmers used levees to con-

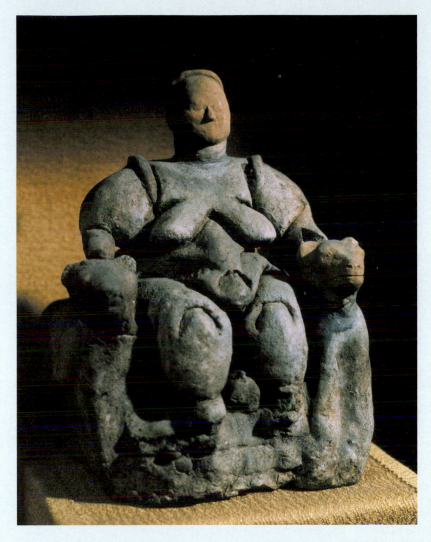

8.31   *Female Fertility Figure*, found at Çatal Hüyük, c. 6000 BCE. Terracotta, 7.9" high. Anatolia (modern Turkey).

trol floods as early as 3000 BCE. Some researchers believe that as early as 2100 BCE, the Xia Dynasty brought centralized rule to a large region of China. Other researchers, however, dispute the existence of this dynasty.

The earliest traces of the Greek civilization emerged on islands in the Aegean Sea around 2500 BCE. Once again, fertility was a concern, as seen in the *Idol from Amorgos* (Fig. 8.2), from the Cycladic culture.

Era/Event	Date	Artwork
Paleolithic Era	**25,000 BCE**	Venus of Willendorf
Mesolithic Era	**10,000**	
Settlements in China and Chile	**8000**	
Çatal Hüyük		
Neolithic Era	**7000**	
Settlements in India	**6000**	Female Fertility Figure at Çatal Hüyük
	4000	
Birth of Mesopotamia		
Unification of Egypt	**3100**	
Old Kingdom	**2500**	Idol from Amorgos
Civilizations in Crete		
Irrigated farming in Andes	**2000**	
Shang Dynasty—China	**1600**	
	1000	
	200	Kidder Figure
	100	
Roman Empire		
	50 CE	Initiation Rites of Dionysos, Villa of Mysteries
Romanesque Era	**1000**	Mother and Nursing Child
Cahokia Civilization		Relief Carving from the Kandarya Mahadeva Temple
Moche and Chavin cultures		Moche Pottery Depicting Sexual Intercourse / Moche Pottery Depicting a Woman Giving Birth Assisted by Midwives
Gothic Era, Europe / Aztec Empire	**1400**	van der Weyden: Virgin and Child in a Niche

Era/Event	Date	Artwork
Ming Dynasty—China		van Eyck: Wedding Portrait
Mughal Dynasty—India		Masaccio: Expulsion from Paradise / Aztec Marriage Couple
Benin Kingdom—Africa	**1700**	Utamaro: A Pair of Lovers
Captain Cook's voyages in Oceania		Krishna and Radha in a Pavilion
U.S. Revolutionary War		
French Revolution		
	1800	God Te Rongo and His Three Sons
		Figure of a Deity: A'a Rurutu
		Potawatomi Male Figure (Love Doll)
		Ingres: Grande Odalisque
		Manet: Olympia
Russian Revolution	**1900**	
		Dogon Primordial Couple
World War I	**1915**	Asante Akua'ba doll
		O'Keeffe: Grey Line with Lavender and Yellow
		Brancusi: Torso of a Young Man
	1925	
World War II	**1939**	Bamana Female Figure, Mali
	1970	Neel: Pregnant Woman
Desert Storm	**1990**	Bourgeois: Blind Man's Bluff
		Kruger: Untitled (Your body is a battleground)
		Hershman: Deep Contact
		Opie: Justin Bond
	1995	Koons: Made in Heaven
	2000	

Art has been used to ensure, teach, and document human fertility, reproduction, sexuality, and sexual issues. Early, small, figurative sculptures of fertility "gods" and "goddesses" from the Stone Age and early Greek cultures were likely used to aid human fertility. Similar figures were found more recently in the Americas, Africa, and Oceania. Murals from Pompeii depicted possible fertility rituals.

Sculptures and paintings have witnessed, documented, and commemorated the coupling and marrying of human beings. Images depicting lovemaking and sexuality are numerous. Some push the limits of cultural taboos. Hinduism teaches that sexuality and sexual acts reflect the relationship between humans and the divine. Gender relationships within cultures can be seen in artworks depicting the female body. Some were meant for male consumption. Other artworks complicate the usual formula of the male gaze upon the female body. High-technology, mass media, and personal choices are often presented in sexual wrappings. Sexual imagery can be realistic or abstracted.

Examples of pregnancy, childbirth, and offspring images from different cultures were examined.

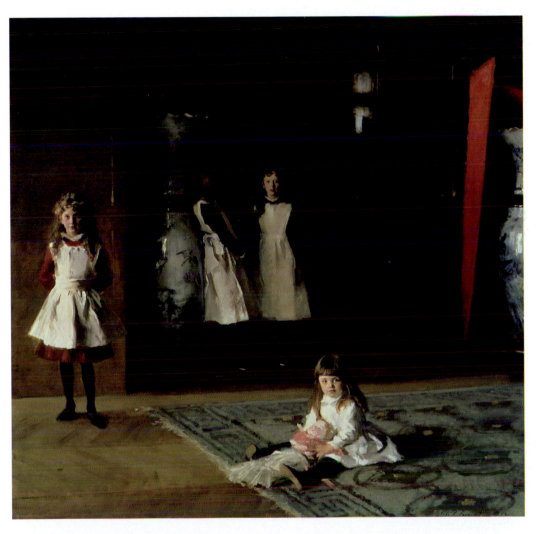

8.32   JOHN SINGER SARGENT. *The Daughters of Edward Darley Boit*, 1882. Oil on Canvas, 87" × 87". Museum of Fine Arts, Boston. From left to right, Mary, Florence, Jane, and Julia.

FOOD FOR THOUGHT

Much of the art in this chapter comes from cultures in which human reproduction was actively promoted or even ritually aided. Having children was seen as an absolute good. Early pregnancy was common, and large families were a blessing and a source of pride. See Figure 8.32.

However, in the last several decades, that attitude has changed. Abortion and birth control put more choices along the way to becoming parents. Sexuality has been emphasized more for personal pleasure rather than procreation; however, the threat of sexually transmitted diseases complicates this new attitude. Teenage pregnancy or marriage is not viewed positively in the United States today. As the human population tops six billion, many believe that there are too many people for the planet to sustain. Indeed, the world's most populous country, China, has already legislated population control measures.

- *How do you see these various attitudes reflected around you in the art made today?*
- *What attitudes do you see in images from popular culture—in movies, comics, fashions, dolls, advertisements, magazines, calendar art, billboards, and so on?*
- *How do we determine when a sexual image is being used for oppressive ends?*

Your Thomson Online Resources

 Go to **ArtExperience Online** for the Flashcards, Quiz, and Study Guide for this chapter.

Religion

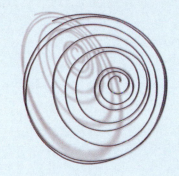

The supernatural realm lies beyond our senses, yet in almost every age and culture, people have attempted to create diagrams, symbols, and pictures that express to some extent their understanding of divinity.

How can humans make pictures of God? How can we account for the earth, ourselves, the stars, the entire cosmos? What kinds of places of worship have humans built, where they can feel a divine presence? What kinds of art have been made in reaction to—or in preparation for—death?

In the next two chapters, we will look at art from world cultures for perspectives on the following topics:

- Understanding the supernatural and communicating with divinity through art
- Using architecture and art to structure spaces that seem divine
- Building large-scale sacred architecture, and its relationship to secular power
- Employing art for creating houses and memorials for the dead
- Incorporating nature into religious and mortuary shrines, through art

CHAPTER 9 | DEITIES AND PLACES OF WORSHIP

CHAPTER 10 | MORTALITY AND IMMORTALITY

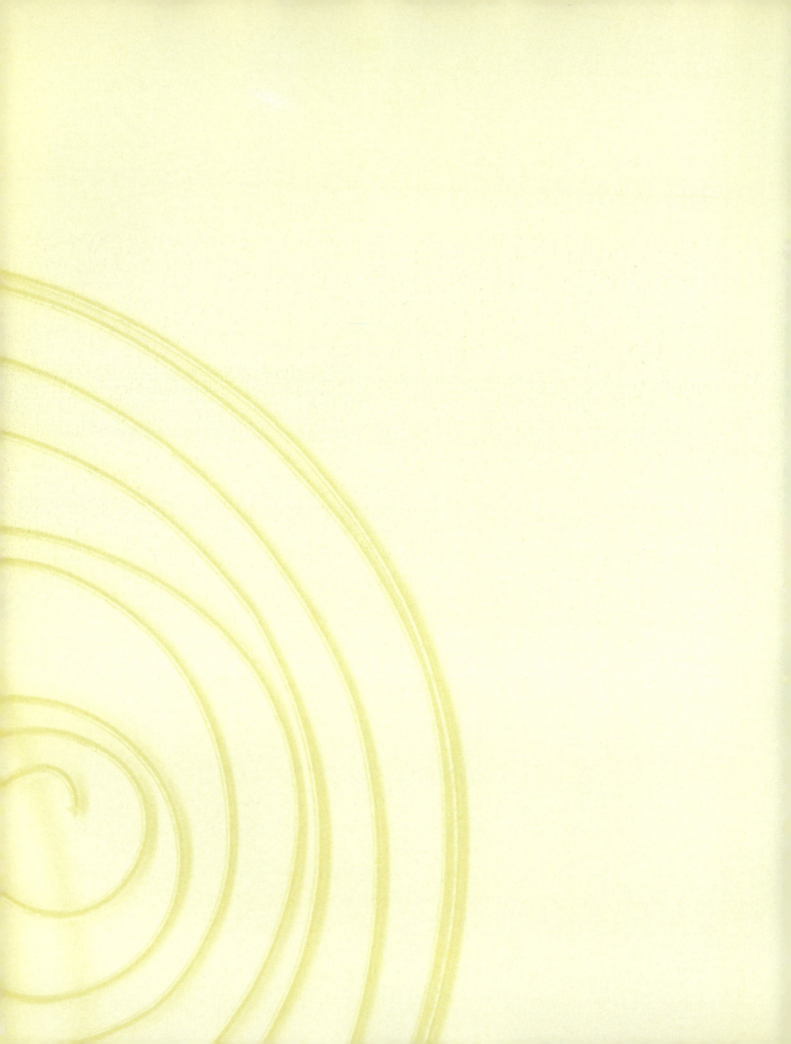

Deities and Places of Worship

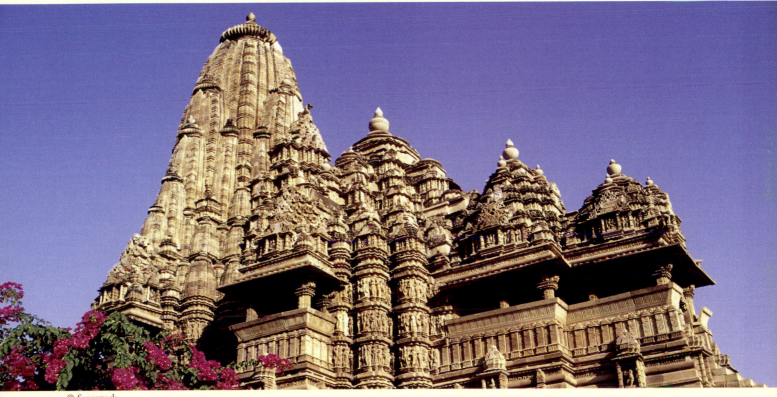

© Superstock

INTRODUCTION

Humans strive constantly to grasp the divine realm, to communicate with it, or to be joined with it. Rituals, oral tradition, sacred writings, meditation, prayer, and music are but a few paths used by humans to connect to the Transcendent. Art is another.

- *What can art tell us about deities of very ancient religions?*
- *How can a spiritual being be shown or symbolized in an artwork?*
- *How can art become a form of prayer? How can it be used to express a prayer?*
- *How do artists depict the cosmos?*
- *What are some visual characteristics of places of worship and sacred structures?*
- *How does the use and design of a sacred space reflect the religious experience there?*
- *How do people use art forms other than architecture in sacred spaces?*
- *How can large-scale sacred architecture also be an expression of political power?*

IMAGES OF SPIRITUAL BEINGS

Artists make images or sculptures of gods and goddesses and other holy beings to aid people in some religions' rituals. The faithful may believe that the deity is actually present in the artwork or is just represented by it.

Simple geometric shapes often symbolize God. The sphere and dome are significant in Islamic architecture, as they stand for the heavens and the oneness of God. In the Hindu religion, the circle can symbolize the unknowable Supreme Being. The triangle stands for the Christian Trinity. Words can also be symbols of God, such as in Islamic calligraphy. In many religions, light is a symbol for God.

Animal features or natural phenomena can represent, act as metaphors for, or symbolize deities. For example, the sun can be a symbol for God and, at other times, can actually be worshipped as a deity itself. In Christian art, Jesus is symbolized by a sacrificial lamb, and the Holy Spirit by a dove or by fire. Other religions are animistic, with natural elements or animals as deities or inhabited by spirits. The earth is often understood to be a female force because of its ability to generate life. Other religions depict God with human attributes, which may include gender.

In many religions, God is not pictured. Most African religions and the Hindu religion recognize a completely unknowable Supreme Being. In the Islamic religion, Allah is very rarely depicted.

Let us now look at a few ways that deities are depicted in artwork.

EARLY DEITIES

The Earth Mother is the original deity in almost all areas of the globe—the giver of life and fertility and the carrier of death. In ancient myths of nomadic cultures, the Goddess existed first. Later, she created her male counterpart, with whom she mated to produce the rest of Creation. As agriculture increasingly replaced hunting and gathering as the primary source of food, the importance of paternity increased, along with land ownership, animal breeding, cities, and hierarchical classes. Powerful goddesses continued to be worshipped in many religions, but alongside important male gods.

The *Snake Goddess,* c. 1600 BCE (Fig. 9.1), probably evolved from the Earth Mother in the Minoan civilization on Crete from 2000 to 1200 BCE. The open bodice and prominent breasts tie this figure to early fertility goddesses. Her intense expression and upraised

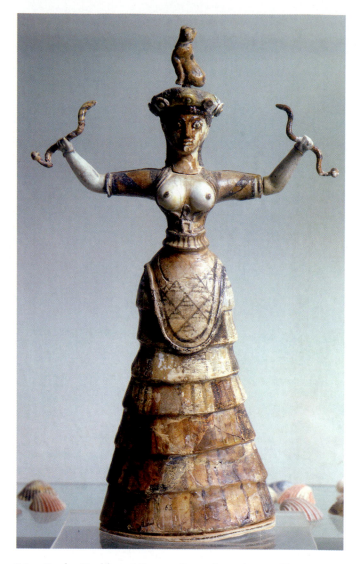

9.1 *Snake Goddess,* Minoan, from the palace at Knossos, c. 1600 BCE. Glazed earthenware, 13½" high. Archeological Museum, Heraklion. © Nimatallah/Art Resource, NY.

arms energize this piece. She holds snakes, which may have represented male sexuality. Female fertility and regenerative powers may also have been connected to the snake's periodic shedding of its skin. The leopard-like animal on her head may have symbolized royalty. Her tiered dress and hairstyle likely represent Minoan fashion.

Connection *For more on early goddesses, see the sections Fertility Goddesses and Gods, and Fertility Figures in Chapter 8.*

The deities of ancient Egyptian religion were mostly personifications of natural forces, such as the daily rising of the sun, the ripening of crops, and the annual flooding of the Nile River. These divine beings required worship and sacrifice from humans, who appealed to them for special needs. Most were represented as animals or as animal-human combinations.

The goddess Hathor, associated with the sky, stars, love, mirth, joy, and beauty, was depicted as a cow or as a combination of a woman and a cow. In *The Goddess Hathor and the Overseer of Sealers, Psamtik,* sixth century BCE (Fig. 9.2), she encompasses and hovers protectively over Psamtik, an Egyptian official. Her horns surround the head of a cobra, signifying royalty, and the sun disk with a crown of feathers, signifying divinity. The side view of this piece shows the entire length of the cow striding forward, with bone and muscle beautifully sculpted. In the front view of her face, we see more stylized features, such as the repeated ridges above the eyes and the radiating pattern in the ears. Psamtik has a standardized face and body that show conventional divisions of breast, rib, and belly, while the arms and hands are presented frontally and symmetrically. His official duties are inscribed on his skirt. The work was likely commissioned by Psamtik as an offering to Hathor.

Connection *In Chapter 10, a hawk representing Horus, the Sky God, is on the coffin case of the Pharaoh Tutankhamen (Fig. 10.3, page 246).*

THE GREEK GODS

The ancient Greeks believed that the beginning of all life on earth was Gaia, the Earth Goddess. Her descendants, the Greek gods on Mount Olympus, had distinct personalities, and formed alliances and enmities among themselves and with humans. They were responsible for many aspects of the natural world and human life, such as love, warfare, and the seasons. The Greek gods appear in human form, as the Greeks considered themselves superior to other religions that worshipped animals or mountains. The earliest images were stiff and frontal, without fluid movement, similar to Egyptian sculpture. Later Classic depictions had convincing anatomy and movement, but were entirely idealized and flawless, conforming to Greek standards of beauty. Our example, *Zeus,* or possibly *Poseidon,* 460–450 BCE (Fig. 9.3), is from the Classic period. Zeus, chief among the Greek gods, is usually shown as a mature

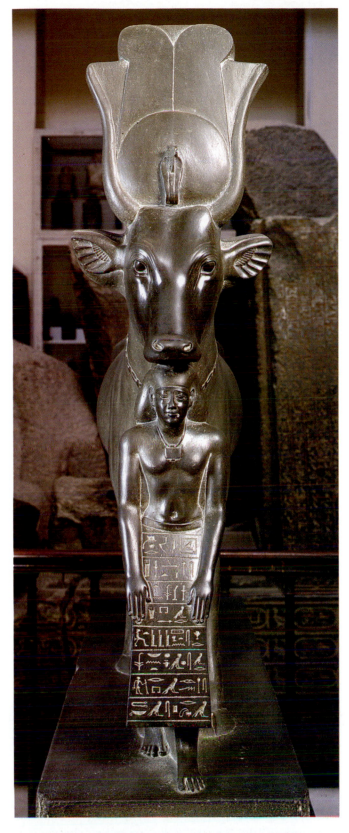

9.2 *The Goddess Hathor and the Overseer of Sealers, Psamtik,* Saqqara, Egypt, Late 26th Dynasty, 6th century BCE. Gray stone; base: 11½" × 43¼"; height of cow to horns, 33". Cairo Museum, Egypt. © Sandro Vannini.

HINDUISM

In the Hindu religion, there are apparently numerous gods, but this is not polytheism because they are all manifestations, or "avatars," of the Unbounded, or Brahman. The Unbounded is one, pure being, pure intelligence, and pure delight, and is therefore unknowable. Although never pictured, Brahman can be partially known through the human senses because all natural things, humans, and spiritual beings reflect Brahman.

The God Shiva, one of the primary avatars, is the source of good and evil, male and female. He is the unity in which all opposites meet. He is the destroyer of life, but also re-creates it. Since the tenth century, *Shiva* has been often depicted in Hindu art as *Nataraja, or Lord of the Dance,* seen here in a sculpture from c. 1000 (Fig. 9.4). Shiva's body is shown as supple, sleek, and graceful. Cobra heads form the ends of his hair, and he stands in perfect balance. As the Lord of the unending dance, he is the embodiment of cosmic

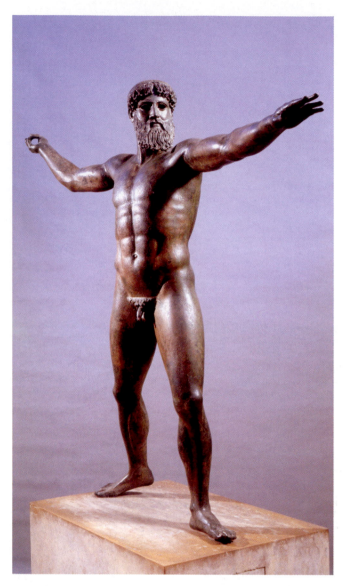

9.3 *Zeus,* or *Poseidon,* Greece, 460–450 BCE. Bronze, 6'10" high. National Archeological Museum, Athens. © Nimatallah/Art Resource, NY.

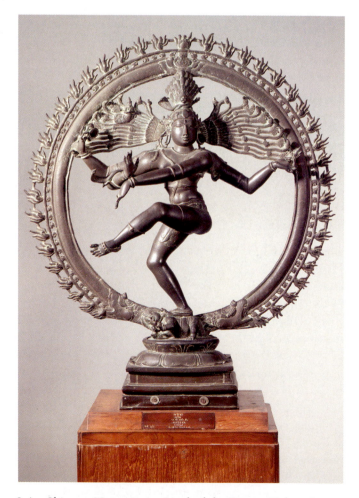

9.4 *Shiva as Nataraja, or Lord of the Dance,* Naltunai Isvaram Temple, Punjai, India, c. 1000. Bronze. © Angelo Hornak/Corbis.

bearded male with an ideal, godlike physique. His right hand probably once held a thunderbolt, an attribute of Zeus, the god of sky and storms. However, he may have held a trident, which is an attribute of Poseidon, the god of the sea. The over-life-size figure appears monumental, muscular, and ideally proportioned. It conveys a sense of action and energy and, at the same time, poise and dignity. Fully extended, the figure's mighty body is balanced between the backward movement of his arm and its anticipated forward movement as he hurls a thunderbolt or trident.

energy, yet the balanced pose also contains the concept of eternal stillness. The multiple arms tell of his power, and his divine wisdom is shown by the third eye in the middle of his forehead. His far right hand holds a small, hourglass-shaped drum, the beating of which stands for creation and the passing of time. The second right arm is ringed by a coiled snake that symbolizes regeneration, while the hand itself forms a *mudra,* a symbolic gesture that is a sign of protection. The far left hand balances a flame that symbolizes destruction, while the other left hand points to his feet. The left foot is elevated in the dance, indicating release from this earth, and the right foot crushes the personification of ignorance. The circle of fire that radiates around *Shiva* shows the unfolding and transformation of the universe, and its destruction.

BUDDHISM

The Buddhist religion follows the teachings of Siddhartha Gautama, a prince born in India near Nepal around 563 BCE. He fled from court life to become a homeless holy man and later achieved enlightenment, or Buddhahood. The Buddha, also known as Sakyamuni (meaning "the sage of the Sakya clan"), contin-

ued to teach for the next forty-five years until his death. Buddhists, like Hindus, hold that humans are perpetually reincarnated, most often into lives of suffering, based on the deeds of their past lives. By following the teachings of Sakyamuni, humans can overcome desires and the cycle of rebirth. Then they can attain nirvana, a transformation of their consciousness from the material world to the eternal realm.

For several hundred years after his death, Sakyamuni was represented by a set of symbols, but never as a human because he had achieved enlightenment (nirvana). In the Hinayana form of Buddhism, one symbol for Sakyamuni was the *stupa* which was a mound tomb. It eventually was transformed into a monument that contained the ashes or relics of a Buddha. An example of an early Buddhist stupa is the *Great Stupa* at Sanchi, third century BCE to first century CE (Fig. 9.5), a solid, dome-shaped mound of earth enclosed in brick and stone. The form of the mound represented the cosmos as the world mountain, the dwelling place of the ancient gods and a sacred womb of the universe. The structure is encircled with a low balustrade wall containing four heraldic gates, all highly adorned with rich carvings. The

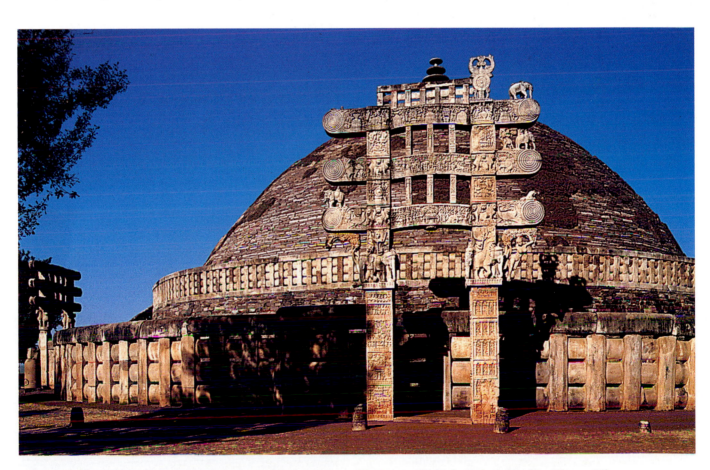

9.5 *Great Stupa,* Sanchi, India, 3rd century BCE–1st century CE. Dome: 50' high. Robert Harding Picture Library.

gates, called *toranas,* are located at the four cardinal points in the circular wall. The balustrades are also densely carved. Pilgrims would come to walk around the stupa clockwise and chant, meditate, and pray as they observed the special meanings of the carvings. The square enclosure on top of the dome symbolized the heavens, surmounted by the mast with umbrellas, called *chatras,* that united the world with the paradises above. The chatras signified the levels of human consciousness through which the human soul ascends to enlightenment.

The eastern torana in front of the *Great Stupa* rises thirty-four feet. The gate contains many scenes showing episodes from the life of Sakyamuni, with Sakyamuni represented only by symbols, such as the empty throne, which represents Buddha's separation from his princely life; footprints, which represent the Buddha's spiritual journey; and the elephant, a bodily form assumed by the Buddha. Additionally, there are sensuous images of the nature deities retained from the early Vedic sculptural tradition. Small stupas carved on the gateway reliefs and resembling the *Great Stupa* symbolize Sakyamuni in his attainment of Buddhahood. The stupa as a symbol of Buddhahood spread throughout Asia, although there were local variations in its design.

Connection *One of the carvings from the Great Stupa at Sanchi is the* Yakshi *(Fig. 13.13, page 345).*

As the later Mahayana sects emphasized a more personal god-like Buddha, images of him in human form were produced, along with the traditional symbols. At first, these figurative sculptures were variations of older Hindu spirits, with certain Buddha-identifying attributes, such as the topknot of hair (a cranial bump indicating

wisdom) and a circle between the eyebrows. Earlobes were long, because Sakyamuni was once a bejeweled prince.

In still later images, the emphasis was on the general serenity of Buddhahood. The red sandstone of the *Seated Buddha,* late fifth to early sixth centuries (Fig. 9.6), has been carved and polished to a smooth, flawless finish. The statue seems to represent a generalized rather than a specific person. The body seems almost weightless. The face is rendered as a perfect oval, and the torso and limbs are simplified into graceful lines and elegant shapes. Clothing is sheer and clinging, unworldly in its draping and perfection. The tall arches of the brow, downcast eyes, and quiet but sensual mouth all speak of a transcendent serenity. The Buddha is seated in lotus position on a throne, under which are carved worshippers around the Wheel of the Law. Abstracted foliage above and around Sakyamuni repre-

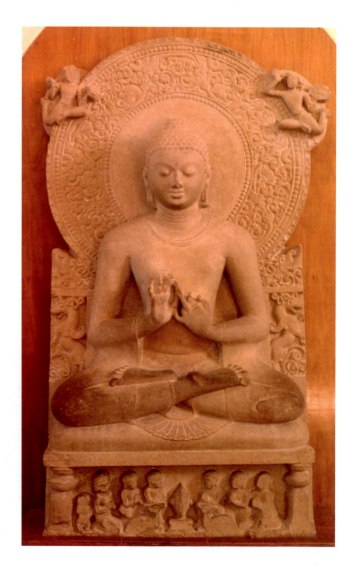

9.6 *Seated Buddha,* from Sarnath, Uttar Pradesh, India, late 5th–early 6th centuries. Sandstone, 63" high. Sarnath Museum. © Borromea/Art Resource, NY.

sents the Tree of Enlightenment. His hands are posed in a preaching gesture.

Over the centuries, Buddhist beliefs became more complex. Bodhisattvas are living beings who have attained Buddhahood but have chosen to remain on earth to help others. While Buddhas in their serenity in nirvana may seem remote to struggling humans, the Bodhisattvas are immediate personal intercessors who give aid. *The Water and Moon Guanyin Bodhisattva*, c. 1100 (Fig. 9.7), is the most powerful Bodhisattva, with a great capacity for salvation. Depictions of *Guanyin* vary radically, with two to twelve arms, often crowned, sometimes with a muscular male body and sometimes with an effeminate body. In our example, the body is graceful and the face beautiful and serene. The elegance of the body and right hand, along with the lavish carving and rich colors, make this sculpture sensually appealing. The diagonals of the figure's right leg and arm balance the verticals of the torso and the left limbs, while the flowing curves of the drapery unite all.

JUDAISM

Judaism is one of the oldest religions of the Western world and is the foundation of Christianity and Islam. The Jews consider themselves the Chosen People and have a special covenant with their God and Creator,

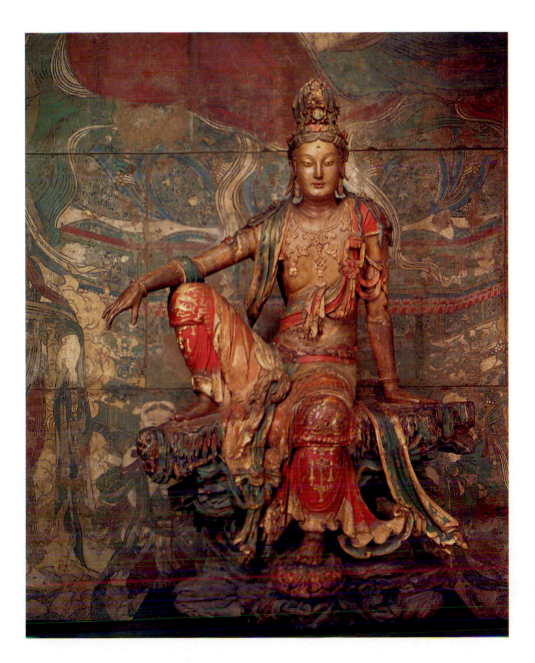

9.7 *The Water and Moon Guanyin Bodhisattva,* China, Song Dynasty, c. 1100. Painted wood, 7'11" high. The Nelson-Atkins Museum of Art, Kansas City. Purchase: Nelson Trust.

Yahweh, who alone is to be worshipped and none other. It was thought by scholars that the making of art images in the Jewish faith was forbidden because of the Second Commandment. However, images have been found in scripture illumination and on the walls of ancient synagogues. In Figure 9.8, we see the interior of the *Synagogue at Dura-Europos* dated 245–256 CE, which is covered with paintings depicting Old Testament themes. Dura-Europos was an outpost in Syria and was probably founded around 323 BCE.

The *Synagogue at Dura-Europos*, originally a private home with a courtyard, was transformed into a place of worship in the second century CE. The paintings on the walls were didactic, illustrating stories found in the Hebrew Bible. The figures have stylized gestures, lack expression, mass, and depth, and mostly stand in frontal rows, as a means to explain a concept or illustrate a story. Yahweh was shown as a hand emerging from the top of the panels, which was an accepted form of iconography.

CHRISTIANITY

Unlike Judaism, the Christian tradition has many kinds of images of God. Some Christians understand God as a single being, while others conceive of God as a Trinity, with three persons in one—the Father, Son, and Holy Spirit. The Father is usually depicted as an aged patriarch, wise, powerful, and judging. The Son was incarnated as Jesus and founded the Christian religion. He is believed by Christians to be the Savior of souls. Images of Jesus range from a babe in arms to a young man in life, death, and resurrection. The Holy Spirit is represented as a symbol, either a dove or a flame of fire.

As an actual historical figure, Jesus is the most commonly depicted of the Trinity. In early images, he was a youthful protecting shepherd, a comforting figure to early Christians, who were often persecuted by Romans. Once Christianity became the official state religion of the Roman Empire in the fourth century, Jesus was depicted as a royal ruler. Images of Jesus as miracle worker, judge, and teacher usually combine a narration of historical events with layers of symbolism.

In the **Renaissance** painting, the *Madonna of the Meadow* (Fig. 9.9) by Raphael Sanzio, c. 1505, Jesus is the robust, beautiful child in the center, with his cousin, St. John the Baptist, at the left, and mother Mary, who towers over both children. Although the children look youthful and sweet, their solemn composure and the

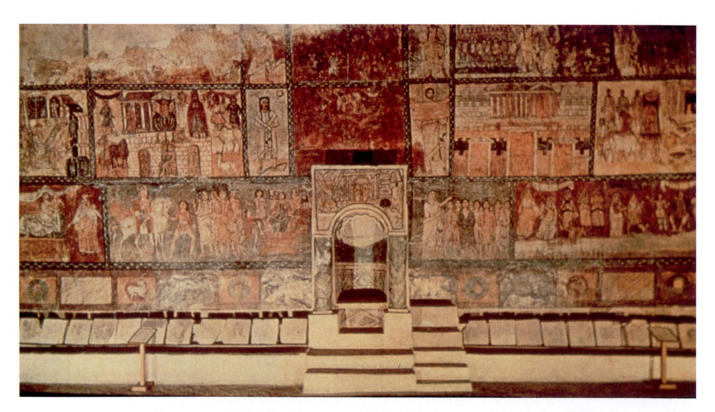

9.8 *Synagogue at Dura-Europos*, interior, with wall paintings of biblical themes, Syria, 245–256 CE. National Museum, Damascus. © Jewish Museum, NY/Art Resource, NY.

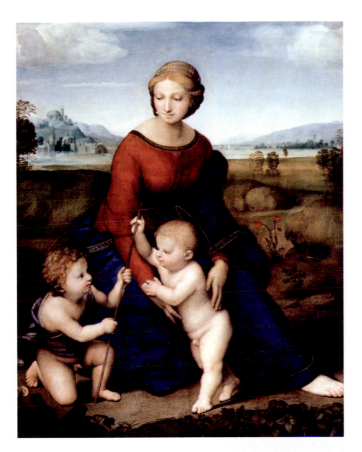

cross they hold portends their roles of savior and prophet. All figures are totally human, but their dignity and serenity seem divine. The blues, reds, and greens add to the sense of harmony. Mary and the two children fit into an implied triangle, a stable, symmetrical, sacred shape recalling the Trinity. Mary's silhouette completely contains the form of Jesus, attesting that she is Jesus' mother and establishing her as a symbol for the Christian church. The large, sheltered body of water in the background implies a harbor, and Mary was known as the Port of Salvation.

In contrast, another Renaissance painting, the *Crucifixion* from *The Isenheim Altarpiece,* c. 1510–1515 (Fig. 9.10) by Matthias Grünewald, shows Jesus at death, which for Christians is a moment both of annihilation

9.9 RAPHAEL. *Madonna of the Meadow,* Italy, c. 1505. Panel painting, 44½" × 34¼". Kunsthistorisches Museum, Vienna. © Francis G. Mayer/Corbis.

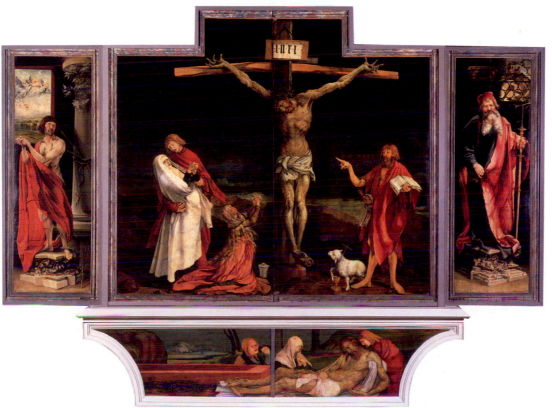

9.10 MATTHIAS GRÜNEWALD. *The Isenheim Altarpiece,* Germany, c. 1510–1515. Oil on wood; center panel: *Crucifixion,* 9'9½" × 10'9", Musée d'Unterlinden, Colmar, France.

and of redemption from sin. The dark, gloomy background obliterates all landscape detail. The grisly details of Jesus' sore-ridden and scraped skin, convulsed body, and drooping head are meant to be a realistic picture of a terrible death. At the same time, the *Isenheim Altarpiece* is a conceptual rather than a realistic representation. The bottom panel, which shows Jesus' body being placed in the tomb, would sit directly above the altar, where the body of Jesus is offered at Christian Eucharistic rituals in the form of bread and wine. The lamb in the *Crucifixion* panel, holding a cross and bleeding into a chalice, symbolizes animal sacrifices conducted by Jews in the past and the current offering of bread and wine. People who were present at the Crucifixion, such as Roman soldiers, are omitted from this painting, while St. John the Baptist is shown, although he had already died. Saints on side panels were associated with cures for the sick. This painting was a form of consolation for hospitalized patients, for they could see the horrendous suffering of Christ and relate it to their own. Also, the dark *Crucifixion* panel opens in the center, revealing three joyful scenes from the life of Jesus—his conception, birth, and resurrection from the dead, all in brilliant colors.

Connection *For an example of a very early image of Jesus, see the* Catacomb of Sts. Peter and Marcellinus *(Fig. 10.15, page 257). Turn to* The Last Judgment *(Fig. 13.17, page 349) to see an image of Jesus as judge.*

GODS FOR SPECIAL PURPOSES

Many religions are polytheistic; that is, they recognize and worship a number of gods, who are responsible for various aspects of earthly life. Mesoamerican cultures often linked the gods associated with corn and water, because water was so essential and corn symbolically stood for all food.

Having a special role as the protector of young corn plants, the maize goddess was called *Xilonen* (Fig. 9.11). In our image of her, dating from 1000–1200, the head is rounded, very humanlike, and grandly adorned. She wears a headdress with ornamental bands and ears of corn, a collar with sun rays, heavy ear pendants, and a jade necklace that symbolizes crop fertility.

Tlaloc was the rain deity who made crops flourish. The most worthy of the human dead were received into Tlaloc's heaven. Images and temples dedicated to Tlaloc were common. We will see a Tlalocan Painting from a temple in Figure 9.34. Tlaloc was traditionally shown

9.11   *Xilonen, Goddess of Young Corn,* Huastec, Tuxpan (Veracruz), Mexico, 1000–1200. Limestone, 33" high. © Gianni Dagli Orti/Corbis.

with distinctive features: circular eyes, twisted serpent nose, fanged mouth, headdress, and large ear ornaments with pendants.

HUMANS RESPOND TO GOD

Humans use religious ceremonies, prayers, and rituals to acknowledge God and to request what they need for earthly or spiritual existence. Many religions require humans to make offerings to the gods, as outward signs of their devotion. Art frequently is part of this process.

CEREMONIES

The Kwakiutl of the Pacific Northwest dwelled in two sites corresponding with summer food gathering and elaborate winter rituals, such as marriages, initiations, feasts, potlatches, and dramatic performances. Special houses were built for the Winter Ceremonies. Performers in full masquerade told their stories and became the supernatural beings of their masks.

Our example is the twentieth-century *Transformation Mask* (Fig. 9.12)—during performance, its character changes from that of an earthly being to that of a supernatural being. At the critical moment in the story-drama, the dancer would turn and manipulate the mask with hidden strings and devices, and then turn back in a completely different mask. This surprising transformation might be the changing of a bear or a sea creature into one of the horrendous cannibal spirits. The intent of this magical event was to make humans fear the supernatural. Besides being superbly carved, the mask is exquisitely painted. Bright, bold colors in undulating shapes create overall harmonious compositions that complement the facial contours. This distinct aesthetic with its flowing, curvilinear style is visible throughout Kwakiutl art forms, both past and present.

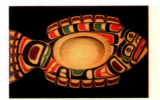

Connection *Figure 7.17, page 153, shows a large contemporary Feast Dish in the tradition of those used in a potlatch.*

Connection *Figure 6.1, page 118 shows the Hamatsu Great Winter Ceremony, with costumed and masked performers.*

OFFERINGS

The Balinese have many days of religious observance, which they commemorate by giving handmade offerings. They regard these offerings as artworks and consider many of their people to be artists. Religion and

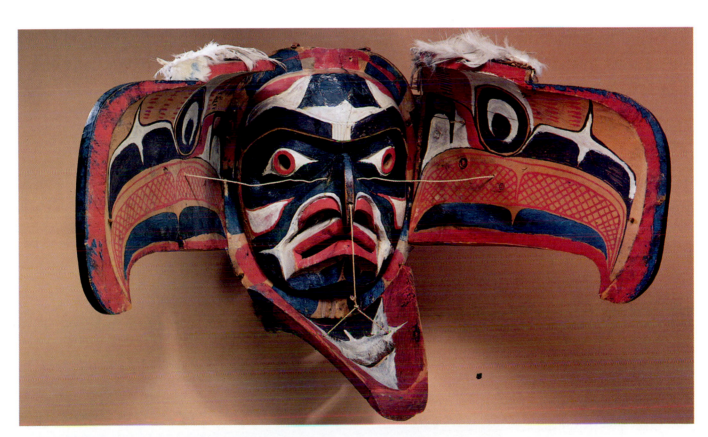

9.12 *Transformation Mask,* Kwakiutl, British Columbia, 20th century. Painted wood American Museum of Natural History, New York.

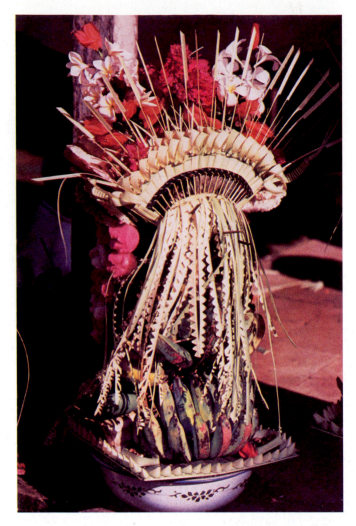

art are integrated components of everyday life. Often, handmade offerings are modest, but on festival days, women make and carry to temples more elaborate offerings, such as the *Offering with Cili-Shaped Crown*, from the mid-1980s (Fig. 9.13). It is an intricate sculpture of fruit, flowers, and cut and woven palm leaves. An ancient symbol of wealth, fertility, and luck, the cili is a simplified woman's head with a large, fanlike headdress radiating from it. In temple rituals, the gods accept the essence of the offering; afterward, any foodstuff that has not touched the ground is eaten in the temple or by the family making the offering. Offerings in the Balinese sense mean to give back in thanks and do not have the connotation of sacrificing something.

Connection Figure 5.8, page 105, shows a Sarad Offering, a large colorful sculpture of dyed rice dough, made for a Balinese temple festival.

In central Mexico, hundreds of believers leave small votive paintings called *retablos* at certain important religious shrines, as a form of prayer and thanks for a divine favor. Pictures, bright colors, and text dramatically record emotional, miraculous events. These artworks also may contain holy cards, pictures of loved ones, diplomas, or legal papers.

The translated text from the *Retablo of Maria de la Luz Casillas and Children* (Fig. 9.14) reads, "I give

9.13   *Offering with Cili-Shaped Crown*, Bali, c. 1985. Flowers, fruit, and palm leaves, approx. 24" tall. Photo Hans Hinz.

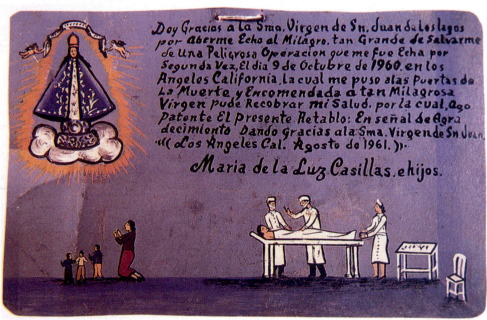

9.14   *Retablo of Maria de la Luz Casillas and Children*, Central Mexico, 1961. Oil on metal, 7" × 10". Durand-Arias Collection. Photo Jorge Durand.

thanks to the Holiest Virgin of San Juan de los Lagos for having made me so great a miracle of saving me in a dangerous operation that was performed on me for the second time on the 9th day of October 1960, in Los Angeles, California. Which put me at the doors of death but entrusted to so miraculous a Virgin I could recover my health, which I make apparent the present retablo: in sign of thanksgiving . . ." (Durand and Massey 1995:164). The Virgin of San Juan de los Lagos is a small statue of Mary, the Mother of Jesus, in a shrine in the central Mexican state of Jalisco. Multiple scenes are common on retablos, and, in this example, we see Maria de la Luz Casillas twice, both as a helpless and vulnerable patient on the operating table in a foreign land and as the supplicant with her children imploring the help of the Virgin. In the retablo, the Virgin looms large in the bleak, gray room, with golden rays, miraculously intervening in a fearful episode.

SACRIFICES

In other cultures, human offerings to God did entail sacrifice, sometimes involving the spilling of human blood. In the various Mesoamerican cultures—Maya, Toltec, Aztec, and others in Central America—the sun was believed to be ever thirsty for blood to stave off the power of the moon and was symbolized by a fiery tongue. In *Shield Jaguar and Lady Xoc,* dated c. 750 (Fig. 9.15), we see an example of a bloodletting ceremony, in which the Mayan ruler holds a torch over his principal wife as she pulls a thorny rope through a hole in her tongue. Those participating in blood sacrifices had to be high ranking, shown by their wrist bracelets, necklaces, crowns, and garb. Their flattened foreheads were signs of beauty, an unnatural effect created by binding boards on the soft skulls of very young children of the nobility. More extreme forms of blood sacrifice were practiced, such as cutting out the hearts of captured warriors or the captains of ball teams. Ballplayers were important members of society, and ball games were important religious rituals in which the ball itself and the opposing teams symbolized the terrible balance between the sun and the moon.

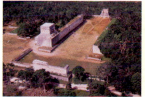

Connection *For more on the Mesoamerican ball games and their meaning, see the Mayan ball court in Figure 16.10, page 438.*

Judeo-Christian religions recognize the offering of foodstuffs and have a history of blood sacrifice. Cain offered farm produce to God; Abel offered an animal and animal fat; the priest Melchizedek prepared a ritual meal for an offering for Abraham. One famous story of sacrifice concerns Abraham, who prepared to kill his son Isaac at the command of God, but at the last minute he was allowed to substitute the slaughter of a ram. The gilded

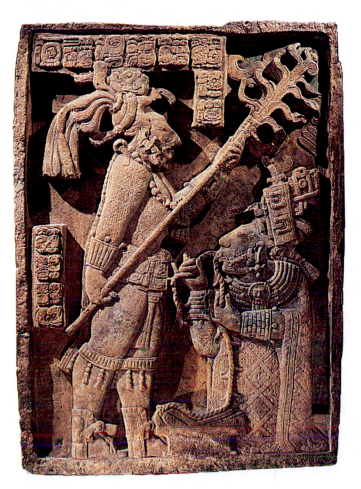

9.15 *Shield Jaguar and Lady Xoc,* Classic Maya, from a palace at Yaxchilan, Chiapas, Mexico, c. 750. Relief. © Justin Kerr.

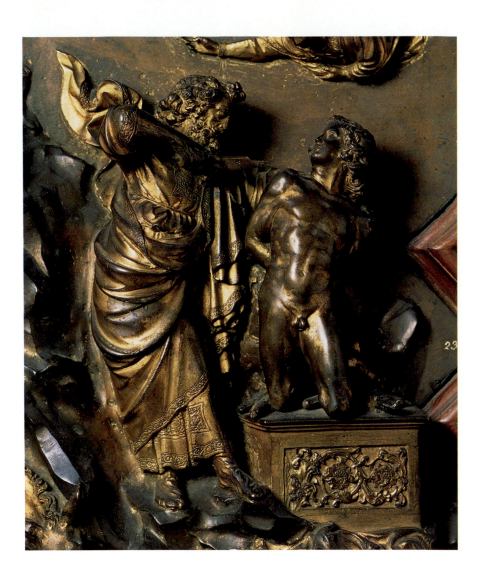

9.16 LORENZO GHIBERTI. *Sacrifice of Isaac* (detail), Florence, Italy, 1401–1402. Gilded bronze, 21" × 17½". Museo Nazionale del Bargello. © Scala/Art Resource, NY.

bronze relief panel, *Sacrifice of Isaac* (Fig. 9.16), sculpted by Lorenzo Ghiberti in 1401–1402, shows the emotionally intense moment when the youthful Isaac is bound on an altar of sacrifice, as his fierce-faced father, Abraham, holds the knife to his son's throat. The curves of their bodies echo each other, with Isaac pulling away as Abraham is poised to lunge forward. The nude body of Isaac is idealized and perfect, increasing the merit of the sacrifice. The intervention of an angel halted the sacrifice, and food, in the form of a ram (not visible in our detail), became an acceptable alternative offering. Although blood sacrifices are no longer offered in mainstream Christian religions, the Eucharistic offering of bread and wine may be celebrated, using many skillfully crafted art items.

PRAYERS

Prayer is a vehicle of communication between human beings and the gods, and it may take many forms. An example of an art object used as a form of prayer is the *Power Figure*, such as the sculpture in Figure 9.17, which would be used to counter the evil influence of enemies, whether human, animal, or spiritual. This example is dated c. 1875–1900. Sculptors carve the power figure with an open mouth, indicating that the sculpture will "speak out" on behalf of anyone beset by evil. Shamans activate them, first by ritually placing medicines in cavities in the figure's abdomen, back, or head. Then they release the figure's power by driving in one metal nail or blade for each request for help. Once effective, the exact nail representing a particular request must be removed. This *Power Figure* is visually dramatic, with its compact form, expressive face, and bristling nails. Power figures are rarely used now, as African religious practices are evolving and rituals may be abandoned or amalgamated into other beliefs.

The Hopi of North America make small sculptures that act as a form of prayer. The Hopi believe that kachinas, or spirits of dead ancestors, dwell in their

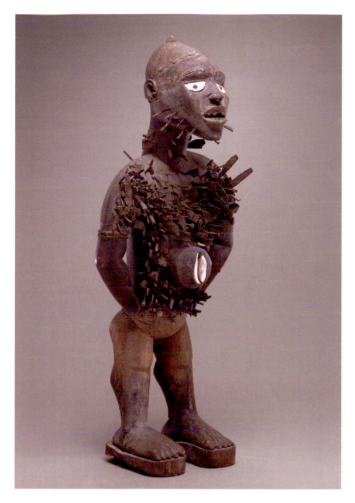

9.17 *Power Figure (Nkisi n'kondi)*, Kongo, Zaire, c. 1875–1900. Wood, nails, blades, medicinal material with cowrie shell, 46¾" high. Detroit Museum of Art. Eleanor Clay Ford Fund for African Art. © 1998 The Detroit Institute of Arts.

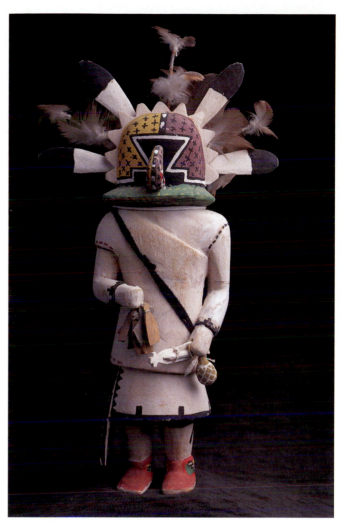

9.18 Jimmie Kewanwytewa. *Ahola Kachina*, Hopi, Third Mesa, Oraibi, 1942. Cottonwood, paint, feathers, wool, 13" high. Museum of Northern Arizona.

community for six months in winter and spring. Kachinas ensure the welfare of the community and sufficient moisture for crops. Male members of the Hopi community perform as kachinas during religious festivals.

Kachina performers also carve dolls that reproduce the costume of specific spirits. Our example, the *Ahola Kachina,* dated 1942, by Jimmie Kewanwytewa (Fig. 9.18), is the primary spirit at an important celebration. It is identifiable by the dome-shaped mask, yellow on one side and brownish gray on the other, covered with small crosses. Other identifying attributes of the costume include the large, inverted black triangle on the face and the feathers from an eagle's tail that project from the head. The colors on the dolls, which look like the performers' costumes, represent sacred directions: north is symbolized by blue or green; west, by yellow; south, by red; east, by white; the heavens, by multicol-

ors; and the nadir, by black. During ceremonies, children receive the dolls to educate them about the individual kachinas and the elaborate costumes and rituals. Women receive them as symbols of fertility. The dolls are hung from rafters in houses as blessings and as prayers for rain and good crops. Older dolls are stiffly posed, but newer ones are more naturally proportioned and often appear in active poses. Bright acrylic colors are now used, and feathers are often carved, as certain birds have become endangered.

THE COSMOS

Artists in various religious traditions have created artworks that map the cosmos, showing the origin of the world, the structure of the universe, spiritual beings, the place of humans in relation to the gods, or a diagram of time. Our first example, a mandala, is a radially balanced, geometric diagram augmented by images of deities, humans, and symbols of the universe. Together, they form a map of the structure and relationships among all entities of the cosmos, in accordance with Hindu or Buddhist beliefs. By meditating on the mandala, people can begin to grasp these cosmic relations and understand their place within them.

The mandala begins with a circle, which symbolizes the void before all creation. Into this emptiness the image of the God will appear. In our example, the *Mandala of Samvara,* dated c. sixteenth century from Tibet (Fig. 9.19), the deity Samvara (also referred to in this work as Cakrasamvara, who rules and sets into motion the universe) erotically embraces his female Buddha consort, Vajravarahi. Samvara, an angry emanation of the Absolute Being, is shown with blue skin and multiple arms, symbols of his power and divinity. He is pictured here with a donkey face, because those

meditating on this image learn the illusory nature of the physical body. Radiating from this center are eight paths, which terminate at the sides or corners of a square. These paths refer to rays of light, the cardinal directions, and elements, such as fire, water, wind, and earth. Other fierce deities, combinations of animal and human forms, occupy these paths. While the inner circles contain deities, the large outer circle encloses charnel fields, where vultures, wild dogs, or cremation fires consume the bodies of the dead (there are generally no graveyards in Southeast Asia). The details vividly depict harmful forces. Immediately outside the ring of the charnel fields are eight auspicious signs, such as a lotus blossom and a white conch shell, that represent divine gifts offered to Buddhas. The outermost areas of the mandala are populated with images of monks, mystics, and more deities.

The underlying geometry makes the mandala both simple and complex. During meditation, it can be followed from the outside inward to the center circle,

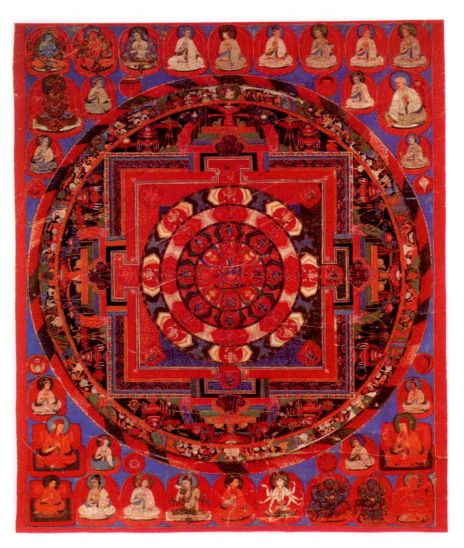

9.19 *Mandala of Samvara (Kharamukha Cakrasamvara Mandala),* Tibet, c. 16th century. Water-based pigments on cotton cloth. 23" high, 18" wide. The Zimmerman Family Collection. Photo Otto Nelson.

indicating stages of increasing enlightenment. In reverse, the mandala represents the emanation of the creative force responsible for all life, which originates from Samvara. The mandala reinforces the belief that the cosmos, including the physical and spiritual worlds, is an uninterrupted whole of continually fluctuating energy states. Red is a common color of Tibetan mandalas and predominates here. The brilliant blue comes from lapis lazuli, an expensive pigment derived from grinding semiprecious stones.

The images on the *Ceiling of the Sistine Chapel,* painted by Michelangelo (Fig. 9.20) from 1508 to

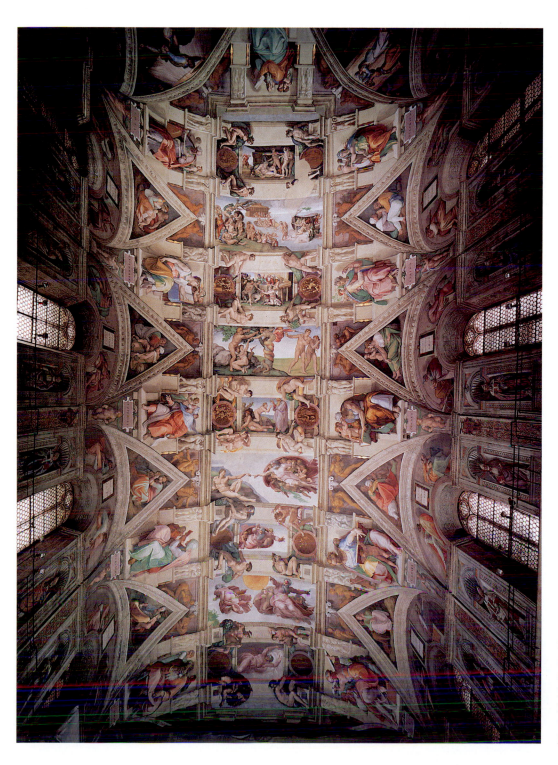

9.20 MICHELANGELO. *Ceiling of the Sistine Chapel,* The Vatican, Rome, Italy, 1508–1512. Fresco, approx. 128' × 45'. Photo Vatican Museums.

1512, present the origin of the universe, of human beings, and of sin. Pope Julius II commissioned the work; more accurately, the pontiff's strong will triumphed and Michelangelo reluctantly acquiesced. The artist felt that he was a sculptor and that painting was a less noble art form. Originally, the work was to consist only of the twelve apostles with some other ornamentation. But as Michelangelo proceeded, he changed the imagery from the apostles to nine scenes from Genesis, along with seven prophets and five sibyls. Illusionistic marble frames subdivide the broad expanse of the ceiling.

At the center bottom of Figure 9.20 is a panel showing God as a powerful-bodied, older man in pink robes, separating the light in the lower right from the darkness in the upper left. Next, God creates the sun and the moon and then separates the water from land. Following are the creation of Adam, then Eve, and original sin, in which Adam and Eve break God's commandment and are expelled from Paradise. The three center panels at the top are concerned with stories of Noah, the patriarch of the human race after a devastating flood destroyed most life on earth. These cosmic moments are depicted in bright, clear colors against plain backgrounds, emphasizing the bodies' dramatic shapes.

The *Creation of Adam* is near the center, and it shows the moment when God transmits the spark of life into the body of Adam, thus creating the human race. God's bursting energy contrasts starkly with the languor of Adam, clearly distinguishing the creator from the created. Yet, human and divine bodies are similarly powerful and similarly posed, indicating the Christian beliefs that humans are created in the likeness of God and that, with God's help, humans can attain heaven.

In other spaces are prophets and learned teachers who pointed to the coming of Jesus (see Figs. 6.17 and 6.18). The nudes may symbolize ideal humans perfected through Jesus. The Mass celebrated in the Sistine Chapel commemorates these events, linking the past to current ritual.

PLACES OF WORSHIP AND THEIR GENERAL CHARACTERISTICS

Since prehistory, people have set aside special places for religious worship. All these places, from simple to grand, are designed to reveal something of the spiritual realm and to provide an experience beyond the normal and mundane. Across cultures and religions, places of worship may

- shelter a congregation

- house sacred objects

- incorporate elements of nature

- provide sites for repeated religious celebrations

- incorporate symbolic geometry in their dimensions or the determination of their location

- incorporate the concept of journey or provide a destination for pilgrims

Regarding the first point, it is sufficient to say that places of worship were often designed to house a large group of people, all of whom are participating at the same time in ritual observances. The other five characteristics are explained more fully here.

HOUSING SACRED OBJECTS

Many places of worship were built specifically to house a sacred image, text, or artifact of a religion. In the Jewish religion, the Temple of Solomon contained the sacred scriptures called the Torah and other sacred objects. The most holy structure, called the *Ark of the Covenant*, was a special tabernacle that held these sacred objects and is depicted in Figure 9.21. Moses constructed the *Ark* according to instructions from Yahweh, so that the prophet could communicate with and receive revelations from him during the exodus from Egypt. Our image is a mosaic from the fourth century CE, which depicts the *Ark* in the center of the composition. Sanctuary implements, including elaborate seven-branched candelabra, flank the tabernacle.

Because the Jewish peoples seldom had a permanent homeland in the early years of their history, a tent was likely their early place of worship as well as a temporary temple. Later, King Solomon built the Temple in Jerusalem, which was destroyed in 586 BCE. Part of the wall remains, and Jews from all over the world still go there to pray. In more recent centuries, the synagogue has evolved as a community house of worship, assembly, and study. Even modern synagogues, however, still house sacred objects: each con-

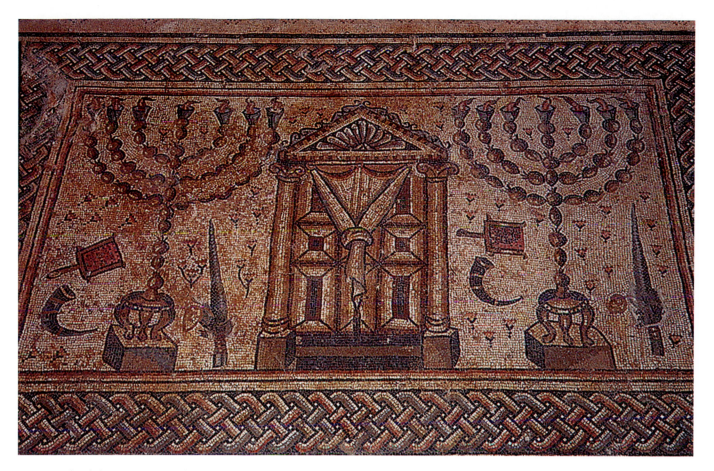

9.21 *Ark of the Covenant* and sanctuary implements, Hammath, near Tiberias, 4th century. Mosaic. Israel Antiquities Authority, Jerusalem. Photo: Zev Rodovan, Jerusalem.

tains an Ark, scrolls of the Law, an eternal flame, and a candelabrum.

Connection *The Roman Emperor Titus led troops into Jerusalem and destroyed the Second Temple in 70 CE. Relief carvings on the Arch of Titus commemorate the emperor's victory in Jerusalem and depict his soldiers carrying the booty from the Temple in a victory parade. See Figure 11.16, page 289.*

Other religions also house sacred objects in their places of worship, as we shall see later in this chapter. Often, these are specially constructed buildings, such as temples or churches. In some cases, however, formal structures are not necessary. For example, among many African religions, shrines that hold sacred objects are part of ordinary houses. Thus, spiritual forces are woven into everyday life.

INCORPORATING ELEMENTS OF NATURE

Places of worship can be natural sites: mountains, springs, and sacred trees or groves. Mountains have been meeting places between heaven and earth or dwelling places of divine beings. Rocks can be seen as containers or symbols for spirits and deities. The earth and water are the sources or sustainers of life. Trees may be seen as sources of truth and symbols of the cosmos, existing simultaneously in the underworld, the earth, and the heavens. Fire, light, and the sun are divine symbols or sometimes spirits themselves.

The *Ziggurat at Ur* (Fig. 9.22), dated c. 2150–2050 BCE, is a sacred artificial mountain erected by the Sumerians of the city of Ur to honor their special deity from among the Sumerian pantheon of gods. Its corners point toward the four points of the compass, reflecting the movement of the sun. The word *ziggurat*

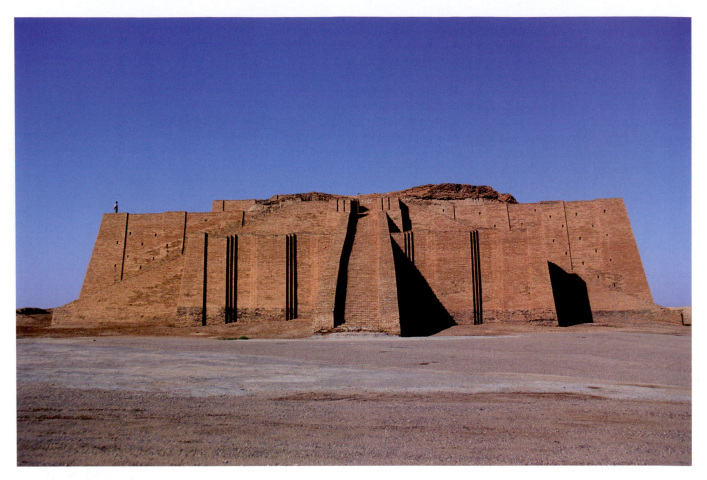

9.22 *Ziggurat at Ur* (partially reconstructed), Third Dynasty of Ur, Iraq, c. 2150–2050 BCE. Hirmer Fotoarchiv. Photo Erwin Bohm.

itself means "mountain" or "pinnacle." Surrounded by flat land, this terraced tower of rubble and brick seemed to reach into the heavens. The *Ziggurat at Ur* has three broad staircases, each with one hundred steps, leading to a temple-shrine forty feet above the ground, dedicated to protective gods and goddesses and attended to by special orders of priests and priestesses.

The Shinto religion in Japan teaches that forests and enormous stones are sacred dwellings of the gods of nature, who are called the *Kami*, all connected to growth and renewal. Our example, the *Main Shrine at Ise* (Fig. 9.23), is located in a forest, on a holy site. Through ritual, the Kami are prevailed upon to enter the shrine, where their powers are worshipped and their aid solicited. A mirror placed inside facilitates their coming into the shrine.

The *Main Shrine at Ise* is made of natural materials, primarily wood and thatch. It is rebuilt every twenty years to exactly the same specifications, so what we see in Figure 9.23 is both a new building and a structure that dates from c. 685. With each rebuilding, the builders observe careful rituals and express gratitude as

they take wood from the forest. Boards taken from the same tree are placed together in the building of the shrine. The wood is left plain and unpainted to retain its natural character, and it is carefully fitted and joined with wooden pegs. The golden color of the wood emphasizes the striking geometry in the architecture.

Connection *Compare the basic design of the Shinto shrine to the* Toba Batak House *(Fig. 7.28, page 159).*

PROVIDING SITES FOR SACRED CEREMONIES

Places of worship are sites where sacred ceremonies are performed. Sometimes there is no special architecture, only the use of the arts—music, dance, singing, literature, or the visual arts. In the southwestern United States, the making of sand paintings has constituted an essential part of Navajo religious ceremonies for centuries. These impermanent paintings are made directly on clean-swept floors of houses and are destroyed in the course of the ceremony. Very few have ever been

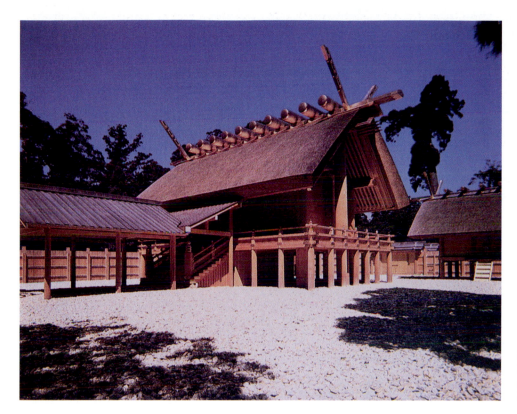

9.23 *Main Shrine at Ise* (exterior), Japan, c. 685, rebuilt every 20 years. Kyodo News International.

photographed or documented; however, the rituals are fixed, and certain symbols must be repeated each time. To cure illness, ensure success in hunting, or promote fertility, the artist-priest chants and prays while making the painting using the natural elements of colored sand, crushed stones, charcoal, and pollen. The person in need sits in the center of the painting to receive the supernatural power. Sometimes ceremonies are performed for the earth itself.

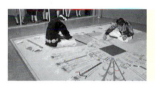

Connection *An example of a Navajo sand painting can be seen in Fig. 3.14 on page 65.*

USING GEOMETRY SYMBOLICALLY

Many cultures use geometry and symmetry to symbolize divinity, all-encompassing totality, perfection, and timelessness. Such geometry may determine the placement or orientation of religious sites, or a building's plan, layout, or elevation.

Stonehenge, dated c. 2000 BCE (Fig. 9.24), in Wiltshire, England, was built at a time when religion and science were not separate but were a single, unified means of understanding natural forces. Thus, *Stonehenge* is likely an altar for religious rituals as well as an astronomical device that maps solar and planetary movement upon the earth. The stone arrangement marks the midsummer solstice, essential to an agrarian civilization dependent on successful crop planting. Other Neolithic stone arrangements in the area align with *Stonehenge,* creating a larger network that may have mapped force fields within the earth.

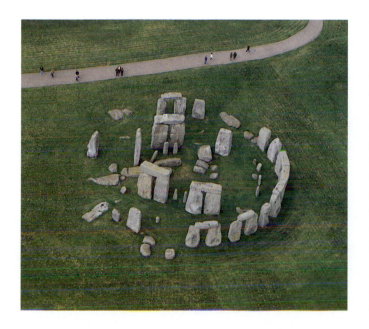

9.24 *Stonehenge,* Wiltshire, England, c. 2000 BCE. Diameter: 97'; upright stones with lintel, approximately 24' high. Pubbli Aer Foto.

The first building phase of *Stonehenge* was a gigantic circular ditch, with rubble piled to create an outer bank. The later core of *Stonehenge* consists of a ninety-seven-foot-diameter ring of colossal sarsen stones, twenty-four feet high with their capping lintel. An inner ring of bluestones in turn surrounds a horseshoe-shaped stone arrangement and, finally, an altar stone in the center. A heel stone, separate from the circle, marks the solstice. Builders dragged the stones twenty-four miles, pounded and rubbed them to shape, and likely set them in place using ropes and earthen ramps. *Stonehenge* includes several large rings of holes dug into the ground that conceptually connect the center stones to the surrounding earth.

Centuries later, simple geometric shapes formed the basis of a Roman building that alluded to divine qualities of perfection and completion. The *Pantheon*, 118–125 (Fig. 9.25), is a shrine to the chief deities of the Roman Empire. A 142-foot-diameter sphere fits into the interior space, making the width of the building equal to its height. The dome, a perfect hemisphere, is the top half of that sphere. A thirty-foot circular opening at top (the *oculus,* or eye) creates a shaft of sunlight that dramatically illuminates the interior. Squares are inscribed in the dome and wall surfaces and are the basis of the pattern on the marble inlay floor. The entire structure is symmetrical, both inside and out, and creates the impression of loftiness, simplicity, and balance.

PROVIDING DESTINATIONS FOR PILGRIMAGES

A pilgrimage is a journey to a shrine or sacred place for believers hoping to receive special blessings or deepening of faith. The concept of journey is both metaphoric

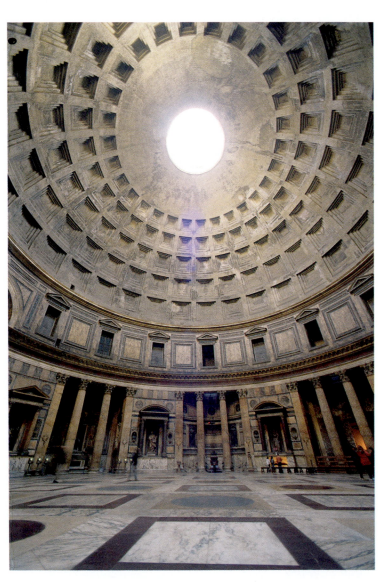

9.25 *Pantheon*, Rome, Italy, 118–125. Concrete and marble; 142' from floor to opening in dome. Henri Stierlin.

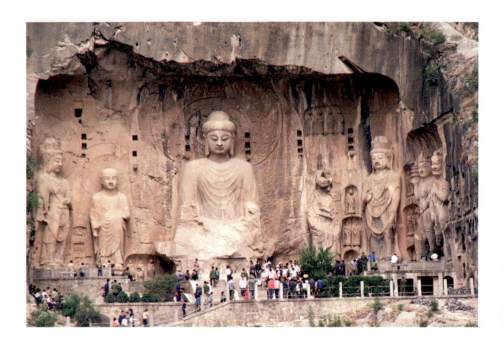

9.26 *Shrine to Vairocana Buddha*, Longmen, Luoyang, Valley of the Yellow River, China, c. 600–650. Natural rock carving, 50' high. © Lowell Georgia/Corbis.

and actual, as the soul's spiritual search for understanding has been likened to a physical journey. Almost all major religions incorporate the concept of pilgrimage into their belief systems; for example, Hindus and Buddhists journey to shrines; Jews, to Jerusalem; Christians, to various sites such as Lourdes; and Muslims, to Mecca. Our first example is from the Longmen caves in China, a huge complex of cave-shrines housing thousands of sacred statues, which is a Buddhist pilgrimage destination. At Longmen, 1,352 caves have been carved into the limestone mountains, with over 97,000 statues and 3,600 inscriptions dedicated to Buddha. The largest of these is the monumental *Shrine to Vairocana Buddha*, dated c. 600–650 (Fig. 9.26), who is the universal principle dominating all life and all phenomena.

He is attended by demons and lesser Buddhas who govern their own worlds, a model used by tyrant emperors in China to justify their rule. In fact, the carvings at the Longmen caves were supported by imperial patronage. The Buddha at the center is serene, massive, and volumetric, with drapery defined with a few simple curves, to enhance the colossal scale of the carving.

Notre Dame du Haut (Fig. 9.27), a Catholic chapel in the Vosges Mountains of France, built between 1950 and 1955, is a pilgrimage destination. The design recalls praying hands, the wings of a dove, and the shape of a boat, all Christian symbols of divine generosity to humans. The shape of the structure resembles sculpture. To accommodate very large crowds on holy days, the church was fitted with an outdoor altar and pulpit (visible toward the right in this photograph), so that services could be conducted for 12,000 pilgrims on the lawn. Then, the building's exterior becomes a monumental sculptural backdrop for the religious event. The interior of *Notre Dame du Haut* is a relatively small space with limited seating, almost mystically dark and cave-like, with deep-set, square, colored-glass windows piercing the walls.

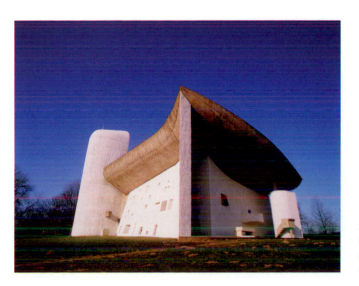

9.27 LE CORBUSIER. *Notre Dame du Haut*, Ronchamps, France, 1950–1955. © Archivo Iconografico, S.A./Corbis. © 2004 Artists Rights Society (ARS), New York/ADAGP, Paris/FLC.

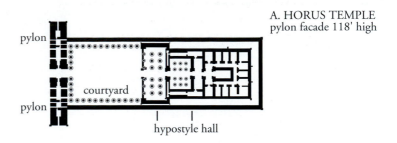

A. HORUS TEMPLE
pylon facade 118' high

pylon

courtyard

pylon

hypostyle hall

B. ACROPOLIS
Parthenon approximately 60' high

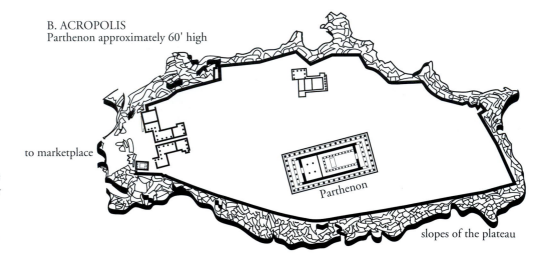

to marketplace

Parthenon

slopes of the plateau

9.28　Comparison of the plans of various places of worship. Notice that all plans are drawn to the same scale and vary tremendously in size. Heights vary tremendously also; they are indicated next to each plan. A. *Horus Temple* (top left), B. *Acropolis* (middle left), C. *Chartres Cathedral* (lower left), D. *Pyramid of the Sun* (top center), E. *Kandarya Mahadeva Temple* (right), F. *Masjid-i-Shah* (lower center). See Figure 9.38 for the plan of the Buddhist temple compound, the *Altar of Heaven,* which is too large to be shown at scale here.

C. CHARTRES CATHEDRAL
north tower 377' high

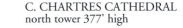
0   100   200   300
⊢────┴────┴────┴───⊣ FEET

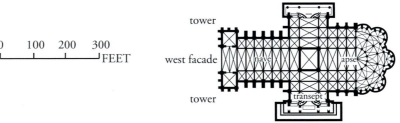

tower

west facade   nave   apse

tower   transept

TEMPLE COMPLEXES AND LARGE-SCALE SACRED ARCHITECTURE

Some religious sites are more grand, extensive, and complex than what we have already seen. They are some of the most famous works of art in the world. They all incorporate the general characteristics of sacred sites that we saw at the beginning of this chapter. When a religion has become firmly established and tied to political power, these expensive, labor-intensive, long-term proj-

ects are possible. Thus, grand places of worship are expressions of temporal power, religious power, and broad cultural values. With imposing size and lavish detail, these structures are spectacles. In ceremonies, the individual is reduced to spectator, part of the throng that adds to the religious importance of the site.

First, compare the plans of six of the seven major sites we will study (Fig. 9.28). All are drawn to the same scale. Even the smallest, the *Kandarya Mahadeva Temple,* is imposing with its 130-foot height. The largest, the *Pyramid of the Sun* in Central

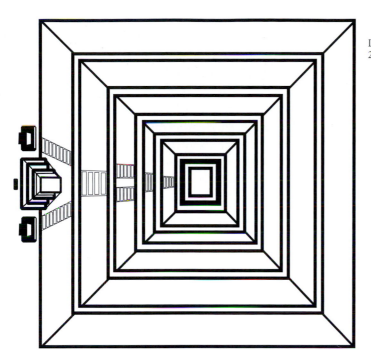

D. PYRAMID OF THE SUN
215' high

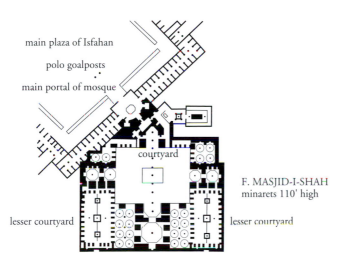

main plaza of Isfahan

polo goalposts

main portal of mosque

courtyard

lesser courtyard

lesser courtyard

F. MASJID-I-SHAH
minarets 110' high

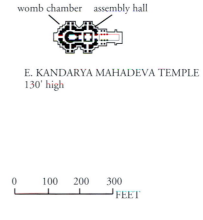

womb chamber   assembly hall

E. KANDARYA MAHADEVA TEMPLE
130' high

0   100   200   300
FEET

Mexico, is truly enormous. The plans also reveal how important geometry is in these designs to suggest perfection, completion, balance, and formality. Symmetry is an excellent visual metaphor for political power and divinity.

The plan of the seventh major site, the Buddhist *Altar of Heaven,* is shown in Figure 9.38. The temple compound is integrated into the design of a quarter-mile-wide park and will be discussed in that context.

Let us begin our study of religious compounds and large-scale sacred architecture with the Greeks.

THE GREEK TEMPLE

In studying Greek temple design, we will use the Parthenon in Athens as our example.

Athens is situated on a plain surrounded by mountains, with a high plateau in the center dedicated to the city's patroness, Athena. This plateau, the Acropolis, forms a dramatic setting for temples and is a mountain to climb in the pilgrimage journey. Smaller buildings, clustered along the steep approach, contrast dramatically with the large temples and open space at the top (see plan). It is visually impressive from many surrounding viewpoints.

Temple Design

The *Parthenon* (Fig. 9.29) is a good example of a standard **Classical** Greek temple. Following a three-hundred-year precedent, it is a two-room structure with pediments above the short sides and a colonnaded porch all around. It is more graceful and refined than older temples, but, like them, was covered using the post-and-lintel system. This particular style (or "order") of temple was called **Doric** and could be easily identified by its column. The Doric column had no base, a simple cushion capital, and a shaft that was fluted, or carved from top to bottom with thin, vertical channels. High-quality marble blocks were carefully stacked and finished so that the columns originally appeared seamless.

In designing the *Parthenon*, the architects Iktinos and Kallikrates often treated it more like a piece of sculpture than architecture. Like a pedestal, the steps form the base for the structure. They are higher at the middle of each side and lower at the corners, to counteract the illusion of sagging in the middle. Thus, the *Parthenon* contains optical illusions. The corner columns are thicker and placed closer to neighboring columns to compensate for the glaring bright sky behind them that would make them seem thinner. Outer columns lean slightly toward the middle of the building to make the *Parthenon* more visually cohesive. The shaft of the Doric column swells slightly at the middle, called *entasis*, to give the column a feeling of organic flexing.

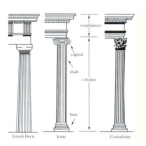

Connection *Greek columns appear on the Roman Colosseum in Figure 16.9, page 438. See also Figure 2.36, page 50, for diagrams of the Doric, Ionic, and Corinthian orders.*

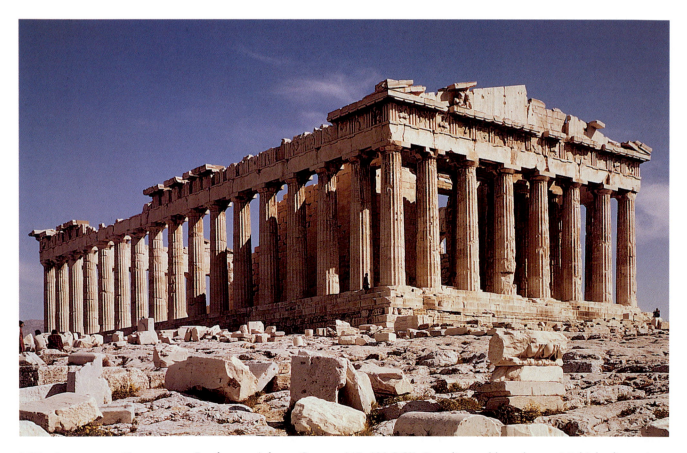

9.29 IKTINOS AND KALLIKRATES. *Parthenon*, Athens, Greece, 447–432 BCE. Pentelic marble; columns 34' high, dimensions of structure 228' × 104'. © Photodisc Green/Getty Images.

Sculpture and Relief Carving

The *Parthenon* had two interior rooms for housing sacred objects and the treasury, rooms that only a few priests entered. Religious ceremonies took place outside, so originally the exterior was richly adorned with sculpture and brightly painted. Large sculptures of the gods stood in the pediment and near the roof (see Fig. 6.6), and a long band of sculpture (three feet six inches high, 524 feet long), called a *frieze*, girded the top outside walls of the *Parthenon*'s two inner chambers. Carved c. 440 BCE, the frieze shows a long procession of Greek worshippers climbing up to the *Parthenon*, with marshals, youths, maidens, musicians, jar carriers, horsemen, and charioteers, some bringing animals for sacrifice. At the beginning of the procession, the worshippers are raucous and unorganized, like our *Horsemen* (Fig. 9.30). Gradually, the worshippers become solemn and orderly as they approach the gods. This is probably a depiction of the special Panathenaic Festival procession, which occurred every four years to bring a new ceremonial tunic to robe an ancient wooden statue of Athena.

The carving on the sculptural frieze is very high quality, an especially amazing feat given that the sculpture is almost twice the length of a football field and was completed in less than a decade. Overlapping, crisscrossing diagonals—horses' legs, waving hands, drapery—communicate the bustle early on. Gods and humans are similarly rendered as rounded and lifelike, with carefully carved muscles. They are dignified, composed, well proportioned, and idealized. The frieze is carved more deeply at the top and more shallowly at the bottom to make it clearer to viewers below.

Mathematical Proportions and Greek Philosophy

In their science, geometry, art, religion, and philosophy, the Greeks were engaged in a search for perfection. For example, they believed that certain geometric ratios and certain musical intervals resonated with the cosmic order and were in tune with the heavens. Thus, builders used a consistent set of proportions to determine the length and width of parts within the *Parthenon*, and they balanced horizontal and vertical elements to give the structure a quality of self-containment. By not being overwhelming in size, the *Parthenon* also reflects the Greek idea of the value of the individual.

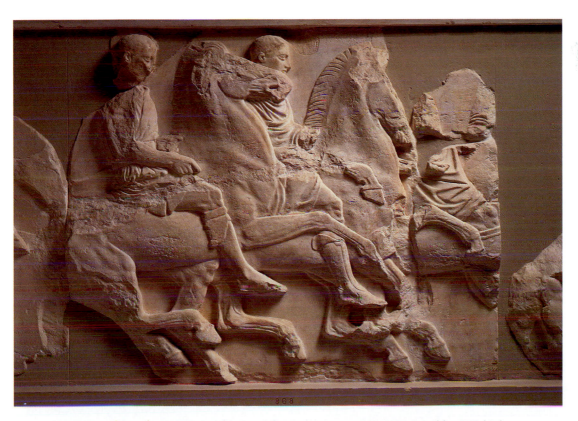

9.30 *Horsemen* (from the Parthenon frieze), Athens, Greece, c. 440 BCE. Marble, 37" high.
© Nimatallah/Art Resource, NY.

THE EGYPTIAN TEMPLE

Egyptian temple design remained relatively constant for 3,000 years, and so the study of one will illustrate the qualities of many.

Setting and History

Protected by the desert, life in ancient Egypt was unusually stable. Natural cycles, such as night and day and the annual flooding of the Nile River, provided powerful symbols for the Egyptian religion. The Egyptians used symbolic geometry to demarcate sacred alignments in the landscape. East-west marked the path of the sun god, Re, symbolizing life, death, and resurrection. The north-south axis paralleled the Nile River. Generally, cult temples, which were used to worship gods, were located on the east bank of the Nile, like the rising sun, while funerary temples were on the west. Cult temples were often parts of large sacred cities. Successive pharaohs would add new temples to the complex or expand existing ones.

Connection Other than cult temples, much Egyptian architecture, such as the Mortuary Temple of Hatshepsut *(Fig. 10.5, page 248)*, consists of tombs and funerary temples.

Temple Design

The *Horus Temple at Edfu*, which is located on the west side of the Nile, housed the sacred cult image of the sun falcon, Horus. Because cult temples were believed to be the actual dwellings of the gods, they were modeled after the residences of nobles and pharaohs (see plan, Fig. 9.28). Courtyards and halls were like reception rooms leading to the sanctuary, which corresponded to the private family bedrooms. For purity, amulets protected the temple's foundations, and its outer edges were walled.

The *Great Pylon of the Horus Temple at Edfu*, built c. 237–57 BCE (Fig. 9.31), is a temple front entrance, with two large, symmetrical, geometric "mountains" flanking the large doorway. The image may have been derived from the Nile River flowing between cliffs. Visually, the pylons both define the entrance and act as barriers. The lower classes of the Egyptian population were forbidden to enter. Statues and carvings animated the great surfaces, and they were painted to make the temple facade very colorful. The four vertical niches once held tall poles with flying banners.

All doorways and open areas were aligned to create a straight-line path that continues throughout the temple, suggesting the flow of the Nile River and echoing

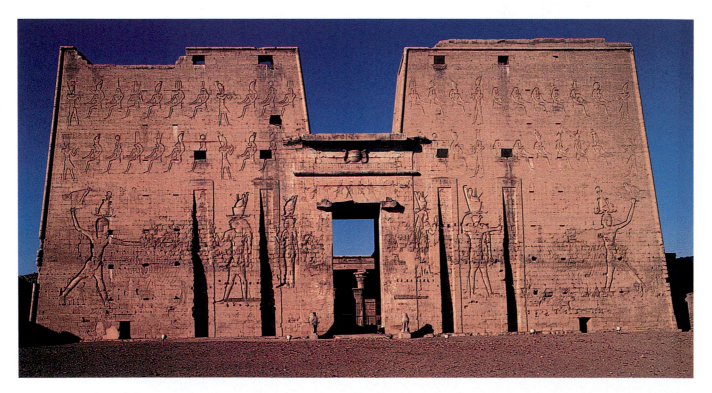

9.31 *Great Pylon of the Horus Temple at Edfu*, Egypt, c. 237–57 BCE. The pylons are 118' high and the facade is 230' wide. Unlike most Egyptian cult temples, this one is located on the west side of the Nile River. Ronald Sheridan Ancient Art & Architecture.

the Egyptians' sanctified experience of nature. The temple floor was painted to depict a river, and the ceiling was decorated with sun rays and the stars of the night sky. Two covered rooms are located beyond the entrance courtyard at Edfu (see plan). They were hypostyle halls, with parallel rows of columns that supported the ceiling. In the *First Hypostyle Hall* at Edfu (Fig. 9.32), the columns are huge and closely spaced, clogging the interior space. The stone roof necessitated closely spaced supports. The concept of the passageway is again emphasized, as the space is not really usable as a room. The shapes of the columns and capitals were probably derived from the bundles of reeds used to build the very early Egyptian buildings. To express divine permanence and power, Egyptians translated that original organic material into massive and monumental granite and limestone. The stone capitals often resemble lotus buds, blossoms, or palm fronds. The shafts of the columns swell like the flexing of organic materials. At Edfu, the columns of the hypostyle hall are fifty feet tall; at another temple site, Karnak, the central columns in the hypostyle hall are sixty-six feet high, and the capitals at the top are twenty-two feet in diameter, large enough to hold one hundred people. The massive stones are held in place solely by their tremendous weight.

The temple became darker with each succeeding room, and rooms became smaller, with lower ceilings. To help protect its purity, the sacred image of Horus was kept in the sanctuary at the very back, sealed by heavy doors covered with bronze or silver and decorated with precious stones. The holiest areas were

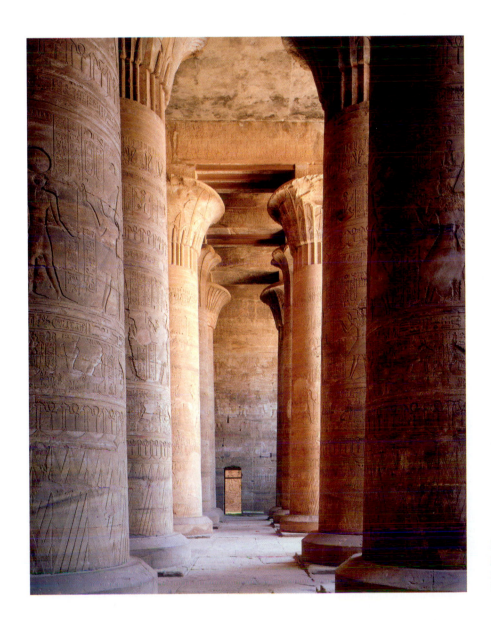

9.32 *First Hypostyle Hall, Horus Temple at Edfu,* Egypt, c. 237–57 BCE. The roof slabs are 50' from the floor.
© Scala/Art Resource, NY.

opened only on special occasions and could be approached only by a very few. The sacred image of Horus did not always reside in darkness, however. On certain special feast days, such statues were taken out and rejoined with the sun to recover their vigor.

THE MESOAMERICAN TEMPLE

Mesoamerican temples often took the form of a pyramid with a small structure on top. The pyramid or the mound was a frequent holy site throughout the Americas, from Illinois to Peru.

History and Setting

Thirty miles north of today's Mexico City, the Teotihuacános, a pre-Aztec people, built a vast religious center in a large city high on a plateau surrounded by mountains, a center that reached its peak from 100 to 400. Teotihuacán, or "Place of the Gods," had 200,000 residents, enormous temples, and numerous and lavish palaces, and governed a wide area. Unlike in previous rambling Mesoamerican cities, the streets of Teotihuacán were rigidly laid out on a grid oriented to north, south, east, and west, and even a river through

the town was channeled to conform to that grid. The main north-south corridor, the *Avenue of the Dead*, formed the religious center of the city, with more than one hundred temples in two miles. The incredible scale of the Avenue of the Dead dwarfs any of the places of worship we have seen so far. The plan of the architectural design shows the pyramids as solid masses, with plazas as voids that were often the same size as the bases of the pyramids. Ball courts were also included.

The very building and growth of Teotihuacán directly led to its decline, as forests were leveled to fire kilns to make plaster, resulting in soil erosion, failure of rains, and the decline of the city.

Temple Designs

In the middle of the *Avenue of the Dead* was the *Pyramid of the Sun*, begun before 150 (Fig. 9.33) and probably dedicated to sun worship. It was aligned east-west and along the rising of the star cluster Pleiades on the days of the equinox, and once had a temple on top. The pyramid is quite simply staggering in size, covering 7.5 acres and rising 215 feet. The Teotihuacános did not use the wheel and had no beasts of burden, so peo-

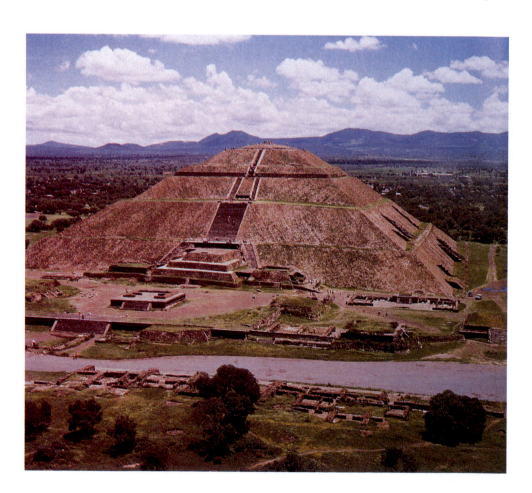

9.33 *Pyramid of the Sun*, with the *Avenue of the Dead* in the foreground, Teotihuacán, Mexico, begun before 150. Pyramid is 768' along one side of the base. Photo courtesy Ester Pasztory.

ple carried the 2.5 million tons of earth, stone, and rubble to the site. Probably 3,000 laborers worked thirty years to complete the pyramid. The ledges, tiers, vertical insets, and square corners visually separate the pyramid from the rounded mountains that surround it. To prevent erosion, it was built with a relatively low profile, with embedded stone walls set perpendicular to the outer face.

The entire earthen mound was once covered with huge clay bricks faced with stone, and finished with a coat of smooth, white, polished lime plaster. It must have looked like a gleaming white mountain, with certain parts painted in color. Ceremonies with splendid pageantry were likely held on the steps and ledges.

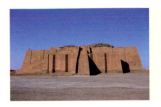 **Connection** *Compare the similarities between the* Pyramid of the Sun *and the* Ziggurat at Ur *(Fig. 9.22, page 220), seen earlier in this chapter.*

Temple Painting

Early temples had sculptural ornamentation, but after the third century, paintings were used, like the restored copy of the *Tlalocan Painting* (Fig. 9.34), from a palace in Teotihuacán. A large frontal figure at the center is a water god with green water droplets springing from her hands. Plants populated with butterflies and spiders grow from her head, while two priests, shown symmetrically and smaller in scale, attend and make offerings. The colors in this restored version are bright, with an especially intense red background. The deity is distinguished by her larger size, frontality, and the profusion of symmetrical patterns that ornament her.

THE HINDU TEMPLE
Theology and Temple Design

Hinduism is based on two belief systems. The first is nature-based and venerates the various spirits responsible for the incredible abundance of plant and animal life in India. From this came the concept of reincarnation, an infinitely repeating cycle of death and life. Around 1500 BCE, invaders brought the second belief system—an understanding of the cosmos in symbolic, geometric terms. The circle stood for the totality of the universe; the square was that divine force made physical in life on earth; a vertical pole was the pillar between heaven and earth, a link that also ensured their separation. A good person would eventually break the cycle of rebirth and death and move into a changeless, timeless union with the Supreme Consciousness, Brahman.

Temple architecture gives form to these spiritual beliefs. The earliest temples were cave temples carved into mountains, like opening the earth's womb to find the divinity enshrined inside. Other temples were freestanding, thick-walled cubes, containing a womb-chamber that housed the cult image or symbol of the deity. A heavy tower, like an abstract mountain, covered it, and a few relief sculptures adorned the exterior. Worshippers brought offerings, meditated, and made sacrifices individually, but remained outside. Priests tended to the deities housed inside and acted as intermediaries for the

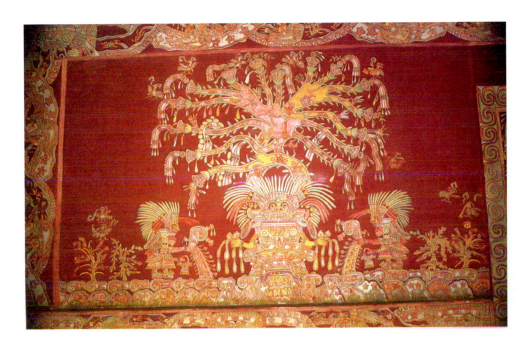

9.34 *Tlalocan Painting,* from Tepantitla compound, Teotihuacán, Mexico. Copy by Agustin Villagra. Original: pigment on stucco. Photo by Mary Ellen Miller.

worshippers. There is no collective service in the Hindu religion, and the temple is the dwelling of the deity.

Later Hindu temples and precincts became much more elaborate, but the same basic formula of womb-chamber and mountain remains. In now-deserted Khajuraho, an important political capital in the tenth and eleventh centuries, was a grouping of thirty temples, symbolizing abundance and proliferation. One was the *Kandarya Mahadeva Temple* (Fig. 9.35), dedicated to Shiva in his manifestation as Mahadeva, who maintains all living things. The *Kandarya Mahadeva Temple* is still an artificial mountain that surmounts the small, dark womb-chamber. The basic shapes are symbols of male and female sexuality, representing sexual energy and the procreative urge. Then, almost lifelike, they break down into multiplying, cascading forms that are fantastic in their variety and number. Several attached porches and a front assembly hall add to the proliferating forms.

Despite the multiplicity of forms, visual unity is maintained because of the basic mountain-like form and because of the simple umbrella shape (which represents the Unbounded) that surmounts the tallest tower, above the womb-chamber. Thus, the temple exterior was an instrument of meditation on reincarnation. Up close, the relief carvings become more readable, with images of deities and of smaller shrines. Many are openly erotic, because the Hindu religion believes that carnal bliss reflects divine union with the Unbounded.

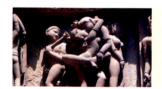

Connection *Figure 8.17, page 185, shows an erotic scene from the Kandarya Mahadeva Temple.*

Geometry and its Significance

The plan of the temple (Fig. 9.28) is a mandala, a geometric drawing that symbolizes the universe, which we saw in Figure 9.19. Four porches on the temple pointing in the cardinal directions mark the four sides. Then the squares and circles, which have cosmic meaning, are repeated, rotated, and overlaid, and then expanded into space to create the fantastic compilation of shapes that proliferate to become the outer layer of the temple, which still relates to the inner sanctum.

THE GOTHIC CATHEDRAL

The imposing, mystical **Gothic** cathedral is one of the most famous forms of a Catholic church. Christians believed that the body and earth are profane and sinful, while the soul is sacred. They saw the church building as the heavenly Jerusalem on earth. Abbot Suger, a leading cleric during this era, remarked upon entering a Gothic church, "I see myself existing on some level . . . beyond our earthly one, neither completely in the slime of earth nor completely in the purity of Heaven." Gothic cathedrals were all funded by and built in cities, indicating the rise of cities and monarchies and a decline in feudalism. The modern humanist view that values the individual was beginning to develop at this time.

Plan and Design

Gothic cathedrals towered over the towns around them, which is evident in *Chartres Cathedral* (Fig. 9.36), built between 1194 and 1220. The spires symbolized the church's role linking heaven and earth. Flat, blank walls are almost nonexistent. Large windows are filled with

9.35 *Kandarya Mahadeva Temple,* Khajuraho, India, 10th–11th centuries. This is one of 30 temples at this site, dedicated to Shiva, Vishnu, or Mahavira. Main tower is 130' high. © Brian A. Vikander/ Corbis.

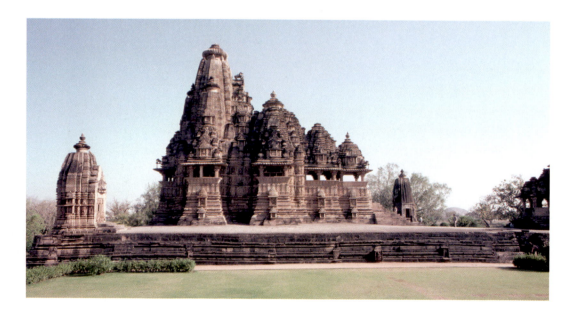

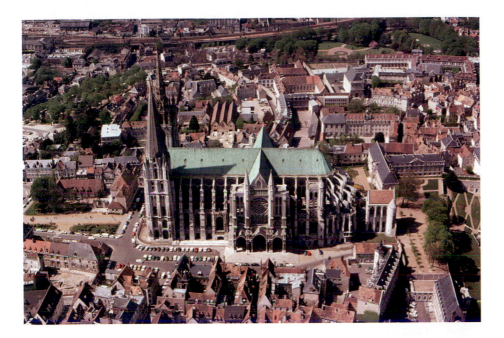

9.36 *Chartres Cathedral*, Chartres, France. South tower 344' high, north tower 377' high; the cathedral itself is 427' long. A rose window is visible at the middle of the church. Although parts of the west front date from 1145–1170, most of the exterior of this structure was built between 1194 and 1220. © Marc Garanger/Corbis.

tracery, a lacy stone framework that holds sections of glass in place. Blank spaces are covered with figurative sculptures or decorative carvings, showing Jesus, saints, rulers, and sometimes demons. Flying buttresses create a visual pattern of forms that jog in and out, as can be seen in Figure 9.36. Towers, arches, buttresses, and arcades create vertical lines that continue from ground to roof. The plan of *Chartres* is symmetrical, while its shape (Fig. 9.28) is a cross, symbolizing Jesus' crucifixion as the act of salvation that redeemed sinful humanity.

The emphasis on verticality continues inside. Long lines rise from the floor, up the piers, and between the windows, and flow gracefully up the pointed groin vaults. The vaults seem to billow overhead rather than being stone structures that weigh tons.

Window Design

The large stained-glass windows were not only incredible technical achievements but also powerful symbols of heavenly radiance. Previously, churches tended to be very dark, but these windows fill the Gothic church with muted light. The flying buttresses on the outside make the enormous windows possible, because the buttresses and not the walls are holding up the vaults above.

The *Rose Window*, from 1233, on the north transept of Chartres (Fig. 9.37), shows rings of Old Testament prophets and kings surrounding Mary with her child Jesus. This illustrates the Christian concept that the Old Testament culminated in the birth of Christ. Mary's central location indicates the raised status of women. (In fact, the church is dedicated to Mary.) The female model was now Mary, mother of the savior Jesus, rather than

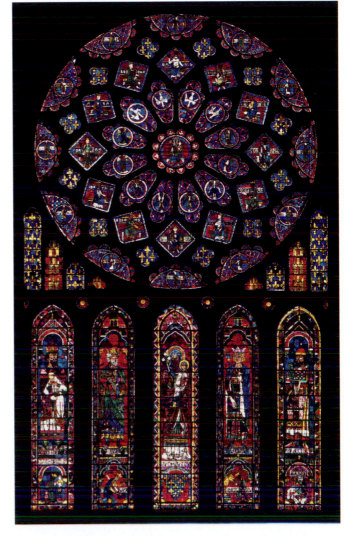

9.37 *Rose Window,* from the north transept of *Chartres Cathedral*, Chartres, France, 1233. © Angelo Hornak/Corbis.

sinful Eve. Geometry was used to locate the various small scenes in this window by inscribing and rotating squares within a circle. The window is shaped like a blooming rose, a symbol of Mary.

Connection *For an example of the English style of Gothic architecture, see the* Chapel of Henry VII, *Figure 10.17, page 259.*

THE BUDDHIST TEMPLE

Distinct versions of Buddhist temples sprang up in India, Southeast Asia, Indonesia, China, Japan, and Korea. For now, we will confine our discussion to just one Buddhist temple compound from China, the *Altar of Heaven*, and to one temple within it, the *Temple of Heaven*.

The *Altar of Heaven* (Fig. 9.38), constructed over the fifteenth and sixteenth centuries, is a large, tree-filled temple compound located in Beijing, south of the palace core. Surrounded by a four-mile wall, the compound is square at its southern end and semicircular at its northern end. To the Chinese, the round shape symbolized the heavens, while the square represented the earth.

The major structures and roadways of the complex are laid out on a north-south axis. Altars and temples face south, the source of temperate weather and abundance, while the north was the source of evil influences. Temple complexes were also carefully sited relative to the forces of wind and water (*fengshui* means "wind and water"), because wind disperses the breath of life and must be stopped by water. All structures are symmetrical and enclosed by walls, railings, terraces, or gates, expressing the Chinese values of seclusion and order.

Design of a Pagoda Temple

Three or four times a year, the emperor used the *Temple of Heaven* (Fig. 9.39), built in 1420 and restored in 1754, to officiate at religious-political ceremonies, mostly dedicated to the earth and crops. The temple is a lofty, three-tiered pagoda, a cone-shaped structure distinguished by its layers of eaves and gilded orb on top. Its shape is a geometrically simplified mountain form, like the Hindu temple. The entire structure is 125 feet high and nearly 100 feet across. The wide eaves provide shelter from bright sun and rain. The colors and patterns in this wooden building are brilliant. It has a gently curving, violet-blue tile roof, similar to the color of a dark blue sky. The outside walls are deep red, offset with bands of gleaming gold. The interior is red lacquer with foliage patterns in gold and blue and

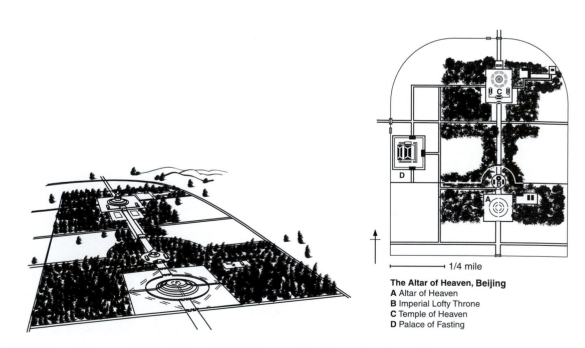

The Altar of Heaven, Beijing
A Altar of Heaven
B Imperial Lofty Throne
C Temple of Heaven
D Palace of Fasting

1/4 mile

9.38 *Altar of Heaven,* Beijing, China, 15th–16th centuries. Plan and artist rendering.

contains green and white beams. Twenty-eight tall posts on the interior entirely support the roof. There are no walls, only door-like partitions pierced with latticework. The four central posts represent the four seasons, while other columns represent months of the year and the division of day and night. In the center of the stone floor is a marble slab with a design incorporating the dragon and phoenix, symbols of the emperor and empress.

The *Temple of Heaven* sits atop three terraces surrounded by richly carved, lacelike, white marble balustrades. Worshippers circumnavigate the round structure at different levels to symbolize the achievement of wisdom. The temple's symmetry and order contrast strikingly with expanses of wooded areas.

THE ISLAMIC MOSQUE

The religion of Islam requires that its adherents pray five times a day while bowing toward Mecca, the birthplace of the prophet Mohammed. On Friday, men are required to attend collective prayer services in mosques, a word derived from the Arabic *masjid,* which means "prostration." The faithful ritually cleanse themselves and then assemble on beautifully patterned rugs facing Mecca for prayer, sermons, and readings from the Quran, or Koran, the Islamic book of sacred texts.

It is thought that the plan of Mohammed's house in Medina influenced the design of early mosques, which were simple courtyards with shaded areas. On the wall facing Mecca was the *mihrab,* a special marker niche. A stepped pulpit called the *minbar* was usually located next to the *mihrab.* The tall minarets could be seen from afar, giving hope to weary travelers. There are no icons, statues, or images in Islamic worship or in mosques.

Later Developments in Mosque Design

One of the most beautiful mosques ever constructed is located in ancient Persia, or present-day Iran. Shah Abbas I (the Great) sought to make Persia an important center and undertook an ambitious urban renewal

9.39 Round hall from the *Temple of Heaven*, Beijing, China, begun 1420, restored 1754. Wood with tile roof. © Liu Liqun/Corbis.

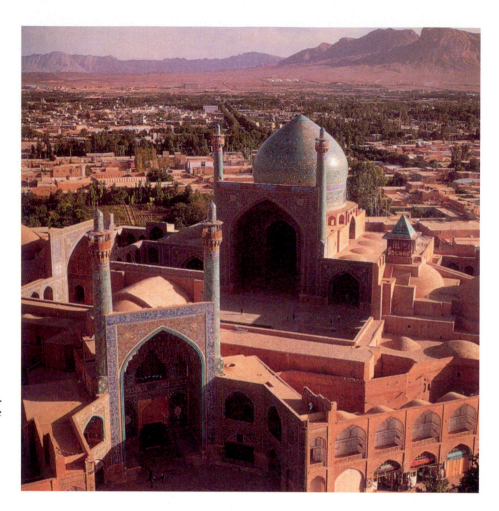

9.40 *Masjid-i-Shah*, or *Royal Mosque*, Isfahan, Iran, 1612–1637. The arch of the main portal, to the left in this picture, is 90' high; the minarets are 110' high. © Roger Wood/Corbis. See also Fig. 5.16 and accompanying text for more on the dome design.

program in the capital city, Isfahan. With the *Masjid-i-Shah*, or *Royal Mosque* (Fig. 9.40), dated 1612–1637, the individual parts of the mosque became elaborate and were given separate identity. The portals, for example, became separate, large structures distinguished by elaborate decoration and pattern to awe and draw in the viewer. The once-simple courtyard evolved into a two-story arcade covered with blue-patterned tiles, with four huge, porch-like portals, where schools of Islamic theology could be assembled. The covered prayer hall is physically and conceptually separate from the open courtyard. Worshippers move through a series of interlocking areas to leave the profane world and enter the sacred realm. The single minaret has multiplied to four.

Connection *Like temples and churches in other religions, different mosque designs were developed in various regions of the world. For example, see the Grand Mosque in Mali, Africa, Figure 1.22, page 20, and also the Badshahi Mosque in Pakistan, Figure 1.23, page 21.*

Pattern

Ornamentation in Persian mosques is profuse and serves several purposes: (1) it symbolizes Allah in its suggestion of infinity and creation; (2) it enhances the sacred character of the mosque; (3) it identifies and makes visually distinct the various parts of the mosque, so that portals, porches, windows, domes, and the mihrab are easily recognizable; and (4) the ornamentation disguises the mosque's mass, although not the form. The mosque walls seem to be merely thin screens of incredible color and delicate pattern, rather than thick, heavy, massive brick walls.

In mosques, patterns come from many sources. Windows are covered with decorative screens that break up the light into patterns as it reflects off the patterned tiles. Reflecting pools amplify or distort pattern, depending on the water movement. Text passages on mosque walls are a favored form of decoration. Calligraphic lettering was stylized to become very elegant and, in some instances, almost indistinguishable from geometric or foliage patterns. Tiles produce rich color and elaborate patterns. The panels on either side of the

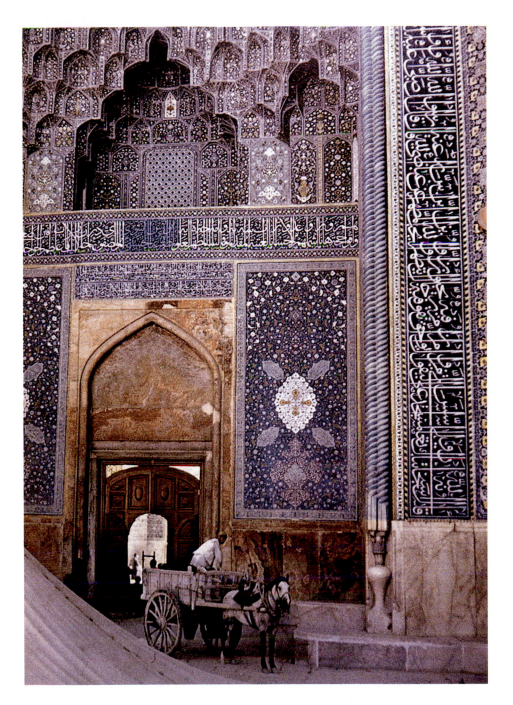

9.41 *Masjid-i-Shah*, or *Royal Mosque* (detail of the main portal), Isfahan, Iran, 1612–1637. Photo: Wim Swaan, Getty Research Library.

doorway in Figure 9.41 resemble Persian weavings and tapestries. In the Islamic world, weavings serve utilitarian functions in the home, palace, and mosque, but they are also high aesthetic achievements and signs of favor. As treasured portable objects, they recall the early nomadic Arabs and the founding of Islam. The *mukarnas (muqarnas)*, or vaults, in the upper left in Figure 9.41, are also pattern elements. The hanging quarter-domes break up the structure and disguise the mass of the building.

The entire complex is unified by the enormous, patterned turquoise dome that dominates the Isfahan skyline. The circular dome stands for the heavens and symbolizes the oneness of Allah.

Connections The Taj Mahal (Fig. 10.18, page 260), is an Islamic structure decorated with carved and inlaid stones.

Figure 5.16, page 109, is a diagram of the dome of the Masjid-i-Shah that shows its patterned mosaic decoration.

Religions developed as major civilizations flourished around the world. The Middle East was an area of great cultural growth, with many amazing works of art. Babylon was a center of religious worship, with tall ziggurats topped by temples, not unlike the earlier *Ziggurat at Ur* (Fig. 9.22). Between 1792 and 1750 BCE, Hammurabi recorded his Code of Law, covering the tax system, fair wages and prices, property rights for women, and criminal punishment (see illustration in this box). In 1350 BCE, the Assyrians conquered the Fertile Crescent, including Babylonia and, later, Egypt. They built extensive roads, developed a political system of provinces and governors, and established libraries of cuneiform tablets.

The Hebrew people went to Egypt in 1800 BCE because of drought in Canaan and were put in bondage. In 1250 BCE, Moses led the Exodus, and by 1000 BCE, they conquered the people of Canaan and established Jerusalem. Their religion was monotheistic and became the roots of Judaism, Christianity, and Islam.

On the island of Crete, the Minoan civilization flourished through seafaring and trade. The Minoans produced a number of fertility figures and goddesses, like the *Snake Goddess* (Fig. 9.1). Around 1200 to 800 BCE, another maritime culture, the Phoenicians, prospered in small city-states in present-day Lebanon, with colonies in Carthage and North Africa and an active trade economy. They are also known for their alphabet, based on sounds of the human voice.

The Persians lived east of the Crescent Valley from 550 to 330 BCE, with their capital at Persepolis. Their religion included the teachings of Zoroaster, which were written down in the book *Avesta*.

The Egyptians had three long-lived kingdoms. During the Old Kingdom, 2700–2200 BCE, the Great Pyramids and Sphinx were built. From 2100 to 1800 BCE, Egypt was ruled by invaders, but later recovered. In the New Kingdom, 1600–1100 BCE, remarkable temples were built that were similar in style to the later *Horus Temple at*

Map 3 The Assyrian and Persian Empires. Courtesy of Replogle Globes, Inc., Broadview, IL.

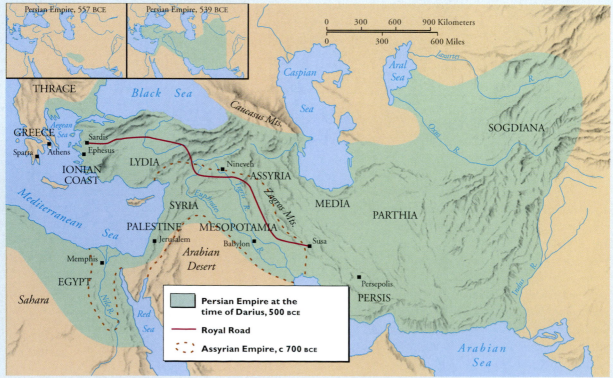

Edfu (Figs. 9.31 and 9.32). The Egyptian religion was polytheistic. The goddess Hathor was one of the deities worshipped. She was represented as a cow, as seen in Figure 9.2.

The Greek civilizations established city-states, the strongest being Athens and Sparta. The ancient Greeks are credited with developing the early forms of democracy. Around 500 BCE, the Golden Age of Greece began, producing great advances in philosophy, the arts, architecture, writing, crafts, medicine, mathematics, and Olympic sports. Art and architectural examples are the sculpture of *Zeus* (Fig. 9.3) and the *Parthenon* (Fig. 9.29). Between 750 and 500 BCE, the Etruscan people ruled what is now central Italy. In 500 BCE, the Romans overthrew them, drove them out, and established the Roman Republic.

In India around 1500 BCE, nomadic peoples formed a new culture that incorporated Hinduism and the Sanskrit language. Later, the sacred text of the *Rig-Veda* was written. In 563 BCE, Siddhartha Gautama was born. He would later become the Buddha, the Enlightened One, founding the religion of Buddhism (see *Seated Buddha*, Fig. 9.6). Begun in the third century BCE, the *Great Stupa* (Fig. 9.5) was built for Buddhist pilgrimages.

From 2000 to 1500 BCE, China was cultivating millet and wheat, using the potter's wheel (to produce black pottery), and domesticating animals. Later, the Shang Dynasty (1500–1122 BCE) was known for developing writing, cultivating silkworms, and producing white pottery, bronze works, and marble, jade, and ivory artworks. The people practiced ancestor worship. Between 1123 and 256 BCE, the Chinese invented the crossbow and perfected lacquer.

In Africa, the Kush people lived in the Sudan between 2000 and 350 BCE. In 732 BCE, they conquered Egypt and ruled for one hundred years. In 600 BCE, they were conquered by the Assyrians.

On the American continent, the Olmec civilization existed on the coast of the Gulf of Mexico between 1200 and 400 BCE. They built great temples, pyramids, colossal heads, and monuments. They also invented an accurate calendar and a counting system. In northern Peru, the Chavín culture existed from

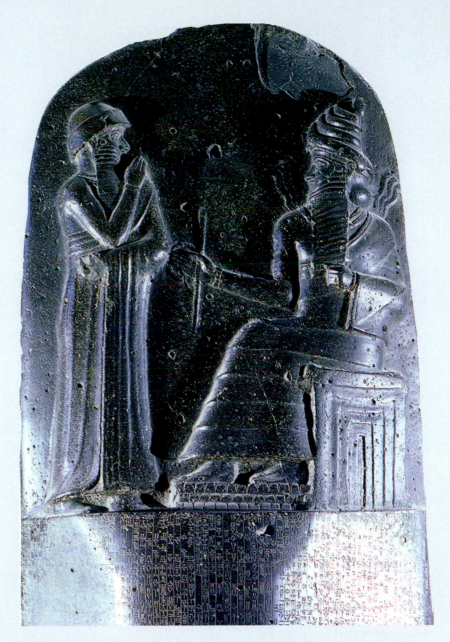

9.42 *Hammurabi Stele*, from Susa (modern Shush, Iran), 1792–1750 BCE. Relief, 28" high. Detail showing the king standing before the sun god and god of justice Shamash, who commanded Hammurabi to record the law. © Réunion des Musées Nationaux/Art Resource, NY.

1000 to 200 BCE. They built temples with stone carvings and produced fine pottery and gold work. Mound builders, farmers, and potters lived in central North America.

Around 2000 BCE, Europe was still in the New Stone Age, with megalithic structures built over a widespread area. Religious rituals were mixed with astronomy and agriculture, as at *Stonehenge* (Fig. 9.24).

History	Date	Art
Old Kingdom—Egypt	2700 BCE	
Middle Kingdom—Egypt	2100	
		Ziggurat at Ur
Babylon	2000	Stonehenge
Early Greek Civilizations		
Neolithic Europe		
Hebrew Culture	1800	
Hammurabi's Code		
Minoan Civilization	1700	
New Kingdom—Egypt	1600	Snake Goddess
Indian Civilization, Hinduism, and Sanskrit / Shang Dynasty—China		
	1400	
	1300	
Assyrians Conquer the Fertile Crescent		
Phoenician Civilization	1200	
Olmec Culture in Mexico		
Chavin Civilization—Peru	1000	
Etruscan Civilization		
	700	
	600	The Goddess Hathor and the Overseer of Sealers, Psamtik
Birth of Buddha		
Roman Republic	500	
Golden Age of Greece		
Persian Empire		
		Zeus (or Poseidon)
		Parthenon
		Great Stupa / Horus Temple
	400	
Roman Empire	100	

History	Date	Art
Birth of Jesus	4	
		Synagogue at Dura-Europos
		Pantheon
	200 CE	Pyramid of the Sun
		Tlalocan Painting
		Ark of the Covenant mosaic
	600	Seated Buddha
Founding of Islam		Main Shrine at Ise
	700	
Crusades: Wars between Christians and Muslims for the Holy Land		Kandarya Mahadeva Temple / Shield Jaguar and Lady Xoc
	1000	Shiva as Nataraja, or Lord of the Dance / Xilonen, Goddess of Young Corn
	1100	The Water and Moon Guanyin Bodhisattva
Gothic Era—Europe		Chartres Cathedral
	1200	
Mali Empire—Africa	1300	
Aztecs Build Tenochtitlan		
	1400	Ghiberti: Sacrifice of Abraham
	1500	Raphael: Madonna of the Meadow / Grünewald: Isenheim Altarpiece / Michelangelo: Ceiling of the Sistine Chapel / Mandala of Samvara / Altar of Heaven
	1600	Masjid-i-Shah, or Royal Mosque
Height of the Asante Empire—Africa		
	1800	
	1900	Power Figure
		Kewanwytewa: Ahola Kachina / Le Corbusier: Notre Dame du Haut / Retablo of Maria de la Luz Casillas and Children / Offering with Cili-Shaped Crown / Transformation Mask
	2000	

In creating images of gods, goddesses, and other holy beings, artists use (1) geometric symbols, especially circles, squares, and triangles; (2) symbols taken from the natural world; (3) animal forms, which may be gods or symbolize gods; and (4) the human body, usually idealized. Religions that worship many gods often assign particular spheres of influence to various deities.

Art is part of the process of communication between humans and God, either as thanksgiving, an act of sacrifice, an offering, or a prayer in a ritual.

Many cultures believe that geometry can be symbolic in architecture and make a site sacred. Most sacred architecture is extraordinary in some way, in location, size, elaborate forms, decoration, or other aspects. It often incorporates elements of nature or the concept of a journey or both.

The materials used in construction and decoration are meaningful. Stone may communicate the idea of eternity or the majesty of mountains, while unadorned natural wood may echo animistic beliefs. Brilliant color, luminosity, or pattern helps relate the idea of transcendence. Very large religious structures are usually spectacular in materials and in scale. They are often expressions of both religious and secular power.

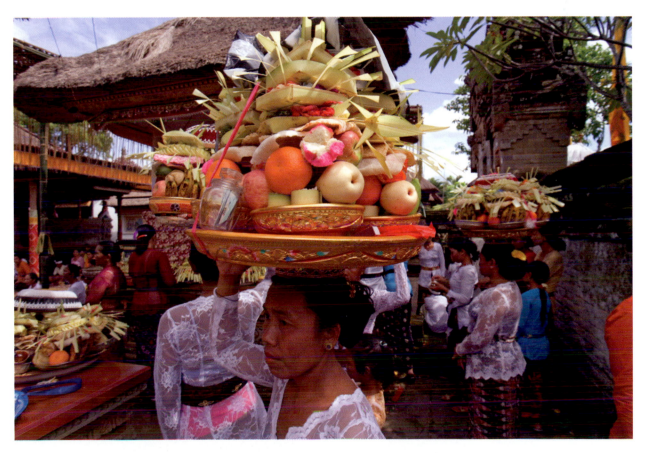

9.43 *Woman Carrying Offerings for the Odalan Festival*, Sukawati Temple, Bali, Indonesia. The offerings are similar to Fig. 9.13, *Offering with Cili Shaped Crown*.

FOOD FOR THOUGHT

Try to visit an important religious site during a ceremony, when people are using it in prayer or preparing for worship. See Figure 9.43. It becomes alive, and other senses are invoked in rituals and processions: the sound of music and singing; the movement of bodies; the smell of incense, sacred oils, candles, and sacrificial fire, and so on.

Think about the many paradoxes and contradictions embedded in the human attempt to give image to the divine. For example, the visible is a vehicle to grasp the invisible. Diagrams of incredible complexity are paths for understanding Oneness. States of powerlessness can be required to come in touch with supernatural power. The material world can be both a divine manifestation and the total opposite of it.

- *Can you think of art examples where contradictions are purposely used to point to the extraordinary in worship?*

- *Why is it that human beings have often attempted to create images of divine or spiritual beings, only later in some cases to have them banned or destroyed?*

- *Do you think that the artists who created images of spiritual beings were divinely inspired?*

- *Could there be worship of a deity without the aid of the arts and architecture?*

- *How has art or architecture been a part of your own religious experience?*

Your Thomson Online Resources

 Go to **ArtExperience Online** for the Flashcards, Quiz, and Study Guide for this chapter.

CHAPTER 10

Mortality and Immortality

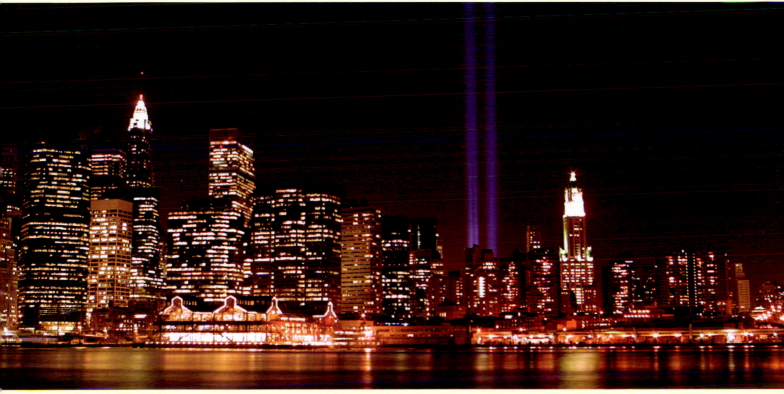

© Gianni Dagli Orti/Corbis

INTRODUCTION

This chapter explores funerary and commemorative art, especially to answer the following questions:

- *What does it mean if a tomb is enormous, lavishly furnished, or both?*
- *By studying a tomb, can you tell what the people thought about the afterlife?*
- *How much do rituals and religions affect tomb design?*
- *How have burial practices evolved over the centuries?*
- *What is the difference between commemorative art and tombs?*
- *What does all this mean for the living?*
- *How are tombs and memorials used for political and social purposes?*
- *Is funerary art different in big cities than in more open environments?*

EARLY TOMBS: MOUNDS AND MOUNTAINS

The very earliest tombs in many cultures were artificial mounds. The Egyptians built pyramids, which were geometric mountains. Others built funeral mounds that look like naturally occurring grass-covered hills, with hidden burial chambers. Some were lavishly furnished. They were often oriented with natural phenomena, such as the movement of the sun. Mound graves can be found in Europe, Asia, the Middle East, and the Americas.

ANCIENT BURIALS

Funerary practices, religion, agriculture, and astronomy were often interrelated among early peoples. In Ireland, the late Stone Age tomb at *Newgrange* (Fig. 10.1), from 3200 BCE, is part of a complex of tombs and monolithic rock structures. It contains 220,000 tons of loose stone with a white quartz–rock facing on one side. Inside, a long passageway leads to a cross-shaped interior chamber with five burials. The passageway has forty-ton stones, some decorated with spirals or geometric patterns, perhaps indicating stars or planets. It is sealed to prevent water seepage. *Newgrange* is oriented so that for about two weeks around the winter solstice, a burst of brilliant morning sunlight radiates down the entire passage, illuminating one patterned stone in the burial chamber. Over time, like other mounds, *Newgrange* eroded and blended into the natural landscape. After the fourth century, *Newgrange* was an abandoned and undisturbed site until 1699, when it was rediscovered by men quarrying for building stone.

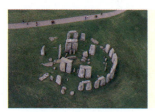

Connection Stonehenge (Fig. 9.24, page 221) is an example of a monolithic rock structure, dating from the same era as New-grange.

Like *Newgrange*, the *Great Pyramids* of Egypt are very old, very large, and oriented to the sun. They are

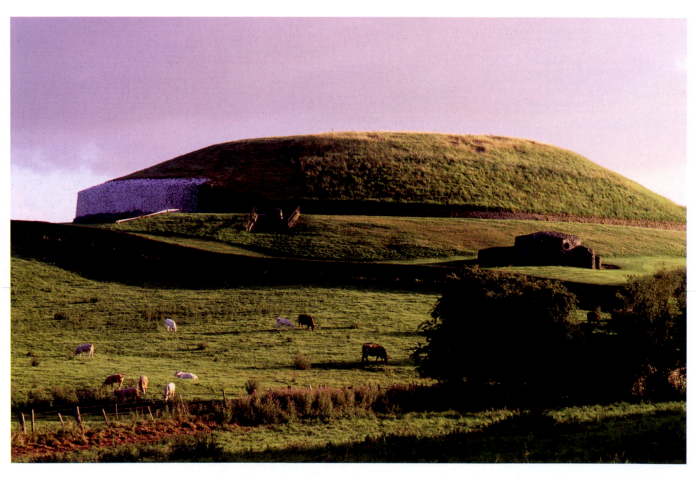

10.1 *Newgrange,* County Meath, Ireland, 3200 BCE. Neolithic.

the tombs of the pharaohs, believed to be descendants of the most powerful god, Re, the Sun God. These artificial mountains on an artificial plain stand dramatically on the edge of the Sahara. They are part of a **necropolis** of tombs and mortuary temples that extends for fifty miles on the Nile's west bank. The largest pyramids were built for pharaohs *Menkaure,* c. 2525–2475 BCE, *Khafre,* c. 2575–2525 BCE, and *Khufu,* c. 2600–2550 BCE (Fig. 10.2). The numbers associated with the very largest, the pyramid of *Khufu,* are often recited, but still inspire awe: 775 feet along one side of the base; 450 feet high; 2.3 million stone blocks; average weight of each block, 2.5 tons. Disassembled and buried in a trench at the base of the pyramid of Khufu were two long, sleek wooden boats, used to navigate the Nile during the pharaoh's lifetime; in death, they were used to bring the pharaoh's body and possessions to the city of the dead on the Nile's west bank.

For the Egyptians, the pyramid created the meeting place between earthly life and eternity. The *Great Pyramids* have interior chambers that are quite small and, when opened in modern times, contained only empty stone crypts. The tombs may have contained provisions, but were robbed shortly after they were sealed. In an effort to thwart grave robbing, which was rampant in ancient Egypt, later pharaohs stopped building enormous, expensive, ostentatious tombs like the pyramids. Instead, the rulers were buried in less-costly chambers cut deep into the sides of mountains, with hidden entrances (see *Tutankhamen,* Fig. 10.3).

FURNISHED TOMBS

Many cultures believed that the afterlife was similar to this life and that the dead continued to "live" in the tomb, using furnishings such as furniture, clothing, utensils, and precious items. Such tombs were usually for the wealthy and powerful.

Egyptian Tombs and Mortuary Temples

The ancient Egyptians provide the supreme examples of furnished tombs. According to Egyptian belief, a human

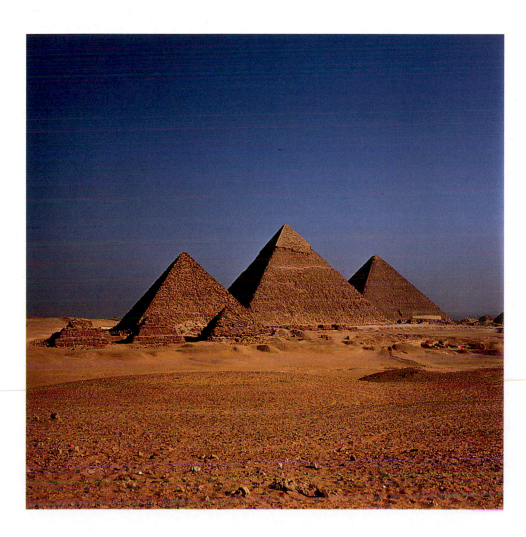

10.2 *Great Pyramids,* Gizeh, Egypt. From left, *Menkaure,* c. 2525–2475 BCE; *Khafre,* c. 2575–2525 BCE; *Khufu,* c. 2600–2550 BCE. © E. Strouhal/Werner Forman/Art Resource, NY.

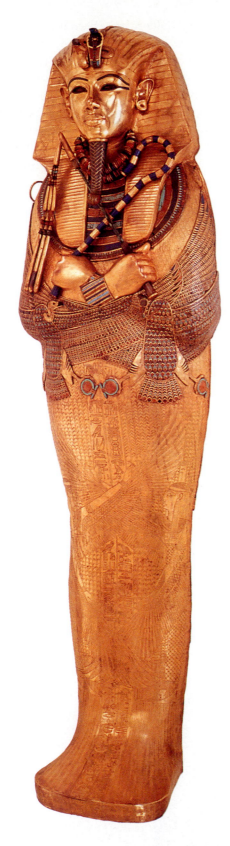

possessed a soul with both a **ba** and a **ka.** The ba was seated in the heart or abdomen and was depicted as a human-headed bird. The ba flies from the body at death, but returns hungry and thirsty seventy days later when mummification is completed. A well-prepared tomb sustains the ba in the afterlife with provisions like water, wine, grains, dates, cakes, and even dehydrated beef and fowl. The ka is the mental aspect of the human's soul, symbolized by two outstretched arms or by an attendant figure that represents the double of the personality. The ka dwells in a lifelike statue of the deceased, which is placed in the tomb. Provisions for the ka would include chairs, beds, chariots, models of servants, kitchen utensils, dishes, and simulated food (unlike the real food the ba required). Combs, hairpins, and ointments were also included, along with games for entertainment. Elaborate tombs have treasures of gold and silver as well as carriages and boats for the ka's journey to heaven. Both the statue and the sarcophagus had a strong likeness of the dead person, so that the ba and ka could easily recognize their destinations. The ba and the ka were thought to enter the tombs through a small chimney or an air vent.

Despite later pharaohs' efforts to hide their tombs, almost all were robbed long ago, except that of King Tutankhamen, which was only partly plundered. Ironically, grave robbers who were stealing treasures from a nearby tomb happened to heap piles of debris on Tutankhamen's tomb entrance, so it remained undisturbed until 1922. Among the amazing treasures found in Tutankhamen's tomb was his *Innermost Coffin,* dated c. 1325 BCE, in Figure 10.3. It is beaten gold, weighing nearly three-quarters of a ton, and is inlaid with semiprecious stones. Two other larger coffin cases of gold fit over it, and together they encased the mummy. To preserve bodies and make them recognizable, they were mummified with natron, a mineral mixture found in the desert. Portraits also were placed in the tomb as substitute spirit receptacles should something happen to the mummy. Pharaohs had several stone statues or effigies in gold, like the *Innermost Coffin.* The wings of the god Horus protectively encircle the coffin, and Tutankhamen holds insignia of his rank. Certain features are standard on Tutankhamen's face: the distinctive eye makeup; the false beard, a symbol of power; the striped head-cloth; the cobra head to frighten enemies. Nevertheless, it is indeed a portrait of Tutankhamen.

The tomb also contained inlaid chests, gilt chairs, and other wooden items covered with gold; carved watchdogs; life-size guardian statues; jewels; and so on.

10.3 *Innermost Coffin of Tutankhamen,* Thebes, Egypt, c. 1325 BCE. Gold inlaid with enamel and semiprecious stones, 6'1" long. Egyptian Museum, Cairo. © Boltin Picture Library.

To provide for the comfort of those of high rank, clay statues of servants were included in the tombs. Because Tutankhamen died unexpectedly before the age of twenty, there was little time to prepare his tomb, as mummification, funerary rites, and burial had to be completed in seventy days. Archeologists believe that his tomb was surely less lavishly furnished than those of pharaohs with long reigns. It is small and its walls were painted, while other rulers' tombs were large, barrel-vaulted chambers with relief carvings.

In tombs, wall paintings and carvings re-created the pleasures and labors of earthly existence. The *Fowling Scene*, a wall painting from the tomb of Nebamun, c. 1400–1350 BCE (Fig. 10.4), shows an Egyptian noble hunting in the marshes along the Nile River. The air is filled with birds painted with care and distinction, and the water is thick with fish. Pattern is important, as seen in the water ripples and the repeated image of birds in the nobleman's hand. The marsh grasses fan out in a beautiful but rigid decoration. Depth is rarely shown in ancient Egyptian paintings, so everything is distributed vertically or horizontally. Pattern elements are visual metaphors for the seasonal cycles of the Nile, the unchanging culture, and the vast desert that surrounds the river valley.

In this wall painting, humans dominate the scene. The noble is shown in the formal manner reserved for exalted persons: head, shoulders, legs, and feet in profile; eyes and shoulders frontal. Size was an important indicator of rank, so the nobleman is larger than his wife and daughter, indicating their lower status.

When high-ranking Egyptians began to hide tombs in hillsides, the funerary temples that formerly were appendages to pyramids were enlarged and emphasized. The *Mortuary Temple of Hatshepsut*, c. 1490–1460 BCE (Fig. 10.5), of the Eighteenth Dynasty, shows this later development. The temple was the monument to her greatness. It once housed two hundred statues of her and many brightly painted reliefs showing her divine birth, coronation, military victories, and other exploits.

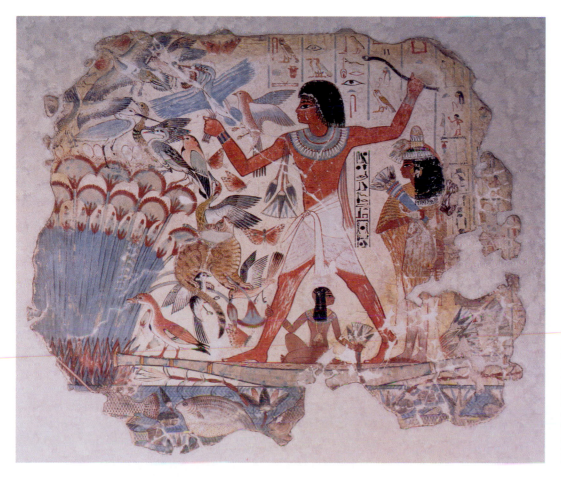

10.4 *Fowling Scene,* Thebes, Egypt, c. 1400–1350 BCE. Paint on dry plaster, approx. 32" high. Wall painting from the tomb of Nebamun. The British Museum, London. Photo © British Museum.

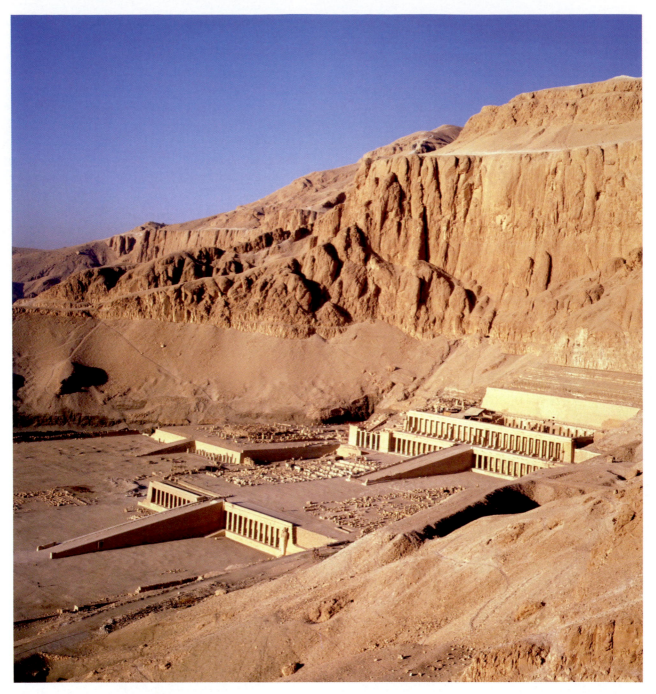

10.5 *Mortuary Temple of Hatshepsut*, Deir el-Bahri, Egypt, c. 1490–1460 BCE. © Dallas and John Heaton/Corbis.

The *Temple* was pillaged and vandalized shortly after her death by her successor, Pharaoh Thutmose III, who was angered that her two-decade rule had delayed his rise to power.

This large temple has an open, light design, without the mass and weightiness of the earlier pyramids. The simple vertical columns echo the cliff's rock formations. A quarter-mile-long forecourt contained a garden with a pool and papyrus and with rows of frankincense trees. The garden was a pleasure in Egyptian life and, thus, was prominent in their afterlife imagery. An inscription from another tomb says: "May I wander around my pool each day for evermore; may my soul sit on the branches of the grave garden I have prepared for myself; may I refresh myself each day under my sycamore."

Etruscan Tombs

The Etruscans were another ancient people whose wealthy members were buried in earthen mounds furnished for the afterlife. Etruria comprised the city-states in what is now central Italy and is discussed more in *Art and History in Context* on page 282. Around the city of Cerveteri are row after row of earthen mounds arranged along "streets" in a necropolis. The Etruscan tombs often had several rooms laid out like modest houses, emphasizing sociability and life's pleasures. These tomb chambers were carved directly out of the soft bedrock called **tufa**. Chairs, beds, or utensils were sometimes carved in relief on the underground rock surfaces.

The freestanding terra-cotta sculpture *Sarcophagus with Reclining Couple,* c. 520 BCE (Fig. 10.6), comes from a tomb in Cerveteri. The clay sarcophagus, with life-size figures, was molded in four pieces. The wife and husband are the same size, reclining together at a banquet, indicating that Etruscan women had more rights than women in most other cultures. The facial features are similar and standardized on both figures, and their hair is represented as a geometric pattern. Their bodies are somewhat flattened and unformed from the waist down. Still, the wife and husband seem lively and vigorous. Their gestures are animated.

In tombs carved into cliffs near the Etruscan city of Tarquinia, the walls were often covered with paintings emphasizing pleasure. One example is *Banqueters and*

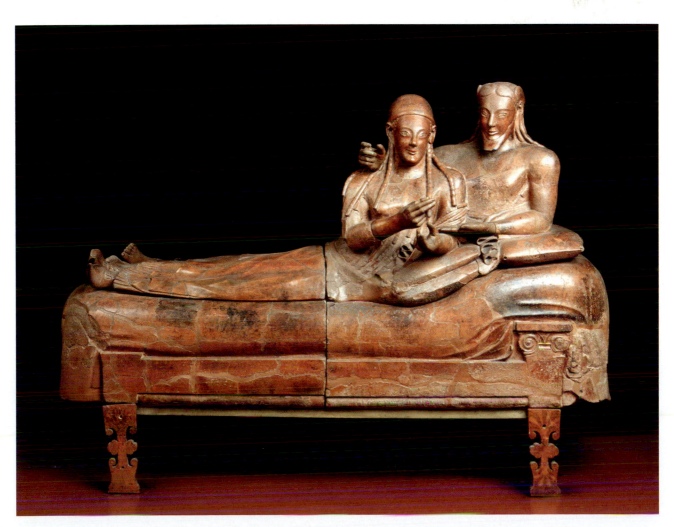

10.6   *Sarcophagus with Reclining Couple,* Etruria (Italy), c. 520 BCE. Painted terra-cotta, 45½" tall. From a cemetery near Cerveteri. Museo Nationale di Villa Giulia, Rome. © Araldo de Luca / Corbis.

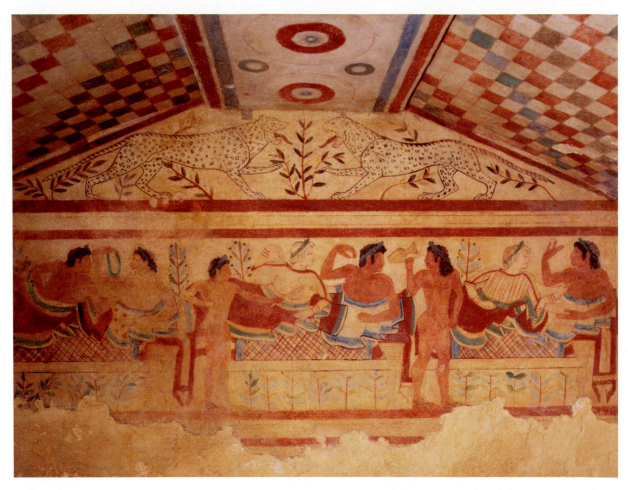

10.7 *Banqueters and Musicians,* Etruria (Italy), c. 480–470 BCE. Mural painting from the Tomb of the Leopards in a cemetery near Tarquinia. Hirmer Fotoarchiv.

Musicians, from the Tomb of the Leopards, c. 480–470 BCE (Fig. 10.7), so named for the leopards near the ceiling. To the left, banqueters recline on couches while servants bring them food and drink. The women are shown with light skin and men with dark, according to conventions of representation at that time. The third figure from the right is a man holding an egg, a symbol of rebirth. To the right, musicians dance across the wall. Oversized hands make lively gestures. Golds, reds, and greens predominate, with ceiling patterns adding to the colorfulness.

Funeral Complex of Shi Huangdi

One of the most extensive tombs ever constructed was that of Ying Cheng, who at age thirteen became the ruler of the Qin state in 259 BCE. By 221 BCE, he had subdued the rival neighboring states to unify China and found the Qin Dynasty. A brutal ruler, he assumed the title *Shi Huangdi,* the "First Emperor." Shi Huangdi accumulated amazing power, ruthlessly homogenizing Chinese culture and eradicating all opposition to his rule (see *Art and History in Context,* page 283). Shi Huangdi built for himself a large, lavish underground funeral palace. In 1974, peasants digging a well uncovered pieces of a huge, buried army of 6,000 life-size clay soldiers guarding the afterlife palace complex. Since then, archeologists have concentrated on excavating and restoring the terra-cotta army only; the tomb is mostly untouched.

The *Soldiers from Pit 1* (Fig. 10.8), from 221–206 BCE, are arranged in eleven columns, with four soldiers abreast in nine of the columns. Only a small percentage of the life-size sculptures are visible! The torsos are hollow, while the solid legs provide a weighty bottom for support and balance. The bodies are standardized: frontal, stiff, and anatomically simplified. Certain features, such as hands, were mass-produced in molds. However, every face is different and sculpted with great

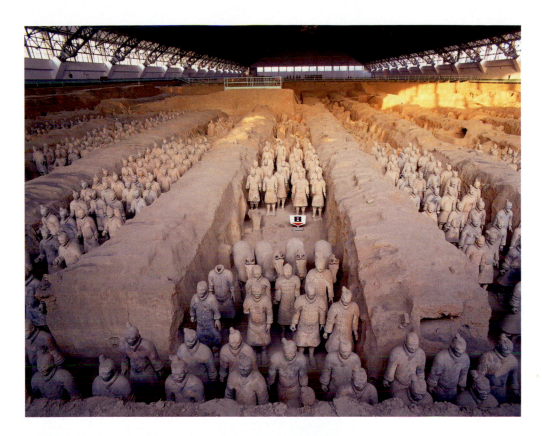

10.8 *Soldiers from Pit 1*, Shaanxi, China, 221–206 BCE. Painted ceramic; average figure height, 5'9". Near the tomb of Shi Huangdi.

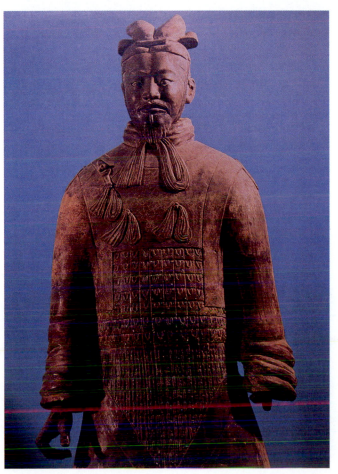

skill and sensitivity, like the *Infantry General* (Fig. 10.9). He is presumed to be the supreme commander because he wears more armor than any other soldier and is five inches taller than the rest. The hair is shown with detailed individualized knotting and braiding, typical of Chinese infantry of the time.

The clay soldiers were outfitted with bronze spears, swords, crossbows, or all three and were originally painted in vivid colors. The army stood on brick "streets" that were fifteen to twenty feet below ground level. Separating the columns were rows of pounded earth that supported wood beams that once covered the entire pit. Fiber mats and plaster were placed over the beams to seal the pits and prevent water seepage. All were hidden under a low, flat mound of dirt.

Royal Tombs of the Moche Civilization

From 150 to 800 CE, the Moche civilization extended for more than four hundred miles along the Pacific Ocean in modern Peru (see *Art and History in Context*, page 268). Moche society was stratified from rich to poor, which is reflected in their burials, ranging from

10.9 *Infantry General*, Shaanxi, China, 221–206 BCE. Painted ceramic, 6'4" tall. From the tomb of Shi Huangdi. Cultural Relics Publishing House, Beijing.

simple shallow pits to elaborate burial chambers on pyramids. Warrior-priests apparently ruled the Moche civilization, judging by their richly furnished graves. The primary reason for warfare in Moche society was to capture prisoners for sacrificial ceremonies. A class of skilled artisans worked full time to create gold and silver metalwork for elite burials, as well as pottery for all classes.

Just recently discovered in the late 1980s, the *Royal Tomb of Sipán* from c. 300 contained several sets of warrior-priest ceremonial gear, including many layers of jewelry, breastplates, weapons, and ornamental feathers. The mannequin in Figure 10.10 is dressed in a small portion of the objects found in the tomb. He is wearing a cloth covered with gilded platelets, shell beads over his wrists and shoulders, and a truly striking helmet on his head. A nose plate is suspended from a hole in the nasal septum. This one is plain gold; others are elaborately decorated. From his waist hang crescent-shaped bells that would have jangled with every step. Figure 10.11 shows the magnificent *Peanut Necklace*, with ten gold and ten silver "beads." The peanut may have been a ceremonial food or a food of honor. The Moche used gold and silver symmetrically, as in the necklace. An identical pair of weapons was found in one tomb, one in gold and one in silver. In another tomb, a gold ingot was found in the deceased's right hand and a silver one in the left. Some nose plates are symmetrically half gold and half silver.

Viking Ship Burial

The Vikings were maritime raiders from Scandinavia with settlements in Iceland, England, northern France,

and Russia in the ninth and tenth centuries. Their tombs reflect how important sea travel was to their civilization. The Oseberg ship burial, located under a mound approximately 20 feet high and 130 feet long and excavated in 1904 near Oslo, Norway, was the tomb of a high-ranking Viking woman. The ninth-century tomb had been robbed centuries ago, but large wooden items were left behind. The *Viking Ship*

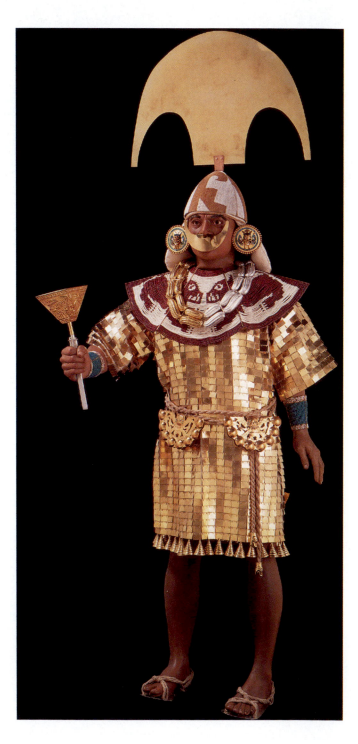

10.10 Mannequin dressed in replicas of some of the objects found in tomb 1, Moche Civilization, Peru, c. 300. The Fowler Museum of Cultural Heritage, University of California at Los Angeles.

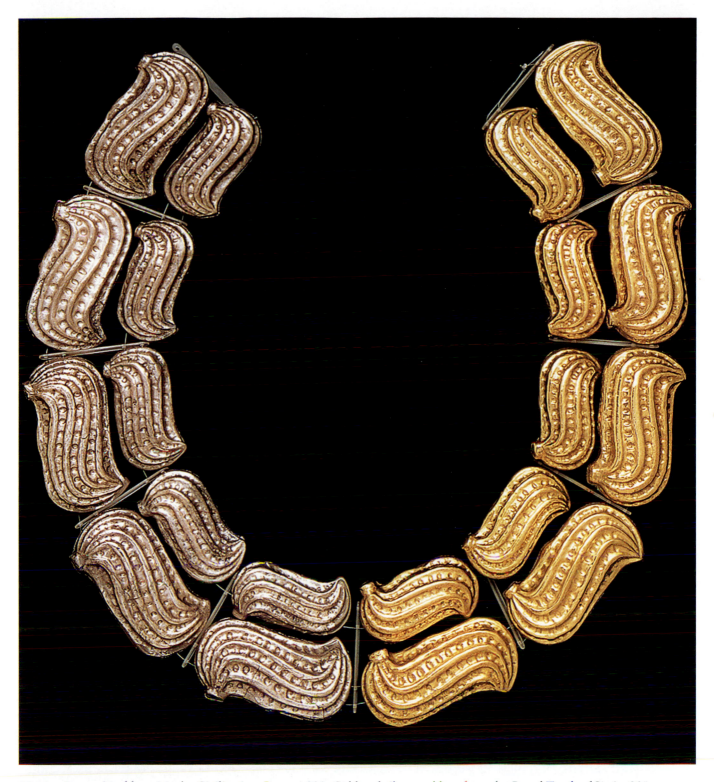

10.11 *Peanut Necklace,* Moche Civilization, Peru, c. 300. Gold and silver necklace from the *Royal Tomb of Sipán,* 20" diameter. Museo Archeológico Nacional Bruning de Lambayeque, Peru. Photo courtesy Fowler Museum, University of California at Los Angeles.

(Fig. 10.12) was probably the private vessel of a wealthy family, intended for use near the coast and on inland waterways. It had a mast and sail plus rowlocks for thirty oarsmen. The graceful curves of the low, wide ship culminate in tall spiral posts at stem and stern; the one at the front is carved like a coiled snake. Rising

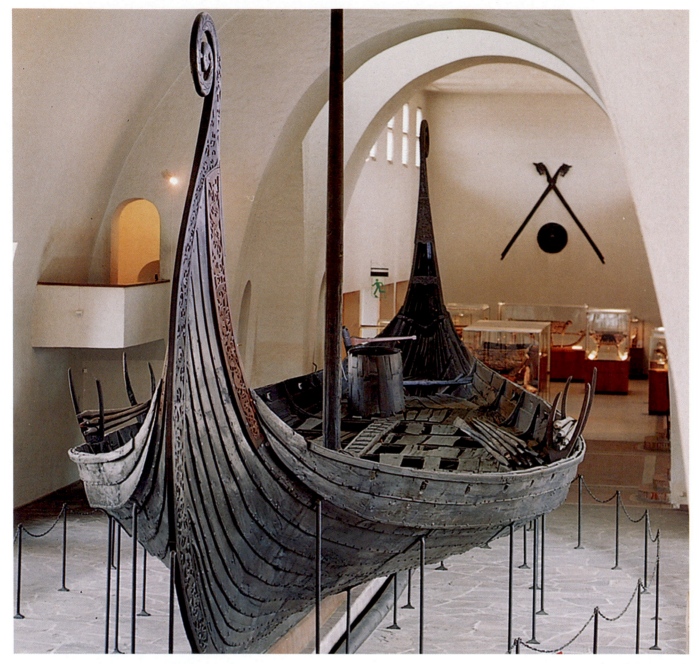

10.12　*Viking Ship*, Norway, early 9th century. Oak, 65' long. From the Oseberg ship burial, Viking Ship Museum, Oslo. Photo University Museum of National Antiquities, Oslo, Norway.

up each post are relief carvings of elongated animal forms interlocked in complex, lace-like patterns. In these intricate carvings, each animal is composed of layered networks of crisscross lines. Other wooden objects were found in the burial, including beds, carts, and sledges, with carvings of imaginary birds or totally unidentifiable beasts. All convey a feeling of wild agitation, firmly contained within the margins of the carving.

DEVELOPMENT OF CEMETERIES AND GRAVE MONUMENTS

During the first millennium BCE, mound tombs were gradually replaced by other funerary art and architecture. Tombs became commemorative structures instead of furnished homes for the afterlife.

The ancient Greeks developed the earliest commemorative funerary architecture in Europe and the Middle East. Although large, magnificent mausoleums were the privilege of the wealthy, cemeteries near Greek (and, later, Roman) cities were laid out for the burial of the merchant and working classes. As populations in cities grew, cemeteries with small plots marked by upright monuments became practical. In ancient Greece, the most common monuments were (1) small columns that supported vases, urns, or small statues; (2) life-size freestanding figures of young men or women; or (3) relief carvings on stone slabs, like the *Grave Stele of Hegeso,* c. 410–400 BCE (Fig. 10.13). Hegeso is the seated woman, whose servant has brought her jewelry. Quiet, everyday moments were often depicted on Greek grave markers. A simple architectural frame encloses the scene. Its straight edges contrast with the curve of the chair and complex drapery

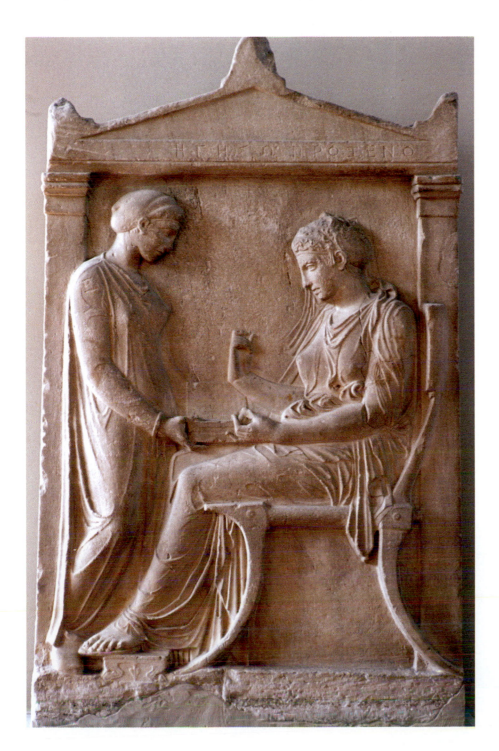

10.13 *Grave Stele of Hegeso,* Athens, Greece, c. 410–400 BCE. Marble relief, 5'2" high. From the Dipylon cemetery. National Archeological Museum, Athens. © Saskia.

folds. The bodies are rounded and naturalistic, but they also are idealized in their proportions and in their serenity and composure. Grave markers such as this were once colorfully painted. *Hegeso's* combination of idealism and naturalism echoes the Greeks' emphasis on humanism, as seen in *Art and History in Context* (page 282).

In ancient Rome, the dead were buried outside the city walls, along roadways entering the city, in highly visible funerary monuments to preserve an individual's fame, family honor, and standing in society. The tomb was the meeting place for the living and the departed, and families would hold feasts at the tomb, putting out food and drink for the dead to enjoy.

Roman family tombs and mausoleums were built in several styles: altar-tombs, towers, modified Greek temples, diminutive Egyptian pyramids, or combinations of these. Almost all featured inscriptions and relief carvings that announced the fame of the individual or family interred there. Tombs of the wealthy had lavish sculpture in dignified, idealized Greek styles. In contrast, the *Funerary Relief of a Circus Official,* dated 110–130 CE (Fig. 10.14), was produced for a working-class person's tomb and is very cramped in style, is full of details, and has numerous characters. The largest figure is the official himself, holding hands with his wife at the far left. In Roman art, the handshake symbolized marriage. The wife is smaller, as she is of lesser status, and stands on a pedestal as a sign that she died before him. The faces of the official and his wife are frank, unflattering portraits. The Romans often produced non-idealized likenesses—in this case, with forehead wrinkles, protruding ears, and a drooping nose and mouth. The official and his wife are crowded to the side to give space for the Circus Maximus. Only one team of horses is shown, but their leaping stance communicates the speed and competitiveness of all the chariot races. The race-course is tilted up and shrunken down behind the chariot, while the charioteer is shown twice, once driving the team and again holding a palm branch of victory. The deceased may be officiating the race, or he may be the charioteer himself, shown in his younger days.

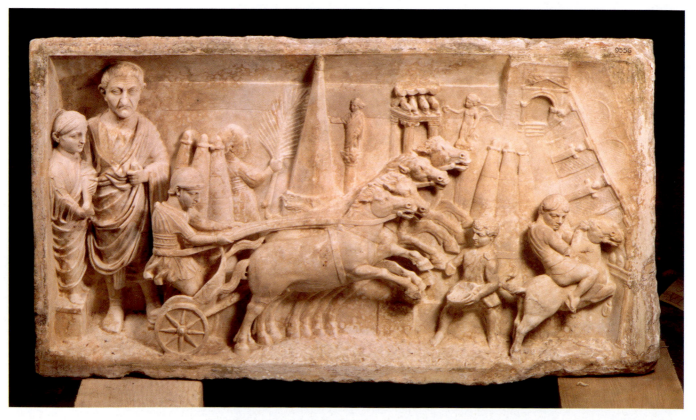

10.14   *Funerary Relief of a Circus Official,* Ostia, 110–130. Marble relief, approx. 20" high. Vatican Museum, Rome. © Scala/Art Resource, NY.

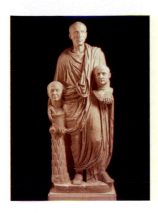

Connection *Realistic portraiture was important because respected ancestors raised the status of the living Romans, as discussed in Art and History in Context, page 268. For an example of nonidealized Roman portraiture, see Statue of Togato Barberini (Fig. 14.12).*

BURIAL IN PLACES OF WORSHIP

In some cultures, a preference arose for being buried in holy sites. This practice could be either a sign of religious devotion or the desire for prestige. The most sanctified places for burial were reserved for those with the greatest wealth, power, or religious standing.

CHRISTIAN BURIALS

Early Christians buried their dead rather than cremating them because they believed the body would be resurrected and rejoin the soul at the end of time. Around Rome, vast underground networks called *catacombs* were dug out of the same tufa as the Etruscan burial chambers. They were used from the second through the fourth centuries, and some were five levels deep. From floor to ceiling, passageways were lined with openings for bodies, which were sealed after burial and decorated with painted plaster or carvings (an unsealed opening is visible in Fig. 10.15). The catacombs became sanctified places during times of persecution from 249–251 and 303–306: martyrs were buried there, fugitives hid from the Romans, and, occasionally, worship services were conducted. Christians refused to recognize the divinity of the emperor or pay token tribute to Roman gods; therefore, the Romans considered them destabilizing to civil order.

Periodically in the catacomb passageways, small rooms were carved out to be used as mortuary chapels. They were often plastered and painted, like the ceiling in the fourth-century mortuary chapel (Fig. 10.15) from the *Catacomb of Sts. Peter and Marcellinus*, in Rome. The style and imagery are very similar to Roman secular painting in which pastoral scenes were common. But here, lambs take on the symbolic meaning of the Christian "flock" of followers protected by

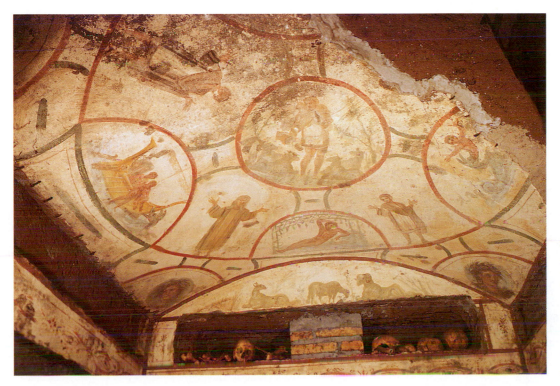

10.15 *Catacomb of Sts. Peter and Marcellinus*, Rome, early 4th century. Ceiling painting from a cubiculum. Fresco. The center circle shows Jesus as the Good Shepherd; surrounding half-circles show scenes from the biblical story of Jonah and the Whale. © Madeline Grimoldi.

Jesus, the Good Shepherd, who is shown in the central circle of the ceiling painting. Decorative motifs of birds, foliage, little angels, and images of the seasons also come from Roman secular painting. The background was usually white, for better visibility in the dark tunnels, with red and green lines dividing scenes. Lively and energetic figures, rendered in quick brushstrokes, occupy the shallow space.

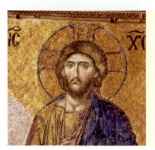

Connection *Later Christian art became much more formalized, rigid in design and awe-inspiring in size, as seen in the detail of the* Deesis Mosaic *from Hagia Sophia in Istanbul (Fig. 2.15).*

Eventually, Christianity became accepted and legalized in 313, and, under the emperor Constantine, it became the official religion of Rome (see *Art and History in Context,* page 283). During his lifetime, Constantine funded the construction of lavish churches over the tombs of famous martyrs, one of which was Old St. Peter's in Rome. St. Peter's tomb lay in the ground, but was marked by six twisting marble columns and four brass candelabra, each ten feet tall and finished in silver.

By the sixteenth century, Old St. Peter's, a deteriorating timber church, was no longer a fitting symbol for the expanded Catholic Church, and so a newer, grander St. Peter's was constructed in stone. The saint's tomb continued to be the focal point of the new church, marked by a new canopy in bronze, called a Baldacchino (Fig. 10.16), designed by Gianlorenzo Bernini between 1624 and 1633. This grand, lavish structure, taller than an eight-story building, recalls the cloth canopies that originally covered tombs of early martyrs, and its curving columns recall those

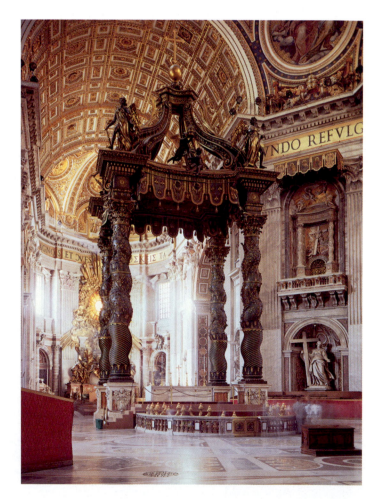

10.16 GIANLORENZO BERNINI. *Baldacchino,* St. Peter's, Rome, Italy, 1624–1633. Gilded bronze, 100' high. © Scala/Art Resource, NY.

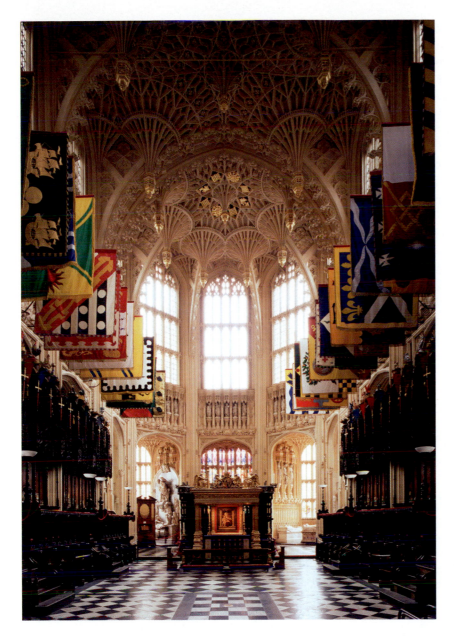

10.17 *Chapel of Henry VII,* Westminster Abbey, London, England, 1503–1519. Interior, toward east. © Corbis.

that Constantine placed in Old St. Peter's. The vine-covered, twisting columns seem to leap up and support the canopy as if it were weightless, instead of tons of bronze (which was stripped from the nearby Pantheon and melted to make the Baldacchino).

Church burials were periodically banned, as tombs rapidly overtook church interiors. However, the rich and powerful continued to enjoy church burials, partly because many churches depended upon the donations that accompanied the burial. (The poor and working classes were buried outside in cemeteries and in rural churchyards.) The *Chapel of Henry VII,* dated 1503–1519 (Fig. 10.17) is a large chapel, almost a separate church on the back of London's Westminster Abbey, built to house the tomb of Henry VII and his wife and to honor his already-deceased uncle, Henry VI. To help atone for his acts of war and royal intrigue, Henry VII donated to various charities and gave funding to Westminster Abbey, where the monks had lobbied heavily for the royal burial, along with its generous endowments. The tomb established the abbey's fame, making it a destination for pilgrims.

The chapel is built in the **English Perpendicular** style, a variation of the **Gothic** style. The ceiling seems to rise up on slender piers between the windows, and then fan out gracefully and drape downward into lacy vaults. Window tracery and carvings add to the overall effect. Sculptures of saints fill the remaining wall space. The height and delicate patterning make a fitting symbol of royal power at the end of the age of chivalry. A carved wooden screen encloses the tombs of Henry VII and his wife, Elizabeth of York, which have bronze effigies atop them. The tombs are directly behind the altar, the most venerable location in the chapel. Westminster Abbey continued to be used for royal burials until the eighteenth century, and it houses tombs of illustrious statesmen, military leaders, artists, and poets as well.

Connection *Compare the French Gothic cathedral emphasis on verticality with the elaborate Perpendicular style of the Chapel of Henry VII. See Chartres Cathedral (Figs. 9.36 and 9.37, page 233).*

ISLAMIC MAUSOLEUMS

The wealthy and powerful among Islamic societies were sometimes buried in mausoleums adjoining mosques. For example, Shah Abbas the Great, a seventeenth-century Persian ruler, was buried in a mausoleum attached to the *Masjid-i- Shah* (see Fig. 9.40).

Possibly the most famous Islamic mausoleum is the *Taj Mahal*, the final resting place of Mumtaz Mahal and a monument to the greatness of her husband, Shah Jahan, ruler of the Mughal Empire in India. The emperor apparently loved her dearly; she may have been his trusted advisor. The *Taj Mahal* (Fig. 10.18), built between 1632 and 1654, sits at the north end of an expansive walled and gated garden, like some in Turkey and Iran. Such gardens symbolized Paradise and were earthly re-creations of it. Canals divide the thirty-five-acre garden into four equal squares, with a large reflecting pool in the center. Those four squares are further subdivided into fours. The canals symbolize the four rivers of Paradise, from the Quran. An inscription

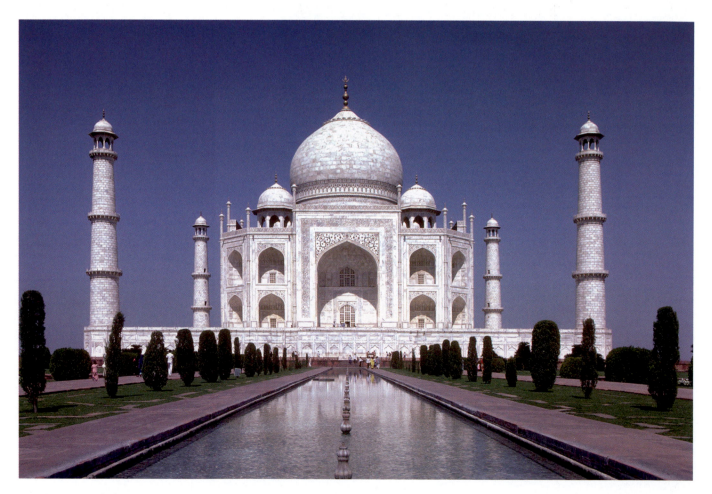

10.18   *Taj Mahal*, Agra, India, 1632–1654. © Sheldan Collins/Corbis.

on the garden's main gate reinforces the link between the garden and Paradise:

> But O thou soul at peace,
> Return thou to the Lord, well-pleased,
>   and well-pleasing unto Him.
> Enter thou among my servants,
> And enter thou My Paradise.
> (THE QURAN SURA 89)

Connection *In the manuscript painting* Babur Supervising the Layout of the Garden of Fidelity *(Fig. 15.15, page 413), we see an example of a walled garden from Persia.*

The *Taj Mahal* itself symbolizes the throne of Allah, a celestial flowering rising above the Paradise garden, buffered from the outside world. A red sandstone mosque and guesthouse flank the white mausoleum. The *Taj Mahal* is a compact, symmetrical, centrally planned structure, on a raised platform and surrounded by four minarets. The huge dome dominates and unites the entire building, but the various parts, from arched portals to windows to porches, maintain their own identity. The *Taj Mahal* seems billowing and light, and, combined with its reflection in the pool, it seems to float. The walls throughout the *Taj Mahal* are decorated lavishly with inlaid or carved floral designs, with onyx, red sandstone, agate, jasper, cornelian, lapis, coral, jade, amethyst, green beryl, and other semiprecious stones.

RELIQUARIES

In some religions, bones, tissues, and possessions of deceased holy persons are kept and venerated. Since the time of the Roman Empire, Christians have sought out the relics of saints and martyrs as they prayed to God. The practice continued in medieval Europe, where pilgrims would visit prominent medieval churches to ask special favors in the presence of a saint's relics. Fragments of clothing or body parts were kept in **reliquaries**, small precious shrines like the *Reliquary Arm,* c. 1230 (Fig. 10.19). Frequently, these shrines were sculptures in the shape of the body part contained within. This example was built to hold pieces of arm bone from an unknown holy person. Clergy used it to bless the faithful or heal the ill. Reliquaries were expensive to produce, as was appropriate because relics were precious. In addition to decorations in silver, gold, and gemstones, this reliquary has scenes from the lives of Saints Peter and Paul. Reliquaries were related as much to the jeweler's craft as to sculpture.

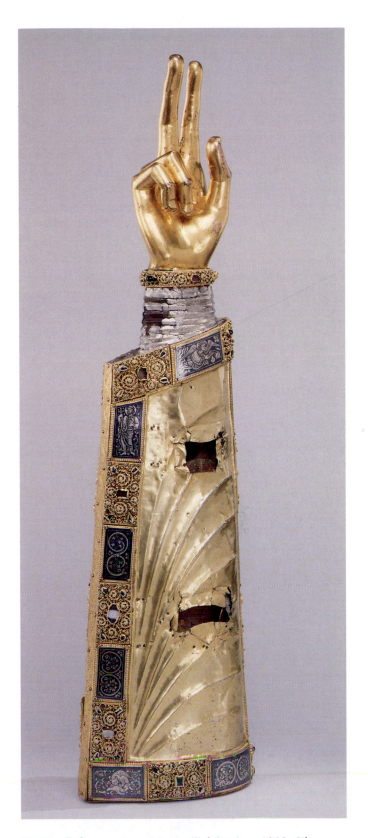

10.19 *Reliquary Arm,* Mosan (Belgium), c. 1230. Silver over oak; hand: bronze-gilt; appliqué plaques: silver-gilt, niello, and cabochon stones; 25½" × 6½" × 4". The Metropolitan Museum of Art, The Cloisters Collection, 1947 (47.101.33). Photograph © The Metropolitan Museum of Art.

Reliquaries from Africa often held the remains of venerated ancestors. Most African religions honor ancestors through ritual and sculptures because they are believed to affect the welfare of the living in many ways. The *Reliquary Guardian Figure* (Fig. 10.20) from Gabon in west-central Africa, was placed on a bag or basket that contained the skulls and long bones of the ancestors who founded a clan. The guardian protected relics from evil and helped obtain food, health, or fertility from these ancestors. The sculpture, combined with the relics, was considered the image of the spirits of those dead ancestors. Offerings were made to them.

This *Reliquary Guardian Figure* and others like it were constructed over flat wooden armatures, and then covered with sheets and wires of brass or copper. The faces were oval and usually concave, with projections to show the elaborate hairstyles traditionally worn in the area. The guardian figure probably evolved from figurative sculptures with hollow torsos in which bones were originally placed, a practice that became impracti-

cal as more bones were accumulated. In their present form, these figures could also be used in dances. These sculptures were extremely influential in the development of twentieth-century European modern art.

Connection *Pablo Picasso was influenced by African sculpture. See Les Demoiselles d'Avignon (Fig. 1.4).*

MODERN COMMEMORATIVE ART

Commemorative art from the past two centuries is varied and includes monuments that deal with personal loss, memorials for groups, and monuments for important political leaders. They express loss, preserve memory, or transform the experience of death. Elements are drawn from fine art, architecture, popular culture, folk art, and craft.

MODERN CEMETERIES

From the middle of the eighteenth century and into the nineteenth century, cemeteries within cities in Europe reached a crisis point. Expanding cities began to overtake neglected churchyards, overcrowded with graves that were seen as unhealthy and sources of pollution. As a result, civil authorities gradually removed control of burial practices from the churches and established new, large, suburban cemeteries that buried the deceased who followed any (or no) religion.

In Italy, the new cemeteries were rigidly organized in tight grids. In contrast, northern Europeans favored the picturesque cemetery, like the *Père Lachaise Cemetery,* opened in 1804 (Fig. 10.21), originally on the outskirts of Paris. Its design was influenced by **Romanticism,** a major art and cultural movement of the nineteenth century that emphasized a return to a simpler, rural way of life, just as the Industrial Revolution was creating ever more packed cities, greater pollution, and mechanization of life. The cemetery was laid out with meandering paths on a hilly site, with massive trees overhead. As families could own plots in perpetuity, they often constructed elaborate and fantastic structures, running the gamut from Egyptian, Greek, Roman, Byzantine, and Gothic to modern art nouveau styles. Urns, columns, and obelisks abound. Their exotic qualities are further manifestations of Romanticism. The famous and the obscure are buried together here, making the cemetery a national tourist attraction, like many burial places in this chapter.

Ophelia (Fig. 10.22), painted by John Everett Millais in 1852, is contemporary with some of the monu-

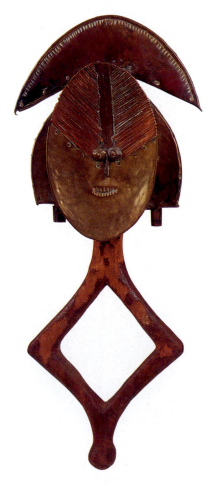

10.20 *Reliquary Guardian Figure,* from the Kota-Obamba regions of Gabon, Africa. Wood, brass, 24" high. Stanley Collection, University of Iowa Museum of Art.

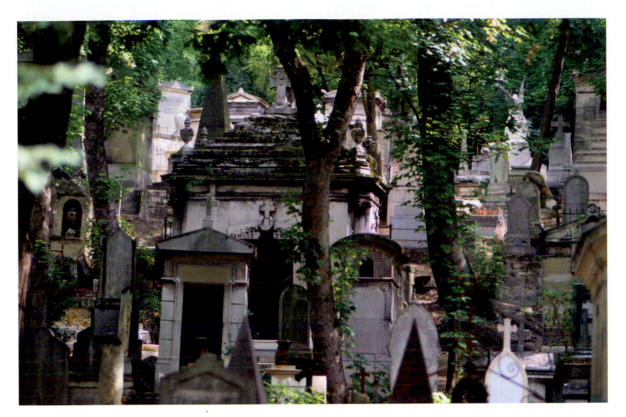

10.21   *Père Lachaise Cemetery,* Paris, France, opened 1804. © Alamy.

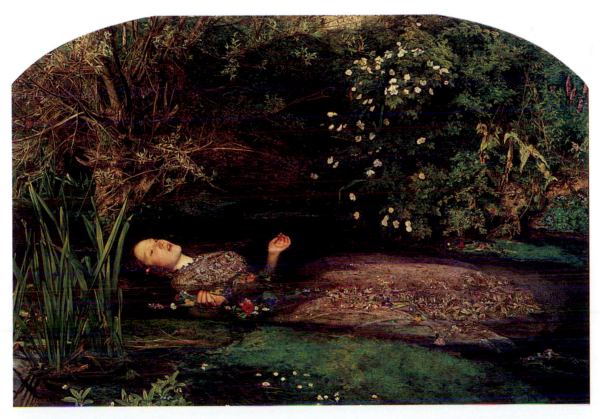

10.22   JOHN EVERETT MILLAIS. *Ophelia,* England, 1852. Oil on canvas, 30" × 44". Tate Gallery, London. Art Resource, NY.

ments in *Père Lachaise Cemetery*. Ophelia, a character in the Shakespearean play *Hamlet*, becomes incapacitated from grief and later drowns. This painting exhibits the same feeling toward picturesque nature that is apparent in *Père Lachaise Cemetery*, with deep color, lushness, accurate detail, and extraordinary delicacy. Ophelia's pose and flower-strewn dress already suggest the casket. The whole scene is lacking in the grisly details of madness and death by drowning, but rather is permeated with tragedy and poetic feeling. At *Père Lachaise Cemetery*, many monuments echo the sensibilities expressed in this painting, with sculptures of family members reaching for each other or lying together in death.

CONTEMPORARY MEMORIAL ART AND PRACTICES

Today's art and rituals of death serve a broad array of social, political, and personal needs.

The Day of the Dead is a popular celebration, mixing Christian and Aztec beliefs. It is celebrated in Mexico and parts of the United States with local variations. Marketplaces become sites for parades and spirited celebrations. In private homes, altars commemorate the family's dead, with burning incense and pictures of the departed placed next to their favorite foods to welcome their returning spirits. Families may spend the night at the graveyard with the deceased, decorating the grave sites and burning hundreds of candles.

Diego Rivera depicted this important ritual celebration in a series of murals about Mexican history and culture in the Ministry of Education building in Mexico City. The painting *Día de Los Muertos*, executed in 1923 (Fig. 10.23), shows the urban observance of the feast day; two other panels depict more traditional rural observances. Great crowds fill the marketplace in a raucous celebration. In the foreground are food vendors and children in skull masks. Hanging under the awning in the background are satirical skulls and skeletons of various characters, including a priest, a general, a capitalist, and a laborer. In Mexico, the carnival atmosphere of Day of the Dead invites political satire and commentary. Rivera painted his figures in a simplified, rounded, monumental style. He insightfully recorded different individuals' personalities, and he captured the crush and excitement of the crowd and the spirit of the event.

Northeast of Australia, on New Ireland and nearby islands, villagers hold memorial festivals to commemorate recently deceased clan members. Both the festivals and the sculptures carved for the occasions are called *malanggan*. Planning takes several months, as special crops must be planted, pigs raised for the feast, and sculptures carved for the occasion. Honoring the dead requires a great expenditure of effort and wealth, which stimulates the local economy and creates stronger alliances among villages and clans. Malanggan also include initiation rites for young men. Although they have evolved due to foreign influence, malanggan rituals continue to be enacted.

Some malanggan carvings are narrative sculptures with intricate openwork carving. Humans and various animals transform into one another or merge ambiguously, but the exact meanings are clan secrets. Less complex is the *Helmet Mask* or *Tatanua*, shown in Figure 10.24, which is used most frequently in dances. Combined with rituals, the fierce and dramatic masks provide an opportunity for spirits to be present in the villages. They are made of painted wood, vegetable fibers, and shells, and the top crest resembles men's traditional hairstyles. The traditional colors for malanggan are red, black, white, and yellow, which have symbolic meaning; for example, red usually means danger.

The Day of the Dead and malanggan rituals commemorate the dead as well as serve social needs. Our

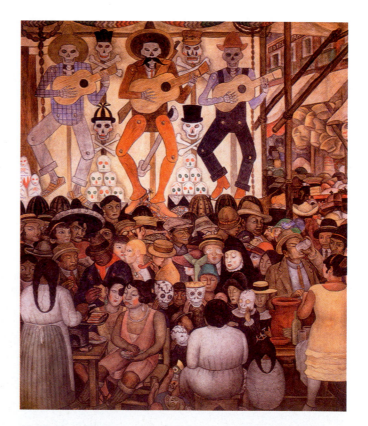

10.23 DIEGO RIVERA. *Día de Los Muertos*, Mexico, 1923. Fresco, detail showing the city fiesta. South wall, Court of the Fiestas, Ministry of Education, Mexico City. Photo © Bob Schalkwijk.

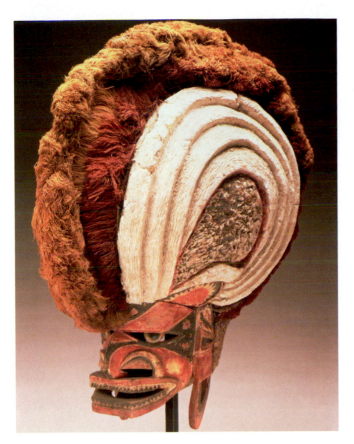

next work functions commemoratively and politically. The *Mausoleum of Mao Zedong* (Fig. 10.25) not only houses the body of the leader of the Communist revolution in China but also asserts the authority of the Communist government after centuries of imperial rule. Mao's historical accomplishments included helping to restore Chinese independence and redistributing land to the peasants.

The major axis of Beijing, the Chinese capital, runs north-south, and official buildings, palaces, public grounds, and city gates were placed along this axis, along with the Forbidden City and the Imperial Palace. This alignment signifies the authority of the imperial dynasties. In front of the Forbidden City is Tiananmen Square, a large, important ceremonial space. The *Mausoleum of Mao Zedong* is deliberately located in the square, on the north-south axis, as the Communist leaders claim to be rightful successors to the emperors.

10.24 *Helmet Mask (Tatanua)*, Oceania, 19th century. Northern New Ireland, Papua New Guinea. Wood, paint, natural fibers, and opercula shells. $15\frac{1}{4}$" $\times$ $9\frac{1}{2}$" $\times$ 12". Museum of Fine Arts, Houston, Texas.

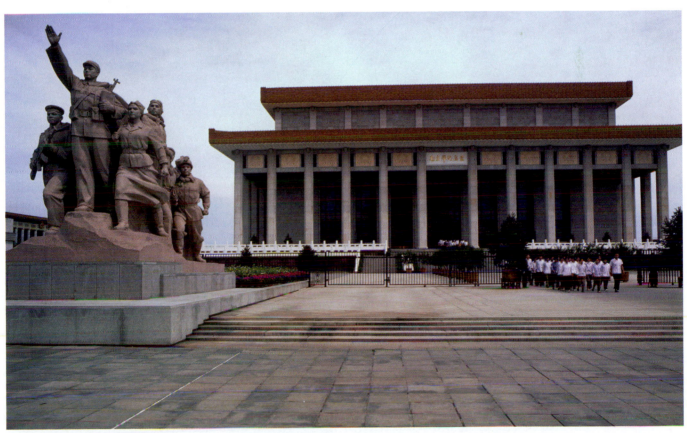

10.25 *Mausoleum of Mao Zedong*, Tiananmen Square, Beijing, China, latter half of the 20th century.

Connections *See the discussion of the elaborate Forbidden City and the Imperial Throne Room in the Hall of Supreme Harmony in Chapter 11 (Fig. 11.11).*

Like the tomb of Mao Zedong, the Vietnam Veterans Memorial (Fig. 11.28) stands on politically significant ground, the Mall in Washington, D.C.

The *AIDS Memorial Quilt,* shown here in 1996 (Fig. 10.26), is a commemorative work with a personal and political impact. The quilt is composed of thousands of individual three-by-six-foot panels, approximately the size of a twin-bed blanket, which would cover the body of one person who died from AIDS. Friends or family make each panel and decorate it, sometimes only with initials, but often more elaborately, with photographs, memorabilia, or details of a life story. The work is organized by a group called the Names Project in San Francisco, and most people contributing quilt pieces have no art training. The format of a quilt is especially appropriate for this collaborative, grassroots product of loving remembrance. After only a few years, the *AIDS Memorial Quilt* had become a vast public spectacle, which communicates the enormity of the epidemic and its toll in the United States alone. The quilt changes every time it is displayed. In Figure 10.26, its proximity to the White House and government buildings means that the disease was recognized publicly as a crisis and a tragedy by the U.S. government.

The tragedies of September 11, 2001, have been memorialized in several ways. For one month in 2002, *Tribute in Light* (Fig. 10.27), designed by three architects and two artists, projected two powerful beams of light into the night sky where the twin towers of the World Trade Center once stood. These temporary "towers" of light appeared architectonic, because each was composed of forty-four high-powered lamps that, combined, resembled a three-dimensional column with fluting. As light, the beams referenced hope and aspiration, but because they were immaterial, they also recalled the transitory nature and vulnerability of earthly things.

Studio Daniel Libeskind has developed models for new construction on the World Trade Center location, as shown in the *Computer-Generated Design to Rebuild the World Trade Center Site,* 2003 (Fig. 10.28). The proposal includes a ring of lower office buildings and one large Freedom Tower, a tapering, twisting seventy-story skyscraper, topped by an openwork cable superstructure and a spire. The Freedom Tower will be 1,776 feet tall, commemorating the year of the Declaration of Independence. The goal of the architect and design teams is to have the tower symbolize the spirit of the United States, while being extremely safe and secure and not competing with the design of the old World Trade Center.

The area in the middle of the ring of buildings will be left open for a tree-covered plaza and permanent memorial to those who died at the site on September 11, 2001. Michael Arad and Peter Walker's design has been chosen for that permanent memorial, *Reflecting Absence* (Fig. 10.28), consisting of two sunken reflecting pools. Access areas beneath the pools feature walls with the victims' names inscribed, a meditation room, and a site for leaving mementos. The sunken pools mark the footprints of the old towers.

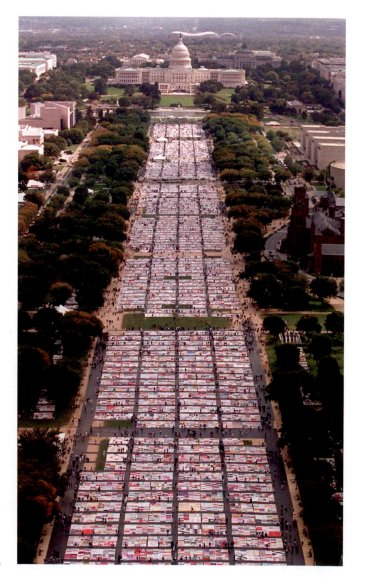

10.26 *AIDS Memorial Quilt.* Displayed on the Mall in Washington, D.C., October 11, 1996. Organized by the Names Project, San Francisco. © AP/Wide World, Ron Edmonds.

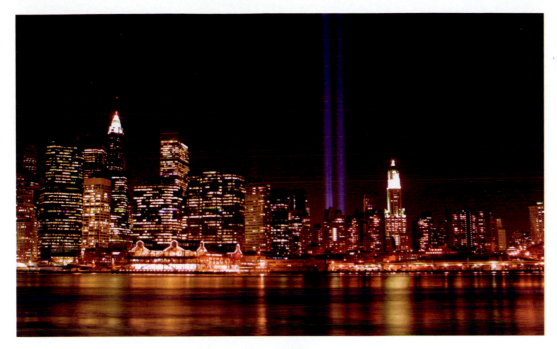

10.27 JOHN BENNETT,
GUSTAVO BONEVARDI,
RICHARD NASH GOULD,
PAUL MYODA, JULIAN
LAVERDIERE, AND PAUL
MARANTZ. *Tribute in
Light*, New York City,
2002. High-power
lamps. World Trade
Center Memorial at
Ground Zero.

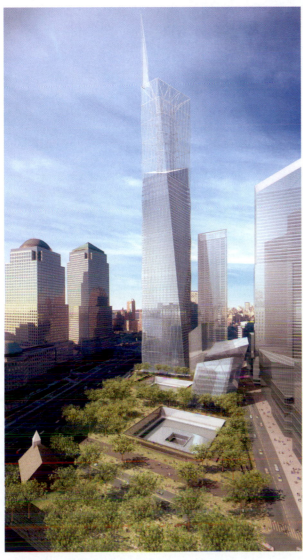

10.28 STUDIO DANIEL LIBESKIND.
*Computer-Generated Design to
Rebuild the World Trade Center
Site*. Selected design for World
Trade Center Site Memorial—
Reflecting Absence by Michael
Arad and Peter Walker, copyright
2004 LMDC. Rendering by dbox.
Courtesy of Lower Manhattan
Development Corp.

Major civilizations and empires emerged or were flourishing around the world at this time. The great wealth and power of these empires produced elite classes who commissioned amazing works of art, among which were monumental tombs and funerary art that preserved their fame.

In Greece, which consisted of independent city-states, 500–338 BCE is considered the Classical Age. In Athens, the *Parthenon* (Fig. 9.29) and other artworks reflect Greek humanism with their idealized yet naturalistic representations of the human figure, as seen in the *Grave Stele of Hegeso* (Fig. 10.13). Athens also developed an early but short-lived form of democracy. Athens fell to Sparta in warfare in 404 BCE. In the fourth century BCE, the Macedonians conquered their Greek neighbors to the south and, under Alexander the Great, invaded Persia and defeated King Darius. Alexander's empire, stretching as far as India and the Middle East, further spread Greek influence.

Much of what we know about the city-states of the Etruscan civilization in central Italy comes from excavations of their tombs and funerary art. Tomb paintings of lively people engaged in feasts, dancing, or enjoying outdoor sports are common, as in the *Banqueters and Musicians* from Tomb of the Leopards (Fig. 10.7). Evidence from texts, artifacts, and art such as the *Sarcophagus with Reclining Couple* (Fig. 10.6) indicates the independence that Etruscan women enjoyed: they attended symposia and sporting events, were equals at banquets with their husbands, owned property independently, and likely had a high rate of literacy. Beginning in 509 BCE, the Romans began chipping away at Etruria and completely overwhelmed the Etruscans by 273 BCE.

Rome was founded as a city in 753 BCE, but by 100 CE its influence had spread into Europe, Asia Minor, and North Africa. At first a republic, Rome became an empire in 27 BCE when Caesar Augustus came to power. His reign was the beginning of the *Pax Romana* (Roman Peace), which lasted for two hundred years and saw the construction of many amazing Roman monuments, including the *Pantheon* (Fig. 9.25), the *Colosseum* (Fig. 16.9) and the *Ara Pacis* (Fig. 11.31). In Rome, an individual's or a family's pedigree was important, evidenced by the many busts of

Map 4   Empires of the World, 500 BCE–500 CE.

ancestors or funerary monuments, as in the *Statue of Togato Barberini* (Fig. 14.12) or *Funerary Relief of a Circus Official* (Fig. 10.14).

Jesus Christ was born during Augustus's reign. Early Christian art, such as the *Good Shepherd* from the *Catacomb of Sts. Peter and Marcellinus* (Fig. 10.15), developed within the influence of Roman art, although Christians were subject to periodic persecutions. In 312, Emperor Constantine made Christianity legal, and eventually it became the religion of the empire. The fragments of the *Colossal Statue of Constantine* (on this page) clearly indicate that he was a powerful ruler, but others found it difficult to hold the huge expanse of the empire together and periodically it was subdivided. Nomadic tribes from northern Europe migrated toward Italy, and the western part of the Roman Empire was overrun by 476 CE. The eastern portion survived for another thousand years as the Byzantine Empire.

In India, the Mauryan Empire united most of the country with a central government between 321 and 185 BCE. The major rulers were Chandragupta and Asoka. The empire included northern and central India (modern Pakistan and part of Afghanistan). The Golden Age of India occurred between 330 and 500 CE during the Gupta Empire, begun by Chandragupta I. During this time, India prospered, and the arts were highly developed.

During the Zhou Dynasty in China, which ended in 256 BCE, Confucianism and Daoism were practiced, and the art of lacquering was developed. From 221 to 206 BCE, Shi Huangdi destroyed rival states and unified China, establishing the Qin Dynasty. To consolidate his power, he had all historical books burned and scholars burned or buried alive to eradicate old traditions. He established a civil service and bureaucratic government that continued for centuries in China. He built the *Great Wall* (see Fig. 11.20), highways, and canals, and standardized weights, measurements, axle widths, currency, and script styles for trade. The life-size ceramic army, the *Soldiers from Pit 1* (Fig. 10.8), that guarded his extravagant tomb is an eloquent visual monument to a ruthlessly ambitious ruler.

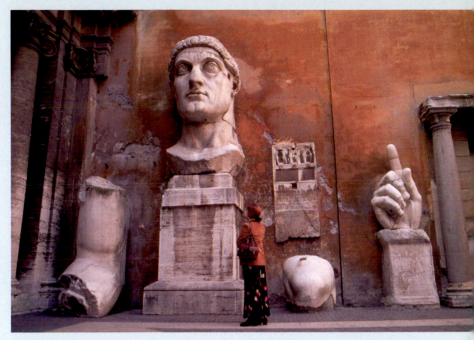

10.29   *Colossal Statue of Constantine*, fragments, Palazzo dei Conservatori, Rome, c. 330 CE.

Shi Huangdi's dynasty ended quickly after his death and was succeeded by the Han Dynasty (202 BCE to 222 CE). Arts included wall painting and sculpture. There was a major expansion of both domestic and foreign trade.

During this period, Egypt was dominated by foreign powers. Further south in Africa, the Great Empire of Ghana was established in 300. The Ghanaians set up trade routes and controlled trade in gold and salt. South of Egypt, the independent state of Kush thrived due to vigorous trade. In 400, the Bantu people settled in South Africa.

In Mesoamerica, the Maya developed writing, a calendar, sophisticated architecture, painting, and sculpture between 250 and 900. In Peru, the Chavin culture flourished between 1000 BCE and 200 CE and developed agriculture and art. Later, the Moche, whose culture dates from 200 to 800, built pyramids, buried their dead in elaborate tombs, and made fine pottery. Their leaders were warrior-priests whose regalia likely inspired awe and fear (see the artifacts from the *Royal Tomb of Sipán* in Figure 10.10 and the *Peanut Necklace* in Figure 10.11).

	BCE 4000	
	3000	Newgrange Burials
Old Kingdom—Egypt		Great Pyramids at Gizeh
Middle Kingdom—Egypt	**2000**	
New Kingdom—Egypt		Mortuary Temple of Hatshepsut
		Fowling Scene
		Innermost Coffin of Tutankhamen
Chavin Culture—Peru Etruscan Civilization	**1000**	
		Sarcophagus with Reclining Couple
Golden Age of Greece		
		Banqueters and Musicians Grave Stele of Hegeso
First Emperor—China Qin Dynasty		Soldiers from Pit 1 Infantry General
Birth of Jesus	**CE 100**	
Roman Empire		Funerary Relief of a Circus Official
Moche Civilization—Peru		
		Royal Tomb of Sipán Peanut Necklace
Constantine, Emperor of Rome		Catacomb of Sts. Peter and Marcellinus, ceiling painting
Byzantine Empire	**500**	
Founding of Islam		
		Viking Ship

Gothic Era	**1000**	
Mali Empire at Height		Reliquary Arm
	1500	
Renaissance Begins		Chapel of Henry VII
Baroque Era Begins	**1600**	
		Bernini: Baldacchino
		Taj Mahal
Age of Enlightenment Colonization of the Americas and Africa	**1700**	
	1750	
Industrial Revolution American Revolution French Revolution South American Revolution		
Mexican Independence from Spain	**1800**	Père Lachaise Cemetery
	1850	Millais: Ophelia
Mexican Revolution Russian Revolution World War I	**1900**	
		Rivera: Día de Los Muertos
World War II		Helmet Mask (Tatanua)
People's Republic of China Established		
	1950	Reliquary Guardian Figure
Vietnam War		Mausoleum of Mao Zedong
Desert Storm		AIDS Memorial Quilt
	2000	
September 11 Terrorist Attacks		Tribute in Light
	2002	Libeskind: Design to Rebuild the World Trade Center

Tombs are among the very oldest works of art, testaments to human mortality and to the persisting faith in immortality. Ancient tombs were often mound-shaped and oriented to the movements of celestial bodies, reflecting the belief that spiritual, agricultural, and scientific concepts were intertwined. The wealthy and powerful have built ostentatious tombs for themselves, to provide for their afterlife or to preserve their fame with future generations.

At tombs, the living are connected with their departed loved ones. Elaborate rituals may accompany a burial and are often continued on certain feast days. Religion is closely tied to burial art and rituals. Tombs and commemorative art reflect a culture's values and ideas about death. Many commemorative monuments serve political and social purposes.

Both ancient Egypt and the Etruscan civilization established elaborate cities of the dead. In eighteenth- and nineteenth-century Europe, new ideas in city planning and landscape design led to the development of the suburban cemetery.

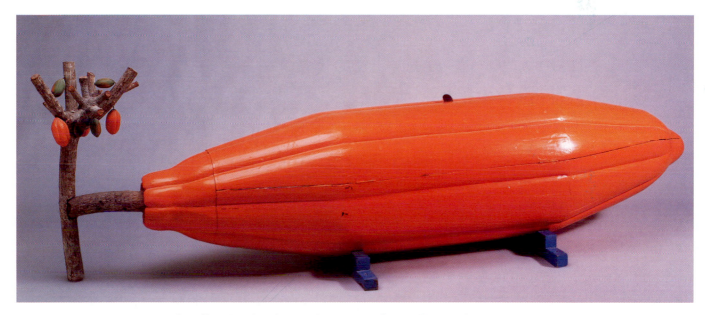

10.30 KANE KWEI. *Coca Pod Coffin*. Wood and enamel paint, 92" long. Ghana, Africa, 1970s. Collection of M. H. De Young Memorial Museum, the Fine Arts Museum of San Francisco. Gift of Vivian Burns, Inc.

FOOD FOR THOUGHT

Birth and death are often linked in art. We saw the rising sun that shone into the tomb at Newgrange, the egg imagery in the Etruscan Tomb of the Leopards, and the continued living of the Egyptian soul in their tombs. We also saw the birth–death link in several works in Chapter 8, Reproduction and Sexuality.

- *Are life and death linked in your experience?*

- *What pictures of death and funeral rituals are in the news media (locally, nationally, and internationally)? What do you see regarding the deaths of celebrities and the deaths of common people?*

- *Is fame a form of life after death, and is that the real purpose of elaborate burials and extravagant tombs?*

- *What visual elements are part of funeral rituals that you know?*

- *Funerary arts can be life-affirming, colorful, and celebratory. Contemporary Ghanaian carpenter and artist Kane Kwei used representational images of food in funerary art to honor the deceased's work in life. The Coca Pod Coffin (Fig. 10.30), was made for a farmer who grew that crop in life. (Kwei also carved an onion-shaped coffin for an onion farmer.) Have you experienced funerary events that were joyful remembrances?*

Research the new World Trade Center buildings and memorial as they are being built. What kinds of political, aesthetic, and security issues are influencing the design? What changes are being made to the original proposals, and why? Do you think this design is an appropriate memorial for the September 11 event and for this site?

Your Thomson Online Resources

 Go to **ArtExperience Online** for the Flashcards, Quiz, and Study Guide for this chapter.

The State

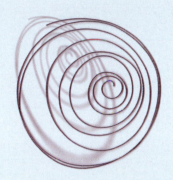

Rulers and governments use art to celebrate and spread their earthly power. Art is also used in war, either in creating weapons and armor for it or in making images that promote it. Art also gives us images of peacemaking and monuments for peace. Art can be an equally strong voice of protest against a government or against a social practice. People who are not in power can use art to affirm their ideas and to protest against warfare, oppression, or political policy.

CHAPTER 11 | POWER, POLITICS, AND GLORY

CHAPTER 12 | SOCIAL PROTEST/AFFIRMATION

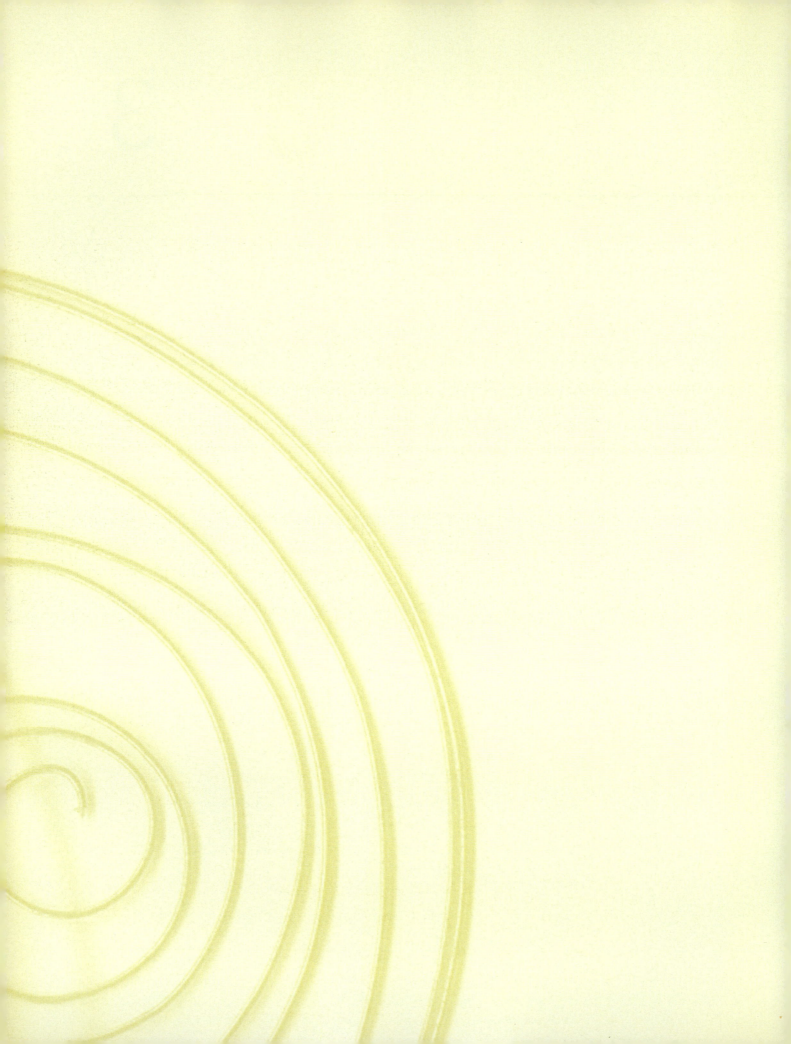

Power, Politics, and Glory

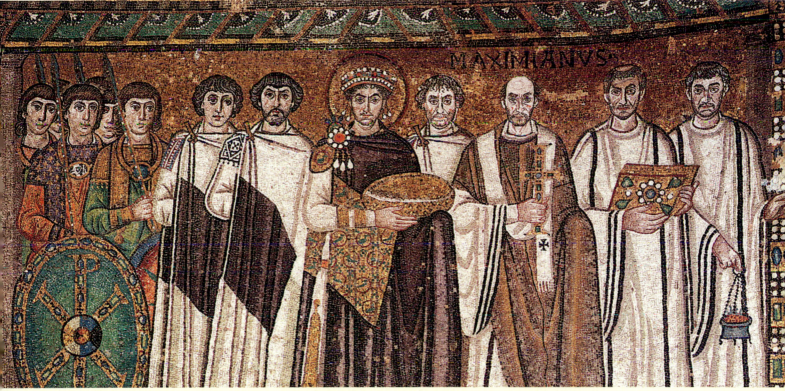

© Superstock

INTRODUCTION

Throughout human history, a vast amount of artwork has promoted, popularized, or propagandized governments as well as those who lead them. Art has depicted war and helped shape our reaction to it. Art has also celebrated peace. Think about the following questions while reading this chapter:

- *In what ways can art be used in the service of the state and rulers?*
- *What kinds of art and architecture have been so employed?*
- *Do politics influence the design of architecture?*
- *Why have the designers of objects of war included aesthetic considerations in their creations?*
- *How has war influenced the form and function of architecture?*
- *How has art documented both war and peace?*

THE GLORY OF THE RULER

The following artistic devices are often used to glorify a ruler's image:

- the idealized image: the ruler's face and/or body are depicted without flaw and often with youthful vigor; the idealized image often includes a wise or dignified demeanor

- symbols: details are included that indicate omnipotence, authority, or divine blessing; some symbols show military or religious power

- compositional devices: the ruler often occupies the center of a picture and may be shown larger than attendants or other figures; the ruler's clothing may attract attention

DIVINE RULERS, ROYALTY, AND SECULAR/RELIGIOUS LEADERS

Many heads of state through history have considered themselves not only royalty but also religious leaders or members of a divine or mythic family. Images helped them to spread and communicate that idea.

An early example of a royal portrait is the Egyptian royal couple, *Menkaure and His Wife, Queen Khamerernebty*, dated c. 2600 BCE (Fig. 11.1). They stand side by side, united by the queen's embrace, placing the same foot forward. Young, strong, and confident, they display the Egyptian ideal of beauty and maturity. Khamerernebty is shown as large as Menkaure, as pharaonic succession was traced through the female line. The compact pose makes the sculpture more durable and permanent, befitting the pharaohs as divine descendants of the Sun God, Re.

The sculpture was carved from a block of slate, a very hard stone. One view was likely sketched on each side, according to the Egyptian canon of proportions, and then carved inward until all four views met. Traces of paint were found on the piece. Menkaure was the pharaoh who built the third and smallest of the *Great Pyramids* at Gizeh (see Fig. 10.2). This shrine-like statue was found in his valley temple.

> **Connection** *Chinese emperors were considered to be divine Sons of Heaven. See the detail of Yan Liben's Portraits of the Emperors in the Art and History in Context section at the end of this chapter.*

Another royal portrait is *Emperor Justinian and His Attendants*, from the Church of San Vitale in Ravenna, Italy, built in the sixth century (Fig. 11.2).

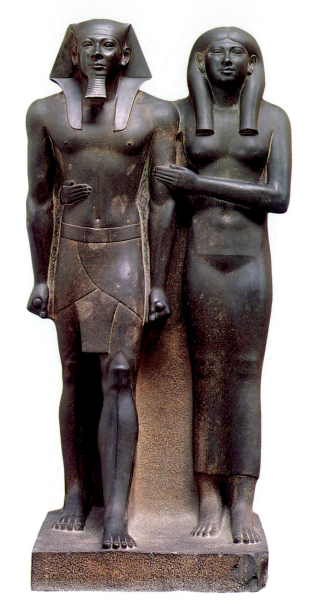

11.1 *Menkaure and His Wife, Queen Khamerernebty,* Gizeh, Egypt, Fourth Dynasty, c. 2600 BCE. Slate, approximately 4'6$\frac{1}{2}$" high. Museum of Fine Arts, Boston.

Justinian dominates this image, just as he dominated the Byzantine Empire, an outgrowth of the old Roman Empire that grew in power from the sixth century onward (see *Art and History in Context* on page 302). A devout Christian, he occupies the center spot between clergy to the right and military and state leaders to the left. As emperor-priest, Justinian wears a purple cloak and a magnificent jeweled crown and carries a golden bowl with bread used in Christian ritual. The solar disk or halo behind his head indicates divine status, a device used in Egyptian, Persian, and late Roman art. The emperor is flanked by twelve figures, alluding to Christ

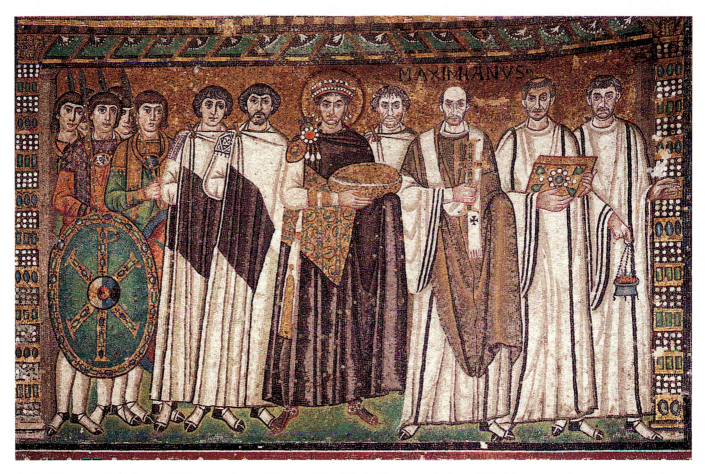

11.2 *Emperor Justinian and His Attendants,* Church of San Vitale, Ravenna, Italy, c. 547. Mosaic on the north wall of the apse. Canali Photobank.

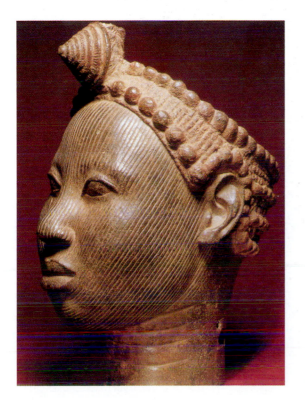

11.3 *Crowned Head of an Oni,* Wunmonije Compound, Ife, Nigeria, 12th–15th centuries. Yoruba. Zinc, brass. Smaller than life size. Museum of the Ife Antiquities, Ife, Nigeria.

and the twelve apostles. The clergy hold sacred objects: the crucifix, the book of Gospels, and the incense burner. Even a soldier's shield displays the **Chi-Rho,** an ancient symbol of Christ. A similar mosaic (not pictured here), *Empress Theodora and Her Attendants,* faces the Justinian mosaic in the church's sanctuary. Theodora, Justinian's wife, was an able and effective co-ruler, and her image indicates her equal rank and power.

In the next example, the head alone carries the exalted qualities of a ruler. In west-central Africa, several superb portrait heads were made in the twelfth to fifteenth centuries, each very much like the *Crowned Head of an Oni* (Fig. 11.3). This head represents a ruler in one of the many early empires emerging in Africa at this time (see *Art and History in Context* on page 303). The delicately detailed portrait is in a naturalistic style that contrasts with the more abstracted art from much of Africa. The face has a remarkable sense of calm and serenity, with beautiful flowing features, making it an outstanding example of an idealized royal portrait. Scholars still debate the exact identity and use of these portrait heads, but many believe each head represents a Yoruba or Benin ruler, who traced their rule back to the mythic first human ancestor. The crown was likely a royal insignia. The lines on the face may indicate scarification or perhaps strings of a beaded veil. Also visible are neck rings that are similar to those worn today among the Yoruba.

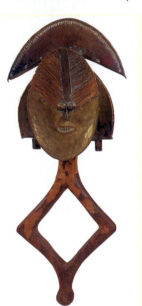

Connections *To see the range of styles in African art, contrast the naturalistic quality of the* Crowned Head of an Oni *with the more abstracted style of the* Reliquary Guardian Figure *(Fig. 10.20, page 262).*

Yoruba leaders today are identified by such headgear as the Great Beaded Crown of the Orangun-Ila, *in Figure 14.25 (page 387). These contemporary crowns are ancient forms that may date back to those worn by the early onis.*

Also from the twelfth century is the portrait head of *Jayavarman VII* (Fig. 11.4), the last great king of the Angkor Empire of the highly civilized Khmer people (in present-day Cambodia). He was a mighty military leader who conquered invaders and fought back rival states; one campaign lasted twenty years. Jayavarman VII was also well known for his amazing building projects, including the great *Temple of Bayon* at Angkor Wat that boasts fifty towers, each side with a large face of Buddha. Yet in this portrait, Jayavarman chose to be represented almost as a mystic, and in fact his own conversion from Hinduism to Buddhism spread that religion in the area. His face is softly modeled with eyes down-turned in meditation, and his gentle smile became famous in Khmer art.

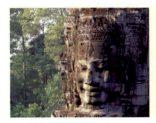

Connection *Jayavarman's likeness may have been the model for the Buddha faces on the* Temple of Bayon at Angkor Wat *(Fig. 6.16, page 129).*

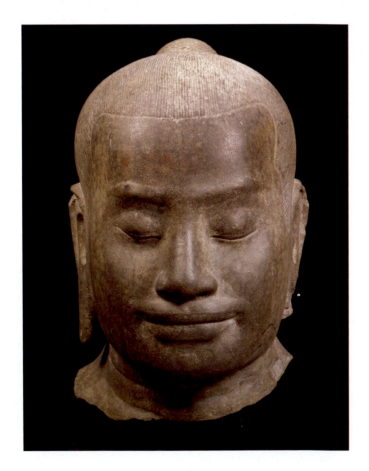

11.4 *Jayavarman VII*, Cambodia, province of Siemreap, Angkor region, late 12th or early 13th century CE. Bayon style. Sandstone head, 41 × 25 × 31 cm. Musée des Arts Asiatiques-Guimet, Paris, France. Photo: Erich Lessing/Art Resource, NY.

Many royal portraits from various cultures use similar attributes that convey an exalted quality: the idealized face/body, the symbolic details, centralized composition, and dignified demeanor.

OBJECTS OF ROYALTY AND PRESTIGE

Royalty have always adorned themselves in elaborate garments, dazzling jewelry, or objects of power. Thrones and orbs also proclaim a ruler's exalted status.

Hawaiian royal objects were made of materials that were taboo to all others in the society, unlike the gold and gems in a European crown, which any wealthy individual could possess. Hawaiians considered feathers sacred and connected with the gods, so only royalty could own or wear them. The *Cloak and Feather Hat* (Fig. 11.5) is magnificent apparel made of red and gold feathers. Although feather work is common in many Pacific islands, the Hawaiian work is the most developed and intricate. Colors have symbolic value, with red representing royalty, while yellow signifies a prosperous future. Hawaiian royalty also enjoyed large, elaborate feathered fly whisks called kahili, which were common objects transformed into luxury items and used for special occasions.

Connection *See* Moctezuma's Headdress *in Figure 11.32 (page 301) to compare Hawaiian and Aztec feather work.*

Among the Mesquakie people around Tama, Iowa, in the mid-1800s, grizzly bear claws were signs of high status, just as diamonds and pearls might be of value in other cultures. The prairie grizzly's nails—over three inches in length—were difficult to acquire and were

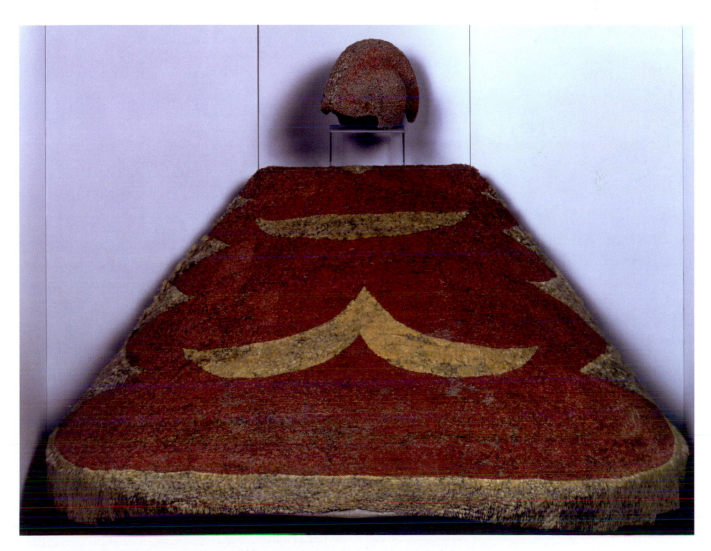

11.5 *Cloak and Feather Hat,* Hawaii, 18th century. Museo de America, Madrid, Spain.

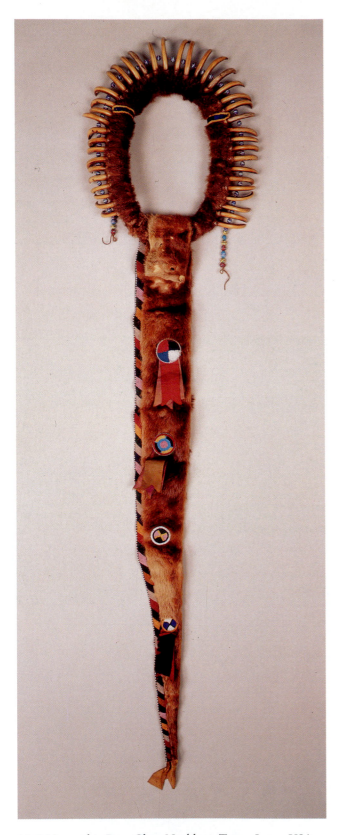

11.6 *Mesquakie Bear Claw Necklace,* Tama, Iowa, USA, c. 1860. Otter pelt, grizzly claws, glass beads, silk ribbon, 16¼" long, 14¼" wide, 3" high. Photo archive of the National Museum of the American Indian. Photo by Carmelo Guadagno.

considered a great trophy. The *Mesquakie Bear Claw Necklace* (Fig. 11.6) represented the strength and tenacity of the bear, which added to the dignity of the owner. The unassembled materials—claws, colored glass beads, otter pelts, and silk ribbons—would be given to those who owned the rights to create the neckpiece. The striking repetition of delicate curves suggests the lethal potential of each claw. The decorated otter pelt is attached to the necklace to become an elegant train.

CONTEMPORARY POLITICAL LEADERS

Images of contemporary political leaders are fundamentally different from those of the past, just as the concept of "ruler" has evolved. Today, almost no rulers openly consider themselves to be of divine descent, and many are not royalty. And with photography, pictures of rulers come to us not as artworks, but as a flood of newspaper or television images. There is a great difference between images that are produced under the ruler's direction and those over which the ruler has little or no control. In 1934, Adolf Hitler commissioned the film *Triumph of the Will* (Fig. 11.7), directed by Leni Riefenstahl, to glorify his rule, his military strength, and the Nazi order of Aryan supremacy. A work of brilliant propaganda, Riefenstahl's film established Hitler as the first media hero of the modern age.

Given unlimited funding by Hitler, Riefenstahl had a staff of over 130 people, sixteen cameras, four sound trucks, and cranes and dollies for dramatic shots. Skillfully edited into the film were speeches, parades, cheering crowds, and the lush music of the popular German composer Richard Wagner. Although the film was a documentary covering a six-day rally celebrating Hitler at Nuremberg, the imagery was entirely staged. Of course, all film and photographic content can be manipulated when shot as well as retouched and altered later. In this case, Riefenstahl carefully set the scene so that Hitler is presented to and worshipped by the masses as Germany's savior. In close-ups of Hitler's smiling face, his charisma is evident. At the end of the film, we see an aerial shot of massive military power in rigid formation under Hitler's control (Fig. 11.7). This utopian image of harmony and strength appealed to those whose lives were in disorder, and human history experienced one of its most horrendous episodes.

One can wonder about Riefenstahl's motivation. Perhaps she was a devout believer in Hitler and Nazi

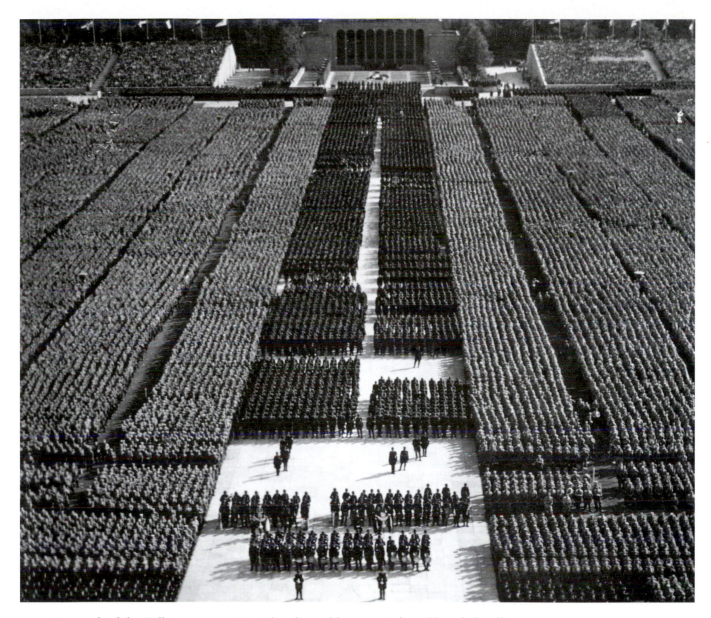

11.7 *Triumph of the Will*, Germany, 1934. Film, directed by Leni Riefenstahl. Kobal Collection.

dogma, or perhaps she was seduced by the opportunity to work in a new art medium with unlimited funds. Whatever the case, Riefenstahl's prototype in film would affect future campaigns for political elections as well as lay the foundation for consumer advertising.

THE POWER OF THE STATE

Palaces, government buildings, and monuments can make the state and the ruler seem powerful and glorious.

PALACES

As official residences of kings, emperors, and religious leaders, palaces visually represent the state's power. Often palaces are seats of government. Palaces frequently have the following qualities:

- Their grand size distinguishes them from ordinary residences.
- They are usually lavishly ornamented.
- Height is often an important element.
- They feature art prominently, often adding symbolic content.

One example of palace art is the mighty *Lamassu* (Fig. 11.8), from 720 BCE, an enormous sculpture from Khorsabad, capital of the Assyrian Empire. The Assyrians, known for their ruthlessness and brutality, dominated the Near East for over three hundred years. With enormous size and glaring stare, two large *Lamassu* guarded the palace gate, to terrify and intimidate all who entered. A form of a divine genie, the winged creature is part lion or bull, with the head of a human being. The horned crown symbolizes the king's divine power. Carved from one large block of stone, the *Lamassu* has five legs to show movement and stability at the same time. From the side, the *Lamassu* appears to be striding forward. The front view, however, shows the beast at a stalwart standstill, blocking the viewer's forward movement. Stylized and natural elements are combined, with hair and wings depicted with linear and repetitive patterns, while the strong, muscular legs and facial features are more naturally rendered.

Connection *We will look at other fantastic animals, and the reasons humans invented them, in Chapter 15, Nature, Knowledge, and Technology.*

An outstanding early example of a palace comes from the Achaemenid civilization in ancient Persia, which produced a body of monumental art of outstanding splendor. The palace of *Persepolis*, begun by Darius I in 518 BCE and destroyed by Alexander the Great in 331 BCE, took fifty years to build (Fig. 11.9). The heavily fortified palace citadel was located on a terraced platform measuring 1,500 feet by 900 feet, with mud walls reaching sixty feet high and sometimes faced with carved stone slabs and glazed brick. Interior spaces were large, wide **hypostyle** halls, with many carved columns supporting the roofs. The windows were made of solid blocks of stone with cutout openings. Stairs were also chiseled from stone blocks and then fitted into place.

The Royal Audience Hall was two hundred feet square and sixty feet high and may have held up to 10,000 people. One hundred tall columns (some visible in the right background of Fig. 11.9) supported a massive wood beam ceiling. On top were elaborate capitals with curving scrolls and foreparts of bulls or lions. Some had human heads. A grand staircase, cut directly from natural rock formations, was covered with reliefs

11.8 *Lamassu*, Khorsabad, Iraq, 720 BCE. Limestone, 14' high. © RMN/Art Resource, NY.

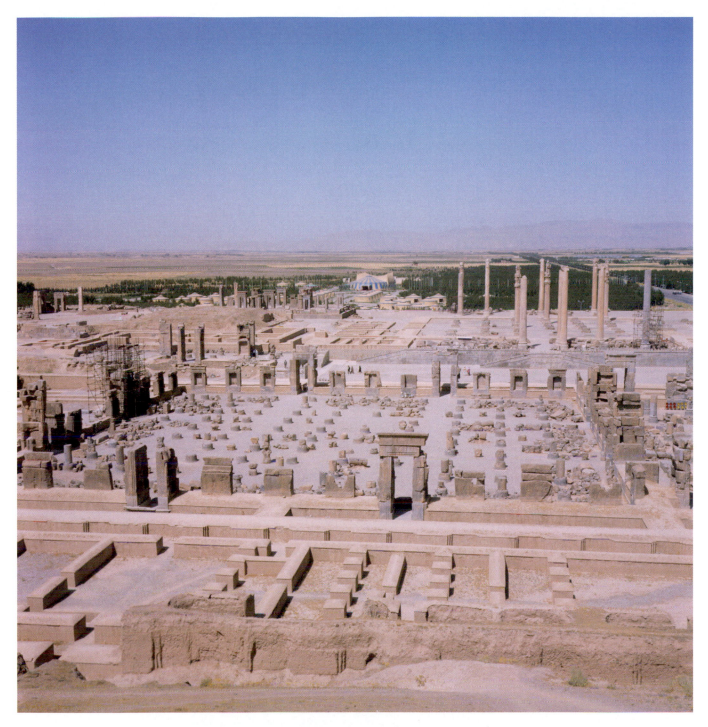

11.9 *Persepolis,* general view, Persia (Iran), 559–330 BCE. Achaemenid.

depicting subjects presenting tribute to the king. Gates at Persepolis had guardian figures like the *Lamassu* (Fig. 11.8).

Like the Persians, the Mayans of Central America created large palaces with high platforms and relief sculpture. Occupied from 514 to 784, but abandoned before the Spanish conquest, Palenque remained com-pletely hidden by tropical flora until it was rediscov-ered in modern times. Palenque was the center of one of several successive empires in Central America (see *Art and History in Context* on page 302). It had the living quarters for the Mayan royalty, a center for reli-gious rites, facilities for astronomical studies, and an administrative precinct.

The *Palace at Palenque* (Fig. 11.10) featured four courts, each surrounded with rooms and galleries, likely used for administrative purposes. A number of thrones were found within the galleries. Built on a thirty-foot-high platform, the complex measures 250 feet long by 200 feet wide. Large, painted stucco masks of human faces once adorned the ends of the terraces. Nearby, a vaulted underground aqueduct brought water to the *Palace*. The seventy-two-foot-high tower adds important verticality to the horizontal design. Large tower windows facing the four cardinal points may have had both astronomical and defensive uses. The profusely decorated interior was covered by parallel rows of corbel arches and vaults. The outer walls were pierced with T-shaped windows and doorways. The thin walls and airy rooms countered the fierce tropical heat.

Chinese royal architecture helped sustain the emperor's rule, because its magnificence supported his claim to be Son of Heaven, father of the people, and the one who maintained Heaven on Earth. The Forbidden City, an enormous palace compound that once had 9,999 rooms, resembles a city unto itself within Beijing. No commoners were allowed to enter. The major structures have gleaming yellow tile roofs and rich vermilion walls. Pure white marble staircases connect one courtyard after another. There were also mansions of princes and dignitaries, lush gardens, artificial lakes, theaters, and a library, laid out in a symmetrical plan. The city's major axis is north-south, with most structures facing south, the source of fruitfulness (north brought evil influences). The *Imperial Throne Room* (Fig. 11.11) is one example of the interior decoration. The majestically high ceiling is covered with elaborate patterns

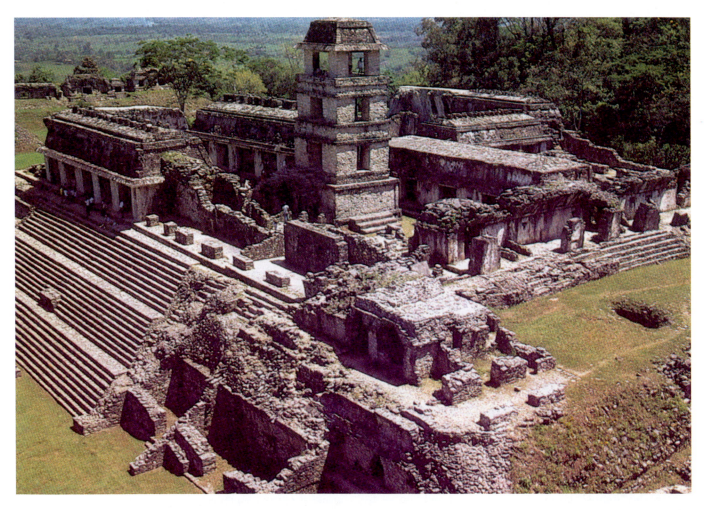

11.10   *Palace at Palenque*, Chiapas, Mexico, 514–784. Maya. Photo by Mary Ellen Miller.

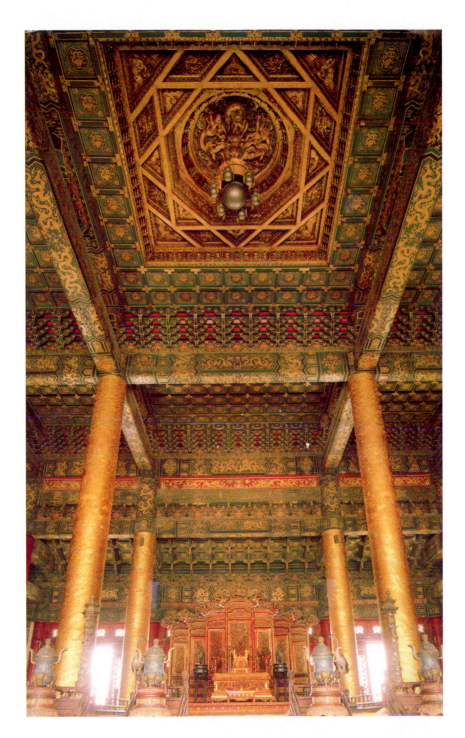

11.11 *Imperial Throne Room*, in Hall of Supreme Harmony, Forbidden City, Beijing. China Photographic Publishing House, Beijing.

subdivided by grids. The focus of the room, the throne, is framed by columns and elevated on a stepped platform.

Connection Other Chinese examples of ambitious royal building projects are the Soldiers from Pit 1 (Fig. 10.8, page 251) from the tomb of Qin emperor Shi Huangdi, and the Great Wall of China (Fig. 11.20, page 292).

Like the Forbidden City, the palace complex at Versailles was both a sign of power and an instrument for maintaining that power. It was built by King Louis XIV of France, the Sun King who identified himself with Apollo. Louis moved his entire court from Paris to Versailles in 1682 in order to better control them. Originally Louis's grandfather's hunting lodge, Versailles was extensively enlarged and remodeled. Approximately

36,000 workers took twenty years to complete it to Louis's liking, with grand spaces, dramatic embellishment, and theatrical display in the **Classical Baroque** style. The connected buildings measure 2,000 feet wide and are surrounded by seven square miles of parks. Over four million tulip bulbs were planted in the parks' flower beds (see illustration on page 381).

Inside, the *Hall of Mirrors* (Fig. 11.12), 240 feet long, connects the royal apartments with the chapel. The ceilings were covered with marvelous frescoes, and the long, mirrored room was embellished with gilded bronze capitals, sparkling candelabra, and bejeweled trees. Just as Louis XIV dominated the French church, nobility, and peasants, he also controlled the arts, fashion, and manners. He established the French Royal Academy of Painting and Sculpture to ensure a steady supply of works that would glorify his person and reign (see page 106).

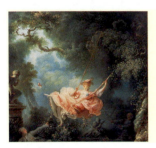

Connection *At Versailles, Louis XIV stripped the nobility of their power, so they occupied their time in games of romance and intrigue, as in Fragonard's* The Swing *(Fig. 14.24, page 386).*

The Palace at Ikere, the residence of a Nigerian ruler, provides another example of artwork that sym-

bolizes kingly power. Olowe of Ise carved the *Palace Sculpture* (Fig. 11.13) showing the senior wife, the queen, standing behind the enthroned king. Women are revered for their procreative power, so the royal female towers over the king while crowning him, because she is the source of his power. His conical crown is topped by a bird, a symbol for the reproductive power of mothers, female ancestors, and deities. The interlocking forms of king and queen visually convey monumentality and elegance. Details, such as the pattern of body scarification, add authenticity to the sculpture. Yoruba aesthetic values are evident: "clarity, straightness, balance, youthfulness, luminosity and character" (Blier 1998:85).

Yoruba kings would seek the best artists to make artwork for their palaces, as a way to increase their prestige. Olowe of Ise spent four years (1910–1914) at Ikere producing around thirty pieces. Songs or poems of praise (**oriki**) were composed about him:

> Handsome among his friends.
> Outstanding among his peers.
> One who carves the hard wood of the iroko
> tree as though it were as soft as a calabash.
> One who achieves fame with the proceeds of his carving.
> (Blier 1998:85)

Thus, across several continents and several centuries, we have seen palaces built with certain distin-

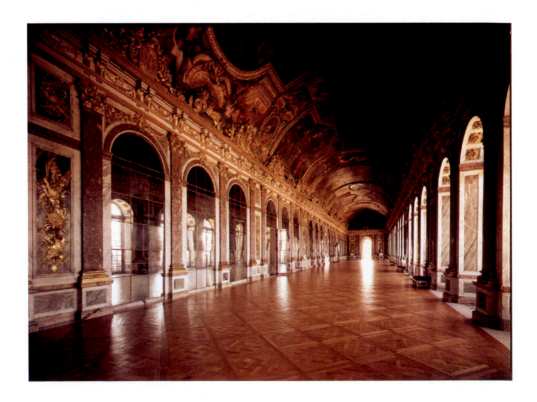

11.12 JULES HARDOUIN MANSART AND CHARLES LE BRUN. *Hall of Mirrors,* Versailles, France, c. 1680. © Scala/Art Resource, NY.

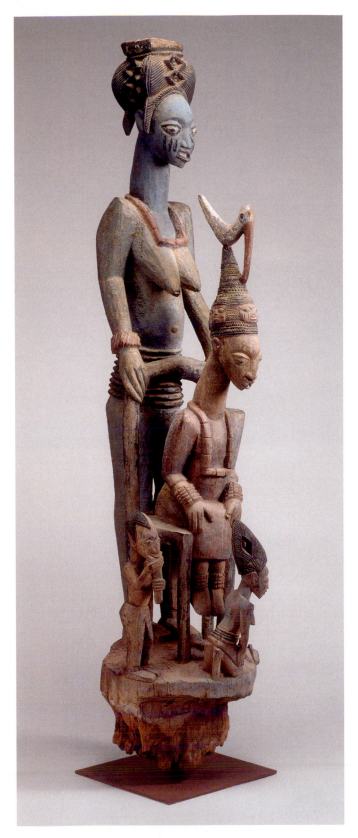

11.13 OLOWE OF ISE. *Palace Sculpture*, Ikere, Nigeria, 1910–1914. Yoruba. Wood and pigment, 60" × 13¼". Photograph by Bob Hashimoto. Reproduction: The Art Institute of Chicago.

guishing features: large size, height, terraces and/or platforms, decorated interiors, and symbolic sculptures.

SEATS OF GOVERNMENT

Social and political pressures help determine which styles of architecture are used in government buildings, as seen in the designing of England's *Houses of Parliament* (Fig. 11.14). In 1836, the old Houses of Parliament burned. A new design was sought that would reinforce England's desires to create a "national identity" and express patriotic spirit. Architect Charles Barry designed the general plan in the **Gothic Revival** style, while A. W. N. Pugin was responsible for suitable ornamentation. They felt that the style of the soaring medieval cathedrals appropriately represented a Christian nation. New building materials, such as cast iron, enabled the Gothic Revival style to flourish on a grand scale.

Pugin and Barry were hotly criticized for breaking away from **neoclassic** architecture, which was widely used for public and government buildings in western Europe and the United States, like the U.S. Capitol Building (Fig. 4.3). The painter John Constable argued that the new Gothic Revival design of Parliament was a "vain endeavor to reanimate deceased art, in which the utmost that can be accomplished will be to reproduce a body without a soul" (Honour and Fleming 1995:621). Pugin, however, felt that Gothic art never died or lost its soul. He believed that Gothic was a principle rather than a style, "as eternally valid as the teaching of the Roman Church" (1995:621). He also reasoned that contemporary Greek temples were mere imitations and had no integrity.

The long, horizontal buildings are topped with Victoria Tower on one end, while the famous clock tower, with Big Ben, is on the other. Ironically, the building's plan is clearly symmetrical with repetitive ornamentation, qualities of Classical architecture. However, the building resembles a medieval church or a castle-fortress, visually housing Parliament in a metaphor of the church's strength and the government's power.

> **Connection** *Chartres Cathedral (Fig. 9.36, page 233) and the* Chapel of Henry VII *in Westminster Abbey (Fig. 10.17, page 259) are two examples of Gothic architecture, which inspired the design of the Houses of Parliament.*

Just as a new architectural style was developed for the *Houses of Parliament,* a new form of architecture evolved on New Zealand in response to political and social needs. In the nineteenth century, the Maori nation was undergoing tremendous change due to

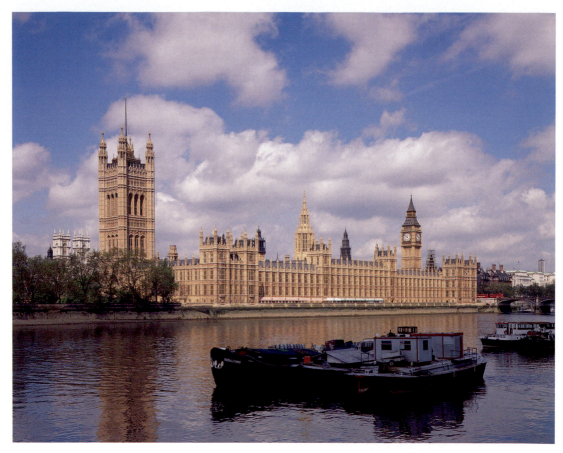

11.14 CHARLES BARRY AND A. W. N. PUGIN. *Houses of Parliament,* London, 1840–1860. 940'
long. © A. F. Kersting.

European colonization. The Maori Meeting House, like *Te Papaiouru Marae* (Fig. 11.15) in Ohinemutu, was an elaborate version of a chief's home and a site for reaffirming old tribal values and clan ties. It represented the body of a powerful ancestor, and, once inside, the living became one with their ancestor. The porch is considered to be the ancestor's brain, the bargeboards are the ancestor's arms and hands, and the roof's ridgepole represents the ancestor's backbone, terminating at the front with a face mask. Inside, the rafters and wall slabs represent the ancestor's ribs and are covered with carved and painted vines that symbolize the clan's generations.

The sculptures on Maori meeting houses are visually overwhelming. These profuse carvings, swirls, lines, and frightening imagery empower clan members, while intimidating any outsiders. The carvings represent mythical first parents and the tribe's history, in this case, Tamatekapua, who was the captain of the canoe that first brought the tribe's ancestors to New Zealand. Inspirational stories about clan heroes, told in the presence of these images, pass on clan history, traditions, and values to the young.

MONUMENTS

A final category of government art is the commemorative monument. These structures are often very large, with architectural elements, sculpture, and inscriptions. Although we are looking at only one monument in this section, later in this chapter are examples that relate to war and peace. In addition, you can find many monuments in cities around the world that commemorate past events, civic leaders, and military heroes.

> **Connection** The Portrait of George (Fig. 12.29, page 328) is a monument to slain San Francisco mayor George Moscone Another example is the Monumental Heads from the Easter Islands (Fig.3.23, page 70).

Roman triumphal arches commemorate military victories or major building projects. The *Arch of Titus* (Fig. 11.16) was built along the Via Sacra (the Holy Road) in Rome, by Titus's brother Domitian, to record Titus's apotheosis. The inscription at the top reads roughly, " . . . dedicate this arch to the god Titus, son of the god Vespasian."

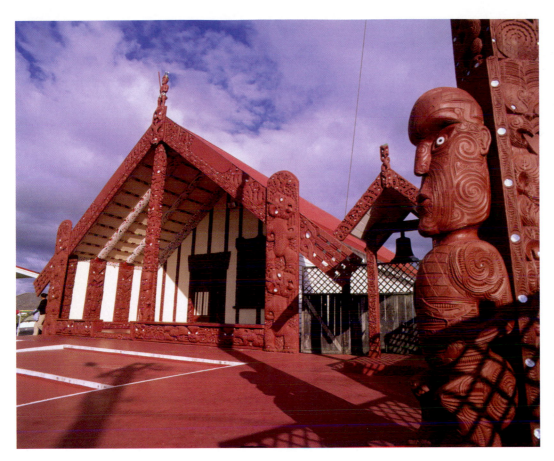

11.15 *Te Papaiouru Marae*, Maori Meeting House, Ohinemutu Maori Village, Rotorua, North Island, New Zealand, late 19th century.

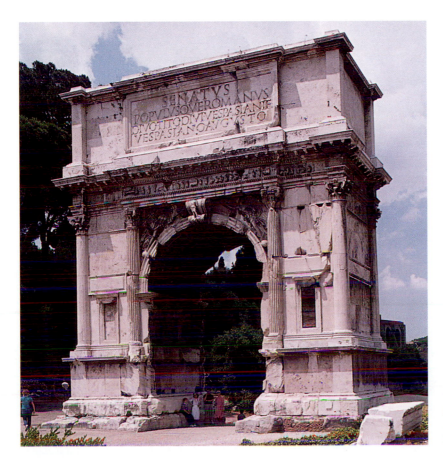

11.16 *Arch of Titus*, Rome, Italy, 81 CE. Marble on concrete, 50' high, 40' wide. Saskia Ltd., Cultural Documentation.

This single-passageway arch (others have two or three) is a mini–**barrel vault.** Engaged columns have both Ionic and Corinthian elements, a Roman synthesis of Greek **orders.** The attic is the uppermost section with the inscription. "Winged victories" in the spandrels symbolize Titus's military successes. Under the vault, one relief depicts Titus being carried up to heaven on the back of an eagle, giving a visual image of his deification. Other relief carvings show his military victories.

WAR

War is part of the history of most civilizations and cultures, and it is part of the story of power, politics, and glory.

WARRIORS, WEAPONS, AND FORTIFICATIONS

Warriors have been depicted in art since 8000 BCE. Warrior images can be found in almost every culture since then. Frequently, fierceness is shown in the following ways:

- Large size of warriors

- Emphasis on armor, weapons, or regalia of power

- Menacing or aloof facial expressions

In the Toltec city of Tula in central Mexico, colossal *Tula Warrior Columns* (Fig. 11.17) stand on a temple platform atop a pyramid dating between 900 and 1000. These sixteen- to twenty-foot-tall figures once held up the temple roof; figuratively, they "supported" the religion. Stiff, blocky, and frontal, they are carved in low relief from four basalt drums attached with dowels and originally painted in bright colors. They wear Toltec garb with elaborate headdresses, and each held *atlatls*—spear-throwers—at their side. Thus, the warriors' attire is more than functional; it is also aesthetic to increase their power and prestige. The warriors' uniformity gives the impression of a formidable army that could crush anything. Stylized butterflies, carved on their chests, were the souls of past warriors.

Before the modern era, the warrior on horseback was greatly feared. Andrea del Verrocchio's colossal

bronze *Equestrian Monument of Bartolomeo Colleoni* (Fig. 11.18) joins the horse's power with the rider's strength and determination. Colleoni was a *condottiere,* or mercenary soldier, who fought many campaigns for the city-state of Venice during the fifteenth century. The fifteen-foot-tall statue is raised on a high pedestal, so that viewers are vulnerably placed under the horse's raised hoof. The animal's tense, bulging muscles, Colleoni's twisted pose, and his scowling face are the very embodiment of aggression.

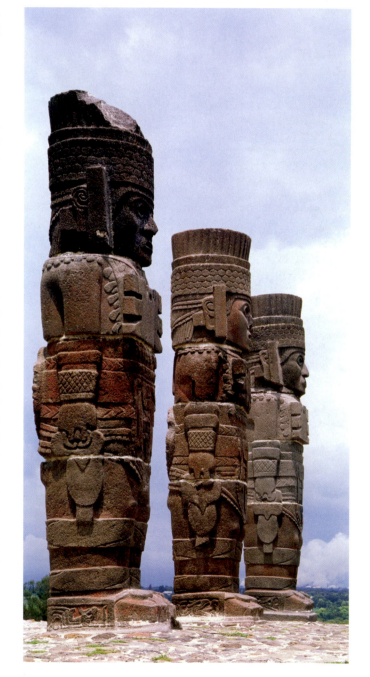

11.17 *Tula Warrior Columns*, Mexico, 900–1000. Toltec. 16' to 20' high. © Superstock.

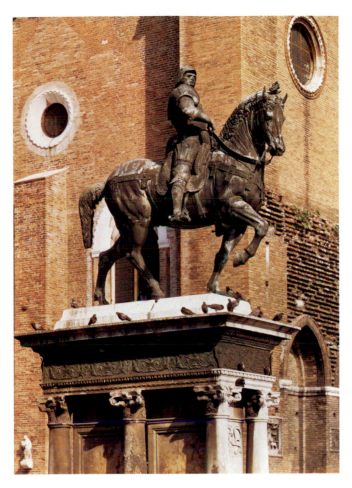

11.18 ANDREA DEL VERROCCHIO. *Equestrian Monument of Bartolomeo Colleoni*, Italy, c. 1483–1488. Bronze, 15' high. Campo Ss. Giovanni e Paolo, Venice. © Scala/Art Resource, NY.

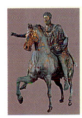

Connection *Compare the Equestrian Statue of Marcus Aurelius (Fig. 1.2) for a non-warrior image of a ruler on horseback.*

The brass *Plaque with Warrior and Attendants* (Fig. 11.19) depicts an impassive Nigerian warrior king from the seventeenth or early eighteenth century. Larger than his two attendants, the king displays classic African figurative proportion, approximately three heads high. His apron and shield have leopard imagery, a regal symbol made more important because of the artistic attention given to it. Dominating the composition are the warrior's spear, helmet, and shield. Often, armor and weapons were protection for both the body and the spirit. The frontal, symmetrical composition of the *Plaque* conveys absolute authority, power, and

strength; the face is aloof. These plaques were documents of kings, warriors, and famous events and were displayed prominently in Benin palaces. The plaques represented the king's power and literally were his image among his people, because he rarely appeared in public except to wage war and to officiate at religious ceremonies.

Outstanding among war architecture is the *Great Wall* of China (Fig. 11.20). Begun in 206 BCE during the Qin Dynasty, with major additions during the Ming Dynasty (1368–1644 CE), this 1,500-mile-long wall is a "wonder of the world." New pieces of it are still being discovered, and the section near Beijing has been restored. The brick-faced wall averages twenty-five feet in height and width, and creates a light-colored, undulating line on the brown and green hills. Strategically placed watchtowers provide points of visual emphasis. The towers contained embrasures for cannons and were used as signal stations, with smoke by day and fires by night.

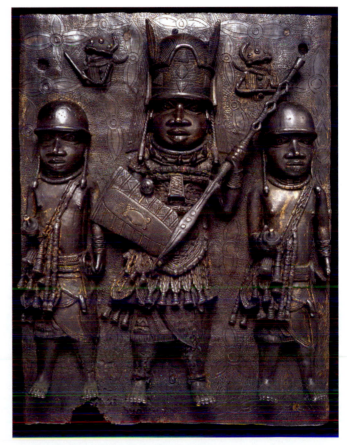

11.19 *Plaque with Warrior and Attendants*, Nigeria, 17th or early 18th century. Benin. Brass, 19¼" high. Peabody Museum of Architecture and Ethnology.

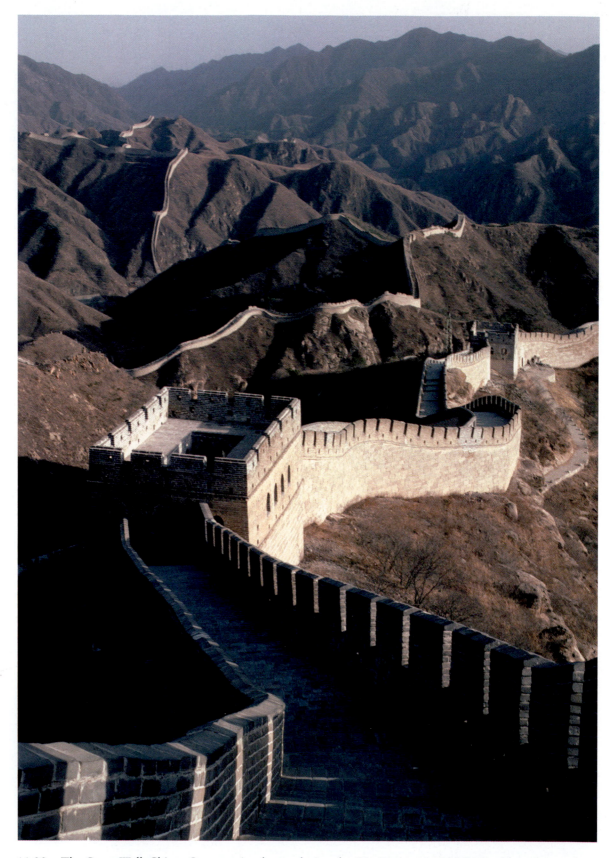

11.20 *The Great Wall*, China. Construction began during the Qin Dynasty in 206 BCE with major work occurring during the Ming Dynasty, 1368–1644 CE. Brick faced, average height 25', 1,500 miles long. © Michael Howell/Index Stock Imagery/Picturequest.

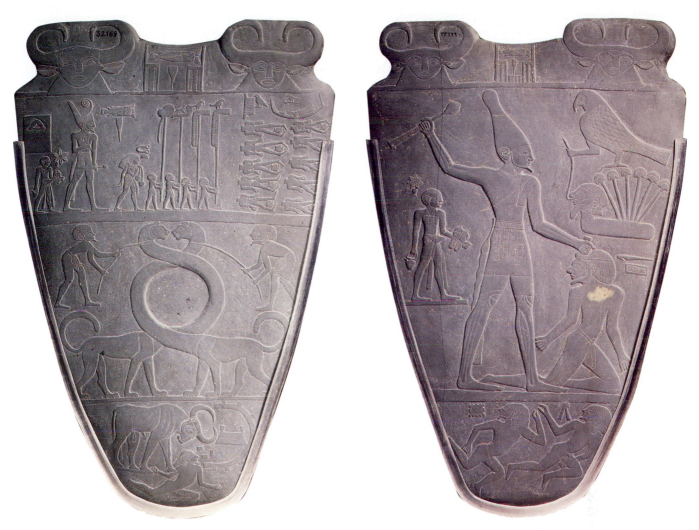

11.21 *Palette of King Narmer*, Egypt, c. 3000 BCE. Slate, 25" high. © Jurgen Liepe, Berlin.

WAR SCENES

Art can present war as a memorable, even glorious, action-filled event. Or art can document battles from various points of view. Finally, art can emphasize the horrors of war.

Glorifying War

The *Palette of King Narmer* (Fig. 11.21), from 3000 BCE, was used for mixing black eye makeup worn by ancient Egyptian men and women. The carving records the forceful unification of Egypt, when Narmer (also called Menes), king of Upper Egypt, was victorious in war over Lower Egypt. At top center, the horizontal fish above a vertical chisel are pictographs for "Narmer." Flanking Narmer's name are two images of Hathor, the cow goddess of beauty, love, and fertility, who was the king's protector. Like *Menkaure* (Fig. 11.1), Narmer is shown in the formal, standardized pose typical of Egyptian art, but here

he is larger than those around him because of his status. Horizontal divisions (or **registers**) separate scenes.

On the right, a large King Narmer, wearing the tall white crown of Upper Egypt, is about to administer a deadly blow to the enemy he grasps by the hair. Behind him is a servant who is carrying his sandals, his bare feet suggesting that this is a divinely predisposed event. The falcon represents Horus, the god of Upper Egypt, standing triumphantly on a head and papyrus, both representing Lower Egypt. In the bottom register are dead prisoners. On the left, the triumphant Narmer wears the cobra crown of Lower Egypt. Preceded by standard-bearers, he inspects the beheaded enemies lined up in rows with their heads tucked between their feet. The intertwined necks of beasts may represent unification of Egypt.

During the Kamakura era, medieval Japan was convulsed by civil war and two invasions by the Mongol emperor Kublai Khan (see *Art and History in Context* on page 303). Warfare and artistry were particularly

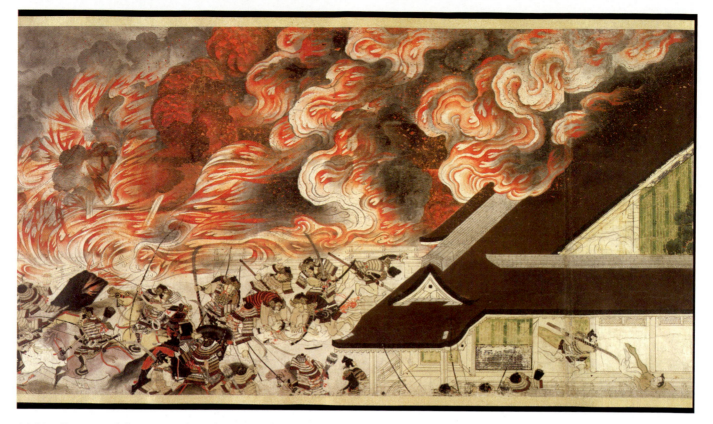

11.22 *Burning of the Sanjo Palace,* from the *Heiji Monogatari,* hand scroll (detail), Japan, Kamakura period, late 13th century. Ink and color on paper, 16¼" high, 22'9" long. Museum of Fine Arts, Boston.

interwoven at this time. The martial arts were elevated to a precise art form, and literature featured long tales of war and battle, unlike the courtly love tales from the period immediately preceding. The *Heiji Monogatari* is an illustrated scroll nearly twenty-three feet long, telling the tale of two feuding clans in the twelfth century. It was to be unrolled one scene at a time and viewed by two or three people. One scene, the *Burning of the Sanjo Palace* (Fig. 11.22), shows the tumult and disorder of warfare. As flames and smoke erupt dramatically, the raiders dash away to the left, trampling their victims or leaving them trapped in the burning rubble. Strong visual contrasts heighten the sense of chaos. Jumbled shapes differ from the clean lines of the palace roof. Groups are juxtaposed with single figures to build and then diffuse dramatic moments.

Nineteenth-Century Battle Scenes

In the preceding examples, the artists had license to exaggerate or even fantasize about the battles and warriors. The nineteenth-century invention of the camera changed that. Along with romanticized photographs of war heroes came horrific battlefield scenes, such as *Dead Confederate Soldier with Gun* (Fig. 11.23), by

Mathew B. Brady (or staff) from 1865. The first to photograph war, Brady made 3,500 photographs covering both sides of the U.S. Civil War. Brady often arranged "props," such as the rifles, to enhance both the composition and the sense of tragedy. Rough textures fill the image, except for the smooth planes of the soldier's face and rifle stock. The fallen tree forms a horizontal barrier separating the dead soldier from the living. His fallen body parallels the guns and rubble in the background behind him.

The *Battle of Little Big Horn* (Fig. 11.24), painted in 1880 by the Sioux artist Red Horse, presents the Native American point of view of Custer's last stand. The Sioux had been given land in a treaty with the U.S. government, but gold prospectors, settlers, and the railroads wanted it revoked. The flamboyant Lt. Col. George Custer attacked the Sioux and their leader, Sitting Bull, thinking this would help Custer to be elected U.S. president. As the painting illustrates, Sioux warriors advance from the right in their last victory as a nation. Custer was defeated, and the dead and wounded from both sides occupy the bottom of the image. Red Horse stacked figures above each other to show both the chaos and the detail of battle.

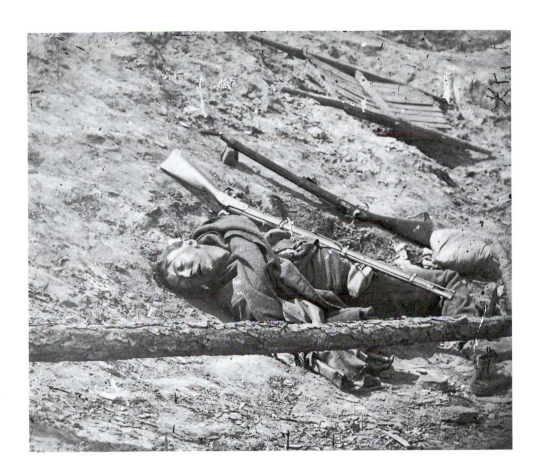

11.23 MATHEW B. BRADY (OR STAFF). *Dead Confederate Soldier with Gun,* USA, 1865. Civil War photograph. Reproduced from the Collections of the Library of Congress.

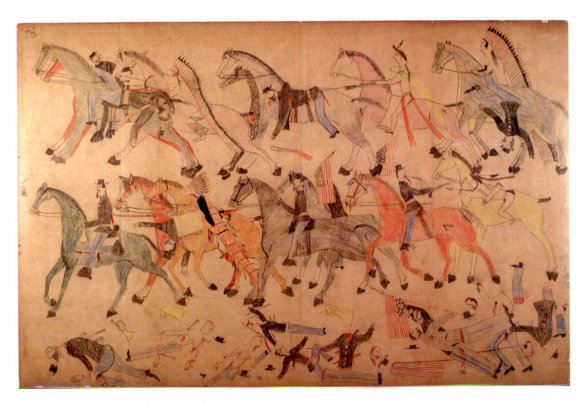

11.24 RED HORSE. *Battle of Little Big Horn,* USA, 1880. Sioux. National Anthropological Archives, Smithsonian Institution, Washington, D.C.

Twentieth-Century Images of War

Although war is still glorified in twentieth-century art, as we saw in Riefenstahl's *Triumph of the Will* (Fig. 11.7), more and more images present the horrific side.

After the revolution of 1917 in Russia, Communist leader Vladimir Lenin saw the advantages of film as a new medium. Sergei M. Eisenstein was commissioned to glorify the collective heroism and martyrdom of the Soviet people in his masterpiece film, *The Battleship Potemkin*, made in 1925 (Fig. 11.25). A great admirer of U.S. filmmaker D. W. Griffith, Eisenstein used many cinematic devices: full views; extreme close-ups; panned shots; iris (blurred edges); traveling (moving from front to back or back to front); flashbacks; and crosscutting (two events interwoven for dramatic effect).

Eisenstein's strength, however, was his editing. He used a rapid form of **montage** that allowed the viewers to piece together the narrative from fleeting images. The Odessa Steps Massacre sequence in *The Battleship Potemkin* shows the horrendous conclusion of a failed 1905 uprising. It lasts four minutes and twenty seconds, but contains 155 separate shots, all from different camera angles, showing Czarist soldiers firing on unarmed people, a mother holding a dead child, the bloodied face of a beaten woman, a baby in a carriage that careens down the steps, a horrified student, and the dreadful aftermath of the dead lying on the stairs of the port. The quick-cut images capture the feeling of terror, panic, and chaos.

One of the greatest twentieth-century paintings, *Guernica* (Fig. 11.26) by Pablo Picasso, dramatized the 1937 destruction of the Basque capital during the Spanish Civil War. German Nazi planes bombarded the city, which burned for three days and left over 1,000 people dead. In Paris, shocked and outraged, Picasso immediately set down sketches for the painting, blending the nightmarish aspects of **Surrealism** with his own style of **Cubism**. The bull represents Fascist Spain, doomed to be tortured and suffer a slow, inevitable death. The gored, dying horse is the Spanish Republic, while the fallen soldier holding the broken sword represents the spirit of resistance against tyranny. Other heads represent shocked witnesses to the suffering and carnage. The electric lightbulb shaped like an eye suggests that the world is being shown its inhumanity. A sense of agony pervades. Picasso himself experienced a conversion after Guernica. In earlier work, he was more concerned with the formalistic elements in art. Subsequently, he said, "Painting is not done to decorate apartments. It is an instrument of war for attack and defense against the enemy."

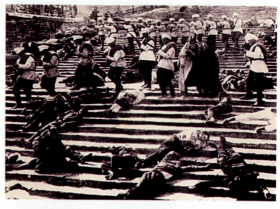

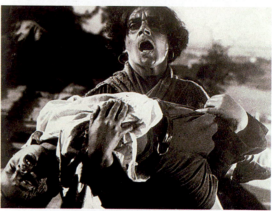

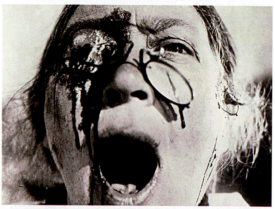

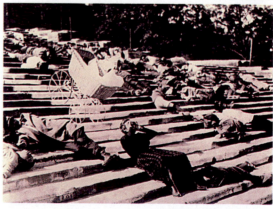

11.25 Sergei M. Eisenstein. *The Battleship Potemkin*, Russia, 1925. Film stills. © Kobal Collection.

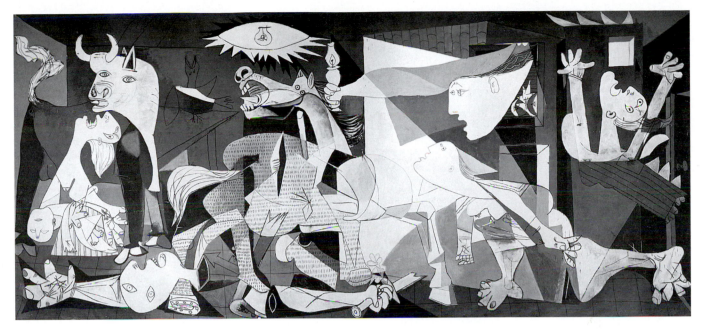

11.26 PABLO PICASSO. *Guernica,* Spain, 1937. Oil on canvas, 11' × 28'8". Prado Museum, Madrid. Institut Amatller d'Art Hispanic © Museo del Prado. © 2004 Estate of Pablo Picasso/Artists Rights Society (ARS), NY.

Connection *Turn to Chapter 12 for examples of protest art against war.*

WAR MEMORIALS

An entire book could be devoted to monumental art dedicated to war victories, battles, and the dying. In this chapter, we have already seen the *Arch of Titus* (Fig. 11.16), which both enhanced the emperor's fame and memorialized his battle victories.

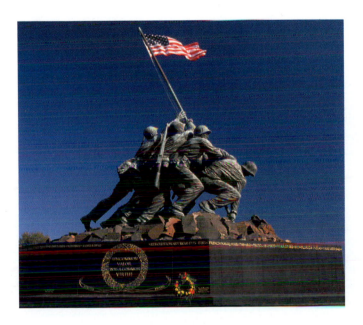

The *USA Marine Corps War Memorial* (Fig. 11.27), sculpted by Felix W. Weldon and dedicated in 1956, commemorates the 6,800 U.S. soldiers who died in the victorious battle for Iwo Jima Island in World War II. This sculpture is a copy of an Associated Press photograph that captured the second flag raising after the Marines' charged up Iwo Jima's Mt. Suribachi. Weldon's bronze sculpture is over life-size, grand, and dramatic. The soldiers form a triangle to indicate strength and solidity, while the numerous diagonals suggest tumbling haste. The past blends with the present, as every day, a real flag is raised and lowered on the memorial.

Built in 1982, the *Vietnam Veterans Memorial* by Maya Lin (Fig. 11.28) is located on the Mall in Washington, D.C. The names of nearly 58,000 Americans who died in the Vietnam War, from 1959 until 1975, are carved in chronological order on its black granite face. Its polished surface reflects the faces of the living and superimposes them on the names of the dead, which forces a personal connection between the two. Family and friends make rubbings of the names and

11.27 FELIX W. WELDON. *USA Marine Corps War Memorial,* Arlington, Virginia, USA, 1954. Cast bronze, over life-size. © Andre Jerry/Picturequest #527094.

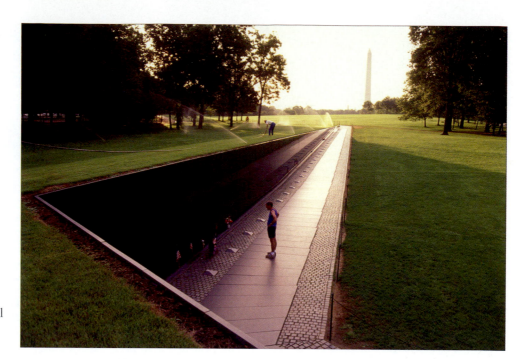

11.28 MAYA YING LIN. *Vietnam Veterans Memorial,* Washington, D.C., USA, 1982. Black granite, 492' long; height of wall at center, 10'1". © Frank Fournier/Contact Press Images.

leave all kinds of remembrances, such as poems or childhood mementos. Visitors meditate or mourn rather than celebrate. This lack of glory made the *Memorial* very controversial, so figurative sculptures of heroic soldiers and nurses were added later near the site. Taken all together, these monuments create a powerful memorial to the Vietnam War.

The long, V-shaped memorial is set into the ground with one end pointing to the Washington Monument, a symbol of national unity, and the other end pointing to the Lincoln Memorial, remembering a nation divided by civil war. This reflects the national anguish over soldiers who died in a war about which the general population was ambivalent. Magazine and newspaper coverage had brought the blunt realities of the war into U.S. homes, as evident in *Brigadier General Nguyen Ngoc Loan summarily executing the suspected leader of a Vietcong commando unit* (Fig. 11.29), a war photograph from 1968 by Eddie Adams. Its harshness contrasts severely with romanticized images of war.

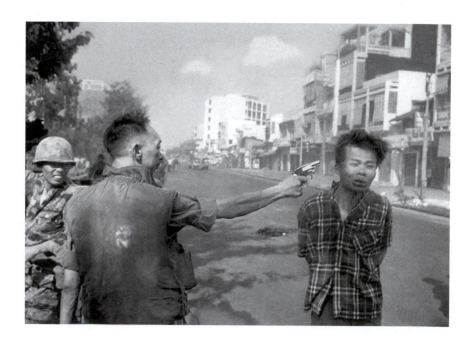

11.29 EDDIE ADAMS. *Brigadier General Nguyen Ngoc Loan summarily executing the suspected leader of a Vietcong commando unit,* Saigon, South Vietnam, February 1, 1968. © AP/Wide World Photos.

PEACE

Winged allegorical figures, doves, women, and pastoral landscapes have symbolized peace in Western art. Gardens, bells, and temples serve as monuments to peace in Asia, Europe, and the Americas.

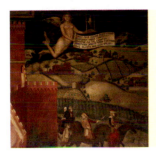

Connection Ambrogio Lorenzetti's Allegory of Good Government *contains a personification of peace and shows the prosperity that comes with peace. See also Figure 12.19.*

ART ABOUT PEACE

Edward Hicks's *The Peaceable Kingdom* (Fig. 11.30), painted between 1830 and 1840, is based on the following biblical passage:

> The wolf also shall dwell with the lamb, and the leopard shall lie down with the kid; and the calf and the young lion and the fatling together; and a little child shall lead them. (Isaiah 11)

Hicks was also inspired by the Quaker William Penn and his treaty with the Indians, which is visible in the background as a copied detail from a famous painting by U.S. artist Benjamin West. This moment came to signify a utopian new world. Hicks's visual metaphors have become standard language for expressing

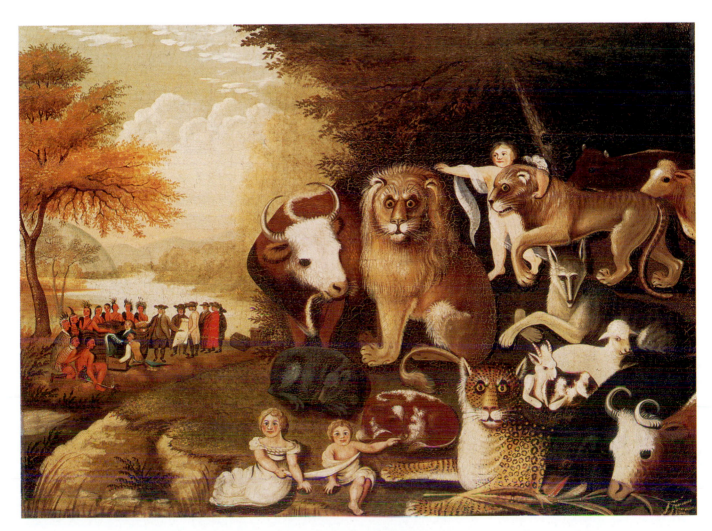

11.30   EDWARD HICKS. *The Peaceable Kingdom*, USA, 1830–1840. Oil on canvas. 17 7/16" × 23 9/16". Brooklyn Museum of Art.

the concept of peace. A luminous sky glows in the background, while lush vegetation frames the foreground figures. The animals are rendered in a flat, decorative, imaginative style. There is a feeling of innocence and peace, without strife and turmoil.

PEACE MONUMENTS AND PEACE OFFERINGS

An example of a peace monument is the *Ara Pacis Augustae* (Fig. 11.31), from 13–9 BCE, built to commemorate Emperor Augustus's stopping of the civil wars between Spain and France. It sits on a podium with twelve steps, enclosed by walls covered with reliefs of the Earth Mother, Tellus; Aeneas, the legendary founder of Rome; and two long processions led by Augustus. Carved foliage and fruit garlands symbolize the golden age of plenty as well as fecundity, ripeness, and peace, all under the rule of Augustus. Sacrificial offerings of animals and humans are indicated. The whole piece was probably brightly painted. Although the *Ara Pacis* celebrates the peace of the Roman Empire, it can also be seen as a victory monument that glorifies the emperor Augustus.

When peace treaties are signed, art and gifts are often exchanged to seal the agreement. Precious objects might also be offered to show submission or to avoid further confrontation. *Moctezuma's Headdress* (Fig. 11.32) is believed to have belonged to the last Aztec ruler, Moctezuma, who may have given it to the Spanish leader Cortés as a peace offering or as a desperate last measure to avoid his own demise. Objects made of feathers are frail, and not many survive long periods. This one is exceptional. The four-foot-high headdress features iridescent green feathers from the quetzal bird's tail and has blue feathers from the cotinga interwoven with small gold disks. Three hundred workers staffed the royal aviaries that produced these feathers. Moctezuma's wives and concubines probably made the piece.

Native Americans created tomahawks and pipes used exclusively for peaceful exchange. The *Presentation Pipe Tomahawk* (Fig. 11.33) is an aesthetically beautiful work meant to be presented as a ritual peace offering. It is made of hickory wood, silver, iron, and lead. The name "Ottokee," a member of the Great Lakes Ottawa tribe in 1820, is engraved in silver inlay on the handle, along with naturalistic fish and an abstract curvilinear pattern. On the head and blade of the tomahawk are engraved an acorn, a heart, and a half moon. The style of the engravings suggests European influences. The pipe tomahawk may have been crafted by European, American, or Ottawan metalsmiths.

Recently in the twentieth century, memorials to peace were constructed in Hiroshima, Japan, and in Los Angeles, California. These "peace parks," not shown here, were built to heal wounds of war. It is hoped such memorials will become a more prominent part of human history.

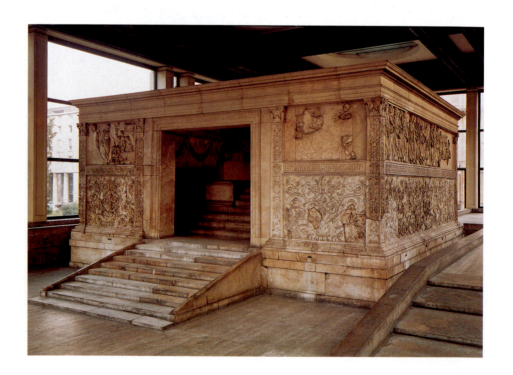

11.31 *Ara Pacis Augustae,* Rome, 13–9 BCE. Marble; outer wall, 34'5" × 38' × 23'. © Scala/Art Resource, NY.

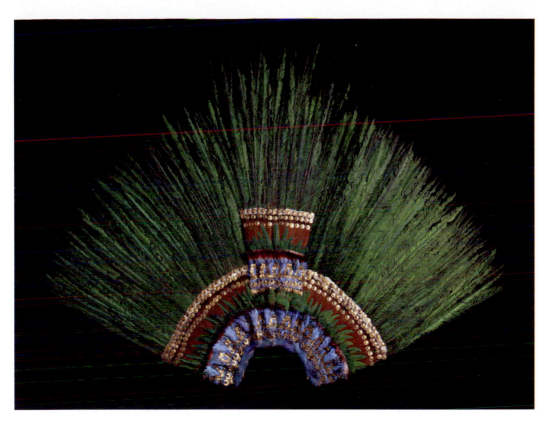

11.32 *Moctezuma's Headdress,* Mexico, c. 1319. Aztec. Quetzal and cotinga feathers, gold plaques. Kunsthistorisches Museum.

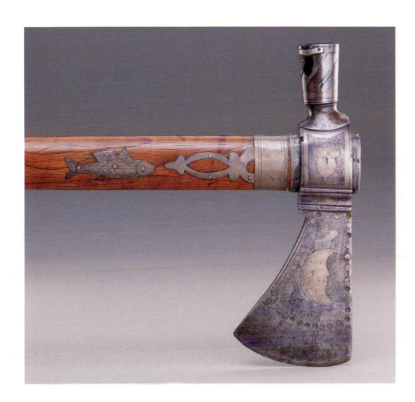

11.33 *Presentation Pipe Tomahawk,* USA, c. 1820. Ottawa. Wood, inlaid metal. 23½" × 8". The Detroit Institute of Arts.

World history from 500–1300 witnessed the rise and fall of many kingdoms, with rulers using art to increase their prestige.

Civilization centers flourished throughout the Americas. The Moche civilization (200–800) of coastal Peru produced great temples of sun brick and had elaborate burials filled with metal, jewels, and ceramic treasures. The Inca civilization in the Andes Mountains was shortly to emerge. North American centers included the Mississippian culture (c. 800) and the Anasazi (1000–1300), who built the famous cliff dwellings in the southwest United States.

Central America saw the succession of many great empires with ambitious architecture and advances in learning, especially in mathematics and astronomy. All were hierarchical societies, governed by a supreme ruler with warrior and priest classes. Teotihuacán reached its height around 600. The old Maya Empire in the Yucatan Peninsula thrived until around 900, with grand temples and palaces, like the *Palace at Palenque* (Fig. 11.10). From the Toltec culture (900–1200) around Veracruz came the *Tula Warrior Columns* (Fig. 11.17). Beginning in the thirteenth century, the Aztec built a powerful empire in central Mexico, with

engineering feats that included irrigation and drainage systems and road building.

During this period, the Byzantine Empire and the expansion of Islam dominated Eastern Europe, the Middle East, central Asia, and northern Africa. One of the great rulers of the Christian Byzantine Empire (476–1453) was Justinian, whose notable churches featured mosaics such as the *Emperor Justinian and His Attendants* (Fig. 11.2). Wealthy Byzantium had many centers for learning and for preservation of ancient knowledge. It began to decline around 1100, due to warfare with Muslims.

The prophet Muhammed founded the Islamic religion in the early seventh century. Islam spread quickly, sometimes through warfare. Muslim armies conquering northern Africa, Spain, and the Middle East within one hundred years and advancing on India beginning in 1000. Important Muslim kingdoms were established in today's Spain, Iraq, and Turkey. The Muslims were known for their accomplishments in algebra, geometry, astronomy, optics, and literature as well as for the creation of great universities and libraries.

Map 5 The Expansion of Islam, the Byzantine Empire, and the Migration of Germanic People into Southern Europe. Courtesy of Replogle Globes, Inc., Broadview, IL.

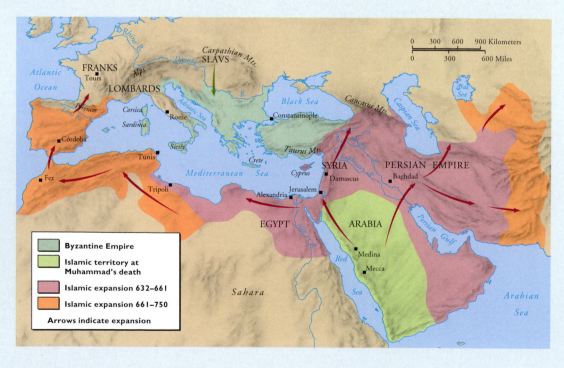

This was the Middle Ages in Europe, beginning with the dissolution of the Western Roman Empire and concluding with the early forms of the modern European nation-states. Until 600, Europe experienced upheaval as Germanic peoples migrated south and east. Once they settled, they founded Christian kingdoms with architecture and art influenced by Rome and Byzantium. Large monasteries and the Catholic Church in Rome were more powerful than any other European government. Almost all art was religious. The Crusades (1095–1291), a series of wars for control of the Holy Land, brought the Germanic Europeans in further contact with Byzantium and the Muslim Empire. Feudalism was the main form of social and economic organization. The Black Death (1347–1351) ravaged Europe, killing one-third of the population. By 1200, a distinctive art form, Gothic, developed in Northern Europe.

Africa also saw the emergence of several early empires. Northern empires were Islamic, while southern empires followed native African religions. Powerful and wealthy Ghana (c. 700–1200) controlled the area's trade in salt and gold. Its ironworks produced powerful weapons. Later in the same area, Mali became a large Islamic empire. Farther south, in Ife, the twelfth century saw the founding of the Yoruba civilization, with its famous *Crowned Head of an Oni* (Fig. 11.3). Also in the south, the Zanj people thrived on trade with China, Arabia, and India from 1200 to 1500, and the kingdom of Zimbabwe flourished, with its great stone buildings.

India experienced a resurgence of Hinduism beginning in the sixth century, and many huge temple complexes were constructed. After 1000, Muslims invaded and established the Mughal Empire in northern India. In the south, strong Hindu dynasties continued, with ambitious building programs. Indian art and architecture spread to Southeast Asia and Indonesia throughout this period. In Cambodia, the Khmer people developed a culture noted for its amazing architecture and sculpture, like *Jayavarman VII* (Fig. 11.4).

The imperial court in China promoted the arts throughout this era, with accomplishments in poetry, literature, music, ceramics, and painting, like the *Portraits of the Emper-*

ors on this page. The dynasties were the Tang (618–906), Song (960–1279), and Yuan (1279–1368). The Yuan was founded by invading Mongolians under Kublai Khan. Inventions included the magnetic compass, paper money, book printing, and gunpowder. After 1368, the Ming Dynasty began an ambitious building program, which included the structures in the Forbidden City (Fig. 11.11 and Fig. 11.35) and the *Great Wall* (Fig. 11.20), and China became an international naval power.

Japanese recorded history begins around the year 600, when the Japanese culture changed due to foreign influences. It imported the Buddhist religion, mathematics, architecture, the arts, and agricultural methods from the Chinese, but eventually modified them. Shinto is the native Japanese religion. Japan produced the world's first novel, *The Tale of the Genji*, by Lady Murasaki Shikibu, illustrated in the handscroll, *Heiji Monogatari* (Fig. 11.22). From the eighth century through the nineteenth, Japan was essentially a feudal state, with a hierarchy of military leaders under the shogun, and experienced periods of internal strife.

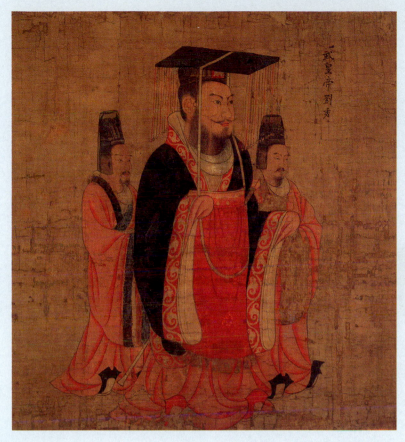

11.34   Yan Liben, *Portraits of the Emperors* (detail), China, 7th century. Ink and colors on silk, 17.5" high. Museum of Fine Arts, Boston.

Chinese emperors were believed to be Sons of Heaven. Their lavish attire, serene expression, and relatively large size all attested to their brilliance.

500 – 1300 CE

Timeline

Left Events	Left Date	Left Art Works
Unification of Egypt	**3200 BCE**	*Palette of King Narmer*
		Menkaure and His Wife, Queen Khamerernebty
	1500	
Assyrian Empire	1000	
Achaemenid Persia	500	*Lamassu* *Persepolis*
Roman Republic		*The Great Wall*
	100	
Roman Empire		*Ara Pacis Augustae* *Arch of Titus*
Teotihuacán	200 CE	
German Migration in Europe	400	
Byzantine Empire Begins	500	
		Emperor Justinian and His Attendants *Palace at Palenque*
Tang Dynasty—China Islam Founded Japan—Historic Era	600	
	700	
	800	
	900	
Yoruba Culture Founded		
Maya–Toltec Culture		
Song Dynasty—China		
Romanesque Era	1000	*Tula Warrior Columns*
Anasazi Culture		*Crowned Head of an Oni*
	1100	
		Jayavarman VII
	1200	
Gothic Era		
Yuan Dynasty—China	1300	*Burning of the Sanjo Palace* *Moctezuma's Headdress*

Right Events	Right Date	Right Art Works
Aztec Empire		
Black Death		
Incan Empire Renaissance in Europe Ming Dynasty—China	1400	
		Verrocchio: *Equestrian Monument of Bartolomeo Colleoni*
Mughal Dynasty— India		
Forbidden City Begun	1500	*Imperial Throne Room*
	1600	
		Hall of Mirrors
Benin Kingdom—Africa	1700	*Cloak and Feather Hat* *Plaque with Warrior and Attendants*
U.S. Revolutionary War		
French Revolution	1800	*Mesquakie Bear Claw Necklace* *Te Papaiouru Marae*, a Maori Meeting House *Presentation Pipe Tomahawk* Hicks: *The Peaceable Kingdom* Barry and Pugin: *Houses of Parliament* Brady (or staff): *Dead Confederate Soldier with Gun* Red Horse: *Battle of Little Big Horn*
Russian Revolution	1900	Olowe: *Palace Sculpture*
World War I		Eisenstein: *The Battleship Potemkin*
World War II		Riefenstahl: *Triumph of the Will* Picasso: *Guernica*
	1950	
		Hiroshima Peace Memorial Park Weldon: *USA Marine Corps War Memorial* Adams: *Brigadier General . . . executing . . .*
Vietnam War		
	2000	Lin: *Vietnam Veterans Memorial*

Art has played a tremendous role in promoting rulers' power. Portraits denote power, and special objects are signs of prestige. Art can glorify rulers' achievements. The state also is glorified in art, especially in palaces, seats of government, and monuments.

A warrior's paraphernalia raises the owner's status, and artistry enhances the spirit and function of the weapon. War scenes can exalt the drama of war, give alternate views of battle, or emphasize the horror of war. War memorials may evoke deep patriotism or private mourning and contemplation. Peace itself is given an image in painting, and beautifully crafted art objects may become peace offerings. Peace memorials may glorify the abundance possible when there is no war.

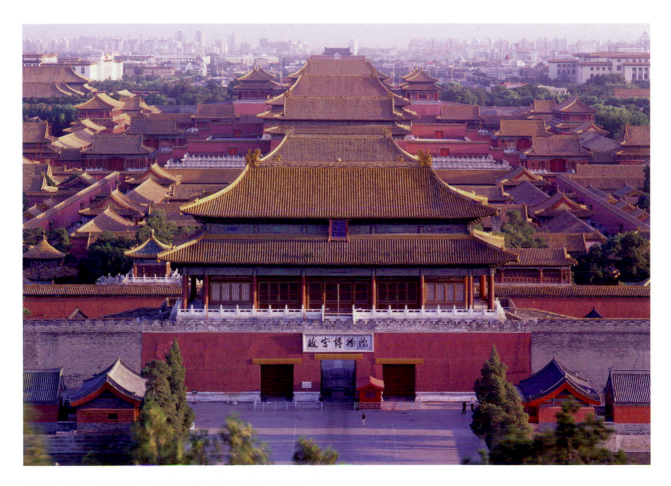

11.35   *Imperial Palace*, Forbidden City, Beijing, China.

FOOD FOR THOUGHT

■ *Many great works of art and architecture have been commissioned by "divinely empowered" individuals or the rulers of modern totalitarian states. For example, the Forbidden City is a huge, lavish compound of palaces, temples, and other structures built for the Chinese Imperial family. See Figure 11.35. Often such great works of art carry a high cost in lives and funds. Can this be justified? Would such grand works of art and architecture ever be created without enormous power behind them?*

- How are war and peace presented now in contemporary mass media—in comic books, television shows, movies, or computer games? Does one group or the other seem to have justice on its side? How are winners and losers presented? Are there instances in which peace is fully imagined or explored?

- Photography is often associated with factual reporting. But the video camera records only one point of view, and that can be edited. Photographers choose which pictures to take and which to ignore. Editors select only a few images to print. Governments can control the press's access to events and thus influence coverage, as happened in the early 1990s during Operation Desert Storm. Is the news factual? Is art factual?

- Research some of the weapons that have been made throughout.

Your Thomson Online Resources

 Go to **ArtExperience Online** for the Flashcards, Quiz, and Study Guide for this chapter.

CHAPTER 12

Social Protest/Affirmation

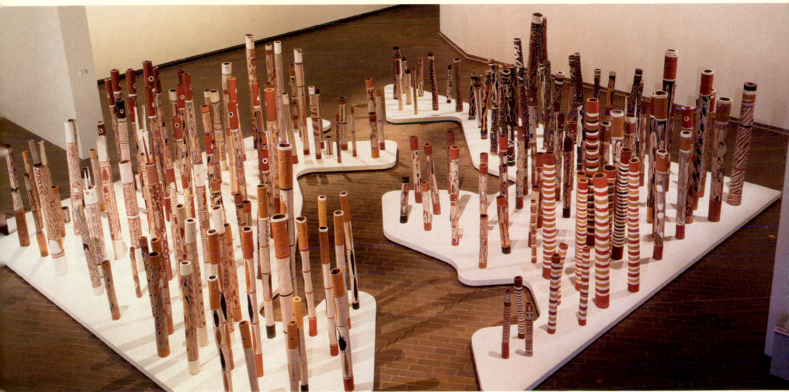

National Gallery of Art, Canberra. © 2007 Artists Rights Society (ARS), New York/VI$COPY, Australia.

INTRODUCTION

Many artists protest injustice with their artwork. They identify villains, honor heroes, and promote causes with emotional and visual impact unequaled by the written word. Protest art is a form of affirmation, because it is based on respect for human dignity and the belief that change is possible.

- *What art has been made in protest of war, and when?*
- *What strategies have artists used to make their work more effective for political and social change?*
- *What is "normal" in society?*
- *What do artists say about all-pervasive normalcy?*
- *What types of social power are used to control or oppress people?*

Two other chapters contain related images. Chapter 11 has artworks about war. Chapter 14 contains art that examines race and gender.

PROTESTS AGAINST MILITARY ACTION

For thousands of years, artists have depicted war, sometimes glorifying the victors, sometimes showing the defeated and those killed or wounded. Not until two hundred years ago, however, did artists begin to make art that protests a particular war or the idea of warfare altogether. One likely reason is that a sizable percentage of past art was made for victorious political or religious leaders. Warfare was one means to gain power, and art was a way to display that power. Especially since World War II, however, growing numbers of artworks have protested full-blown war, police actions, covert operations, and guerrilla activity.

A pivotal piece in the history of protest art is *The Executions of May 3, 1808* (Fig. 12.1), from 1814. The artist, Francisco Goya, based his painting on sketches he had made of the actual event as it happened six years earlier. The citizens of Madrid unsuccessfully rose up against Napoleon Bonaparte's occupational army in 1808. The soldiers captured many of the rioters and executed them a short distance outside the city. Goya individualized the Spaniards trembling, praying, or protesting as they face the firing line, so that we identify with their horror. We particularly focus on the man in white with outstretched arms who is posed like the crucified Jesus, surrounded with light colors against the pervasive gloom. In contrast, Goya has dehumanized the soldiers, with repeated poses and hidden faces. The barrels of their pointing rifles are rigidly organized, like a war machine. Goya's painting goes beyond partisanship and could stand for any mass execution.

Käthe Kollwitz dedicated her art to ending war and poverty. She lived in Germany through the two world wars, losing a son and a grandson in the fighting. In her artwork, however, she frequently turned to past conflicts to show the destructive energy of war. *The Outbreak ("Losbruch")*, dated 1903 (Fig. 12.2), is the fifth in a series of seven prints that tell of the Peasant War in Germany in the early sixteenth century. In the first four prints in the series, we see the causes for the peasant revolt: abuse by the ruling class, poverty, crushingly hard work, rape of the women. In the fifth image, *The Outbreak ("Losbruch")*, the peasants revolt, propelled by their wretched living conditions.

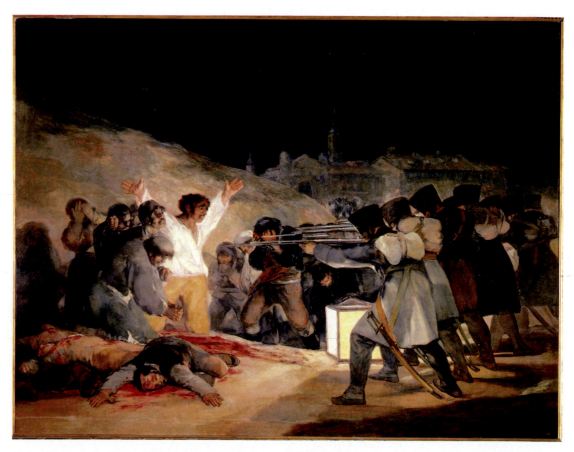

12.1   FRANCISCO GOYA. *The Executions of May 3, 1808*, Spain, 1814. Oil on canvas, 104³/₄" × 135³/₄". Prado, Madrid. © Erich Lessing/Art Resource, NY.

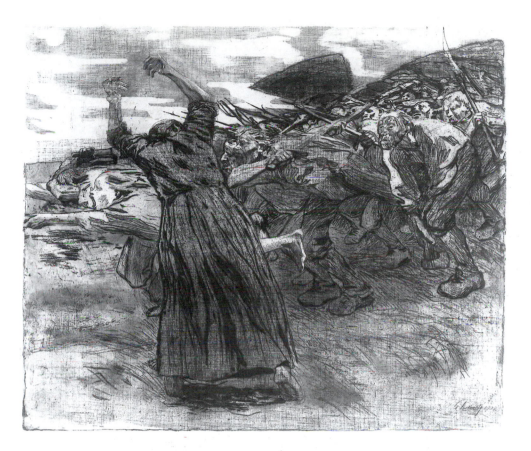

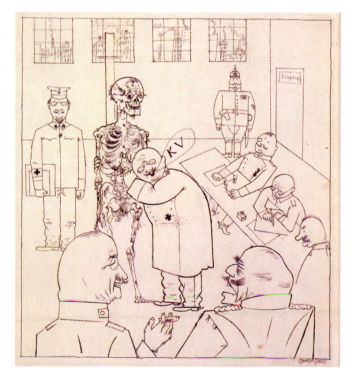

12.2   KÄTHE KOLLWITZ. *The Outbreak ("Losbruch")*, Germany, 1903. Etching, 20" × 23¼". Reproduced from the collections of the Library of Congress, Washington, D.C. © 2004 Artists Rights Society (ARS), New York/VG Bild-Kunst, Bonn.

The composition of the work is remarkable. The peasants group at the right, while already at the left they rush at deadly speed to attack their oppressors with crude weapons and farm tools. The dark woman in front becomes the leader and the conscience for the group. Her upraised arms incite them to action, while her bony, twisted hands and arms are documents to the incredible harshness of the peasants' life. Stark blacks and whites flash across the image, visually conveying the emotional moment.

Kollwitz shows a woman leading the revolt, breaking old stereotypes about women's passivity. This also attests to the misery of the peasants' lives—in the end, the women rose up.

The uprising was unsuccessful, as the forces of the ruling class suppressed the peasants with brutality. The last two prints of the *Peasant War* series show a mother searching for her dead son among piles of bodies, and peasant prisoners bound together awaiting execution.

Fit for Active Service (Fig. 12.3), a 1918 pen-and-ink drawing by George Grosz, exposed the bloated doctors and self-absorbed officers, secure in their bureaucratic assignments, who sent elderly, sick, or very young men to the front lines to fight for Germany

12.3   GEORGE GROSZ. *Fit for Active Service*, Germany, 1918. Pen and ink, 14½" × 13½". The Museum of Modern Art, New York. © Digital Image © The Museum of Modern Art/Licensed by Scala/Art Resource, NY. © Estate of George Grosz/Licensed by VAGA, New York, NY.

near the end of World War I. (All able-bodied men had been sent out much earlier.) With grim wit, the artist's pen outlines the smug, laughing faces of the officers in the foreground. Farther back, two toadying soldiers stand at attention. The seams in their uniforms line up with the floor and the window frames. They are conformists subsumed into the structure, without independent conscience. The doctor at the center seems almost happy, since he has found another body for the front lines. Outside, factories contentedly belch out the machinery of war. In contrast to the spare and flattened manner in which the other figures are portrayed, the skeleton seems the most "human," as it is rounded, detailed, and adorned with rotting organs and tufts of hair.

John Heartfield dedicated much of his art to exposing and condemning the horrors of Nazi Germany. He was born in Germany as Helmut Herzfelde, but later anglicized his name. *Goering the Executioner,* dated 1933 (Fig. 12.4), is a **photomontage,** in which news photographs are combined and manipulated with drawing. It appeared on the front page of the Prague newspaper *AIZ* (*Arbeiter-Illustrierte-Zeitung*). The subject is Field Marshal Hermann Goering, one of the major leaders of the Nazi party. Heartfield pulled Goering's head forward, increasing the thickness of the neck and emphasizing the aggressiveness of his bullying face. Behind him burns the Reichstag, the German parliament building, destroyed in 1933 by an act of terrorism that was likely perpetrated by the Nazis but "officially" blamed on Communists. The Nazis used this excuse to seize absolute power and end any democratic government. Black-and-white elements give the image an unvarnished, blunt quality. Goering's meat cleaver and stained apron have the quality of factual truth, even though the artist added those props. Heartfield's warnings of Nazi bloodshed proved to be prophetically true. Heartfield was forced to leave Germany and spent much of the 1930s and 1940s in England.

In the mid-1930s, Spain was engulfed in a civil war that in many ways was a prelude to World War II. In 1937, David Alfaro Siqueiros painted *Echo of a Scream* (Fig. 12.5) in response to the horror of the Spanish Civil War. Siqueiros symbolized all of humanity with the screaming, helpless, pained child sitting amid the debris and destruction of modern warfare. The sky is filled by the large, detached head—the child's head repeated—a massive cry that symbolizes the combined pain of all the victims we do not see. The dark tones and blue-gray colors of the painting add a somber note to the ugly surroundings. The painting also alludes to urbanization and industrialization, and to the endless piles of waste that are the result of "progress" and "innovation." Siqueiros knew his subject matter firsthand. He was a Mexican citizen who fought in Spain in the International Brigade, composed of volunteers from fifty countries who fought for the Spanish Republic against the Fascists and their German Nazi backers. He was also a political activist and social reformer.

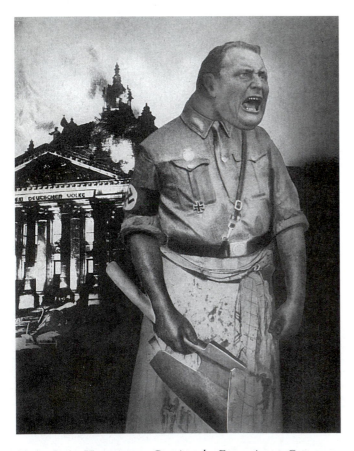

12.4 JOHN HEARTFIELD. *Goering the Executioner,* Germany, 1933. Photomontage cover for *AIZ.* Reproduced from *John Heartfield,* by Wieland Herzfelde (Dresden: VEB Verlag der Kunst, 1964). © 2004 Artists Rights Society (ARS), New York/VG Bild-Kunst, Bonn.

Connection *See Pablo Picasso's* Guernica *(Fig. 11.26, page 297) for another artwork that deals with the Spanish Civil War.*

Later, Robert Motherwell painted the *Elegy to the Spanish Republic XXXIV,* between 1953 and 1954 (Fig. 12.6), part of a series of over 150 paintings that mourned the loss of liberty in Spain after the Fascist forces were victorious. Although the paintings do not

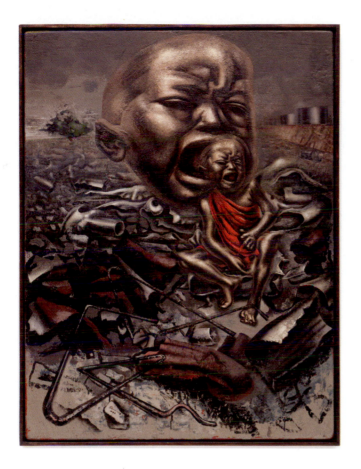

tell a story, Motherwell believed that abstraction communicated, in universal terms, the struggle between life and death and between freedom and oppression. The large size of the painting makes these struggles seem monumental. Motherwell was influenced by the **Surrealist** process of expression called **automatism**, which incorporates intuition, spontaneity, and the accidental when creating artworks, similar to the **Abstract Expressionist** style. His black-and-white forms suggest several Spanish motifs, according to Robert Hughes (1997:496). They are bull's testicles, the patent leather berets of the Guardia Civil, and living forms (represented by the large, ovoid shapes) being crushed by the black bands.

12.5 DAVID ALFARO SIQUEIROS. *Echo of a Scream*, Mexico, 1937. Enamel on wood, 48" × 36". Gift of Edward M. M. Warburg (633.1939). The Museum of Modern Art, New York, NY. © Estate of David Alfaro Siqueiros/SOMAAP, Mexico City/VAGA, New York.

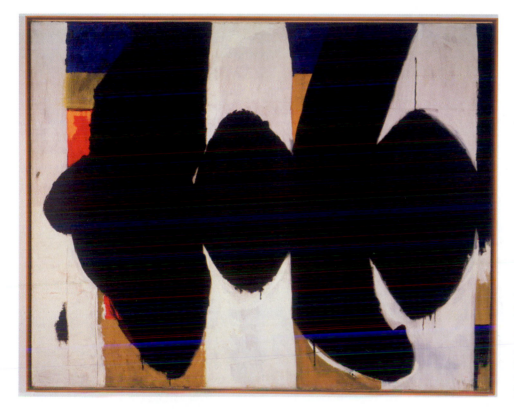

12.6 ROBERT MOTHERWELL. *Elegy to the Spanish Republic XXXIV,* USA, 1953–1954. Oil on canvas, 80" × 100". Albright-Knox Art Gallery, Buffalo, N.Y. © Dedalus Foundation/Licensed by VAGA, New York, NY.

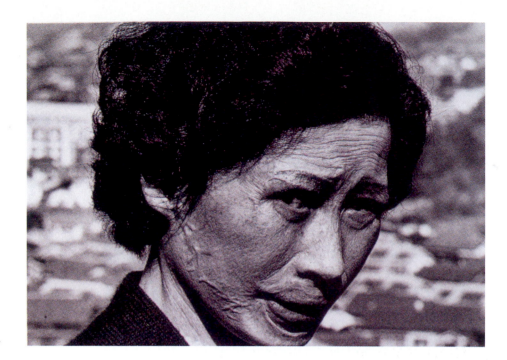

12.7 TOMATSU SHOMEI. *Woman with Keloidal Scars* (from the series *11:02 – Nagasaki*), Japan, 1966. Gelatin Silver Print, 11.5" × 16". Courtesy of the artist.

From the other side of the world, Tomatsu Shomei's *Woman with Keloidal Scars* (Fig. 12.7) is one of a series of photographs of victims of the atomic bombing of Nagasaki, Japan, at the end of World War II. The blast was so powerful that it vaporized the victims who were nearest the center of impact. Those farther away suffered terrible injuries and deformities. Tomatsu's photograph is technically beautiful, with a full range of deep blacks and silvery grays. But the lacy texture is excessive fibrous tissue stretched over the woman's skull. With her pained, fearful expression, her psychological and physical injuries still seem fresh, although inflicted long ago. Yet there is a strange sense of normalcy, as if she were out sightseeing. Tomatsu made this series to document past horrors and to protest against U.S. troops stationed in Japan for decades. Since World War II, some Japanese have pushed for complete, permanent demilitarization of the country.

Leon Golub's painting, *Mercenaries I* (Fig. 12.8), from 1976, shows two "guns for hire" dangling a bound victim between them, using brute power to bolster a repressive government. These professional fighters are devoid of any ideological stance; they are simply paid thugs. The mercenaries are flattened figures against

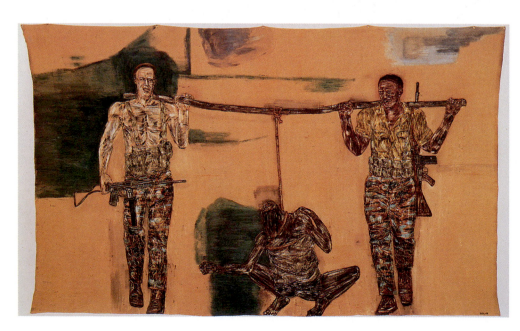

12.8 LEON GOLUB. *Mercenaries I*, USA, 1976. Acrylic on canvas, 116" × 186½". The Broad Art Foundation. © Leon Golub/Licensed by VAGA, New York, NY. Courtesy Ronald Feldman Fine Arts.

the flat background. They are pushed aggressively to the foreground, and we, the viewers, are dwarfed by the nearly eleven-foot height of the painting. Looking up, we share the same view as the victim, who has no identifying traits and could be anyone, even us. The paint, applied thickly at first, has been scraped repeatedly so that the surface seems raw and nasty. The flesh looks particularly repulsive, both on the cruel faces of the mercenaries and on the tortured victim. The colors are jarring and acid.

Golub worked from news photographs and insisted that his images realistically report atrocities occurring regularly in the world. His images have an immediacy to them because of the news and because of entangled global politics and economies.

FIGHTING FOR THE OPPRESSED

Artists who fight for the rights and affirm the values of economically or politically repressed peoples use several strategies to make their points most forcefully. These include beauty, illustration, narrative, humor, and shock. Most social protest works are designed generally to affect public consciousness, rather than to prescribe specific changes.

STRATEGIES FOR PROTESTING OPPRESSION

Interestingly, beauty and excitement can be very effective elements in protest art. In Eugène Delacroix's *Liberty Leading the People,* painted in 1830 (Fig. 12.9), Liberty has been personified as a partially nude woman—apparently flesh and blood—but reminiscent of a Greek goddess in her profile and in her idealized body. Energized and oblivious to danger, she carries a rifle and the flag of the French Revolution. She forms the peak of a triangle made up of merchants, students, laborers, soldiers, and even young boys who emerge from the smoke, debris, and dead bodies to move toward the light that surrounds Liberty.

The lower and middle classes revolted many times against European ruling classes in the late eighteenth

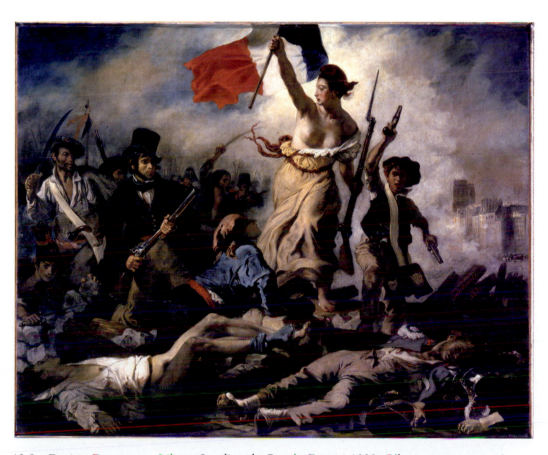

12.9   EUGÈNE DELACROIX. *Liberty Leading the People,* France, 1830. Oil on canvas, approximately 8'6" × 10'8". Louvre, Paris. © Réunion des Musées Nationaux/Art Resource, NY.

and early nineteenth centuries. This painting is a homage to the Paris revolt in 1830. Delacroix's painting mixes realistic, idealistic, and romantic elements. Realistic are the faces of the men, who look like Parisians of the day, and the details of the clothing, weapons, and the Paris skyline in the background. Ideal elements include the glowing, goddess-like figure of Liberty, and the belief that revolution will lead to a better way of life. The work is romantic in its portrayal of fighting as thrilling, dangerous, and liberating. Compare this work to Siqueiros's *Echo of a Scream* (Fig. 12.5), where warfare is not romanticized.

One of the most direct ways to make social protest art is to illustrate the oppressive situation. At the beginning of the twentieth century, sociologist and artist Lewis Hine photographed miserable labor conditions and slum housing in the United States. He was particularly known for exposing child labor in mines and textile mills, where children were doing the lowest-paying, most tedious jobs. *Leo, 48 Inches High, 8 Years Old, Picks Up Bobbins at 15¢ a Day,* from 1910 (Fig. 12.10), shows a young boy who dodges under textile looms to pick up loose thread spools. Children in these jobs ran the risk of injury or death from moving machinery. They typically worked ten- to twelve-hour shifts in the mills, six days a week, making schooling impossible. Child laborers were destined to remain illiterate, poor, and overworked. Hine fully documented the youthfulness of the child laborers by giving his photos long titles, yet in some ways, they were unnecessary. Hine's composition emphasizes the large scale of the weaving machines—their great length and height—that dwarf the child. Leo seems very young and apprehensive. The factory is gloomy, littered, and staffed by women, another underpaid group. Hine's pictures are harder to forget than wordy ideological arguments, pro or con, on labor conditions.

Hine worked with the National Child Labor Committee, a private group dedicated to protecting working children, and the loosely organized Progressive Movement of the early twentieth century, which sought reform for a number of problems resulting from urbanization and industrialization. He lectured and his images were published in magazines, making his work unusually successful in changing both public opinion and public policy. Child labor was eventually outlawed in the 1930s.

Ben Shahn used narrative as a protest strategy in *The Passion of Sacco and Vanzetti,* dated 1931–1932 (Fig. 12.11), to tell the story of Nicola Sacco and Bartolomeo Vanzetti, Italian immigrants who were active in labor organizations, avoided the draft in World War I, and were political anarchists. They were arrested and convicted for robbery and murder, despite several witnesses who testified that they were elsewhere at the time of the crime. Many claimed that Sacco and Vanzetti were convicted because of their politics, as the judge allowed the prosecution to make inflammatory

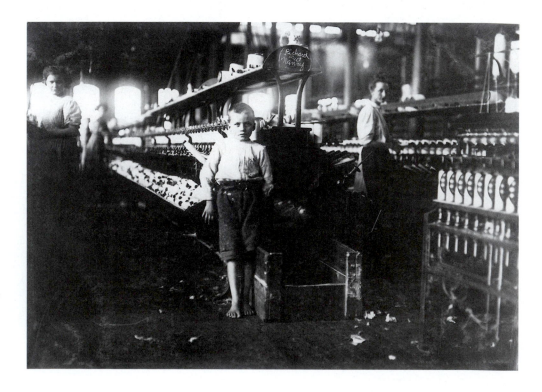

12.10 LEWIS HINE. *Leo, 48 Inches High, 8 Years Old, Picks Up Bobbins at 15¢ a Day,* USA, 1910. Photograph, 8½" × 11". University of Maryland Library, College Park, Maryland. Reproduced from the collections of the Library of Congress.

statements about their political beliefs during the trial. In his painting, Shahn collapses time, showing simultaneously the courthouse steps, the framed portrait of the judge who presided over the original trial, and the ashen faces of Sacco and Vanzetti as they lie in their coffins. Prominent in the middle are three commissioners who declared the trial to have been legal, thus allowing the executions to take place. The commissioners are dour and righteous, bolstered by institutional rigidity. The harsh colors express Shahn's distress at the death of the two men, whom Shahn and many others felt were heroes.

Jacob Lawrence also used narrative to recount the accomplishments, challenges, and oppressions of the African community uprooted to the Western Hemisphere by slavery. He made thirty-one paintings about Harriet Tubman and twenty-two on John Brown. The paintings reconstruct the past with lengthy, narrative titles to make the story clearer and to inspire African Americans today. Our example is *No. 36: During the Truce Toussaint Is Deceived and Arrested by LeClerc. LeClerc Led Toussaint to Believe That He Was Sincere, Believing That When Toussaint Was Out of the Way, the Blacks Would Surrender* (Fig. 12.12). It is one of forty-one paintings made from 1937 to 1941 on

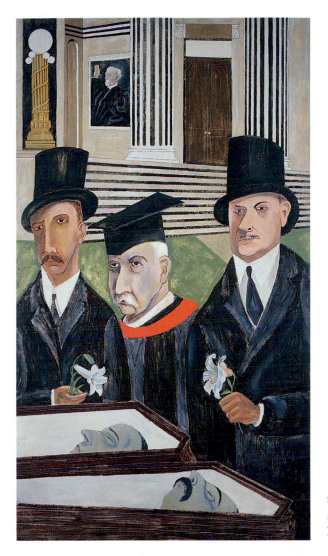

12.11   BEN SHAHN. *The Passion of Sacco and Vanzetti*, USA (Lithuanian born), 1931–1932. Tempera on canvas, 84½" × 48". The Whitney Museum of American Art, New York.

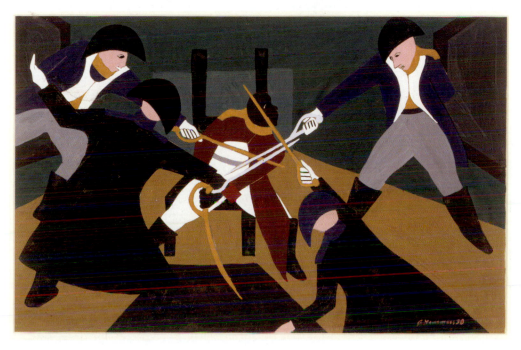

12.12   JACOB LAWRENCE. *No. 36: During the Truce Toussaint Is Deceived and Arrested by LeClerc. LeClerc Led Toussaint to Believe That He Was Sincere, Believing That When Toussaint Was Out of the Way, the Blacks Would Surrender*, USA, 1937–1938. Tempera on paper, 11" × 19". Photograph courtesy of Gwendolyn Knight Lawrence/Art Resource, NY © 2004 Gwendolyn Knight Lawrence/Artists Rights Society (ARS), New York.

François-Dominique Toussaint-L'Ouverture (or "Louverture"), a slave who led a revolt in Haiti that resulted in the abolition of slavery there in 1794. Toussaint then established a semiautonomous black government, resisting French, English, and Spanish attempts to control Haiti. He was eventually captured by French forces and died a year later in a French prison. Haiti finally overcame the French in 1804 and became the first black-governed country in the Western Hemisphere.

Lawrence completed forty-one preliminary drawings and then worked on all the paintings simultaneously, so that the series has formal cohesion with its bold, flat, simplified style. Colors are limited, with black and white punctuating the images, giving them strength and starkness. *No. 36* shows the French soldiers' crossed swords that pin Toussaint in the center. The floor tilts up, and the walls of the room trap him at the intersection of colors. The black chair reads like bars of a prison. Broad sections of yellow and green in the background unify the image, while the center, with its greatest density of detail, provides a forceful focal point. In his use of space and color choices, Lawrence was influenced by Cubism as well as the bright patterns of handmade rugs.

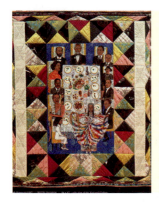

Connection *Lawrence trained in Harlem during the Harlem Renaissance and was influenced by the vibrant community of artists, writers, and performers, as shown in Faith Ringgold's* The Bitter Nest, Part II: The Harlem Renaissance Party *(Fig. 3.48). An example of a Cubist work is Pablo Picasso's* Guernica *(Fig. 11.26).*

The Rent Collection Courtyard, sculpted in 1965 (Fig. 12.13), narrates instances of injustice from Chinese history in several scenes. Although the work is officially credited to an anonymous team of sculptors, the over one hundred life-size figures were made by Ye Yushan and others at the Sichuan Academy of Fine Arts. Here, a bent, aged peasant farmer is bringing his harvest to the landlord to pay his taxes. Excessive taxation kept peasants in poverty, often forcing them to mortgage their future crops and sell their children into servitude. In another vignette from the work, not shown here, the landlord's thugs drag a peasant to prison while one thug kicks kick the peasant's wife, pleading on the ground with an infant in her arms. In the final scenes, the peasants are rising in revolt.

Realistic details and life-size figures make viewers feel as if they are witnessing the actual event. The poses make clear where our sympathies should lie, with the aged, bowing peasant in strong contrast to the relaxed, haughty, well-dressed landlord. The *Courtyard* was meant to validate the existing Chinese Communist government, which instituted land reforms in the 1950s that eliminated the powerful landlords. It was first displayed in the courtyard of a landlord's mansion (Liu Wencai in Dayi) where the events depicted actually took place.

Connections *Contrast the idea of the anonymous artist working at the service of others with the notion of art stars and the artist as genius in Chapter 5, Who Makes Art?*

The Rent Collection Courtyard *is similar to the* USA Marine Corps War Memorial *in Figure 11.27 (page 297) in that both are highly realistic, both memorialize past events, and both affirm the existing government of each nation. They do, however, commemorate different kinds of events.*

Shocking ugliness can be used in the service of protest art. In *The State Hospital,* from 1966 (Fig. 12.14), artist Edward Kienholz criticizes the way society deals with people it deems incompetent. The outside of this work, not shown here, is a grim, boxlike cell with a locked, grimy door. Inside, a naked mental patient is strapped to his bed. His mattress is filthy and the bedpan is streaked with excrement. His head is replaced by a fish bowl with two black fish swimming aimlessly inside. Encircled in neon is the cartoon balloon above his head that shows another image of himself. The patient is completely isolated and has no life beyond this room. Kienholz's props are actual institutional objects: the bed frame, the urinal, the rolling table (barely visible at left). The strongest impact, however, comes from the pathetic body of the patient—his bony knees; his sagging, exposed genitals; his leathery skin. As in *The Rent Collection Courtyard,* the realism makes the sculpture seem more immediate to the viewer.

To look inside, one has to peer through a barred window, which makes everyone on the outside part of "normal" society that supports such institutions in which the powerless are mistreated. Looking through the window, viewers take on the role of guards or surveillance cameras. Kienholz drew on his experiences as an employee in a mental hospital, where he saw, for example, a staff member repeatedly hit a patient in the stomach with a soap bar wrapped in a towel, so there would be no surface bruises.

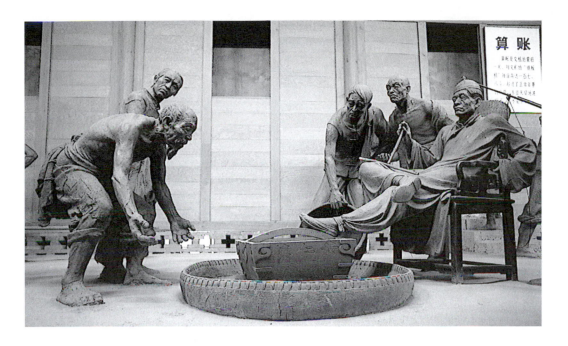

12.13   YE YUSHAN AND
A TEAM OF SCULPTORS
FROM THE SICHUAN
ACADEMY OF FINE ARTS,
CHONGQING. *The Rent
Collection Courtyard*
(detail), China (Dayi,
Sichuan), 1965. Clay,
life-size figures.

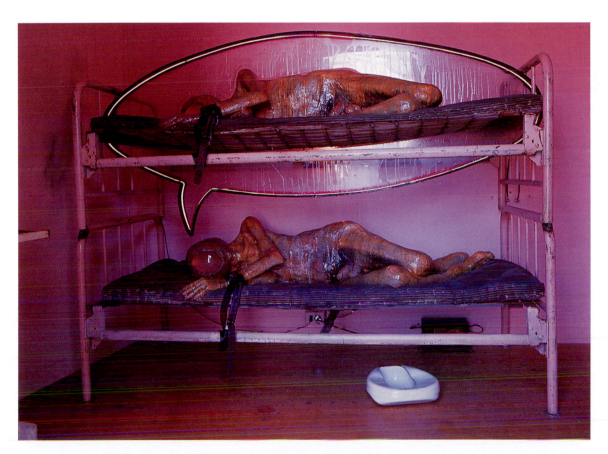

12.14   EDWARD KIENHOLZ. *The State Hospital* (detail), USA, 1966. Mixed media, 8' × 12' × 10'. Moderna
Museet, Stockholm. © Edward Kienholz.

Cildo Meireles made *Insertions into Ideological Circuits: Coca-Cola Project* (Fig. 12.15) in the 1970s in response to Brazil's military government, which supported itself by "selling" the country to foreign investors, mostly from the United States. Much of the natural environment as well as the cultures of indigenous peoples in Brazil were being destroyed because of such policies. Meireles and others wanted to affirm Brazil's autonomy and resist becoming a market for foreign goods, but art that was openly critical of the government was repressed. So Meireles took empty Coca-Cola bottles, screen printed subversive messages on them, and then returned them for refilling. The added writing on the bottles is almost invisible when they are empty. Only the person holding the bottle close while drinking the soda can easily read the message. Using Coca-Cola bottles as vehicles for political messages was clever in many ways: first, because Coca-Cola is everywhere; second, because Meireles took advantage of the already-existing system of reusing bottles; and third, because Coca-Cola is a popular symbol for U.S. culture.

> **Connection** Some would say that writing "Yankees go home!" on Coca-Cola bottles is not art. Others would argue that an artist's job is to increase the viewer's awareness. For more, see Chapter 4, Deriving Meaning.

Humor is another strategy for effective protest. In *Sun Mad*, dated 1981 (Fig. 12.16), Ester Hernandez takes familiar imagery from popular, commercial culture and subverts it. For decades, the raisin growers around Hernandez's hometown heavily used insecticides that contaminated the groundwater the local population used for drinking and bathing. Hernandez took the packaging of the best-known raisin producer, Sun Maid, and changed the usual image of healthy eating into a message of death. Her grimly humorous work is effective because the raisin industry advertising is so successful and we know the original image.

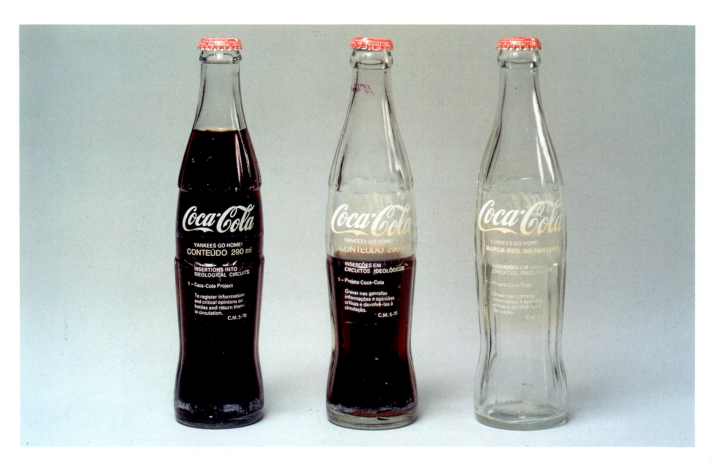

12.15   CILDO MEIRELES. *Insertions into Ideological Circuits: Coca-Cola Project*, Brazil, 1970. Screen print on Coca-Cola bottles. Courtesy of the artist and Galerie Lelong, New York.

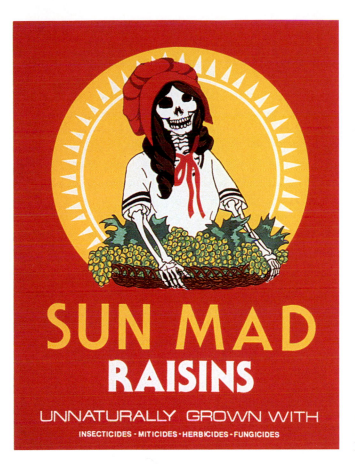

Hernandez chose an art form that allows her to reach many people, just as advertising does. This work is a color screen print that has been reproduced and widely disseminated on T-shirts and postcards. Even though Hernandez was reacting to a specific instance of contamination, her work reaches out to everyone who ingests pesticide residue or to farmworkers who were sprayed with pesticides while working in the fields.

Yinka Shonibare uses historical quotes, clothing, and humor to protest the colonial past and to show the complexity of world trade and culture in his *Mr. and Mrs. Andrews Without Their Heads,* 1998 (Fig. 12.17). A contemporary British artist of Nigerian origin (Nigeria was a British colony), Shonibare has created a three-dimensional parody of the famous eighteenth-century painting in which the landed gentry show off their estate. In his version, Shonibare has beheaded the aristocrats, recalling the fate of the ruling class during the French Revolution. The most complex aspect of the piece, however, is the printed cotton cloth, the kind

12.16   ESTER HERNANDEZ. *Sun Mad,* USA, 1981. Color serigraph, 22" × 17". © 1981 Ester Hernandez.

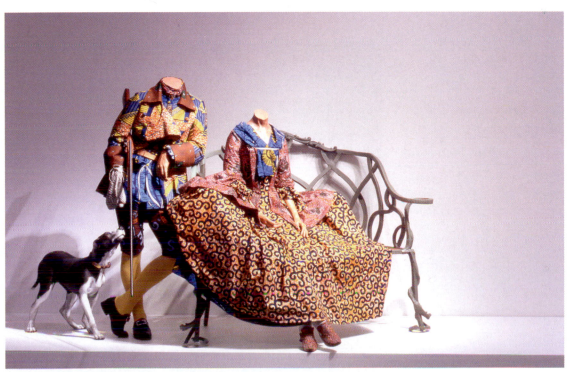

12.17   YINKA SHONIBARE. *Mr. and Mrs. Andrews Without Their Heads,* British, of Nigerian descent, 1998. Wax-print cotton costumes on mannequins, dog mannequin, painted metal bench and rifles, 65" × 224" × 100". Courtesy Stephen Friedman Gallery, London. Collection of the National Gallery of Canada, Ottawa, Canada.

associated with idealized African culture, which Mr. and Mrs. Andrews are wearing. The cloth is not African at all, but is made in the batik method that the Dutch and English manufacturers learned in Indonesia and then sold in West Africa. Shonibare shows that all cultures are intertwined and hybridized, and although many people may like the idea of cultural purity, it does not exist.

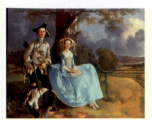

Connection *Shonibare based his sculpture on the eighteenth-century painting by British artist Thomas Gainsborough,* Mr. and Mrs. Andrews *(Fig. 2.10).*

Some art dealing with past injustices and oppressions is met with mixed responses, even from those who are descendants of the oppressed. Kara Walker is an African American artist who creates life-size, cutout silhouette figures based on racist imagery of the slave era in the United States. Petticoated plantation mistresses, slaves with their masters' heads under their skirts, bastard children, black women squeezing out multiple babies between their legs, slaves being tortured or murdered—all are depicted as elegant flat shapes,

both humorous and shocking. The imagery is based on fact and fantasy, primarily from pulp fiction sources dealing with subjugation and titillation. In works like *"They Waz Nice White Folks While They Lasted" (Says One Gal to Another),* from 2001 (Fig. 12.18), Walker's cutouts are enhanced with projections in darkened galleries, so that viewers participate in the action by casting their own shadows on the wall, joining the animated and raucous silhouettes hung there. Walker has received many letters of protest from black people who believe that she should refrain from presenting negative images of African Americans. Walker responds that she makes these images because they are controversial and should be discussed.

AFFIRMING THE VALUES OF THE OPPRESSED

When a group of people is oppressed, their way of life tends to be discounted or ridiculed. Art is an especially effective tool for affirming the lifestyles and values of downtrodden groups.

When Ambrogio Lorenzetti painted the fresco *Allegory of Good Government: The Effects of Good Government in the City and in the Country,* dated 1338–1339 (Fig. 12.19), Italy was a patchwork of city-states regularly thrown into turmoil by competing political fac-

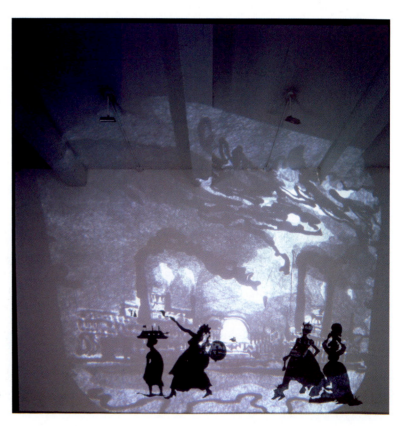

12.18   KARA WALKER. *"They Waz Nice White Folks While They Lasted" (Says One Gal to Another).* Cut paper and projections on wall, 14' × 20'. USA, 2001. Courtesy of Sikkema Jenkins & Co., New York City.

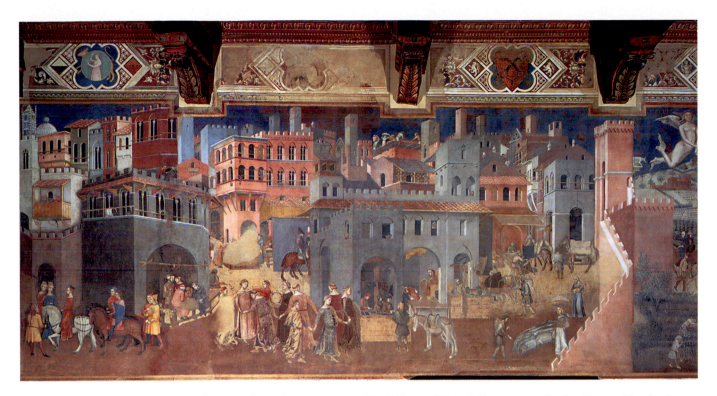

12.19 AMBROGIO LORENZETTI. *Allegory of Good Government: The Effects of Good Government in the City and in the Country* (detail), Italy, 1338–1339. Fresco. Sala della Pace, Palazzo Publico, Siena, Italy. © Scala/Art Resource, NY.

tions, overthrown governments, and petty tyrants. In contrast, Lorenzetti showed how common citizens prosper when Justice, Prudence, Temperance, and Fortitude reign, represented by hovering allegorical figures. In a climate of security, businesses flourish, culture thrives, and the fields are fruitful. This late-**Gothic** painting is full of delightful details of everyday life in fourteenth-century Italy. The sweeping panorama was a remarkable achievement in Italian painting of the era. It still attests to the right of people to live free of tyranny.

Likewise, in Northern Europe, power was concentrated in religious and secular rulers, but their absolute authority was being questioned (see *Art and History in Context* on page 350), while the idea developed of the worth of the ordinary individual. In 1527, Hans Holbein the Younger painted the portrait of the Christian humanist *Sir Thomas More* (Fig. 12.20), who was a scholar, author, and statesman. An independent thinker, More saw that his daughters received a classical education normally reserved for young men. He invented the

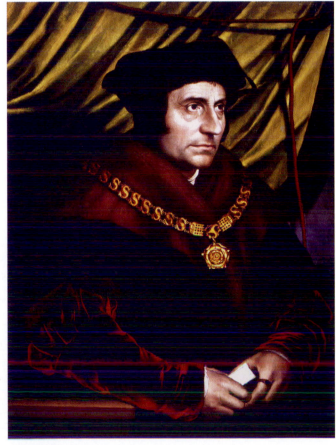

12.20 HANS HOLBEIN THE YOUNGER. *Sir Thomas More*, Flanders, 1527. Oil on oak panel, 29½" × 23¾". Frick Collection, New York.

term *utopia* and wrote a book envisioning a state practicing religious tolerance and free of political and economic oppression. He criticized the Catholic Church for its abuses and secular power. But it was his opposition to King Henry VIII of England's divorce and remarriage that cost him his life, despite the fact that he held the highest political office. Holbein's portrait shows More's intelligent eyes and ordinary mien, under the richness of the regal robes. The work, as well as More's life, affirmed the importance of the individual's conscience even when it opposes authority.

Art can affirm the history and culture of a people even as that culture is being attacked and eradicated. The Aztec *Codex Borbonicus* (Fig. 12.21) is a religious calendar that was made during the period of the Spanish conquest, either just before or just after the fall of the Aztec empire (see *Art and History in Context*, page 330). The *Codex Borbonicus* and the handful of other manuscripts that have survived from this era preserve the pre-Columbian culture. This image depicts calendar **glyphs** surrounding the large image of two gods, Quetzalcoatl (light and sun) and Tezcatlipoca (moon and destruction), who are devouring a man. Traces of Aztec culture survive in Central America to the present day.

Aboriginal artists have used art to affirm their cultural values, which have been suppressed by Australians of European descent. Because of colonization, many Aborigines lost their land or were killed. While the rest of the country was celebrating the two hundredth anniversary of Captain Cook's "discovery" of Australia, the Aboriginal population commemorated "Invasion Day." Forty-three artists collaborated to make *The Aboriginal Memorial*, installed in 1988 (Fig. 12.22). The work is composed of two hundred logs, one for each year of settlement, hollowed out as traditional Aboriginal coffins. They are memorials to all the native peoples who died as a result of European settlement and were never given proper Aboriginal mortuary rites. Artists painted the logs with their important clan Dreamtime symbols, affirming traditional Aboriginal culture, which was undermined and, at times, outlawed. Poles reach as high as ten feet and seem like living growths springing up with vibrating patterns and vigorous animal imagery (Caruana 1993:206).

Connections For more on Aboriginal culture and Dreamtime imagery, see Witchetty Grub Dreaming in Figure 7.2 (page 151).

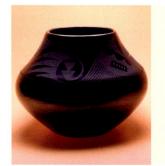

Like the Australian Aboriginal artists, many contemporary Native American artists continue to reference traditional imagery and art processes in the work they produce today, as in the late-twentieth-century Bowl by Maria Martinez (see Fig. 3.41).

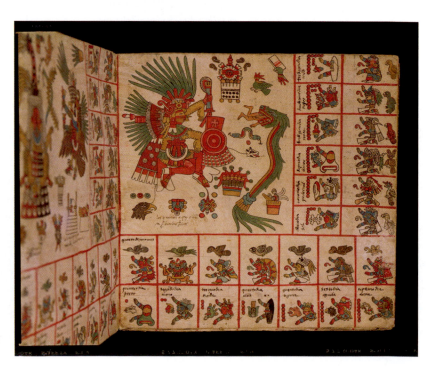

12.21 *Codex Borbonicus*, early 16th century. Detail depicting Quetzalcoatl and Texcatlipoca. Paint on vellum, 39 cm × 40 cm. Aztec. Bibliothèque de l'Assemblée Nationale, Paris, France.

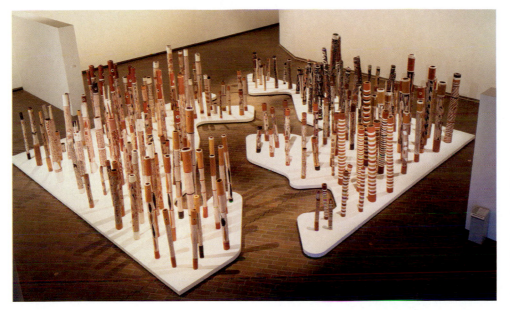

12.22 PADDY DHATANGU, DAVID MALANGI, GEORGE MILPURRURRU, JIMMY WULULU, AND OTHER ARTISTS FROM RAMINGINING. *The Aboriginal Memorial*, Australia, 1988. Natural pigments on 200 logs; heights: 16" to 128". National Gallery of Art, Canberra. © 2004 Artists Rights Society (ARS), New York/VI$COPY, Australia.

Puerto Rican–born Pepón Osorio's mixed media installation, *The Scene of the Crime (Whose Crime?)*, 1993–1999 (Fig. 12.23), affirms the worth of Puerto Rican culture in New York, while protesting how the people are depicted in mass media. He has re-created a "typical" Puerto Rican house, cluttered with kitsch statuettes, inexpensive religious objects, plastic plants, sentimental family photos, trophies, covers of *TV Guide*, and so on. Police tape and bright lights indicate a crime has happened, and a mannequin corpse lies face down at the back of the installation, but everything is remote and no details are given. A welcome mat in front reads: "Only if you can understand that it has taken years of pain to gather into our homes our most valuable possessions; but the greater pain is to see how in the movies others make fun of the way we live." Because much is obscure or just out of sight, viewers' reactions are based on stereotypes or narratives from mass media, including assumptions of drugs and crime in the culture, or class-based condemnations of the décor. Like Kara Walker (see Fig. 12.18), Osorio at times has received negative responses, some from Latino viewers who want to distance themselves from these cultural stereotypes.

Mona Hatoum is an artist of Palestinian descent who has lived in London since 1975, when she was forced to flee the fighting in Beirut. Her work deals

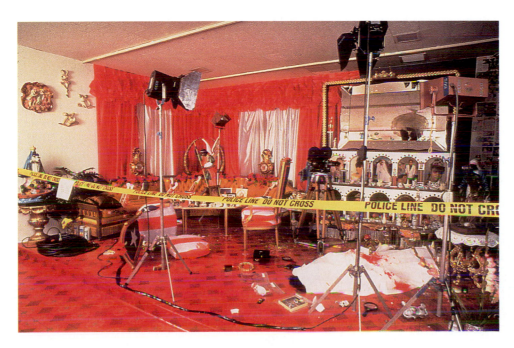

12.23 PEPÓN OSORIO. *The Scene of the Crime (Whose Crime?)*, Puerto Rico/USA, 1993–1999. Mixed media installation, dimensions variable. Bronx Museum of the Arts. Purchased through funds from the H. W. Wilson Foundation and the National Endowment for the Arts, 1999.1.4. Courtesy Ronald Feldman Fine Arts, New York.

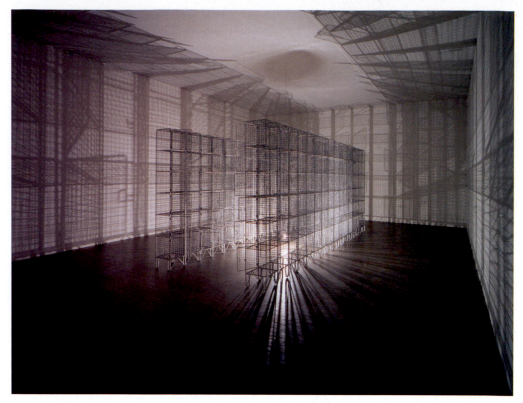

12.24 MONA HATOUM. *Light Sentence,* Palestine/England, 1992. Mixed media, dimensions variable. Musée National d'Art Moderne, Centre Georges Pompidou. © Courtesy the artist and Jay Jopling/White Cube (London). © CNAC/ MNAM/Dist. Réunion des Musées Nationaux/ Art Resource, NY.

poetically with personal identity, the body, surveillance, and control. *Light Sentence,* 1992 (Fig. 12.24), is an installation of wire mesh lockers in a dark room, stacked to human height. In the middle, a bare light-bulb swings around, casting wildly rocking shadows so that the cell-like room seems to sway. The swinging bulb is like a sometimes-blinding prison searchlight, implying surveillance. Lockers should hold private possessions safely, but here everything is exposed. The piece suggests animal cages in an experimental laboratory and connotes the oppressively uniform high-rise housing for low-income people. *Light Sentence* reveals the instability that those without power endure.

QUESTIONING THE STATUS QUO

The status quo is the existing state of affairs, which appears natural or inevitable instead of constructed and evolving. In this section, artists take a critical look at the "normal," at all those underlying and ingrained systems, beliefs, and ways of operating within a culture.

THE SOCIAL ENVIRONMENT

William Hogarth satirized the English upper classes in a series of six paintings called *Marriage à la Mode,* dated c. 1745, a comedy mixed with criticism and condemnation. In the second of the six images, *Breakfast Scene* (Fig. 12.25), the wall clock indicates past noon, but the couple is just meeting over the breakfast table in their lavish mansion. The disheveled, bored husband has been out all night. The puppy sniffs at his pocket where another woman's lingerie hangs. The young wife stretches after a night of cards and music at home. The overturned chairs indicate that the evening became a bit raucous. The paintings on the walls indicate a taste for sexual intrigues, despite the presence of classical busts and religious images for propriety. At left, a servant rolls his eyes, clutching unpaid bills.

The young man is a penniless nobleman whose father arranged this marriage to the daughter of a wealthy merchant. For her part, the arranged marriage brings status and a title, Lady Squanderfield. She casts a flirting glance at her husband, but he is completely unresponsive. A vacuum of unconcern separates them. The series ends miserably with infidelity, scandal, and death by duel. Hogarth's paintings were turned into inexpensive prints that were enormously popular and received widespread distribution among the English middle class.

Magdalena Abakanowicz's *Backs,* dated 1976 to 1982 (Fig. 12.26), consists of eighty slumping, hollow backs that are more than life-size, but without legs, heads, and hands. They hunch forward, immobile, in

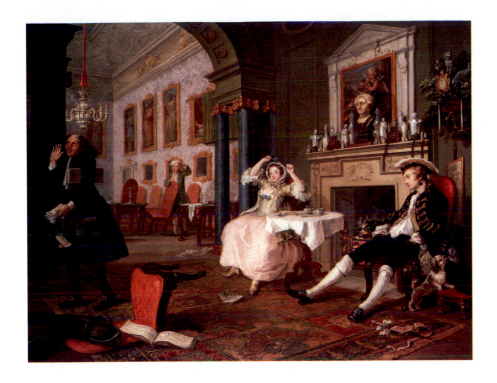

12.25 WILLIAM HOGARTH. *Breakfast Scene* (from the series *Marriage à la Mode*), England, c. 1745. Oil on canvas, 28" × 36". National Gallery, London. © National Gallery Collection; By kind permission of the Trustees of the National Gallery, London/Corbis.

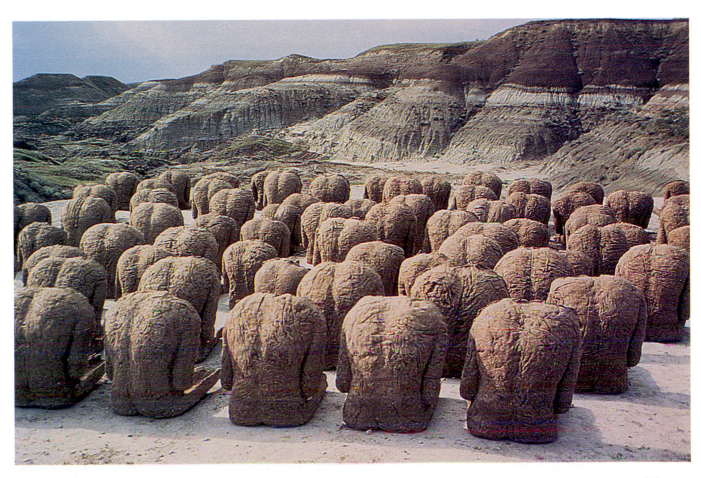

12.26 MAGDALENA ABAKANOWICZ. *Backs,* Poland, 1976–1982. 80 pieces, burlap and glue, each over life-size. © Magdalena Abakanowicz. Courtesy of Marlborough Gallery, New York.

lines all facing the same direction. *Backs* alludes to the human condition in times of great distress. Abakanowicz lived in Poland during World War II, saw her mother's arm shot off at the shoulder, and witnessed death, pain, and destruction. In postwar Soviet-dominated Poland, she encountered many hardships in her struggle to make artwork.

Backs suggests the modern malaise of uniformity, of loss of self and of individuality. Organic fibers were pressed into the same plaster mold to make all eighty backs, so that each is very similar to the others. However, small degrees of individuality emerge in the twist of the fiber and in the slight variations created as each back was removed from the mold. The thick, matted fibers resemble wrinkled skin, knotted muscles, and visceral tissue. Their organic quality emphasizes our phys-

icality and our ties to the natural world. The weary backs also suggest endurance, strength, and survival.

Jenny Holzer focused on the mass of implicit beliefs that are widely accepted in the United States today, in *Untitled (Selected Writings)*, dated 1989 (Fig. 12.27). Holzer wrapped electronic signs around the spiral interior of the Solomon R. Guggenheim Museum in New York City and placed a circle of red granite benches below. The stream of words jumps out from the darkened interior of the museum, starting at the bottom, and then swirling up until they disappear at the top of the spiral. The phrases seem familiar, but as a whole, they sound contradictory or even a little idiotic. As Holzer herself says, "They're about how we drive ourselves crazy with a million possibilities that are half correct" (Auping 1992:55). "A sincere effort is

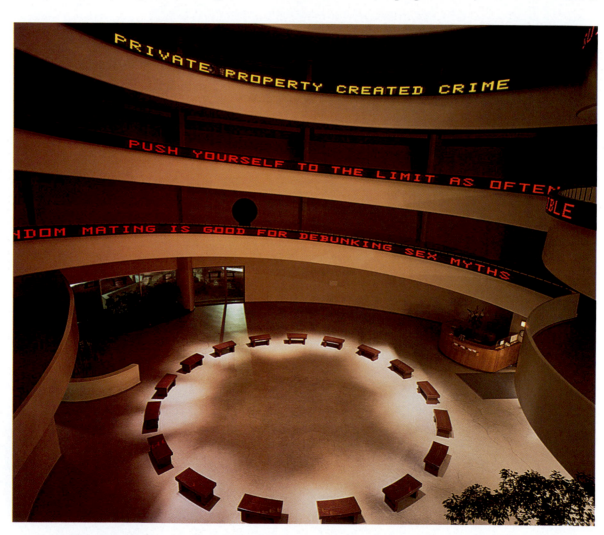

12.27 JENNY HOLZER. *Untitled (Selected Writings)*, USA, 1989. Extended helical LED electronic signboard, with selected writings; 17 Indian Red granite benches. Installation view at Solomon R. Guggenheim Museum. Photo by David Heald, courtesy Solomon R. Guggenheim Museum. © 2004 Jenny Holzer/Artists Rights Society (ARS), New York.

all you can ask" is countered with "Enjoy yourself because you can't change anything anyway." Another example is, "Protect me from what I want," written in a culture where money can buy almost anything. The electronic signs flash words like a mass media attack, and then they quickly slip away almost before we can grasp them. In contrast, the words carved in the stone benches below are permanent, but just as conflicting. The sheer number of phrases, the speed at which we see them, and their contradictory messages destroy thought, although we normally think of words as the carriers of meaning.

ART VERSUS POLITICS

In Chapter 11, Power, Politics, and Glory, we saw art that promoted the personal glory of a ruler or the power of a state. In this section, we will see art that pokes at the political status quo.

The political cartoon has a long history of challenging politics and society in Western nations. In France, Honoré Daumier was especially known for his pointedly satirical caricatures, until an 1835 government crackdown outlawed works like the lithograph, *The Legislative Belly* (Fig. 12.28), from 1834. Here, members of the French legislature are mean-spirited,

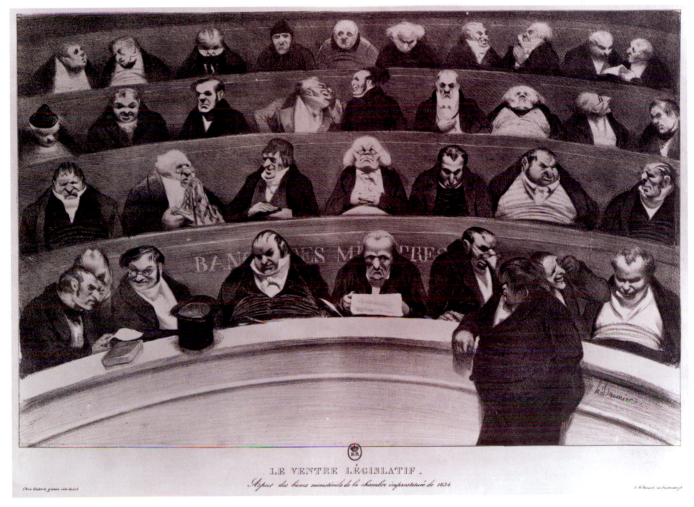

LE VENTRE LÉGISLATIF.
Aspect des bancs ministériels de la chambre improstituée de 1834

12.28 HONORÉ DAUMIER. *The Legislative Belly*, France, 1834. Lithograph; image: 11" × 17"; sheet: 13¹¹/₁₆" × 20³/₁₆". Bibliothèque nationale de France, Paris. Giraudon/Art Resource, NY.

sleeping, or arrogant. The curving walls echo their fat bellies. Although Daumier depicted specific politicians (who would have been recognized by the French public at that time), his great composition and caricatures are an indictment to corrupt lawmakers at any time, in any place.

Portrait of George, dated 1981 (Fig. 12.29), by Robert Arneson, is a bust portrait of George Moscone, a popular mayor of San Francisco in the late 1970s. Moscone's smiling face is distinct and lively, animated by splattered colors. The bust sits on a column casually covered, graffiti-like, with phrases recalling Moscone's background, some of his more memorable sayings, and events from his life and death. Moscone and another politician were assassinated in 1978 by a disgruntled San Francisco city supervisor named Dan White, who had disagreed with Moscone on most political points, including issues concerning homosexuals.

The bust was made for a new civic center in San Francisco. Arneson's *Portrait of George* departs from the status quo of bland, bronze portrait heads of political leaders that are common in parks and in lobbies of public buildings. This sculpture is irreverent, colorful, and very large. Bullet holes apparently pierce the pedestal and a yellow, phallic Twinkies snack cake is prominent. At his trial, Dan White received a light sentence for his crimes, because his lawyers argued that he was unbalanced at the time of the shooting from eating too many Twinkies. Many San Franciscans protested the sentence, and there was a night of rioting. Because Arneson's sculpture was a vivid reminder of the murder and riots, *Portrait of George* was officially removed from the civic center after one week because the pedestal was deemed crude and inappropriate. The work was later sold to a private collector.

In South Africa for many years, the economic and political status quo was based on apartheid, a system of laws and social standards that repressed the native population. William Kentridge created charcoal drawings and film animations based on the causes and injustices of apartheid. Kentridge's work, however, goes beyond the specifics of the South African situation. The *Drawing from Mine*, from 1991 (Fig. 12.30), shows the white businessman with tangled financial tapes wrapped around sculptural heads of Africans, very much like the *Crowned Head of an Oni* (Fig. 11.3). Kentridge's art points out the moral difficulties that attend all instances of power, ownership, and oppression on a grand scale. This charcoal drawing and others were photographed repeatedly, while Kentridge drew and erased, to create the short film sequence called *Mine*.

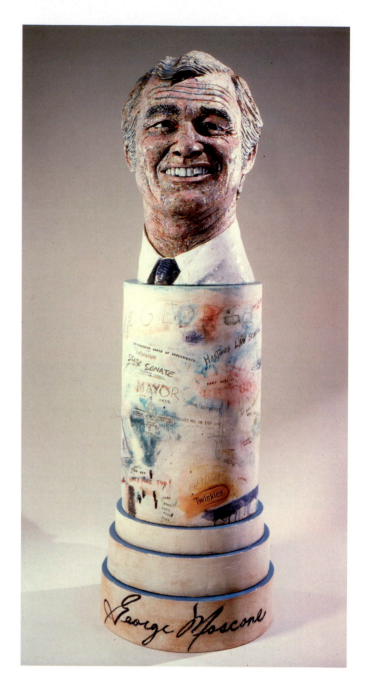

12.29 ROBERT ARNESON. *Portrait of George*, USA, 1981. Glazed ceramic, 94" × 29" × 29". Private Collection. Art © Estate of Robert Arneson/VAGA, New York, NY. Courtesy of George Adams Gallery, New York.

Connection *Another artwork that protests against apartheid in South Africa is Hans Haacke's* MetroMobiltan *in Figure 4.7 (page 90).*

Our last example of protest art is from contemporary El Salvador, with Miguel Antonio Bonilla's *The Knot* (Fig. 12.31), from 1994. The two ominous figures

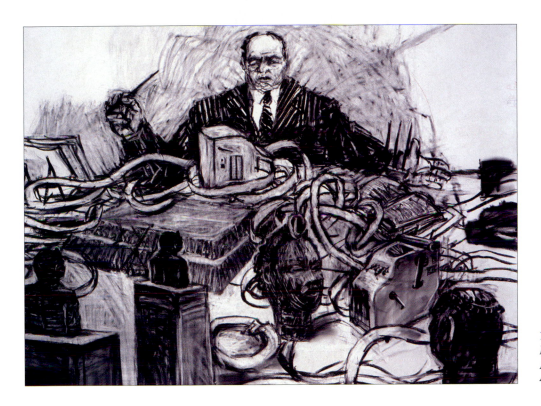

12.30 WILLIAM KENTRIDGE. *Drawing from Mine*, South Africa, 1991. *Mine* is a 5 min. 49 sec. film. Charcoal.

represent the country's police and politicians, who conspired in the 1980s to create an oppressive regime in El Salvador. The knot that connects them seems to be made of two extended, elongated phalluses. In this way, Bonilla referred to the chauvinism in his culture that allows factions to oppress others and also causes domestic violence. Bonilla took a political risk in this painting because of its criticism of the political status quo. He also took artistic risks, making the painting purposefully ugly and shocking. The style of this work was contrary to prevailing Salvadoran aesthetics for painting at that time.

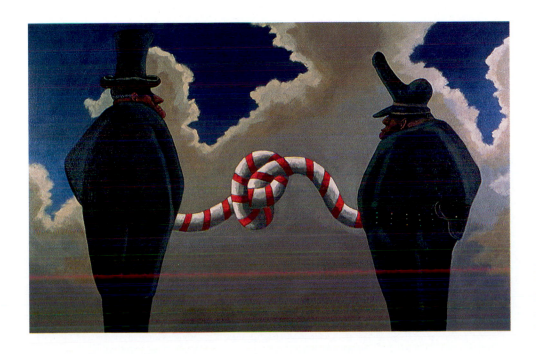

12.31 MIGUEL ANTONIO BONILLA. *The Knot,* El Salvador, 1994. Acrylic on canvas, 51" × 78". Museum of Latin American Art.

The world in 1300 was still a patchwork of relatively autonomous, relatively isolated regions. Two hundred fifty years later, much of that had changed.

China during this period was ruled by two dynasties: the Yuan dynasty of the Mongolian invaders, which ended in the mid-1300s, and the native Ming dynasty, known for its territorial expansion as well as its amazing building program, which included rebuilding the Great Wall and constructing the Forbidden City. Wealth was distributed to lower classes through the Civil Service and land ownership. This was a period of stability, prosperity, religious tolerance, and a high standard of living. Chinese ships traveled to India and Africa, and the Portuguese landed at China's ports in 1514.

Islam continued to expand in Asia, Africa, and southeastern Europe. Around 1280, the mighty Ottoman Empire was established with Turkey as its center, and it expanded its territories in North Africa and the Middle East. Many Ottoman rulers were art patrons, great builders, and conquerors. They generally tolerated other religions. Likewise, the Mughal Empire in India was known for its ambitious building program, its humane rulers, and its illuminated manuscripts. The Safavids ruled Persia after 1500.

At this time, Europe saw the end of the Middle Ages and the beginning of the Renaissance. The rise of Christian humanism in the fourteenth and fifteenth centuries brought an emphasis on reason, human abilities, and intellectual achievement, as exemplified by scholars such as *Sir Thomas More* (Fig. 12.20). This humanistic tradition has continued to grow, and, because it promotes the inherent worth and dignity of all human beings, it is the basis for much social protest art. Small areas of Italy had republican governments, notably Florence and Siena, as shown with the *Allegory of Good Government* (Fig. 12.19). In Italy, the era brought increased prosperity and the rediscovery of Greco-Roman culture.

Beginning in 1300, the secular power of the Catholic Church slowly declined in Europe. The Church's religious authority was challenged in the 1500s when the Protestant

Map 6 Patterns of World Trade. Courtesy of Replogle Globes, Inc., Broadview, IL.

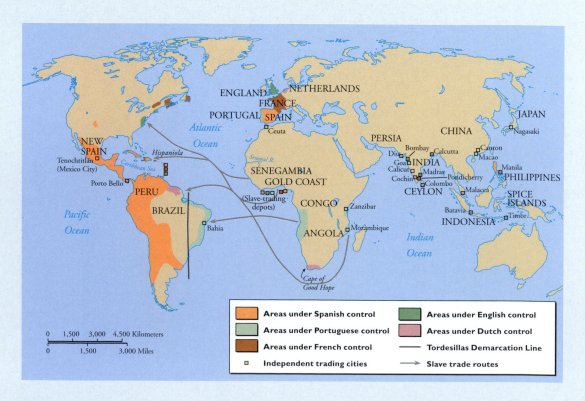

▮ Areas under Spanish control	▮ Areas under English control	
▮ Areas under Portuguese control	▮ Areas under Dutch control	
▮ Areas under French control	—— Tordesillas Demarcation Line	
▫ Independent trading cities	→ Slave trade routes	

Reformation divided European Christians between the Protestants and Catholics.

This was the beginning of the age of exploration and expansion. European sailors undertook amazing voyages of discovery, most notably in the Americas in 1492. Advanced civilizations had flourished earlier in Central America, especially the Maya/Toltec culture, with hieroglyphics, ball courts, and palaces. In 1500, the Aztecs dominated central Mexico and had a complex society with accomplishments in painting, architecture, astronomy, and cosmology. The Aztec *Coatlicue* (see history box illustration) is a colossal freestanding sculpture of a deity representing sacrificial death as well as the potential for new life. The *Codex Borbonicus* (Fig. 12.21) is an example of Aztec book-making and painting accomplishments that also shows the culture's calendar system. In 1519, the Spaniards conquered the Aztecs and attempted to wipe out their culture; later, they also conquered the Incas of Peru and established a large colonial empire in America.

Other adventurers circled the globe, visiting ports in Asia and India. Trade expanded greatly in the 1500s and reached many parts of the world. For Europe, the spice trade with Southeast Asia and the slave trade with Africa were important. Other traded commodities included fur, fish, timber, tobacco, rice, silver, gold, sugar, cacao, coffee, diamonds, tea, silk, cotton, and ivory (see map).

The Kingdom of Zimbabwe flourished from 1300 to 1450 in Africa. Other central areas of Africa remained free of Europeans, but African slaves from coastal areas were brought to Europe and the Americas beginning in the 1500s. England, Portugal, and France as well as Spain established American colonies. In still-isolated Australia, the Aboriginal peoples were growing in population and developing long-distance trading among themselves.

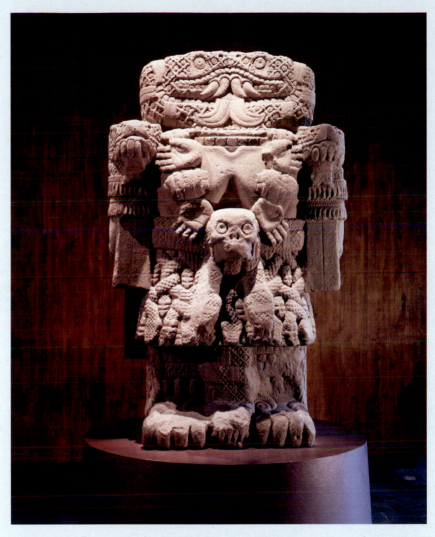

12.32   *Coatlicue.* Tenochtitlán, Mexico, c. 1487–1520. Aztec. Andesite, 11'6" high. Museo Nacional de Antropología, Mexico City.

Thus we have seen the beginnings of slavery, the expansion of Islam and European colonization taking hold as long as 700 years ago. The resulting injustices and conflicts are still the subject of contemporary artworks, such as Yinka Shonibare's *Mr. and Mrs. Andrews Without Their Heads* (Fig. 12.17), Kara Walker's *They Waz Nice White Folks While They Lasted* (Fig. 12.18), and William Kentridge's *Drawing from Mine* (Fig. 12.30).

1300 – 1550 CE

Timeline

1000 CE		
Chola Kingdom—India		
Yuan Dynasty—China		
Maya/Toltec Culture in Mesoamerica		
	1300	Lorenzetti: *Allegory of Good Government*
Black Death in Europe		
Ming Dynasty—China		
Great Wall of China rebuilt		
Renaissance in Europe	**1400**	
Ottoman Empire in Turkey, North Africa, and Middle East		
Christopher Columbus		*Coatlicue*
	1500	
		Codex Borbonicus
		Holbein: *Sir Thomas More*
Portuguese arrive in China		
Spanish conquest of the Aztecs and Incas		
Martin Luther and the Reformation		
European colonies in the Americas		
Slave trade begins: Africa, Europe, and the Americas		
Spice trade—Dutch East Indies and Southeast Asia		
Mughal Empire in India	**1600**	
	1700	
Japan closed to Westerners		
Rise of merchant class in Japan		
		Hogarth: *Breakfast Scene*

	1800	Goya: *The Executions of May 3, 1808*
		Daumier: *The Legislative Belly*
Displacement of Native Americans from Western U.S.		
		Delacroix: *Liberty Leading the People*
Aboriginal decline in Australia		
	1850	
Colonial rule established in Africa		
Civil War, U.S.		
End of slavery in U.S.		
	1900	Kollwitz: *The Outbreak ("Losbruch")*
		Hine: *Leo, 48 Inches High . . .*
		Grosz: *Fit for Active Service*
Harlem Renaissance	**1920**	
Great Depression	**1930**	Shahn: *The Passion of Sacco and Vanzetti*
Stalin and the U.S.S.R.		Heartfield: *Goering the Executioner*
		Lawrence: *No. 36: During the Truce Toussaint Is Deceived . . .*
Spanish Civil War		Siqueiros: *Echo of a Scream*
World War II	**1940**	
U.N. Universal Declaration of Human Rights	**1948**	
People's Republic of China		
Cold War, 1950–1990		Motherwell: *Elegy to the Spanish Republic XXXIV*
Civil Rights Movement, U.S.	**1960**	
		Shomei: *Woman with Keloidal Scars*
Cesar Chavez and the United Farm Workers		
		The Rent Collection Courtyard

	1970	Kienholz: *The State Hospital*			Kentridge: *Drawing from Mine*
Six-Day War—Israel		Golub: *Mercenaries I*	Apartheid ends— South Africa		Hatoum: *Light Sentence*
		Meireles: *Insertions into Ideological Circuits*			Bonilla: *The Knot*
Islamic Revolution in Iran		Abakanowicz: *Backs*	World Conference on Global Warming		Osorio: *The Scene of the Crime (Whose Crime?)*
	1980	Hernandez: *Sun Mad*		**2000**	
Nicaraguan Civil War		Arneson: *Portrait of George*			Walker: *"They Waz Nice White Folks . . ."*
		The Aboriginal Memorial			
		Holzer: *Untitled (Selected Writings)*	USA Patriot Act		
Iraqi invasion of Kuwait	**1990**				
		Shonibare: *Mr. and Mrs. Andrews Without Their Heads*			

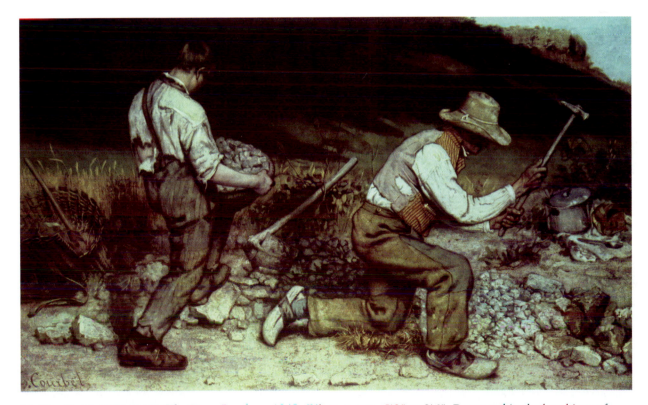

12.33   GUSTAVE COURBET. *The Stone Breakers*. 1849, Oil on canvas, 5'3" × 8'6". Destroyed in the bombings of Dresden, Germany, in World War II.

SYNOPSIS

Art can depict the cruelty and destruction of war and can expose cynical military leaders. Even abstract art can express the human struggle for liberty against totalitarian forces.

Artists have protested many forms of oppression, such as the exploitation of laborers, repressive governments, and acts of betrayal. Art has been used to protest colonization and pollution as well as to affirm indigenous values.

"Normal" conditions are reexamined by artists and, in many cases, found wanting. Half-truths, stultifying bureaucracies, police states, and upper-class greed and mindlessness are all targets for artistic critique. Other artists look at consumerism, oppressive patriarchy, the status of women, and institutionalized discrimination.

FOOD FOR THOUGHT

Here are a few questions to think about in relation to protest art.

■ *Is protest art in galleries or museums reaching a wide enough audience to be effective?*

■ *What about artwork that is sympathetic to a repressed group, like the 1849 painting of Stone Breakers by Gustave Courbet (Fig. 12.33)? The hardships endured by the lowest classes in France are depicted here. Who would have been the audience for this painting?*

■ *With protest art, the artist often has a clear political message to deliver, presents it in a persuasive way, and hopes to cause change. Is that different from propaganda?*

■ *Can propaganda be art?*

Finally, some recent artists and art writers have been critical of social protest work such as Hine's Leo, 48 Inches High . . . because it did not change the existing power structures, even if it did change public opinion about child labor. The wealthy remained insulated, powerful, and privileged, able to gaze upon people like the mill workers, who cannot see them in return. The wealthy might be moved to "reform" the situation out of their own benevolence. Or they might not. What do you think of criticisms such as this?

Your Thomson Online Resources

 Go to **ArtExperience Online** for the Flashcards, Quiz, and Study Guide for this chapter.

Self and Society

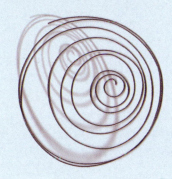

In this section, the artworks deal with the human body, social structures, and the world around us. The next four chapters explore the following major topics:

- Idealizing body types as seen in art and mass media in different cultures.
- Revealing the nature of humans in general and individual personalities in particular through figurative art.
- Examining attitudes about race and gender that are made evident through art.
- Investigating social and economic distinctions that are reflected in art.
- Defining changing concepts of "family" as portrayed in art.
- Revealing through artwork the shifting relationship of humans to animals and humans to the land.
- Expanding knowledge about ourselves and the world around us through art.
- Making art that entertains, pleases, or diverts us.
- Learning about visual culture in relationship to contemporary art.

CHAPTER 13 | THE BODY

CHAPTER 14 | RACE, GENDER, CLAN, AND CLASS

CHAPTER 15 | NATURE, KNOWLEDGE, AND TECHNOLOGY

CHAPTER 16 | ENTERTAINMENT AND VISUAL CULTURE

The Body

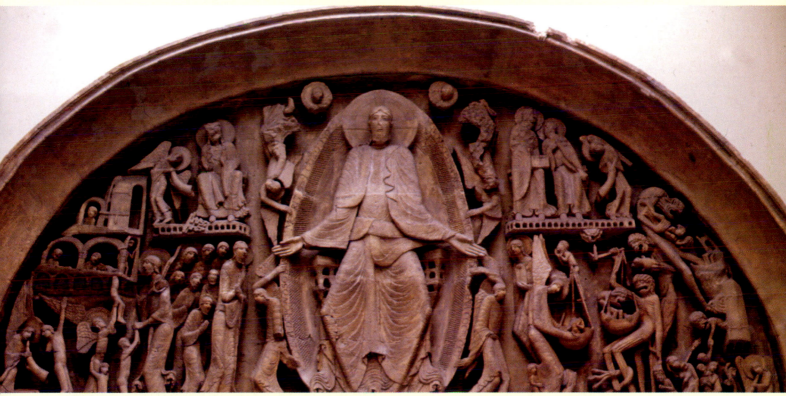

Photograph by Dominique Darbois.

INTRODUCTION

The body is very personal: this is my body, this is me. The body is very social: we study each other; we use our bodies to communicate attitudes; the ways we dress and walk are meaningful to the group. Through art, different cultures show their concept of the individual, as well as human nature in general and larger social trends.

- *How does portraiture reveal the individual?*
- *What do depictions of the body indicate more broadly about human nature?*
- *What are the boundaries between the self and the world?*
- *What is the experience of sickness and death?*
- *How is the human body used in art, both as material and as tool?*

DEPICTING THE BODY

The following sections, "Portraits" and "Self-Portraits," reveal personal aspects of an individual. Later, in "The Physical Body," artworks reflect ideas about human nature in general.

PORTRAITS

In Oscar Wilde's nineteenth-century novel *The Picture of Dorian Gray*, Gray remained handsome and youthful in appearance throughout his life. However, hidden in a closet, Gray's portrait aged, becoming ugly and blemished because of his reckless, dissolute life.

Like this example from literature, a successful portrait in art is usually considered someone's likeness, not only in face but also in character. Faces are important to humans and, in fact, are the very first things to which newborn children respond. Humans are extremely perceptive in determining—or imagining—another person's state of mind by nuances in facial expressions. As adults, we continue to study our own faces and the faces of others for hints of character and experiences.

Connection Chapter 14 includes portraits used to strengthen clan ties, like the **Statue of Togata Barberini** *(Fig. 14.12, page 376).*

The first attribute of a portrait is usually individualized features, which we can see in the famous bust of Queen Nefertiti, from the Egyptian New Kingdom's Eighteenth Dynasty (Fig. 13.1). Notable features include Nefertiti's perfectly symmetrical face, her long, thin nose, fully proportioned lips, flat ears, and long, graceful neck as well as the tall royal crown. These features have made her both easily recognizable and famous through the ages. Likely sculpted by the artist Thutmose c. 1350 BCE, *Nefertiti* displays the new aesthetic canon, which is eased, flowing, naturalistic, and elegant, different from the rigid, abstract style found in the art of the past. This canon, called the Armana style, was begun by Amenhotep III, Nefertiti's father-in-law. She was married to Akhenaten, the pharaoh who broke with Egyptian tradition and started a short monotheistic religion.

Nefertiti's beauty as rendered in this painted limestone portrait has influenced the Western aesthetic of

13.1 *Nefertiti*, Egypt, c. 1350 BCE. Portrait bust. Approximately 1'8" high. Aegyptisches Museum, Staatliche Museen zu Berlin, Berlin, Germany. Photo: Vanni/Art Resource, NY

feminine beauty, in both the past and the present. Her name reflects this, as it translates to "The Beautiful One has come."

Connection Another ancient head modeled with refined, portrait-like sensitivity is the **Jayavarman VII** *(Fig. 11.4, page 278).*

The *Study for the Portrait of Okakura Tenshin*, painted in 1922 (Fig. 13.2), records the face of a shrewd, intelligent individual who was at the center of social, political, and aesthetic controversies in Japan during his time. Okakura was a writer, aesthete, educator, and art curator who lived from 1862 until 1913, a time when rulers of Japan were ending three hundred years of isolation and embarking on a period of rapid Westernization. Eastern-influenced music, literature, religion, and medicine were suppressed and replaced with Western modes. The one exception was the visual arts, in which traditional and Western styles—and mixtures of the two—flourished. Traditional Japanese paintings and prints were popular and sold well not only in Japan but also in the West. They influenced a number of Western artists, such as Vincent van Gogh (see Fig. 13.3).

Okakura and a U.S. scholar, Ernest Fenollosa, wrote the first Western-style history of Japanese art and established a Japanese museum, an academy of art, and art appreciation societies, which were essentially Western cultural institutions. Before this, the Japanese aesthetic

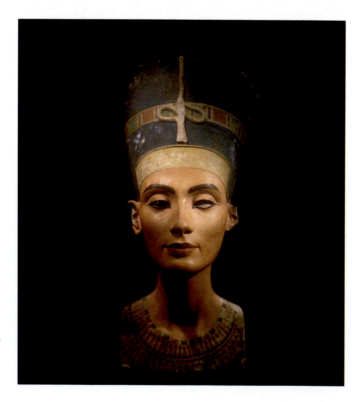

tradition did not include these concepts and institutions. Later, Okakura wrote *The Ideals of the East*, in which he created the concept of Asia as the East in contrast to the West. Eventually, he moved to the United States and became an assistant curator in the Japanese and Chinese Department of the Boston Museum of Fine Arts.

The very style of *Study for the Portrait of Okakura Tenshin* reflects much of the controversy that raged around Japanese art during his time. Japanese-style contour lines and flat shapes are apparent here, especially in Okakura's left hand and sleeve. But the face and hat are rendered with Western chiaroscuro—that is, by dark and light shading. Okakura smokes a West-

ern cigarette while wearing traditional Japanese garb. Okakura believed that only the combination of modernism and tradition meant progress in art. His face is the focal point of the composition, sitting atop the triangular shape of his body, and his features make a great study of shrewdness, toughness, and perception.

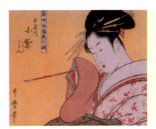

Connection *For an example of a face rendered in traditional Japanese style, with outlines only, see Komurasaki of the Tamaya Teahouse (Fig. 14.31, page 393).*

Often artists reveal as much about themselves as they do about their subjects. In the *Portrait of Dr. Gachet*, dated 1890 (Fig. 13.3), Vincent van Gogh painted a free-thinking, eccentric, homeopathic doctor with the foxglove flower to symbolize his profession. Gachet's portrait is also a vehicle for van Gogh to

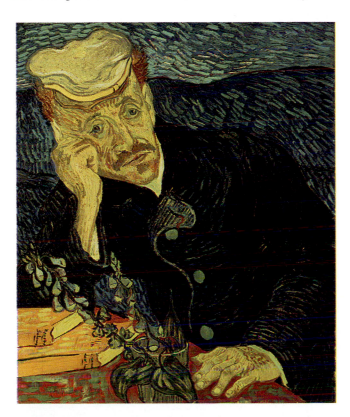

13.3   VINCENT VAN GOGH. *Portrait of Dr. Gachet*, Netherlands, 1890. Oil on canvas. 26¼' × 22'. Photo courtesy Christie's. Copyright © Christie's Images, Inc./Christies Images—All rights reserved.

13.2   SHIMOMURA KANZAN. *Study for the Portrait of Okakura Tenshin*, Japan, 1922. Pigment on paper, 53½" × 26". Art Museum, Tokyo National University of Fine Arts and Music.

make observations about modern urban life in general, which van Gogh found to be full of suffering. With a melancholy face and pose, Gachet leans on two nineteenth-century novels about tragic and degenerate life in Paris. Van Gogh himself found life in Paris to be unhealthy and miserable, and he took refuge in his art, in the countryside, and in medical help. At this time, van Gogh was painting at a feverish pace, but was less than two months away from his own suicide. Thick paint animates the entire surface, with emphatic dashes and tight swirls that model form, increase color saturation, and indicate van Gogh's own agitation and intensity. Thus, Gachet's likeness was both an image of Gachet and a reflection of van Gogh's own inner state.

In *Fanny (Fingerpainting)*, dated 1985 (Fig. 13.4), artist Chuck Close has painted an elderly woman's head in great detail, at an enormous scale (more than nine feet high). Her face fills the foreground space of the painting, pushing toward us her lizard-like eyelids, her watery eyes and cracked lips, and the sagging skin of her neck. With this painting, we can stare curiously at a person's face, an action considered impolite in U.S. culture.

The pose is ordinary, like that on a driver's license. Her nonidealized features are lit unflatteringly from both sides, leaving dark shadows at the center of her face. But the scale and surface make her face forceful and imposing. The artist works from photographs. Like his photographic sources, this painting is in sharp focus in certain areas, with soft focus in others. The center of the face is clear, but all points closer (the tip of the nose) and more distant (the hair, base of the neck, and shoulders) fall out of the camera's depth of field and are blurred. The expression on the woman's face also makes evident the photographic source: her eyes are focused on the camera that is close to her nose, and she seems both tolerant of and slightly affronted by the camera.

In the 1992 series called *Faces*, Nancy Burson also gave us the opportunity to indulge our curiosity about

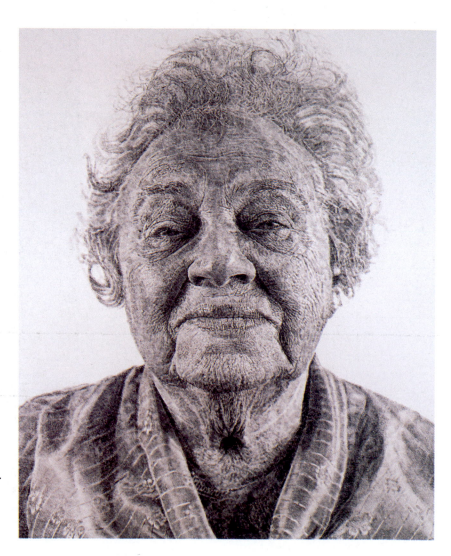

13.4   CHUCK CLOSE. *Fanny (Fingerpainting)*, USA, 1985. Oil on canvas, 120" × 84". Washington, D.C., National Gallery of Art, donation of Lila Acheson Wallace.

other people's faces. She used a cheap plastic camera to make grainy, fuzzy photographs of children with unusual faces due to genetic conditions, accident, or disease. The low-quality lens produced surprisingly beautiful images, with blurred edges, softened highlights, and grainy but luminous shadows. Burson's photographs reveal some aspects of the children's personalities, such as friendliness, dreaminess, caution, concern, curiosity, and boldness. Our untitled example (Fig. 13.5) shows the boy at the left obligingly posing and encouraging the other to do so also, while the other boy remains reluctant and suspicious of manipulation. Framing makes the child at the left seem to be moving, while the other appears more pinned at the center.

Burson's photographs act as a mirror to the viewers, who reveal themselves in their reactions to the images. Burson noted that people who dwell on disaster see these children as disasters, whereas others react to them as they would to other children. Thus, degrees of "normal" and "abnormal" are more the viewers' judgments than objective standards.

Full-body portraits include posture and body type, which may reveal more about the sitter's personality. *Leigh under the Skylight,* painted in 1994 (Fig. 13.6), is one of Lucian Freud's many full-body portraits. During

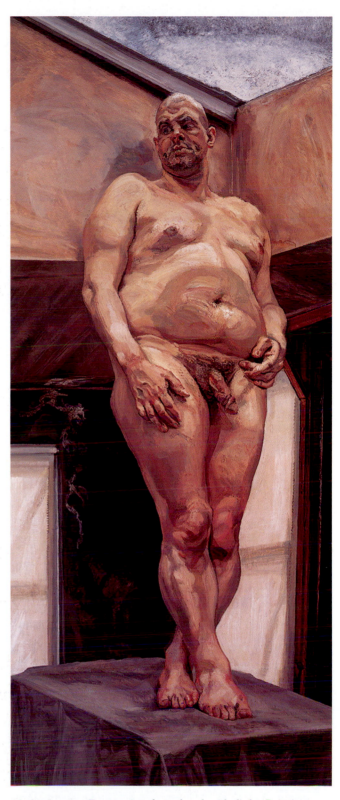

13.6 LUCIAN FREUD. *Leigh under the Skylight,* Britain, 1994. Oil on canvas, 90" × 48". New York, Acquavella Contemporary Art. By permission of the Artist.

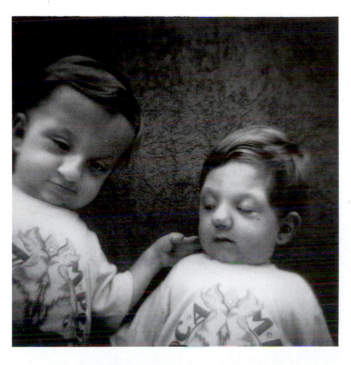

13.5 NANCY BURSON. Untitled image from *Faces,* USA, 1992. Silver gelatin print, 15" × 15". Twin Palms Publishers, Santa Fe, New Mexico. Courtesy of the Artist.

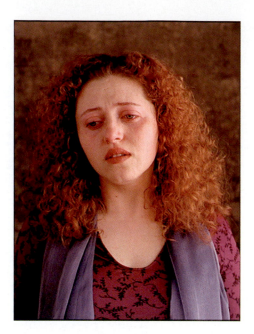 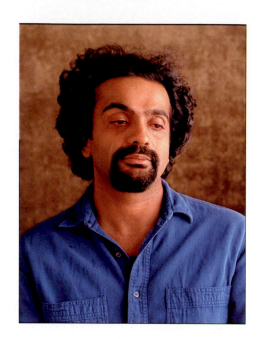

13.7 BILL VIOLA. *Dolorosa* (production stills from the video installation), USA, 2000. Photo by Kira Perov. Courtesy of the Artist.

the long process of sitting for a painting in Freud's studio, the sitters unintentionally reveal clues about their most intimate selves, primarily through their poses and facial expressions. The figure of Leigh is massive, and from the low point of view assumed by the artist, he appears to be almost gigantic. Yet the flesh is soft. The crossed legs, deeply lined face, and furrowed brow communicate a sense of tightness. The figure appears almost stuffed up against the space of the skylight, wary and exposed. The paint is thick and buttery below the knees and the top of the belly, but congealed and clotted around the jaw, nipples, navel, and genitals. The excess of texture is both fascinating and repulsive. This full-size nude is definitely a portrait of an individual man, in contrast to the full-size nude *Doryphoros* (see Fig. 13.14), which is a depiction of "Man."

Video allows artists to make moving portraits. Bill Viola's *Dolorosa* (Fig. 13.7) consists of two flat-panel monitors arranged like a diptych or a double-frame portrait showing a weeping man and woman. At first glance, the videos look like paintings, because the color is so saturated, the picture so sharp, and the movement so excruciatingly slow. Only after a few minutes of study do we see the subtle changes in their faces, expressing a deep, almost unbearable sorrow. Viola made this work and more than twenty others in a series titled *The Passions*, based on Renaissance and Baroque paintings of figures in sorrow, ecstasy, or astonishment. Rather than restage the old paintings, Viola sought to expand their emotional and spiritual dimensions. Viewers can study faces as never before.

SELF-PORTRAITS

We will look at four artists who have made many pictures of themselves. Rembrandt van Rijn made at least sixty-two self-portraits. Frida Kahlo painted herself fifty-five times, which represents almost one-third of the artwork she did in her entire lifetime. Cindy Sherman has photographed herself hundreds of times in various guises and settings. Likewise, Mariko Mori has made multiple images of herself that cross the boundaries between fine art, consumer culture, and kitsch.

Rembrandt's records of his face can be strong, vulnerable, cloddish, or sophisticated, and range from youth through old age. The paintings are emotional barometers as well, showing happiness, worry, sorrow, humor, or resignation. In *Self-Portrait,* painted in 1669 (Fig. 13.8), Rembrandt records both a human face and a human soul. His lit face emerges from the void of the background. Light seems both to reflect off the surface of his face and to emanate from inside his head. His eyes express gentleness, pain, and knowledge. The left side of his face is in soft shadow, a fitting visual metaphor for a man of wisdom facing his own death. In fact, Rembrandt died later that year. Earth tones, blacks, dull reds, and luminous yellows predominate in this painting. The paint surface is rich and thick. Rembrandt studied himself in a country where both religion and the state promoted individualism (see *Art and History in Context* on page 360).

In her fifty-five self-portraits, Frida Kahlo conducted a long inquiry into her inner and her outer being. Her face stays almost the same in all her paintings: distinc-

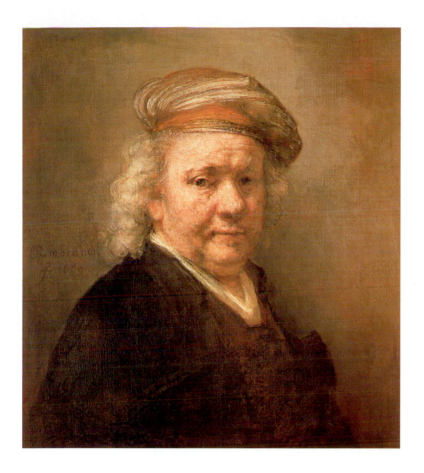

13.8 REMBRANDT VAN RIJN. *Self-Portrait*, Netherlands, 1669. Oil on canvas, 23¼" × 20". The Hague, Mauritshuis. © Scala/Art Resource, NY.

tive, unemotional, and with an unblinking gaze that looks back. She surrounds herself with signs and images of the different factors that shaped her life, such as her ancestry, her physical body, her nearly fatal accident and chronic pain, the indigenous Mexican culture, the landscape, the Christian religion, and her relationship with Diego Rivera, a prominent Mexican artist. In *Self-Portrait with Monkey*, painted in 1938 (Fig. 13.9), Kahlo's face is central, studying us as we study her. Her long hair is braided and pulled on top of her head in traditional Mexican style, to show her identification with the peasant culture. Lush foliage from the Mexican landscape surrounds her head. For Kahlo, the monkey was her animal alter ego. In other self-portraits, Kahlo uses such symbols as hummingbirds, which stood for the souls of dead Mayan warriors, and blood, which alludes to the crippling injuries she suffered in a bus accident, to Mayan bloodletting ceremonies, and to the Christian crown of thorns.

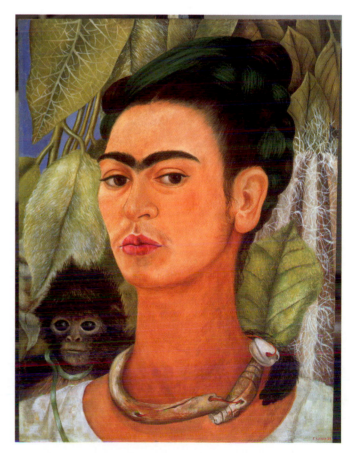

13.9 FRIDA KAHLO. *Self-Portrait with Monkey*, Mexico, 1938. Oil on masonite, 16" × 12". Albright-Knox Art Gallery, Buffalo, N.Y. Bequest of A. Conger Goodyear, 1966.

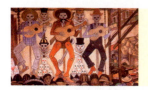

Connections *For an example of Diego Rivera's work, see* Día de Los Muertos *(Fig. 10.23, page 264).*

A Mayan relief depicting a bloodletting ritual, Shield Jaguar and Lady Xoc, *appears in Figure 9.15, page 213.*

Kahlo's and Rembrandt's self-portraits show the inner self of a unique, deeply feeling person. Cindy Sherman photographed herself hundreds of times, but the cumulative effect is one of fragmentation, not of piecing together a unique individual. Each image of Sherman reflects a socially prescribed or media-disseminated role. Our example, *Untitled Film Still #35* (Fig. 13.10), is one of a series of sixty-nine fake film stills she made between 1977 and 1980. They were all black and white, eight by ten inches, the exact format of B-movie stills. She wears a wide range of costumes and poses in all kinds of settings, with a vast array of props, as if unaware of the camera. Yet Sherman often reveals the mechanics of her self-portraiture; in this picture, the shutter release cable that Sherman operates is visible on the floor at the left.

In the photos, Sherman is sometimes almost unrecognizable as she reenacts roles for women that are given to us by the media, such as the sweetheart next door, the housewife, the girl left behind, or the vulnerable hitchhiker from a slasher film. In *Untitled Film Still #35,* Sherman appears as a poor woman who is hardened, trapped, sullen, and sexy. The grimy setting and costumes seem to be taken from the 1930s. The kick marks on the door allude to an atmosphere of violence. This image is the reversal of the independent, single, working girl who becomes the happy homemaker. Sherman suggests that we have no built-in sense of identity, but rather compose ourselves from pieces of popular culture. The *Film Still* self-portraits are collectively a portrait of familiar female stereotypes, as represented through the media.

Connections *To read what critics have said about Sherman's work, turn to pages 90–91).*

Japanese-born Mariko Mori is an artist and a former fashion model and fashion designer living in both New York and Tokyo. She creates photographs and performances "starring" herself in various roles, such as geisha or cyberchick, which she sees as total fabrications. Embracing the commercial world that uses mod-

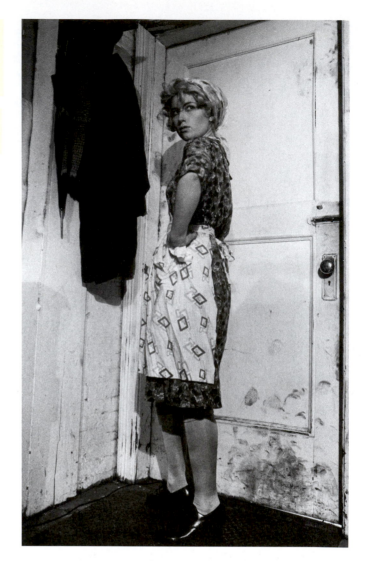

13.10 CINDY SHERMAN. *Untitled Film Still #35,* USA, 1979. Gelatin Silver Print, 8" × 10". Collection of Eli and Edythe Broad, Los Angeles. Courtesy of the Artist and Metro Pictures.

els to sell messages, she sees her artwork as part of pop culture and wants to connect art with movies and fashions. In *Birth of a Star,* she photographed herself as a teen rock star in a shiny, plastic, plaid skirt and spiked purple hair, surrounded by computer-manipulated floating bubbles. Afterward, she translated that same image into *Star Doll,* 1998 (Fig. 13.11), an edition of ninety-nine dolls. Because her identity is a totally fabricated hybrid, her work raises the question, "What is 'self'?" Mori's work collapses distinctions among the categories of art, toy, fashion, kitsch, frivolity, and serious inquiry.

THE PHYSICAL BODY

Artists use the body to address ideas about the essence of humanity.

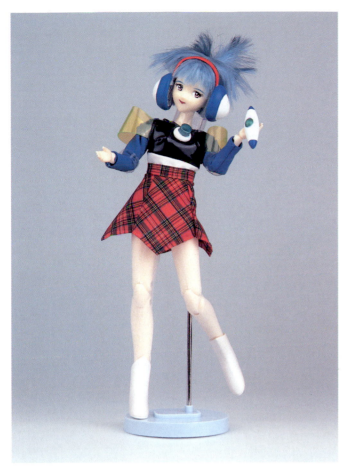

13.11 MARIKO MORI. *Star Doll*, 1998 (edition for Parket 54, 1998–1999). Multiple of doll, 10¼" × 3" × 1⁹⁄₁₆" (irreg). Publisher: Parkett, Zurich and New York. Manufacturer: Marmit, Tokyo. Edition: 99. © 1998 Mariko Mori and Parkett.

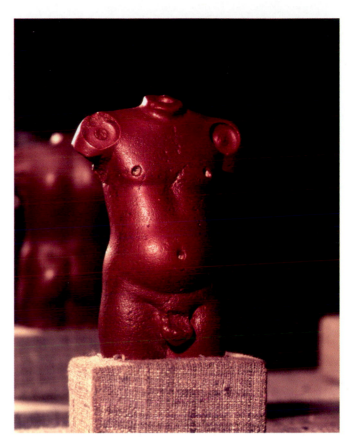

13.12 *Torso*, India (Harappa, Pakistan), c. 3000 BCE. Red sandstone, 3½" high. National Museum, New Delhi. © Borromeo/Art Resource, NY.

The Idealized Body

Our first four examples present the human body in ideal terms, although that varies from culture to culture. *Torso*, dated c. 3000 BCE (Fig. 13.12), is a carving from the ancient Harappan civilization that was centered on the Indus River in what is now Pakistan. The sculpture is an idealized version of the human body, with a supple, rounded form. The arm sockets suggest that the figure originally included several arms, possibly representing a youthful deity. The somewhat distended stomach suggests a yogic breathing posture. The stone has been so sensitively shaped that it gives the impression of living flesh, smooth muscle, and a little pad of fat. The outlines and forms are smooth and curving, suggesting grace, flexibility, sensuality, and even vulnerability.

Yakshi, dating from the first century BCE in India (Fig. 13.13), continued the rounded form and sensuality of the *Torso*. Yakshi is a nature spirit who represents

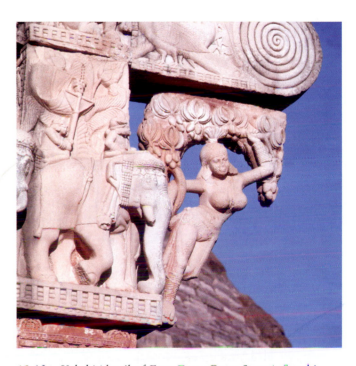

13.13 *Yakshi* (detail of East Gate, Great Stupa), Sanchi, India, early Andhra period, 1st century BCE. Sandstone, approx. 5' high. Robert Harding.

fertility; her breasts are exaggerated to emphasize her powers—her touch caused trees to flower. Her nearly nude body is curving and rounded and can be seen through her transparent skirt with the hemline draping across her shin. *Yakshi* twists with incredible flexibility, looking natural in a pose that would leave a human totally off balance. Jewelry adorns her lower arms and legs, giving interest to the less-curving features of her body. Her belt visually emphasizes her broad hips in contrast to her small waist. For the next several centuries, India produced an enormous amount of splendid figurative sculpture, and the twisting pose and voluptuous form appear often. Thus, in India, sensuality is an important and central characteristic of human nature.

Protagoras said, "Of all things, the measure is man," and the ancient Greeks had a great respect for the human mind and body, esteeming the arts, sciences, philosophy, and athletics. The democratic government, although limited, meant that individuals were self-governing. Athlete, philosopher, scientist, statesman, playwright, and warrior were all ideal occupations for men. The Greeks believed that humans were capable of near perfection, defined as a fit body guided by a keen mind. Emotions were generally considered less important than the intellect and should be properly contained. Nudity was common in art and in athletic events, both of which glorified the unclothed, idealized human form. *Doryphoros,* which means "Spear-bearer," is dated 450–440 BCE (Fig. 13.14). This sculpture by Polykleitos is a slightly larger-than-life-size nude male that reflects the Greeks' deep appreciation of the human body. The figure is idealized in a number of ways: (1) in the balanced pose; (2) in the internal proportions; (3) in the restrained emotions; and (4) in the roles depicted—youth, athlete, and warrior.

The pose is simple, balanced, and understated. The statue's straight leg and arm create a vertical line on the left, balanced by the bent leg and arm on the right. Balance is also expressed across the body. The straight leg and bent arm are tensed, versus the hanging arm and flexed leg, which are relaxed. The action is minimal and at the same time complex in its subtleties, with small twists, stretches, and compressions. This **contrapposto** (counterbalanced) stance is the way many people stand, and so the sculpture re-creates an image of a living, flexing body.

Polykleitos invented and applied a now-lost system of mathematical and geometric proportions, called the Canon, which harmonized one body part with another in his sculptures. *Doryphoros* was originally conceived as a sculpture that would illustrate and demonstrate the

Canon. A few of the simpler proportions of the Canon are still known; for example, the length of the longest finger equaled the length of the palm of the hand, and together they were used as a measure for the length of the arm. The breast nipples are one head-length below

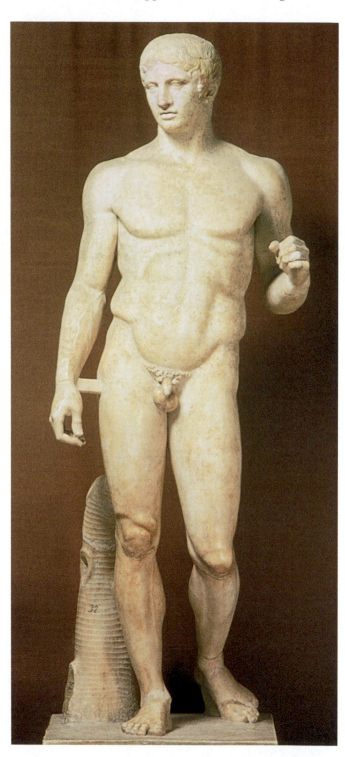

13.14   POLYKLEITOS. *Doryphoros (Spear-bearer),* Rome, c. 450–440 BCE. Marble after a bronze original, 6'11" high. Museo Nazionale, Naples. Saskia Ltd.

the chin, and the navel is another head-length below the nipples. This system also determined the placement of all the muscles. Polykleitos and the Greeks of his era believed that mathematical proportions resulted in a harmonious figure that was morally and aesthetically good. (In fact, the body is blocky, the result of the application of the Canon.)

Polykleitos' total combination of balance, proportion, restraint, and youthful heroism made *Doryphoros* one of the most famous nudes of its time as well as the Roman era and the Italian Renaissance.

> **Connections** *See* **Zeus/Poseidon** *(Fig. 9.3, page 204) to compare the similarity between images of gods and humans in Greek Classical art.*
>
> *The original* **Doryphoros** *was executed in bronze, using the lost wax process. For more, see page 72.*

It is interesting to compare *Doryphoros* with the *Male Torso* (Ancestor figure) in Figure 13.15, which was likely carved in the twentieth century in the Baule area of Africa. Internal proportions, idealized character, harmony of parts, and restraint are important elements here as in *Doryphoros*, but the visual result is very different. In most traditional African sculpture, the front view of the human figure was sculpted symmetrically; arms are in parallel positions, legs both on the ground, head facing forward. This formal, frontal pose contributes to the dignified, almost solemn aspect of the sculpture. In contrast, the side view features counterbalanced curves: the abdomen and knees project forward, balanced by the buttocks to the back. The straight neck and back interrupt the curves. The distinctive silhouette of the head is the focus for the entire work. This sculpture is likely the depiction of an ancestor.

In some African traditions, the head and neck were considered the most important parts of the body, and thus were apportioned one-third the height of the entire figure. The torso occupied another third, and the legs the last third. The sculptor's first cuts set these proportions. The major forms were sculpted next, and, finally, decorative patterns enlivened the surface. The patterns represent scarification and carefully combed, braided, twisted, or beaded hair. The pattern elements are all confidently carved without mistakes or reworking, because African sculptors generally were well trained as apprentices. The *Male Torso* combines naturalistic and abstracted features; for example, the chest and legs are relatively naturalistic compared to the stylized hands. This echoes tendencies in

African sculpture as a whole, which runs the gamut from realistic to very abstract.

Less-Than Perfect Humanity

Having looked at idealized human forms, we turn now to some works that present a less-idealized image of humanity. The first is *Laocoön and His Sons,* dated

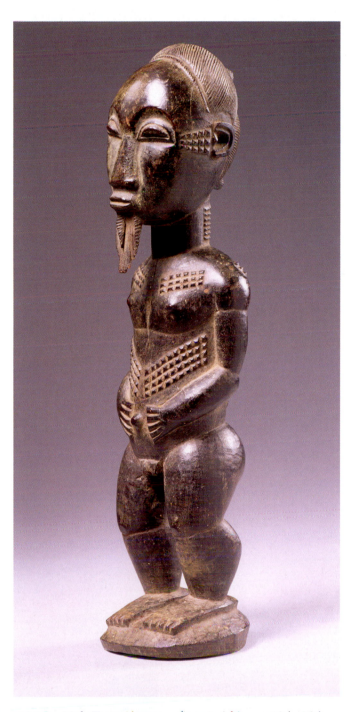

13.15 *Male Torso* (Ancestor figure), Africa, c. 19th–20th century. Wood, 20½" high. Baule. The British Museum, London.

300 to 100 BCE (Fig. 13.16). In the two or three centuries that followed the making of the "perfect" image of *Doryphoros,* the Greeks turned to depicting humans engaged in violent action, vulnerable to age, injured, diseased, and subject to feelings of pain, terror, or despair. Two cults were particularly influential in **Hellenistic** Greece: Stoicism, in which individuals were urged to endure nobly their fate and state in life; and Epicureanism, which advocated intelligent pleasure seeking in life because death was the end of existence. Both philosophies imply a kind of resigned acceptance of fate and a withdrawal from the Classic Greek ideal of the active, heroic, involved person.

Laocoön and His Sons shows these changing concepts of the human body and human nature. In *Laocoön,* the human bodies are impressively muscular, an inheritance of the Classical Greeks. But the balance of mind and body, and the contained emotion, has here burst apart in a scene of high drama and sensationalism. Laocoön was a Trojan priest who tried to warn his fellow citizens against accepting the Trojan Horse as an apparent token of surrender from the Greeks who had been warring against them. Greek warriors hid in the horse, and they overcame the Trojan forces once the horse was inside the fortifications. The gods, who sided with the Greeks against the Trojans, sent sea serpents to strangle

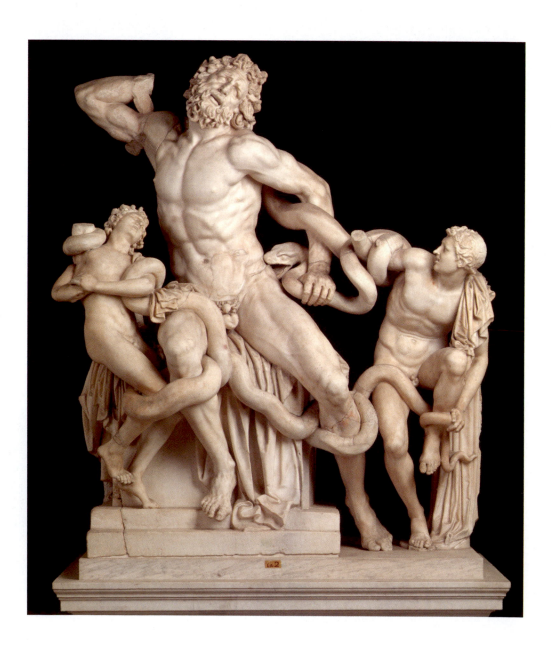

13.16 AGESANDER, ATHENODORUS, AND POLYDORUS OF RHODES. *Laocoön and His Sons,* Greece, late 2nd–early 1st century BCE. Marble, 7'10" high. Hellenistic (Roman patronage). Vatican Museums, Rome. © Araldo de Luca/Corbis.

and kill Laocoön and his sons, even as they were making offerings at an altar. The story seems to be one of great injustice, as a virtuous man helping his fellow citizens is cruelly crushed by the gods. Human vulnerability and lack of control of one's fate are well demonstrated.

The figures are like a group of actors on a stage, all facing forward as if performing for an unseen audience (which is common of Hellenistic sculpture). Their struggles are theatrical. Their bodies are idealized, but the father's is overdeveloped and muscle-bound, more spectacular than heroic. Emotionality is increased by the deeply cut sculpture and Laocoön's dramatic reach into the surrounding space. The textures and surfaces vary from skin to hair, and cloth to serpent.

In medieval Europe, human nature was held in very low esteem. Medieval Christians saw a great split between the purity of God's divine realm and the natural world, a transitory place of sin and corruption. The mortal body was given over to appetites and lusts that led humans into sin and endangered their immortal

souls. Salvation with God was possible only through the Church. In *The Last Judgment,* dated c. 1130 (Fig. 13.17), from the main entrance of the Church of St.-Lazare, human bodies are depicted as miserable, frail, and pitifully unattractive. The scene illustrates the end of time, when every person rises from the ground to be judged forever as worthy of heaven or condemned to hell. In the lower section of this carving, the cowering humans rise from their box-like graves and huddle in line until a pair of large hands, like oversized pliers, clamps around their heads. All are then plucked up and deposited on the scales of Judgment, where they risk being snatched by demons and stuffed in hell for eternity. The saved ones clutch fearfully at the robes of the angels.

Because human nature was considered so base, the Greek nude was inconceivable, and the concept of a naturalistic body as beautiful and good had long since disappeared. The body in medieval art was distorted to communicate moral status. Thus, naked humans are puny. Good angels are elongated and serene, their

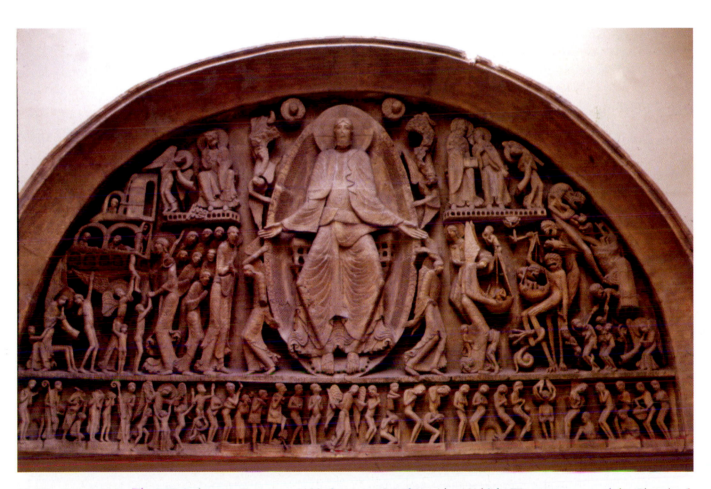

13.17 GISLEBERTUS. *The Last Judgment,* France, c. 1130. Stone carving, 21' wide, 12' high. West tympanum of the Church of St.-Lazare, Autun, Burgundy. The bottom band shows humans raised from the dead on the last day, while Heaven is shown on the upper left, and the scales of Judgment and Hell are on the upper right. Ronald Sheridan/Ancient Art & Architecture.

anatomical distortions emphasizing their distance from earthly beings. The demons, however, seem to have been modeled on a flayed human corpse, with the exposed ribs and muscles of a tortured body, while their faces grimace horribly. Their claw feet are beast-like, and indeed the human body was associated with animals, which were seen as even more distant from God. Jesus is depicted in a grand manner reigning over heaven and earth, frontal and symmetrical, and much larger than all others.

Attitudes about human nature shifted again in Europe as the Renaissance flourished in Italy. Humanistic philosophy of this time celebrated the glory of humanity: Italian philosopher Giovanni Pico della Mirandola declared in the fifteenth century, "There is nothing to be seen more wonderful than man," reflecting an attitude very similar to the Greeks'. Michelangelo Buonarroti, the famous painter, sculptor, and architect of the Italian **Renaissance**, believed that the human form was the most perfect and important subject to depict. He believed that his work was an echo of God's divine creation of humanity. Like most other Italian artists of that time, he was strongly influenced by Hellenistic and Roman sculptures that were being excavated in central Italy, for example, *Laocoön and His Sons* (Fig. 13.16). The nude as an ideal form became popular again.

But Renaissance nudes were different from the Classical nudes. On the one hand, the body was seen now as a work of God and deserving of respect and honor. Yet the medieval beliefs persisted regarding the enduring soul versus the corruptible body. *David*, dated 1501 to 1504 (Fig. 13.18), represents the Israelite youth who fought the giant warrior, Goliath, saved his people, and later became the greatest king of the Old Testament. Michelangelo chose the moment that the young David first faces Goliath. Tension is apparent in his frown, tensed muscles, and protruding veins. The sculpture is not self-contained, in contrast to *Doryphoros* (see Fig. 13.14); the turning figure of David is "completed" by the unseen Goliath. The head and hands are oversized, indicating youthful potential still maturing and a greater potential violence, all attributes that differ from the restrained, relaxed *Doryphoros*. David's inner tension speaks of the core of being, the soul, that is separate from the body. The body is ennobled and emphasized, but only as a vehicle for expressing the soul.

David reflects some broad trends. During the Renaissance, there was also a growing interest in scientific inquiry and the study of human anatomy. Michelangelo, Leonardo da Vinci, and other Italian artists performed dissections to assist them in rendering muscles. Also, David versus Goliath was a popular story in the republic of Florence, the city-state in central Italy for which this sculpture was made. Florence was ruled by a group of wealthy families rather than by a single leader,

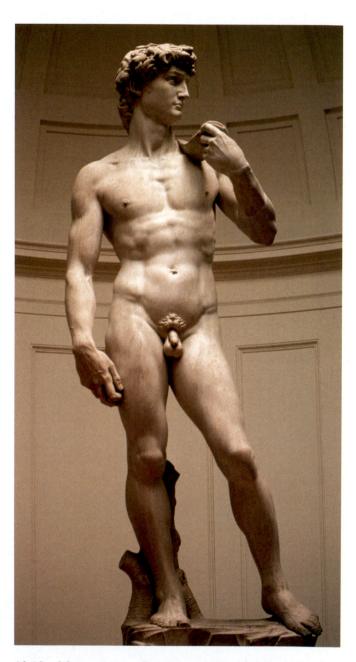

13.18 MICHELANGELO BUONARROTI. *David*, Italy, 1501–1504. Marble, 14'3" high. Galleria dell'Accademia, Florence, Italy. © Michael S. Yamashita / Corbis.

and Florentines saw themselves as much more self-determining than citizens of other areas ruled by tyrants.

Connections *See Andreas Vesalius's* Fourth Plate of Muscles *(Fig. 15.21, page 417) for more on Renaissance scientific studies of anatomy.*

Ambrogio Lorenzetti's Allegory of Good Government *(Fig. 12.19, page 321) was a tribute to republican governments in Siena, a city-state in central Italy.*

By the nineteenth and twentieth centuries, religious models for human nature held less sway in Europe and were increasingly challenged and displaced by concepts of human nature based on scientific inquiry. This shift was apparent in artwork, also. One indicator was the training of young artists, who now studied in academies, where art training was standardized and systematized. New technologies, such as photography, changed the understanding of the human body and the way art was made. With photography, human movement could be stopped and observed as never before. *Handspring, a flying pigeon interfering, June 26, 1885* (Fig. 13.19) is a study of the human body in action made by Eadweard Muybridge and subsequently published with other such studies in the book *Animal Locomotion*. Muybridge invented a special camera shutter and then placed twelve cameras so outfitted in a row. When the athlete performed the handstand, his movements broke the series of strings stretched across his path, thus progressively triggering each of the twelve cameras.

For Muybridge, the human body was an object of detached, scientific study and not a powerful presence like *David* or the *Male Torso* from Baule. With Muybridge, the concept of the human body was altered and was recognized as being modified by time and space. Muybridge made similar studies for all kinds of human and animal movement. He also developed a cylindrical device that allowed his images to be mounted, rotated, and viewed to give the illusion of motion. In this respect, his work was a precursor of cinema.

THE LIMITS OF THE SELF

Is the individual person a discrete entity? What are the boundaries between the self and the environment, between the self and the spiritual realm, or between the self and technology?

Many Oceanic cultures of the South Pacific conceive of the person as an amalgam of life forces, physical substances, and ritual knowledge that come from

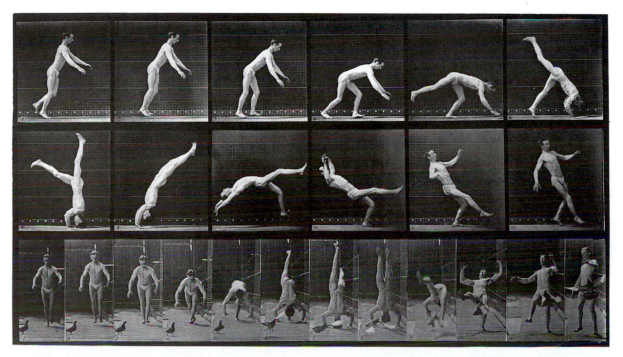

13.19 EADWEARD MUYBRIDGE. *Handspring, a flying pigeon interfering, June 26, 1885*, England/Scotland/USA, 1887. Print from an original master negative, Plate 365 of *Animal Locomotion*. International Museum of Photography at George Eastman House, Rochester, New York.

many sources. That amalgam, which is at this moment a particular person, is in fact constantly changing and transforming and also in danger of coming apart.

Ritual tattooing was one way of strengthening the individual and was used throughout the more eastern islands of the South Pacific. On the Marquesas Islands, the entire body was tattooed, while tattooing was confined to the buttocks and thighs of the women of Fiji and of the men of Samoa, Tahiti, and Tonga. Extensive tattooing subjected a person to severe pain for a long time, but the result was generally seen as a kind of ritual empowerment. Extra eyes, for example, gave the tattooed person more power and decreased vulnerability. Tattooing is often part of initiation rites that gradually harden the human body for adulthood.

The tattoos of *Tomika Te Mutu of Coromandel* (Fig. 13.20), a nineteenth-century Maori tribal chief, were seen as an extra protective shell and a new ritual skin. Tattooing was effective in war, as it distracted and confused opponents. The tattoos also identified the individual. Among the Maori, facial tattoos were often considered more memorable than the person's natural features, which is true of Tomika Te Mutu. The chiseled whorls emphasize his scowl, piercing vision, hot breath, and fierce mouth. Traditional Maori tattooing is done with chisels, which gouge deep grooves in the skin. Curves and spirals are like the patterns in Maori woodcarving.

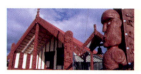 **Connection** Turn to Figure 11.15, page 289, to see Maori woodcarving on a traditional meeting house.

If ritual beliefs can shape the concept of the human being, scientific discoveries and technological advances can do so, also. A vast range of environmental factors influence the living body. The human being is seen now as permeable and as an integrated part of the total world.

In *Unique Forms of Continuity in Space* (Fig. 13.21), cast in 1931, artist Umberto Boccioni dissolves the conventional belief that the skin layer defines the body's outer edge. To him, the body is a mass of wave energy defined by its movement through a fluid atmo-spheric medium. Significantly, the body is considered less as a human and more as a form that is continuous with others in space. Muscle and bulk are implied, but the sculpture resembles a map of aerodynamic turbulence and the distorting effects of air currents on forms. Boccioni was part of an art movement called **Futurism**, which celebrated violence, speed, energy, motion, force, and change, which reflected his contemporary world.

The body can also be affected by a host of internal forces. In *The Scream* (Fig. 13.22), painted by Edvard Munch in 1893, the distorted body is the vehicle for expressing inner terror, anxieties, and pressures. Realism has been abandoned to give form to these internal emotions. At this time, Sigmund Freud had propagated his theories of repression and neurosis as both social and personal ills, which influenced Munch and other artists. The central character glances back at distant figures, but it is unclear whether they are part of the scene or disinterested bystanders. Whatever the situation, fear in the mind has twisted the body and reduced the face to a near skull. The figure stands in complete

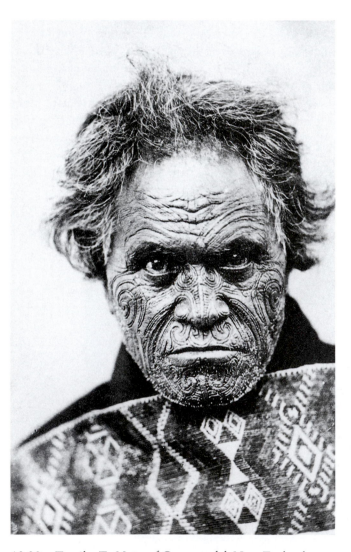

13.20 *Tomika Te Mutu of Coromandel,* New Zealand, 19th century. Maori chief. Photo by John Hillelson.

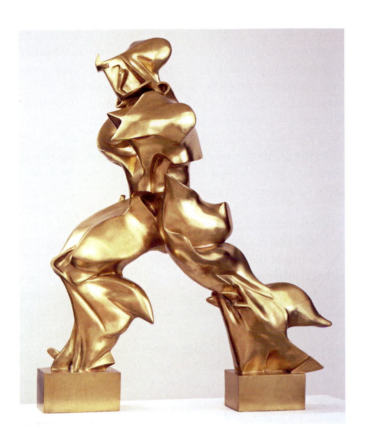

13.21 UMBERTO BOCCIONI. *Unique Forms of Continuity in Space,* Italy, 1913. Bronze (cast 1931), approx. 43" high. The Museum of Modern Art, New York; acquired through the Lillie P. Bliss Bequest. © Digital Image © The Museum of Modern Art/Licensed by SCALA/Art Resource, NY.

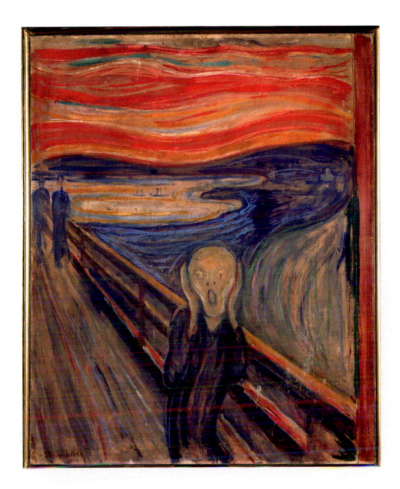

13.22 EDVARD MUNCH. *The Scream,* Norway, 1893. Oil painting, 35³/4" × 29". National Gallery, Oslo, Norway. © Erich Lessing/Art Resource, NY. © 2004 The Munch Museum/The Munch-Ellingsen Group/Artists Rights Society (ΛRS), New York.

physical and emotional isolation, cupping its hands over its ears and screaming at a pitch that reverberates in the landscape and in the sky. The colors are emotionally distorted and heightened.

In an era of consumerism, people often gauge their worth by the purchases they can make, not by character, deeds, fate, or karma. Body shape becomes something that can be bought, too. In the 1956 collage *Just What Is It That Makes Today's Homes So Different, So Appealing?* (Fig. 13.23), by Richard Hamilton, we see the aestheticized body ideals of the late twentieth century: the buff, muscular man of amazing sexual prowess (the Tootsie pop) and a super-thin, sexy woman with a fashion-model pout on her face. The faces and bodies have been molded through implants, plastic surgery, and the latest abdominal workout machine. In addition, the couple's attractiveness is enhanced by their acquisition of trendy props, which in the 1950s included modern furniture, the latest appliances, and new media products. Hamilton took his imagery from popular magazines and billboards. The rug is a designer version of a Jackson Pollock action painting, which we will see at the end of this chapter. The cluttered composition, with all things new and

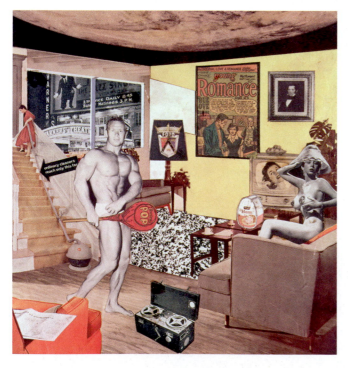

13.23 RICHARD HAMILTON. *Just What Is It That Makes Today's Homes So Different, So Appealing?* England, 1956. Collage, 10¼" × 9¾". Kunsthalle Tubingen, Germany. Bridgeman Art Library © 2004 Artists Rights Society (ARS), New York/DACS, London #NUL 108077.

chic, makes everything seem arbitrary and faddish. Hamilton's lampoon of modern consumer culture reveals the effectiveness and ridiculousness of advertising, because it projects ideal body images that are so extreme, images to which we can never (but must always try to) measure up.

> **Connection** *Hamilton's work is fine art with mass media imagery, and he is critical of both. For more, see "Fine Art, Popular Culture, and Kitsch," in Chapter 1.*

Installation artist Jin Soo Kim was born and raised in South Korea, trained as a nurse, and immigrated to the United States at age twenty-four. Much of her work has consisted of Environments, in which she transforms discarded refuse into works that allude to the human body and to self, as evident in the installation view of her 2003 exhibition at the Chicago Cultural Center (Fig. 13.24). Organic and architectural forms blur, as objects covered in gauze bandages "bleed" rust, while wrapped ropes and furniture resemble skeletons and viscera. Pieces of furniture seem to become creatures. All forms together suggest a vulnerable, living, interconnected environment of bodies and the things humans build. Kim's work suggests that the human body is completely one with its surroundings. She also suggests that the human "self" is not just the body or a person's character, but also the objects that one carries through life.

SICKNESS AND DEATH

Intra-Venus, dated from 1992 to 1993, is a series of large-scale photographs that the artist, Hannah Wilke, made with her husband, Donald Goddard, as she struggled with and eventually succumbed to cancer. In this series, both cancer and its medical cures transform and ravage Wilke's body. In many cases larger than life, the photographs present her body to us as it weakened, bloated, and bled. The size makes the physical reality of sickness apparent; it is "in your face." In one bust-length portrait, we see her bald scalp, mottled skin, and bleeding, pus-filled tongue, all resulting from her cancer treatment. Yet many of the images show that her body possessed a kind of monumental beauty and that Wilke was still a person of humor and strength.

In three panels from *Intra-Venus* (Fig. 13.25), Wilke assumes three poses derived from images of sexually attractive nudes taken from fine art and from magazines, such as *Playboy.* Her glance implies the presence of a sexual partner, as she poses herself as the object of voyeurism. Her posture speaks of narcissistic pleasure. She is Venus, the goddess of love and beauty,

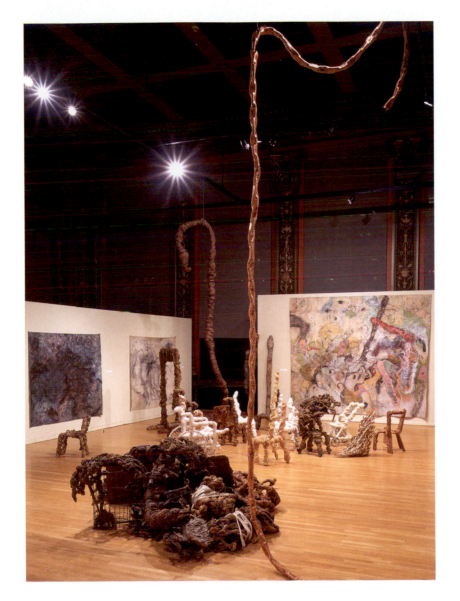

13.24   JIN SOO KIM. Installation view of various artworks at Chicago Cultural Center, 2003. Sculptural works date from 1983–2003. On walls left to right: *Winter*, 1986; *Untitled XV*, 1990; and *Untitled (from Environment D)*, 1984, all acrylic and charcoal on canvas. Photo by Tom Van Eynde, Courtesy Chicago Department of Cultural Affairs, Jin Soo Kim.

even with the ravages of disease and surgery. Wilke reclaims sexuality for herself in sickness and, thus, challenges conventional ideas of attractiveness. In doing so, her last work continued her earlier art. Before the onset of cancer, her body conformed to "fashion model" looks, and she frequently used her body in her artwork to undermine or critique how female beauty is currently defined and consumed in the United States.

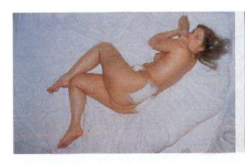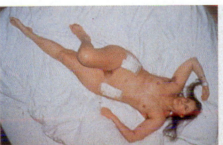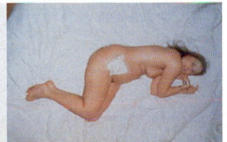

13.25   HANNAH WILKE. *Intra-Venus,* USA, 1992–1993. Chromogenic supergloss photographic prints (13); each panel: 26" × 39½". Courtesy Ronald Feldman Fine Arts, New York.

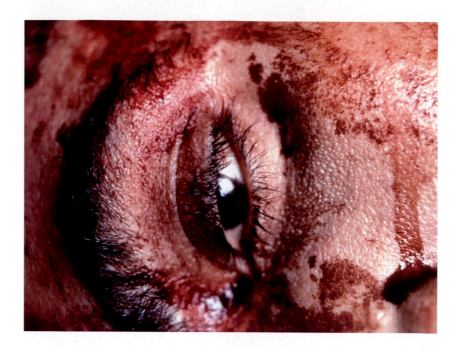

13.26 ANDRES SERRANO. *The Morgue (Hacked to Death II)*, USA, 1992. Cibachrome, 49¹/₂" × 60". Musée d'Art Contemporain de Montréal. Courtesy Paula Cooper Gallery, New York.

Connection *For more about the sexual meaning of gaze and gender roles in images, see* Olympia *by Edward Manet (Fig. 8.19, page 187).*

The Morgue (Hacked to Death II), dated 1992 (Fig. 13.26), is one of a series of twenty large-scale photographs by Andres Serrano, showing close-up details of the bodies of people in morgues who have died as a result of accidents, violence, or disease. The location is not important, however, as Serrano's images block out the surroundings. In some images, it is not clear if the person is lying on the side of a road or asleep in bed. No body is shown in entirety, so the individuals have no identity. They are close and intimate to the viewer.

The Morgue (Hacked to Death II) is a disturbing image, not only for its content, but because it is impossible to see this death as distant, as one would see a death on the evening news. We can see each hair as it grows out of the person's pores, study the dirt ground into the skin, trace the blood where it flowed and congealed. We cannot miss the dull, unfocused eye in dead center of the image. Serrano's framing, focusing, and manipulation of tones is artful and aesthetic; the refinement and beauty of the image jar with its content.

Connection *Compare this image of death with those from war, such as Mathew Brady's* Dead Confederate Soldier with Gun *(Fig. 11.23, page 295).*

THE BODY IN ART AND AS ART

The body is not only depicted in art. It is used in making art, or it is transformed to become artwork itself.

THE BODY AS ART MATERIAL

The human body is material for art making. It can be painted or sculpted, or it can be part of a performance or spectacle. In all these instances, the living body energizes, personalizes, or adds emotional content to the artwork. We have already seen an example of body art in the tattooed face of *Tomika Te Mutu* (see Fig. 13.20), where his skin is the canvas upon which the artwork is made. The marks on the face of the *Male Torso* (Ancestor figure) from Baule (see Fig. 13.15) may be scarification patterns. In both cases, the body art has great cultural significance.

The Mayan *Head from the Tomb of the Temple of Inscriptions* from Mexico (Fig. 13.27), dated mid to late seventh century, shows how the human body is plastic and moldable, a kind of raw material from which works of art can be made. To the Mayans, a flat, sloping forehead was beautiful and aesthetically pleasing, so they bound and compressed infants' heads to deform the shape as they were growing. Hair was bluntly cut at different levels and woven with jade ornaments, cotton threads, and flowers. The stair-step cut on the sides and the top plume of hair were common designs. The resulting human head was a living artistic creation, the image of which is reproduced in this stucco sculpture in the

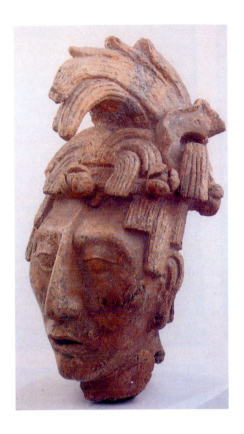

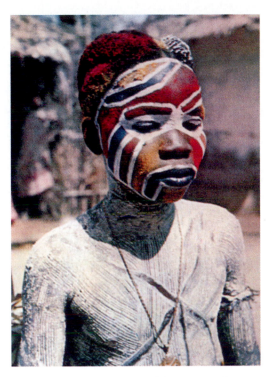

13.27 *Head from the Tomb of the Temple of Inscriptions*, Mexico, mid–late 7th century. Stucco, 17" high. Maya. Palenque, Chiapas, Mexico. Museo Nacional de Antropología, Mexico City. Photo © 2004 Metropolitan Museum of Art, New York.

13.28 *Ngere Girl Prepared for a Festival*, Africa, late 20th century. Body painting. Photograph by Dominique Darbois.

round, which was once brightly painted. This portrait sculpture of a ruler known as Shield II (or *Pacal II* in Mayan) was found next to his tomb.

Body ornamentation is an art form in many traditional African cultures, where rituals are the supremely important events for the community, governing all aspects of life, death, everyday survival, and interaction with the spirit world. In many of these cultures, body painting is equivalent to wearing masks or costumes. Among the Ngere people in the late twentieth century, girls after initiation paint their torsos white and their faces in brilliant colors, as in *Ngere Girl Prepared for a Festival* (Fig. 13.28). The patterns of color are similar to the way the face can be abstracted and broken down into parts in sculpture, while the parallel lines in the white paint echo both chisel marks and sculptural hair patterns. Body painting, like tattooing, makes the living body into a work of art, expands its power and its protection, announcing the status of the person in the community—in this case, an initiated girl.

Ana Mendieta created a number of outdoor performances that dealt with her body directly or the trace of her body on the earth. Individual works in the series, called *Silueta* (Silhouette), were performed in Iowa and in Mexico from 1973 until 1980 and exist now only as documentary photographs. In *Arbol de la Vida, No. 294*, dated 1977 (Fig. 13.29), Mendieta made herself

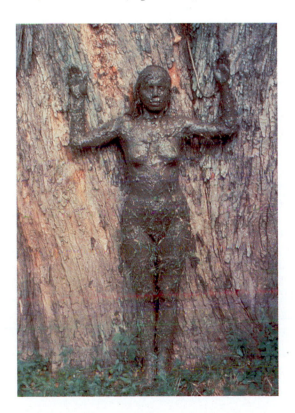

13.29 ANA MENDIETA. *Arbol de la Vida, No. 294*, Cuba/USA, 1977. From the series *Arbol de la Vida/Silueta* (Tree of Life/Silhouette). Color photograph documenting the earth/body sculpture with artist, tree trunk, and mud, at Old Man's Creek, Iowa City, Iowa. Collection Ignacio C. Mendieta. Courtesy of Gallery Lelong, New York.

into a body sculpture covered with mud and straw. She posed against a tree in a manner reminiscent of ancient fertility goddesses, leaving traces of mud on the bark. The site of her performance was very dramatic, with a massive tree growing at the edge of a deeply cut creek bed. In other works in the *Silueta* series, Mendieta sculpted the mud or used stones or flowers to trace the outline of her body on the earth. It was important to use her living body in these performances because they became like rituals in which the energy of her living being was joined with that of the earth, which she believed was a force that was omnipresent and female.

Connection *Review the discussion of ancient fertility goddesses, such as* Idol from Amorgos *(Fig. 8.2, page 173).*

In some cases, the artist relinquished control in a performance. Yoko Ono wrote scripts that set up situations for artworks, but the exact outcome of the pieces was determined by chance or by spontaneous audience participation. In a 1964 performance of *Cut Piece* (Fig. 13.30), Yoko Ono entered an empty stage clothed in a black dress and sat/knelt in a traditional position for Japanese women. She held aloft scissors and then placed them in front of herself, as if preparing for *seppuku* (ritual suicide). She then invited and encouraged audience members to cut away her clothing. As the performance proceeded, she sat without showing emotion. Long pauses occurred during the performance. Ono was influenced by John Cage, a composer who believed that the silences between sounds were as important as the music. More and more skin showed until she was nearly nude and bare chested, and the performance ended as she gasped and covered herself.

Cut Piece alludes to a number of ideas: the traditional male sexual prerogative over the female body; the display of the body for the consuming gaze; violation and control; and the herd mentality among humans. Roles are confused in the piece: Ono, apparently the violated, also set up the situation. Yet the audience members acted freely, as it was beyond her control to dictate what they did. The artist's body and the actions of the audience are the art piece, not the photo document we see in this book. The physical presence of real bodies, the quality of spectacle, the uncertainty, and the palpable experience of time passing are potent elements that still photography cannot convey.

Ono was part of the **Fluxus** movement in New York, which sought to create a kind of anti-art or non-art. In Fluxus, art was conceived as an artist-initiated experience rather than an object, like a painting or sculp-

ture. For both Ono's and Mendieta's work, photodocumentation is all that remains.

Connection *In Chapter 16, the section titled "Art and Dramatic Productions" provides more discussion of performance art.*

THE BODY AS AN ART TOOL

The first and most important tools of artists are their bodies: their fingers, hands, and arms, guided by their minds. In making works of art, artists continually touch the entire surface of their works. This is obvious with sculptors who model clay with their hands. But even painters work the entire surface of their images with sensitive brushes and often adjust or finish their work with their fingertips. Although the touch of photographers and computer artists may leave no mark on their works, their hands are nonetheless essential and

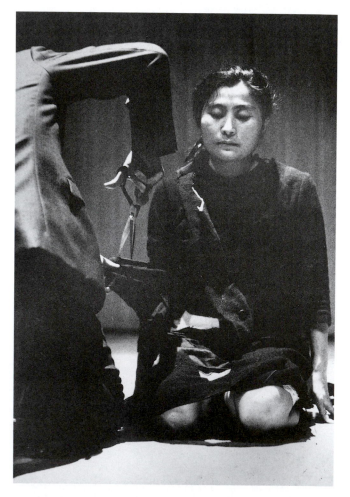

13.30 YOKO ONO. *Cut Piece*, Japan/USA, 1964. Photo documentation of performance at Yamaichi Concert Hall, Kyoto. Collection of the artist, courtesy Studio One.

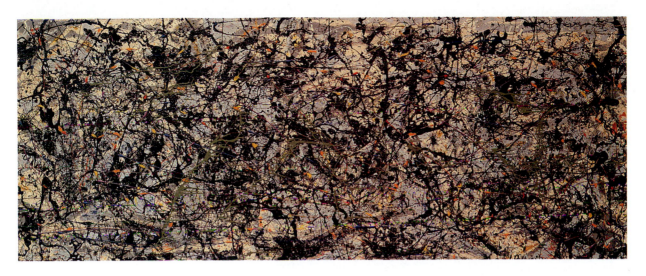

13.31 JACKSON POLLOCK. *Lucifer,* USA, 1947. Oil, aluminum paint, and enamel on canvas, approx. 3'5" × 8'9". Collection of Harry Ward and Mary Margaret Anderson. © 2004 Pollock-Krasner Foundation/Artists Rights Society (ARS), New York.

present. In *Fanny (Fingerpainting),* which we saw in Figure 13.4, artist Chuck Close created the woman's enormous head in detail, showing the texture of her hair, skin wrinkles, her watery eyes, and the cloth of her dress. The entire work was painted with the artist's hand and fingerprints. Although it looks like a photograph, the face in fact is a mass of smudges, a record of everywhere the artist touched. The mark of the hand relates to fossils and the handprints in prehistoric cave paintings and to the first marks we made as children.

When Jackson Pollock painted *Lucifer* (Fig. 13.31) in 1947, the motion of his entire body was very significant. This style of painting is called "gestural abstraction" or "action painting." The "action" came from the movement of the artist himself, as seen in Figure 13.32, which shows Pollock in his studio. The canvas was laid down on the ground, and Pollock poured, dripped, and flung paint upon it as he stood at the edges or walked across the surface. He lunged and swirled about in furious outbursts, which were followed by periods of reflection. His body movements were fixed and recorded in the paint surface, which is a rhythmic mesh of drips, congealed blobs, and looping swirls.

Pollock's act of painting and the painting itself were frequently described in quasi-combat terms. He saw the canvas on the ground as a plane of action, but when hanging on the wall in front of the viewer, it became a plane of confrontation. Pollock believed his spontaneous, energetic painting style fit the mood of the United States immediately after World War II. He also believed that the power of his unconscious mind

was being released in action painting and that his painting style was a burst of primal energy and a release from civilized constraints. The action painter was seen as being an isolated genius, almost always male, whose work had no morals and no narrative, just pure paint and pure body action. Pollock as a painter of action reflected the ideas that made the cowboy or the "rebel without a cause" so appealing. His paint handling was seen as sophisticated and a mark of artistic genius.

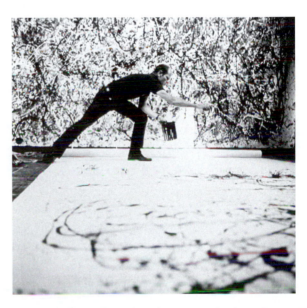

13.32 Jackson Pollock in his Long Island Studio, 1950. Photo © Hans Namuth, Ltd.

This era saw the increased development of centralized states, in some cases formed around ethnic units. Also, beginning in 1700, the world population grew dramatically for four reasons: (1) better immunity to diseases that had been spread by the first explorers, (2) a period of climate warming, which improved agricultural conditions, (3) new food sources through trade, and (4) the invention of gunpowder, which allowed rulers to control larger areas with their armies and to create more stability.

The Ottoman Empire in Turkey and the Middle East continued to flourish, in spite of unsuccessful bids to conquer areas of central Europe. Africa's heartlands continued to be self-ruling and relatively isolated, although the coastal regions were engaged in the slave trade with Europe. The Asante Kingdom was established in western Africa in 1680. Likewise, in Southeast Asia, Dutch and English traders continued in the lucrative spice trade, but the inland areas were generally unaffected and self-ruled.

Map 7 Latin America in the Eighteenth Century. Courtesy of Replogle Globes, Inc., Broadview, IL.

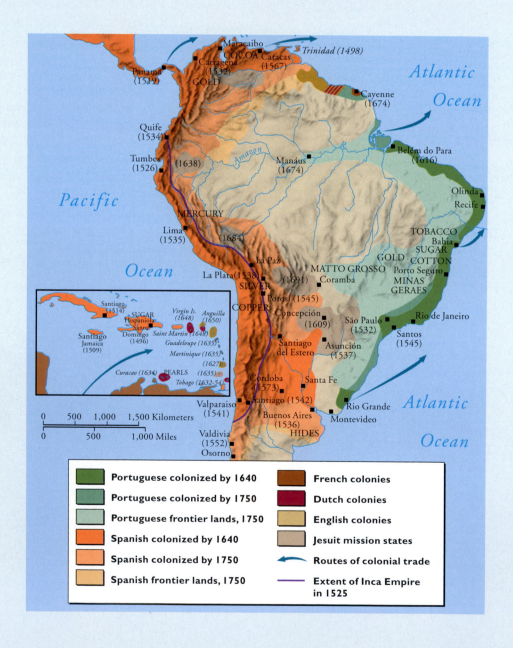

Portuguese colonized by 1640
Portuguese colonized by 1750
Portuguese frontier lands, 1750
Spanish colonized by 1640
Spanish colonized by 1750
Spanish frontier lands, 1750
French colonies
Dutch colonies
English colonies
Jesuit mission states
Routes of colonial trade
Extent of Inca Empire in 1525

The Mughal Empire continued in India, and Akbar (1556–1605) oversaw a period of humane rule, peace, and prosperity. Mughal artists excelled at miniature painting. The empire subsequently weakened throughout the eighteenth century. After a long peasant uprising that ended in 1644, China also saw a period of remarkable tolerance, prosperity, and unity, especially under the reign of Kangxi (1661–1722). Japan continued to be ruled by local warlords until 1603, when Tokugawa Ieyasu unified Japan under his command and closed the country to foreigners. The Japanese merchant class grew in number and wealth for the next few hundred years. Japanese art was distinguished by painted scrolls, screens, and gardens.

Europe had already embarked on a period of global expansion. With the exception of limited access to a few ports, Europeans were kept out of China, Japan, and India. However, they rapidly colonized the Americas. North America was divided into English, French, and Spanish colonies. The population in the English colonies continued to be mostly European, both racially and culturally. Spanish rule was the most extensive, covering western North America, Central America, and most of South America, except for Portuguese Brazil. At this time, Latin America (see map) began to emerge as a cultural entity, although it was composed of many individual states. Latin American societies were multiracial, reflecting intermarriage among native populations, Europeans, and Africans since the 1500s. Because Latin America was more remote, European rulers exercised less direct control, and large, local landowners developed extensive power.

In Europe itself, 1560–1650 was a period of crisis as a result of religious wars between Catholics and Protestants, competition for colonial lands, and hardship caused by crop failures. In response to the unrest, new centralized powers emerged after 1650. In some cases, these were absolute rulers who governed all aspects of their country with tight control—for example, Louis XIV of France, Peter the Great of Russia, and the rulers of Prussia. Louis XIV lived in his lavish palace, *Versailles* (see image in history box), a fitting setting for his absolute rule as the Sun King, which also helped him to control the nobility.

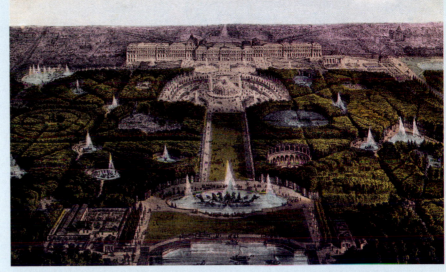

13.33   *Versailles*. Anonymous 17th-century painting. © Bettmann/Corbis.

The Habsburgs ruled Austria, but the nobility maintained considerable power. England developed a constitutional monarchy. The Baroque style of art dominated European art at this time. One strong influence on the Baroque era was the heroic sculptures and paintings of Michelangelo, as seen in *David* (Fig. 13.18)

This was also the period of the Enlightenment, which saw advances in philosophy, science, literature, and human rights. Increasingly, learned people believed that men were entitled to life, liberty, the pursuit of happiness, property ownership, and individual rights. The rising support for human rights eventually led to the curtailing of the power of kings and contributed to the American Revolution in 1776 and the French Revolution in 1789.

The beliefs of the Enlightenment contributed to the power and prosperity of the Dutch middle class, which Rembrandt (see Fig. 13.8) depicted in many paintings. The Netherlands were Calvinist Protestant, a religion that believed industriousness and spirituality were the measure of an individual. Humanist philosophy flourished in leading Dutch universities, and learning was valued in upper and middle classes. Power in the country was distributed among wealthy bourgeois families, rather than concentrated in a monarchy.

Timeline

Context	Date	Artwork
Indus River Civilizations	**3000 BCE**	*Torso* (Harappa)
	1350	
Egypt, Eighteenth Dynasty		*Bust of Nefertiti*
Olmec Civilizations	**900**	
Classical Greece	**400**	Polykleitos: *Doryphoros*
Hellenistic Greece		
Mauryan Dynasty founded in India		
	100	*Laocoön and His Sons*
		Yakshi
Mayan Civilization	**600 CE**	*Head from the Tomb of the Temple of Inscriptions*
	1100	Gislebertus: *The Last Judgment*
Renaissance—Europe		
	1500	
Reign of Akbar—India		Michelangelo: *David*
Tokugawa Shogunate—Japan		
Thirty Years War—Europe, 1618–1648		
Louis XIV of France	**1650**	Rembrandt: *Self-Portrait*
Kangxi of China		
Enlightenment		
	1700	
Latin American Independence Movement		
Victorian Era—England	**1850**	
		Tomika Te Mutu
Freud and Psychoanalysis		Muybridge: *Handspring*
	1890	
		van Gogh: *Portrait of Dr. Gachet*
		Munch: *The Scream*
	1900	*Male Torso* (Ancestor figure), Baule

Context	Date	Artwork
End of the Ottoman Empire		Boccioni: *Unique Forms of Continuity in Space*
World War I	**1920**	Kanzan: *Study for the Portrait of Okakura Tenshin*
	1940	Kahlo: *Self-Portrait with Monkey*
		Pollock: *Lucifer*
	1950	
Death of Stalin		
Khrushchev era—Soviet Union		
	1960	Hamilton: *Just What Is It . . . ?*
		Ono: *Cut Piece*
Death of Mao Zedong—China	**1970**	
		Mendieta: *Arbol de la Vida, No. 294*
	1980	Sherman: *Untitled Film Still #35*
		Close: *Fanny (Fingerpainting)*
		Ngere Girl Prepared for a Festival
Tiananmen Square Uprising—Beijing		
Reunification of Germany	**1990**	Burson: Untitled image from *Faces*
Creation of the European Union		
		Freud: *Leigh under the Skylight*
		Wilke: *Intra-Venus*
		Serrano: *The Morgue (Hacked to Death II)*
Digital Video, Digital Imaging		
Mandela becomes president of South Africa		Mori: *Star Doll*
	2000	Viola: *Dolorosa*
		Kim: *Installation*

In portraiture, we might intimately encounter either a unique individual or a person who conforms to mass media types. The body has been idealized in art and alludes to a range of ideas about human nature. Other artwork emphasizes the tragic or the debased in human nature. The body can be measured and studied like a machine.

Increasingly, humans include themselves as part of the larger physical, spiritual, and technological world. This dissolving of boundaries transforms the human body, first at the skin layer and then below the skin with the very structure of the skeleton and muscles. Physical and psychological pressures can distort the body. More frequently, there is a strong tie between the human body and the things that humans build.

In artwork that deals with sickness and death, the horrible and the beautiful often are mixed.

The body can be either art material or art tool. It is malleable and can be scarred, sculpted, or painted. It is a primary element in performance art. It is the most wonderful art-making tool we have.

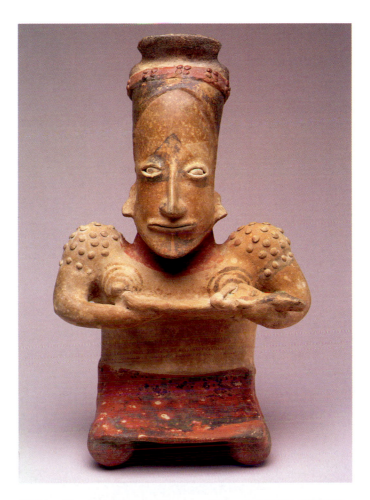

13.34 *Kneeling Woman Nursing a Baby*, 100 BCE—300 CE. Jalisco, Mexico. Earthenware with polychrome slip. Height 13". Tattooing or scarification is indicated on the shoulders. Notice also the distinctive headdress.

FOOD FOR THOUGHT

A number of the artworks we studied in this chapter seem to fall outside strict definitions of art. In the United States, we generally do not consider tattooing as art, nor body painting or hair styling. Yet probably we have all seen examples of piercing, tattooing, hair cutting, and styles of dressing that seem like artistic expressions. In some cases, the boundary between art and fashion is hard to determine. Other cultures have practiced scarification and tattooing as ritual empowerment or to enhance the appearance of their bodies. See Figure 13.34. With footbinding (Fig. 14.11) and cranial deformation (Fig. 13.28), the body's bone structure is altered.

■ *What do you think are the most powerful ways in which individuals use their bodies to express themselves visually in your world today? Does art aid in keeping this balance?*

Science and medicine are meant to serve humans and their bodies. However, the fascination with scientific measurement and comparison can result in disaster. For example, in the late nineteenth century, criminologists believed that certain skull shapes indicated which individuals were capable of deviant behavior; thus, you could be condemned if you had bumps in the wrong places. Also, at times, some medical cures have caused huge amounts of suffering.

■ *What social tools do we have to keep science and medicine in check? How do they affect artists and their art?*

Your Thomson Online Resources

 Go to **ArtExperience Online** for the Flashcards, Quiz, and Study Guide for this chapter.

Race, Gender, Clan, and Class

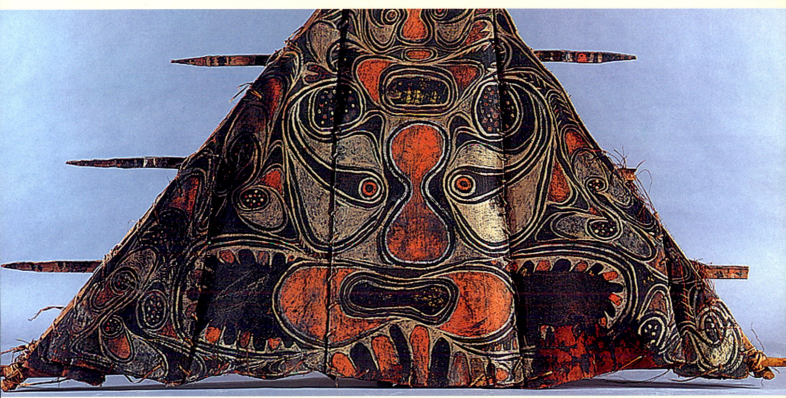

The Rijksmuseum Amsterdam.

INTRODUCTION

All persons are born with race and gender characteristics, class standing, and genealogy that will affect their lives. These characteristics contribute to personal identity, but on the downside, they may also trigger prejudice and discrimination.

- *How does art help forge racial identity?*
- *How is gender tied to ideas of what is beautiful or what is heroic?*
- *How does art promote or reinforce gender roles?*
- *How does art identify a clan?*
- *When are ancestors important to a clan, and how does art help to make that relationship possible?*
- *How does art show us the ways different classes live?*
- *How does art reflect the tastes, ideas, and needs of different classes?*
- *Why does possession of a certain kind of art indicate a person's class status?*

RACE AND ART

This section contains a number of artworks that deal with race. Some help form a cohesive identity for a racial group, while others challenge negative attitudes.

ART THAT PROMOTES ETHNIC HISTORY AND VALUES

These works of art examine or illustrate the history or values of a certain ethnic group.

In the 1800s and early 1900s in Russia, Jews were considered outsiders because of laws and traditions originated and maintained both by the Jews themselves and by the Russians. The Jews actively maintained their own identity, and Russian law also enforced separateness—Jews were allowed to live only in certain areas and were restricted from attending universities. That separateness was often passively accepted, but at times Jews suffered from anti-Semitic terrorism. Even so, Russian Jews were often cultural innovators and, in many cases, were known throughout Europe as artists, musicians, and writers.

Marc Chagall was a prominent Jewish artist who grew up in Russia but spent most of his long life in Paris, France. Many of his paintings imaginatively recreated Jewish village folklife at the turn of the twentieth century in Russia, which was in fact disintegrating due to political, religious, and economic pressures. Chagall's imagery was a personal, sometimes incoherent, reordering of bits and pieces of his experience, including folktales, festivals, marriages, funeral practices, and suffering and death caused by anti-Semitism. In *Over Vitebsk,* dated 1915–1920 (Fig. 14.1), Chagall painted a large, solitary figure floating over his own village, representing thousands of Eastern European Jewish refugees who fled to Russia, displaced by World War I. In Yiddish, "passing through" is expressed as wandering "over the village," which Chagall painted literally by means of the floating figure, the refugee. A sense of rootlessness and upheaval pervades the picture. The space in the foreground of the picture appears fractured, and Chagall used the cubist device to represent instability. The picture contains Chagall's memories of Vitebsk, its architecture, its streets, its icy winter landscape. The colors are **Fauvist,** an art movement

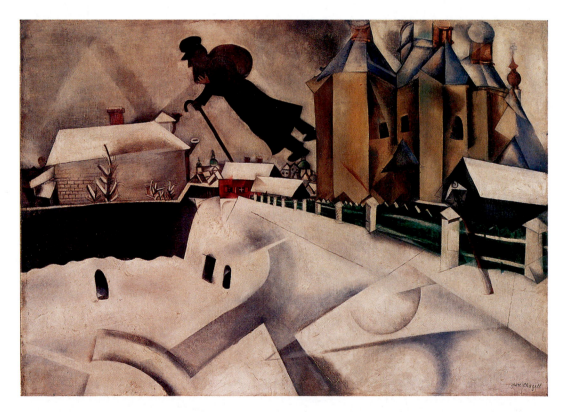

14.1 MARC CHAGALL. *Over Vitebsk* (after a painting of 1914), Russia/France, 1915–1920. Oil on canvas, 26½" × 36½". The Museum of Modern Art, New York. Acquired through the Lillian P. Bliss Bequest, 1949. © MOMA/Art Resource, NY/© 2004 Artists Rights Society (ARS), New York/ADAGP, Paris.

that originated in Paris in which color was exaggerated in paintings for greater power and expression.

James VanDerZee was a commercial studio photographer whose works are a record of the Black Renaissance of Harlem, generally dating from 1919–1929 (he continued to photograph the Harlem residents through the 1940s). VanDerZee's photographs contrast strongly with the two kinds of images of African Americans from that time. The most common were crude racial caricatures of African Americans from postcards, comics, magazines, picture books, and greeting cards. On the other hand, a few photographers depicted African Americans as helpless victims of racism and their situation as a problem to be solved. In contrast, VanDerZee's African Americans are autonomous, healthy, and self-aware. They were the black middle class, like the women pictured in *Society Ladies*, photographed in 1927 (Fig. 14.2). His subjects were intellectuals, merchants, and writers who demanded full participation for blacks in U.S. politics and culture. The furniture and trappings of comfort surround his well-dressed sitters. Their poses convey a variety of emotions, including confidence, humor, directness, and dreamy wistfulness.

VanDerZee was influenced by films of the 1920s and 1930s and encouraged sitters to take poses from the films. At times, VanDerZee provided costumes and props that allowed his sitters to expand their personalities. He manipulated and retouched his images. The results were self-assured, proud portraits that cannot be seen as racial caricatures or images of victims.

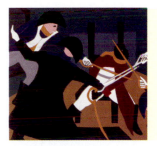

Connection *Another artist of the Harlem Renaissance, Jacob Lawrence, painted the history of African Americans in the Western Hemisphere. For more, see* No. 36, During the Truce Toussaint *... (Fig. 12.12, page 315).*

Art That Criticizes Racism

Unflattering images of African Americans have been common in popular culture over the past 150 years—for example, the pickaninny, Little Black Sambo, and Uncle Tom. Another is Aunt Jemima, a domestic servant

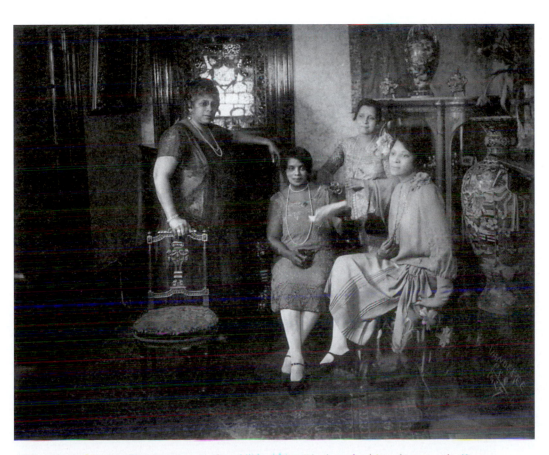

14.2 JAMES VANDERZEE. *Society Ladies,* USA, 1927. Black-and-white photograph. Donna Mussenden VanDerZee.

whose title of "aunt" was a commonly used term of subordination for African American domestic servants, nannies, and maids. Aunt Jemima is a caricatured jolly, fat woman who has been used recently to sell commercially prepared pancake mix. In the 1972 mixed-media piece *The Liberation of Aunt Jemima* (Fig. 14.3), Betye Saar uses three versions of Aunt Jemima to question and turn around such images. The oldest version is the small image at the center, in which a cartooned Jemima hitches up a squalling child on her hip. In the background, the modern version shows a thinner Jemima with lighter skin, deemphasizing her Negroid features. The older one makes Jemima a caricature, while the new one implies she is more attractive if she appears less black.

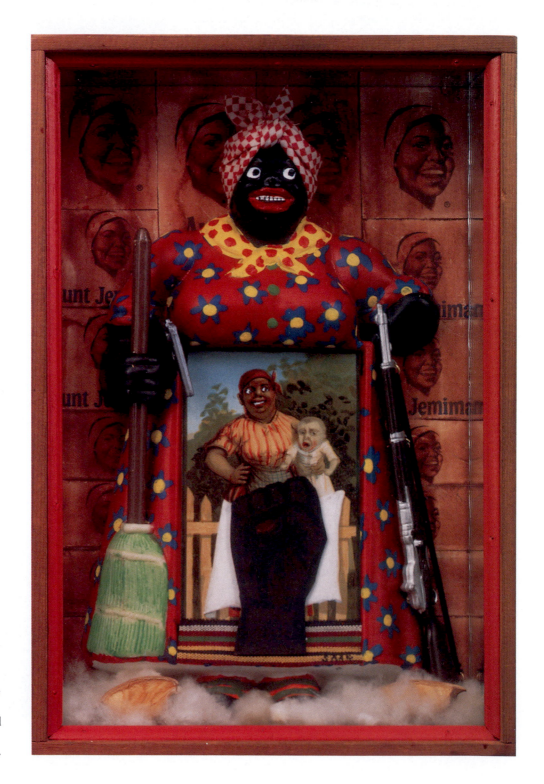

14.3 BETYE SAAR. *The Liberation of Aunt Jemima,* USA, 1972. Mixed media, 11³/₄" × 8" × 2³/₄". University Art Museum, University of California, Berkeley. Purchased with the aid of National Endowment for the Arts funds.

The middle Jemima is the largest figure and the most emphasized. Her checked and polka-dotted clothing is very bright and colorful. Her black skin makes her white eyes and teeth look like dots and checks, too. This Jemima holds a rifle and pistol as well as a broom. A black-power fist makes a strong silhouette shape in front of all the figures, introducing militant power to the image. The idea of Aunt Jemima, in any of its forms, can no longer seem innocuous. Saar enshrined these images in a shallow glass display box to make them venerable. Symmetry and pattern are strong visual elements.

In *The Artifact Piece,* performed in 1986 (Fig. 14.4), Native American artist James Luna challenged the way contemporary American culture and museums have presented his race as essentially extinct and vanished. In this performance piece, Luna "installed" himself in an exhibition case in the San Diego Museum of Man in a section on the Kumeyaay Indians, who once inhabited San Diego County. All around were other exhibition areas with mannequins and props showing the long-lost Kumeyaay way of life. Among them, Luna posed himself, living and breathing, dressed only in a leather cloth, with labels around him pointing out his scars from wounds suffered when drunk and fighting.

Various personal items were displayed in a glass case, including contemporary ritual objects used currently on the La Jolla reservation where Luna lives, recordings by the Rolling Stones and Jimi Hendrix, shoes, political buttons, and other cultural artifacts. The mixture of elements revealed a living, developing culture.

In this striking piece, Luna challenged the viewer to reconsider what museums teach about cultures and what constitutes a cultural artifact. Museum artifacts may be simply the things that, by chance, happened to survive. In other cases, some objects are kept, while others are ignored or destroyed. Thus, we learn less about Native American culture than we learn about the white culture's ideas about Native American cultures. In addition, museums and museum visitors often discount living cultures of today, and are only interested in preconceived idea of "cultural purity." "Authentic Indians" are those who are long dead. Native Americans who are alive today are less interesting to museums, because they are cultural mixtures who may wear Reeboks rather than moccasins. Luna sees himself in a new way. Although he still considers himself a warrior, he is a new one who uses art and the legal system to fight for Native Americans. In *The Artifact Piece,* Luna also touches on the effects of alcohol on Native Americans.

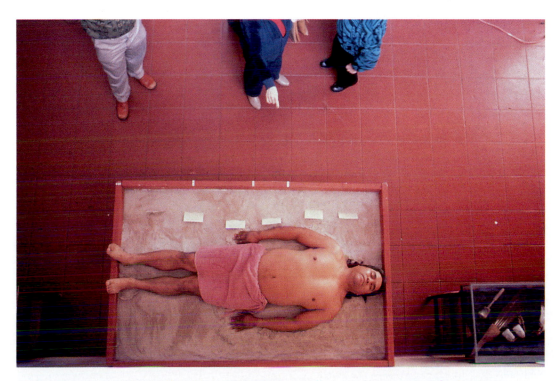

14.4   JAMES LUNA. *The Artifact Piece,* USA, 1986. Installation/performance at the San Diego Museum of Man. Museum of Man, San Diego.

WHO IS LOOKING AT WHOM?

In the United States, hundreds of images are produced every day that deal with other cultures, so we develop ideas about foreign or ethnic groups from the mass media images we consume. But who is making those images of others, and why? And what about the viewer? The position of the viewer is a privileged position, "consuming" the images of other people without directly interacting with them. Chapter 8 covered the gaze in reference to sexuality. Now we return to it in a political sense, to see how it may reflect power relationships in the world.

Tseng Kwong Chi turned around the act of looking in a series of photographic self-portraits, such as *Disneyland, California*, photographed in 1979 (Fig. 14.5). While Western industrial countries have produced a wealth of images of peoples from the rest of the world, Tseng Kwong Chi produced images of Asians looking at the West and made them for a Western audience. In his many self-portraits, he posed in front of tourist sites in the United States, such as the Grand Canyon, Mount Rushmore, and the Statue of Liberty. In all his images, he wore a Mao jacket to emphatically identify himself as Chinese,

rather than Japanese, Korean, or any other Asian ethnicity. He took his own picture—the shutter release cable is evident—to show that he was the author of his own image. He appears as a tourist, but with mirror glasses. We cannot see his eyes, while he critically appraises what he sees of the West from an Asian point of view. He is unyielding and severe next to the goofy, grinning Mickey Mouse. We, the viewers of this photograph, have been displaced from our positions of power, as Tseng has taken on the role of the noninteractive viewer.

Tseng's rigid pose is repeated in all the self-portraits in this series to emphasize his unmistakable, unique individuality from picture to picture. This was done to counter the stereotypes that Asians are all alike, that they shun any show of public individuality, or that they avoid making themselves stand out.

Connection *We also encounter the issue of the gaze in Lewis Hine's* Leo, 48 Inches High . . . *(Fig. 12.10, page 314; see especially the Food for Thought section of Chapter 12). In Chapter 8, review the section on "The Feminine Body and the Gaze" (page 185).*

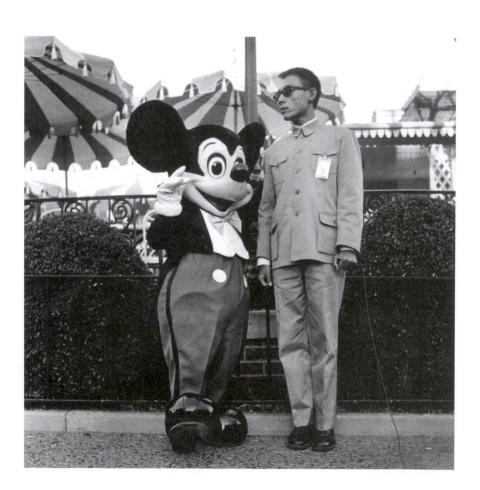

14.5 TSENG KWONG CHI. *Disneyland, California*, China/USA, 1979. Gelatin Silver Print, 36" × 36". Photograph by Tseng Kwong Chi © Muna Tseng Dance Projects Inc., New York.

GENDER ISSUES

Every culture sets up standards that define and limit acceptable behavior for women and for men. Artwork from different eras and cultures often gives us clues about those social restrictions and, in some cases, is actually part of making them.

ART AND RITUAL PERPETUATING GENDER ROLES

We will begin by examining gender concepts, ritual, and art among the Sepik people of New Guinea in the South Pacific, focusing on the early twentieth century, before foreign influences had seriously disrupted the indigenous social order and religion. Men dominated women in much of Sepik life, and art and rituals reinforced and dramatized this relationship. Sepik art also made men powerful in war.

These rituals, called "Tambaran," took place in large, decorated cult houses that were generally A-frame in design. The large cult houses were eighty to one hundred feet high, and were very difficult and dangerous to build. When finished, the men believed that the spirits accomplished the "miraculous" feat. At the same time, the house affirmed the men's own strength, creativity, and domination. The cult houses were gendered; that is, the Sepik men saw the ridgepole as phallic and the interior of the house as the belly of a woman, so the house itself was a reenactment of the sexual act that results in birth. Men saw their rituals as creating men from infants, usurping women's procreative power. Unlike the Western notion that an individual exists from birth, many South Pacific peoples believed that a person's very being was built through a lifetime of ritual experiences.

Men invested their vigor into the paintings and carvings that hung in the cult house. The men who made the paintings did not own them, but in fact had to give them away to pass their spirits on to those at lower stages of initiation. The paintings do not explain the Tambaran cult or illustrate it; rather, they become effective or invigorated in cult rituals.

In our example, *Painting from a Cult House* at Slei (Fig. 14.6), from the early twentieth century, the curves create multiple faces, with gaping, tooth-filled mouths, large noses, and numerous eyes. Faces can be read stacked or superimposed on each other. The curves and spirals fill the triangular shape of the painting—cramped and small at the edges, swelling into large, aggressive forms in the middle. The colors—black, red, and off-white—are bold, with high contrast from dark to light. Major forms, such as mouths and eyes, are outlined repeatedly in alternating black and white lines, resulting in vibrating patterns that express the idea of fearsome vigor. The paintings were made on bark or natural fibers from trees in the area.

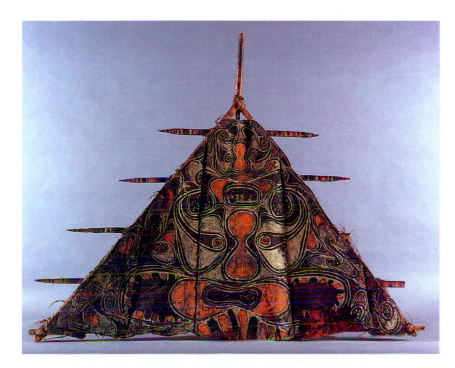

14.6 *Painting from a Cult House,* Slei, Middle Sepik Region, Papua New Guinea, c. 20th century. Palm leaves on a bamboo frame, painted with earth pigments, 44" × 61½". Museum der Kulturen, Basel, Switzerland.

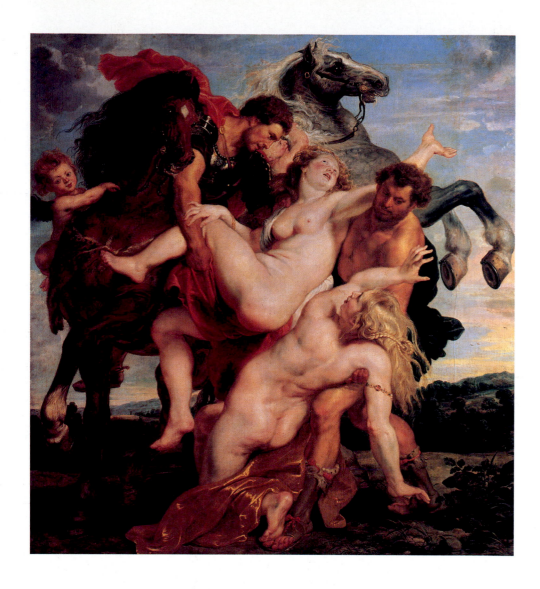

14.7 PETER PAUL RUBENS.
*Abduction of the Daughters
of Leucippus,* Flanders, 1617.
Oil on canvas, 7'3" × 6'10".
Alte Pinakothek, Munich.
© Scala/Art Resource, NY.

GENDER REFLECTED IN ART AND ARCHITECTURE

Gender roles are often revealed in art and are reflected in architecture and fashion.

Our first work, *Abduction of the Daughters of Leucippus,* painted by Peter Paul Rubens in 1617 (Fig. 14.7), is another example of European painting dealing with sexual exotica, like the *Grande Odalisque,* which we saw in Chapter 8. The scene comes from Greek mythology. Castor and Pollux were twin sons of Zeus, and they captured a philosopher's two daughters as they were out horseback riding. Aided by Cupids who hold the horses' reins, the two immortals lower the women, who resist with dramatic but ineffective, fluttering gestures. Interestingly, this painting is also commonly referred to as *Rape of the Daughters of Leucippus,* as an old

meaning of *rape* was "the carrying away of someone by force."

Blue skies, shimmering cloth, and a variety of textures add to the rich surface of the image and the sensual color harmonies. The composition places all figures in a diamond shape, which is compact and yet expressive of movement because of its instability. Darks predominate on the left, acting as a foil to the lighter areas in the center and at the right. The forms are modeled in color and lit with a glow. Various textures, such as armor, satin, flesh, and hair, are all expertly painted.

Through poses, behavior, and clothing, the painting indicates what was considered masculine and feminine during that era. All figures represent ideal body types for their time. The women's voluptuous, soft fleshiness was considered sexually attractive and a sign of health and wealth. Outdoor activity was appropri-

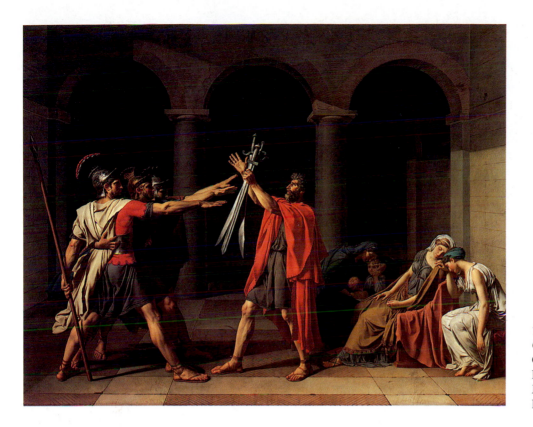

14.8   JACQUES-LOUIS DAVID. *Oath of the Horatii*, France, 1784. Oil on canvas, 10'10" × 14'. Louvre, Paris. © Réunion des Musées Nationaux/Art Resource, NY.

ate for the darker-skinned, muscular men versus the pale women who occupy the domestic interiors. The painting also represents current ideas of gender behavior. Men had privilege over women's bodies. Women learned to be helpless, and they relied on social structures to protect their virtue. The expressions of the men are subdued and determined, while the women's bodies and faces are much more emotional. The men are at least partially clothed—one is in armor—while the women are unclothed and displayed. Western art history has numerous examples of the female nude providing pleasure for male viewers, legitimized because it was "art."

All kinds of trappings can serve as indicators of masculinity or femininity. In *Oath of the Horatii*, painted in 1784 (Fig. 14.8), Jacques-Louis David represents a scene from the early history of ancient Rome, in which three brothers vow to represent the Roman army in a fight to the death against three representatives of an opposing army. Their father hands them their swords, reminding them of the manly virtues of courage and patriotism, while their sisters swoon at the right, in dread and sorrow at the anticipated killing (one of the sisters was to marry a representative of the opposing army). Heroic actions are a mark of mas-

culinity, reinforced by the women's passivity. In a moment of male bonding, forged in the face of danger, the three brothers become a single force, a part of each other, and each willing to die for the others and for an external cause.

There are other gender indicators. The male dress is rendered in angular lines that contrast with the soft curves of the female attire. The men hold weapons as their job is war, while women's jobs are concerned with children. The architecture's symmetry and the composition's overall balance suggest the orderliness of this world. The images both reflect the "reality" of gender roles and create that "reality." They spring to some extent from existing social conditions, but they also entrench those conditions and make them seem natural, not just social conventions.

In this painting, the classical architectural background is an indicator of masculinity, which was popular during the French Revolutionary era when this painting was executed. The use of classical elements in art and architecture at this time formed a style called **Neo-Classicism,** which was a revival of Greek and Roman aesthetics after the ruins of Pompeii were discovered. Also at this time, French citizens were about to overthrow the oppressive, parasitic French monarchy

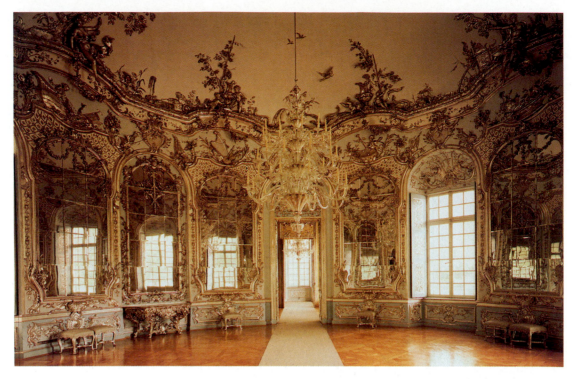

14.9 FRANÇOIS DE CUVILLIÈS. *Hall of Mirrors*, Germany, 1734–1739. Amalienburg, Nymphenburg Park, Munich. © Scala/Art Resource, NY.

and aristocracy. The nobility favored decorative architecture called **Rococo,** such as that seen in the *Hall of Mirrors* at the Amalienburg hunting lodge in Munich, Germany, dated 1734–1739 (Fig. 14.9), by François de Cuvilliès. Rococo architecture was seen as female, with its emphasis on the delicate, the curving, the colorful. Square walls and ceilings dissolve in curves, and these curves themselves dissolve under the abundance of nature-based decoration and the reflecting mirrors, crystal, and silver. The ceiling appears to be an open sky, with birds flying from branch to branch of gold-leafed stucco trees. All elements—the architectural shell, the precious materials, the detailed, graceful decorations—contribute to the entire exquisite effect. The French middle class, on the verge of revolt, chose the clean, simple, austere architecture that we see in the background of *Oath of the Horatii* to distinguish themselves from the aristocracy and to serve as an appropriate symbol for their ideas.

Indeed, in Western culture, architecture is gendered; that is, different styles come to come be associated with certain qualities, and those qualities in turn are associated with masculinity or femininity. This goes back at least as far as the ancient Greeks, who saw the Doric Order as masculine and the Ionic as feminine. Although the architecture behind the Horatii was considered manly while the *Hall of Mirrors* was considered feminine and elegant, there is nothing inherent in these styles that requires them to be understood in this way. In another situation, the Horatii background might be seen as bare and oppressive and the *Hall of Mirrors* considered uplifting and stirring to the imagination. The gendered associations of Western architectural styles continue, as writers commonly associate the modern, bare, high-rise skyscrapers of the late 1960s and 1970s with masculinity.

Connection The Doric and Ionic Orders are illustrated in Figure 2.36. The Swing (Fig. 14.24, page 386) is a Rococo painting by Jean-Honoré Fragonard and reflects the same sensibilities as the Hall of Mirrors.

CRITIQUING GENDER ROLES

In many cultures, people change their bodies to enhance their femininity or masculinity, usually by dieting, plastic surgery, implants, scarification, and various bindings that mold body parts, most often the skull, waist, neck, or feet. These practices can be widely accepted at times. But in times of cultural change, they can become very controversial.

In her work, artist Hung Liu has examined foot binding, practiced in China from the Song Dynasty (960–1279) until the beginning of the twentieth century. Many Chinese women's feet were bound from birth to artificially confine their growth, distorting them into small, twisted fists that were sexually attrac-

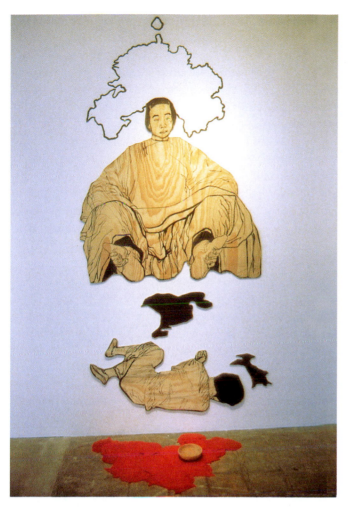

14.10 HUNG LIU. *Trauma*, China/USA, 1989. Ink on plywood cutouts, acrylic on wall, felt cutout, and wooden bowl, 108" × 52" × 26". Courtesy of the Artist.

tive to men. With bound feet, walking was extremely difficult, but the mincing steps were considered delicate and lovely. Bound feet left women handicapped, which also ensured that they remained subservient. Many women resorted to prostitution when the Chinese Communist government came to power and mandated physical labor for all able-bodied people.

Liu ties oppressive gender practices to broader political repression. In *Trauma,* dated 1989 (Fig. 14.10), the woman at the center publicly shows her bound feet. Although bound feet were considered erotic in private, public exposure was a shameful act. Below her is an image of a dead Chinese student, killed by Chinese government forces when they violently crushed the demonstrations for freedom in 1989 in Tiananmen Square. Liu sees the killings in Tiananmen Square as a shameful event for China. The outline map of China behind the woman's head is upside down, while its reflection below, cut out of red felt, becomes a bloodstain on the floor below the student. The bowl is a symbol Liu sometimes uses. It is a vessel often emptied and filled, but never in exactly the same way. Poetically, the empty bowl represents China and the artist herself, emptied and then refilled by the cycles of history. Because of their long history, the Chinese commonly make associations between contemporary events and events of the distant past, a habit of thought that is evident in Liu's work.

The Guerrilla Girls' *Do women have to be naked to get into the Met. Museum?* (Fig. 14.11) seeks to correct a specific kind of gender discrimination. In 1986,

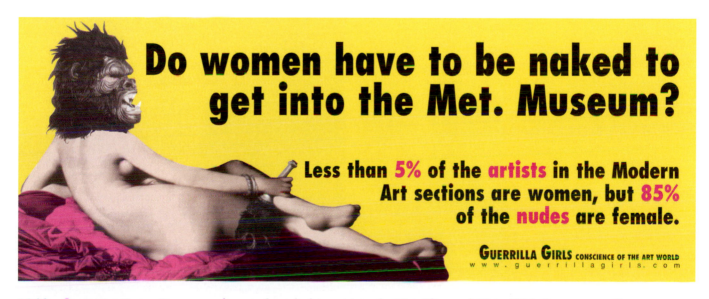

14.11 GUERRILLA GIRLS. *Do women have to be naked to get into the Met. Museum?* USA, 1986. Street poster. Courtesy www.guerrillagirls.com.

when the poster was made, high-profile art exhibitions in prestigious museums often included very few women artists. In other words, a naked woman painted by a man might be shown in a museum, but a painting by a woman artist was not likely to be. On the poster, the woman's body is that of the *Grande Odalisque* (see Fig. 8.19 in Chapter 8, Reproduction and Sexuality), whose aesthetically pleasing elongated torso reclines on cushions, on display for male viewers to enjoy and "consume." However, her head has been obscured by a gorilla mask, like those the Guerrilla Girls wore in public appearances to maintain their anonymity and to liken themselves to revolutionary guerrillas who seek to overthrow a dominant power.

The Guerrilla Girls is a collective of anonymous women artists and arts professionals protesting racial and gender discrimination in the art field. Their mass-produced, inexpensive posters feature text, image, and humor presented with a strong graphic design sensibility. The Guerrilla Girls in masks would show up at galleries and museums hosting high-profile art events where women were underrepresented. The purpose of their work is to cause exposure, embarrassment, and, eventually, change. The Guerrilla Girls also protest the fact that women artists have fewer exhibition opportunities, have fewer tenure-track teaching jobs in universities, make approximately 33 percent of the income from art that male counterparts earn, are infrequently discussed in scholarly works, and so on. Later posters have been concerned with both gender and racial imbalances in museums, exhibitions, and teaching opportunities.

CLAN

A clan is a group of people joined by blood or marriage ties. It could be as small as two people or extend to groups of families who share a common ancestor and recognize one member as leader.

THE EXTENDED FAMILY

Art helps solidify extended families in three ways: (1) art makes major ancestors available to the living clan members, (2) art depicts important events in the clan's history, and (3) art is an important element in rituals that bring the entire clan together.

Ancestors

For many, the founding members of a clan have a major impact on the prestige of the living people and

on their ability to function with power and authority. Ancient Romans believed their ancestry was tremendously important. They preserved portraits of their ancestors and venerated their memory, as a way of establishing their own importance as they went about the business of living. At first, these ancestor portraits were simply death masks, made by pressing soft wax on the face of a deceased family member shortly after death. However, the wax masks deteriorated after a few years and looked like death, with sagging tissue and sunken eyes. Around the first century BCE, affluent Romans began having copies of the death masks made in marble for permanence, and so the face could be sculpted to appear energetic or even monumental.

The *Statue of Togata Barberini* (Fig. 14.12) is an excellent example of Roman portrait sculpture made to worship an ancestor and to glorify the lineage. Here, Togata Barberini is holding portrait busts that boast of his lineage. All three faces are factual, unflattering

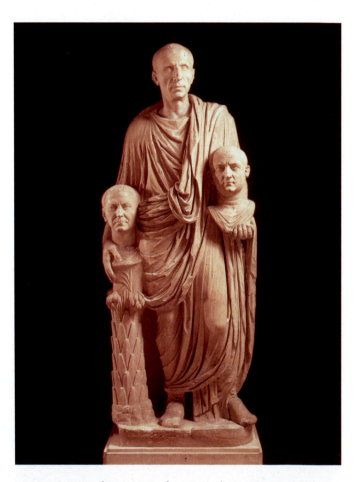

14.12 *Statue of Togato Barberini*, Early 1st Century CE, Marble. 65" high. Palazzo Barberini, Rome, Italy. © Gianni Dagli/Corbis.

records of appearance. Personality also comes through in the expressions. Ancestor portraits were treated with respect and were frequently copied for various family members; having a unique art object was not important. For large sculptures like this, the portraits were individually made and often were inserted into mass-produced and standardized marble bodies. Prominent Romans kept sculptures and busts in a shrine in the family home and brought them out at funerals and family ceremonies as status symbols.

Among the Zapotec people of Oaxaca in southern Mexico, ancestors were so important that the living interred the dead in tomb chambers under their houses and consulted them on pressing problems. By displaying their ancestors' leg bones, the rulers ensured their right to rule. These underground tombs were lavishly decorated, houselike crypts, with sculpture and painting to make ancestors available to the living. Tombs were reopened when a clan leader died, and important rituals were held there to transfer that leader's power, wealth, and energy to the living. Figure 14.13 shows *Portrait Heads from Tomb 6*, from the town of Lambityeco, in Oaxaca. They are life-size heads sculpted in

stucco, and date from 640–755. The heads seem very lively and create a strong presence. The male head on the left has a goatee, a beaded necklace, and earrings, and his hair is pulled up and tied in a bun above his forehead. Lines through his eyebrows and below his eyes are actually ancient symbols or glyphs that identify him. The wife's head, to the right, is lined with age. Her hair is styled with ribbons very much like that of Zapotec women today. The faces have individualized features and are definitely portraits. They likely represent the founding parents of a clan. Both were important as lineage was traced through the male and female sides. These portrait heads are located on the lintel above the entrance to the tomb and probably represent the first ones buried within.

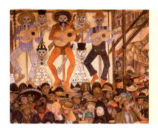

Connection *Among the present-day Zapotec, belief in the power of the dead continues. They celebrate* Día de Los Muertos, *as in Diego Rivera's painting (Fig. 10.23, page 264).*

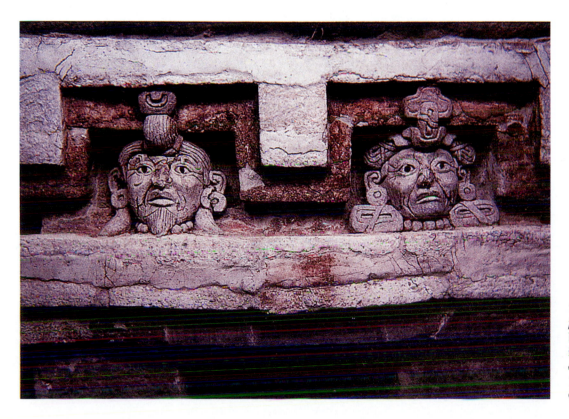

14.13 *Portrait Heads from Tomb 6*, Lambityeco, Oaxaca, Mexico, 640–755. Stucco, each head $10^{1}/_{2}$" × $11^{1}/_{2}$". Photo by Arthur G. Miller.

Clan History

Art is also instrumental in preserving clan history, which helps ensure clan cohesion and thus increases its power.

The *Interior House Post*, dated c. 1907, in Figure 14.14, was one of four carved by Arthur Shaughnessy for the Raven House of the John Scow clan of the Northwest Coast of North America. The Raven House, completed in 1916, was a lineage house, built when a new lineage was founded because of death or marriage. When first built, these houses were used for festivities when the new leader assumed his ceremonial name. Guests would be invited to several-day celebrations called potlatches, with elaborate singing and masquerades. Later, the interior was subdivided to create living quarters for several clan families.

The carvings in lineage houses were visual aids that accompanied the telling of clan legends and history. The carvings were concentrated in significant areas, specifically around doorways, on totem poles that stood in front of the houses, and on the house posts, as we have seen. The carvings might represent specific ancestors (like animals in European family crests) or important deities, or a human in animal form. House posts both physically support the house and symbolically represent the spiritual and mythical foundation of the clan.

The top of our *Interior House Post* has a mythical thunderbird with imposing, spread wings, representing a chief. Its powerful curved beak and curved ears suggest supernatural powers. Extra eyes are placed on the wings and torso, again to imply power. The feathers

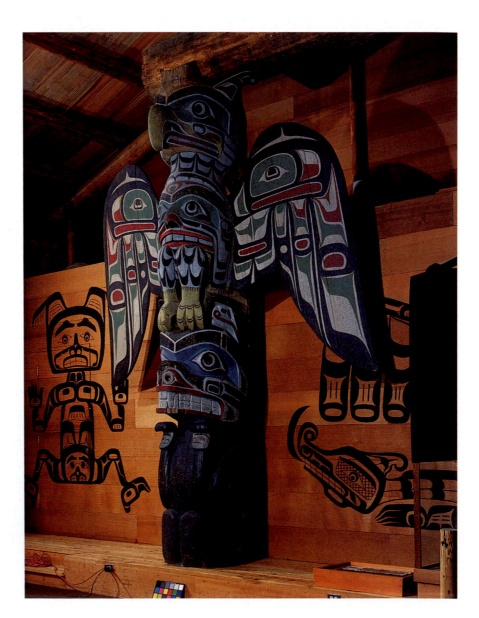

14.14 ARTHUR SHAUGHNESSY. *Interior House Post*, Gilford Island, British Columbia, Canada, c. 1907. Carved and painted red cedar, 180" × 132" × 34". Kwakiutl. Seattle Art Museum. Gift of Mr. John H. Hauberg.

are examples of formline design, typical of much Northwest Coast art. The intention of the Northwest Coast artist is not to invent new forms, but to invest old ones with new life and energy. The formline (Fig. 14.15) divides and merges, creating a continuous flowing grid that beautifully unifies the overall decoration. The ovoid is always convex on its upper side with the lower side slightly concave; the shape possibly was inspired by the elliptical spots on a ray fish. We also see two examples of the "U form" (Holm 1995:29, 37–41). Black emphasizes the major shapes, while red, white, green, and yellow are added for brightness and high contrast. For this *Interior House Post,* Shaughnessy used formline design extensively in the thunderbird's wings, painted with newly available commercial paint for brighter colors. Older works were painted with natural pigments, so their color is less saturated.

The figure below the thunderbird is a bear, a common figure on family crests, often associated with an elder or a high-ranking person. It has bared teeth, an upturned nose with circular nostrils, and compact arms and legs. Bodies were usually compressed, but heads were oversized, often one-third the total figure. Essential features were emphasized in a highly stylized manner, while less important features were understated or even omitted. In this example, the bear's claws are given prominence—an extra face is painted on each paw—while the torso is generalized, without musculature or surface detail. The claws and muzzle were sepa-

rate pieces added to the trunk, again increasing the dynamism of the carving.

Connection *For more on the potlatch, see* Halibut Feast Dish *by Stan Wamiss (Fig. 7.17, page 153).*

Art Used in Clan Rituals

Clan ties are strengthened through rituals, and art is often an essential part of those rituals. Among the Asmat people of Irian Jaya, of Western New Guinea, the living engaged in elaborate rituals to pass on the life force of the deceased clansmen to the rest of the group. They carved and erected tall poles called *Bis* or *Bisj Poles* (Fig. 14.16), up to sixteen feet high, which were named and which represented the deceased clansmen, now called ancestors. The large openwork projections on the top figures are penises, representing power

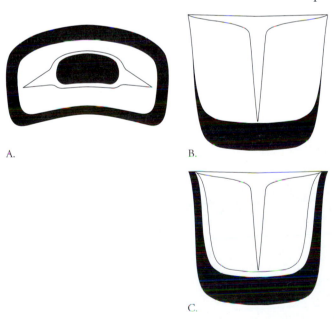

14.15   Examples of formline design in Northwest Coast art. A: ovoid form; B: typical U complex with semiangular curves; C: split U with outline (after diagrams by Bill Holm).

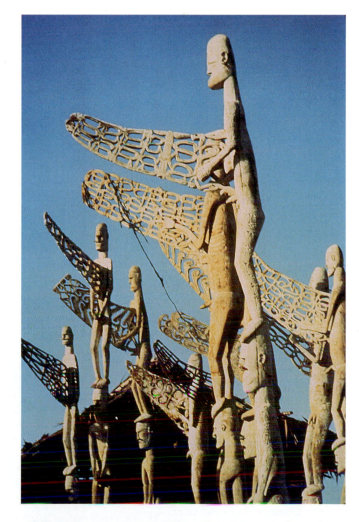

14.16   *Bisj Poles,* Buepis Village, Fajit River, southwest New Guinea, c. 19th–20th century. Wood and paint, approx. 16' high. Asmat. Photograph by Tobias Schneebaum.

in warfare and in fertility. The height and intricate carving make the poles impressive. The negative and positive shapes and snarling faces speak of bristling warlike energy. Sometimes poles were painted in high-contrast colors. As recently as the 1950s, the Asmat were headhunters, and part of their rituals involved avenging a clansman's death, as they believed that death is not natural, but caused by enemy warfare or magic. After the men carved and painted the *Bisj* poles, the ritual feast prepared them for actual headhunting. Warriors stood before the poles and bragged about their power and received the strength of the ancestors for success in headhunting. These rituals were also tied

to fertility, as successful warriors were rewarded with sexual favors. After the rituals, the poles were traditionally left to rot in groves of sago palms, where they would pass their vitality on to the plants that provide a staple food for the Asmat.

Art, ritual, and clan identity are intertwined among the Yoruba people of west-central Africa. The Epa Festival is held every other year for three days in March to promote fertility and the well-being of the community. The *Epa Headdress called "Orangun"* (Fig. 14.17), sculpted by Bamgboye of Odo-Owa, was used in masquerades to honor the family. The base of an Epa headdress is a helmet that fits on top of the performer's

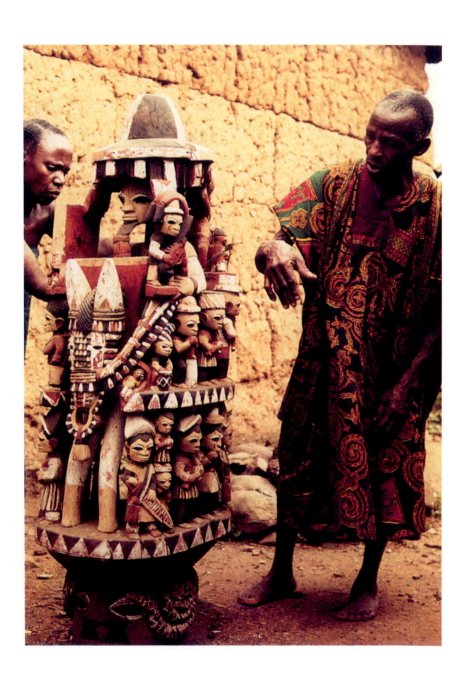

14.17 BAMGBOYE OF ODO-OWA. *Epa Headdress called "Orangun,"* Erinmope, Nigeria, 1974. Wood and paint. Yoruba. Photo by John Pemberton III.

head, and it is carved with grotesque Janus-like faces, front and back. Above the helmet is a large structure with an equestrian figure, the nomad warrior chief who founded several towns. Other characters represent important members of the household. Although such masks weigh more than fifty pounds, young dancers would perform athletically in them.

THE NUCLEAR FAMILY

In highly industrialized societies, where individuals have great mobility, the extended family has lost much of its strength, and the clan has dwindled to the nuclear family. Artists have examined the nuclear family to find its strengths, its changes, and its points of tension.

The Family, dated 1962 (Fig. 14.18), by the artist Marisol, presents us with a mother and her children arranged as if sitting for a photographer. Feelings of both mutual affection and personal awkwardness emanate from the three older children, as they present themselves to the world as family members and as individuals. The mother in the center is dignified, solid, and thoughtful, but not elegant. She links all the figures and elements. The doors and decoration behind suggest the domestic setting, but they seem generally poor. Marisol's figures are blocks of wood, drawn on and minimally carved, each maintaining its own separateness while interlocking with the group. The shoes and doors are real, found objects that Marisol incorporated into her work. *The Family* contrasts with the uniformity, happiness, and

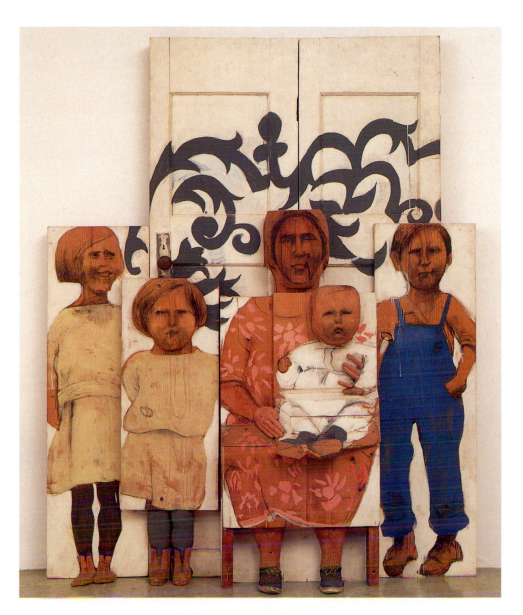

14.18 MARISOL. *The Family*, USA, 1962. Painted wood and other materials in three sections; overall, 6'10" × 65½" × 15½". Advisory Committee Fund (231.1962.a–c), The Museum of Modern Art, New York. © The Museum of Modern Art, New York/Art Resource, NY. Art © Marisol Escobar/Licensed by VAGA, New York, NY.

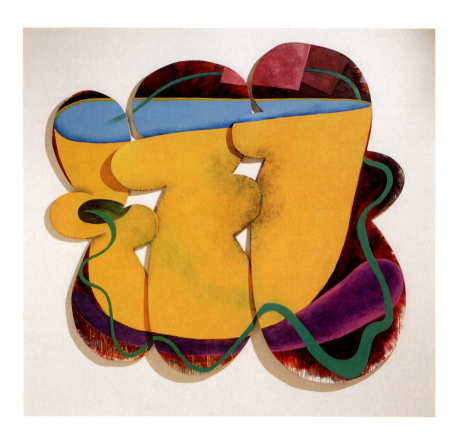

14.19   ELIZABETH MURRAY. *Sail Baby*, USA,
1983. Oil on three canvases, 126" × 135".
Walker Art Center, Minneapolis, Minnesota.

affluence of the nuclear family as it was commonly presented on U.S. television in 1962, with shows like *Leave It to Beaver* and *Father Knows Best*.

Artists sometimes allude to their subject without presenting it literally. Such is the case with *Sail Baby*, dated 1983 (Fig. 14.19), by Elizabeth Murray, which is a painting about family life. Three rounded canvases suggest the bouncy, energetic bodies of infants or children. The bright colors recall the palette of childhood. The yellow shape becomes a cup, referring to the role of parents, the domestic sphere, and feeding. The grouping of the three shapes suggests the closeness of siblings, all with similarities and, at the same time, each a unique individual. The ribbon of green reflects their relatedness and the intimacy of their lives. The artist, in fact, has said that this painting is about her own siblings and her children, while her other abstract paintings refer to different family relationships, such as mother-daughter and husband-wife.

As the twentieth century drew to a close, the definition of family had been expanded. *Baby Makes 3* (Fig. 14.20), from the late 1980s, is by General Idea, the Canadian collective of three artists, A. A. Bronson, Felix Partz, and Jorge Zontal, who had been working together since 1968. General Idea presented a homosexual approach to the nuclear family, showing three men in bed in the clouds, looking tranquil and impish.

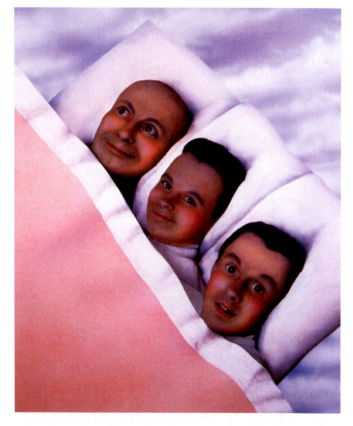

14.20   GENERAL IDEA. *Baby Makes 3*, Canada, 1984–1989. Lacquer on vinyl, 78¾" × 63". By permission of General Idea.

The work both pokes fun at the idea of the happy nuclear family and also shows how gays and lesbians re-create such family and social structures. *Baby Makes 3* also alludes to recent discoveries in science that suggest methods other than heterosexual reproduction to generate a biological family. The image appeared on the cover of *File,* which was General Idea's parody of *Life* magazine. General Idea critiqued many aspects of popular culture that so heavily promote the heterosexual nuclear family. They created their own versions of TV dinners, postage stamps, boutique items, videos with commercials, and so on.

CLASS

A group of people sharing the same economic, social, or ruling status comprises a class. Class boundaries are rigid in some cultures, while in others, people can easily move up or down the "social ladder."

Class becomes like a very large extended family where individuals often find their identity and their social circle. Art and class structure can be linked in several ways: (1) members of different classes may be depicted with distinctive body styles and poses; (2) artwork can show the environment, accoutrements, and activities that mark members of a certain class; and (3) a work of art can be a status item, the possession of which indicates the class of the owner.

CLASS STATUS AND BODY STYLES

In ancient Egypt, the human body was sculpted in different ways, depending on the class of the person. Upper classes, consisting of the pharaoh and his family, the nobility, and the priests, were depicted in formal, highly standardized ways that indicated immediately their importance in the social hierarchy. The four gigantic statues at the *Temple of Ramses II* at Abu Simbel, dated c. 1275–1225 BCE (Fig. 14.21), are examples of official images of the pharaoh. Befitting his

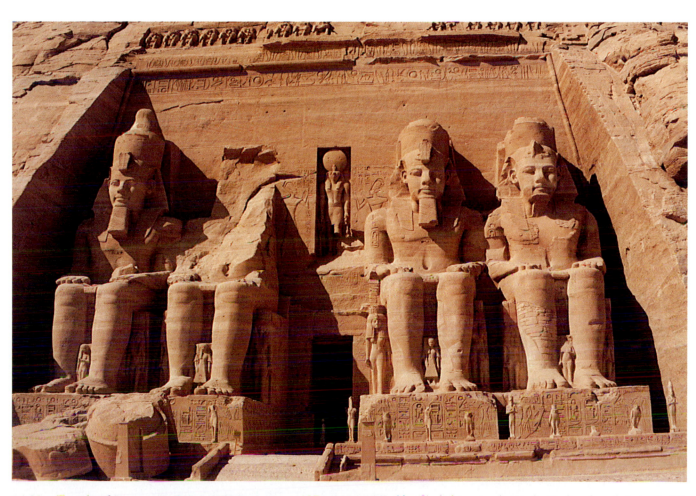

14.21   *Temple of Ramses II*, Egypt, XIX Dynasty, c. 1275–1225 BCE. Abu Simbel (now relocated). Each colossal statue is 65' high. John P. Stevens/Ronald Sheridan Ancient Art & Architecture Library.

semidivine status, he is enormous. The repetition of the image reinforces the idea of his imposing grandeur and divinity. Another eight standing statues are just inside the doorway, each standardized, each thirty-two feet high. The seated pose is frontal, composed, and symmetrical, according to the Egyptian aesthetic, with few breakable parts. The expressionless face and staring eyes look outward in timeless serenity. The body of Ramses II is well developed and flawless, frozen forever in idealized, youthful prime. Smaller figures at Ramses' knees and feet are members of his family, their smaller size indicative of their lesser rank. Enormous projects of this kind were very costly and demanded the skills of the best carvers, reinforcing the status of the very highest classes.

The colossal statues of Ramses II were intended to be permanent memorials to him, as befitting his rank. In 1968, the statues were moved to higher ground and affixed to artificial cliffs to avoid their being submerged in the back pools of the new Aswan Dam. Their permanence remains.

By contrast, the *Seated Scribe*, dated c. 2500–2400 BCE (Fig. 14.22), is a portrait of an Egyptian court official of much lesser rank than the pharaoh. The sculpture is limestone, a relatively soft, inexpensive stone considered to have an unattractive finish, so the work was

painted. The result is more lifelike and thus less eternal and permanent than the monumental stone image of Ramses II at Abu Simbel. As befitting those of lower class, there is much less formality and idealization in the portrait of the scribe. His pose is more relaxed, and the figure is cut away from all backing stone. His face is expressive and personalized, rather than eternally calm and divine. He seems intelligent, alert, and aware. His body shows the effects of age, with sagging chest muscles and a potbelly, attributes that would be considered disrespectful in a portrait of a pharaoh.

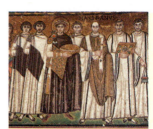

Connection *The Egyptians were not the only people to create idealized images of their leaders. See images of rulers in Chapter 11, such as* Emperor Justinian and His Attendants *(Fig. 11.2, page 277).*

CLASS ACTIVITIES AND LIFESTYLES

Art records not only the lifestyles of the rich and famous but also the more mundane existence of the lower classes. We will look at a cross-cultural selection of images that reflect class activities and class lifestyles. It is important to remember that the great majority of these images are made by the ruling class or middle class, often of themselves but also of classes below them.

The Ruling Class

Upper-class and ruling families in Europe in the last millennium have used art to define and maintain their high rank. Portraits were often records of high positions, as only the wealthy could afford to commission or own an oil painting.

The title of *Las Meninas* (Fig. 14.23), painted by Diego Velazquez in 1656, means "Maids of Honor," which by itself marks the upper class. At the center of the composition is the blond Infanta Marguerita, the daughter of King Philip IV and Queen Mariana of Spain, the focus of considerable attention and energy. She is shown almost casually in the painter's studio. This informal image was not meant for public display, but for the king's private office. Although the Infanta is not painted in a throne room or with a crown, we can understand her exalted position through many elements in the painting. Her location at the center of the picture, the light that floods her, and her glowing white dress all mark her as the most important figure. As the presence of

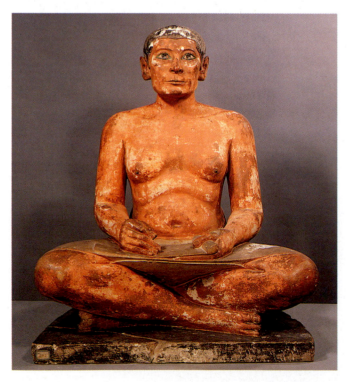

14.22 *Seated Scribe*, Egypt, V Dynasty, c. 2500–2400 BCE. Painted limestone, approx. 21" high. From a mastaba tomb at Saqqara. Louvre, Paris. © RMN/Art Resource, NY.

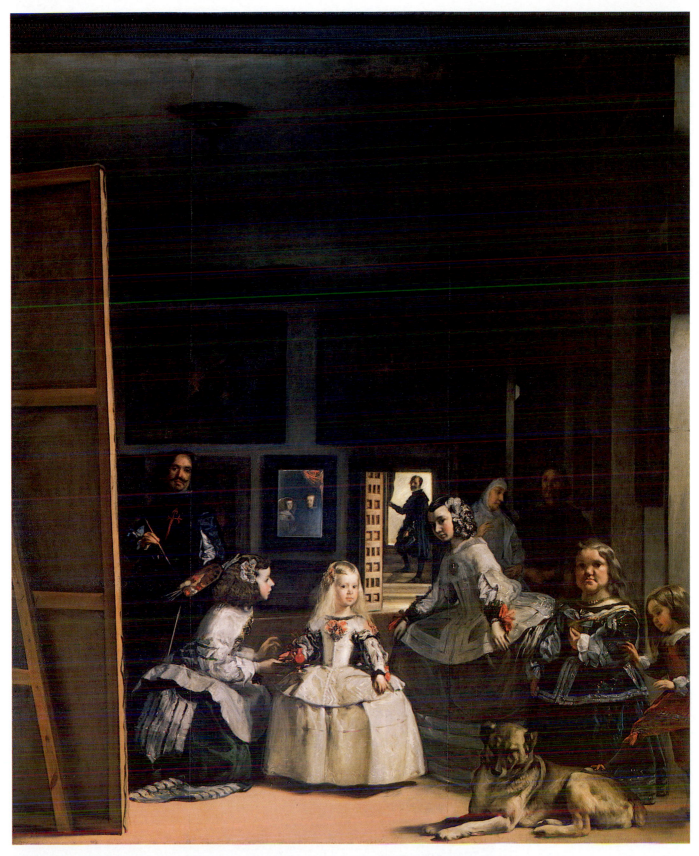

14.23 DIEGO VELAZQUEZ. *Las Meninas*, Spain, 1656. Oil on canvas, approx. 10'5" × 9'. Museo Nacional del Prado, Madrid. Institut Amatller d'Art Hispanic. © Museo del Prado.

servants is also a sign of rank, she is attended by two young ladies in waiting, two dwarfs, and two adult chaperones, male and female, in the shadowy right background. Her royal parents are reflected in the mirror against the back wall; presumably, they are standing where the viewer of the painting would be.

The space of the painting is majestic: light floods the foreground; the room is grand; the deep space extends back in the distance. The space is also made complex by mirrors. One we see but the other we cannot, although its presence is implied by the fact that Velazquez peers outward, presumably into a mirror, to paint himself. Velazquez is the standing figure at the left of the painting, working on a large canvas, perhaps this very picture.

Size is important. This painting is ten and one-half feet by nine feet. A physical object this large is a sign of rank and a mark of distinction, as well as is owning, possessing, or commissioning such an artwork. Diego Velazquez was a celebrated and famous artist. His prestige is an important addition to the royal commissions.

Sometimes class was indicated by its members' activities. *The Swing* (Fig. 14.24), painted by Jean-Honoré Fragonard in 1766, shows the frivolous sexual escapades of the French aristocratic class in the mid-eighteenth century. During that period, they enjoyed tremendous wealth and privilege and had few responsibilities, as most of their power had been assimilated by the French king and most of their duties assumed by an

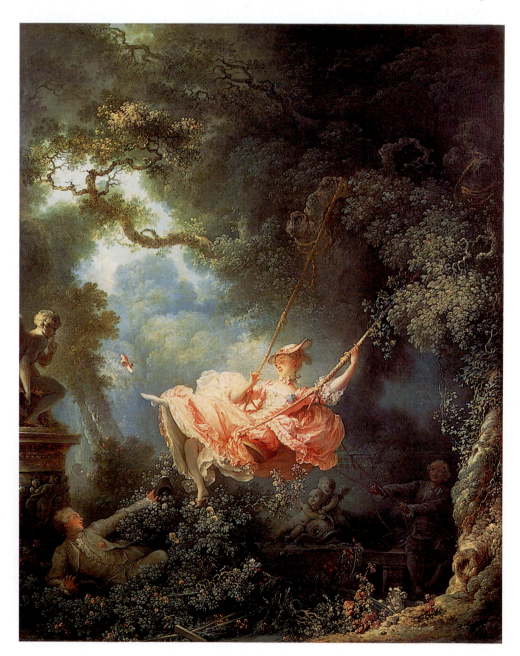

14.24 JEAN-HONORÉ FRAGONARD. *The Swing*, France, 1766. Oil on canvas, 35" × 32". Photo Wallace Collection, London.

ever-growing middle class. The aristocracy was effectively transformed into a leisure class, with little to do but become embroiled in their own intrigues.

In *The Swing*, a young, aristocratic woman enjoys a moment of swinging, assisted by the bishop in the shadows who pulls the ropes. Hidden among the bushes in the lower left is a young nobleman, enjoying a peek up the woman's skirt as she playfully kicks off her pink shoe at a statue of Cupid. All details speak of the wealth and the lack of purpose of the aristocracy: the lush parks of their beautiful estates sprinkled with statuary, their rich clothing, the complete frivolity of their days' activities, and their interest in sexual intrigues. Fragonard's rich colors, delicate details, and sensual textures lend sweetness to the scene, and a sense of fragility. In fact, the aristocratic class was shortly to be brutally eliminated by the French Revolution, which began in 1789 (see *Art and History in Context,* page 396).

Dress and other paraphernalia are often a sign of rank. We see this often among royalty and nobility as well as with members of the military and even the Boy or Girl Scouts. Priests of most religions dress distinctively to show their status. We could look at hundreds of examples in art where class hierarchy is made apparent by dress, but we will view just one, the *Great Beaded Crown of the Orangun-Ila* (Fig. 14.25), from the Yoruba people of Nigeria in Africa. The image shows not only the crown but also the robe and staff that are signs of rank. Crowns such as this one are worn by high-ranking territorial chiefs and are similar

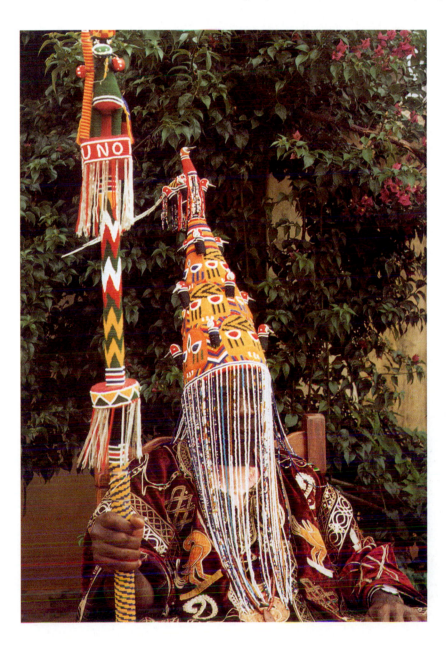

14.25 BEADWORKERS OF THE ADESINA FAMILY OF EFON-ALAYE. *Great Beaded Crown of the Orangun-Ila,* Ila Orangun, Nigeria, 20th century. Yoruba. Photograph by John Pemberton III, 1971.

to the headgear worn by priests and the supreme ruler. Rank is made apparent through dress in a number of ways: (1) the shape of the clothing or headgear, (2) the materials used, and (3) the meaning of the decorative symbols. The conical shape of the crown is a highly significant Yoruba symbol. It represents the inner self, which, in the case of those of rank, is connected with the spirit world. The cone shape is repeated in the umbrella that protects the chief from the sun and in the peaked-roofed verandas where he sits while functioning as the ruler. Beads have been used in Yoruba crowns at least since the 1550s and likely even earlier. The birds on the chief's crown and robe represent generative power, closely associated with women's reproductive abilities and the life-giving, stabilizing structure of Yoruba society. The long, white feathers at the top of the crown are from the Okin, called the royal bird by the Yoruba people.

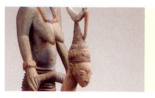

Connection *For an example of the conical shape used in Yoruban art, see the* Palace Sculpture *by Olowe of Ise (Fig. 11.13, page 287).*

The Working Class

The middle class flourishes in cities, where the dense population provides opportunities for commercialization and specialization for merchants, skilled workers, laborers, restaurateurs, entertainers, and others.

Kaifeng, the longtime capital of China, had 260,000 households in the year 1105. Scenes of its urban culture are recorded in the scroll painting, *Spring Festival Along the River* (Fig. 14.26), by Zhang Zeduan, from the late eleventh or early twelfth century. A painting this size was undoubtedly commissioned by a member of the aristocracy, and so this image represents an upper-class concept

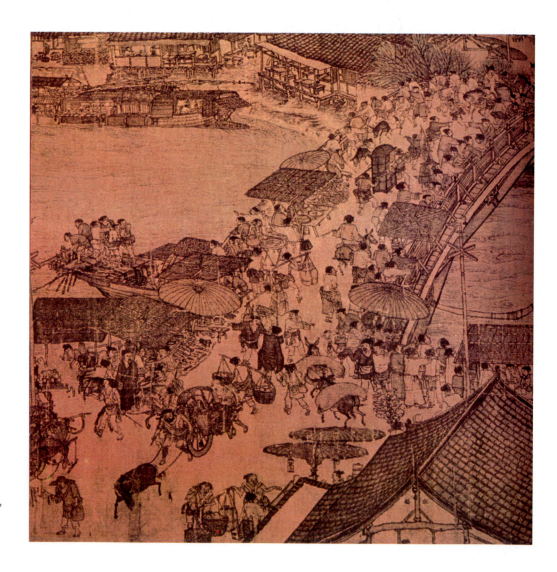

14.26 ZHANG ZEDUAN. *Spring Festival Along the River* (detail), China, late 11th–early 12th centuries. Handscroll, ink on silk, 10" high × 207" long. The Palace Museum, Beijing.

of middle-class life. Our example here shows the ideal working class, animated with crowded, bustling activity. Details show merchants selling goods in booths, people eating in restaurants, farmers delivering produce, and so on. Friendly neighbors were helpful and involved with each other. For example, onlookers shout advice and gesture from the bridge and banks as boatmen steer their vessel under the Rainbow Bridge. Each small scene is rendered with the same amount of detail and similar color, and the accumulated scenes give a picture of busy, contented, unassuming middle-class life.

The Kitchen Maid (Fig. 14.27), painted by Jan Vermeer in 1660, shows a maid in a modest home in the Netherlands of the seventeenth century. In this painting, the working class is elevated in dignity. The mundane tasks of pouring milk and arranging bread seem almost sacred. The gentle light bathes, outlines, and gives a strong sense of the physical presence of a humble woman, an image with such simplicity and directness that she almost personifies virtue. Her work seems healthy and life sustaining. The woven basket, the crust of the bread, the earthen jug, the texture of the wall seem burnished with age and glowing. The color harmonies of cream, gold, and rust are earthen versions of the strong primary colors red and yellow.

Vermeer often painted ordinary scenes from everyday life, a category of paintings called **genre painting**. This was part of an overall tendency in the Netherlands of the seventeenth century to emphasize and elevate middle-class domestic life, where music, reading, and culture flourished and basic needs were met. The maid, from an even lower social level, is treated with the

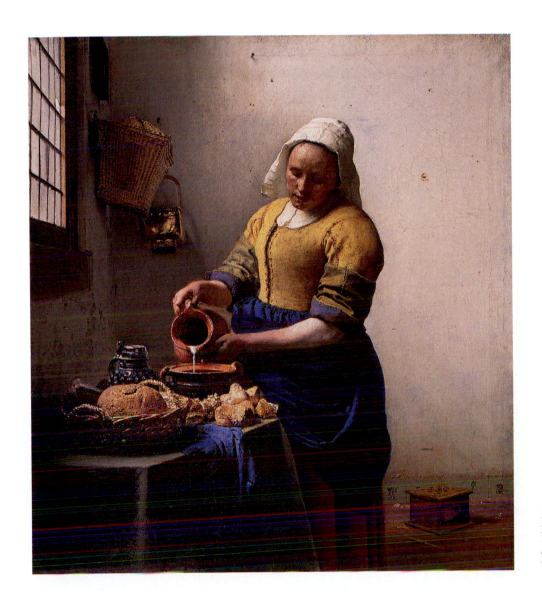

14.27 Jan Vermeer van Delft. *The Kitchen Maid*, Netherlands, 1660. Oil on canvas, approx. 17" × 15". The Rijksmuseum Amsterdam.

same grace and dignity. The sphere of women was the home, and *The Kitchen Maid* reflects the ideals of womanhood at that time: virtue, modesty, hard work. As a middle-class country without a king or an aristocracy, the Netherlands focused on the family and family life and the individual. Portraits were common, as were moralizing genre scenes that criticized such vices as laziness, drunkenness, and lust.

Connection *The* Self-Portrait *(Fig. 13.8, page 343) by Rembrandt van Rijn reflects the same sense of individual worth and the sacredness of a modest life as does Vermeer's* Kitchen Maid.

In *La Grande Jatte*, dated 1884–1886 (Fig. 14.28), Georges Seurat painted a middle class that was enjoying the increased wealth and leisure that accompanied nineteenth-century industrialism. The very creation of parks was the result of the affluent middle class's desire to reintroduce nature into increasingly crowded cities.

The painting shows a collection of strangers outdoors on a modern holiday. Unlike villagers attending a local festival, the groups do not know each other. The figures are proper, composed, and orderly. Details of middle-class dress are carefully recorded. Almost all figures are shown rigidly from the side, front, or back. Diagonals are reserved for the left side of the painting and are stopped by the orderly verticals on the right. Shadows mass in the foreground, and light in the back.

The painting reflects the growing emphasis on and awareness of science. The woman in the right foreground holds a monkey on a leash, and the similarity between the monkey's curved back and the bustle on her dress shows an awareness of Charles Darwin's theories of evolution and the resulting social Darwinism, which placed women closer on a continuum to the rest of nature than men were placed. Also, Seurat was influenced by the science of color and optics, especially the works of the scientist Eugène Chevreul, as he painted with small dots of intense colors laid side by side in a style called **Pointillism.** Chevreul the-

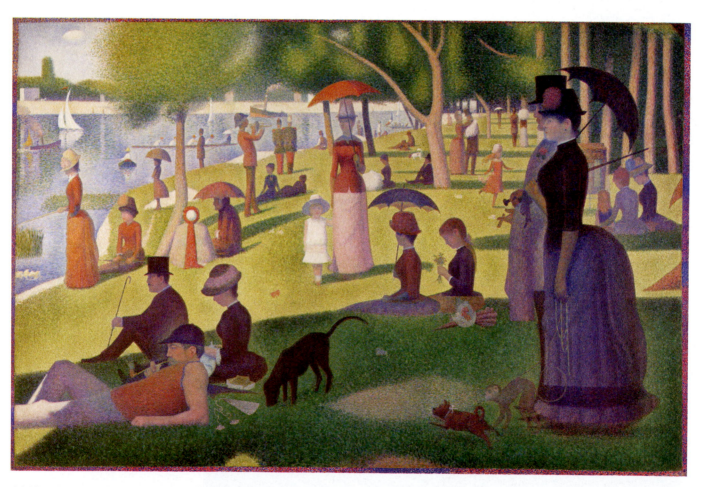

14.28 GEORGES SEURAT. *La Grande Jatte* (also called *A Sunday on La Grande Jatte—1884*), France, 1884–1886. Oil on canvas, approx. 6'9" × 10'. The Art Institute of Chicago, Helen Birch Bartlett Memorial Collection. Photo © The Art Institute of Chicago. All Rights Reserved.

orized that contrasting colors applied that way could intensify each other. The dots of bright colors eliminated muddy mixtures, and, in fact, this painting up close is a somewhat dizzying and disorienting mass of small colorful dots. So labor-intensive was this process that it took Seurat more than two years to complete the work.

The Poor

Art provides us a record of the poor, their way of life and their struggles. Art itself, however, is often an upper- or middle-class luxury, so often artworks represent how the more affluent classes saw the very destitute. An example of such art is Honoré Daumier's *Third Class Carriage*, which appears in *Art and History in Context* on page 397.

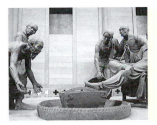

Connection *For an example of how the poor might view the rich, see* The Rent Collection Courtyard *(Fig. 12.13, page 317), which shows an instance of exploitation and oppression.*

Migrant Mother, Nipomo Valley (Fig. 14.29), photographed by Dorothea Lange, is one of many workers who were starving at a migrant camp Lange visited in 1936. Lange's field notes tell us about the woman: "Camped on the edge of a pea field where the crop had failed in a freeze. The tires had just been sold from under the car to buy food. She was 32 years old with seven children." The woman's face and pose express both strength and desperation. Skin, clothes, and hair show signs of poverty and hard times. Fear and uncertainty permeate the scene, made more acute because we also see the emotional ties of the family and the fear of the children. *Migrant Mother, Nipomo Valley* is an example of documentary photography, which purports to record facts objectively and in a straightforward manner. In reality, we know that this family posed for Lange, that she made several exposures of them, and that she edited her prints for the most effective image. Nevertheless, it is important that we understand the photograph to be factual, whether or not it was staged or manipulated.

Lange was a New York commercial photographer who was hired by California and federal agencies to

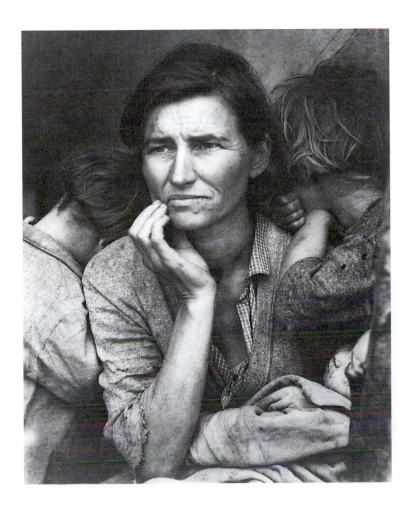

14.29 DOROTHEA LANGE. *Migrant Mother, Nipomo Valley,* USA, 1936. Gelatin Silver Print. From the Collections of the Library of Congress.

document migrant farmworkers during the Great Depression in the United States. Her photographs were especially effective because she made her subjects so human and so immediate. Her photographs were credited with improving conditions for migrant workers in California. The black-and-white photograph was an especially effective medium to use to express conditions of poverty, to concentrate on the facial expression, and to lend the aura of truth.

Connections Many other U.S. artists took up the cause of the poor or laboring classes throughout the nineteenth and twentieth centuries. Turn to Ester Hernandez's memorable print, Sun Mad (Fig. 12.16, page 319).

For more on Migrant Mother, Nipomo Valley and the apparently objective nature of photography, see Chapter 4, Deriving Meaning, especially pages 84, 85 and 95.

ART OBJECTS THAT INDICATE CLASS STATUS

Finally, different kinds of art are often indicators of class. Art objects are made for and reflect the needs and tastes of specific classes. We could have chosen from many examples to illustrate this concept, but we will focus first on two from the era of the Tokugawa Shogunate (1573–1868) in Japan. We will conclude

with an example from the United States of the twentieth century.

Historically in Japan, classes were kept rigidly distinct. The ruling class consisted of the imperial family and the warriors, who divided the land and were its feudal rulers, led by the shogun. The very poorest class consisted of the peasants, who farmed the land that belonged to the warrior class. In addition, a middle class of urban dwellers began to emerge, starting in the mid-1600s and continuing into the twentieth century. This class was composed primarily of merchants, manufacturers, and laborers, and the largest concentration of them was in the city of Edo, known today as Tokyo. As each group was kept separate and distinct, they all developed their own cultural spheres. For example, the emperor and warrior class preferred a restrained, sophisticated, understated style of theater known as Noh, while the middle class favored the more expressive Kabuki theater.

Likewise, different art styles developed for each class. The warrior-rulers built for themselves splendid stone castles that were both fortresses and self-aggrandizing monuments. Because of the stone construction, rooms in these castles were large, gray, and dimly lit. The warrior-rulers commissioned large screens, sliding doors, and wall paintings to lighten and decorate the dark, drab interiors. For example, *Uji Bridge,* from the sixteenth or seventeenth century (Fig. 14.30), is a large screen more than five feet tall. The bridge arcs across

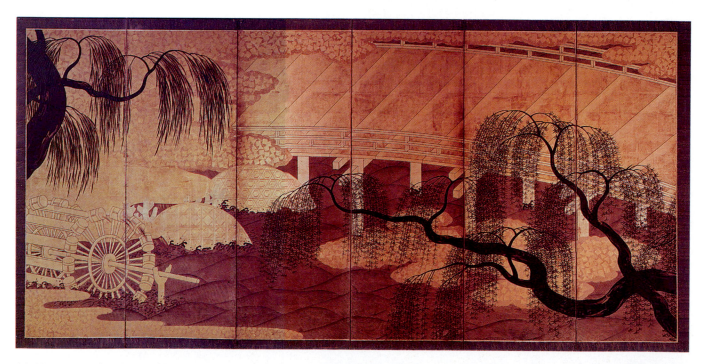

14.30 *Uji Bridge,* Japan, Momoyama period, 16th–17th centuries. Six-fold screen, color on paper, 62" high. Tokyo National Museum.

the top of the screen, partly obscured by mists. In the foreground, the river rolls past a water wheel. Dramatic willow branches contrast with budding leaves. The dark branches stand in stark contrast to the golds and reds of the background. The painting expresses qualities of simplicity and beauty, perishable with the passing of the moment.

The artwork of the middle class was likely the ukiyo-e print (see *Art and History in Context* box, page 396). These prints were modest in size and produced in large numbers, so that the cost of each was within the reach of the middle-class merchant. They were kept in drawers and therefore did not require a castle to house them. The ukiyo-e prints were eclectic in style, combining Japanese, Chinese, and, later, Western styles. Because they were inexpensive to produce, the artist who drew the original design was able to be innovative. For lavish screens like the *Uji Bridge*, artists had much less latitude in the designs they produced.

Ukiyo-e prints showed generally one of three subjects: famous Kabuki actors, beautiful young women,

and landscapes. *Komurasaki of the Tamaya Teahouse* (Fig. 14.31), designed by Kitagawa Utamaro in 1794, is an example of the beautiful woman theme, showing the courtesan Komurasaki. The image is beautiful, but fleeting and simple. The woman is charming, but human existence is transitory; thus, the beautiful can add a melancholy note, making humans ache all the more for life's passing. This wistfulness is a quality of many Japanese images, as we saw even with the *Uji Bridge* screen. The colors are exceedingly delicate, with yellow ochres, olive tones, dull reds, grays, and blacks—not blazingly bright. The line quality of the prints was splendid—elegant and fine, curving and graceful (or, in the case of prints of the energetic Kabuki actors, vigorous and even wild). The lines in the face and hair are especially refined, while the folds of the drapery are expressed in bold marks and curves. Geishas and courtesans were depicted in ways that would make them outlets for male desires; the market for these pictures was married men who would see in these women

14.31 KITAGAWA UTAMARO. *Komurasaki of the Tamaya Teahouse*, Japan, 1794. Multicolor woodblock print from the series "A Collection of Reigning Beauties," 10" × 15". Tokyo National Museum.

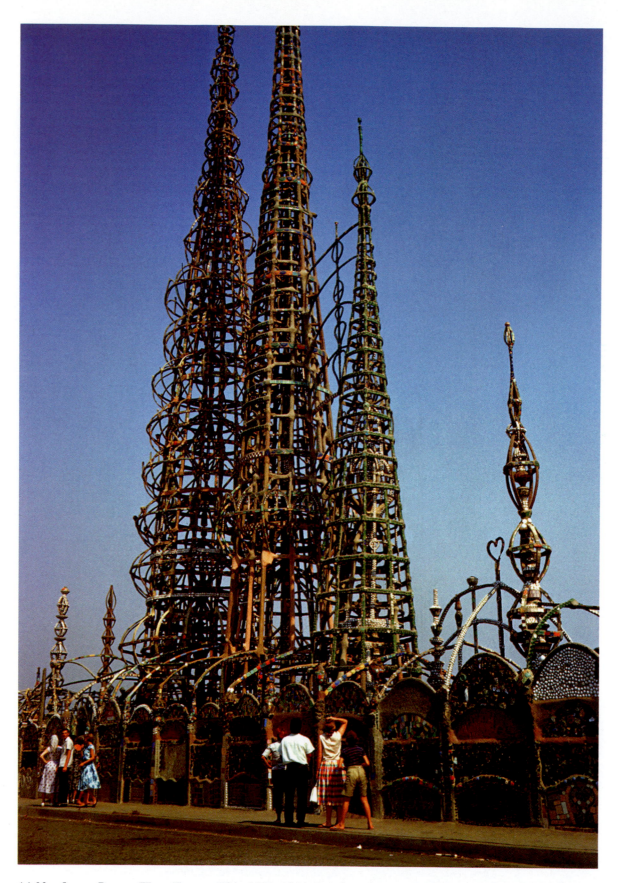

14.32 SIMON RODIA. *Watts Towers*, USA, 1921–1954. Reinforced concrete with mixed media and found materials, 100' high. Los Angeles, California. © Bettmann/Corbis.

for hire a fleeting beauty and an erotic perfection that they desired. Especially famous courtesans and geishas would be depicted in popular prints, and their images circulated and collected.

Connection *You can read more about Japanese prints with* A Pair of Lovers *(Fig. 8.14, page 183). The production of such prints is discussed in Chapter 3,* Media, *on page 62 and with Figure 3.8.*

Our last example, *Watts Towers* (Fig. 14.32), was made by a working-class man for a working-class neighborhood in Los Angeles. Beginning in the 1920s when he was in his late forties, Simon Rodilla (also called Simon or Sam Rodia) labored for more than thirty years in his backyard to erect a nine-part sculpture, more than one hundred feet high. It was an amazing artistic and physical effort. The tower forms rise dramatically against the sky, while the openwork pattern adds an element of rhythm. The *Watts Towers* are constructed of rods and bars shaped into openwork sculptures. The concrete coating on the *Towers* was encrusted with ceramic pieces, tiles, glass, seashells, mirror pieces, and other shiny or broken castoffs, creating a glittering mosaic-like surface. An immigrant from Italy, Rodia wanted to construct a monument to pay tribute to his adopted land.

Rodia was not academically trained as an artist, and his work does not reflect the major art trends of his day. His work was not made for an upper-class audience. As a result, many critics place *Watts Towers* in categories outside of fine art. It has been variously described as folk art, outsider art, or naive art. The dense and shimmering surfaces have caused some to relate his work to crafts and decorative arts. Some have even called it "kook" art, claiming that Rodia was trying to make a transmitter to contact aliens. Some of these descriptors ("naive," "kook," "decorative," etc.) have more or less pejorative connotations, while "folk" suggests an art category of less value than fine art. But there is no denying the power and memorability of the *Watts Towers*.

Connection *Another work of "folk art" is the Retablo of Maria de la Luz Casillas and Children (Fig. 9.14, page 212). Read about that work and then review the discussion of "Fine Art, Popular Culture, and Kitsch" in Chapter 1.*

The period 1750–1850 brought major changes in the history of humankind. In 1760, the Industrial Revolution was beginning in Europe—power machinery replaced hand labor and steam engines replaced water wheels and spinning mills. People moved to the cities to work in factories, and a middle class grew and gained power. This was also the Age of Enlightenment, which fostered ideas of personal liberty.

Europeans divided the entire Americas through colonization. The French claimed land from Canada through the Great Lakes and down the Mississippi River to the Gulf of Mexico. Britain controlled the thirteen colonies, and Spain claimed Florida, Texas, New Mexico, Arizona, and California as well as vast territories in Central and South America. Britain also maintained colonies throughout Asia and Africa.

In 1775, the American Revolution against England began, followed by the French Revolution in 1789 in which the monarchy was overthrown. In art, the revolutionary spirit was presented in Neo-Classical terms, as seen in *Oath of the Horatii* (Fig. 14.8). By contrast, the art that had been made for the nobility is Rococo, as in *The Swing* (Fig. 14.24) The gap in wealth and lifestyles between the rich and the poor in France can be seen by comparing *The Swing* with the *Third-Class Carriage* by Daumier in this box.

George Washington became the first president of the United States, while

Map 8   Napoleon's Grand Empire. Courtesy of Replogle Globes, Inc., Broadview, IL.

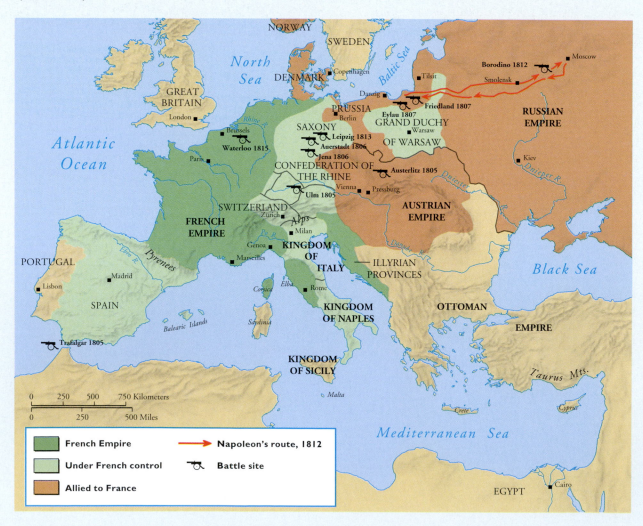

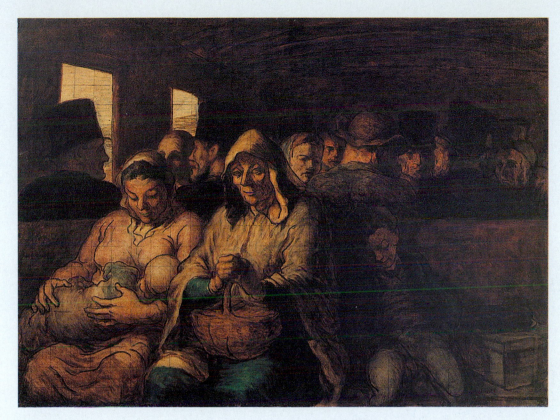

14.33   HONORÉ DAUMIER.   *Third-Class Carriage*, France, 1862. Oil on canvas, 25¹⁄₄" × 35¹⁄₂". The Metropolitan Museum of Art, New York. Havemeyer Collection, bequest of H. O. Havemeyer, 1929.

Napoleon took control of France and conquered an empire (see Map 8). In 1812 in South America, Simón Bolívar and José de San Martín fought for independence from Spain. In the 1800s, Eli Whitney invented the cotton gin, workers formed the first trade unions to fight for their rights, and Karl Marx and Friedrich Engels wrote the *Communist Manifesto.*

In India, Great Britain set up colonial rule, and, later, Queen Victoria would become the Empress of India. Also during this time, Japan saw the rise of its merchant class, and color woodblock prints called ukiyo-e were made that appealed to their tastes and financial means. One example is *Komurasaki of the Tamaya Teahouse* (Fig. 14.31). The Japanese

middle class also developed theatrical forms that were distinct from those of the ruling class.

The Manchu Dynasty ruled in China during this period. Between 1839 and 1842, the Opium Wars broke out between China and Britain. Britain had smuggled opium from India into China causing mass addiction to the drug, which in turn greatly affected China's economy. Britain won the war and gained Hong Kong plus five ports in China for trade.

In Africa, during the 1700s and 1800s, the Dutch, Portuguese, and other Europeans colonized vast territories. Toward the latter part of this period, the empires of Zimbabwe and Asante came to an end.

1750 – 1850 CE

— Timeline

Old Kingdom, Egypt	**2700 BCE**	
	2500	*Seated Scribe*
	2000	*Temple of Ramses II*
Roman Empire	100	
	75	*Statue of Togato Barberini*
Tang Dynasty—China	**600 CE**	
Historic Era—Japan		
	640	*Portrait Heads from Tomb 6*
Teotihuacán—Mexico	700	
	1000	Zhang Zeduan: *Spring Festival Along the River*
Renaissance Begins	1400	
	1500	
	1600	*Uji Bridge*
	1617	Rubens: *Abduction of the Daughters of Leucippus*
	1656	Velazquez: *Las Meninas*
	1660	Vermeer: *The Kitchen Maid*
Age of Enlightenment	1700	
England, France, Spain colonize the Americas		
Dutch and Portuguese colonize Africa		
	1734	de Cuvilliès: *Hall of Mirrors*
Industrial Revolution	1760	
American Revolution	1775	
	1776	Fragonard: *The Swing*
		David: *Oath of the Horatii*
French Revolution	1789	
	1794	Utamaro: *Komurasaki of the Tamaya Teahouse*
South American Revolution	1800	
First trade unions established		
Britain colonizes India		
Opium Wars between Britain and China	1839	

Communist Manifesto		
	1862	Daumier: *Third-Class Carriage*
	1863	
	1884	Seurat: *La Grande Jatte*
Women's suffrage begins in1900; movement continues to present day		
	1900	Adesina Family: *Great Beaded Crown of the Orangun-Ila*
		Bisj Poles
	1907	Shaughnessy: *Interior House Post*
	1908	
World War I		*Painting from a Cult House*
	1921	Rodia: *Watts Towers*
	1927	VanDerZee: *Society Ladies*
World War II		
	1936	Lange: *Migrant Mother, Nipomo Valley*
	1949	Chagall: *Over Vitebsk*
Vietnam War		
	1962	Marisol: *The Family*
Feminist Movement	1970	
	1972	Saar: *The Liberation of Aunt Jemima*
	1974	Bamgboye of Odo-Owa: *Epa Headdress called "Orangun"*
	1979	Tseng Kwong Chi: *Disneyland, California*
	1983	Murray: *Sail Baby*
	1984	General Idea: *Baby Makes 3*
	1986	Luna: *The Artifact Piece*
		Guerrilla Girls: *Do women have to be naked to get into the Met. Museum?*
	1989	Hung Liu: *Trauma*

Art can preserve racial identity and the history and values of an ethnic group, or it can expose racial oppression.

Gender roles are reinforced or challenged in artworks. Art can be a vehicle to protest unequal pay and opportunities for women in the art world.

The very identity of a clan is often supported by artwork that preserves clan history. The nuclear family is depicted in art as a complex entity. Art can show us the closeness of siblings or the shifting definitions of family.

In art from various cultures, class rank and distinction are often made clear through the amount of space occupied and the quality of the furnishings. Poverty and fear mark the figures from the lowest classes, while middle and upper classes enjoy leisure and comfort. Classes also develop their own styles of artwork.

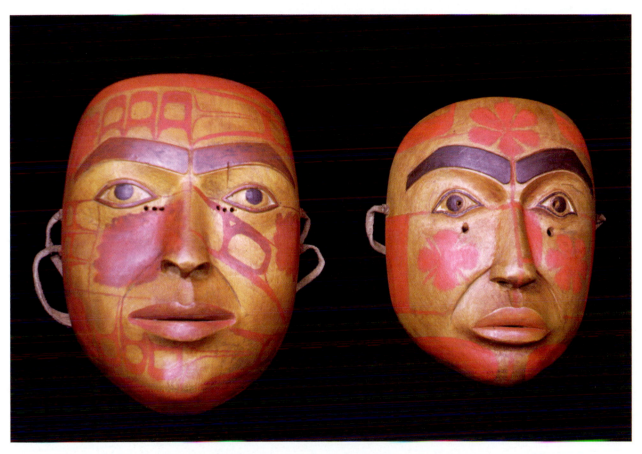

14.34   *Two Haida Masks of Women*, 1882, Haida, Northwest Coast. Painted wood.

FOOD FOR THOUGHT

Art throughout the ages has reflected racial, gender, clan, and class distinctions. These categories often intersect; for example, the Two Haida Masks of Women (Fig. 14.34) reflect racial/ethnic art traditions, contain specific clan symbols, and display appropriate body decoration for Haida men or women.

The following questions ask you to examine race/gender/clan/class distinctions in your culture today.

- *Glorifying racial identity may have positive results. Racial glorification mixed with ideas of racial superiority leads to disaster. When does art that promotes what is beautiful about a people get confused with art that promotes superiority?*

- *The gender-based culture of the Sepik people may seem very distant from our culture in the United States today. Consider, however, if contemporary art and advertising reinforces gender roles in the United States today.*

Although we did not study aging in this chapter, what images of elderly people do we get from fine art and popular art? Almost every art form is a reflection of the class for whom the art is made. We see repeatedly that the most lavish works are made for upper classes, while more modest works are for the lower classes. What about access to art? In many cases, the wealthy are the only ones who can afford to purchase high-profile art or develop collections around well-known artists. Most private collections are closed to the public, but some private collections eventually end up in museums.

- *Does the museum redress the class-related issues of ownership and access to art?*

- *Who controls what art gets into museums?*

- *Are there any forms of art that transcend class?*

- *Art is made by humans for humans, so shouldn't everyone feel comfortable with it, no matter of what clan or class?*

Your Thomson Online Resources

 Go to **ArtExperience Online** for the Flashcards, Quiz, and Study Guide for this chapter.

CHAPTER 15

Nature, Knowledge, and Technology

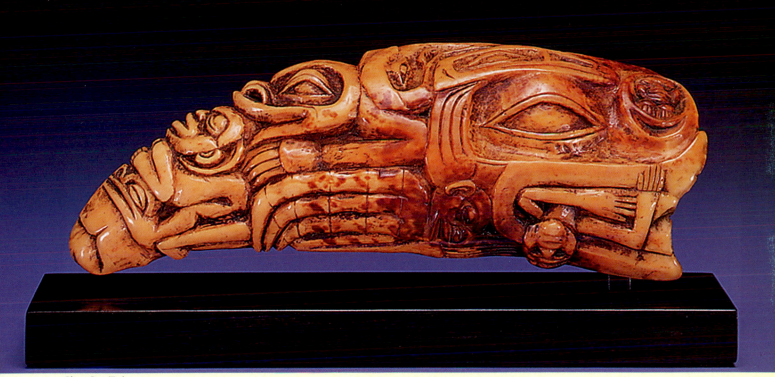

Photo Pam Taylor.

INTRODUCTION

Art can imitate, praise, or criticize the world around us. That world consists of animals and plants as well as human constructs: our knowledge systems, our technology, our cities. For this chapter, the basic questions are:

- *What do we consider ideal in nature?*
- *How do animals in art reflect desirable or despicable qualities in humans?*
- *What do we know about the world around us through art?*
- *How does art advance knowledge?*
- *What are our attitudes regarding the things humans have constructed in the world?*
- *How is technology helping us, and how is it hurting us?*

NATURE

Our natural world consists of the earth and its flora and fauna. The relationship of humans and animals is very complex. We hunt them, love them, and eat them. They are part of industry, as we breed some and extinguish others. We identify with animals and project our highest aspirations and deepest fears onto them. Likewise, people use landscape imagery, both the wild and the cultivated, to project their own ideals.

ANIMALS

Animals appear in art in every culture, in forms both real and imagined. Animals were likely the subjects of humans' first drawings. They figure in myths and religious narratives, such as "Noah and the Ark" and the *Ramayana*. Humans have recorded animal likenesses and have invented bizarre creatures from parts of other living beings.

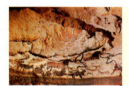 **Connection** *The cave drawings at Lascaux (Fig. 7.1, page 142) are among the oldest existing drawings made by humans.*

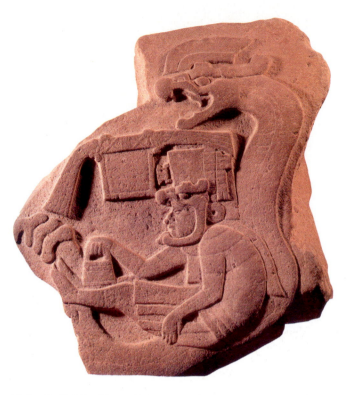

15.1 *Relief*, La Venta (Mexico), 6th century BCE. Basalt, 38½" high. Olmec. Museo Nacional de Antropología, Mexico City. The Metropolitan Museum of Art, New York.

Fantastic Creatures

Fantastic creatures are the product of human imagination, fear, and desire. Because they really do not exist, their human creators can assign a meaning and purpose to them. These creatures still feed popular imagination today, as mermaids, giant insects, and werewolves thrive in film and popular fiction.

Fantastic creatures can express various forms of power. The limestone *Relief*, dated sixth century BCE (Fig. 15.1), comes from the Olmec culture of ancient Mexico, which produced many instances of animal imagery that combine natural and fantastic elements. Here, a warrior or priest is seated and wearing an elaborate jaguar-serpent helmet with the extended jaw of the creature forming the chinstrap. Towering over him is a large serpent with heavy brows and a crest like some sort of imaginary bird. Undoubtedly, the animal attributes protect the man as well as combine with him to create heightened powers.

The ancient Greeks invented several fantastic creatures that usually were threats to humans or represented degraded human nature. Harpies were woman-headed birds who lured and fed on men. Centaurs were man-headed horses known for their lustfulness. Satyrs

were men with goat or horse attributes and were prone to drunkenness and sexual excess. Medieval Europeans were especially interested in fantastic animals, like the satyrs and centaurs from antiquity, and made up several of their own. Medieval beasts, however, often acted like humans in narratives that had a moralizing purpose, or were demons in warnings about hell.

The unicorn is a horse with some goat features and a long, single horn projecting from its forehead. Ancient Greeks and Romans first described it, but it was very popular in late medieval literature. "Unicorn" horns were expensive, prized possessions (they were actually the spiral tusk of a narwhal, an arctic whale) that could purify water and remove poison. Another common belief was that the unicorn could elude all hunters. However, when it saw a virgin, it put its head on her lap and could easily be caught. The virgin was taken to represent Mary, and the unicorn became a symbol for Christ.

The Unicorn in Captivity, dated late fifteenth century (Fig. 15.2), is the last image in six tapestries. Our

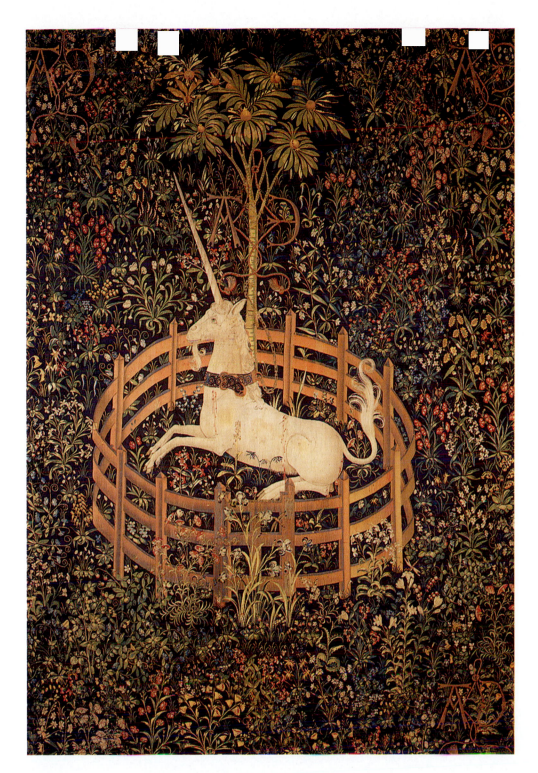

15.2 *The Unicorn in Captivity*, South Netherlandish, 1495–1505. Wool warp, wool, silk, silver, and gilt wefts, 12'1" × 8'3". Gift of John D. Rockefeller Jr., 1937. The Metropolitan Museum of Art, New York, Cloister Collection.

example shows the unicorn as a brilliant white horse captured in a paradise garden, surrounded by an abundance of decorative flowers and plants. The details are delightful, all distributed in a flat pattern that fills the space from top to bottom with carefully rendered, colorful flowers. The unicorn has a lively and soulful expression on its face. It is surrounded by a fence, wears a jeweled collar, and is chained to a pomegranate tree.

The unicorn represented at least two different sets of meanings in these tapestries. One is that of Jesus, believed to be the source of spiritual life, who was hunted by men, was brutally killed, and then rose back to life. Or, the images may represent true love in the Age of Chivalry, with the unicorn (man) enduring terrible ordeals to win his beloved. The collar represents a chain of love, mentioned in medieval allegories as a sign that a gentleman submits to his lady's will. The pomegranates dripping red juice onto the unicorn may symbolize Christ's sacrifice and human fertility. Multiple meanings were common in the medieval era, as a way to acknowledge the complexity of life.

The *Shaman's Amulet,* dated c. 1820–1850 (Fig. 15.3), shows the combination of animal forms as a source of power and protection among the peoples of the Northwest Coast of North America. A shaman was a person with supernatural powers, believed to be a bridge among the human, animal, and spirit worlds. The amulet was a visible sign of the shaman's power, and it extended that power. The most prominent animal is the sea serpent, whose head is to the right, swallowing a human. This indicated that the shaman could take on the forms of certain animals and could operate in both the animal and human realms. Other animals include a bear, for its strength, and a bird, for its ability to fly.

All details are contained within the smooth, arching outline of the amulet. Many internal forms, such as folded arms, lines of feathers, and the serpent's mouth, echo the outer curves. A dark patina gives depth to the work. Its shape and size enabled it to fit easily in the hand.

Another example of fantastic creatures comes from Thailand, a country with monsoon rains, thick jungles, and abundant animal life. Plants, birds, and beasts abound in traditional Thai art and are associated with forces in nature. Most images have more than one meaning. Monkeys, for example, are common wild animals in Thailand, and they are metaphors for humans, who aspire to be gods. In many Hindu and Buddhist tales, they also indulge in behavior unfit for humans or gods, such as lust and drunkenness, and thus present the realistic side of human nature in contrast to the idealized.

Mask of Hanuman (Fig. 15.4) is a headpiece representing the white monkey-hero and loyal follower of the deity Rama in the Thai story *Ramakien* (called the *Ramayana* in India). Performers wear this mask when representing this fantastic creature, a divine monkey with white fur, jeweled teeth, and a white crest of hair that shone like diamonds. His heroic exploits were

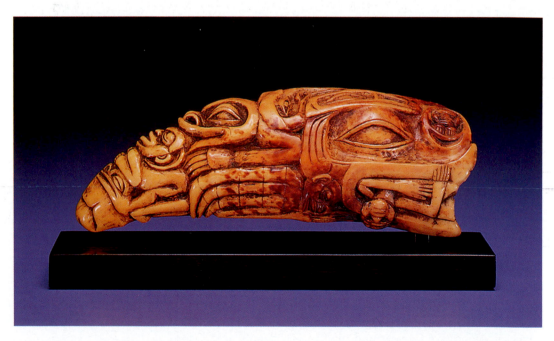

15.3 *Shaman's Amulet,* Alaska/British Columbia, c. 1820–1850. Sperm whale tooth, 6½" long. Tlingit. Indiana University Art Museum, Bloomington, Raymond and Laura Wielgus Collection (RW 60–197). Photo by Michael Cavanagh/Kevin Montague.

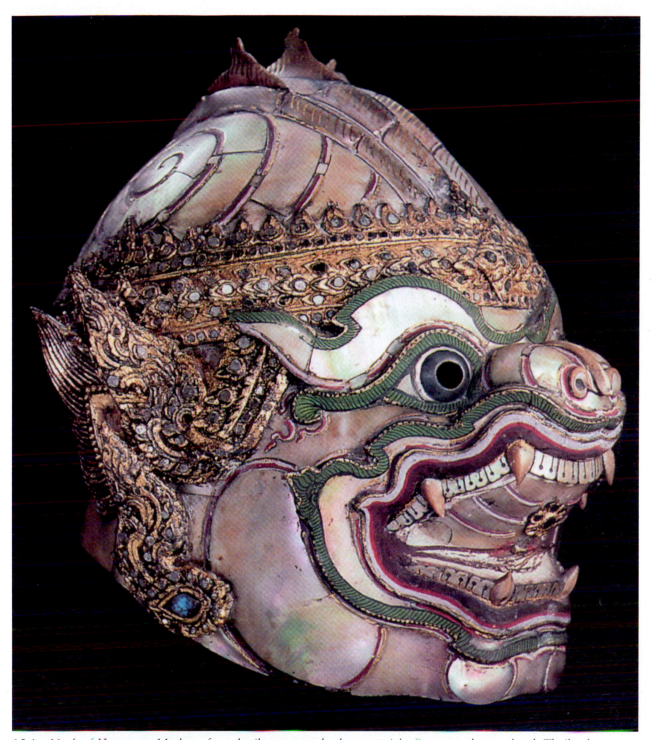

15.4 *Mask of Hanuman.* Mother-of-pearl, gilt, gems, and other materials; fits over a human head. Thailand. National Museum of Bangkok. Photo Pam Taylor.

many, including helping rescue Rama's wife from a demon and bringing a mountain of medicinal plants to cure the wounded in battle. The *Mask of Hanuman* is equally fantastic, covered with gleaming, iridescent mother-of-pearl. Red, black, and green dramatically outline his facial features. His bulging eyes and snarling mouth are visually arresting, alert, and ferocious. Gold serpents curl at his ears. Hanuman is modeled from an actual monkey, the leaf-eating langur from India (Taylor 1994:35–38).

The monkey is again a stand-in for human behavior in Chris Ofili's 1999 painting, *Monkey Magic—Sex, Money and Drugs* (Fig. 15.5). Here the monkey holds an empty turquoise vessel and tries to capture three powerful elements of life: sex, money, and drugs, represented by three clumps of dried elephant dung attached to the canvas. Thick beads of paint and layers of glitter make the surface colorful and shining, to emphasize the imagined rather than the real. A British artist of Nigerian descent, Ofili uses dried elephant dung to reference the African ritual use of it. His paintings often rest on balls of dung, seeming to come up from the earth rather than hang on the wall.

Connection *Examples of fantastic creatures appear in previous chapters. They include serpents (Laocoön and His Sons, Fig. 13.16, page 348), human-headed winged bulls (Lamassu, Fig. 11.8, page 282), and totem animals (Interior House Post, Fig. 14.14, page 378).*

Observed Animals

Animals are magnificent creatures, and, in many instances, their likenesses—without embellishment—are sufficient justification for a work of art.

An ancient set of stone reliefs shows how people admire animals and, at the same time, desire to destroy them. In the detail entitled *Ashurbanipal II Killing Lions*, c. 650 BCE (Fig. 15.6), the lion's muscles, veins, and bones show its tremendous strength, fierceness, and agility. Although they greatly admired the beauty of the living lion, the Assyrian elite slaughtered the animals in a public spectacle, the royal lion hunt. Lions in cages were released in an enclosed arena, where the king, Ashurbanipal, accompanied by bowmen and spearmen, would face them to show his courage. Other scenes show a large number of lion carcasses piled behind the king, or wounded lions slowly dying. Assyrians believed that the longer a man or beast took to die, the higher the layer of heaven that was attained in the afterlife. The Assyrians made many such relief carvings to cover the mud-brick palace walls. They boasted the king's power not only in lion hunts but also in battle campaigns and in accompanying the gods.

The Nazca culture, a pre-Incan civilization in southwestern Peru, produced huge animal drawings on a rocky, arid plain, with no wind and essentially no rainfall. A casual footprint or scrap of litter will remain undisturbed for years. The Nazca drawings were made at least 1,400 years ago by scraping the brown surface of the desert floor, revealing lighter-colored sand beneath. The earliest drawings were of animals, such as

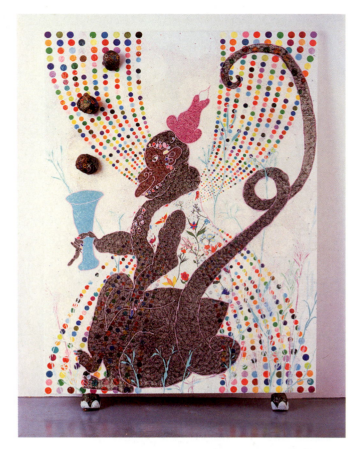

15.5 CHRIS OFILI. *Monkey Magic—Sex, Money and Drugs*, Great Britain, 1999. Acrylic, collage, glitter, resin, pencil, map pins, and elephant dung on canvas, 96" × 72". Museum of Contemporary Art, Los Angeles. Purchased with funds by the Broad Art Foundation. Courtesy Chris Ofili—Afroco and Victoria Miro Gallery.

birds, whales, monkeys, or dogs. Our example, *Spider* (Fig. 15.7), dates from around 200–600. Later drawings consisted of large geometric shapes, spirals, and long, straight lines that extend for miles or radiate from center points. Many drawings were made right on top of previous ones.

The Nazca drawings are remarkable for their regularity. All lines are a standard width and executed as a continuous path. The Nazca people probably used rudimentary surveying instruments and string to plot the paths. The drawings are so large and the plain so flat that most drawings can only be seen from the air. Some long, straight lines may have been used for astronomical sightings, while others may have been paths that connected the plain's various shrines. In this arid area, the animal drawings may have been messages or offerings to water gods residing in mountains. Even today in areas of Peru and Bolivia, the spider is highly regarded because it both augurs weather changes and may foretell rainfall.

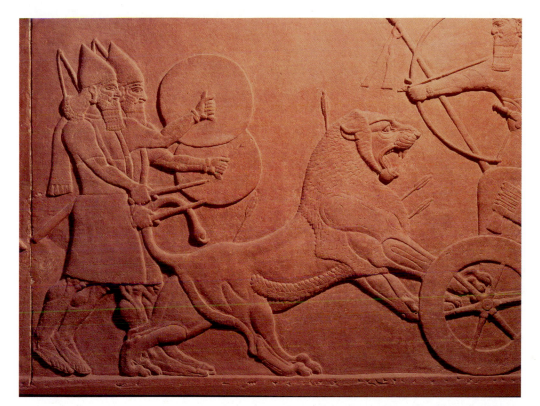

15.6 *Ashurbanipal II Killing Lions*, Assyria, c. 650 BCE. Limestone relief, approx. 60" high. From the Palace of Ashurbanipal, Nineveh (northern Iraq). The British Museum, London. Photo: The British Museum, London.

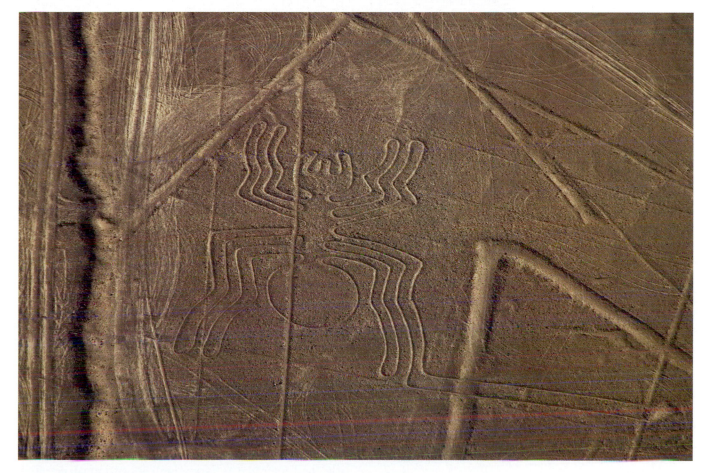

15.7 *Spider*, Nazca, Peru, c. 200–600. Large drawing created when brown surface rocks were scraped away to reveal yellowish surface below. Henri Stierlin.

Vessel in the Form of a Monkey, made between 800 and 900 (Fig. 15.8), is from the pre-Columbian Veracruz culture in Mexico. Animal-shaped vessels were common in many Mesoamerican and South American cultures. The monkey's squatting pose, with its arms overhead grasping its own tail, and its facial structure are so convincingly naturalistic that its species can be identified: it is a spider monkey. The artist has captured the animated expressions and energy of the animal. In addition, small rocks sealed inside in hollow pockets rattle when the vessel is shaken, mimicking the monkey's chatter. Monkeys were kept as pets and were featured in Mesoamerican mythology. They were also linked to dancers, because of their quick, agile movements, or to uninhibited sexuality (Pelrine 1996:75). The monkey in this example has pierced ears, like humans. On the formal side, the vessel can be enjoyed for its design: the monkey's belly in front and the expanded back become the vessel. The opening is behind the monkey's head. Rounded belly shapes contrast with angular forms of the arms, as do the concentrated facial details with the smooth abdomen. Protruding forms, negative spaces, and dark hollows all add to the vessel's visual richness.

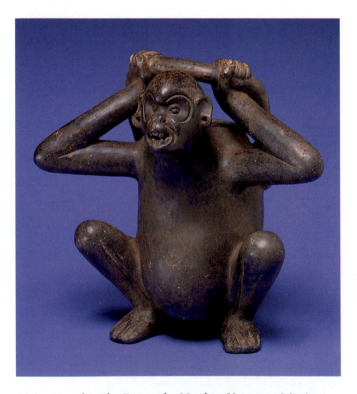

15.8 *Vessel in the Form of a Monkey,* Veracruz, Mexico, late Classic period, 800–900. Clay, 8¹/₂" high. Indiana University Art Museum, Bloomington, Raymond and Laura Wielgus Collection, IUAM 100.7.4.75 (RW 62–233). Photo by Michael Cavanagh/Kevin Montague.

THE LAND

This section contains landscapes, flowers and gardens, and earthworks, which are gigantic sculptures using the earth as their base.

Landscape Imagery

A landscape image is different from the actual outdoors. Landscape images are composed translations of reality that often have deeper social or religious meanings.

In China and Japan, landscape paintings were especially popular among upper- and middle-class urban populations, especially in noisy and polluted areas. The booming city of Suchou, wealthy from the European silk trade and tourists, had one park so overcrowded that a local artist called it "squalid," with "visitors flock there like flies swarming on meat" (Cahill 1966:87). Such paintings as Sheng Maoye's *Beyond the Solitary Bamboo Grove* (Fig. 15.9), from the seventeenth century, made pristine nature once again available. Landscapes were displayed in homes on large, hanging silk scrolls; fans or smaller albums were made for private viewing. Our example shows the subtle blur of misty mountains, an isolated hut, and the distinctive silhouettes of various trees, all rendered by subtle washes of ink and light color. Inspiration for paintings often came from poetry or the beliefs of Daoism (or Taoism), which held that nature was a visible manifestation of the Absolute Dao, the ultimate substratum from which all things come. Nature also reflected Daoism in its rhythms, changes, and transformations. Chinese landscapes are carefully composed imaginary scenes. Artists practiced their brushwork for years to achieve a sense of effortlessness and spontaneity, qualities valued in Daoism.

Landscape paintings were particularly common in the United States and in Europe in the nineteenth century. Landscapes tended to have a nationalistic look. For example, German landscapes sometimes were marked by melancholy or morbidity. English landscapes, however, tended to emphasize the open-air expansiveness of farm scenes. John Constable's *The Haywain,* from 1821 (Fig. 15.10), shows a broad meadow in the distance, with a farm scene in front. The composition seems casual, direct, natural, and unstudied. Tranquility pervades all, as a warm mellow light washes over the greens, golds, and browns of the land, and brilliant clouds play against the blue sky.

Constable's work appealed especially to Europeans who had migrated in large numbers to industrial cities and missed contact with nature. Before painting large

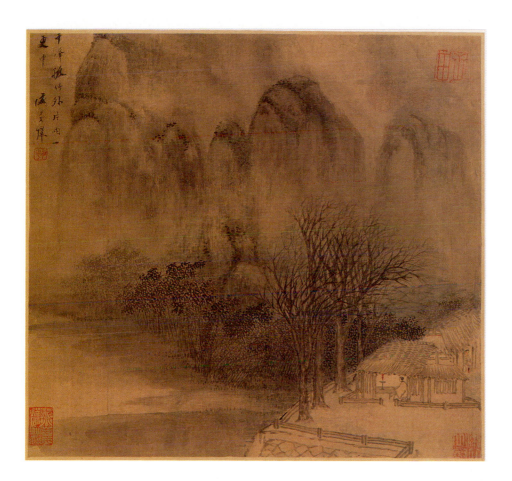

15.9 SHENG MAOYE. *Beyond the Solitary Bamboo Grove*, China, c. 1625–1640. Ink and color on silk, 11¼" × 12". From an album of six leaves; landscapes inspired by Tang poems. The Metropolitan Museum of Art, New York. Purchase, The Sackler Fund, 1969 (69.242.4).

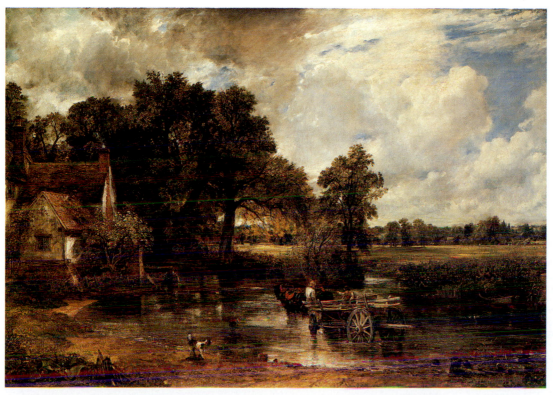

15.10 JOHN CONSTABLE. *The Haywain*, England, 1821. Oil on canvas, 4'3" × 6'2". The National Gallery, London.

canvases, Constable made numerous outdoor studies that he saw as being scientific (meteorology was his avocation). His work also grew from **Romanticism**, which elevated nature and immediate experience. In his works, he used stippling, in which small dabs of bright color and white are applied to reproduce shimmering light. His method was important later to Impressionism.

One Impressionist, Claude Monet, is especially well known for his paintings of nature. He painted almost exclusively outdoors to capture the subtle qualities of light and reflection, and even planted his own water garden at his home in Giverny, France. In *Water Lily Pool* (Fig. 15.11), from 1900, the colors are dazzling; by mixing vivid strokes of pure color, Monet achieved the effect of sunlight upon water. In Monet's later career, his paintings approached abstraction, as brushstrokes became more important than imagery. The Impressionists' emphasis on observation paralleled the ideas of scientists and philosophers of the day, who posited that reality was only that which could be sensed, measured, and analyzed (see *Art and History in Context*, page 448).

Landscape painters in the United States were influenced by European models, but they produced more images of pristine, untouched nature than the Europeans did. Even photographers in the United States were influenced by undeveloped areas of the Midwest and West. Ansel Adams was particularly well known for grand and romantic photographs of remote landscapes, like *Clearing Winter Storm, Yosemite National Park, California, 1944* (Fig. 15.12). In our example, the mist- and cloud-covered mountains are the focal point, while the texture of clouds and trees balance each other. The center seems to recede into infinite space.

Adams worked very hard to get his negatives, exploring, studying, and waiting for just the right moment. In this case, the light caught the waterfall while the surrounding cliff was in dark shadow. Finally, Adams manipulated his prints in the darkroom to achieve the full range of tones, from brilliant white to darkest black. His splendid photographs raised public support for national parks and for the environmental movement in general.

Flowers and Gardens

Art gives us framed, composed, distilled, and transcendent images of flowers. And gardens are living sculptures, exotic refuges arranged for human enjoyment. Water is frequently a central motif in a garden of any size. Paintings of gardens attempt to capture that same sense of pleasure and release.

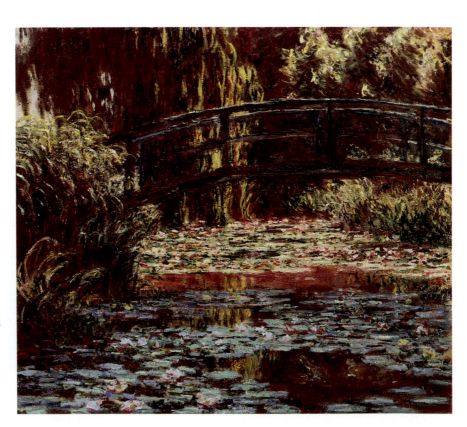

15.11 CLAUDE MONET. *Water Lily Pool*, France, 1900. Oil on canvas, 35' × 39³⁄₄". The Art Institute of Chicago. Mr. and Mrs. Lewis Larned Coburn Memorial Collection. © 2004 Artists Rights Society (ARS), New York/ADAGP, Paris.

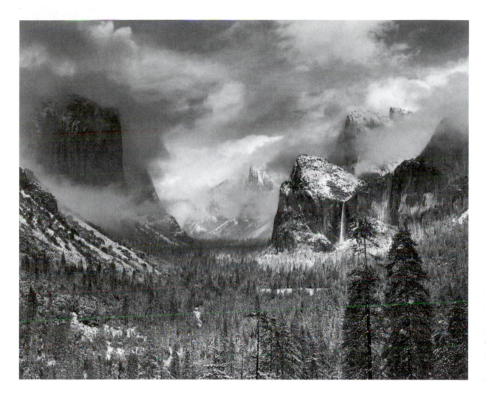

15.12 ANSEL ADAMS. *Clearing Winter Storm, Yosemite National Park, California, 1944,* USA, 1944. Photograph. Copyright © 1993 by the Trustees of the Ansel Adams Publishing Rights Trust/Corbis. All rights reserved.

Flowers are sources of beauty and vehicles for greater understanding. In Japan, flower arranging is considered an important art form, on the level of painting, calligraphy, and pottery. Flower paintings were particularly popular in both China and Japan. An example from China is *Apricot Blossoms,* dated early thirteenth century (Fig. 15.13), by Ma Yuan, a lyric painting with lines of poetry by Empress Yang, which read: "They greet the wind with artful charm;/Boasting pink beauty moist with dew." Ma Yuan's brushwork is refined. The blossoms are outlined in elegant curves, while the ink strokes that make the branch are crisp and angular. The twisting branches bend and display themselves in an off-balance, irregular composition that

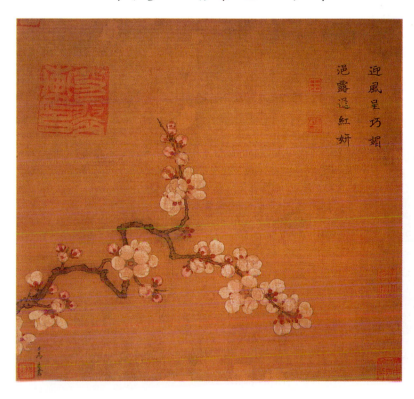

15.13 MA YUAN. *Apricot Blossoms,* China, Southern Song Dynasty, early 13th century. Album leaf with ink and color on silk, 10' high. National Palace Museum, Taiwan.

captures the unexpected forms in nature. Branch and poem both seem to be suspended in the space. The rich golden background and the delicate blossoms contrast with the dark branch. The beauty of the blossoms is simple and timeless, but the flowers last only a short time.

Ma Yuan was a professional court painter who collaborated with Empress Yang on other works as well. Such painters produced many small works, with poems penned by the emperor or his circle, to be given away as gifts and favors. Both poetry and painting were believed to have the capacity to express ineffable beauty. Ink wash paintings look simple, but they require long practice. Also, artists had to know how to paint the essence of apricot blossoms, to suggest the whole experience of the short-lived blooms, including their smell and their movement in the wind.

Flower paintings have also been very popular in the West. In Jan Bruegel's *Little Bouquet in a Clay Jar*, dated c. 1599 and also known as *Iris Bouquet* (Fig. 15.14), the bouquet fills the frame with a joyful display of vitality, not only in the fresh flowers but also in insects that abound. Bruegel layered his paint to create bright, subtle mixtures that captured the silkiness and

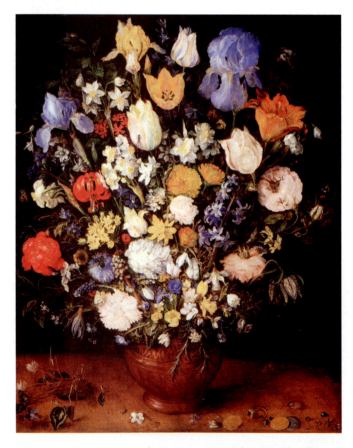

15.14 JAN BRUEGEL. *Little Bouquet in a Clay Jar*, Flanders, c. 1599. Oil on panel, 20" × 15¾". Kunsthistorisches Museum, Vienna. © Archivo Iconographico, S.A./Corbis.

translucency of petals. He claimed that they were lovelier than gold and gems, proving it with rings and coins at the lower right. Bruegel's flower arrangements never existed in real life. He combined local meadow flowers and exotic varieties in a single vase and included specimens that bloom in different climates and in different seasons. Yet he painted only from life, using a magnifying glass, sometimes waiting months for a certain bloom. Bruegel's flower paintings are like little pictures of paradise. Since medieval times, flowers had been sacred symbols: the iris, for example, represented Jesus, while the rose stood for Mary. The symbolism may have enriched the meaning of the painting for Bruegel's patrons.

Gardens were very popular among the ruling classes of Persia, central Asia, and Mughal India, all areas under Islamic rulers (these areas are modern-day Iraq, Iran, Afghanistan, Pakistan, and northern India). The painting, *Babur Supervising the Layout of the Garden of Fidelity*, c. 1590 (Fig. 15.15), illustrates many key concepts of Islamic gardens that represent Paradise. Water is channeled in four directions, representing the rivers of Paradise. The four resulting squares can be repeated or subdivided and yet maintain the integrity of the original layout. The proliferation of squares represents the abundance of Allah's creation. The outer wall provides privacy and protects the trees and birds from surrounding desert. The English word *paradise* comes originally from ancient Persian words for "walled garden."

Babur Supervising the Layout of the Garden of Fidelity is a book illumination from the memoirs of Emperor Babur, a botanist who took great interest in planning many gardens throughout the lands that he ruled. Here, he is dressed in gold and is directing engineers and workmen. For Babur, the gardens helped establish his identity and secure his power. Originally a minor prince, he conquered much of central Asia and northern India, claimed to descend from Genghis Khan and Tamerlane (Timur), and established gardens, which was a prerogative of princes. In addition, Babur believed his rule created order out of the chaos, and the garden's symmetry was a sign of that.

Connection Review the discussion of the Taj Mahal (Fig. 10.18, page 260) for more on Islamic gardens symbolizing Paradise.

In Japan, there are different traditions for gardens. One kind is planned around a pond or lake, and features rocks, winding paths, and bridges to delight the viewers with ever-changing vistas. A second tradition is exemplified in the *Ryoanji Zen Garden of Contemplation*, c. 1488–1499 (Fig. 15.16), in a courtyard of a

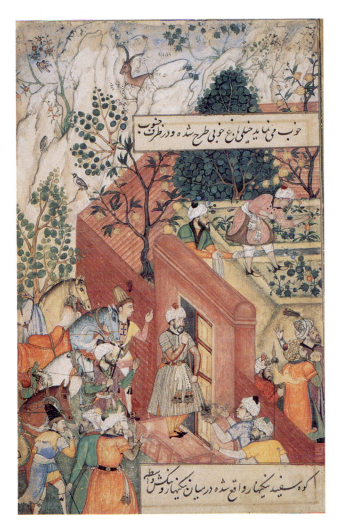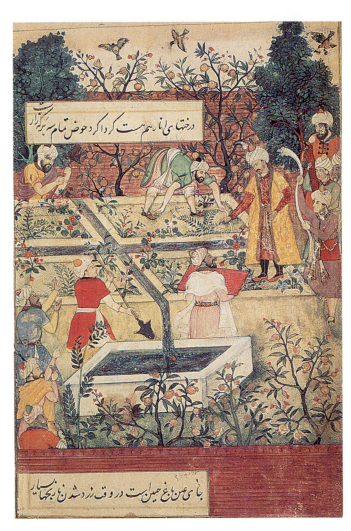

15.15 BISHNDAS (PORTRAITS BY NANHA). *Babur Supervising the Layout of the Garden of Fidelity,* India, c. 1590. Manuscript painting, gold and gouache on paper, 8³/₄" × 5³/₄". Mughal. Victoria and Albert Museum, London (IM 276–1913).

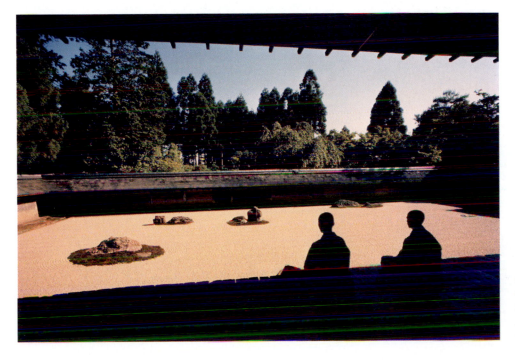

15.16 *Ryoanji Zen Garden of Contemplation,* Japan, c. 1488–1499. Walled garden, 99' wide × 33' deep. Daijuin Monastery, Kyoto. © Paul Chesley, Stone/Getty Images.

Buddhist temple in Kyoto. The rock garden reflects Zen Buddhist beliefs that the world is full of change and disorder, but meditation can lead to an understanding of the oneness of the universe. Visitors do not walk through the garden, but sit along the edge meditating on the raked quartz gravel that represents the void both of the universe and of the mind, while the dark rocks represent material substances and worldly events that float through those voids. The garden also represents an ocean journey with gravel raked to signify waves and boulders now standing for mountains. The fifteen large rocks, each of a distinctive shape and outline, are arranged such that visitors can see only fourteen at once from any angle. The fifteenth can be seen through the mind's eye after spiritual enlightenment. The *Ryoanji Zen Garden of Contemplation* is small, but because the largest boulder is at the front and the smaller at the back, there is an optical illusion of greater depth.

Earthworks and Site Pieces

The earth itself is sculptural material. Hundreds of years ago, native peoples of North America used dirt to construct large ceremonial mounds. Mounds and pyramids were relatively common in the ancient world, but the North American mounds are unique in being animal-shaped, like the *Serpent* (or *Snake*) *Mound*, c. 900–1300 (Fig. 15.17), in Ohio. The serpent's body follows a natural ridge near a small river. The distended jaw of the 1,400-foot-long serpent is pointing to the upper right. Its body is rhythmically curved and ends with its spiraling tail. An oval shape inside the serpent's jaw, measuring almost 79 by 158 feet, encircles a plateau topped with what may have been a stone altar. The builders must have had a great admiration for the snake to stamp its form so dramatically on their landscape, especially since they themselves never enjoyed an aerial view of it. Much labor was required to dig and carry earth to the site. In 1846, the snake's body was five feet high and thirty feet wide, but it has since eroded to four feet by twenty feet.

Contemporary **earthworks** are large-scale environmental pieces in which the earth itself is an important component. Earthwork artists not only use natural materials but also are responsive to their sites. The monumental scale of their work is an attribute of both

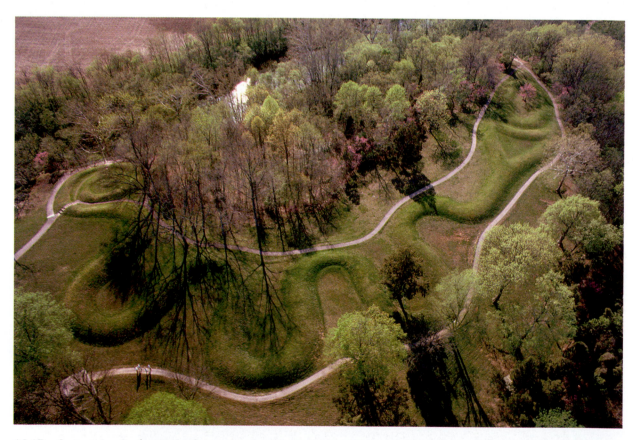

15.17 *Serpent* (or *Snake*) *Mound*, near Locust Grove, Ohio, c. 900–1300. Earthen sculpture, 1,400' long. Native American. © Richard A. Cooke/Corbis.

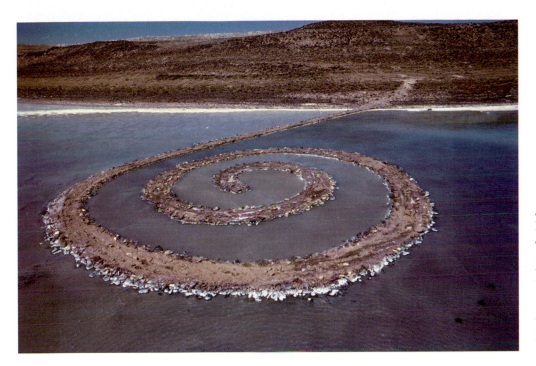

15.18 ROBERT SMITHSON. *Spiral Jetty,* USA, 1970. Earthwork; black rocks, salt crystals, earth, red water (algae), 1,500' long × 15' wide × 3½" high. Great Salt Lake, Utah. Courtesy James Cohan Gallery, New York. Art © Estate of Robert Smithson/Licensed by VAGA, New York.

ancient and modern art. There is a minimalist emphasis on simple shapes. Robert Smithson's *Spiral Jetty,* 1970 (Fig. 15.18), was made of rocks, dirt, salt, and water, extending into the flat, still surface of the Great Salt Lake. Smithson thought the spiral suggested an incredible potential force, like a dormant earthquake or a raging cyclone immobilized. Located in a remote site, *Spiral Jetty* was seen by few people and now is often invisible because of the rising lake level.

Smithson was interested in moving his art outside the gallery and away from traditional art materials. He saw his earthworks as unifying art and nature. Human design is, of course, evident in this work. Less evident is what went into making the piece, which involved heavy earth-moving equipment, engineering skills, and a number of workers.

The Lightning Field, 1971–1977 (Fig. 15.19), by Walter De Maria, consists of a large, flat plain

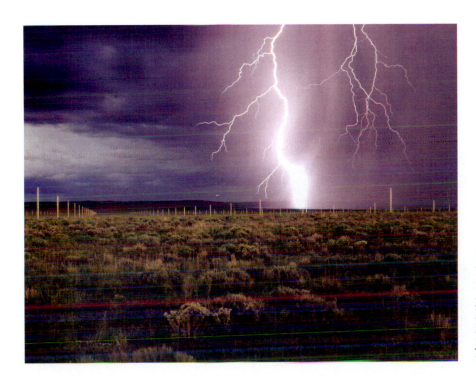

15.19 WALTER DE MARIA. *The Lightning Field*, USA, 1971–1977. 400 stainless steel poles, average height: 20'7"; land area: 1 mile × 1 kilometer in New Mexico. Photograph by John Cliett. © Dia Center for the Arts.

surrounded by mountains in New Mexico, and four hundred stainless steel poles arranged in a rectangular grid measuring one kilometer by one mile. The work requires some effort and endurance on the part of viewers. Like *Spiral Jetty, The Lightning Field* is remotely located. To see it, one must get permission from the Dia Foundation, which commissioned the work. Once on-site, the viewer waits for whatever happens. On clear days, the shiny, pointed poles catch the sun and glow against the natural vegetation. On stormy days, an occasional bolt of lightning may strike a pole, creating a fleeting, but dramatic, visual effect. *The Lightning Field* is better known through photographs that document it in different conditions than it is by actual experience. In this respect, the work is also a conceptual piece, existing primarily in the mind of the viewer, who contemplates the contrast between constructed and natural elements, the slow passage of time in the desolate environment, and the imagined experience of the work as known through various photographs.

Ecological Concerns

Artists who deal with the land and with landscape often have ecological concerns as part of their motivation to make art. We already saw this with Ansel Adams' *Clearing Winter Storm, Yosemite National Park, California*, 1944 (Fig. 15.12). And very possibly the creators of the *Serpent Mound* (Fig. 15.17) believed that the land was sacred.

Today, however, ecological concerns are clearly political and social issues. *The Social Mirror*, 1983 (Fig. 15.20), by Mierle Laderman Ukeles, focuses on the problem of waste caused by growing populations and consumerism. Ukeles had a clean New York City garbage truck fitted with gleaming mirrors, which transform it into a piece of sculpture. *The Social Mirror* also has a performance element, as in this photograph taken when the truck was part of a parade. The mirrors reflect the faces of the public, making them aware that they make trash and are responsible for its impact. The mirrors also glamorize the garbage truck and raise the status of sanitation workers, whose labor is not respected but is absolutely necessary. All of Ukeles's work since the mid-1970s has focused on ecological issues of maintenance, recycling, waste management, and landfill reclamation.

KNOWLEDGE

Humans systematically study and examine the world in an attempt to understand (and often control) its course. Although all art is a kind of knowing, this section focuses on art that deals directly with a body of knowledge. The first group consists of informative images, in which art helps explain a specific body of learning. The second group provides glimpses into areas of intuited knowing. Finally, art critiques what we consider knowledge.

These same ideas—scientific knowledge, intuited knowledge, or critiqued knowledge—are found in other historical and cultural areas. Finally, the wars of the twentieth century caused many to question the use of knowledge for destructive purposes.

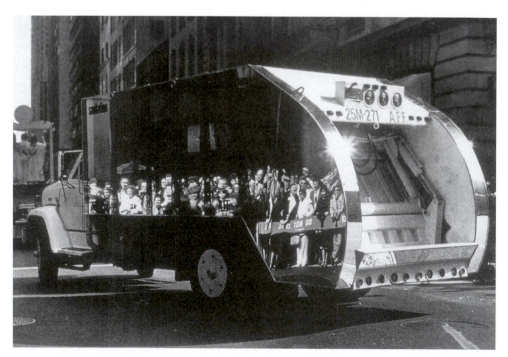

15.20 MIERLE LADERMAN UKELES. *The Social Mirror,* USA, 1983. 20-cubic-yard New York City garbage collection truck fitted with hand-tempered glass mirror with additional strips of mirrored acrylic. The New York City Department of Sanitation. Photo: Michael James O'Brien, courtesy of Barbara Gladstone Gallery. Courtesy Ronald Feldman Fine Arts, New York.

INFORMATIVE IMAGES

There are numerous examples of art that illustrate a specific body of knowledge. In the Low Countries in 1543, Andreas Vesalius of Brussels published *De Humani Corporis Fabrica*, a study of bones, muscles, and internal organs based on the dissection of human bodies, which is considered the beginning of modern science. Before that time, Western knowledge of the human body was based on ancient Greek, Roman, and medieval Arabic writings. Vesalius's studies corrected errors in old sources and added a tremendous amount of new knowledge. Important here, however, is that Vesalius created a major work of Western science and art.

The Fourth Plate of Muscles, dated 1543 (Fig. 15.21), shows that Vesalius gradually stripped the cadaver's outer muscles, but left them partly attached to make clear their relation to deeper muscles just exposed. Nonetheless, the body is standing as if alive and turning on one leg, because Vesalius wanted to show the living, moving body instead of the separated parts of the dead. Altogether, there are eight plates of muscles that make a lurid and fascinating narrative of dismemberment. In *The First Plate of Muscles*, the body stands like a classic statue, with an aura of grandeur mixed with a sense of pathos. Our *Fourth Plate* is both fascinating and horrible. By the time we arrive at the seventh and eighth plates, the disjointed cadaver is dangling on ropes. The works comment both on the wonder of the human body and on its inevitable disintegration.

De Humani Corporis Fabrica is a collaborative work. Vesalius created sketches and notes, which other artists polished. An unknown artist drew the landscape backgrounds, and an unknown professional made the engravings. Another famous illustrated study, also a collaborative work, is John James Audubon's *Birds of America*, a very large book that contained 435 plates. Robert Havell Jr. made most of the printing plates from Audubon's original watercolor studies. *Birds of America* is an outstanding work, both artistically and scientifically. *Carolina Paroquet*, 1827–1838 (Fig. 15.22),

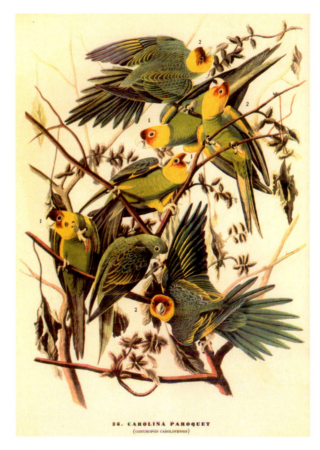

15.22 JOHN JAMES AUDUBON. *Carolina Paroquet*, USA, 1827–1838. Watercolor, 29½" × 21¼". Original for Plate #26 of *Birds of America*. North Carolina Museum of Art.

15.21 ANDREAS VESALIUS OF BRUSSELS. *The Fourth Plate of Muscles*, Flanders, published in 1543. Engraving from *De Humani Corporis Fabrica*.

shows several birds in scientific detail, with all the markings and in their habitat. Audubon eliminated the background to emphasize the birds' defining silhouettes. The birds are arranged in two arcs, one that echoes and one that opposes the direction of the main branch. The entire work is a decorative pattern that is enhanced by the bright colors.

Drawings in the service of science continue to be made. Even though photography might seem to be an adequate substitute for them, artist drawings can emphasize details that either do not stand out in photographs or become lost in the wealth of detail. Medical books are still enhanced with drawings, and medical illustrations are essential aids for study. Drawings also are used in studies of plants and insects and for very small items.

Our next example is an educational aid. *Hunter and Kangaroo*, c. twentieth century (Fig. 15.23), is from the Aboriginal people of Australia. The painting on bark shows the instant that the hunter's spear is about to enter the animal. The animal is shown in x-ray style, meaning that both external silhouette and internal organs are evident, to assist the hunter with the kill. We can see the kangaroo's backbone, heart, and intestines. The kangaroo is larger than the hunter, because it is the subject of the painting. This work, and others like it on bark and on the walls of cave shelters, was meant to be educational and, perhaps, ritually powerful. The hunter's body implies movement and energy. The specific form of cross-hatching associated paintings with individual clans and endowed the painted objects with spiritual force.

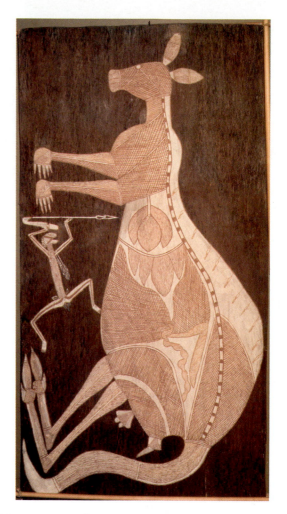

15.23 *Hunter and Kangaroo*, Australia, c. 20th century. Paint on bark, 51" × 32". Aboriginal. Oenpelli, Arnhemland. Private collection, Prague. © Werner Forman/Art Resource, NY.

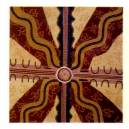

Connection Other Aboriginal paintings transmit knowledge from one clan member to another, as we saw in Paddy Carroll Tjungurrayi's Witchetty Grub Dreaming (Fig. 7.2, page 143).

Some works of art are experiential in a way that is both conceptually interesting and educational. For example, the Optical Art (or Op Art) style was popular in the United States and Europe in the 1960s. Bridget Riley's *Current*, 1964 (Fig. 15.24), is a precisely painted pattern of undulating lines that affect our visual perception. The work seems to pulsate and flicker, similar to experiments by psychologists who test the limits of visual perception to better understand how our vision works. The painting is also related to mathematics, as each line is a sinusoidal curve, in which the

interval between each dip increases as your eyes move away from the central horizontal axis. *Current* makes evident that our vision is physiological, because our eyes tire and hurt if we stare at the image too long. Its large size means that, up close, the work encompasses our entire visual field, both the sharp foveal vision at the center and our peripheral vision at the edges.

Connection Georges Seurat also relied on the science of optics in his work La Grande Jatte (Fig. 14.28, page 390).

ART AND INTUITED KNOWLEDGE

For humans, the "world" consists not only of the external environment but also of the internal realm of the mind and the metaphysical world. Art also deals with knowledge that humans can intuitively grasp without

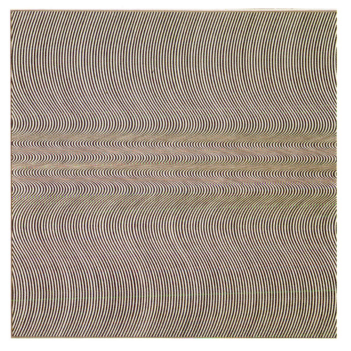

15.24 BRIDGET RILEY. *Current,* Great Britain, 1964. Synthetic polymer paint on composition board, approx. 58¹/₂" × 58¹/₂". The Museum of Modern Art, New York. © Digital Image The Museum of Modern Art/Licensed by Scala/Art Resource, NY.

necessarily being able to articulate it. This kind of knowing is the product of dreams, visions, and speculative guessing. It is not necessarily systematic, organized, or scientific.

Surrealism was an early-twentieth-century art movement in Europe and the United States that explored the unconscious, especially through dream imagery. Surrealism developed in part as a reaction to increased industrialization and to the horrors of World War I (see *Art and History in Context,* page 449). Surrealists posited that this unconscious or dream world is at least as real as, and probably more important than, the ordered and regimented external world in which humans function. For example, watches are devices of knowing and a means of maintaining external order. However, in his painting *The Persistence of Memory,* 1931 (Fig. 15.25), Salvador Dali presents watches that are limp and useless. The landscape stretches out, vast and empty. The sky glows in splendid blues and golds, while the still water reflects the sun-bathed cliffs like a flawless mirror. Nothing makes "sense," but Dali has painted everything with rigorous detail and convincing realism so that book-learned knowledge fades in importance, and we enter the eerie scene with a kind of intuited knowing. Swarming ants and a fly allude to the horror dimension in dreams.

Other works of art refer to knowledge that cannot be clearly articulated in words. Although Mark Rothko started as a figurative painter, he abandoned imagery that reflected the physical world for abstractions that hint at a sublime moment or transcendent state of being. This series of paintings contained large rectangles, sometimes only vaguely defined, against a field of other colors. Shapes and background emerge, float, and

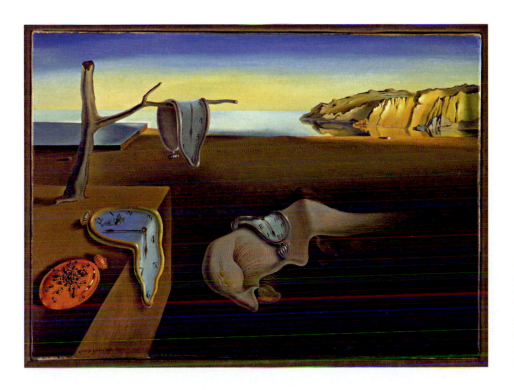

15.25 SALVADOR DALI. *The Persistence of Memory,* Spain, 1931. Oil on canvas, 9¹/₂" × 13". Museum of Modern Art/Licensed by SCALA/Art Resource, NY. © 2004 Salvador Dali, Gala-Salvador Dali Foundation/Artists Rights Society (ARS), New York.

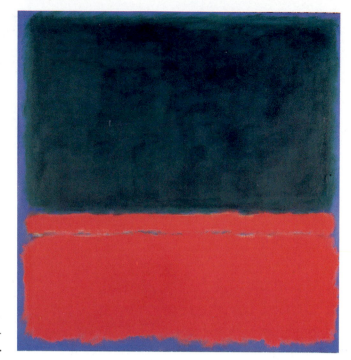

15.26 MARK ROTHKO. *Green, Red, Blue*, USA, 1955. Oil on canvas, 81½" × 77¾". Milwaukee Art Museum. Gift of Mrs. Harry Lynde Bradley (m1977.140). © 1998 Kate Rothko Prizel & Christopher Rothko/Artists Rights Society (ARS), New York.

glow, as in *Green, Red, Blue*, 1955 (Fig. 15.26). Rothko first applied thin "veils" of paint that soaked into and stained the canvas. He then applied many layers on top to create shapes that seem present and yet hard to define, hovering in a space that is real and yet not wholly knowable.

Rothko turned to abstraction as a means to address these broad and fundamental feelings/ideas, because figurative or narrative imagery was too specific and too limiting. In addition, Rothko's abstractions were meant to provide a kind of direct physical experience to the body. Another 1950s painter, Robert Motherwell, expressed these ideas in this way:

It is the social world that tends to appear irrational and absurd. . . . Nothing as drastic as abstract art could have come into existence save as the consequence of a most profound, relentless, unquenchable need. The need is for felt experience—intense, immediate, direct, subtle, unified, warm, vivid, rhythmic. If a painting does not make a human contact, it is for nothing. (O'Hara 1965:45, 50)

THE CRITIQUE OF LEARNING

Gods of the Modern World, 1932–1934 (Fig. 15.27), painted by José Clemente Orozco, is a strong critique of sterile knowledge. It is a warning against the aca-

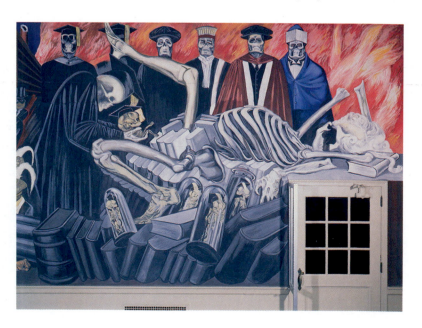

15.27 JOSÉ CLEMENTE OROZCO. *Gods of the Modern World*, Mexico, 1932–1934. Fresco, 126" × 176". Twelfth panel in a cycle of murals entitled *An Epic of American Civilization*. Baker Memorial Library, Dartmouth College, Hanover, New Hampshire. Commissioned by the Trustees of Dartmouth College, Hanover, New Hampshire.

demic who is completely occupied with research or learning that has no value outside academia. The black-clad university scholars line up like midwives to watch a skeleton give birth to miniature scholar-skeletons and stacks of obscure books. Orozco believed that sterile education passes for knowledge, but it actually keeps the young busy without giving them any real wisdom or understanding. The lurid red background suggests urgency, as if the world is on fire, but no guidance or concern can be found among the "learned." Their posture is aloof, frontal, stiff, and unresponsive. The style of the work is very striking. The rhythm of the lines is strong, from the verticals of the academic robes, to the black and white of the skeleton's ribs, to the swaying parade of book spines below. Significantly, this painting is in the library of a prestigious U.S. college, to be seen by all students and professors.

In *Breaking of the Vessels,* 1990 (Fig. 15.28), artist Anselm Kiefer looks at knowledge on many different levels. The piece consists of a three-tiered bookshelf filled with massive volumes whose pages are made of sheets of lead. The books sag perilously, some about to fall from the shelf. Glass shards from the books have fallen, and their shattering has covered the floor all around. Above, written on a half-circle of glass, are the Hebrew words *Ain Soph,* meaning "the Infinite." Dangling copper wires connect thick stumps projecting from the sides. The piece is seventeen feet high and weighs over seven tons. The shattered glass covers several square yards of floor all around.

The piece contrasts the infinity and clarity of the spiritual realm with the thick, dull, ponderous containers of human knowledge. Human knowledge, as contained in and symbolized by the books, is limited and sagging under its own weight. Visually, the heavy lead pages are like the blackened pages of burned books. The knowledge contained within them seems inaccessible to most people; the book format hides knowledge rather than exposes it. The books seem as though they might even be rotting away, ready to crash to the floor. The sheer mass of the sculpture becomes a metaphor for the accumulated struggles to acquire and preserve human knowledge. But books and their contents disintegrate. The work alludes to the fact that all human endeavor is cyclical like nature; it is subject to periods of decline and entropy that eventually lead to regeneration.

The title *Breaking of the Vessels* refers to mystical Hebrew writings (the Kabbalah) that tell of the awesome, uncontainable Divine essence whose power filled and shattered the fragile vessels of the universe upon Creation. The title symbolizes the introduction of evil

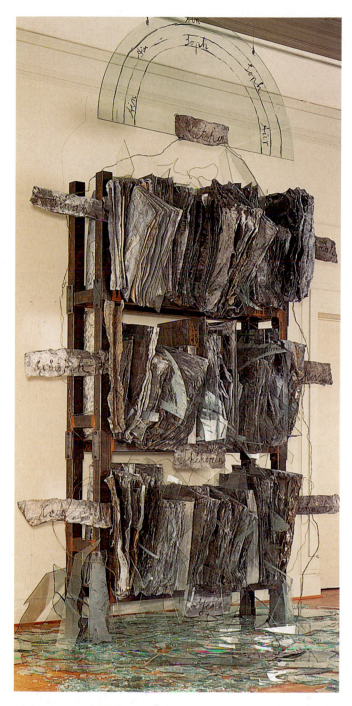

15.28 ANSELM KIEFER. *Breaking of the Vessels.* Lead, iron, glass, copper wire, charcoal, and aquatec, 17' high. Germany, 1990. St. Louis Art Museum. Courtesy Gagosian Gallery.

into the world. It also refers to the atrocities of *Kristallnacht* (the Night of Crystal or the Night of Broken Glass), when the Nazis vandalized and terrorized Jewish neighborhoods in Germany and Austria in November 1938.

TECHNOLOGY

Technology is the last component of the outside world in this chapter. The first artworks regard technological advances as good, healthy, exciting, and even aesthetically pleasing. The second group evaluates our constructed world for both its positive and negative impacts.

TECHNOLOGICAL ADVANCES

In *Farm Scene*, c. 1000–1240 (Fig. 15.29), we see that technology has long been part of human history and has often made life easier. A farmer and his wife operate a foot-driven pump that diverts water to flood their rice field. Beneath a shed, a water buffalo turns a larger pump for similar results. A boy fishes in the background, a boat is moored to a riverbank, and a footbridge spans the water between clumps of land. Pumps, bridges, boats, and fishing poles—all pieces of technology—fit comfortably into the overall scene. Well-placed trees shade all workers, and the generous river waters stretch out for long distances in the background. Human handiwork and nature seem in harmony. The emphasis on horizontal lines, the orderly diagonals in space, the blended ochres, greens, and browns all turn what could be a scene of hard labor into an image of peaceful coexistence.

When we consider technology today, however, we most likely think of the world since the Industrial Revolution of the nineteenth century and more recent

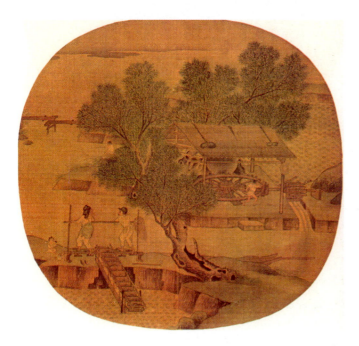

15.29 *Farm Scene*, China, Song Dynasty, c. 1000–1240. Ink and color on silk. C.C. Wang, New York.

developments in transportation, manufacturing, and communication (see *Art and History in Context*, page 426). Technology advanced rapidly in the early twentieth century, causing cities to expand and producing structures in shapes and sizes never seen before. Particularly striking were bridges, factories, skyscrapers, ocean liners, and fast trains. These forms inspired many artists, among them Fernand Léger, who was also influenced by Cubism. His painting *The City*, dated 1919 (Fig. 15.30), was a tribute to geometric industrial structures and the precision and efficiency of machines, all of which struck Léger as forms of beauty. The city of Léger's painting is rendered in abstract forms, but speaks of its concrete, steel, electrical power, and transportation systems. The repetition of colors and shapes suggests the staccato of city sounds. Letterforms refer to billboard advertisements. The colors are bright and artificial. Other shapes resemble a jumble of roofs and walls, bridge trestles, or factory smokestacks. Even humans are robotlike, as their bodies are composed of geometric volumes. The space seems shallow, as all forms are compressed and pushed forward, in contrast to the open horizon and distant spaces in paintings of rural scenes.

David Smith's *Cubi XXVI*, 1965 (Fig. 15.31), is abstract art imitating some qualities of machines. Smith used industrial fabrication to create this stainless steel sculpture and others in this series. He learned this technology as a factory worker. His works are marked by a machine aesthetic, and thus his processes and materials are the same as those that would be used to make a locomotive. The large, geometric shapes of stainless steel cubes, rectangles, and cylinders look machine-manufactured, with clean edges, flawless welding, and precise fits. They resemble mass-produced items. The structure, unsoftened, is bluntly emphasized. Strong, balanced forms seem to defy their weight. The metal surfaces, however, were abraded to give them a spiral pattern that seems to dissolve the solidity of the volumes. Smith emphasized gesture, so that the sculpture seems to be striding along, like an animated stick figure of a walking person. The forms suggest vectors in space, some in opposition to others. The work also suggests forces suspended and in movement, like components of a machine.

EVALUATING THE CONSTRUCTED WORLD

We have already seen Ukeles's *Social Mirror*, which dealt with consumerism and its impact on the land. The following artists present technology to us in a way that makes clear its mixed impact.

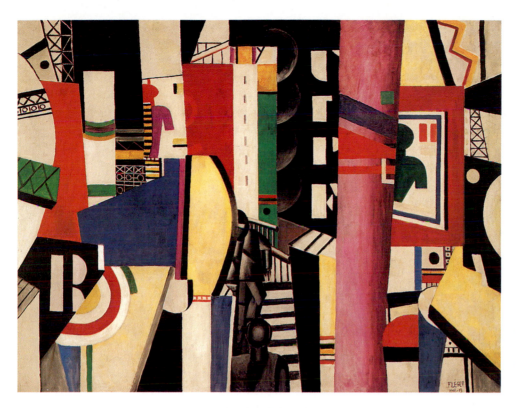

15.30 FERNAND LÉGER. *The City*, France, 1919. Oil on canvas, 91" × 117½". Philadelphia Museum of Art. © 2004 Artists Rights Society (ARS), New York/ADAGP, Paris.

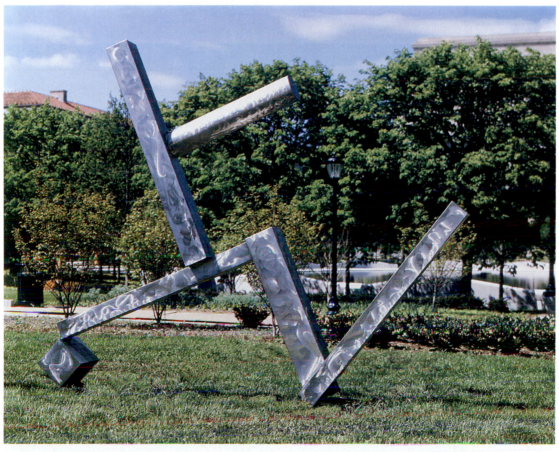

15.31 DAVID SMITH. *Cubi XXVI*, USA, 1965. Steel, approx. 10' × 12'6" × 2'3". Alisa Mellon Bruce Fund. Image © National Gallery of Art, Washington, D.C. Art © David Smith/Licensed by VAGA, New York, NY.

In *The Fighting Temeraire Tugged to Her Last Berth to Be Broken Up,* 1838 (Fig. 15.32), Joseph Mallord William Turner distinguishes between innovation and progress. He painted the tall, shimmering, white form of the elegant sailing vessel against the new powerful tugboat, which is squat, dark, and smoky. By this time, sailing vessels were obsolete for war or commerce, superseded by more modern technology. Turner marked the *Temeraire*'s passing by the splendid glowing sunset (marred by the tug's smoke!)—both ship and sunset were soon to be lost forever. Turner was famous for his facility with paint; thick blobs become an array of golden clouds, brushy strokes blend where mist meets blue sky. The scene is a conflict between light and darkness, and light is just about to be eclipsed.

Without a doubt, Turner was romanticizing archaic technology, responding to the latest innovation that seemed ugly to him. He painted this work in his old age, as a sign of his own life drawing to a close. The beautiful colors and expressive handling of the paint convey the poignant feeling of beauty and loss, transforming an otherwise nondescript harbor scene along the Thames River in London into a picture of poetic beauty.

Jean Tinguely's *Homage to New York,* 1960 (Fig. 15.33), looked like a whimsical, playful, absurd machine. Tinguely constructed it with the help of an engineer, using junkyard machine parts. The work was designed so that it would destroy itself in one evening in the gardens of the Museum of Modern Art in New York City, which it did, but not according to plan. A fire in some parts necessitated the unscheduled participation of the

New York City Fire Deparment. Tinguely was mocking the machine, and yet celebrating it for qualities very different from Léger's *The City.* To Tinguely, the machine was not magnificent because of its clean design or its efficiency, but for its unexpected results. Machines never work in exactly the way that we expect them to, nor can we anticipate all the results of using them. Tinguely's satirical work references the frenzy of the machine age and, by extension, the city of New York at that time, which in some ways could be seen as a large machine, absurd in its size, its complexity, its haphazard workings, and its entertainment value.

Connection Homage to New York *was both an environmental sculpture and a happening. For more on such works, see the sections "Engaging All the Senses" and "Chance/Improvisation/Spontaneity" in Chapter 2.*

For us now, technology includes computers and televisions. For nearly forty years, artist Nam June Paik has been exploring what that means and its impact on us as humans. *Megatron,* 1995 (Fig. 15.34), is composed of over two hundred video screens divided into two groups, displaying video clips, digital distortions, and animation sequences. Paik's images are from high and popular culture, from East and West, and include scenes from the Olympic Games, experimental art events, rock concerts, and Korean rituals as well as sexual images, scenes of aggression, and, sometimes, simply a wall of white screens or a display of national flags. Visually, the piece is very dense, as images are juxtaposed or tumble one

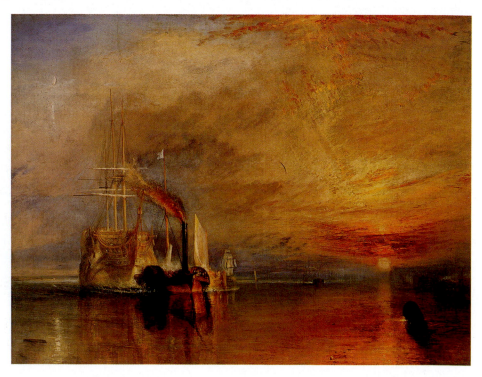

15.32 JOSEPH MALLORD WILLIAM TURNER. *The Fighting Temeraire Tugged to Her Last Berth to Be Broken Up,* England, 1838. Oil on canvas, 35¼" × 48". The National Gallery, London. © The Tate Gallery/Art Resource, NY.

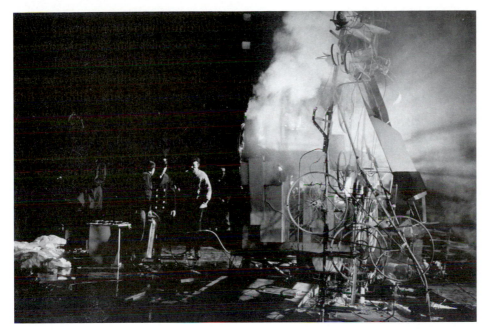

15.33 JEAN TINGUELY. *Homage to New York: A Self-Constructing, Self-Destructing Work of Art*, Switzerland, 1960. Mixed media sculpture. Photograph of the work as it self-destroyed in New York City on March 17, 1960. Photo by David Gahr. © 2004 David Gahr © 2004 Artists Rights Society (ARS), New York/ADAGP, Paris.

after another. Pictures are even nested inside each other, as can be seen in the upper left, in which the large shape of a flying bird is composed of smaller images. *Megatron*'s visual assault is matched by the cacophonous sound track. Yet over time, the piece may have a lulling or perhaps hypnotic effect.

The viewer is restricted to the role of spectator, dwarfed and essentially silenced by the forceful presence of *Megatron*. The accumulation of screens and the large size of *Megatron* speak of the imposing presence of the mass media in everyday life, a feature in the home, in business, in sports, in entertainment, in commerce, and so on, where again the viewer is a spectator only. The making of *Megatron* was itself a technological feat, as images are fed by laser disc players and controlled by seven computers in such a way that sequences rarely repeat. In this way, the piece reflects our everyday lives, in which we are bombarded by disjointed but familiar images while flipping through television channels, zipping past freeway billboards at sixty-five miles per hour, or surfing the Internet.

This piece and others by Paik are about the act of perception, how reality is presented, and how we as viewers reintegrate the random images. To Paik, the recombinations and dislocations of images are potentially playful and constructive. He sees his pieces as creative ways of thinking about the reshaping of our lives and becoming engaged in the diversity and variety in contemporary culture.

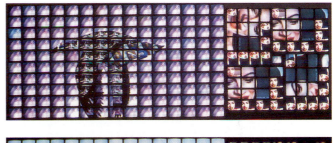

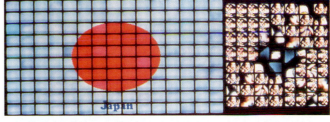

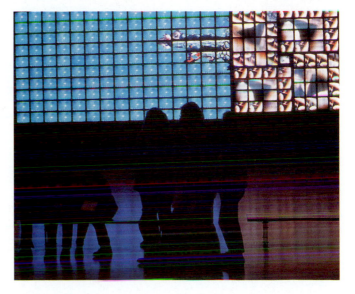

15.34 NAM JUNE PAIK, in collaboration with Shuya Abe. *Megatron* (three views), Korea, 1995. Eight-channel video and two-channel sound installation in two parts, overall size 12' × 33' × 2'. Courtesy Holly Solomon Gallery, New York.

Three major trends marked this period: industrialism, modernization, and nationalism. Older western European nations continued to build their colonial empires in Africa and Asia. The years from 1850 to 1914 marked the high point of colonialism, even with increased resistance and colonial independence movements. Colonies provided raw material for industrialized nations. The Industrial Revolution, which had already begun in Great Britain, spread to other areas of western Europe and the United States. The Industrial Revolution brought amazing advances in technology as well as profound social changes, including the development of a large middle class and an industrial working class, the creation of factories, great increases in population, and mass migration into urban areas, as reflected in Fernand Léger's *The City* (Fig. 15.30). Scientific advances were important, especially in medicine and physics. Science also influenced art, especially Impressionism and Futurism. Claude Monet's style of painting

in *Water Lily Pool* (Fig. 15.11) is based in part on optics.

The newly powerful middle class enjoyed greater educational opportunities and leisure time, as seen in Renoir's *The Luncheon of the Boating Party*, but the working class was oppressed. Karl Marx coauthored the *Communist Manifesto* in 1848, and the labor movement was agitating for fair wages, safe working conditions, and reasonable hours for workers. Civil rights movements for racial and gender equality grew in power throughout this period.

Nationalism is devotion to one's country, especially promoting that country's interests and culture above all others. Nationalistic fervor saw the formation of modern nations in South America, central Europe, and the Balkans. In the United States, the Civil War (1861–1865) both split and then reinforced the national identity.

In 1868, the old shogun rulers of Japan were overthrown. Emperor Meiji rose to

Map 9   World War II in Asia and the Pacific. Courtesy of Replogle Globes, Inc., Broadview, IL.

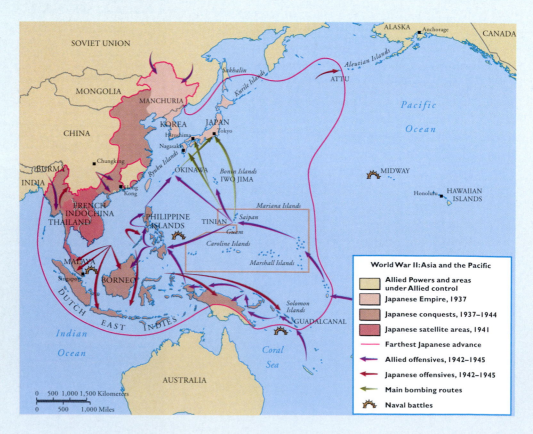

power and began the rapid industrialization of Japan and modernization of its society. In 1874, Japan began a period of expansion in Asia, following the model of Western colonial empires. Japan envisioned itself as the dominant power in Asia.

The Great War (World War I) broke out in 1914 and lasted until 1918. Its causes were many, including increased friction among European nation-states, entangling alliances, internal conflicts caused by ethnic groups that had not yet achieved nationhood, and competition for colonies and trade. The war and the terms of the peace treaty embittered Germany, one of the losing nations. Art movements such as Dada and Surrealism developed in response to the horrors of World War I, the crumbling social order, and increased industrialization, as seen in Salvador Dali's *The Persistence of Memory* (Fig. 15.25). Other artworks were more pointedly critical, like José Clemente Orozco's *Gods of the Modern World* (Fig. 15.27).

Imperial rule was beginning to crumble. The 1912 revolution in China ended centuries of dynastic rule. The Russian Revolution of 1917 created a Communist state and ended the rule of the czars. The centuries-old Ottoman Empire, centered in Turkey, was broken up in 1919. Unfortunately, totalitarianism in other forms was on the rise. All people were subject to the absolute authority of the state in Stalinist Russia and Nazi Germany in the 1930s, and there was a rise of dictatorships in Latin America. Fascism dominated in Spain and Italy as well.

The 1930s and 1940s were periods of great hardship and destruction. The Great Depression was a decade of severe financial difficulty for industrialized nations, and many people suffered. The depression's unemployment and homelessness, coupled with extreme nationalism and the rise of totalitarian regimes, led to World War II. A bloody prelude to that war was the Spanish Civil War, waged by Fascists and Republicans/Communists from 1936-1939, each side heavily aided by foreign countries. Beginning in 1931, Japan, Italy, and Germany began seizing lands around them, until war was declared in Europe in 1939 and in the Pacific in 1941. When the amazingly destructive war finally ended in 1945, at least 17

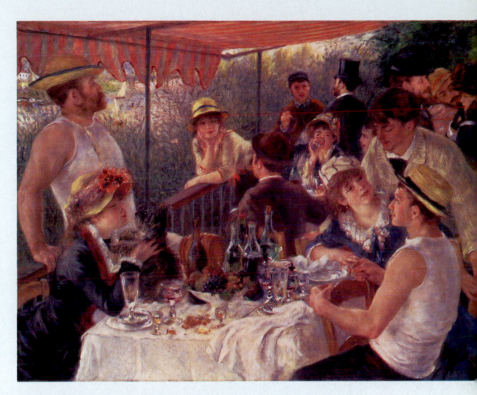

15.35   PIERRE AUGUSTE RENOIR. *The Luncheon of the Boating Party*, France, 1881. Oil on canvas, 51" × 68". The Phillips Collection, Washington, D.C. The European middle class enjoyed greater leisure time in the late 19th century, including pleasurable outings in nature, as we see in this painting.

million soldiers and perhaps as many as 40 million civilians were dead, including the millions who died in German concentration camps.

The years immediately following World War II saw the founding of the United Nations, the destruction of old European colonial empires, and the establishment of Communist China (1948). Also established was the modern state of Israel, which displaced the Palestinians.

Thus, we see that today's trend toward globalization was already under way in 1850, as the foundations were laid for the global economy, global trade and resources, and global political entanglements. Nevertheless, many areas of the world remained unindustrialized. For example, in central Australia, artists in the Aboriginal culture produced works such *Hunter and Kangaroo* (Fig. 15.23). Within industrialized nations, artworks such as Ansel Adams' *Clearing Winter Storm, Yosemite National Park, California, 1944* (Fig. 15.12) glorified the beauty of the natural land.

— Timeline

Domestication of horse and camel	**4000 BCE**
	3500
Wheel appears—Mesopotamia	
Bronze casting in Sumeria	
	2000
First library in Sumeria	
First libraries in China	**1700**
China: The Silk Trade	**600**
	300
Library at Alexandria	
Paper first used in China	**100 CE**
Elephants first used in warfare	
Printing invented in China	**200**
Islamic libraries established	
Temple libraries in Japan	
	800
	1000
Moslem paper mills in Spain	
Medieval universities	
	1300
Renaissance in Europe	**1400**
Gutenberg's press	
	1500
	1600

Ashurbanipal II Killing Lions
Relief (Olmec)

Spider (Nazca)

Vessel in the Form of a Monkey
Serpent (or Snake) Mound
Farm Scene

Ma Yuan: *Apricot Blossoms*
The Unicorn in Captivity

Ryoanji Zen Garden of Contemplation
Vesalius: *The Fourth Plate of Muscles*
Sheng Maoye: *Beyond the Solitary Bamboo Grove*
Bruegel: *Little Bouquet in a Clay Jar*
Bishndas: *Babur Supervising the Layout of the Garden of Fidelity*

Industrial Revolution begins	
Steam locomotive—Europe	**1800**
Early experiments in photography	
Invention of dynamite	
Edison and the light bulb	
Labor Movement	
Women's Rights Movement	
First flight, Wright Brothers	**1900**
World War I	
	1920
Great Depression	
Early experiments with computers	
World War II	**1940**
	1960
	1970
Desktop publishing	**1980**
Digital imaging	
The Internet	**1990**
	1999

Shaman's Amulet
Constable: *The Haywain*
Audubon: *Carolina Paroquet*
Turner: *The Fighting Temeraire*
Monet: *Water Lily Pool*
Hunter and Kangaroo
Léger: *The City*
Orozco: *Gods of the Modern World*
Dali: *The Persistence of Memory*
Adams: *Clearing Winter Storm, Yosemite National Park, California, 1944*
Rothko: *Green, Red, Blue*
Tinguely: *Homage to New York*
Riley: *Current*
Smith: *Cubi XXVI*
Smithson: *Spiral Jetty*
De Maria: *The Lightning Field*
Ukeles: *The Social Mirror*
Kiefer: *Breaking of the Vessels*
Paik: *Megatron*
Ofili: *Monkey Magic—Sex, Money and Drugs*

Artists use animals to reflect many human qualities and the human need for power. Art also shows us how much we admire animal beauty.

The land—its natural state and what we do with it—is of acute interest to artists. Landscape paintings and photographs are popular in many cultures. Humans also love to arrange plants, rocks, water, and ground into gardens that become pieces of the earthly paradise. Plant forms are also admired in art, and flowers are symbols for the beauty and fleeting nature of life. The ground itself is sculptural material in site-specific work. Other artists examine the negative impact that human technology has had on the environment.

Art is a means to deliver knowledge, either as single illustrations or in books. Some art communicates knowledge that cannot be clearly articulated; some is intended to give us the experience of the sublime. Artists also make judgments on the value of esoteric knowledge.

Finally, technology is examined in art. Artists working in many media show us the good and the bad results of our fascination with machines.

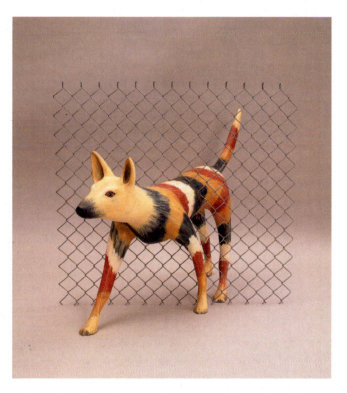

15.36   LIN ONUS. *Dingoes: Dingo Proof Fence* (detail from the series *Dingoes*). Synthetic polymer on fiberglass, wire, metal, 37 1/2" high. Aboriginal. Australia, 1989. National Gallery of Australia, Canberra. © 2004 Artists Rights Society (ARS), New York / VI$COPY, Australia.

FOOD FOR THOUGHT

It is possible to think of humans as distinct and separate from nature and technology, or as part of these larger systems. Networks are the basis of human existence on the cellular level and in the nervous, lymphatic, and circulatory systems. However, our body's survival depends on (and is sometimes threatened by) larger networks such as the earth's ecosystems and by technological systems that we have constructed, such as transportation and energy grids. Databases construct our legal and financial identities. Our bodies are composed of the same materials as the animals, plants, dirt, and the stars. Is the real "you" in your body, or the virtual self of the Internet?

- *How much do we model the systems we make—whether the freeways or the Internet—upon systems within our own bodies?*

- *Because of ecological changes, medicines, and machines, how are we different from humans of centuries ago? How is that reflected in art?*

- *Compare the earliest artwork produced by humankind with the most recent. What conclusions can you draw?*

- *Are humans separate from animals and technology, or are we all evolving together?*

- *Is the human sphere separate from the animal realm? Consider the long-term relationships that can exist between humans and horses, or between humans and dogs.*

- *In some cases, a group of people feel such an affinity with an animal that they use it to represent themselves and their interests, as in Lin Onus' Dingoes: Dingo-Proof Fence (Fig. 15.36). This work upholds the wild animals' right to the land, which also supports the aboriginal way of life in Australia. Can you think of other art of animals that functions in this way?*

Your Thomson Online Resources

 Go to **ArtExperience Online** for the Flashcards, Quiz, and Study Guide for this chapter.

Entertainment and Visual Culture

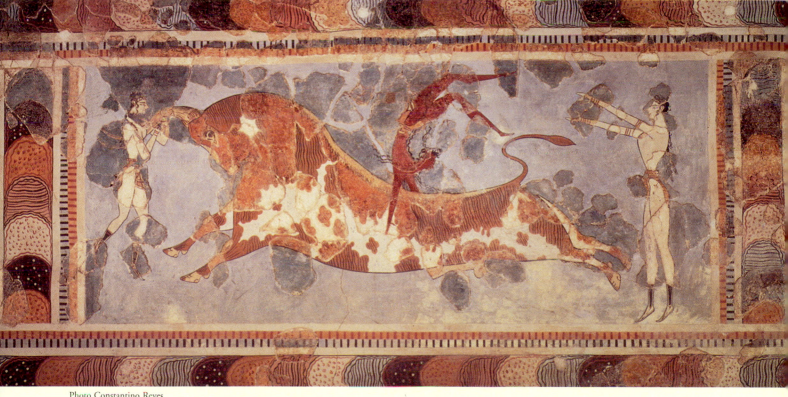

Photo Constantino Reyes.

INTRODUCTION

The art in this chapter is intertwined with the performing arts, popular culture, and entertainment. Artistic buildings enhance many leisure activities, like concerts, sporting events, and exhibitions.

*Some forms of art and entertainment can be analyzed together as part of **Visual Culture** which is the totality of images and visual objects produced in industrial and postindustrial nations, and the ways that those images are disseminated, received, and used.*

- What are the basic concepts associated with visual culture?
- How has architecture facilitated the performing and visual arts?
- In what areas do the visual and performing arts overlap?
- What forms of art are very close to entertainment forms?
- What kinds of imagery have artists made that depict forms of entertainment?

THE SCOPE OF VISUAL CULTURE

Visual media are huge in everyday life. Images come to us from art, advertising, information design, gaming, news organizations, science, and education. Researchers in biology, medicine, and astronomy are making visualizations of things that are not visible. Surveillance is part of the public space. Ordinary people are constantly making and circulating images with cell phones and camcorders. Visual culture scholars study visual media of all sorts as well as the "centrality of vision and the visual world in producing meanings, establishing and maintaining aesthetic values, gender stereotypes and power relations within cultures" (Rogoff 1998:14). Image competes with word as our main mode of communication and of understanding the global culture. Scholars also maintain that our eager consumption of images fills our lives with virtual experiences that replace real life.

"Seeing" is not simply the physical workings of our eyes, but a cognitive process that is associated with pleasure, anxiety, power, and fantasy. Vision is associated with the **gaze** (discussed on page 197 in relation to gender and on page 366 in relation to race). Who is looking? Who is being looked at? What power relationships are implied in that visual event?

Visual culture is also concerned with **spectacle,** or any kind of public show on a grand scale. This event could be the opening ceremonies for the Olympic Games, the miles of neon lights on the Las Vegas strip, a celebrity making an entrance, or a Hollywood blockbuster movie with special effects and enhanced sound. The value of these objects or events lies in their images.

Visual culture is transnational. In some cases, it may not make sense to identify the source of some art by geography. If an artist grew up in Tokyo, now lives in Paris, and makes art installations in Rio de Janeiro, is that art Japanese, French, or Brazilian? Pictures reflect the complexity, ambiguities, and contradictions of the world today. No one "world picture" comes through the study of visual culture; rather, we experience multiple viewpoints and meanings may shift from person to person, and from country to country. Things are becoming more complex rather than simple (see *Art and History in Context* on page 452).

Connection Chapter 4 provided more in-depth discussion for deriving meaning, or multiple meanings, from artworks.

Visual culture sits at the intersection of art history, anthropology, and sociology. It is a field of very broad inquiry, but some of it touches quite directly on art and popular culture. Why is there high and low art in Western cultures? How is the border between the two areas changing all the time? Why might the art of one culture be considered "more advanced" than the art of another? Why are some images considered good art or bad art, or good entertainment or bad entertainment? To the visual culture scholar, an image is valuable "in the circulation of the image, its proliferation and durability in the whole sphere of visual culture" (Mitchell 2001:18).

Visual culture studies more than just art and entertainment, which are the subjects of this chapter. Yet art, popular culture, and entertainment provide a good introduction to visual culture studies. Some of the artworks in this chapter predate the industrial era and, thus, are technically not part of the visual studies field. However, these examples are important for our historical understanding of art and entertainment.

ARCHITECTURE FOR ENTERTAINMENT

Structures built for culture and entertainment are significant parts of visual culture. Museums and performance spaces must function well and comfortably accommodate their audiences. In addition, these spaces must meet the aesthetics, expectations, and values of the audience for the activities that happen inside.

Art and architecture give visual form to sports activities, which helps to move the meaning of these activities beyond one of simple leisure or game playing. Sports often have political or religious implications, not only in long-past cultures but also today; for example, sports commentators talk of personalities and human drama rather than simply describing the play-by-play.

"HOUSES" FOR THE ARTS

In early art we can find precedents for what we see today in our visual environment. Ancient Greek comedies and tragedies were originally part of ritual festivals dedicated to the deity Dionysos. They were first performed in natural settings, in the hollows of hills. Eventually, magnificent theaters were designed to add visual significance to these dramas, like the *Theater at Epidauros* (Fig. 16.1), designed by Polykleitos the Younger around 350 BCE. It is a theater of great size (387 feet in diameter) and formal grandeur that suggests the Classical Greek ideal shape, the circle. The *theatron*, or seating area, could accommodate 12,000 spectators on its fifty-five tiers of stone benches, which rise at a high

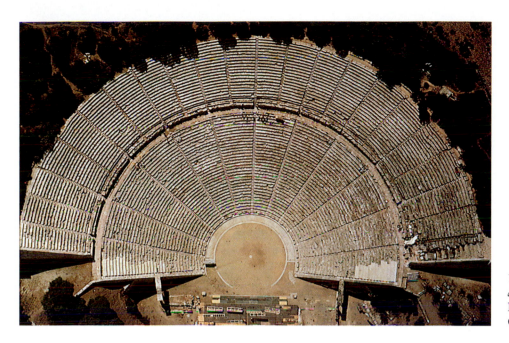

16.1 POLYKLEITOS. *Theater at Epidauros*, Greece, c. 350 BCE. Hellenic Ministry of Culture.

angle for clear views and good acoustics for all. Stairs connect each section for easy access. At the very center was the orchestra platform, a circle in which the chorus would dance near or around the altar of Dionysus. Behind the orchestra is a long, rectangular structure used for the stage, backed by the **skene,** a building that provided a backdrop for the plays and contained dressing rooms and scenery. These ritual plays included music and dance, with actors wearing elaborate costumes with oversized masks to emphasize the characters' emotions and amplify voices through megaphone-like mouths.

Not only dramas but also opera, ballet, and art exhibitions were housed in structures specifically designed to magnify the importance of the event and to heighten the audience's enjoyment of a special occasion. In the nineteenth century, houses for the arts were often very ornate or built in the Classical style to resemble a Greek temple. In that era, it was important to link art back to the Classics, to amplify their importance. Today, houses for the arts continue to be made, but in styles that reflect modern values of innovation, bold movement, or future potential. The *Opera House* (Fig. 16.2) in Sydney, Australia, stands on the harbor's edge

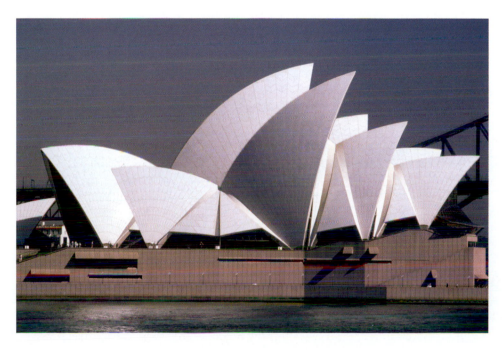

16.2 JOERN UTZON. *Opera House*, Sydney, Australia, 1959–1972. Reinforced concrete; highest shell 200' high. © Roger Ressmeyer/ Corbis.

to greet visitors arriving by air, land, or sea. The Danish architect Joern Utzon thought of it as "functional sculpture." Called **organic architecture,** this style was rooted in the work of Frank Lloyd Wright (see Fig. 16.3). Utzon was also influenced by the platform architecture of Mesoamerica. The cascading vaults suggest the billowing of the sailboats in Sydney Harbor, and they are faced with gleaming ceramic tile, adding jewel-like reflections to the fluid forms. Windows are covered by two laminated layers of amber glass, creating a quiet interior with spectacular views of the surrounding harbor. The concert halls, theaters, auditoriums, and recording studio are all lined with rich natural woods, both for aesthetics and acoustics. The Sydney *Opera House* took twelve years to complete, due to controversy over the original design, cost overruns, scandals, and Utzon's resignation.

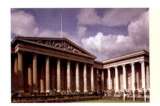

Connection The British Museum *(Fig. 6.8, page 127) is an example of a nineteenth-century house for the arts built to resemble a Greek templee.*

Frank Lloyd Wright's *Solomon R. Guggenheim Museum* (Fig. 16.3) is another example of organic architecture, here designed to exhibit art. Its rounded form encloses a ramp that spirals around an empty center that is ninety feet wide. Certainly the museum creates a striking visual image. The viewer takes an elevator to the top and then walks down past individual bays with paintings, allowing closer focus on small groups of artworks. Yet, critics point out that this space does not work well for showing paintings and sculptures. Artwork can be seen only up close or from all the way across the central open well. There is no in-between vantage point, and some works suffer. Rather than choosing their own course, viewers must see the works in the predetermined order. Because the floor slopes, the exhibition space does not work well for sculptures, and paintings appear askew against the curved wall.

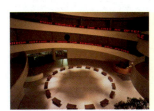

Connections For a view of the inside of the Solomon R. Guggenheim Museum, *see Jenny Holzer's installation* Untitled (Selected Writings) *in Figure 12.27 (page 326).*

Frank Gehry's *Walt Disney Concert Hall* (Fig. 16.4), 2003, in Los Angeles, is a recent entry among world-class music centers. His design echoes many of the basic ideas of visual culture. Trained as a sculptor, Gehry creates buildings that are often irregular, colliding, sculptural, and perhaps even disorienting because they are asymmetrical or have no apparent central point. The concert hall's structural systems are disguised under the curving stainless-steel surface. Gehry has said, "I approach each building as a sculptural object, a spatial container, a space with light and air, a response to context and appropriateness of feeling and spirit. To this container, this sculpture, the user brings

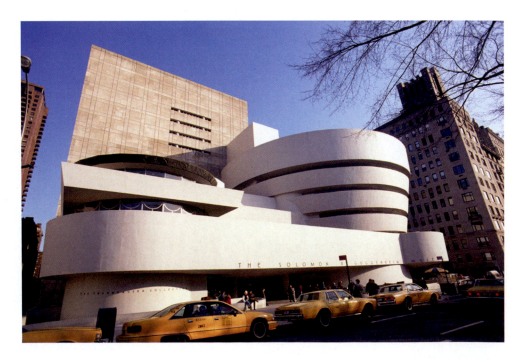

16.3 FRANK LLOYD WRIGHT. *Solomon R. Guggenheim Museum,* New York City, USA, design begun in 1943, structure completed in 1959. © Alan Schein/Corbis.

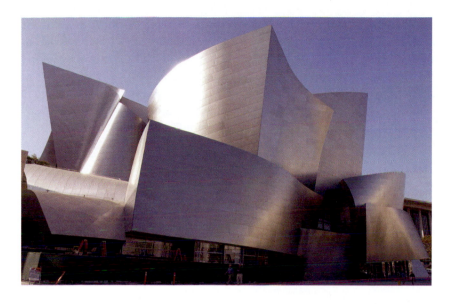

16.4 FRANK GEHRY. *Walt Disney Concert Hall*, USA, 2003. Los Angeles, California. Photo by Al Seib. © Lucy Nicholson/Reuters Newmedia Inc./Corbis.

his baggage, his program, and interacts with it to accommodate his needs. If he can't do that, I've failed" (www.pritzkerprize.com). Such architecture is called **Deconstructivist** because of its many unique viewpoints that do not coalesce into a unified whole. It is also **Neo-Modernist,** with its emphasis on abstract form.

OTHER VISUAL AND PERFORMING ART ENVIRONMENTS

Throughout the ages, art spaces have been combined with structures that serve other uses. Ancient Greeks had art galleries near their temple complexes. In medieval churches in Europe, treasuries held precious artworks from nearby and far-off lands. Today, government buildings all over the world may contain galleries highlighting the artwork of the nation.

In the Roman Empire, many rulers spent public funds to build bathhouses, theaters, amphitheaters, circuses, arenas, and stadiums for the pleasure of their subjects, and they adorned those structures with art. The *Colosseum* in Rome (see Fig. 16.9) is one example, but first let us look at another form of recreational architecture that continues to be popular: the spa. At one time, Rome had over nine hundred bathhouses, ranging from imperial baths to no-frills public baths, where Romans improved their health and socialized. Features included workout rooms, steam rooms, massage rooms, swimming pools, and warm, hot, and cold baths. Imperial baths boasted libraries, art galleries, restaurants, bars, gymnasiums, and shady walkways, and offered theater performances, public lectures, athletic contests, and so on. Excavations of bathhouse sites have revealed much ancient sculpture. The *Baths of Caracalla* (Fig. 16.5), built between 211 and 217 by the emperor of the same name, could serve 1,600 clients. Once covering fifty acres, the baths had brick-faced

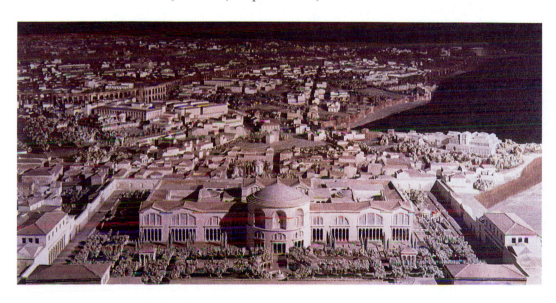

16.5 *Baths of Caracalla.* Reconstruction model. Reconstruction in Museum of Roman Civilization, Rome.

concrete walls 140 feet high supporting the huge vaulted ceiling. It was an imperial bath, and so the interior was palatial, decorated lavishly with stucco ceilings, marble facing, mosaic floors, and colossal statuary. The water for the baths came from the aqueduct, another brilliant Roman invention. Heated air circulated through hollow floors and walls to warm the rooms.

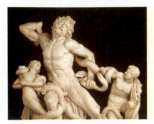

Connection *In the sixteenth century, the Greek sculpture* Laocoön and His Sons *(Fig. 13.16, page 348) was discovered buried in the ruins of an imperial Roman bath.*

In the United States from the nineteenth century to today, the large city park offers a variety of diversions, like the Roman baths without the spa. *Central Park* (Fig. 16.6), in the middle of Manhattan, is a retreat from bustling New York City. The long, narrow park is considered an outstanding example of landscape architecture, and in 1965 it was declared a National Historic Land-

mark. Designers Frederick Law Olmsted and Calvert Vaux worked with the natural setting rather than completely reshaping it. Hog farms, open sewers, and hovels had to be removed before millions of flowers, trees, and shrubs could be planted. Trails, roads, and bridges were added within the natural rolling terrain. The park today features all kinds of entertaining places and events:

- The Metropolitan Museum of Art
- Sheep Meadow, now used for free musical concerts
- Delacorte Shakespeare Theater (free)
- The Ramble (wilderness area trails)
- Zoo and the Children's Zoo
- Wollman Rink and Lasker Rink and Pool
- Chess and Checker Pavilion
- the Harlem Meer, a small lake with a boathouse
- Fort Fish and Fort Clinton, blockhouses from the Revolutionary War and the War of 1812
- sculptures honoring statesmen, writers, children, animals, birds, and military events

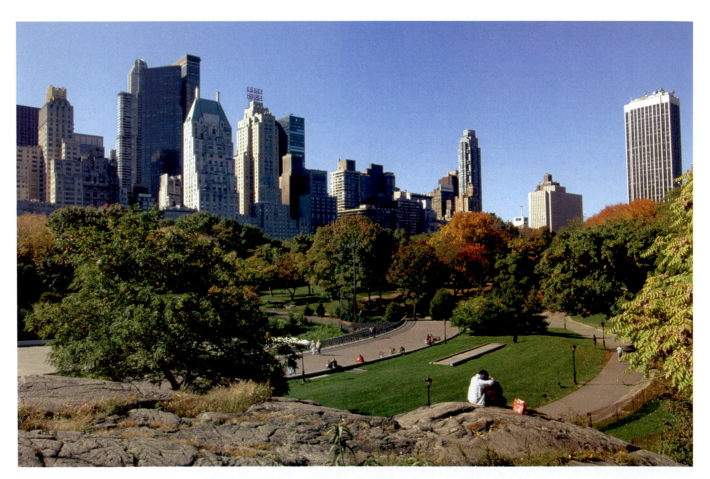

16.6   FREDERICK LAW OLMSTED AND CALVERT VAUX. *Central Park*, New York City, USA, 1857–1887.
© Michael S. Yamashita /Corbis.

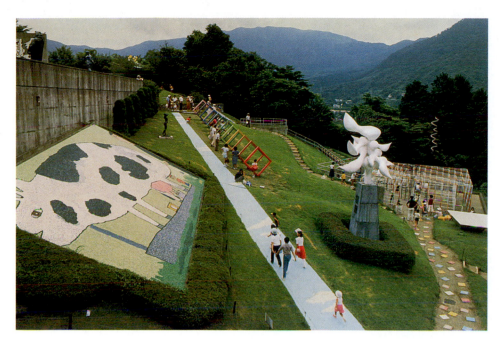

16.7 *The Hakone Open-Air Museum*, Hakone National Park, Japan, opened in 1969. © Courtesy Japan National Tourist Organization.

■ tennis courts, baseball diamonds, football and soccer fields, children's playgrounds, a cafeteria, bike and bridle paths, and many gardens

Connection *The formal gardens of European palaces like Versailles were one inspiration for large urban parks in the United States. See Art and History in Context on page 361.*

The Hakone Open-Air Museum (Fig. 16.7), opened in 1969, is a museum set in nature, located in Japan's scenic Hakone National Park. The exquisitely manicured lawns, woods, and gardens complement the many contemporary outdoor sculptures displayed there, all against the breathtaking beauty of the Hakone Mountains. Indoor galleries feature sculptures and paintings by famous twentieth-century Japanese and European artists.

Art mixes with the gambling, tourism, and entertainment industries in Las Vegas (see *Art and History in Context*, page 453). Las Vegas, Nevada (Fig. 16.8), is visual culture made into a city. It is a dense site of images and reproductions, including Paris's Eiffel Tower, the Sphinx and pyramids of Egypt, the Venetian waterfront, the New York City skyline with the Statue of Liberty, a medieval castle, and so on. If fake cityscapes abound, so do fake Elvis Presleys. Original and copied art are featured in galleries and in the casinos. Neon art and illuminated signs glow through the night. A huge visual spectacle, Las Vegas is a site of tourists' fantasies and desires for glamour and wealth, often satisfied through copies and representations, through the act of looking and being looked at.

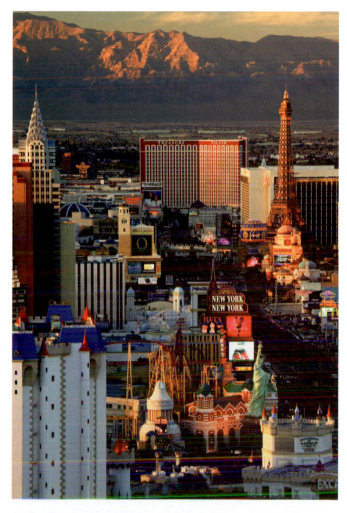

16.8 *Las Vegas*, 2004. Sunset, elevated view. Photo by Adam Jones.

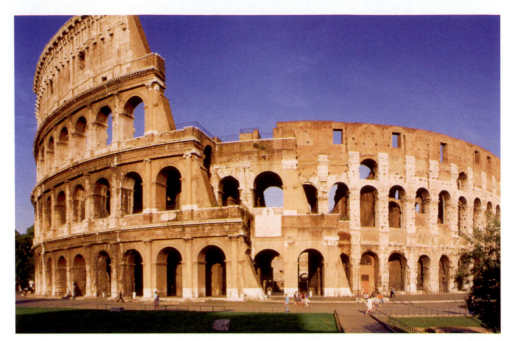

16.9 *Colosseum*, Rome, 70–82 CE. © Richard Glover/Corbis.

SPORTS ARENAS

Architecture provides a framework and an appropriate setting for the drama and spectacle of sports events.

In its original condition, the *Colosseum*, or the Flavian Amphitheater (Fig. 16.9), was a feast for the eyes. This huge structure covering six acres was faced with rich veneers of marble, tile, plaster, and bronze. The 160-foot-high outer wall is encircled by four horizontal bands, three with arches flanked by Greek Classical columns—a monumental celebration of Greco-Roman architecture. Emperors who succeeded the infamous tyrant Nero built it between 70 and 82 CE, on the site of an artificial lake in Nero's private park, where his colossal statue stood (hence, the name *Colosseum*).

Inside, a complex design of ramps, arcades, vaults, and passageways efficiently moved more than 50,000 spectators. Admission was always free to all; however, the seating was reserved by rank. The hot sun was blocked by a huge cloth canopy managed by a special detachment of the navy. The center area could be covered with sand for chariot races, hunting sports, and gladiator games, or filled with water to enact mock sea battles. Complex underground passages, rooms, and elevators were added later so that animals, scenery, and prisoners could make dramatic entrances to the spectacles. The *Colosseum* was dedicated to blood sports, and thousands of humans and animals perished in the gruesome games, which continued until 523.

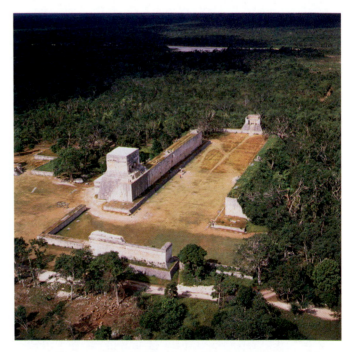

16.10 *The Great Ball Court*, Chichén Itzá, Mexico, 11th–13th centuries. Stone, 567' × 228', I-shaped. Maya-Toltec. Photograph © 1990 The Metropolitan Museum of Art, New York.

On the North American continent, the Maya culture developed a ball sport that was a form of ritualistic entertainment. *The Great Ball Court* in Chichén Itzá, Mexico (Fig. 16.10), from the eleventh to thirteenth centuries, measures 567 feet by 228 feet. The I-shaped court had walls twenty-seven feet high with two stone rings mounted near the top. As in contemporary soccer, the players had to use their heads and bodies to project the hard ball, which took much strength and skill through the long, arduous game. The Maya people saw the ball game as a metaphor for the epic journey through the Underworld taken by the hero twins, the Sun and the Moon, with underlying meanings about the conflict between good and evil and the cycles of heavenly bodies. The game ended when the ball passed through the stone ring, and then one player (or perhaps one team) became a human sacrifice to the gods.

The dramatic ball court is a fitting setting for the ritualistic game. It features the Temple of the Jaguar on the long east wall and another temple at the far north end. Phenomenal decorative reliefs cover the walls. The acoustics of the court are also amazing. A person standing in one temple can hear a conversation taking

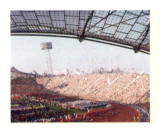

Connection *The same qualities of grandeur and spectacle seen in the* Colosseum *and* The Great Ball Court *are present in many sports arenas today, including the* Olympic Stadium at Munich *(Fig. 2.43, page 56).*

place in the temple at the other end. Similar ball courts existed at most major urban centers of the Maya and other Mesoamerican peoples, with some variations in the designs. Many still stand.

ART THAT ILLUSTRATES LEISURE ACTIVITIES

Throughout history and across cultures, artists have recorded the spectacles, leisure activities, and forms of entertainment in their cultures.

SPORT IMAGERY

The vase painting *Ball Players* (Fig. 16.11) shows some of the very ballplayers who would have competed on the Maya ball court in Figure 16.10. Team members are covered with elaborate dress and heavy padding, especially on the chest and knees. This was eye-catching attire that also provided necessary protection from the hard ball. Patterns and insignia cover the players' clothing, and they are adorned with earrings and a large animal headdress, showing that ballplayers enjoyed considerable status in Maya society. In usual Maya fashion, the painting combines outlined, dark silhouette forms and patterned areas. The figures, though stylized, seem powerful and lithe.

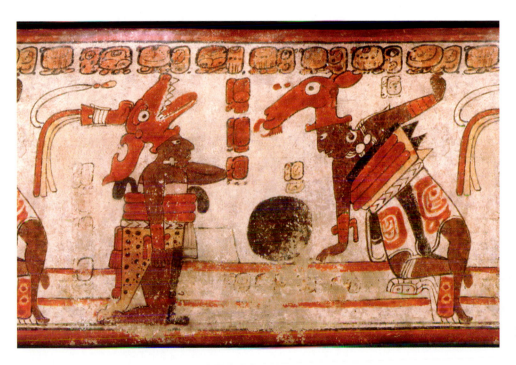

16.11   *Ball Players*, Mexico, 11th–13th centuries. Vase painting. Maya. © Justin Kerr (K2022).

Also from Mexico comes the *Acrobat* (Fig. 16.12), from the ancient village of Tlatilco located outside Mexico City, discovered in 1940. Graves contained burial offerings that included figurines of females, ballplayers, musicians, dancers, and acrobats. Clearly these artifacts indicate that these ancient peoples prepared for an afterlife full of entertainment. The *Acrobat*, from 1200–600 BCE, has a relatively naturalistic face framed with a stylized incised hair treatment. The contorted, truncated body has detailed extremities, seen in the articulation of the feet and toes. The head is disproportionately large, with a concentrating, straining expression. Compositionally, the bent arms and legs create diagonals that frame the face.

From the Minoan culture on the island of Crete comes the wall painting *Bull Jumping* or *Toreador Fresco* (Fig. 16.13), dating from c. 1550–1450 BCE. The fresco is part of a group of murals with bulls as subject matter, located in the ruins of the palace at Knossos. It may refer to the mythical Minotaur, half-man and half-bull beast, to whom young men and women were sacrificed. The bull also symbolizes fertility and strength. The contestants demonstrate their courage with every leap and tumble, as they face the fury of the bull and all he stands for.

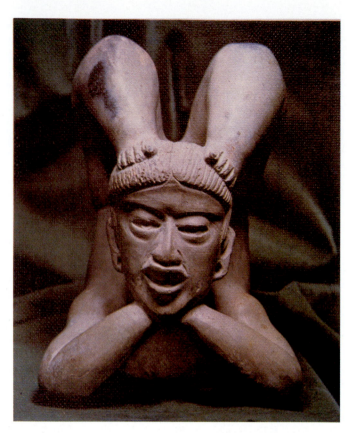

16.12 *Acrobat*, Mexico, Early Pre-Classical, 1200–600 BCE. Light clay, 10" × 6½". National Museum of Anthropology, Mexico City. Photo Constantino Reyes.

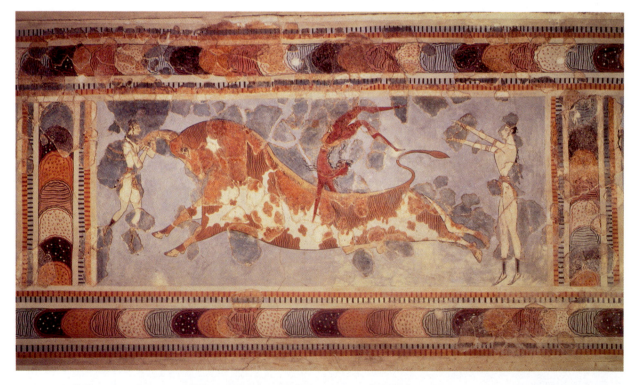

16.13 *Bull Jumping*, Crete, c. 1550–1450 BCE. Wall painting, 24½" high. Palace complex at Knossos. © Scala/Art Resource, NY.

The style of Minoan art is distinctive. The overall forms are flowing, undulating, and floating, as if referring to the ocean that surrounds the islands. The massive bull seems graceful and the figures seem weightless, as if suspended in water. In ancient Mediterranean civilizations, gender was often indicated by dark (male) and light (female) skin tones.

MUSIC AND DANCE IMAGERY

Artworks that depict music and dance can tell us about the musical forms of cultures now long lost, and about the social, political, and religious framework into which music fits. The sculpture and two paintings in this section give visual form to performing events.

In the Cycladic Islands off Greece, sculptures of male musicians were found buried in graves along with plank marble goddess figures like that in Figure 8.2. The *Harp Player*, from c. 2500–1100 BCE (Fig. 16.14), is smoothly carved with clear, well-defined forms. Precise attention was given to the hands and fingers, as in his thumb that plucks invisible strings. The upper torso, arms, and head are exaggerated or stylized. The proportions of the musician figures appear standardized, with a fixed ratio of height to width, perhaps reflecting the mathematical relationship of musical intervals. The *Harp Player* is better viewed in profile, rather than from the front.

An Egyptian wall painting of *Musicians and Dancers* (Fig. 16.15), in the tomb of Nebamun, dated c. 1400 BCE, shows ancient forms of entertainment that were enjoyed by the living as well as the dead. Traditionally, living relatives celebrated the anniversaries of the dead in their tombs, some of which were quite large

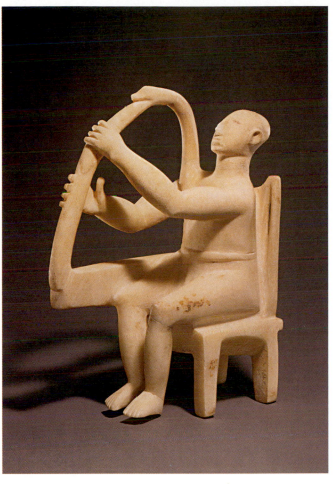

16.14 *Harp Player*, Cycladic culture, c. 2500–1100 BCE. Marble, approx. 14" × 3". Metropolitan Museum of Art, New York, Rogers Fund, 1947 (47.100.1). Photograph © 1996 The Metropolitan Museum of Art.

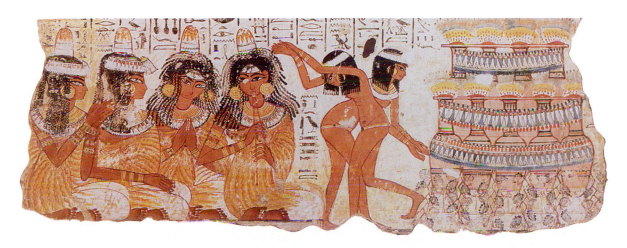

16.15 *Musicians and Dancers*, Egypt, c. 1400 BCE. Fresco, 12" × 27". From the tomb of Nebamun, Thebes. The British Museum, London.

and elaborate and featured fresco wall paintings. In *Musicians and Dancers,* four finely dressed women sit casually, with one playing an oboe-like instrument while others clap in rhythm. The cone on top of each woman's head was made of perfumed animal tallow, which would melt and run down their bodies, covering them with fragrant grease. To the right are barely clad dancers and stacked wine jars.

The painting style of this fresco is relaxed as well, which contrasts with depictions of high-ranking Egyptians. The ladies' hair is loose, the soles of their feet are shown, and two face the viewer head-on rather than in the typical Egyptian profile. The lively dancers are smaller, indicating their lesser rank in the Egyptian social hierarchy. The whole scene gives the feeling of levity and pleasure meant both for the spirit of the deceased and for the living.

Centuries later in seventeenth-century Holland, Judith Leyster painted a young boy engrossed in playing his flute (Fig. 16.16). Leyster was a prolific artist whose work was well known at the time, a rare accomplishment for a woman in a predominantly male art world. *Boy Playing a Flute,* from 1630–1635, is considered her masterpiece. Leyster captures the pride and the enthusiasm of the young musician as he glances at his

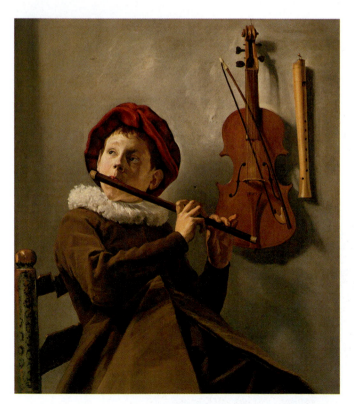

16.16   JUDITH LEYSTER. *Boy Playing a Flute,* Netherlands, 1630–1635. Oil, 28½" × 24¼". National Museum, Stockholm, Sweden. Nationalmuseum, Stockholm.

audience, likely looking for their approval. The mellow tones of the painting suggest the soft tones of the flute. In the shallow space, the boy is balanced compositionally with the instruments hanging on the wall.

Holland at the time was predominantly middle class and Protestant, so music was not written for grand productions for the nobility or for elaborate rituals for the Catholic Church. Leyster painted the boy as an ordinary child, playing for his own pleasure and that of his family, in a middle-class home graced with several musical instruments.

ENTERTAINMENT/ART

This section contains works that straddle the borders dividing art, popular culture, and entertainment. In addition to their striking visual elements, most of these artworks also have components of sound, music, movement, or dance.

ART AND DRAMATIC PRODUCTIONS

The visual arts have long been part of dramatic productions, especially in masks, puppetry, set design, costumes, and graphics. Theater has in turn influenced the visual arts, particularly **Performance Art**.

Puppetry is an art form at least four thousand years old. Japan has a traditional form of "doll drama" called *Bunraku* (Fig. 16.17), which was originally performed by traveling troupes. Doll dramas continue today. The naturalistic puppets are one-half life-size with articulated hands, heads, eyes, brows, and mouths. Only male characters have articulated legs, because female puppets wear long robes. Wearing elevated sandals, the master puppeteer, whose face we see, holds the puppet up and works the head and facial features with one hand and the doll's right hand with the other. Assistants covered in black control the left hand and the feet. Lengthy practice and discipline are required to get all actions precisely synchronized, as they work in full view of the audience. The puppeteers are accompanied by a singer-narrator and a musician playing a three-stringed instrument called a *samisen.* The singer describes the scenes, voices all the roles, and makes comments to enhance the drama. Japan recognizes Bunraku plays and artists as national treasures.

Puppetry took a new form in the mid-1990s on the Broadway stage with Disney's *The Lion King* (Fig. 16.18), which featured a unique combination of human-puppet characters, created and directed by Julie Taymor.

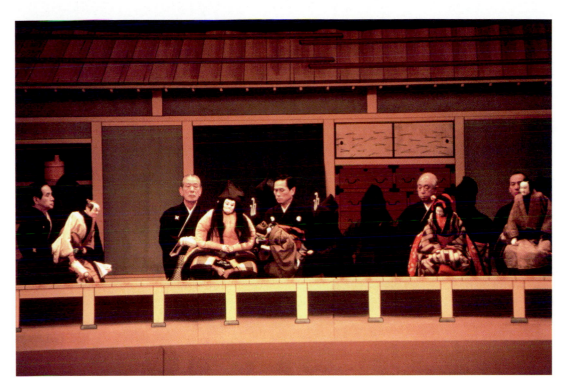

16.17 *Bunraku* performance on stage, Japan, c. 20th century. © Michael S. Yamashita/Corbis.

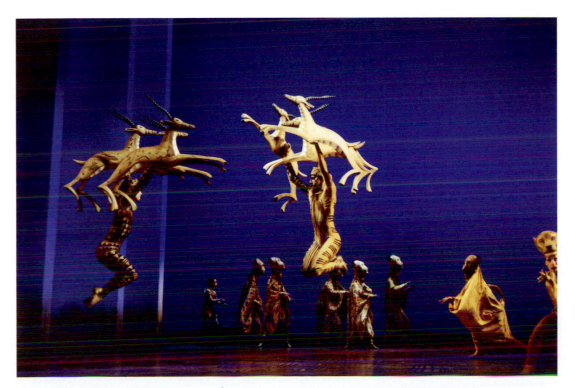

16.18 JULIE TAYMOR (designer and director). Scene from *The Lion King*, New York City, USA, opened mid 1990s. © Robbie Jack/Corbis.

Her background includes Indonesian masked dance, Bunraku puppetry, and Western opera. Because the puppeteer-actors are visible, both the story and the process of telling the story unfold simultaneously. This is especially appropriate because the animal-characters endure humanlike rites of passage and a search for identity. In our example, the dancers perform high, graceful leaps, mimicking antelopes' movements, and their costumes are coordinated with those of the puppets.

Visual artists have produced graphics for the performing arts. Henri-Marie-Raymond de Toulouse-Lautrec lived in the cabaret and theater district of Montmartre, Paris, in the 1880s. There he became friends with artists, entertainers, street people, and prostitutes, many of whom became the focus of his work. His street posters reached a wide audience, who probably did not attend the Paris galleries and salons. A favorite subject was *Jane Avril* (Fig. 16.19), a singer and dancer at the famous cabaret Moulin Rouge. This 1899 poster captures the provocative entertainer as she sings her song, inviting the public to come and see more. Avril's sensuous silhouette

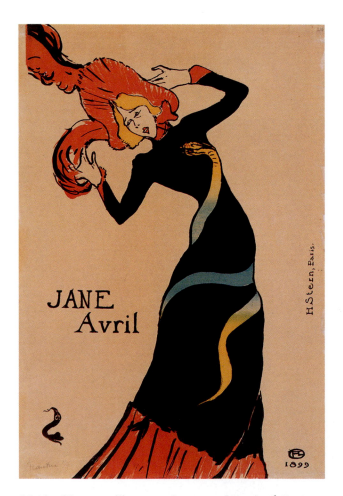

16.19 HENRI DE TOULOUSE-LAUTREC. *Jane Avril*, Paris, France, 1899. Lithographic poster, 22" × 14". © Erich Lessing/Art Resource, NY.

is composed of simple, fluid shapes filled with bright, flat colors. The coiling snake emphasizes her curves and suggests that she is a temptress, like Eve to Adam. Her written name balances the negative space and at the same time visually supports her exaggerated back bend. Toulouse-Lautrec was influenced by shallow space, decorative color, and the fluid contour line of Japanese prints. His work strongly influenced later graphic designers.

Set design is another area of significant overlap between the visual arts and performing arts. In 1958, U.S. artist Robert Rauschenberg, choreographer Merce Cunningham, and composer Morton Feldman created an innovative and provocative work entitled *Summerspace* (Fig. 16.20), with John Cage as musical director, first performed at the American Dance Festival. All components were performed together but were also independent of one another, with aspects of improvisation and chance. Cunningham conceived of space as a continuum, without a focal point for the dancers. Conceptually, this was like some abstract painting in which there is no figure that is more important than the background. Cunningham was also influenced by Albert Einstein's theory of relativity, which posited that there are no fixed points in space. Rauschenberg designed the sets and costumes to echo the dance that had no center point but moved from all points on the stage. The dancer's costumes were covered with dots (or points) like the set, giving each element equal visual importance.

In recent years, the performing arts have had a great influence on the visual arts, especially in **performance art,** a visual art form that incorporates live action and mixed media and is presented before an audience. The first performances were 1960s "Happenings" organized by Allan Kaprow, who believed that art, like life, should be unstable, transitory, and ambiguous. What *happened* was what was important. This opposes much previous Western thought, which regarded artworks as pure, transcendent, universal objects meant to endure. Kaprow felt that art should mesh with life, rather than interpret life experience. During happenings, participants and audience were often one and the same.

For *Household*, Kaprow set the happening to begin at a specific time in a dump area in Ithaca, New York, close to Cornell University. It began as male participants built a tower of garbage, while women built a nest of twigs and string, suggesting the traditional domain of each gender. From inside the nest, the women began screeching at the men, who brought a wrecked car and smeared it with strawberry jam. The women left their nest and began licking the jam off the car (Fig. 16.21) while the men destroyed the nest. Afterwards, the men wiped the jam off the car with

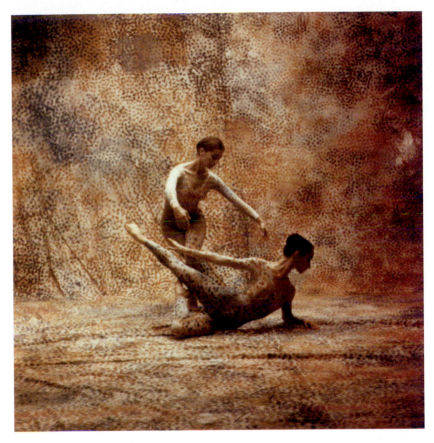

16.20 *Summerspace.* Music by Morton Feldman, choreography by Merce Cunningham, set and costumes by Robert Rauschenberg; John Cage, Musical Director of the Cunningham Dance Company. Premiered at the American Dance Festival at Connecticut College, New London, Connecticut. Dancers: Viola Farber (standing) and Carolyn Brown. Photo by Richard Rutledge.

white bread and ate it, while the women retaliated by decimating the men's tower. The event continued with violence until the men demolished the car and set it on fire. In silence, all participants watched the car burn, and then departed without words. *Household* was bizarre, surreal, and ambiguous like a dream, and Kaprow welcomed individual interpretations.

ART, MUSICAL INSTRUMENTS, AND DANCE

The visual arts and music also overlap, but in ways different from visual art and theater. Historically, artists have made musical instruments and continue to do so today. Aspects of dance recall the visual arts, and artists have provided props for dancers.

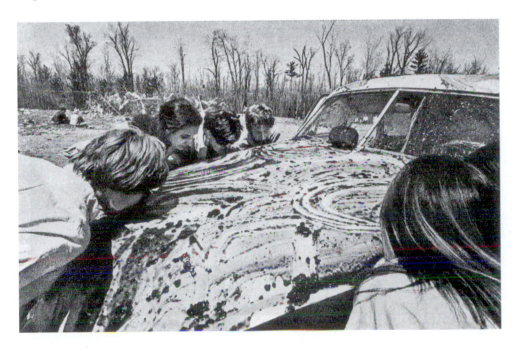

16.21 ALLAN KAPROW. *Household*, May 1964. Performance "Happening." Commissioned by Cornell University, New York. © 2004 Allan Kaprow. Used by permission of the J. Paul Getty Museum, Los Angeles.

One example of an artwork that is also a musical instrument is the beautifully crafted *Lyre* (Fig. 16.22) of wood, lapis lazuli, and gold and shell inlay. It was found in the royal Mesopotamian tomb of Queen Puabi, dated c. 2685 BCE. Similar to a harp, the instrument's wooden sound box and body are composed of clean rectangles and subtle curves, with decorative sculpture and scenes as accents. The stunning blue-bearded bull is made of gold and lapis lazuli, an imported semiprecious stone. It is naturalistic with highly stylized details, such as the outlined eyes and patterned beard. Bearded bulls were symbols of royalty.

Beneath the bull's head are four scenes made of shell inlaid in bitumen. They may depict a fantastic banquet, illustrate fables, or depict the myth of Gil-gamesh. Characters include a young man flanked by two human-headed bulls, and four-legged creatures acting as servants: a lively dog with a dagger carries a table, followed by a lion with a platter and a large jar. Below them, a donkey musician plays a lyre like the one it adorns. Such a grandly made lyre is both a visual and musical work of art.

The drum is nearly universal across cultures. In Melanesia, men make and use very large drums as well as small ones like the *Asmat Hand Drum* (Fig. 16.23). It is carried in one hand, while the lizard skin head is struck with the other. Drums were used in ceremonies for a boy's initiation, to placate ancestor spirits who died because of an enemy raid, and for magical rites. The slender, hourglass-shaped drums were usually decorated

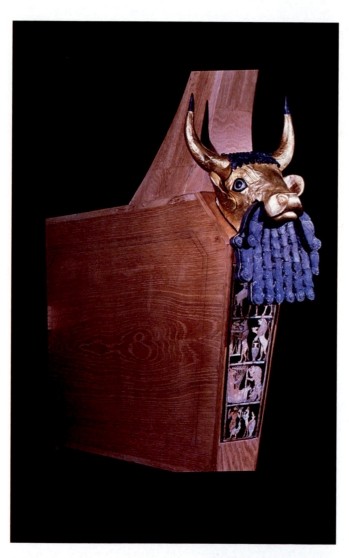

16.22 *Lyre*, Ur (Iraq), c. 2685 BCE. Wood, gold and shell inlay, lapis lazuli, 5'5" high. Sound box from tomb of Queen Puabi. University of Pennsylvania Museum.

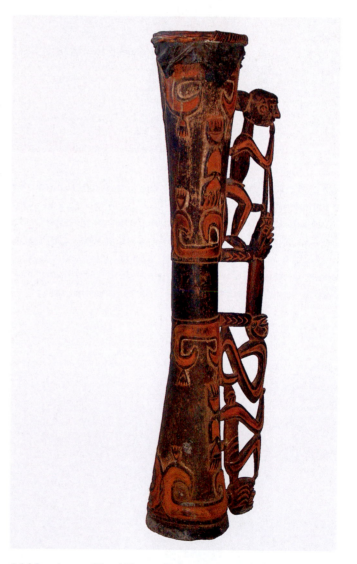

16.23 *Asmat Hand Drum*, Indonesia, c. 1950. Painted wood, lizard skin, rattan, 45" high. Southwest Asmat coast. From the collection of Tobias Schneebaum, New York, N.Y. Photo by Tobias Schneebaum.

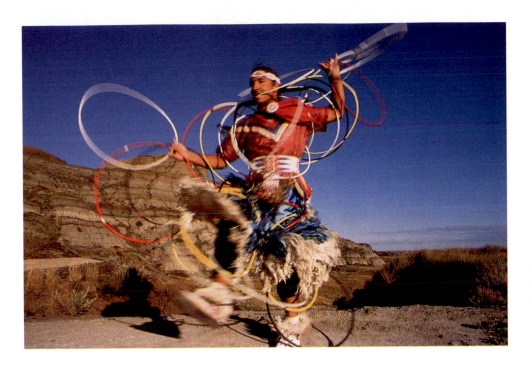

16.24 KEVIN LOCKE. Performing the *Open Circle Dance*, USA, 20th century. Sioux. © 1995 Bruce Wendt Productions/Makoche Recording Company. Photo by Bruce Wendt Courtesy Makoche Recording Company.

with ancestral and head-hunting symbolism, represented in the figures on the handles.

The North American Sioux *Open Circle Dance* (Fig. 16.24) was part of the annual celebration of the springtime rebirth of nature. The dancer performs to a rapid rhythm, using twenty-eight hoops made of wood or reeds. All movements have spiritual significance and together are visualizations suggesting the unity of all things in the universe as well as individual growth, change, and metamorphosis. Some parts of the dance re-create the image of an eagle soaring in flight, suggesting that parts of nature (including human beings) belong to the spiritual world in the heavens. Another configuration represents the caterpillar, which, during the dance, will become a graceful butterfly. The rigorous performance climaxes with the "Hoops of Many Hoops," when all things of the universe come together as part of a hopeful Sioux prophecy for peace among all people. This dance is an elaborate variation of older forms that has been developed because of the interest of tourists. Once again, entertainment, art, and ritual mix.

The Dogon people in Mali connect the dance, costume, and the *Kanaga* mask (Fig. 16.25). The performers are members of a male masked society called the

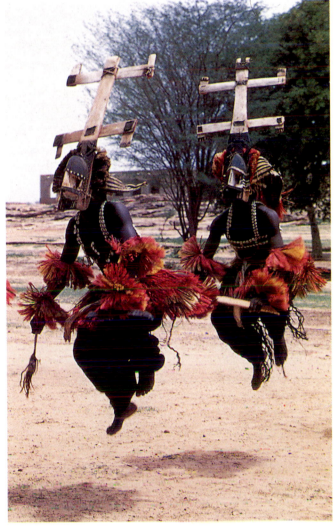

16.25 *Kanaga Masked Dancers*, Mali, 20th century. Dogon. Hutchison Library.

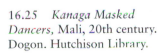

awa, who, in their dance, tell their culture's story about how death entered the world. The masking and the red color of the costume are believed to catch, manipulate, and rechannel vital forces that could pose potential danger to the community if unleashed. Kanaga masks are worn three days after a death in the community, when the spirit of the deceased is believed to leave the body. The masks, carved by the performers, have several interpretations, such as a bird in flight, a mythological crocodile, or a god in the act of creation.

FILM, TELEVISION, AND CARTOONS

Art and entertainment really overlap in film, television, and cartoons, where at times the same work easily can be classified in any or all of these media. Film, television, and cartoons are all based on sequential images. Narrative is a key element in most. All are dependent upon technology, specifically commercial printing, photography, analog recording, and digital imaging. Film and television are fertile areas of investigation for visual culture scholars, because of the embedded social messages and, in the case of Hollywood films, the quality of spectacle. Many films and television programs have influenced fine artists.

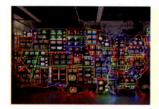

Connection Nam June Paik's multi-imaged Electronic Superhighway (Fig. 3.38, page 77) is a good example of art that refers to entertainment technologies.

Cartoons have a long history in drawing, print-making, and newspapers, where they entertain or promote political causes (like Honoré Daumier's political cartoon in Fig. 12.28). In comics, the sequential images tell a story. First introduced in Sunday supplements in newspapers over a century ago, early comics were marked by great experimentation. *Gasoline Alley* (Fig. 16.26) is part of a later development in comics, with more elaborate storytelling and memorable characters. Although most of the time *Gasoline Alley* was concerned with humble yet humorous domestic issues, occasionally the writer/artist Frank King lavished beautiful graphic arabesques and visual fantasies over the comic space. Our example, with a boy and his Uncle Walt doodling designs with a compass, echoes concurrent developments in abstraction in art. Once considered solely popular culture, comics have recently been featured in major exhibitions at top art museums, and some artists work in the comic-strip format. Comics of

course continue today, and many future classics may be wrapped up with the news in your daily paper.

The motion picture was born of the marriage of photography and electricity. Early experiments in film soon led to elaborate productions with experienced actors. Film quickly became distinct from theater. The movable camera removed all boundaries from the staged space, and sequences could be shot on soundstages or anywhere in the world. Sound was added to the action in 1927, which made or broke many actors' careers.

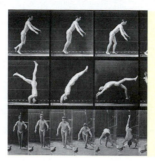

Connection An example of Eadweard Muybridge's sequential images, which are early experiments to capture motion with photography, is Handspring, a flying pigeon interfering, June 26, 1885 (Fig. 13.19, page 351).

Many films are considered classics, even works of art, in addition to their entertainment value. It is beyond the scope of this book to cover film history. However, we will look at *Gone with the Wind* (Fig. 16.27), an excellent example of the type of entertainment that came out of the MGM studios during the 1930s and 1940s. This grandiose and expensive production, romantic and melodramatic, essentially promotes conventional values. With a lush musical score and symphonic accompaniment, the epic story of the Old South dealt with love and family conflict amid the hardships and horrors of the Civil War. Big-screen color played an important part in the magnificence of this motion picture, not only in depicting the grandeur and glory of the Old South but also in conveying the mood of the film. The color red bombards the senses in the picture, underscoring the fiery spirit and burning desires of Scarlett, the blood of the dead soldiers, and the city of Richmond and Southern life in general going up in flames. *Gone with the Wind* continues to be popular and has been recently restored and re-released.

Television is everywhere, adding more layers to our complex visual culture. Television in essence "shrank" the world as people could witness events from far-off places right in their living rooms on the small screen. Television became broadly popular in the 1950s. Most

Connection For more on the recently re-released version of Gone with the Wind, and the controversy it sparked, see the section "Restoration" in Chapter 6, page 128.

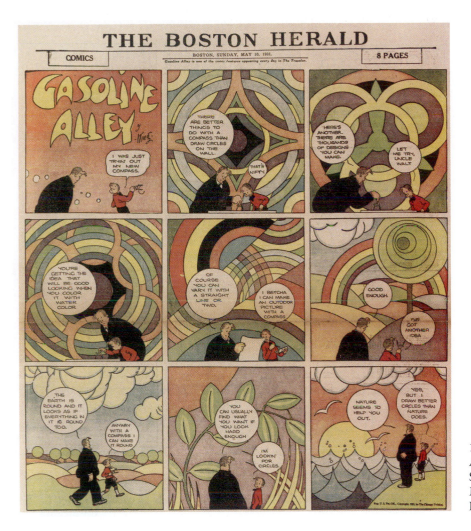

16.26 FRANK KING. *Gasoline Alley*, USA, 1931. Newspaper Sunday page, detail, published May 10, 1931. 23" × 17". Private Collection.

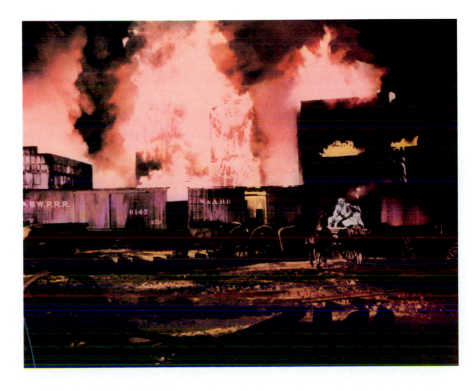

16.27 *Gone with the Wind*, USA, 1939. MGM film, starring Clark Gable and Vivian Leigh. Copyright Metro Goldwyn Mayer.

of the early television shows evolved from radio programs, such as the quiz show, talk show, travelogue, and "sitcom," or situation comedy. Later programming expanded to investigative reporting, political coverage, educational programs, music videos, reality TV, and makeover series.

One icon of American family humor is *I Love Lucy* (Fig. 16.28). Performed and filmed before a live audience, this sitcom was rated number one in its time. Even the 1953 inauguration of President Dwight D. Eisenhower drew fewer viewers than the episode showing the birth of little Ricky. Although the scripts were undoubtedly effective, much of the humor was communicated through facial expression, gesture, and body language. Notice how clearly the idea of conflict and outraged surprise is communicated in Figure 16.28. Still in syndication, *I Love Lucy* remains a popular favorite.

Television and movies have borrowed from art and vice versa. From 1995 through 2003, U.S. artist Matthew Barney created the *Cremaster* cycle of films, juxtaposing historical and autobiographical imagery with bizarre creatures, bodily orifices, and so on. Rather than presenting a narrative, the ravishing imagery promotes personal, free-associative meanings. Much of the films' content deals with gender identity, and many characters have mutant, ambiguous, or partially formed genitalia. Audiences are either repulsed or fascinated. All *Cremaster* films borrow from Hollywood types; for example, *Cremaster 1* references the Busby Berkeley musical extravaganza. Barney also creates individual artworks related to

his films, such as *Cremaster 1: The Goodyear Chorus* (Fig. 16.29), a color print, based on a film still.

Animation grew out of flip books, in which a series of drawn images seem to move as book pages are flipped rapidly. Early animation features gained a wide following beginning in the 1930s. Animation is labor-intensive; for example, an average of 14,000 drawings are required for a ten-minute animation sequence. **Traditional animation** is drawn on transparent sheets, so that foreground action figures can be separated and moved across an unchanging background. **Claymation,** a relatively early form of animation, uses clay sculptures that are photographed while being moved in tiny increments. **Computer animation** is a new form that allows characters to be plotted as a series of points and vectors and made to move with mathematical computation. Disney and Warner Brothers were two pioneers in the animation industry, but other studios and independent producers now exist.

Hayao Miyazaki's *Spirited Away* (Fig. 16.30), 2002, is considered to be an animation movie masterpiece. The story concerns Chihiro, a ten-year-old girl separated from her parents in a fantastic and sometimes frightening land. In the process of reuniting with them, she grows up. Miyazaki created scenes with fantastic structures and broad vistas that are amazingly beautiful, are often vast and ornate, and draw from a variety of historical and global sources. Likewise, lush landscapes abound. Miyazaki is known for his elaborate hand-drawn architectural interiors and diverse characters.

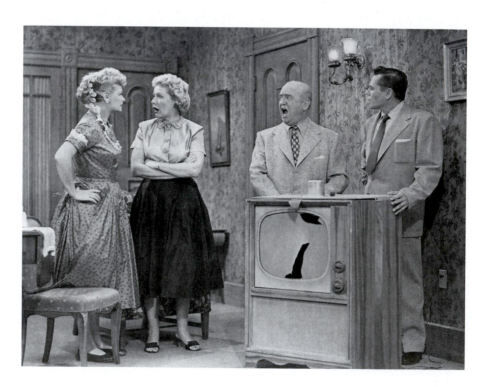

16.28 *I Love Lucy,* USA, c. 1950s–1960s. Television video, situation comedy (sitcom). CBS Entertainment, A Division of CBS, Inc. Images of Lucille & Desi Arnaz are licensed by Desilu, Too, LLC.

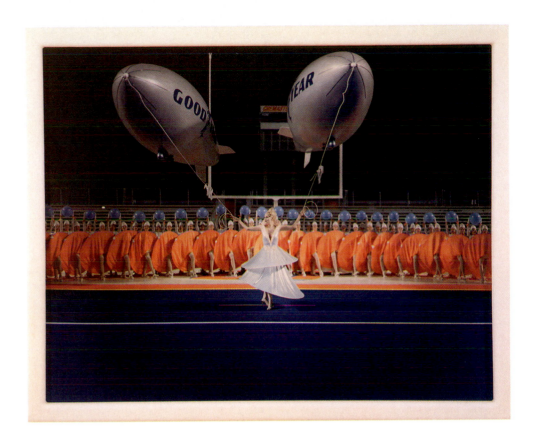

16.29 MATTHEW BARNEY.
*Cremaster 1: The Goodyear
Chorus*, USA, 1995. Color
print in self-lubricating plastic
frame, 43¾" × 53¾". Photo
by Michael James O'Brien,
Courtesy Barbara Gladstone
Gallery.

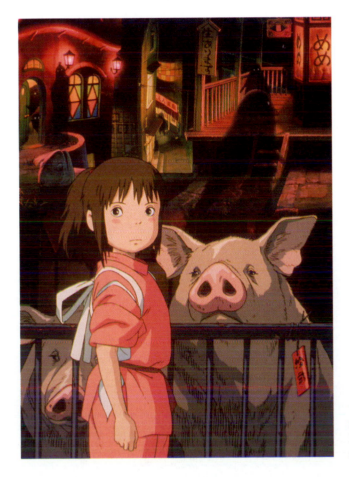

16.30 HAYAO MIYAZAKI. Still
from *Spirited Away*, Japan,
2002. Feature-length animated
movie.

At the end of World War II, the United States and the Soviet Union emerged as competing superpowers. The cold war (1950–1991) saw a massive arms buildup, pitting the United States and its western European allies against the Soviet bloc, consisting of the Soviet Union and its Central and Eastern European allies. The period also saw several major regional wars (the Korean War, the Vietnam War) as well as other conflicts in Latin America, Cuba, and Africa. In Latin America, dictatorships were common through the 1950s and 1960s; some were replaced later with democracies. The 1960s saw the founding of modern African states.

In addition to weapons of war, cold war competition centered on cultural superiority and superiority in technology. Abstract expressionist paintings like Helen Frankenthaler's *Spring Bank* were promoted in the United States as emphasizing individual self-expression over art made in service of the state, such as the social realism of the Soviet bloc and China. This emphasis can be seen in all kinds of Western artwork from this era, such as Utzon's Sydney *Opera House*

(Fig. 16.2), *Summerspace* (Fig. 16.20), and Kaprow's *Household* (Fig. 16.21). Technological competition was seen in the arms race and the race for space (moon landings, satellites, and space stations).

Communist China was the third major force in world politics, but communism itself underwent huge changes in this era. In 1975, China began a program of modernization to become a major manufacturer in goods and electronics. After 1991, the Soviet bloc disintegrated, and the Communist system was discarded or modified. Several states in Eastern Europe, the Balkans, and central Asia became independent.

The Middle East has experienced intense unrest throughout this period. The Arab-Israeli conflict is ongoing. The independence of India (Hindu) and the creation of Pakistan (Moslem) produced tensions that are still present. An Islamic revival and resistance to Western culture have resulted in the mixing of religion and civil government, seen, for example, in the fundamentalist revolution in Iran and the war in Kosovo. The unrest has spread, causing such events as the destruction

Map 10 The World Today

of the World Trade Center, bombings and violence in Indonesia, and the Iraqi war.

For nations like the United States, this is the postindustrial era, so called because technology has advanced, sending most traditional industrial production overseas. Other forms of capitalism, like the entertainment "industry," are growing in importance, starting as long ago as early television productions like *I Love Lucy*, (Fig. 16.28). Tourism supports many art, cultural, and entertainment sites around the world. *Las Vegas, Nevada* (Figure 16.8) perhaps panders most blatantly to tourists. The trend toward globalism continues, with events in one part of the world often having profound effects everywhere.

The technology revolution has created a need for governments to invest in education, communication systems, and transportation and has spurred the desire for open markets and international cooperation. Open trade agreements, such as the European Union and the North American Free Trade Agreement (NAFTA), exist in many areas. The World Trade Organization (WTO), created in 1994, is an international body that enforces trade treaties and laws. The global trade community has created opportunities as well as conflicts, economic hardships, and environmental problems.

Culture now can be and is exported globally, as with Miyazaki's *Spirited Away* (Fig. 16.30). By 1980, anthropologists could find no group of people on the entire planet who did not listen to radio. Nevertheless, older art forms continue, although modified, as with the *Asmat Hand Drum* (Fig. 16.23), Locke's *Open Circle Dance* (Fig. 16.24), and the *Kanaga Masked Dancers* (Fig. 16.25). In fact, older art forms often influence newer productions such as the Broadway play, *The Lion King* (Fig. 16.18). Blockbuster exhibitions have brought the superstar phenomenon to art. The convergence of technologies (telephone, television, satellite communications, personal computers) means new possibilities for the future. People in industrial nations widely use digital technology for writing, information access, sound-mixing, video editing, and still image manipulation.

The global culture has brought changes to the natural world. AIDS and other new, quick-spreading diseases have caused alarm. With global warming and destruction of rain forests and habitats, the earth's environment is changing.

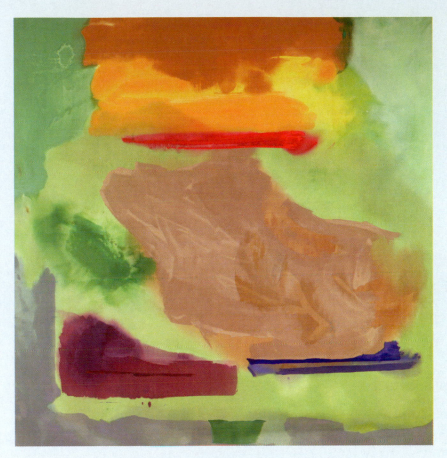

16.31   HELEN FRANKENTHALER. *Spring Bank*, USA, 1974. Acrylic on canvas, 273½ × 269½ cm. Musée National d'Art Moderne, Centre Pompidou, Paris, France.

1950 CE – PRESENT

– Timeline

Left timeline

Context	Date	Work
	2685 BCE	*Lyre*
	2500	*Harp Player*
Pipes and chimes in Chinese tombs		
		Bull Jumping
	1400	*Musicians and Dancers*
	1000	*Acrobat*
	400	Polykleitos: *Theater at Epidauros*
Early museum—Alexandria		
	100	
Three orchestras/829 members—Han Dynasty		
	70 CE	*Colosseum*
	100	
Roman art placed in baths, temples, gardens, villas, and forums	200	*Baths of Caracalla*
Early theater in India based on Sanskrit epics		
	900	First fully developed Chinese opera
	1200	*The Great Ball Court*
Noh theater—Japan		*Ball Players*
Shakespeare, the Globe	1600	Leyster: *Boy Playing a Flute*
Precolonial masquerades in Africa		
Bunraku and Kabuki theater—Japan		
	1700	
Beginnings of modern museums		
Opera at high point in Europe	1800	
Peking Opera		
Zoetrope—precursor to film		
Telegraph invented		
	1850	Olmsted and Vaux: *Central Park*
First art museums in West	1870	
Telephone lines installed in New England		Toulouse-Lautrec: *Jane Avril*

Right timeline

Context	Date	Work
First film screenings	1900	
Hollywood—film capital	1920	
First commercial radio broadcast		
Beginning of global music culture		
		King: *Gasoline Alley*
		Gone with the Wind
	1940	Wright: *Solomon R. Guggenheim Museum*
Television broadcasting begins		
Cold war	1950	*Asmat Hand Drum*
Color television and color movies		
Korean War		
Space programs begin in U.S. and U.S.S.R.		*I Love Lucy*
	1960	
End of European colonies in Africa		
		Utzon: *Opera House*, Sydney *Hakone Open-Air Museum*
		Feldman, Cunningham, and Rauschenberg: *Summerspace*
		Kaprow: *Household*
		Kanaga Masked Dancers
Vietnam War		
	1970	
Technological and Industrial Revolution—China	1980	
VCR and cable networks		
	1990	Taymor: *The Lion King*
Operation Desert Storm		
Expansion of the *Las Vegas* strip		
Digital video		
Internet		Barney: *Cremaster 1: The Goodyear Chorus*
		Locke: *Open Circle Dance*
War on terrorism	2000	
iPod introduced		Gehry: *Walt Disney Concert Hall*
		Miyazaki: *Spirited Away*

SYNOPSIS

Visual culture studies the totality of visual media, examining the range of messages embedded in them. Visual media include art and entertainment and the areas where they overlap. Architecture provides a physical and visual framework that enhances theater, opera, art exhibitions, and sports events.

Some art illustrates forms of entertainment. Other artworks can be categorized as either art or entertainment in and of themselves. Still other artworks are props or instruments in theater, music, or dance performances.

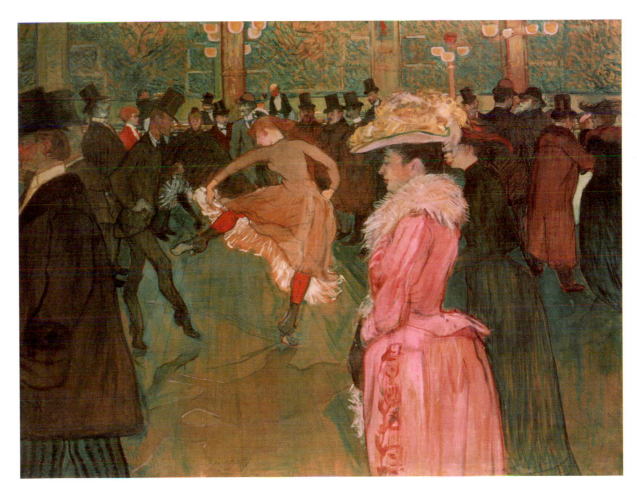

16.32   HENRI TOULOUSE-LAUTREC. *At the Moulin Rouge: The Dance*, France, 1890. 45½" × 59." In memory of Frances P. McIlhenny, 1986. Philadelphia Museum of Art, Philadelphia.

FOOD FOR THOUGHT

Visual culture is said to have replaced reality itself. For example, "pictures" from outer space are visualizations in which certain colors and spaces represent radio frequencies. To the average viewer, are these pictures reality?

Reproductions are a kind of virtual reality. They exist in Las Vegas in the New York, New York, casino that shrinks, edits, and reproduces the New York City skyline. Is this different from learning about art from a textbook, where all you see are shrunken, edited reproductions of the actual objects?

- *Have the new technologies, such as television and the computer, changed the practice of the artist for better or worse? Have they changed the practice of viewing art?*

- *Has Western art come full circle? Has art begun to leave the museum and opera house and intermingle more with life, as it does in some non-Western cultures?*

- *How much should "life" be a part of art?*

And finally, consider the carnival and dance hall, which are sites of entertainment where classes mix and social restrictions are loosened. We already saw this phenomenon with the Diego Rivera's Dia de Los Muertos celebrations in Mexico (Fig. 10.23), with their raucous carnival atmosphere and political satire. Halloween also is carnival-like, as children and adults dress up as their fantasies or their fears. In Henri de Toulouse-Lautrec's At the Moulin Rouge: The Dance (Fig. 16.32), staid and properly-dressed patrons mix among dancers doing wild jigs. All these forms of entertainment have something of a subversive quality.

- *What are some ways that social order is turned upside down in art and entertainment?*

Your Thomson Online Resources

 Go to **ArtExperience Online** for the Flashcards, Quiz, and Study Guide for this chapter.

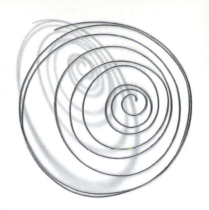

Postscript

WHERE DO YOU FIND ART AND HOW CAN YOU USE IT IN YOUR LIFE?

The overall purpose of this book has been to inquire into human creativity, and therefore our own creativity. We have seen that art is something that human beings have to do, through the ages, throughout the world. And what about you? Art is already part of your life. With a little effort, you can make it even more enriching for you. Here are some suggestions on how you may do that.

Seeing Original Artwork. One of the most thrilling ways to enjoy art is to see it in person! Nothing can describe the awesome feeling of standing in front of the *Great Pyramids* at Gizeh, or walking through the Mayan ruins at *Chichén Itzá,* or experiencing the space in the church of *St. Peter's* in Rome. If distant travel is not possible, you probably have many opportunities to see original artwork within a reasonable drive from your home. Here are some places to seek out art.

- **Museums and Galleries:** Almost all communities of any size support museums and galleries, ranging from modest to grand. Although local museums may not display the most famous "masterpieces," they contain works of real value that are rewarding to study and may surprise the first-time visitor. When you are in a city in the United States or abroad where a major museum or an archeological site is located, such as the Metropolitan in New York City or the tomb of Shi Huangdi in Shaanxi, China (Fig. 10.8), make it a point to spend some time there.

- **Schools:** Student art is extraordinarily inventive, spontaneous, and expressive. Art exhibits can be found in the hallways and libraries of elementary and secondary schools. On a professional or near-professional level, you can find art at most colleges and universities. Undergraduate and graduate student art is often high-quality, exciting work. Art department galleries show the work of faculty and professional artists both to enrich the art program and to expose the academic community to this art. These exhibits are often free and open to the public. Large universities sponsor major exhibitions, like the art of the Peruvian Moche at a University of California at Los Angeles gallery (Fig. 10.10). A phone call to the school is all it takes to find out about the schedules of the exhibits.

- **Civic Buildings, Private Institutions, and Corporations:** Often, government buildings have been designed by accomplished architects, and the buildings are examples of fine works of architecture. In your area, post offices, courthouses, and the like may have distinctive designs as well as housing paintings, sculptures, and art treasures. Other places to look for art in your community are banks, libraries, and hospitals. Many of these institutions have their own collections to enhance their interiors. Often, libraries will have exhibition space available and will host artworks by local artists. Some hospitals collect art. For example, an impressive collection of contemporary artwork can be

457

found in the University Hospitals of the University of Iowa in Iowa City. Many corporations have large art collections displayed in their corporate offices.

- **Public Art:** Since the 1930s, the United States has had a great tradition of art in public places. More recently, the Percent for the Arts Programs have incorporated art into all new government-funded buildings and in redevelopment areas where private investors are receiving tax abatements. You may be able to find excellent art in transportation centers, at bus stops, and along jogging paths, river walks, and historic trails.

- **Historic Homes, Mansions, and Palaces:** The homes of historic or celebrated people sometimes become museums for public viewing, such as *Monticello,* which was built by Thomas Jefferson. This house is full of art treasures and Jefferson's own amazing inventions. Also, the Palace of *Versailles* and the *Forbidden City* are now open to everyone, examples of magnificent opulence originally known to only a few. In the United States are several mansions formerly belonging to wealthy entrepreneurs who bequeathed their estates as museums. Every city and town has a chamber of commerce that can aid the visitor in finding these interesting sites.

- **Places of Worship:** Churches, temples, synagogues, and mosques are rich places to look for art. Besides their architectural designs, they likely are decorated with both old and contemporary artworks. A place of worship may have exquisite stained-glass windows, as seen in the twelfth-century *Chartres Cathedral* (Fig. 9.36), fine paintings, sculptures, or elaborate tile work.

- **Parks:** Many parks are designed by landscape architects, so the gardens, walks, lakes, and so on are carefully planned. The *Boboli Gardens* in Florence, Italy, boast two museums. The well-known *Central Park* in New York City (Fig. 16.6), planned in the nineteenth century, has an art museum, several theaters, a zoo, and many more features. It is also the home of several commemorative sculptures. The open-air park brings art and nature into one enjoyable and relaxing environment. Most community parks are free to the public or charge a small parking fee to help with maintenance.

- **Art Online:** Art is available in many forms on the Internet. Most museums and many galleries have Web sites where you can find information about current exhibitions and permanent collections. Commercial galleries also have Web sites focused on the sale of artwork. Artists have their own Web sites that feature their work. To find artists' Web sites, inquire at arts organizations or do a Web search on art resources or media art centers. They will likely have links to artists' pages or feature recent artists' projects.

Art in Everyday Life. The art in our everyday lives is art in the broadest sense of the word, consisting of aesthetic objects that surround us. You may be aware of some of this, but much is taken for granted. Your home is both aesthetic and functional and is on a continuum with the nineteenth-century Sioux *Tipis* (Fig. 7.29) and Frank Lloyd Wright's *Fallingwater* (Fig. 7.30). Your utensils, dishes, and furniture have aesthetic and design qualities, whether they were mass produced or made by an artist/craftsperson. Notice the quality of light in your room, or the ceramic bowl that holds your serving of soup. Make choices about the space you live in, and the shapes and colors with which you surround yourself. To enjoy art more, make a conscious effort to see it and observe it both in your life and your environment. You might be surprised at how often art is right in front of you!

Develop your own artistic expression. All human beings have the potential to be creative. One of the best ways to enjoy art is to make art, even if you are not an art student or if you question your skills. Studio classes are available for the taking and can be found at local art museums, schools, and community centers. If you would rather study art than make it, look for art history courses available at colleges and museums. If you would rather not take a formal course in studio work or art history, then try it on your own. Many fine artists and learned persons in the world are self-trained. Whatever you choose, have a great time!

Living with Art in Your Home. Start or continue your own collection of work you enjoy and like to look at. There are several resources from which to draw your collection, and the first is right in your home. Frame some work of your own or that of a family member. Children are prolific artists and will have several selections from which to choose. The figure below shows a *Dinosaur Eating a Man* drawn by a young artist. You can purchase art at a reasonable price from student exhibitions and art sales at art schools and departments. Students are both encouraged and gratified when their work is purchased.

Seek out artists in your area and make an appointment to see their work in their studios. Some artists are open to barter or to swapping services in place of a cash transaction.

Many museums have museum stores where reproductions of major works are sold at affordable prices. Sculpture replicas are also available. If you prefer original art, some museums have sales and rental galleries. Of course, galleries are another outlet where you can purchase original art.

Arts and Crafts Fairs are fun and great for purchasing artwork directly from the artists. The artists set up displays of their work and sell it directly to the public. They are usually happy to talk about their work. Many of the artists are working on the site, which makes these fairs all the more interesting and enjoyable.

Congratulations! You have finished this book. The authors wish you well as you personally continue your exploration into the art world, which is inherently *your* world.

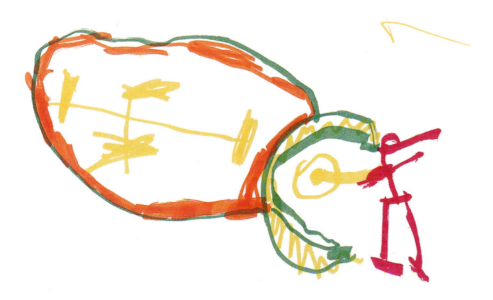

JULIA ROSE LAZZARI-DEAN. *Dinosaur Eating a Man.* Markers on paper, 8" × 6". USA, 1997. Collection of Margaret Lazzari and Mike Dean.

Pronunciation Guide for Proper Names of Persons and Places

(Note: For art terms, their pronunciations, and their definitions, see the Glossary)

A

Abakanowicz, Magdalena	ah-bah-kah-NOH-vich, mag-dah-LAY-nah
Abbot Suger	AB-ot SOO-zhayr
Achaemenid	ah-KEE-meh-nid
Akua'ba	ah-KOO-ah-bah
Allah	AL-luh
Ara Pacis Augustae	AY-rah PAH-chees oh-GUS-tie
Ariadne	ar-ee-AD-nee
Ashanti	eh-SHAN-tee
Ashurbanipal	AH-shure-BAH-nee-PAHL
Asoka	ah-SHOH-kuh or ah-SOH-kuh
Assyria	ah-SEER-ee-ah
Athens	ATH-enz

B

Babur	BAH-ber
Babylonia	bab-eh-LOH-nee-eh
Baule	bau-LAY
Benin	be-NEEN
Bernini, Gianlorenzo	bair-NEE-nee, jahn-loh-REN-zoh
Bisj Poles	bizh
Boccioni, Umberto	boh-CHOH-nee, oom-BAIR-toh
Bourgeois, Louise	boorzh-WAH, lweez
Brahma	BRAH-mah
Brancusi, Constantin	brahn-KOO-see, KOHN-stahn-teen
Bruegel, Jan	BROY-gul, YAHN
Bruegel, Pieter, the Elder	BROY-gul, PEE-ter
Buonarroti, Michelangelo	bwoh-nar-ROH-tee, mee-kay-LAN-jay-loh
Byzantium	bih-ZAN-tee-um

C

Caracalla	kar-eh-KAL-eh
Çatal Hüyük	chah-TAHL huh-YOOK
Chagall, Marc	shah-GAL, mark
Chartres	SHAR-tr'
Chichén Itzá	chee-CHEN eet-ZAH
Cicciolina	chee-choh-LEE-nah
Colleoni	co-lay-OH-nee
Colosseum	kah-leh-SEE-um
Constantinople	kon-stan-te-NOH-pel
Cuvilliès, François de	kyu-vee-YAY, fran-ZWAH duh
Cuzco	KOOS-koh
Cycladic	sik-LAD-ik

D

Dali, Salvador	dah-LEE or DAH-lee, sal-vah-DOHR
Daoism	DAU-izm
Darius	duh-RYE-us
Daumier, Honoré	DOH-mee-ay, on-ohr-AY
David, Jacques-Louis	dah-VEED, ZHAK loo-EE
Degas, Edgar	deh-GAH, ed-GAR
Delacroix, Eugène	del-uh-K(R)WA, oo-ZHEN
Dionysos	die-uh-NEE-sus
Dogon	DOH-gahn
Doryphoros	doh-RIFF-oh-rus
Dürer, Albrecht	DOO-ruhr, AL-brekt

E

Eisenstein, Sergei	EYE-zen-stine, sair-gay
Etruscan	eh-TRUSS-can
Euphrates River	yoo-FRAY-teez
Eyck, Jan van	IKE, yahn vahn

F

Fragonard, Jean-Honoré	frag-uh-NAR, zhan on-ohr-AY

G

Gabon	gah-BOHN
Garnier, Charles	gar-NYAY, sharl
Ghiberti, Lorenzo	ghee-BAYR-tee, loh-REN-zoh
Gislebertus	gheez-lay-BERT-oos
Gizeh	GHEE-zah
Gogh, Vincent van	go, vin-SENT van
Golub, Leon	GOL-ub, LEE-on
Goya, Francisco	GOY-yah, fran-SIS-koh
Grande Jatte	Grahn ZHOT
Grosz, George	GROHS, jorj
Grünewald, Matthias	GRU-nuh-valt, mah-TEE-as
Guanyin	gwahn-YEEN
Guernica	GWAR-nih-kah
Guggenheim	GOO-ghen-hime

H

Hakone	hah-koh-neh
Hammurabi	ham-uh-RAH-bee
Hanuman	hahn-oo-MAHN
Harappan	har-RAP-an
Hardouin-Mansart, Jules	ar-DWAN-man-sar, zhool
Hatshepsut	hat-SHEP-soot
Hesperides	hes-PER-i-deez
Hogarth, William	hoh-GARTH

I

Ikere	i-KEE-ree
Iktinos	EEK-tee-nos
Imhotep	im-HOH-tep
Inca	ING-kah
Ise	EE-say

K

Kabuki	kah-BOO-kee
Kachina	kah-CHEE-nah
Kahlo, Frida	KAH-lo, FREE-dah
Kandarya Mahadeva	gan-darh-ree-ah mah-hah-DAY-vuh
Kaprow, Allan	KAP-ro, al-un
Katsushika Hokusai	kat-s'-SHEE-kah HOH-k'-sye
Khufu	koo-foo
Kitagawa Utamaro	kee-tah-gah-wah oo-tah-mah-roh
Kollwitz, Käthe	KOHL-vits, KET-uh
Krishna	KRISH-nah
Kristallnacht	KRIS-tal-NAHCHT
Kusama, Yayoi	koo-SA-ma, yay-yoy-ee
Kwakiutl	kwah-kee-OOT-'l

L

Lange, Dorothea	lang, dor-uh-THEE-ah
Laocoön	lay-AH-koh-on
Lascaux	las-KOH

Le Brun, Charles	leh-BRUN, sharl
Le Corbusier	leh kor-byoo-see-AY
Le Nôtre, André	leh NOHTr', an DRAY
Le Vau, Louis	leh VOH, lwee
Léger, Fernand	lay-ZHAYR, fer-NAN
Leonardo da Vinci	lay-o-NAR-doh da VEEN-chee
Leyster, Judith	LIE-stur, YOO-dit
Lin, Maya Ying	lin, MY-ah yeeng
Lorenzetti, Ambrogio	loh-rent-SAYT-tee, am-BROH-joh

M

Ma Yuan	ma yoo-an
Mali	MAH-lee
Mamluk	MAM-look
Maori	MAH-oh-ree
Mao Zedong	mau zee-DONG
Marisol	mah-ree-SOL
Masaccio	muh-SAT-choh
Masjid-i-Shah	MUS-jid-i-shah
Maya	MAH-yah
Menkaure	men-KOW-ray
Mesopotamia	mess-oh-poh-TAME-ee-uh
Michelangelo	mee-kay-LAN-jay-loh
Millais, John Everett	mil-AY, jan EV-ruht
Minoan	mi-NO-en
Moche	MOH-chay
Moctezuma	MOCK-teh-SOO-mah
Mori, Mariko	moh-ree, mah-ree-koh
Mu Qi	moo kee *or* moo chee
Mughal	MUH-ghel
Munch, Edvard	mungk, ED-vard
Muybridge, Eadweard	MY-brij, ED-wurd

N

Nam June Paik	nahm joon pahk
Notre Dame du Haut	NOHTr' dahm doo OH

O

Odalisque	OHD-'l-isk
Olmec	AHL-meck
Orozco, José Clemente	oh-ROHS-coh, ho-SAY cleh-MEN-tay

P

Palenque	pah-LENG-kay
Palladio, Andrea	pul-LAY-dee-oh, an-DRAY-uh
Papua New Guinea	PAHP-uh-wah noo GHIN-ee
Père Lachaise	PAYR la-SHAYZ
Pericles	PER-i-kleez
Persepolis	per-SEP-uh-lis
Phoenician	fi-NISH-un
Polykleitos	pal-ee-KLIY-tos
Pompeii	pom-PAY
Poseidon	po-SYE-den
Potawatomi	PAHD-eh-WAHD-eh-mee
Protagoras	proh-TAG-eh-res

Q

Qin	chin
Quetzalcoatl	ket-SAHL-kwaht-'l
Quran	koo-RAN

R

Radha	RAD-uh
Ramayana	rah-MAH-yuh-nuh
Raphael	rah-fay-el

Rembrandt van Rijn	REM-brant van RIYN
Renoir, Pierre Auguste	ren-WAR, pee-AYR oh-GOOST
Riefenstahl, Leni	REE-fen-stahl, len-EE
Rivera, Diego	ree-VAY-ra, dee-AY-go
Ryoanji	ryoh-an-jee

S

Saarinen, Eero	SAR-uh-nen, EER-oh
Sacsahuaman	sack-say-hwua-MAHN
Safavids	suh-FAH-weedz
Safdie, Moshe	SAHF-dee, MOSH-eh
Sanchi	SAHN-chee
Sanzio, Raphael	SAHN-zee-oh, rah-fay-el
Seurat, Georges	sue-RAH, zhorzh
Shi Huangdi	SHI(r) HWANG-dee
Shiva Nataraja	SHIH-vah nah-tah-RAH-jah
Siddhartha Gautama	sid-AR-tha ghu-TAW-mah
Sioux	SOO
Siqueiros, David	see-KAYR-ohs
St. Lazare	SAHN lah-ZAR

T

Tenochtitlán	tah-NOHCH-tee-TLAHN
Teotihuacán	tay-oh-tee-hwah-KAHN
Tinguely, Jean	tan-GLEE, zhon
Tlaloc	TLAH-lohk
Tlingit	TLING-git
Toulouse-Lautrec, Henri de	too-LOOZ low-TREK, on-REE deh
Toussaint L'Ouverture, François	too-SAN loo-vur-TOOR, fran-ZWAH
Trajan	TRAY-jan
Tutankhamen	too-tahn-KAHM-un

U

Ukeles, Mierle Laderman	oo-KEL-leez, murl LAD-er-man
Utzon, Joern	UT-zone, YOHR-'n

V

van Rijn, Rembrandt	van RIYN, REM-brant
Velasquez, Diego	vay-LAS-kas, DYAY-go
Veracruz	ver-eh-KROOZ
Vermeer, Jan	ver-ME(U)R, yan
Verrocchio, Andrea del	vur-ROHK-kyoh, an-DRAY-uh del
Versailles	vair-SYE
Vesalius, Andreas	vih-SAY-lee-us, AN-dree-as

W

Warhol, Andy	WOR-hal, AN-dee
Wilke, Hannah	WILL-key, Han-nah
Willendorf	VILL-en-dorf

X

Xilonen	shi-LOH-nen

Y

Yahweh	YAH-wah
Yakshi	YAK-shee
Yoruba	YOH-roo-bah

Z

Zapotec	zah-peh-TEK
Zeus	zoos
Zhou	joe
Zimbabwe	zim-BAH-bway
Zoroaster	ZOR-oh-as-ter

Glossary

A

Abstract Art An art style developed in Western cultures in the second to fifth decades of the twentieth century. Its imagery ranged from somewhat abstract to nonobjective forms. Its roots are accredited to Cubism.

Abstract Expressionism An art movement that emerged after World War II that emphasized spontaneous artistic self-expression, non-representational imagery, and distinct point application; most abstract expressionist works were paintings.

abstracted texture The treatment an artist gives to the element of texture in his or her work that is a distortion, a simplification, or an exaggeration of an actual texture.

Abstraction Visual imagery in art that does not copy reality. This might be achieved by simplifying, distorting, or exaggerating objects from nature, or it may be expressed in completely nonobjective forms.

academy An institution developed in various cultures to set strict standards and guidelines for artists. Some academies began in France and Japan in the seventeenth and eighteenth centuries.

accent Special attention given to any element of a composition in order to attract the viewer's eye to it. This may be done by giving an element a brighter color, isolating it, or enlarging it in order to accent it. Any visual device may be used in an accent.

achromatic (ak-ruh-MAT-ik) Without color, consisting only of grays.

acropolis (ah-KRAH-pul-us) The highest ground in an ancient Greek city; originally fortified and, later, the site of temples.

acrylic A water-soluble, permanent synthetic paint that was developed in the 1960s.

actual shape Clearly defined positive areas, not ambiguous.

actual space Areas that exist in reality.

actual texture Surface qualities that exist in reality and can be felt.

additive color system Color that is created by mixing light rays. When the three primary colors (red, blue, and green) are mixed, a white light is produced. Cyan, yellow, and magenta are the secondary colors in this system.

adobe (ah-DOH-bee) Sun-dried brick made of straw and clay.

aerial perspective The blurring of forms, colors, and values as they recede into the background. This is sometimes referred to as *atmospheric perspective,* as receding forms in space take on the colors and tones of the natural atmosphere.

Aesthetics (es-THET-iks) A branch of Western philosophies that is concerned with the meaning of beauty. The notion of what is beautiful is a cultural value and, therefore, has an enormous range of meaning.

afterimage A phenomenon that occurs after staring at an area of color for a while, then glancing at a white ground. The eye will see the complementary color.

agora (AG-uh-ruh) An open square surrounded by colonnades and porticos where markets and places of business were located in an ancient Greek or Roman city.

alla prima (ah-la PREE-mah) A technique in painting in which pigment is laid directly on the surface without any underpainting.

ambient light The light all around us in the world.

amphitheater (am[p]-feh-THEE-et-er) An oval or circular arena surrounded by tiers of seats.

amulet (AM-yoo-let) A charm worn to protect one from evil.

analogous colors Colors that are close to each other on the color wheel.

Ancestor Dreaming A system of spiritual beliefs for the Aboriginal people in Australia that accounts for creation and the cosmos.

animation a series of drawings that vary slightly from one to the next, so that the figures within the drawings appear to move.

animé A contemporary style of animation that originates in Japan.

animism The belief that all things in nature contain a spiritual force or soul.

anthropomorphic Giving human characteristics and attributes to a non-human being.

apotheosis (ah-poth-ee-OH-sus) The raising of human beings to a divine level, or to be deified.

appliqué (ap-leh-KAY) Designs made of cutout material joined (usually by sewing) to another piece of material.

apse (aps) Vaulted, semicircular area at the end of a building; usually seen in Roman basilicas, churches, and mosques.

arabesque (ar-ah-BESK) Intricate interlocking surface decorations usually of spiral forms, knots, and flora. There is no suggestion of human forms in the designs.

arcade A line of arches placed side by side on piers or columns that may be freestanding or attached to a wall.

arch A curved structure made of stone or brick that supports weight over an opening, such as a door or window.

architectural systems Organized structures that result in functional and durable buildings. These systems must endure the forces of gravity and weather as well as forces within the building itself.

architecture The science and art of designing buildings and other structures that are both aesthetic and functional.

armature The underlying framework on which clay, wax, or plaster is placed; used in making sculpture.

Art Nouveau (ar noo-VOH) A Western art movement in the early twentieth century that included art forms that were based on natural forms and could be mass-produced in the age of technology and industrialism.

artifact An object made by one or more human beings and usually categorized by time and culture.

ashlars Precisely cut, regularly shaped, and fitted stone used in masonry constructed without mortar.

assemblage (ah-sem-BLAHZH) Sculptures made from various found objects or prefabricated parts that are put together.

asymmetry Balance that is achieved in a composition by giving dissimilar objects equal visual weight and attention.

atlantid (at-LAN-tid) *See* **caryatid.**

atlatl (AHT-[uh]-lat-[uh]l) A stick thrower, or a device that aids the throwing of a stick or spear.

atmospheric perspective *See* **aerial perspective.**

atrium (AY-tree-um) The entrance room with an open skylight in a Roman house. Also, the attached, open-colonnaded court at the entrance of a Christian basilica.

attic The uppermost story in a structure.

avant-garde (av-an[t]-GAR) Late-nineteenth- and twentieth-century artists who develop new concepts in their work.

avatar (av-uh-TAR) In Hinduism, the manifestation of a deity, or an aspect of a deity.

B

ba Part of the human soul, in ancient Egyptian beliefs. *See also* **ka.**

balance Visual equilibrium in a composition; achieved by organizing the weight and attention of all elements in an artwork. Types of balance are *symmetrical, asymmetrical, radial,* and *crystallographic.*

baldacchino (bal-dah-KEE-no) A canopy placed over a throne or an altar, sometimes resting on columns.

balustrade (BAL-us-trade) A railing supported by short pillars.

bargeboards Boards that conceal roof timbers projecting over gables; often decorated.

Baroque style (bah-ROHK) Sculpture and art in seventeenth- and eighteenth- century Western cultures (specifically in Europe) characterized by exaggeration, overstatement, and a flare for artifice and the theatrical.

barque (bark) A small sailing ship.

barrel vault *See* **vaulting.**

bas relief (bah reh-LEEF) *See* **relief.**

base The lowest part of an Ionic or a Doric column.

basilica (beh-SIL-i-keh) A Roman colonnaded hall consisting of a nave and two side aisles, sometimes with an apse attached to the short ends; usually a place of business or government. The Christians adapted this plan for their worship space.

bay A division of interior space that is usually defined by architectural supports, such as columns or buttresses.

belfry A tower that houses a bell.

bestiary (BES-tee-air-ee) A type of medieval natural history book with actual and mythical animals, along with descriptions and moral and religious interpretations.

binder A liquid or wax that holds pigment particles together and dries to create a paint layer.

bitumen A natural, tar-like substance.

black figure style Greek pottery that has been decorated with dark figures placed on a lighter background of red clay.

bodhisattva (boh-dih-SAHT-vah) In Buddhist beliefs, those humans who have attained the level of Buddhahood but choose to postpone their achieving Nirvana to remain on Earth to help others.

bronze An alloy of copper and tin.

Buddhism An Asian religion with the belief that the rejection of personal desires will lead to Nirvana.

bust A sculpture of a human being that includes only the head and shoulders.

buttressing A mass of brick or stone that supports a wall or an arch; a *flying buttress* is a buttress placed some distance from the structure it is supporting, and it is connected to the main structure with an arch.

C

calligraphy (keh-LIG-reh-fee) Handwriting that is considered exceptionally beautiful.

canon (KAN-on) A rule of proportion that meets the requirements of a specific cultural aesthetic.

cantilever (kant-el-EE-ver) A structure in architecture that extends or protrudes horizontally beyond its support.

capital Uppermost element on a column, serving as a transition from the shaft to the lintel.

cartouche (kar-TOOSH) An oblong oval or scroll shape that usually contains glyphs or a heraldic device.

caryatid (kar-ee-AYT-id) A supporting element, like a column, that is carved to represent a female figure. A male supporting figure is called an *atlantid.*

caste system In Hindu societies, the social system in which rank is determined by the family into which one is born.

catacombs (KAT-eh-kohmz) Subterranean chambers used for the burial of the dead.

cathedral (keh-THEE-drel) A church that is the official seat of a bishop.

cenotaph (SEN-uh-taff) A coffinlike monument commemorating a person who has died, but is buried at a different location.

centaur (SEN-tar) A half-man, half-horse creature, from fables.

ceramic Pottery and objects made of clay.

Chi-Rho (ki roh) The initials of Christ's name in Greek.

chiaroscuro (kee-ar-eh-SK[Y]OOR-oh) In a drawing, the use of various tones (black, white and grays) to create the illusion of volume.

chroma (KRO-ma) Brightness or dullness of a hue, or intensity.

cili An ancient symbol of wealth, fertility, and luck. It appears in the shape of a woman's head with a large, fanlike headdress radiating from it.

cire perdue (seer per-DOO) *See* **lost wax.**

city-state An autonomous political entity, consisting of a city and its surrounding territory.

Classical The art of ancient Greece during the fifth century BCE, based on ideal proportion grounded in the human figure. The term also refers to a style that is clear and rational. Western art aesthetics are heavily influenced by Classical Greek art, seen in Roman, Romanesque, Renaissance, and Neoclassical styles.

Classical Baroque The Baroque style that also contains classical characteristics, especially in architecture. *See* **Baroque style.**

claymation A method of animation using clay figures in place of drawings.

clerestory (KLEER-stor-ee) An area of wall that contains windows and that rises above roof areas that surround it.

cloisonné (kloiz-eh-NAY) A method of fusing enamel in metal compartments with the application of heat.

coffer A recessed panel in a ceiling, vault, or dome.

collaboration Arrangement in which two or more artists work together on one artwork.

collage (kuh-LAZH) A two-dimensional composition in which paper, cloth, or other materials are glued to a surface.

colonnade (kol-uh-NADE) A row of columns that supports an entablature or arches.

color wheel A circular arrangement of the hues of the spectrum.

column A cylinder consisting of a base, shaft, and capital (top element) that usually supports a roof. However, freestanding columns sometimes function as monuments. *See* **Orders.**

complementary colors Hues that are located directly opposite each other on the color wheel.

composition The unified organization of the elements of an artwork in such a way that harmony and balance are achieved.

concentric Spheres or circles having the same center.

conceptual Artwork whose primary purpose is to convey an idea or a concept in any medium. Printed text is often included.

contained style In a sculpture, all the forms are kept within the overall outer shape.

conté (KON-tee) A hard wax crayon used for drawing. Traditional conté comes in browns, black and white; more recently, it has been available in an array of colors.

contour line The outline of a shape.

contrapposto (kon-trah-POS-toh) A standing position in which the body weight rests on one leg, with the other leg posed forward, giving the human form an s-shaped curve.

cool colors Generally, blues, greens, and purples.

corbel (KOR-bul) Stones or bricks stacked so that each new layer projects beyond the layer below it; corbels can be arranged to create a corbeled arch or corbeled vault.

Corinthian (kuh-RIN-thee-en) *See* **Orders.**

cornice (KOR-niss) A projecting horizontal member that crowns a structure.

cosmos A systematic, orderly, harmonious universe.

C-print A non-archival color print made from a negative.

craft A category of art that requires special manual skills and is often functional in origin.

crayon A small stick used as drawing material, with pigment held together by a wax binder.

cross-hatching *See* **hatching.**

cross vault *See* **vaulting.**

crystallographic balance (kris-teh-leh-GRAF-ik) Visual equilibrium in which equal emphasis is given to all the elements in a two-dimensional composition so that there is the same visual weight wherever the viewer looks.

cubiculum (koo-BIK-yoo-lum); *pl.* **cubicula** A small room that opens onto the atrium of a Roman house; or, a small room in a catacomb that serves as a mortuary chapel.

Cubism An art movement that represents multiple viewpoints or facets on a two-dimensional picture plane. Analytical Cubism broke down forms, while Synthetic Cubism used collage and assemblage to represent parts of objects in order to visually play with illusions and reality.

cuneiform (kyoo-NAY-uh-form) A system of writing with wedge-shaped characters, used in the ancient Near East.

curvilinear Consisting of visual elements that are made up of or allude to curved lines.

D

Dada An art movement characterized by works with fantastic or incongruous imagery.

daguerreotype (deh-GARE-[e]-o-type) A photographic process invented in the nineteenth century for fixing an image on a silver-coated metal plate.

damascene (dam-eh-SEEN) Ornamentation created on a metal surface, such as iron or steel, using wavy patterns or inlaid work of precious metals.

damask (DAM-esk) An elaborately patterned fabric woven on a Jacquard loom.

dealer A person whose business is to buy artwork directly from the artist and then sell it, or take artwork on consignment.

deconstruction A method for analyzing works of art developed in the late twentieth century, in which artworks are treated as texts that can have a variety of meanings, based on the person who perceives them, emphasizing subjectivity.

Deconstructivist Architecture A contemporary architectural style in which building parts are disassembled and reassembled in an almost sculptural fashion, without regard to the function of the building.

decorative (space) Pictorial space in a two-dimensional work that remains true to the picture plane and shows very little depth.

dharma (DAR-muh) In Hinduism, the laws and duties intended to guide the behavior of people of various castes.

digital art Art that is made with the assistance of electronic devices, or intended to be displayed on a computer.

diptych (DIP-tik) A two-paneled painting, often hinged.

distemper A painting process using pigments mixed with egg yoke, egg white, glue or size.

distortion The changing of an accepted perception of a form or object so that it may be barely or not at all recognizable.

dome A hemisphere used to cover an open interior space, made of an arch rotated 360 degrees on a vertical axis.

Doric *See* **Orders.**

drum A cylindrical stone that is stacked with others to create the shaft of a column.

drypoint An etching, which is a kind of printmaking, in which the design is scratched into the surface of a metal plate.

dymaxion A term invented by R. Buckminster Fuller by combining the words *dynamic, maximum,* and *tension,* to describe his view of architecture that is economical and does more with less.

dynasty A powerful group or family that rules a territory or nation for an extended period.

E

earthenware Ceramic ware made of slightly porous clay fired at a low temperature.

eave The edge of the roof that overhangs the wall.

eclectic Consisting of many varied elements.

effigy mound Ceremonial earthen mound, shaped like an animal, built by Native North American peoples.

egg tempera Paint created by grinding dry pigment into egg yolk, which is the binder.

elements (formal) That which makes up an artwork. The elements are line, value and light, color, shape, space, texture, volume and mass, time, and motion.

emphasis A device in art that draws the attention of the viewer to one or more focal points in an artwork.

enamel A glossy, often colorful surface, fused onto the surface of metal, glass, or pottery.

encaustic (en-KAH-stik) A paint medium in which pigments are mixed into heated beeswax.

engaged column A column partly embedded in a wall.

English Perpendicular Style *See* **Gothic.**

engraving The process of incising or scratching lines on a hard material, such as wood or a metal plate.

entablature (in-TAB-leh-chur) In classical Greek architecture, the part of the building that is above the capital of the supporting columns. It consists of three parts: the architrave, the frieze, and the pediment.

entasis (EN-teh-sis) An apparent swelling or bulging in the shaft of a Doric column.

Environmental art A form of art that surrounds and affects the viewer; it may be in an interior space or out in nature.

ephemeral arts Artworks that are fleeting or transitory and are not permanent. Examples include the masquerade from Africa, and twentieth-century Performance Art or a Happening.

Epicureanism (ep-i-kyoo-REE-en-izm) An ancient Greek philosophy that advocated intelligent pleasure-seeking in life, because death was the end to existence.

equestrian An artwork that depicts a figure mounted on a horse.

etching The creation of lines or areas on glass or a metal plate, using acid that eats into the exposed surface but leaves coated, protected areas unchanged. When etched plates are inked, they can be used in printmaking.

Eucharist (YOO-keh-rist) The Sacrament of Holy Communion in the Christian faith. The ritual involves the symbolic transformation of bread and wine into the sacrificial body and blood of Jesus Christ.

Expressionism An art movement in early-twentieth-century Europe that focused on capturing the subjective feeling toward objective reality. The movement developed a bold, colorful, and vigorous style, especially in painting.

F

façade (feh-SAHD) The front facing of a building.

faience (fay-ANS) Earthenware or pottery decorated with highly colored designs.

Fauvism (FOH-vizm) An early-twentieth-century art movement in Europe led by Henri Matisse that focused on bright colors and patterns. The term comes from the French word *fauve,* meaning "wild beast."

Feminism Artwork or art criticism based on the idea that women should have political, economic, and social rights that are equal to those of men.

fengshui(FUNG-shway) The science and art of arranging architecture and furnishings to allow for a good flow of energy. The term comes from the Chinese words for *wind* and *water*.

fetish An object that is empowered with magic that can heal and protect; also known as a *power figure*.

feudalism (FYOOD-el-izm) An economic and political system in rural societies in which the land is owned and controlled by a few warrior-rulers, and the rest of the people work the land as peasants.

filigree (FIL-eh-gree) Delicate ornamental work.

finial (FIN-ee-el) A crowning ornament or knob.

flute, fluting Narrow vertical channels carved from top to bottom into the shafts of columns.

Fluxus A late-twentieth-century art movement that sought to create a kind of anti-art or non-art; art was conceived as an artist-initiated experience rather than an object.

flying buttress *See* **buttressing.**

focal point Main area of visual concentration in an artwork.

form The total appearance and organization of the physical and formal qualities of an artwork.

formal analysis The study of artwork that focuses on the elements of the language of art and the principles of composition.

formal qualities All that makes up an artwork, such as the formal elements (line, value and light, color, shape, space, texture, volume and mass, time, and motion), the medium, proportion, size, and subject matter.

formalism A method for analyzing artworks based solely on their formal qualities.

forum A central, open space surrounded by public buildings in ancient Roman cities.

found objects Actual everyday objects, such as shoes, tools, and so on, that are incorporated into artworks.

freestanding sculpture Sculpture in the round, intended to be seen from many viewpoints.

French Gothic *See* **Gothic.**

French Impressionism An art movement in early-twentieth-century France in which artists sought to capture the changing effects of light and color as the eye perceives them.

fresco A painting made on plaster; in *true fresco,* water-based pigments are painted directly on a wet lime plaster ground and bind with the plaster when dry; in *dry fresco,* the paint is applied to dry plaster.

frieze (freez) A decorative band in the central section of the entablature in classical Greek architecture, or a decorative band on a building.

frontal Sculpture whose focal point or emphasis is placed on the front side of the piece.

futurists *See* **Italian Futurists.**

G

gable *See* **pediment.**

gallery In Christian church architecture, an upper story over an aisle opening onto a nave. In secular architecture, a large room in which items of art are displayed.

gargoyle (GAR-goil) A carving of a grotesque human figure or animal that is incorporated into a roof to function as a waterspout.

genre painting (ZHAH[n]-reh) Paintings that contain subject matter of everyday life.

genres (ZHAH[n]-reh) Various categories of paintings, as well as arts in general.

geodesic dome (jee-oh-DEES-ik) A dome shape made of framework consisting of interlocking polygonal units, developed by R. Buckminster Fuller.

geometrical Objects, lines, or shapes based on mathematical concepts, such as the circle, square, or rectangle.

gesture A quickly sketched image that captures the essence of the form of the subject.

gild, gilding (gild) Coating or layering a surface with gold, gold leaf (a very thin layer of gold), or a gold color.

glaze In painting, a thin layer of glossy, transparent color applied on top of previously painted, dry areas of the painting; in ceramics, a hard, waterproof, often glossy coating fired onto the clay surface of pottery or sculpture.

glyph (glif) A figure or character that has symbolic meaning and is most often carved in relief.

Gothic The history, culture, and art of western Europe from the twelfth through the fourteenth centuries. Local variations include French Gothic and the English Perpendicular Style.

gouache (gwash) Painting with opaque watercolors.

graffito; pl. graffiti Writing or drawing written or painted on public walls.

Greek Revival A style of architecture that visually echoes Greek Classical architecture. This style was popular in nineteenth-century Europe and United States.

grillwork Metalwork, usually of iron, that adorns windows and doors while also protecting the building against intruders.

groin vault *See* **vaulting.**

guilds (gilds) Organizations of merchants, artisans, and craftsmen that developed in medieval Europe.

H

handscroll An Asian horizontal painted scroll that is unrolled from the right to the left to view individual scenes and read text.

Happening An art event that is planned by the artist and that may be performed spontaneously and solicit participation of its audience. This art form was invented by Allan Kaprow.

harmony The quality of relating the visual elements of a composition through the repetition of similar characteristics. A pleasing visual interaction occurs through harmony.

hatching The placing of lines side by side to create values and tones. Lines that are layered and cross over the layer beneath create cross-hatching.

Hellenistic The culture that flourished around Greece, Macedonia, and some areas bordering the Mediterranean Sea from around 323 to 31 BCE.

hieratic (hi-uh-RAT-ik) A system of proportion of figures or subject matter in a work of art that gives emphasis to what or who is considered to be the most important; for example, the largest figure would be the most important or highest in rank.

hieroglyphic (hi-ro-GLIF-ik) Ancient picture writing, especially that used by the Egyptian culture.

hilt The handle of a sword, dagger, knife, or tool.

Hinduism The dominant religion of India whose basic beliefs encompass the cycle of reincarnation and the striving to achieve Nirvana.

hip roof A roof with sloping ends and sides.

horizon line In linear perspective, a horizontal line that represents eye level.

hue The pure state of color that the eye sees in the spectrum.

Humanism A system of thought in which the efforts, values, and achievements of human beings are the focus.

hydria (HI-dree-ah) A Greek ceramic water jar, usually with two handles.

hypostyle hall (HI-puh-style) A large hall in which rows of columns support the roof.

I

ibex (EYE-beks) A wild goat with long, back-curving horns found in Eurasia and North Africa. This animal is found in prehistoric iconography.

icon A visual image, pictorial representation, or symbol that may have religious or political connotations.

iconoclasm (eye-KON-uh-klazm) The act of destroying religious images or opposing their veneration.

iconography (eye-keh-NOG-reh-fee) The study of visual images and symbols within their cultural and historical contexts.

idealism An artistic interpretation of the world as it should be according to respective cultural aesthetics. Generally, all flaws and imperfections found in nature are removed.

illumination A hand-printed manuscript that has been decorated with drawings or paintings.

imago mundi (im-AG-o MUN-dee) Image of the world.

imam (eye-MAM) A leader of collective worship in Islam.

impasto (im-PAHS-toe) Paint that has been thickly applied to the ground.

implied line A drawn line having missing areas that are visually completed by the viewer.

impluvium (im-PLOO-vee-um) A small pool that collects rainwater; located in the atrium of a Roman house.

Impressionism A late-nineteenth-century painting style, originating in Western Europe, that attempts to capture subtle light qualities with small strokes of strong color.

incise To cut into a surface with a sharp instrument.

inlay To piece together or insert materials, such as ivory or colored wood, into a surface.

installation An art piece usually of mixed media that is designed for a specific space.

intaglio (in-TAH-lee-oh) A printmaking process in which lines are incised or etched into a metal plate, which is then inked and wiped so that the ink remains only in the incised lines.

intensity Brightness or dullness of a hue, or chroma.

intermedia The mixing and overlapping of any materials and/or disciplines in an artwork.

International style A style developed in the thirteenth and fourteenth centuries in Europe with characteristics of French Gothic and Sienese art. Later, in the twentieth century, a style of architecture based on simple geometric forms without adornment.

invented texture An imaginary surface quality created by the artist.

Ionic (EYE-on-ik) *See* **Orders.**

Islam The religion of Muslims as revealed to the prophet Mohammed and recorded in the Holy Koran, or Quran.

isometric projection A perspective system for rendering a three-dimensional object on a two-dimensional surface by drawing all horizontal edges at a 30-degree angle from a horizontal base. All the verticals are drawn perpendicularly from the horizontal base.

Italian Futurists Artists in Italy who, beginning in 1909, were influenced by Cubism and intrigued with light and movement. They were also fascinated with the sensation of speed and with the mechanics of the machine age, as well as the dangers of war.

iwan (EE-wan) A vaulted, recessed area that opens into a courtyard in Islamic architecture.

J

jamb (jam) The vertical side or post of a doorway.

Jihad (jee-HAHD) A holy war in the Islamic religion.

Judeo-Christian Characteristic of cultures whose roots are made up of both the Jewish and Christian traditions.

juxtapose To place contrasting elements, images, or ideas side by side.

K

ka Part of the spirit or soul of a human being in ancient Egyptian culture. *See also* **ba.**

kachina (kuh-CHEE-nuh) A spirit doll of the Pueblo culture in North America.

kami (kah-mee) Spirits or deities in the Shinto religion, believed to dwell in nature and in charismatic people.

karma (KAR-muh) The consequences of the actions of this life, which influence the next reincarnation.

kitsch (kich) Works that are done in what is considered to be poor taste.

kiva (KEE-vuh) An underground, circular ceremonial structure of the Pueblo culture in North America.

Koran (koo-RAN) The sacred book of the Islamic religion; also *Quran.*

kou A native Hawaiian wood from which ceremonial bowls are carved.

L

labret (LA-bret) A mouth ornament.

labyrinth (LAB-eh-rinth) A maze.

lacquer A resinous varnish that adds a rich sheen to a surface.

lamassu (lah-MAH-soo) A winged, human-headed bull, from Assyria.

laminated Composed of layers of glued or fused material.

landscape Art depicting natural land formations and scenes.

lapis lazuli (LAP-is LAHZ-eh-lee) A semiprecious stone with a deep blue color.

lei (LAY-ee) A Hawaiian necklace usually made of feathers or flowers.

limner (LIM-[n]er) A painter or a draftsman.

line An element in art with length but negligible width.

linear perspective *See* **perspective.**

lintel (LINT-el) In architecture, a horizontal member spanning an opening, and usually carrying a weight from above.

lithography (lith-OG-reh-fee) A form of printmaking, invented in the nineteenth century, based on the principle that water and oil do not mix.

lost wax [*cire perdue*] A sculptural method in which a cast is made from a wax model by coating the model with an investment material that can be heated to high temperatures. The wax melts away, leaving a negative mold of the model, into which molten metal is poured or clay is pressed, leaving a positive form of the original wax model.

lotus A water lily. In some cultures, the flower was thought to induce a state of contented forgetfulness.

low key Any values or tones and colors that have a value level of middle gray or darker.

luau (LU-au) A Hawaiian feast.

luminosity The quality of radiating or reflecting light.

M

malagan or **malanggan** (mah-lah-gan *or* mah-lang-gan) The carvings and ritual pieces created to honor the dead in Papua New Guinea; also, the festivals for which the carvings are made.

mana (MAH-na) Supernatural power or influence that flows through some individuals or resides in some objects.

mandala (MUN-duh-luh) A design with geometric elements that delineates deities, the universe, and wholeness in Hinduism or Buddhism.

masjid (MUS-jid) Mosque.

masquerade (mas-ker-ADE) A ceremony or a festive gathering in which masks and costumes are worn.

mass (volume) An area of occupied space. *Mass* usually refers to a solid occupying a space, while *volume* may refer to either a solid mass or an open framework occupying a space.

Mass The Roman Catholic Eucharistic ritual consisting of prayers, ceremonies, offerings, and the consecration of bread and wine.

mausoleum (maw-seh-LEE-um) A stately tomb usually built above the ground.

medieval (meh-DEE-vel) Of or like the period between ancient and modern times.

medium, media Traditional and nontraditional materials used to make art, such as charcoal, paint, clay, bronze, video, or computers.

megalith (meg-ah-LITH) A huge stone, especially one used in ancient or Neolithic monuments or tombs.

menorah (meh-NOR-eh) A Jewish candelabrum with seven branches (a traditional symbol of Judaism) or with nine branches (used during the festival of Hanukah).

Mesoamerica (mes-oh-eh-MER-i-kah) The Central American regions of Mexico, Guatemala, El Salvador, and Belize.

Mesolithic (mes-oh-LITH-ik) The middle Stone Age, between the Paleolithic and Neolithic eras, marked by the earliest use of local and permanent food sources.

metaphor An image or visual element that is primarily descriptive of one thing, but is used to describe something else.

Middle Ages A period between ancient and modern times, often used in reference to Europe from the fifth through the fourteenth centuries.

mihrab (MEE-rahb) In a mosque, a niche in the wall that faces Mecca.

minaret A prayer tower that is part of an Islamic mosque.

minbar (MIN-bar) The pulpit for the imam, in an Islamic mosque.

Minimalism A nonobjective art movement in the twentieth century in the United States in which artists reduced their images and objects to pure form. These images and forms were called *primary structures.*

mixed media The mixing of art materials and forms in creating an artwork. *See* **intermedia.**

moai (moh-eye) A large, stone figure from the Easter Islands (Rapa Nui).

Modernism A period of Western art, primarily in the twentieth century, during which innovation and self-critical practice were emphasized.

module, modular A composition that incorporates modules, or distinct visual units or sections.

monochromatic An artwork that contains the hue, tints, and shades of only one color.

monolith A large, single block or column.

montage (mahn-TAHZH) A composite picture created by combining several separate pictures or separate clips from movies or videos.

mortise and tenon (MORT-is and TEN-en) A technique for joining pieces of wood. A *mortise* is a notch or a slot made in a piece of wood. A *tenon* is a projection made on a separate piece of wood to fit precisely into the mortise to create a joint.

mosaic (mo-ZAY-ik) An image or decoration created by covering a surface with small pieces of variously colored material, such as metal, glass, or stone.

mosque (mosk) An Islamic place of worship.

motif (mo-TEEF) A repeated design or image in a composition that takes on visual significance.

mudra (MOO-druh) A hand gesture with symbolic meaning in Hindu and Buddhist art.

muqarna or **mukarna** (moo-KAR-na) Numerous niches and niche fragments, or hanging vaults, clustered in a honeycomb-like pattern, that appears in Islamic domes, arches, portals, and window openings.

mural Images painted directly on a wall, or covering a wall.

Muslim A follower of the Islamic religion.

N

nadir The lowest point.

narrative An artwork that relates a story.

natural pattern Repeated elements that resemble each other, but are not exactly alike; the interval between elements may be irregular.

Naturalism A style of art with imagery that resembles what we see in the world around us.

nave The tall, center aisle of a church or a basilica, usually flanked with side aisles.

necropolis (neh-KROP-eh-lis) The city of the dead.

negative space Voids within an artwork.

Neolithic (nee-oh-LITH-ik) A period of the Stone Age in which humans used polished stone tools and developed agriculture; the New Stone Age.

neophyte (nee-oh-FITE) A new convert to a faith or a belief.

niche (nich) A recess in a wall, usually designed to hold a decorative or votive object.

nirvana (nir-VAH-nah) The ultimate release from the cycle of reincarnation in the Buddhist and Hindu faiths, achieved by the expulsion of individual passion, hatred, and delusion. The attainment of total peace.

nkisi n'kondi ([n]kee-see [n]kon-dee) A carved power figure of the Kongo people from central Africa, used by a shaman to bestow good or inflict harm on someone.

nonobjective Artwork that has no imagery that resembles the natural world.

O

obelisk (OB-eh-lisk) A tall, four-sided monolith that is tapered at its apex into a pyramid form.

oblique projection A three-dimensional object rendered two-dimensionally with the front and back sides parallel.

obsidian (ob-SID-ee-en) A dark, volcanic glass.

oculus (AH-kyoo-lus) The round opening in the center of a dome.

odalisque (OH-deh-lisk) A Turkish harem girl.

one-point perspective A drawing in which all front-facing planes are shown as parallel to the picture plane, and all other planes recede to a single point.

onion dome A pointed dome whose middle diameter swells outward, creating a smaller diameter at its base.

Op Art A 1960s style of art that created unusual visual vibrations with contrasting colors or closely placed lines.

Orders In Classical Greek architecture, an Order consists of a column with a base, a shaft, a capital, and an entablature that is decorated and proportioned to the Classical Greek canon. The types of Orders are: Doric, Ionic, Corinthian, Tuscan, Roman Doric, and Composite.

Organic architecture A style of American architecture developed by Louis Sullivan and Frank Lloyd Wright that incorporated flowing natural forms in its design.

organic shape A shape that seems to be drawn from nature or that is like nature; not geometric.

orthogonals (or-THOG-eh-nelz) The converging lines that meet at the vanishing point on the horizon line in linear perspective.

P

pagan A follower of a polytheistic religion, or an irreligious or a hedonistic person.

pagoda (peh-GO-deh) A multistoried, Asian, towerlike temple with upward sweeping roofs over each story.

paint Colored pigment ground with a binder, having a semiliquid or paste consistency.

Paleolithic (pay-lee-oh-LITH-ik) Old Stone Age, dating from 25,000 to 8000 BCE; the era of hunters and gatherers.

palmette (pal-MET) Decorative drawing or relief sculpture in palm leaf shapes.

papyrus (peh-PI-rus) A tall water plant, abundant around the Nile River, used for making an early form of paper.

parapet (PAR-eh-pet) A low wall or railing.

parchment (PARCH-ment) Animal skin, usually of a goat or sheep, specially prepared to be used as paper.

pathos The power to provoke compassion.

patriarch The male head of a family or family line.

patron A person who supports the artist and the arts.

pattern In art, a repetition of any element in the composition.

pedestal (PED-es-tel) The base of a column or colonnade in Classical architecture, or a base on which a sculpture or a vase may be placed.

pediment (PED-eh-ment) A low, pitched gable resting on columns, a portico, a door, or a window.

pendentive (pen-DENT-iv) The triangular concave sections that are created when a dome is supported by a base of arches.

Performance Art Influenced by the "Happening," performance art consists of live-action events staged as artworks.

peristyle A colonnade around the inside and/or the outside of a court or room.

Perpendicular Style An English Gothic style of architecture that has strong vertical emphasis and dense ornamental vault ribs that serve only for decoration; also known as the "Tudor" style.

perspective A system of rendering the illusion of three-dimensional depth on a flat, two-dimensional surface.

pharaoh (FA-ro) Title of kings in ancient Egypt.

photojournalism News reporting in which photographs are more important than the text.

photomontage A composition of many photographs, or of one using many prints to create a new image.

photomural (fo-to-MYOOR-el) A very large photograph installed as a mural.

piazza (pee-AT-za) An open court or plaza.

pictograph (PIK-to-graf) A picture or picture-like symbol used in early writing to convey an idea or information.

picture plane The flat, two-dimensional surface of a drawing, a print, or a painting.

pier A solid stone or masonry support, not a column.

pigments Colors in powder form, mixed with binders to create paint.

pilaster A pier that projects somewhat from a wall. Also, a rectangular column that would be designed after one of the Classical Orders.

pillar Any freestanding, column-like structure that does not conform to the Classical Orders. A pillar may or may not be cylindrical.

pinnacle Usually a pointed or conical ornamentation that is placed on a spire or a buttress.

plan A diagram showing the ground plan of a building.

Pointillism An art movement in Europe in the early twentieth century in which artists applied daubs of pure pigment to a ground to create an image. The paint daubs appear to blend when viewed from a distance.

polyptych (POL-ip-tik) Four or more separate panels, hinged together to create an artwork, often for an altar.

pommel A knob that is attached to the hilt of a knife or sword.

Pop Art An art movement in the mid-twentieth century that used popular commercial items as subject matter, including newspapers, comic strips, popular and political personalities, Campbell's soup cans, and Coca-Cola bottles. Usually created as satire, these artworks glorified the products of mass popular culture and elevated them to twentieth-century icons.

porcelain High-fired, lightweight, white ceramic ware.

portal An opening, a door, an entrance, or a gate.

portico (POR-ti-ko) A porch or covered walkway, with columns on one side supporting the roof.

post and lintel A method of construction that uses posts to support a crossbeam that can bear the weight of the roof.

Postimpressionism The late-nineteenth-century movement in European painting that followed Impressionism, in which artists emphasized their subjective viewpoint or the formal qualities of the painting.

Postmodernism The late-twentieth-century movement in art, based to some extent on deconstructivism and accommodating a wide range of styles.

power figure A carved figure that is empowered with magic, which can heal and protect. *See* **fetish** and **nkisi n'kondi.**

Precisionism An art movement in the United States in the first half of the twentieth century that was concerned with rendering human-made environments and the beauty of precise and perfect machine forms in a clear and concise manner. The style of painting was flat and decorative.

primary colors In any medium, those colors that, when mixed, produce the largest range of new colors.

print In printmaking, an image created by pressing an inked plate onto a surface; in photography, a photograph usually made from a negative.

proportion The size relationship, or relative size, of parts of objects or imagery to a whole or to each other.

pueblo (PWEB-lo) A type of communal housing built by Native Americans, primarily in the Southwest.

putto (POOT-toh); *pl.* **putti** (POOT-tee) A young, plump, child-angel used as subject matter in Italian sculpture and painting.

pylon (PIE-lan) A truncated pyramid form usually seen in Egyptian monumental gates.

Q

Quran (koo RAN) Variation of *Koran.*

R

radial balance Visual equilibrium achieved when all the elements in a composition radiate outward from a central point.

rampart (RAM-part) An earthen embankment, usually with a parapet, used as fortification for a castle or fort.

Realism A nineteenth-century style of art that depicts everyday life without idealism, nostalgia, or flattery.

rectilinear (rek-teh-LIN-ee-er) Consisting of straight lines set at 90-degree angles in a composition.

Reformation (ref-or-MAY-shun) A sixteenth-century European movement aimed at reforming the Catholic Church, but resulting in the establishment of the Protestant churches.

register A band that contains imagery or visual motifs; often, several registers are stacked one above the other to convey a narrative sequence.

relic A sacred fragment of an object, a deceased saint, or an ancestor.

relief Sculpture that is partly projecting from a flat surface. When the sculptural form is at least half round or more, it is called a *high relief;* when it is less, it is called a *low* or *bas relief.*

reliquary (REL-i-kwer-ee) A vessel or receptacle designed to house a holy relic.

Renaissance (ren-eh-SAHNZ) A rebirth of learning and the arts in the fourteenth through the seventeenth centuries in Europe, along with the revival and study of ancient Greek and Roman cultures.

render To depict or execute in an art form.

repetition Use of the same element over and over again in a composition; similar to pattern.

representational art Art that presents nature, people, and objects from the world in a recognizable form.

retable (reh-TAY-bel) An architectural wall or screen behind and above an altar. It is usually richly decorated with painting, sculpture, or carved ornamentation.

retablo (reh-TAH-blo) A small votive painting.

rhythm A form of repetitive beats that are usually seen in a composition as a pattern. This is accomplished by repeating one or more of the formal elements in the organization of a work.

ribbed vault *See* **vaulting.**

ridgepole The beam running the length of the building, located under the highest point of a gabled roof.

roach A Native American headdress made of animal fur and worn on a shaven head.

Rococo (ro-ko-KO) The style of art, architecture, music, and decorative arts from early-eighteenth-century Europe, made primarily for the upper class.

Romanticism An art movement in nineteenth-century Europe that focused on the intuitive, emotional, and picturesque, a spirit that was felt between human beings and nature. It rejected the carefully planned and rationalized compositions of the Renaissance and added a sense of mysticism to art.

roof comb A decorative architectural element that crowned Mayan temples and palaces.

rose window A large, circular, stained-glass window in a Gothic church, composed of many segments.

rotunda (ro-TUN-dah) A round building, hall, or room, usually roofed with a dome.

rubble Broken bits and pieces of brick and gravel that was used as fill in Roman architecture.

S

saltcellar A dish or a container designed to hold salt.

samurai (SAM-uh-rye) In feudal Japan, a member of the warrior class.

sanctuary A sacred or holy place in a church or temple.

sanskrit (SAN-skrit) The classic Indo-Aryan language from the fourth century BCE; still used in some Buddhist rituals.

sarcophagus (sar-KOF-eh-gus) A coffin.

sarsen A type of sandstone monolith found in ancient ruins, such as Stonehenge in England.

saturation The intensity or brightness of a color.

scale The size of an object or image that is measured by its relationship to other objects and images that are recognized for their normal or actual size.

scarification (skar-i-fi-KAY-shun) The cutting or scratching of the skin in various designs that will heal as permanent body decoration.

scrollwork An architectural ornamentation that echoes the form of a partially unrolled scroll. Ionic and Corinthian columns have scrollwork in their capitals.

secondary colors Colors that result when any two primary colors are mixed in a particular medium.

secular Of nonreligious matters.

semiotics The study of signs and symbols in written and verbal communication.

seppuku (seh-POO-koo) A Japanese ceremony of taking one's life.

serigraphy (seh-RIG-reh-fee) A printmaking technique in which ink is applied to a stencil that has been temporarily adhered to a stretched cloth.

shade The addition of black to a hue.

shah (shah) A title of the former rulers of Iran.

shaman (SHAH-men) A person, priest, or priestess who is empowered to use magic to cure and heal, imbue an object with magic, control spirits and commune with ancestors, and foretell the future.

shape A flat, two-dimensional element with a defined outline and usually without interior detail.

Shinto (SHIN-to) A major Japanese religion, with emphasis on ancestor and nature worship.

Shiva (SHEE-veh) Hindu god of destruction and reproduction.

shogun (SHO-gun) Any of the various hereditary leaders of Japan until 1867, who were the real rulers instead of the emperors.

shrine A receptacle for holy objects; a holy place or site; a site of the entombment of a saint; a place devoted to a deity or a holy person.

silk screen *See* **serigraphy.**

simulated texture Texture rendered in a composition to look like the actual or natural texture.

skeletal In architecture, relating to a framework of steel that is covered with a "skin" of glass or other light materials.

space An area in which objects or images can exist.

spandrel (SPAN-drel) The area between two arches or alongside one arch, or the space between the ribs of a vault.

spectrum The breakdown of white light into its components of red, orange, yellow, green, blue, indigo, and violet.

sphinx (sfinks) A figure made up of a human head and a lion's body, likely of Egyptian origin.

spire A pointed roof of a tower or steeple.

squinches The spatial areas created when a dome is placed on a square or a polygonal base.

stained glass Pieces of colored glass arranged to create an abstract composition or representational image.

stainless steel Steel alloyed with chromium, which is virtually rust-free and corrosion-free.

stele (STEE-lee); *pl.* **stelae** (STEE-lee) A stone slab or tablet that is carved with images and/or inscriptions usually in commemoration of a person or an event.

still life An assembled composition of objects set up by the artist to use as subject matter for an artwork.

stoa (STO-ah) A roofed colonnade in ancient Greek architecture that may or may not be attached to another structure.

Stoicism (STO-i-siz-em) Indifference to pleasure or pain.

Structuralism For art, the study of systems and art world structures as a way to understand the art that they produce.

stucco (STUK-oh) A plaster material that may be used for reliefs and architectural ornamentation, such as moldings and cornices. It is also a wall covering made of a thin layer of cement.

stupa (STOO-pah) A dome-shaped Buddhist shrine.

style Specific recognizable attributes and characteristics that are consistent and coherent in the artwork within a historical period, within a cultural tradition, or of an individual artist.

stylization The distortion of an image or a figure according to an artistic convention or canon.

subject matter The specific idea of an artwork.

subtractive color system Mixing of pigment to create a color.

subtractive method (sculpture) A technique in which a sculptural material, such as clay or wood, is carved away to produce a form.

sultan (SULT-n) A former ruler of Turkey, or a Muslim ruler.

support A surface upon which a two-dimensional artwork, such as a painting, is made.

Surrealism (ser-REE-el-izm) An art movement in early-twentieth-century Europe influenced by the work of Sigmund Freud. Fantastic and dreamlike imagery drawn from the subconscious was executed through automatic drawing similar to doodling.

suspension (bridge) A bridge in which the deck is suspended by ropes or cables that are attached to two piers.

sutra (SOO-trah) A documented sermon or a dialogue of the Buddha.

symbol A visual element that represents something else, often an abstract concept like peace.

symbolic geometry The use of geometry to demarcate sacred alignments in nature; the use of geometric shapes in art and architecture to symbolize divine attributes.

symmetry Balance has achieved by distributing equal weight evenly throughout a composition. If an imaginary line could be drawn vertically down an artwork that has symmetrical balance, one side would mirror the other.

sympathetic magic A form of ritual or prayer that is directed to an image or an object in order to bring about a desired result, such as a successful hunt.

syncretism (SIN-kreh-tizm) The blending of different religious beliefs and rituals.

T

tabernacle A sacred place that holds the Holy Eucharist in the Christian religion.

taboo Forbidden for general use; usually applied to sacred rituals, places, or objects.

tapestry A heavy fabric woven with designs or images, intended as a wall hanging or furniture covering.

tempera (TEM-per-ah) Painting with pigments mixed with size, casein, or egg yolk.

tensile strength (TEN-sil) The degree to which a material can withstand stretching, stress, or tension.

terra-cotta (TER-eh KOT-ah) A low-fired ceramic clay, such as that found in red-earth flowerpots.

tertiary colors (TUR-shee-er-ee) Colors that result from the mixing of one primary color and a neighboring secondary color.

tetrahedron (teh-trah-HEE-dren) A solid contained by four plane faces.

thatch A roof covering made of straw or reeds.

three-dimensional Having or appearing to have height, length, and depth.

three-point perspective A drawing in which only one point of each volume is closest to the viewer, and all planes recede to one of three points.

tone See **value.**

tooth The surface texture of paper.

torana (TO-rah-nah) Gateway in the stone fence surrounding a stupa, located at the cardinal points.

torso The trunk of the human body from the shoulders to the hips.

totem The emblem or symbol of a family clan.

Tourist Art Art that is based on a particular ethnic tradition, but is specifically created to sell to tourists.

tracery The ornamentation of the upper part of a Gothic window. *Plate tracery* was carved through solid stone, while *bar tracery* was incorporated in the mullions of a window.

transept (TRAN-sept) The crossing arm (space) that intersects the nave (forming a cross) in a basilica or a church.

triptych (TRIP-tik) A three-paneled painting.

triumphal arch A freestanding Roman arch commemorating an important event.

trompe l'oeil (tromp-LOY) Illusionistic painting that fools viewers into believing that they are seeing actual three-dimensional objects instead of their representation.

truss Wooden or metal beams arranged in connected triangles to make a framework.

tufa (TOO-feh) A porous rock formed from deposits of springs. The material can be easily carved when first exposed to air, then hardens with age.

two-dimensional Having or appearing to have height and length, without significant depth.

two-point perspective A drawing in which no planes are parallel to the picture plane, but all recede to one of two points on the horizon.

tympanum (TIM-peh-num) In architecture, a half-circular space below an arch, and above a doorway or window.

U

ukiyo-e (oo-kee-yo-ay) A kind of Japanese print or painting; literally, "pictures from the floating world."

unity A quality achieved in an artwork when the artist organizes all the compositional elements so that they visually work together as a whole.

V

value The relationship of lights and darks in a composition; sometimes referred to as *tone.*

Vanitas (VAH-nee-tas) A style of Dutch painting in which the theme is the transitory nature of earthly things along with the inevitability of death.

variety Opposing or contrasting visual elements in a composition that add interest without disturbing its unity.

vaulting A system of masonry roofing or ceiling construction based on the principle of the arch. There are several types of vaults: The *barrel* vault is a single arch extended in depth from front to back, forming a tunnel-like structure; a *groin* or a *cross* vault is formed with two barrel vaults positioned at 90-degree angles so as to cross or intersect one another; a *ribbed* vault is a variation of the groin vaulting system in which arches diagonally cross over the groin vault forming skeletal ribs; a *dome* is formed by rotating arches on their vertical axis to form a hemispheric vault.

Veda (VAY-dah) One of the four ancient books of Hinduism, with chants, hymns, and sacred formulas.

vellum (VEL-um) A fine kind of parchment.

video; video art Art made with recording cameras and displayed on monitors, and having moving imagery.

vignette (vin-YET) A decorative design that might be used on a page of a book or in a drawing, print, or painting; the outer edges of the composition are softened or blurred.

visual texture The rendering of illusionary texture on a surface or a ground. This texture may be simulated, abstracted, or invented.

volume See **mass.**

voussoir (voo-SWAR) Wedge-shaped stone used to build an arch or a vault.

W

walik A horizontal sculpture used as part of malagan rituals.

warm colors Generally, reds, oranges, and yellows.

woodcut A kind of printmaking done by cutting away nonprinting areas from the surface of a woodblock.

Y

Yakshi (yah-shee) A lesser Hindu and Buddhist female divinity, associated with fertility and vegetation; the male counterpart is the Yaksha.

yin-yang Ancient Chinese symbol of balance and harmony.

Z

Zen A variation of Buddhism, practiced mostly in Japan, Vietnam, and Korea, that seeks intuitive illumination of the mind and spirit, primarily through meditation.

ziggurat (ZIG-oo-rat) A terraced, flat-topped pyramid surmounted by a temple, from the ancient Near East.

Bibliography

Abbate, Francesco, ed. *Precolumbian Art of North America and Mexico.* Translated by Elizabeth Evans. London: Octopus Books, 1972.

Abbott, Helen, et al., eds. *The Spirit Within: Northwest Coast Native Art from the John H. Hauberg Collection.* New York: Rizzoli, 1995.

Abiodun, Rowland, Henry J. Drewal, and John Pemberton III, eds. *The Yoruba Artist: New Theoretical Perspectives on African Arts.* Washington, DC: Smithsonian Institution Press, 1994.

Adachi, Barbara. "Living National Treasures." *Japanese Encyclopedia.* Tokyo: Kodansha, 1983, pp. 60–61.

Adams, Laurie Schneider. *A History of Western Art.* New York: McGraw-Hill, 1997.

Albarn, Keith, Jenny Miall Smith, Stanford Steele, and Dinah Walker. *The Language of Pattern: An Inquiry Inspired by Islamic Decorations.* New York: Harper and Row, 1974.

Alva, Walter, and Christopher B. Donnan. *Royal Tombs of Sipan.* Los Angeles: The Fowler Museum of Cultural Heritage, University of California, Los Angeles, 1993.

American Film Institute. "Preservation." *American Film Institute.* http://afionline.org (accessed July 16, 1998). Andah, Bassey W. "The Ibadan Experience to Date." In *Museums and Archeology in West Africa,* edited by Claude Daniel Ardouin. Washington, DC: Smithsonian Institution Press, 1997.

Anderson, Richard L. *Calliope's Sisters: A Comparative Study of Philosophies of Art.* Englewood Cliffs, NJ: Prentice Hall, 1990.

Ardouin, Claude Daniel, ed. *Museums and Archeology in West Africa.* Washington, DC: Smithsonian Institution Press, 1997.

Arnason, H. H. *History of Modern Art.* Englewood Cliffs, NJ: Prentice Hall, 1986.

Atkins, Robert. *Art Speak: A Guide to Contemporary Ideas, Movements, and Buzzwords, 1945 to the present.* New York: Abbeville Press, 1997.

Auping, Michael. *Jenny Holzer.* New York: Universe Publishing, 1992.

Baines, John, and Jaromir Malak. *Cultural Atlas of the World: Ancient Egypt.* New York: Facts on File, 1994.

Barrie, Dennis. "The Scene of the Crime." *Art Journal* 50, no. 3 (Fall 1991): 29–32.

Barrow, Terrence. *An Illustrated Guide to Maori Art.* Honolulu: University of Hawaii Press, 1984.

Barrow, Tui Terrence. *Maori Wood Sculpture of New Zealand.* Rutland, VT: Charles E. Tuttle, 1969.

Baumann, Felix, and Marianne Karabelnik, eds. *Degas Portraits.* London: Merrell Holberton, 1994.

Beaver, R. Pierce, et al., eds. *Eerdmans' Handbook to the World's Religions.* Grand Rapids, MI: William B. Eerdmans, 1982.

Beck, James, and Michael Daley. *Art Restoration: The Culture, the Business and the Scandal.* New York: W. W. Norton, 1993.

Becker, Carol. "Art Thrust into the Public Sphere." *Art Journal* 50, no. 3 (Fall 1991): 65–68.

Beckwith, John. *Early Medieval Art.* New York: Praeger, 1973.

Benton, Janetta Rebold. *The Medieval Menagerie: Animals in the Art of the Middle Ages.* New York: Abbeville Press, 1992.

Benton, Janetta Rebold, and DiYanni, Robert. *Arts and Culture: Volume II.* Upper Saddle River, NJ: Prentice Hall, 1998.

Bernadac, Marie-Laure. *Louise Bourgeois.* Paris: Flammarion, 1996.

Berrin, Kathleen, ed. *The Spirit of Ancient Peru: Treasures from the Museo Arqueológico Rafael Larco Herrera.* London: Thames and Hudson, 1997.

Bersson, Robert. *Worlds of Art.* Mountain View, CA: Mayfield, 1991.

Bertelli, Carlo. *Mosaics.* New York: W. H. Smith, 1989.

Bianchi, Emanuela. *Ara Pacis Augustae.* Rome, Italy: Fratelli Palombi Editori, 1994.

Blake, Nayland, Lawrence Rinder, and Amy Scholder, eds. *In a Different Light: Visual Culture, Sexual Identity, Queer Practice.* San Francisco: City Light Books, 1995.

Blier, Suzanne Preston. *The Royal Arts of Africa.* New York: Harry N. Abrams, 1998.

Bluemel, Carl. *Greek Sculptors at Work.* New York: Phaidon, 1969.

Blunden, Caroline, and Mark Elvin. *The Cultural Atlas of the World: China.* Alexandria, VA: Stonehenge Press, 1991.

Blunt, Wilfrid. *Isfahan, Pearl of Persia.* London: Elek Books, 1966.

Boardman, John. *Greek Art.* London: Thames and Hudson, 1996.

Boyd, Andrew. *Chinese Architecture and Town Planning 1500 B.C.– A.D. 1911.* London: Alec Tiranti, 1962.

Brainard, Shirl. *A Design Manual.* Upper Saddle River, NJ: Prentice Hall, 1998.

Brotherston, Gordon. *Painted Books from Mexico: Codices in UK Collections and the World They Represent.* London: The British Museum Press, 1995.

Brown, Kendall H., et al. *Light in Darkness: Women in Japanese Prints of the Early Shwa (1926–1945).* Los Angeles: Fisher Gallery, University of Southern California, 1996.

Buehler, Alfred, Terry Barrow, and Charles P. Mountford. *The Art of the South Sea Islands.* New York: Crown, 1962.

Burson, Nancy. *Faces.* Santa Fe, NM: Twin Palms, 1993.

Burton, Rosemary, and Richard Cavendish. *Wonders of the World.* Chicago: Rand McNally, 1991.

Bushnell, G. H. S. *Ancient Arts of the Americas.* New York: Praeger, 1965.

Cahill, James. *The Lyric Journey: Poetic Painting in China and Japan.* Cambridge, MA: Harvard University Press, 1966.

Cameron, Elisabeth L., with Doran H. Ross. *Isn't S/he a Doll? Play and Ritual in African Sculpture.* Los Angeles: UCLA Fowler Museum of Cultural History, 1996.

Canaday, John. *Mainstreams of Modern Art.* New York: Holt, Rinehart and Winston, 1959.

Cantrell, Jacqueline Phillips. *Ancient Mexico: Cultural Traditions in the Land of the Feathered Serpent.* Dubuque, IA: Kendall/Hunt, 1984.

Carpenter, T. H. *Art and Myth in Ancient Greece.* London: Thames and Hudson, 1991.

Caruana, Wally. *Aboriginal Art.* London: Thames and Hudson, 1993.

Casson, Lionel. *Ancient Egypt.* New York: Time-Life Books, 1971.

Caygill, Marjorie, and John Cherry. *A. W. Franks: Nineteenth Century Collecting and the British Museum.* London: The British Museum Press, 1997.

Center for African Art. *ART/artifact: African Art in Anthropology Collections.* New York: Prestel Verlag, 1989.

Chandra, Pramod. *The Sculpture of India 3000 BC–AD 1300.* Washington, DC: The National Gallery of Art, 1985.

Chicago, Judy. *Through the Flower: My Struggles as a Woman Artist.* Garden City, NY: Doubleday, 1975.

Chui, Hu. *The Forbidden City, Collection of Photographs.* Beijing: China Photographic Publishing House, 1995.

Clark, Kenneth. *Animals and Men: Their Relationship as Reflected in Western Art from Prehistory to the Present Day.* New York: William Morrow, 1977.

Clark, Kenneth. *The Nude: A Study in Ideal Form.* Princeton, NJ: Princeton University Press, 1956.

Clearwater, Bonnie. *Mark Rothko: Works on Paper.* New York: Hudson Hills Press, 1984. Distributed by Viking Penguin.

Cocke, Thomas. *900 Years: The Restorations of Westminster Abbey.* London: Harvey Miller, 1995.

Coe, Michael, Dean Snow, and Elizabeth Bensen. *The Cultural Atlas of the World: Ancient America.* Richmond, VA: Stonehenge Press, 1990. Coe, Michael D. *The Maya.* New York: Thames and Hudson, 1982.

Collcutt, Martin, Marius Jansen, and Isao Kumakuro. *Cultural Atlas of the World: Japan.* Alexandria, VA: Stonehenge Press, 1991.

Collier's. *Photographic History of World War II.* New York: P. F. Collier and Son, 1946.

Collignon, Maxime. *Manual of Mythology in Relation to Greek Art.* New Rochelle, NY: Caratzas Brothers, 1982.

Colton, Joel. *Great Ages of Man: Twentieth Century.* New York: Time-Life Books, 1968.

Colvin, Howard. *Architecture and the After-life.* New Haven and London: Yale University Press, 1991.

Compassion and Protest: Recent Social and Political Art from the Eli Broad Family Foundation Collection. New York: Cross River Press, a Division of Abbeville Press, 1991.

Corbin, George A. *Native Arts of North America, Africa, and the South Pacific.* New York: Harper and Row, 1988.

Cotterell, Arthur. *The First Emperor of China.* New York: Holt, Rinehart and Winston, 1981.

Cowart, Jack, et al. *Georgia O'Keeffe: Art and Letters.* Washington, DC: The National Gallery of Art, 1987.

Craven, Roy C. *Indian Art: A Concise History.* London: Thames and Hudson, 1997.

Crimp, Douglas. "The Photographic Activity of Postmodernism." In *Postmodern Perspectives: Issues in Contemporary Art,* edited by Howard Risatti, 131–139. Englewood Cliffs, NJ: Prentice Hall, 1990. Culbertson, Judi, and Tom Randall. *Permanent Parisians: An Illustrated Guide to the Cemeteries of Paris.* Chelsea, VT: Chelsea Green, 1986.

Cunningham, Lawrence S., and John J. Reich. *Culture and Values: A Survey of the Western Humanities, Volume II.* Fort Worth, TX: Harcourt Brace College Publishers, 1998.

Cuttler, Charles D. *Northern Painting from Pucelle to Bruegel: Fourteenth, Fifteenth and Sixteenth Centuries.* New York: Holt, Rinehart and Winston. 1968.

Davies, J. G. *Temples, Churches and Mosques: A Guide to the Appreciation of Religious Architecture.* New York: The Pilgrim Press, 1982.

Dawson, Barry, and John Gillow. *The Traditional Art of Indonesia.* London: Thames and Hudson, 1994.

de Franciscis, Alfonso. *Pompeii: Civilization and Art.* Naples, Italy: Edizioni Interdipress, 1997.

DeMott, Barbara. *Dogon Masks: A Structural Study in Form and Meaning.* Ann Arbor, MI: UMI Research Press, 1982.

Denyer, Susan. *African Traditional Architecture.* New York: Africana Publishing, 1978.

Derson, Denise. *What Life Was Like on the Banks of the Nile, Egypt 3050–30 BC.* Alexandria, VA: Time-Life Books, 1996.

Desai, Vishakha N., and Darielle Mason. *Gods, Guardians and Lovers: Temple Sculptures from North India* A.D. 700–1200. New York: The Asia Society Galleries; Ahmedabad: Mapin Publishing, , 1993.

Dewald, Ernest T. *Italian Painting.* New York: Holt, Rinehart and Winston, 1965.

de Zegher, M. Catherine. *Inside the Visible: An Elliptical Traverse of 20th Century Art.* Cambridge: MIT Press, 1996.

Dickerson, Albert I., ed. *The Orozco Frescoes at Dartmouth.* Hanover, NH: The Trustees of Dartmouth College, 1962.

Drewal, Henry John, and John Pemberton III, with Rowland Abiodun. *Yoruba, Nine Centuries of African Art and Thought.* New York: Center for African Art, 1989.

Duiker, William J., and Jackson J. Spielvogel. *World History.* 4th ed. Belmont, CA: Thomson/Wadsworth, 2004.

Durand, Jorge, and Douglas S. Massey. *Miracles on the Border: Retablos of Mexican Migrants to the United States.* Tucson and London: University of Arizona Press, 1995.

Ebrey, Patricia Buckley. *Cambridge Illustrated History of China.* London: Cambridge University Press, 1996.

Edwards, Jim. *Precarious Links: Emily Jennings, Hung Liu, Celia Munoz.* San Antonio, TX: San Antonio Museum of Art, 1990.

Edwards, I. E. S. *The Treasures of Tutankhamun.* New York: Penguin Books, 1977.

Elkins, James. *Visual Studies: A Skeptical Introduction.* New York: Routledge, 2003.

Encyclopedia Americana. S.v. "Central Park," by Harry L. Coles; "China: Theater," by Chia-pao Wan; "Globe Theater," by Bernard Beckermen; "Japan: Doll Drama," by Donald Richie; "Disneyland and Disney World," "Epcot," "Palenque," by Pedro Armillas; "Zoological Gardens," by William Bridges. Danbury, CT: Grolier, 1986.

Encyclopedia Britannica Online. S.v. "Animal Behaviour: Behaviour of Animals in Groups." *http://www.eb.com:180/cgi-bin/g?DocF=macro/5000/62/94.html* (accessed May 19, 1998).

Etienne, Robert. *Pompeii: The Day a City Died.* New York: Harry N. Abrams, 1992.

Ezra, Kate. *Art of the Dogon.* New York: The Metropolitan Museum of Art, 1988.

Fagan, Brian M. *Rape of the Nile.* Kingston, RI: Moyer Bell, 1992.

Fagg, William. *Yoruba: Sculpture of West Africa.* New York: Alfred A. Knopf, 1982.

Feder, Norman. *American Indian Art.* New York: Harry N. Abrams, 1995.

Feest, Christian F. *Native Arts of North America.* New York: Oxford University Press, 1980.

Fichner-Rathus, Lois. *Understanding Art.* Englewood Cliffs, NJ: Prentice Hall, 1994.

Fiero, Gloria. *The Humanistic Tradition.* Madison, WI: WCB Brown and Benchmark, 1995.

Fiodorov, B., ed. *Architecture of the Russian North, 12th through 19th Centuries.* Leningrad: Aurora Art Publishers, 1976.

Fisher, Robert E. *Mystics and Mandalas: Bronzes and Paintings of Tibet and Nepal.* Redlands, CA: The University of Redlands, 1974.

Flaherty, Thomas H. *Incas: Lords of Gold and Glory.* Alexandria, VA: Time-Life Books, 1992.

———. *The American Indians: The Spirit World.* Alexandria, VA: Time-Life Books, 1992.

———. *The Mighty Chieftains.* Alexandria, VA: Time-Life Books, 1993.

Flaherty, Thomas H., ed. *Aztecs: Reign of Blood and Splendor.* Alexandria, VA: Time-Life Books, 1992.

Fleming, William. *Arts and Ideas.* 3rd ed. New York: Holt, Rinehart and Winston, 1970..*Frank Gehry: Pritzker Architect Prize Laureate 1989.* http://www.pritzkerprize.com/gehry.htm (accessed April 13, 2004).

Frankfort, Henri. *The Art and Architecture of the Orient.* New Haven, CT: Yale University Press, 1970.

Furst, Peter T., and Jill L. Furst. *North American Indian Art.* New York: Rizzoli, 1982.

Gardner, Joseph L. *Mysteries of the Ancient Americas.* Pleasantville, NY: Reader's Digest, 1986.

Gardner, Paul. *Louise Bourgeois.* New York: Universe Publishing, 1994.

Getty, Adele. *Goddess, Mother of Living Nature.* London: Thames and Hudson, 1990.

Getz-Preziosi, Pat. *Early Cycladic Sculpture: An Introduction.* Malibu, CA: J. Paul Getty Museum, 1994.

Gilbert, Creighton. *History of Renaissance Art Throughout Europe.* New York: Harry N. Abrams, 1973.

Gillon, Werner. *A Short History of African Art.* New York: Penguin Books, 1991.

Goggin, Mary-Margaret. "'Decent' vs. 'Degenerate' Art: The National Socialist Case." *Art Journal* 50, no. 4 (Winter 1991): 84–93.

Goodman, Susan Tumarkin, ed. *Russian Jewish Artists in a Century of Change 1890–1990.* Munich: Prestel-Verlag, 1995.

Gowing, Lawrence. *Lucian Freud.* London: Thames and Hudson, 1982.

Graves, Eleanor. *Life Goes to War: A Picture History of World War II.* Boston, MA: Little, Brown, 1977.

Graze, Sue, Kathy Halbreich, and Roberta Smith. *Elizabeth Murray: Paintings and Drawings.* New York: Harry N. Abrams, in association with the Dallas Museum of Art and the MIT Committee on the Visual Arts, 1987.

Greenberg, Clement. "Avant-Garde and Kitsch." *Partisan Review* 6 (Fall 1939). Reprinted in Greenberg, *Art and Culture: Critical Essays.* Boston: Beacon Press, 1961.

Gregory, Richard L. *Eye and Brain: The Psychology of Seeing.* 5th ed. Princeton, NJ: Princeton University Press, 1997. *Grolier Encyclopedia.* S.v. "Pacifism and Non-violent Movements," "Gandhi's Campaigns." 1996.

Grube, Ernst J. *The World of Islam.* New York: McGraw-Hill, 1977.

Gruzinski, Serge. *The Aztecs: Rise and Fall of an Empire.* New York: Harry N. Abrams, 1992.

"Guernica." www.web.org.uk/picasso/guernica.html (accessed March 15, 2004).

Guiart, Jean. *The Arts of the South Pacific.* New York: Golden Press, 1963.

Guilbaut, Serge. *How New York Stole the Idea of Modern Art: Abstract Expressionism, Freedom, and the Cold War.* Translated by Arthur Goldhammer. Chicago and London: University of Chicago Press, 1983.

Hadington, Evan. *Lines to the Mountain Gods.* New York: Random House, 1987.

Hanson, Allan, and Louise Hanson, eds. *Art and Identity in Oceania.* Honolulu, HI: University of Hawaii Press, 1990.

Harle, J. C. *The Art and Architecture of the Indian Subcontinent.* London: Penguin Books, 1986.

Harris, Ann Sutherland, and Linda Nochlin. *Women Artists 1550–1950.* New York: Alfred A. Knopf, 1984.

Hartt, Frederick. *History of Italian Renaissance Art: Painting, Sculpture, Architecture.* Englewood Cliffs, NJ: Prentice Hall, 1969.

Hawthorn, Audrey. *Kwakiutl Art.* Seattle and London: University of Washington Press, 1979.

Hay, John. *Masterpieces of Chinese Art.* Greenwich, CT: New York Graphic Society, 1974.

Heartney, Eleanor. "Pornography." *Art Journal* 50, no. 4 (Winter 1991): 16–19.

Helm, Mackinley. *Mexican Painters: Rivera, Orozco, Siqueiros, and Other Artists of the Social Realist School.* New York: Dover, 1941.

Hershey, Irwin. *Indonesian Primitive Art.* New York: Oxford Press, 1991.

Heusinger, Lutz. *Michelangelo.* Florence, Italy: Scala; New York: Riverside, 1989.

Hillier, J. *Japanese Colour Prints.* London: Phaidon, 1991.

Hoffman, Katherine. *Concepts of Identity: Historical and Contemporary Images and Portraits of Self and Family.* New York: HarperCollins, 1996.

Holm, Bill. *Northwest Coast Indian Art: An Analysis of Form.* Seattle: University of Washington Press, 1995.

Holt, Elizabeth Gilmore, ed. *Literary Sources of Art History: An Anthology of Texts from Theophilus to Goethe.* Princeton, NJ: Princeton University Press, 1947.

Holt, John Dominis. *The Art of Featherwork in Old Hawaii.* Honolulu: Topgallant, 1985.

Honour, Hugh, and John Fleming. *The Visual Arts: A History.* Englewood Cliffs, NJ: Prentice Hall, 1995.

Hooks, Bell. *Art on My Mind: Visual Politics.* New York: New Press, 1995.

Hopkins, Jerry. *Yoko Ono.* New York: Macmillan, 1986.

Howard, Jeremy. *Art Nouveau: International and National Styles in Europe.* Manchester, UK: Manchester University Press, 1996.

Hughes, Robert. *American Visions.* New York: Alfred A. Knopf, 1997.

Hulton, Paul, and Lawrence Smith. *Flowers in Art from East and West.* London: British Museum Publications, 1979.

Huntington, Susan L., and John C. Huntington. *Leaves from the Bodhi Tree.* Seattle: University of Washington Press, 1990.

Identity and Alterity: Figures of the Body 1895–1995. Edited by Manlio Brusatin and Jean Clair. Venice, Italy: Marsilio, 1995. Exhibition catalog of La Biennale di Venezia 46, esposizione internazionale d'arte.

Indych, Anna. "Nuyorican Baroque: Pepón Osorio's *Chucherías.*" *Art Journal* 60, no. 1 (Spring 2001): 72–83.

Internet Medieval Sourcebook. www.fordham.edu/halsall/sbook.html (accessed March 30, 2004).

Ivory: An International History and Illustrated Survey. New York: Harry N. Abrams, 1987.

J. Paul Getty Museum Handbook of the Collections. Malibu, CA: J. Paul Getty Museum, 1991.

Janson, H. W. *History of Art.* New York: Harry N. Abrams, 1995.

Jellicoe, Geoffrey, and Susan Jellicoe. *The Landscape of Man.* London: Thames and Hudson, 1987.

Jonaitis, Aldona. *From the Land of the Totem Poles.* New York: American Museum of Natural History, 1988.

Jones, Alexander. *The Jerusalem Bible.* Garden City, NY: Doubleday, 1966.

Jones, Amelia, ed. *Sexual Politics: Judy Chicago's Dinner Party in Feminist Art History.* Berkeley: University of California Press, 1996.

Kaplan, Janet A. "*Give and Take* Conversations." *Art Journal* 61, no. 2 (Summer 2002): 68–97.

Kaprow, Allen. *Assemblage, Environments and Happenings.* New York: Harry N. Abrams, 1961.

Kessler, Adam T. *Empires Beyond the Great Wall: The Heritage of Genghis Khan.* Los Angeles: Natural History Museum of Los Angeles County, 1994.

Kettering, Alice McNeil. "Gentlemen in Satin: Masculine Ideals in Later Seventeenth-Century Dutch Portraiture." *Art Journal* 56, no. 2 (Summer 1997): 41–47.

Kienholz, Edward, and Nancy Reddin Kienholz. *Kienholz: A Retrospective.* New York: Whitney Museum of American Art, 1996.

Kirsh, Andrea. *Carrie Mae Weems.* Washington, DC: The National Museum of Women in the Arts, 1993.

Kitchen, K. A. *Pharaoh Triumphant: The Life and Times of Ramesses II.* Cairo, Egypt: American University in Cairo Press, 1982.

Koons, Jeff. *The Jeff Koons Handbook.* New York: Rizzoli, 1992.

Kopper, Phillip. *The Smithsonian Book of North American Indians before the Coming of the Europeans.* Washington, DC: Smithsonian Books, 1986.

Kulka, Tomas. *Kitsch and Art.* University Park: Pennsylvania State University Press, 1996.

Kundera, Milan. *The Unbearable Lightness of Being.* Translated by Michael Henry Heim. New York: Harper and Row, 1984.

Kuroda, Taizo, Melinda Takeuchi, and Yuzo Yamane. *Worlds Seen and Imagined: Japanese Screens from the Idemitsu Museum of Art.* New York: The Asia Society Galleries; Abbeville Press, 1995.

Laude, Jean. *African Art of the Dogon.* New York: Viking Press, 1973.

Lauer, David A., and Stephen Pentak. *Design Basics.* Fort Worth, TX: Harcourt Brace College Publishers, 1995.

Lazzari, Margaret, and Clayton Lee. *Art and Design Fundamentals.* New York: Van Nostrand Reinhold, 1990.

Lee, Sherman E. *A History of Far Eastern Art.* New York: Harry N. Abrams, 1973.

Levenson, Jay A. *Circa 1492.* New Haven, CT: Yale University Press, 1991.

Levi, Peter. *The Cultural Atlas of the World: The Greek World.* Alexandria, VA: Stonehenge Press, 1992.

Lewis, Bernard. *Islam and the Arab World.* New York: Alfred A. Knopf, 1976.

Lewis, Phillip. "Tourist Art, Traditional Art and the Museum in Papua New Guinea." In *Art and Identity in Oceania,* edited by Allan Hanson and Louise Hanson. Honolulu: University of Hawaii Press, 1990.

Lincoln, Louise. *Assemblage of Spirits: Idea and Image in New Ireland.* New York: George Braziller, 1987.

Linker, Kate. *Love for Sale: The Words and Pictures of Barbara Kruger.* New York: Harry N. Abrams, 1990.

Lion King: The Broadway Musical ("Circles of Sound," by Lebe M, "New Visions for Pride Rock," by Eileen Blumenthal and Julie Taymor). *Stagebill,* 1998.

Lippard, Lucy R. *Mixed Blessings: New Art in a Multicultural America.* New York: Pantheon Books, 1990.

Lippard, Lucy. *The Pink Glass Swan: Selected Feminist Essays on Art.* New York: New Press, 1995.

Lossing, Benson J. *Mathew Brady's Illustrated History of the Civil War.* Washington, DC: Fair Fax Press; Barre Publishing, 1912.

Lowe, Sarah M. *Frida Kahlo.* New York: Universe Publishing, 1991.

Lundquist, John M. *The Temple: Meeting Place of Heaven and Earth.* London: Thames and Hudson, 1993.

Lyle, Emily, ed. *Sacred Architecture in the Traditions of India, China, Judaism and Islam.* Edinburgh: Edinburgh University Press, 1992.

Machida, Margo. "Out of Asia: Negotiating Asian Identities in America." In *Asia America: Identities in Contemporary Asian American Art.* New York: The Asia Society Galleries; New Press, 1994.

Mackenzie, Lynne. *Non-Western Art: A Brief Guide.* Upper Saddle River, NJ: Prentice Hall, 2001.

Malone, Maggie, and Hideko Takayama. "A Japanese Buying Spree: The Tycoon Who Spent $160 Million at Auctions." *Newsweek,* May 28, 1990, p. 75.

Mann, A. T. *Sacred Architecture.* Rockport, MA: Element, 1993.

Marcus, George E. "Middlebrow into Highbrow at the J. Paul Getty Trust." In *Looking High and Low,* edited by Brenda Jo Bright and Liza Bakewell. Tuscon: University of Arizona Press, 1995.

Mariani, Valerio. *Michelangelo the Painter.* New York: Harry N. Abrams, 1964.

Matilsky, Barbara C. *Fragile Ecologies: Contemporary Artists' Interpretations and Solutions.* New York: Rizzoli, 1992.

Matt, Leonard von, Mario Moretti, and Guglielmo Maetzke. *The Art of the Etruscans.* New York: Harry N. Abrams, 1970.

McLanathan, Richard. *The American Tradition in the Arts.* New York: Harcourt Brace and World, 1968.

Mead, Sidney Moko. *Te Maori: Maori Art from New Zealand Collections.* New York: Harry N. Abrams, 1984.

Media Scape. New York: Solomon R. Guggenheim Museum, 1996.

Miller, Kimberly J. "Battle for Iwo Jima." http://www.usmc.mil (accessed 1997).

Miller, Arthur G. *The Painted Tombs of Oaxaca, Mexico: Living with the Dead.* Cambridge: Cambridge University Press, 1995.

Miller, Mary Ellen. *The Art of Mesoamerica from Olmec to Aztec.* New York: Thames and Hudson, 1986.

Mirzoeff, Nicholas, ed. *The Visual Culture Reader.* London and New York: Routledge, 1998.

———. *An Introduction to Visual Culture.* London; New York: Routledge, 1999.

Mitchell, W. J. T., ed. *Art and the Public Sphere.* Chicago and London: University of Chicago Press, 1992.

Mitchell, W. J. T., and Margaret Dikovitskaya. *An Interview with W. J. T. Mitchell, Gaylord Donnelley Distinguished Service Professor of English and Art History, University of Chicago, 11 January 2001.* http://humanities.uchicago.edu/faculty/Mitchell/Dikovitskaya_interviews_Mitchell.pdf.

Monod-Bruhl, Odette. *Indian Temples.* London: Oxford University Press, 1951.

Morgan, William N. *Prehistoric Architecture in the Eastern United States.* Cambridge, MA: MIT Press, 1980.

Moynihan, Elizabeth B. *Paradise as a Garden in Persia and Mughal India.* London: Scolar Press, 1979.

Munroe, Alexandra. *Japanese Art After 1945: Scream Against the Sky.* New York: Harry N. Abrams, 1994.

Murray, Jocelyn. *The Cultural Atlas of the World: Africa.* Alexandria, VA: Stonehenge Press, 1992.

Murray, Peter, and Linda Murray. *The Art of the Renaissance.* New York: Praeger, 1963.

Nagle, Geraldine. *The Arts-World Themes.* Madison, WI: Brown and Benchmark, 1993.

Nemser, Cindy. *Art Talk: Conversations with 15 Women Artists.* New York: HarperCollins, 1995.

Newhall, Beaumont. *History of Photography from 1839 to the Present Day.* New York: Museum of Modern Art, 1964.

Newland, Amy and Chris Uhlenbeck, eds. *Ukiyo-e to Shin Hanga: The Art of Japanese Woodblock Prints.* New York: Mallard Press, 1990.

Newton, Douglas. *New Guinea Art in the Collection of the Museum of Primitive Art.* New York: Publishers Printing–Admiral Press, 1967.

Nochlin, Linda. *Women, Art, and Power and Other Essays.* New York: Harper and Row, 1988.

Norwich, John Julius, ed. *Great Architecture of the World.* New York: Bonanza Books, 1979.

Nou, Jean-Louis, Amina Okada, and M. C. Joshi. *Taj Mahal.* New York: Abbeville Press, 1993.

Ocvirk, Otto G., Robert E. Stinson, Philip R. Wigg, Robert O. Bone, and David L. Clayton. *Art Fundamentals: Theory and Practice.* Madison, WI: Brown and Benchmark, 1998.

Of Sky and Earth: Art of the Early Southeastern Indians. Edited by Roy S. Dickens. Dalton, GA: Lee Printing Company, 1982. Published in conjunction with the exhibition shown at the High Museum of Art, Atlanta, GA.

O'Hara, Frank. *Robert Motherwell.* New York: Museum of Modern Art, 1965.

Ohashi, Haruzo. *The Japanese Garden: Islands of Serenity.* Tokyo: Graphicsha, 1997.

Oliver, Douglas L. *The Pacific Islands.* Honolulu: University of Hawaii Press, 1989.

O'Neill, John P., ed. *Mexico: Thirty Centuries of Splendor.* New York: Metropolitan Museum of Art, 1990.

Pacific: A Companion to the Regenstein Halls of the Pacific. Edited by Ron Dorfman. Chicago: Field Museum of Natural History, 1991. Field Museum Centennial Collection.

Papanek, John L. *Mesopotamia: The Mighty Kings.* Alexandria, VA: Time-Life Books, 1995.

Papanek, John L., ed. *Africa's Glorious Legacy, Lost Civilizations.* Alexandria, VA: Time-Life Books, 1994.

———. *Ancient India, Land of Mystery.* Alexandria, VA: Time-Life Books, 1994.

Pasztory, Esther. *Aztec Art.* New York: Harry N. Abrams, 1983.

Pelrine, Diane M. *Affinities of Form: Arts of Africa, Oceania and the Americas from the Raymond and Laura Wielgus Collection.* Munich: Prestel-Verlag, 1996.

Pendlebury, J. D. S. *A Handbook to the Palace of Minos at Knossos.* London: Macmillan, 1935.

Penny, David W. *Art of the American Indian Frontier: The Chandler-Pohrt Collection.* The Detroit Institute of Art. Seattle: University of Washington Press, 1992.

Perani, Judith, and Fred T. Davidson. *The Visual Arts of Africa: Gender, Power and Life Cycle Rituals.* Upper Saddle River, NJ: Prentice Hall, 1998.

Perchuk, Andrew. "Hannah Wilke [exhibition at] Ronald Feldman Fine Arts." *Artforum* (April 1994): 93–94.

Phipps, Richard, and Richard Wink. *Invitation to the Gallery.* Dubuque, IA: Wm. C. Brown, 1987.

Pierson, William H., and Martha Davidson. *Arts of the United States: A Pictorial History.* New York: McGraw-Hill, 1960.

Preble, Duane, Sarah Preble, and Patrick L. Frank. *ArtForms.* Upper Saddle River, NJ: Prentice Hall, 1999.

Ragghianti, Carlo Ludovico, and Licia Ragghianti Collobi. *National Museum of Anthropology, Mexico City.* New York: Newsweek (Simon and Schuster), 1970.

Ramseyer, Urs. *The Art and Culture of Bali.* Singapore and Oxford: Oxford University Press, 1986.

Rawson, Jessica, ed. *The British Museum Book of Chinese Art.* London: Thames and Hudson, 1992.

Reilly, Maura. "The Drive to Describe: An Interview with Catherine Opie." *Art Journal* 60, no. 2 (Summer 2001) 83–95.

Rhodes, Colin. *Outsider Art, Spontaneous Alternatives.* World of Art. New York: Thames and Hudson, 2000.

Richter, Anne. *Arts and Crafts of Indonesia.* San Francisco: Chronicle Books, 1994.

Risatti, Howard, ed. *Postmodern Perspectives: Issues in Contemporary Art.* Englewood Cliffs, NJ: Prentice Hall, 1990.

Rochfort, Dennis. *Mexican Muralists.* New York: Universe Publishing, 1993.

Ross, Doran H. "Akua's Child and Other Relatives: New Mythologies for Old Dolls." In *Isn't S/he a Doll? Play and Ritual in African Sculpture,* by Elisabeth L. Cameron, 43–57. Los Angeles: UCLA Fowler Museum of Cultural History, 1996.

Rowland, Anna. *Bauhaus Source Book.* New York: Van Nostrand Reinhold, 1990.

Roy, Christopher. *Art and Life in Africa: Selections from the Stanley Collection, Exhibitions of 1985 and 1992.* Iowa City: University of Iowa Museum of Art, 1992.

Rubin, Barbara, Robert Carlton, and Arnold Rubin. *Forest Lawn: L.A. in Installments.* Santa Monica, CA: Westside Publications, 1979.

Santini, Loretta. *Pompeii and the Villa of the Mysteries.* Narni-Terni, Italy: Editrice Plurigraf, 1997.

Sasser, Elizabeth Skidmore. *The World of Spirits and Ancestors in the Art of Western Sub-Saharan Africa.* Lubbock: Texas Tech University Press, 1995.

Saunders, J. B. de C. M., and Charles O'Malley. *The Illustrations from the Works of Andreas Vesalius of Brussels.* New York: Dover, 1950.

Sayre, Henry M. *The Object of Performance: The American Avant-Garde since 1970.* Chicago: University of Chicago Press, 1989.

Schmitz, Carl A. *Oceanic Art: Myth, Man and Image in the South Seas.* New York: Harry N. Abrams, 1971.

Schwarz, Hans-Peter. *Media-Art-History.* Munich: Prestel-Verlag, 1997.

Seaford, Richard. *Pompeii.* New York: Summerfield Press, 1978.

Setton, Kenneth M., et al. *The Renaissance, Maker of Modern Man.* Washington, DC: National Geographic Society, 1970.

Sharer, Robert, and Sylvanus Morley. *The Ancient Maya.* Stanford, CA: Stanford University Press, 1994.

Sharp, Dennis. *A Visual History of Twentieth Century Architecture.* Greenwich, CT: New York Graphic Society, 1972.

Shearer, Alistair. *The Hindu Vision: Forms of the Formless.* London: Thames and Hudson, 1993.

Sickman, Lawrence, and Alexander Soper. *The Art and Architecture of China.* New Haven, CT: Yale University Press, 1971.

Silva, Anil de, Otto von Simons, and Roger Hinks. *Man Through Art, War and Peace.* Greenwich, CT: New York Graphic Society, 1964.

Simmons, David. *Whakairo Maori Tribal Art.* New York: Oxford University Press, 1985.

Simon, Joan, ed. *Bruce Nauman.* Minneapolis: Walker Art Center, 1994.

Sitwell, Sacheverell. *Great Palaces.* New York: Hamlyn, 1969.

Skinner, Charles Montgomery. *Myths and Legends of Our Own Land.* Philadelphia and London: J. B. Lippincott, 1924.

Skira, Albert. *Treasures of Asia: Chinese Painting.* Cleveland, OH: World, 1960.

Slatkin, Wendy. *Women Artists in History: From Antiquity to the Present.* Upper Saddle River, NJ: Prentice Hall, 1997.

Smith, Bradley, and Wan-go Wen. *China: A History in Art.* New York: Doubleday, 1979.

Snellgrove, David L., ed. *The Image of the Buddha.* Paris: UNESCO (United Nations Educational, Scientific and Cultural Organization); Tokyo: Kodansha, 1978.

Solomon-Godeau, Abigail. "The Other Side of Vertu: Alternative Masculinities in the Crucible of Revolution." *Art Journal* 56, no. 2 (Summer 1997): 55–61.

Sontag, Susan. *Against Interpretation and Other Essays.* New York: Farrar, Straus and Giroux, 1966.

Spayde, Jon. "Cultural Revolution." *Departures* (September/October 1995): 115–123, 154–157.

Sporre, Dennis J. *The Creative Impulse: An Introduction to the Arts.* Upper Saddle River, NJ: Prentice Hall, 1996.

Staccioli, R. A. *Ancient Rome: Monuments Past and Present.* Rome: Vision, 1989.

Staniszewski, Mary Anne. *Believing Is Seeing: Creating a Culture of Art.* New York: Penguin Books, 1995.

Stanley-Baker, Joan. *Japanese Art.* London: Thames and Hudson, 1984.

Sterling, Charles. *Still Life Painting: From Antiquity to the Twentieth Century.* 2nd ed. rev. New York: Harper and Row, 1980.

Stewart, Gloria. *Introduction to Sepik Art of Papua New Guinea.* Sydney, Australia: Garrick Press, 1972.

Stewart, Hilary. *Looking at Indian Art of the Northwest Coast.* Seattle: University of Washington Press, 1979.

Stierlin, Henri. *Art of the Aztecs and Its Origins.* Translated by Betty and Peter Ross. New York: Rizzoli, 1982.

Stierlin, Henri. *The Pharaohs, Master-Builders.* Paris: Terrail, 1992.

Stokstad, Marilyn. *Art History.* Upper Saddle River, NJ: Prentice Hall, 1995.

Stooss, Toni, and Thomas Kellein, eds. *Nam June Paik: Video Time–Video Space.* New York: Harry N. Abrams, 1993.

Stuart, Gene S., and George E. Stuart. *Lost Kingdoms of the Maya.* Washington, DC: National Geographic Society, 1993.

Sullivan, Michael. *Art and Artists of Twentieth-Century China.* Berkeley: University of California Press, 1996.

Sutton, Peter C. *The Age of Rubens.* Boston: Museum of Fine Arts, Boston: 1993.

Swann, Peter C. *Chinese Monumental Art.* New York: Viking, 1963.

Tadashi Kobayashi. *Ukiyo-e: An Introduction to Japanese Woodblock Prints.* Tokyo: Kodansha, 1992.

Tallman, Susan. "General Idea." *Arts Magazine* (May 1990): 21–22.

Tannahill, Reay. *Food in History.* New York: Stein and Day, 1973.

Tansey, Richard G., and Fred S. Kleiner. *Gardner's Art Through the Ages.* Fort Worth, TX: Harcourt Brace College Publishers, 1996.

Taylor, Pamela York. *Beasts, Birds and Blossoms in Thai Art.* Kuala Lumpur, Malaysia: Oxford University Press, 1994.

Taylor, Simon. "Janine Antoni at Sandra Gering." *Art in America* 80 (October 1992).

Tello, J. C. "Arte Antiguo Peruano." *Inca: Revista de Estudios Antropolico.* Vol. 2. Lima, Peru: Universidad de San Marcos de Lima, 1924.

Terrace, Edward L. B., and Henry G. Fisher. *Treasures of Egyptian Art from the Cairo Museum.* London: Thames and Hudson, 1970.

Thomas, Nicholas. *Oceanic Art.* London: Thames and Hudson, 1995.

Thucydides. *The Peloponnesian War.* Translated by Rex Warner. Baltimore: Penguin Books, 1954.

Time-Life Books. *Lost Civilizations: Anatolia—Cauldron of Cultures.* Richmond, VA: Time-Life Books, 1995.

Tom, Patricia Vettel. "Bad Boys: Bruce Davidson's Gang Photographs and Outlaw Masculinity." *Art Journal* 56, no. 2 (Summer 1997): 69–74.

Townsend, Richard F., ed. *The Ancient Americas: Art from Sacred Landscapes.* Chicago: Art Institute of Chicago, 1992.

Tregear, Mary. *Chinese Art.* London: Thames and Hudson, 1991.

Truettner, William H. *The Natural Man Observed: A Study of Catlin's Indian Gallery.* Washington, DC: Smithsonian Institution Press, 1979.

Turner, Jane, ed. *The Dictionary of Art.* New York: Grove, 1996.

Vercoutter, Jean. *The Search for Ancient Egypt.* New York: Harry N. Abrams, 1992.

Vickers, Michael, ed. *Pots and Pans.* Oxford: Oxford University Press, 1986.

Vogel, Susan. *Africa Explores: 20th Century African Art.* New York: Center for African Art, 1991.

Vogel, Susan Mullin. *African Art, Western Eyes.* New Haven and London: Yale University Press, 1997.

Von Blum, Paul. *The Art of Social Conscience.* New York: Universe Books, 1976.

von Hagen, Victor W. *The Desert Kingdoms of Peru.* London: Weidenfeld and Nicolson, 1965.

Vroege, Bas, and Hripsim Visser, eds. *Oppositions: Commitment and Cultural Identity in Contemporary Photography from Japan, Canada, Brazil, the Soviet Union and the Netherlands.* Rotterdam: Uitgeverij, 1990.

Wallach, Alan. *Exhibiting Contradiction: Essays on the Art Museum in the United States.* Amherst: University of Massachusetts Press, 1998.

Wallis, Brian, ed. *Hans Haacke: Unfinished Business.* New York: The New Museum of Contemporary Art; Cambridge: MIT Press, 1986.

Washburn, Dorothy, ed. *Hopi Kachina: Spirit of Life.* San Francisco: California Academy of Sciences, 1980. Distributed by the University of Washington Press. Weibiao, Hu. *Scenes of the Great Wall.* Beijing: Wenjin Publishing House, 1994.

Weintraub, Linda, ed. *Art What Thou Eat: Images of Food in American Art.* Mount Kisco, NY: Moyer Bell, 1991.

Wescoat, James L., Jr., and Joachim Wolschke-Bulmahn. *Mughal Gardens: Sources, Places, Representations and Prospects.* Washington, DC: Dumbarton Oaks Research Library and Collection, 1996.

Wheat, Ellen Harkins. *Jacob Lawrence: American Painter.* Seattle: University of Washington Press, 1986.

Willett, Frank. *African Art.* New York: Thames and Hudson, 1993.

———. *Ife in the History of West African Sculpture.* New York: McGraw-Hill, 1967.

Willis, Deborah, ed. *Picturing Us: African American Identity in Photography.* New York: New Press, 1994.

Willis-Braithwaite, Deborah. *VanDerZee Photographer 1886–1983.* New York: Harry N. Abrams, 1993.

Wilson, David M., and Ole Klindt-Jensen. *Viking Art.* Minneapolis: University of Minnesota Press, 1980.

Wilson, Sir David M., ed. *The Collections of the British Museum.* Cambridge: Cambridge University Press, 1989.

Wingert, Paul S. *An Outline of Oceanic Art.* Cambridge, MA: University Prints, 1970.

———. *Art of the South Pacific.* New York: Columbia University Press, 1946.

Winkelmann-Rhein, Gertraude. *The Paintings and Drawings of Jan "Flower" Bruegel.* New York: Harry N. Abrams, 1968.

Witherspoon, Gary. *Language and Art of the Navajo Universe.* Ann Arbor: University of Michigan Press, 1977.

Wolff, Janet. *The Social Production of Art.* New York: New York University Press, 1984.

Yau, John. "Hung Liu [exhibition at] Nahan Contemporary." *Artforum* (March 1990):162.

Yenne, Bill, and Susan Garratt. *North American Indians.* China: Ottenheimer, 1994.

Yood, James. *Feasting: A Celebration of Food in Art.* New York: Universe Publishing, 1992.

Zarnecki, George. *Art of the Medieval World.* New York: Harry N. Abrams, 1975.

Zelanski, Paul, and Mary Pat Fisher. *Design Principles and Problems.* Fort Worth, TX: Harcourt Brace College Publishers, 1996.

Zelevansky, Lynn, et al. *Love Forever: Yayoi Kusama 1958–1968.* Los Angeles: Los Angeles County Museum of Art, 1998.

Zigrosser, Carl. *Prints and Drawings of Käthe Kollwitz.* New York: Dover, 1969.

Credits

1.CO © Werner Forman/Art Resource, NY **1.01** Metropolitan Museum of Art, New York **1.02** Canali Photobank **1.03** © SCALA/Art Resource, NY **1.04** © SCALA/Art Resource, NY © 2007 Estate of Pablo Picasso/Artists Rights Society (ARS), New York **1.05** © Werner Forman/Art Resource, NY **1.06** © Photo; Juergen Liepe.Bildarchiv Preussischer Kulturbesitz/Art Resource, NY **1.07** © SCALA/Art Resource, NY **1.08** © fotostock/SuperStock **1.09** © 1993 Jaune Quick-to-See Smith **1.10** Edizioni Sipiel, Joseph Cornet **1.11** © Erich Lessing/Art Resource, NY **1.12** © Giraudon/Art Resource, NY **1.13** University of New Mexico Library. Print 999-019¬0013] Mexican Popular Prints, Center for Southwest Research, University of New Mexico Library **1.14** Courtesy Tomio Koyama Gallery, Tokyo ©2001 Takashi Murakami/Kaikai Kiki Co., Ltd. All Rights Reserved. **1.15** Photo courtesy of the Pasadena Tournament of Roses. **1.16** Courtesy of the artist, Pace Wildenstein, NY. Stuart Collection, University of California, San Diego. **1.17** © Erich Lessing/Art Resource, NY **1.18** The Bridgeman Art Library **1.19** © Jacques Faujour, Réunion des Musées Nationaux/Art Resource, NY © 2007 Artists Rights Society (ARS), New York/ADAGP, Paris **1.20** The Museum of Modern Art, New York. Digital Image © The Museum of Modern Art/Licensed by SCALA/Art Resource, NY © 2007 Artists Rights Society (ARS), New York/ProLitteris, Zurich **1.21** © Collection of the Artist, NY. Art Resource, NY © 2007 Frank Stella/Artists Rights Society (ARS), New York **1.22** © Peter Adams/zefa/Corbis **1.23** © Roger Wood/Corbis **1.24** © SCALA/Art Resource, NY **1.25** © Erich Lessing/Art Resource, NY.

2.CO © Superstock **2.02** © Glasgow City Council (Museums)/ The Bridgeman Art Library **2.03** © Tate Gallery, London/Art Resource, NY © 2007 Artists Rights Society (ARS), New York/VG Bild-Kunst, Bonn **2.04** © Foto Marburg/Art Resource, NY **2.05** Photo Katherine Wetzel © Virginia Museum of Fine Arts **2.06** Digital Image © The Museum of Modern Art/Licensed by SCALA/Art Resource, NY © 2007 Artists Rights Society (ARS), New York **2.08** © Erich Lessing/Art Resource, NY **2.09** The Museum of Fine Arts, Houston; Gift of The Brown Foundation, Inc. © 2007 Estate of Louise Nevelson/Artists Rights Society (ARS), New York **2.10** © Art Resource, NY **2.14** Benoy K. Behl **2.15** © Adam Woolfitt/Corbis **2.16** © The Newark Museum/Art Resource, NY **2.17** © Paul Almasy/Corbis **2.18** Courtesy Donald Young Gallery, Chicago. **2.20** © Giraudon/Art Resource, NY **2.22** © Werner Forman/Art Resource, NY **2.23** The Bridgeman Art Library. © 2007 Estate of Giorgio de Chirico, Artists Rights Society (ARS), New York **2.24** Courtesy of Barbara Gladstone Gallery. **2.25** The Philadelphia Museum of Art/Art Resource, NY © 2007 Artists Rights Society (ARS), New York/ADAGP, Paris/Succession Marcel Duchamp **2.26** Courtesy of the Artist. **2.27** © Richard A. Cooke/Corbis **2.28** © Vanni/Art Resource, NY **2.29** © Carol Beckwith/Angela Fisher, Robert Estall Photo Library. **2.30** © Paul Miller/Black Star **2.31** © Wolfgang Kaehler/Corbis **2.32** © Nik Wheeler/Corbis **2.33** Richard A Cooke III/Getty Images **2.35** © Roger Wood/Corbis **2.39** © Vanni Archive/Corbis **2.41** © Bettmann/Corbis **2.43** © Bettmann/Corbis.

3.CO © Smithsonian American Art Museum, Washington, DC/Art Resource, NY. **3.01** © Erich Lessing/Art Resource, NY. **3.02** © Smithsonian American Art Museum, Washinton, DC/Art Resource, NY. **3.03** © The Newark Museum/Art Resource, NY © 2007 The Willem de Kooning Foundation/Artists Rights Society (ARS), New York **3.04** © Nimatallah/Art Resource, NY **3.05** © Erich Lessing/Art Resource, NY. **3.06** © Réunion des Musées Nationaux/Art Resource, NY **3.08** © Réunion des Musées Nationaux/Art Resource, NY **3.09** © The New York Public Library/Art Resource, NY **3.10** © Digital Image, The Museum of Modern Art/Licensed by SCALA/Art Resource, NY © 2007 Estate of Pablo Picasso/Artists Rights Society (ARS), New York **3.11** © Erich Lessing/Art Resource, NY © 2007 Artists Rights Society (ARS), New York/ADAGP, Paris **3.12** © Tate Gallery, London/Art Resource, NY © 2007 Andy Warhol Foundation for the Visual Arts/ARS, New York **3.13** © Erich Lessing/Art Resource, NY. **3.14** © Digital Image © The Museum of Modern Art/Licensed by SCALA/Art Resource, NY **3.15** © Erich Lessing/Art Resource, NY. **3.16** © Alamy Image **3.17** © The Museum of Modern Art/Licensed by SCALA/Art Resource, NY **3.18** © Erich Lessing/Art Resource, NY **3.19** © SCALA/Art Resource, NY **3.20** © Art Resource, NY. Courtesy of the artist. **3.21** © Alamy Images **3.22** © Wolfgang Kaehler/Corbis **3.23** © Erich Lessing/Art Resource, NY **3.24** © AP/Wide World Photos. © 2007 Richard Serra/Artists Rights Society (ARS), New York **3.25** © Art Resource, NY © 2007 Estate of Alexander Calder/Artists Rights Society (ARS) **3.26** © John Bigelow Taylor/Art Resource, NY ART16304 -19.5 **3.28** © Nimatallah/Art Resource, NY **3.29** © Giraudon/Art Resource, NY **3.30** © Cameraphoto/Art Resource, NY © 2007 Artists Rights Society (ARS), New York/ADAGP, Paris/Succession Marcel Duchamp **3.31** Digital Image © The Museum of Modern Art/Licensed by SCALA/Art Resource, NY.Art © Robert Rauschenberg/Licensed by VAGA, New York, NY **3.32** © Erich Lessing/Art Resource, NY **3.33** Photo: Jeanne-Claude. COPYRIGHT CHRISTO 1976. **3.34** Photo by Maria Karras. Courtesy of the Artist **3.35** © HIP/Art Resource. NY **3.36** © Tate Gallery, London/Art Resource, NY **3.37** © Smithsonian American Art Museum, Washington, DC/Art Resource, NY. Courtesy of the Artist. **3.38** Courtesy of Sean Kelly Gallery, NY **3.39** Photo by Walter Pach © MOMA/Art Resource, NY. © 2007 Artists Rights Society (ARS), New York **3.40** © Art Resource, NY **3.41** Courtesy of the artist. © Bridgeman Art Library **3.42** © Réunion des Musées Nationaux/Art Resource, NY © 2007 Succession H. Matisse, Paris/Artists Rights Society (ARS), New York **3.43** © Victoria and Albert Museum, London. Art Resource. Courtesy of the Artist **3.44** © Private Collection/© Bonhams, London, UK/The Bridgeman Art Library **3.45** © Erich Lessing/Art Resource, NY **3.46** © Werner Forman/Art Resource, NY **3.47** Courtesy of the Artist.

4.CO Courtesy www.guerrillagirls.com **4.01** From the Collections of the Library of Congress. **4.02 4.03** © Collection of Harry W. and Mary Margaret Anderson. © 2007 Pollack-Krasner Foundation/Artists' Rights Society (ARS), New York. **4.04** Purchase, Florance Waterbury Bequest, 1969 (69.71)\Collection of the Metropolitan Museum of Art **4.05** © Joseph Sohm/Corbis **4.06** © Réunion des Musées Nationaux/Art Resource, NY. **4.07** ©Georges Pompidou, Paris/Art Resource, NY © 2007 Artists Rights Society (ARS), New York/VG Bild-Kunst, Bonn **4.08** Courtesy of the artist and Metro Pictures. **4.10** Courtesy www.guerrillagirls.com **4.11** The Bridgeman Art Library **4.12** Copyright Shirin Neshat Courtesy Gladstone Gallery, New York **4.13** © Cildo Meireles. Courtesy of the Gallerie Lelong, New York. **4.14** © Art Resource, NY © 2007 Estate of Alexander Calder/Artists Rights Society (ARS) **4.15** © Alison Wright/Corbis **4.16** Seattle Art Museum. Gift of Mr. John H. Hauberg. **4.17** © Smithsonian American Art Museum, Washington, DC/Art Resource, NY © 2007 Estate of Georgia O'Keeffe/Artists Rights Society (ARS) **4.19** Digital Image© The Museum of Modern Art/Licensed by SCALA/Art Resource, NY © 2007 Succession Miro/Artists Rights Society (ARS), New York/ADAGP, Paris.

5.CO © The Bridgeman Art Library **5.01** © Chris Lisle/Corbis **5.02** © Erich Lessing/Art Resource, NY **5.03** © Werner Forman/Art Resource, NY **5.04** © Bridgeman Art Library **5.05** Réunion des Musées Nationaux/Art Resource, NY **5.06** © Smithsonian American Art Museum, Washington, DC/Art Resource, NY **5.07** © Erich Lessing/Art Resource, NY **5.08** © Lindsay Hebberd/Corbis **5.09** © Reuters/Corbis **5.10** © Estate of Robert Smithson/licensed by VAGA, New York, NY. Image Courtesy James Cohan Gallery, New York Collection: DIA Center for the Arts, New York Photo: Gianfranco Gorgoni **5.11** © Estate of Eva Hesse, Photo Credit : Digital

Image © The Museum of Modern Art/Licensed by SCALA/Art Resource, NY **5.12** © The Bridgeman Art Library **5.13** **5.14** © The Bridgeman Art Library **5.15** © The Bridgeman Art Library **5.17** © The Bridgeman Art Library **5.18** The British Museum, London **5.19** © SCALA/Art Resource, NY **5.20** © The Bridgeman library **5.21** Digital Image © The Museum of Modern Art/Licensed by SCALA/Art Resource, NY **5.22** © Werner Forman/Art Resource, NY. **5.23** © Michael S. Yamashita/Corbis **5.24** © Free/ Corbis **5.25** no credit necessary.

6.CO © Andy Goldsworthy. Courtesy of Galerie Lelong, New York **6.01** American Museum of Natural History, New York. **6.02** Carnegie International, Carnegie Museum of Art, Pittsburgh **6.03** © Andrea Jemolo/Corbis **6.04** © Philip James Corwin/Corbis **6.05** Kunsthistorisches Museum. **6.06** © Nimatallah/Art Resource, NY, **6.07** © SCALA/Art Resource, NY **6.08** © Adam Woolfitt/Corbis **6.09** © Tibor Bognár/Corbis **6.10** © Photononstop/SuperStock **6.11** ZKM Music Balcony taken with ZKM's 360° panorama camera, photo: Tom Fürstner/Lydia Lindner **6.12** © Robert Holmes/Corbis **6.13** © Araldo de Luca/Corbis **6.14** © Giraudon/Art Resource, NY **6.15** © Sunset Boulevard/Corbis Sygma **6.16** © age fotostock/SuperStock **6.17** © SCALA/Art Resource, NY **6.18** © Erich Lessing/Art Resource, NY **6.19** © Getty Images **6.20** © Getty Images **6.21** © SEF/Art Resource, NY **6.22** The British Museum, London. **6.23** The Michael C. Rockefeller Memorial Collection, Bequest of Nelson A. Rockefeller, 1979. Metropolitan Museum of Art, New York. (1979.26.1611) **6.24** Photograph by Lee Boltin **6.25** © Andy Goldsworthy. Courtesy of Galerie Lelong, New York.

7.CO Photo © 2004 The Whitney Museum of American Art. © Wayne Thiebaud/Licensed by VAGA, New York, NY. **7.01** Photo Hans Hinz. **7.02** © Jennifer Steele/Art Resource, NY. **7.03** Photo by Pascal James Imperato. **7.04** Courtesy Gil Michaels. © 1988 Sue Coe/Courtesy Galerie St. Etienne, New York. **7.05** Ashmolean Museum, Oxford, U.K. **7.06** Museum of Fine Arts, Boston, William Francis Warden Fund. **7.07** Museo Nazionale Preistorico Etnografico. **7.08** © Newark Museum/Art Resource, NY. Photo by Peter Furst. **7.09** Ernie Wolf III Collection, Los Angeles. Photo by Frank J. Thomas, Los Angeles. **7.10** © 2007 Andy Warhol Foundation for the Visual Arts/Artists Rights Society (ARS), New York. **7.11** The Metropolitan Museum of Art, Rogers Fund 1919. (19.164) Photograph © 1998 The Metropolitan Museum of Art. **7.12** Photo: Shimizu Kohgeisha Co., Ltd. Permission Ryoko-in Management. **7.13** © Réunion des Musées Nationaux/Art Resource, NY. **7.14** © 1981 Center for Creative Photography, Arizona Board of Regents. **7.15** Photo © 2004 The Whitney Museum of American Art. © Wayne Thiebaud/Licensed by VAGA, New York, NY. **7.16** © Edimédia/Corbis **7.17** Courtesy of Just Art Gallery **7.18** Courtesy of the Freer Gallery of Art #F1899.83. **7.19** Photo © Donald Woodman © 2007 Judy Chicago/Artists Rights Society (ARS), New York. **7.20** Art © Estate of Duane Hanson/Licensed by VAGA, New York, NY. **7.21** Courtesy of the artist and Luhring Augustine. **7.22** © Dewitt Johnes/Corbis. **7.23** © Wolfgang Kaehler/Corbis. **7.24** Photo Russell Thompson. The Arkansas Office, Inc. **7.25** Henri Stierlin. **7.26** © SCALA/Art Resource, NY. **7.27** The Nelson-Atkins Museum of Art, Kansas City, Missouri (Purchase: Nelson Trust) 33-521. Photo by Robert Newcombe. **7.28** Royal Tropical Institute, Amsterdam. **7.29** © Werner Forman/Art Resource, NY. **7.30** ESTO © Scott Frances. © 2007 Frank Lloyd Wright Foundation, Scottsdale, AZ/Artists Rights Society (ARS), NY **7.31** © SCALA/Art Resource, NY. **7.32** Photo courtesy of Stephen A. Edwards. **7.33** Comstock **7.34** Courtesy, Pei Cobb Freed & Partners. **7.35** © Robert Holmes/Corbis. **7.36** © Erich Lessing/Art Resource, NY. **7.37** © Private Collection/The Bridgeman Art Library.

8.CO © Victoria & Albert Museum, London/Art Resource, NY. **8.01** © Ali Meyer/Corbis. **8.02** The Ashmolean Museum, Oxford. **8.03** The British Museum, London. **8.04** The British Museum, London. **8.05** Photo © The Detroit Institute of Arts. Cranbrook Institute of Science. **8.06** Photo courtesy Galerie Carrefore, Paris. **8.07** © SCALA/Art Resource, NY **8.8** © North Carolina Museum of Art/Corbis **8.9** Metropolitan Museum of Art, New York, Gift of Lester Wunderman, 1977. (1977.394.15) Photograph © 1993 The Metropolitan Museum of Art. **8.10** Canali Photobank. **8.11** Bodleian Library, University of Oxford, photo Peter Furst. **8.12** © National Gallery Collection; By kind permission of the Trustees of the National Gallery, London/Corbis. **8.13** Museo Arqueologico Rafael Larco Herrera, Lima, Peru. **8.14** © Victoria & Albert Museum, London/Art Resource, NY. **8.15** © Jeff Koons. **8.16** National Museum, New Delhi **8.17** © 2003 Charles Walker/TopFoto/Image Works. **8.18** © SCALA/Art Resource, NY **8.19** © SCALA/Art Resource, NY **8.20** Courtesy of the Artist. **8.21** Courtesy: Mary Boone Gallery, New York. Photo © Zindman/Fremont. © 2007 Artists Rights Society (ARS), NY/VG Bild-Kunst **8.22** Courtesy of Gorney Bravin & Lee, New York, and Regen Projects, Los Angeles. **8.23** The Metropolitan Museum of Art © 2007 The Georgia O'Keeffe Foundation/Artists Rights Society (ARS), New York. **8.24** Hirshhorn Museum, Smithsonian Institution, Washington, D.C. © 2007 Artists Rights Society (ARS), New York/ADAGP, Paris **8.25** Collection Cleveland Museum of Art. Courtesy Cheim & Read, New York. Photo Allan Finkelman. Art © Louise Bourgeois/Licensed by VAGA, New York, NY. **8.26** © Justin Kerr. **8.27** Courtesy of the Robert Miller Gallery, New York. © The Estate of Alice Neel. **8.28** Museo Arqueologico Rafael Larco Herrera, Lima, Peru. **8.29** St. Louis Science Center./Photo © 1985 Dirk Bakker, Detroit Institute of Arts. **8.30** © Erich Lessing/Art Resource, NY. **8.31** The Art Archive/Museum of Anatolian Civilisations Ankara/Dagli Orti. **8.32** © Museum of Fine Arts, Boston, Massachusetts, USA, Gift of Mary Louisa Boit, Julia Overing Boit, Jane Hubbard/The Bridgeman Art Library.

9.CO © Superstock **9.01** © Nimatallah/Art Resource, NY **9.02** © Sandro Vannini. **9.03** © Nimatallah/Art Resource, NY **9.04** © Angelo Hornak/Corbis. **9.05** Robert Harding Picture Library. **9.06** © Borromea/ Art Resource, NY **9.07** The Nelson-Atkins Museum of Art, Kansas City. Purchase: Nelson Trust. **9.08** © Jewish Museum, NY/Art Resource, NY **9.09** © Francis G. Mayer/Corbis. **9.10** Musée d'Unterlinden, Colmar, France. **9.11** © Gianni Dagli Orti/Corbis **9.12** American Museum of Natural History, New York. **9.13** Photo Hans Hinz. **9.14** Durand-Arias Collection. Photo Jorge Durand. **9.15** © Justin Kerr. **9.16** © SCALA/Art Resource, NY **9.17** Detroit Museum of Art. Eleanor Clay Ford Fund for African Art. © 1998 The Detroit Institute of Arts. **9.18** Museum of Northern Arizona. **9.19** The Zimmerman Family Collection. Photo Otto Nelson. **9.20** Photo Vatican Museums. **9.21** Photo: Zev Rodovan, Jerusalem. **9.22** © Michael S. Yamashia/Corbis **9.23** Kyodo News International **9.24** Pubbli Aer Foto. **9.25** Henri Stierlin. **9.26** © Lowell Georgia/Corbis **9.27** © Archivo Iconografico, S.A./Corbis © 2007 Artists Rights Society (ARS), New York/ADAGP, Paris/FLC **9.29** © Photodisc Green/Getty Images **9.30** © Nimatallah/Art Resource, N Y **9.31** © Ronald Sheridan Ancient Art & Architecture. **9.32** © SCALA/Art Resource, NY **9.33** Photo courtesy Ester Pasztory **9.34** Photo by Mary Ellen Miller. **9.35** © Brian A. Vikander/Corbis **9.36** © Marc Garanger/Corbis **9.37** © Angelo Hornak/Corbis **9.39** © Liu Liqun/Corbis **9.40** © Roger Wood/Corbis **9.41** Getty Research Institute, Los Angeles. Wim Swaan Photograph Collection (96.P.21) **9.42** © Réunion des Musées Nationaux/Art Resource, NY. **9.43** © The Image Bank/Getty Images.

10.CO © Gianni Dagli Orti/Corbis **10.01** © Geray Sweeney/Corbis **10.02** © E. Strouhal/Werner Forman/Art Resource, NY. **10.03** Boltin Picture Library. **10.04** Photo © British Museum. **10.05** © Dallas and John Heaton/Corbis **10.06** © Araldo de Luca/Corbis **10.07** © Archivo Iconografico, S.A./Corbis **10.08** © Superstock **10.09** Cultural Relics Publishing House, Beijing **10.10** The Fowler Museum of Cultural Heritage, University of California, Los Angeles. **10.11** The Fowler Museum of Cultural Heritage, University of California, Los Angeles. **10.12** Photo: University Museum of National Antiquities, Oslo, Norway. **10.13** © Saskia. **10.14** © SCALA/Art Resource, NY. **10.15** © Madeline Grimoldi **10.16** © SCALA/Art Resource, New York 1 0.17 © Corbis **10.18** © Sheldan Collins/Corbis. **10.19** The Metropolitan Museum of Art, The Cloisters Collection, 1947. (47.11.33) Photograph © The Metropolitan Museum of Art. **10.20** University of Iowa Museum of Art **10.21** © GETTY IMAGEs/Photodisc Photographer: Philippe Colombi **10.22** © Tate Gallery, London/Art Resource, NY **10.23** Photo © Bob Schalkwijk **10.24** © Bridgeman Art Library **10.25** © Ric Ergenbright/Corbis

10.26 © AP/Wide World, Ron Edmonds **10.27** © Rommel Pecson/Topham/ImageWorks **10.28** Courtesy of Lower Manhattan Development Corp **10.29** © Carmen Redondo/Corbis **10.30** Collection of M.H. DeYoung Memorial Museum, the Fine Arts Museum of San Francisco. Gift of Vivian Burns, Inc. **10 TN.01** Pubbli Aer Foto **10 TN.02** © Gianni Dagli/Corbis **10 TN.03** © Adam Woolfitt/Corbis.

11.CO © Superstock **11.01** Museum of Fine Arts, Boston **11.02** Canali Photobank **11.03** Museum of the Ife Antiquities, Ife, Nigeria **11.04** © Erich Lessing/Art Resource, NY **11.05** © Paul Maeyaert/The Bridgeman Art Library **11.06** Photo archive of the National Museum of the American Indian Photo by Carmelo Guadagno. **11.07** Kobal Collection. **11.08** © RMN/Art Resource, NY. **11.09** © SEF/Art Resource, NY **11.10** Photo Mary Ellen Miller **11.11** China Photographic Publishing House, Beijing. **11.12** SCALA/Art Resource, NY. **11.13** Photograph by Bob Hashimoto. Reproduction: The Art Institute of Chicago. **11.14** © A. F. Kersting. **11.15** © Superstock **11.16** Saskia Ltd., Cultural Documentation. **11.17** © Superstock **11.18** © SCALA/Art Resource, NY **11.19** Peabody Museum of Architecture and Ethnology **11.20** © Michael Howell/Index Stock Imagery/Picturequest. **11.21** © Jurgen Liepe, Berlin **11.22** Museum of Fine Arts, Boston. **11.23** Reproduced from the Collections of the Library of Congress **11.24** National Anthropological Archives, Smithsonian Institution, Washington D.C. **11.25** © Kobal Collection. **11.26** Institut Amatller D'art Hispanic © Museo del Prado. © 2007 Estate of Pablo Picasso/Artists Rights Society (ARS), New York. **11.27** © Andre Jerry/Picturequest **11.28** © Frank Fournier/Contact Press Images **11.29** © A/P/Wide World Photos. **11.30** Brooklyn Museum of Art, Dick S. Ramsay Fund. 40.340. **11.31** © SCALA/Art Resource, NY. **11.32** Kunsthistorisches Museum. **11.33** The Detroit Institute of Arts. **11.34** Museum of Fine Arts, Boston. **11.35** © Yoshio Tomii/SuperStock **11 TN.01** University of Iowa Museum of Art **11 TN.02** © age fotostock/SuperStock **11 TN.03** Photo Wallace Collection, London **11 TN.04** Musei Capitolini, Rome. **11 TN.05** © SCALA/Art Resource, NY.

12.CO National Gallery of Art, Canberra. © 2007 Artists Rights Society (ARS), New York/VI$COPY, Australia. **12.01** © Erich Lessing/Art Resource, NY. **12.02** Reproduced from the collections of the Library of Congress, Washington, D.C. © 2007 Artists Rights Society (ARS), New York/VG Bild-Kunst, Bonn. **12.03** Digital Image © The Museum of Modern Art/Licensed by SCALA/Art Resource, NY. art © Estate of George Grosz/Licensed by VAGA, New York, NY. **12.04** Reproduced from John Heartfield, by Wieland Herzfelde Dresden: VEB Verlag der Kunst, 1964. © 2007 Artists Rights Society (ARS), New York/VG Bild-Kunst, Bonn. **12.05** Digital Image © The Museum of Modern Art/Licensed by SCALA/Art Resource, NY. Art © Estate of David Alfaro Siqueiros/SOMAAP, Mexico City/VAGA New York **12.06** Albright-Knox Art Gallery, Buffalo, N.Y.Art © Dedalus Foundation/Licensed by VAGA, New York, NY. **12.07** Courtesy of the artist. **12.08** The Broad Art Foundation. Art © Leon Golub/Licensed by VAGA, New York, NY. Courtesy Ronald Feldman Fine Arts. **12.09** © Réunion des Musées Nationaux/Art Resource, NY. **12.10** Reproduced from the collections of the Library of Congress **12.11** The Whitney Museum of American Art, New York. Art © VAGA, New York **12.12** Photograph courtesy of Gwendolyn Knight Lawrence/Art Resource, NY © 2007 Gwendolyn Knight Lawrence/Artists Rights Society (ARS), New York. **12.13** China (Dayi, Sichuan), 1965. **12.14** Moderna Museet, Stockholm. © Edward Kienholz. **12.15** © Cildo Meireles. Courtesy of the Gallerie Lelong, New York. **12.16** © 1981 Ester Hernandez. **12.17** Courtesy Stephen Friedman Gallery, Collection National Gallery of Canada, Ottawa, Canada. **12.18** Courtesy of Sikkema Jenkins & Co, New York City. **12.19** © SCALA/Art Resource, NY. **12.20** © HIP/Art Resource, NY **12.21** The Bridgeman Art Library **12.22** National Gallery of Art, Canberra. © 2007 Artists Rights Society (ARS), New York/VI$COPY, Australia. **12.23** Courtesy Ronald Feldman Fine Arts, New York. **12.24** © Courtesy the artist and Jay Jopling/White Cube (London). © CNAC/MNAM/Dist. Réunion des Musées Nationaux/Art Resource, NY. **12.25** © National Gallery Collection; By kind permission of the Trustees of the National Gallery, London/Corbis. **12.26** © Magdalena Abakanowicz. Courtesy of Marlborough Gallery, New York. **12.27** Photo: David Heald, courtesy Solomon R. Guggenheim Museum. © 2007 Jenny Holzer/Artists Rights Society (ARS), New York. **12.28** © Giraudon/Art Resource, NY **12.29** Art © Estate of Robert Arneson/VAGA, New York, NY. Courtesy of George Adams Gallery, New York. **12.30** Courtesy of the artist and Marian Goodman Gallery, New York **12.31** Museum of Latin American Art **12.32** © Gianni Dagli Orti/Corbis **12 TN.01** Courtesy of the Artist **12.33** © Staatliche Kunstsammlungen Dresden/The Bridgeman Art Library **12 TN.02** © Art Resource, NY **12 TN.03** © Art Resource, NY.

13.CO Photograph by Dominique Darbois. **13.01** © Vanni/Art Resource, NY **13.02** Tokyo National University of Fine Arts and Music **13.03** Copyright © Christie's Images, Inc./Christies Images-All rights reserved. **13.04** Washington, National Gallery of Art donation of Lila Acheson Wallace. **13.05** Courtesy of the Artist **13.06** Acquavella Contemporary Art. By permission of the Artist. **13.07** Courtesy of the Artist. **13.08** © SCALA/Art Resource, NY. **13.09** Albright-Knox Art Gallery, Buffalo, N.Y. Bequest of A. Conger Goodyear, 1966. **13.10** Courtesy of the artist and Metro Pictures. **13.11** © 1998 Mariko Mori and Parkett. **13.12** © Borromeo/Art Resource, NY. **13.13** Robert Harding. **13.14** Saskia Ltd **13.15** © Heini Schneebeli/The Bridgeman Art Library **13.16** © Araldo de Luca/Corbis. **13.17** © Ronald Sheridan/Ancient Art & Architecture. **13.18** © Michael S. Yamashita/Corbis **13.19** International Museum of Photography at George Eastman House, Rochester, New York. **13.20** Photo: John Hillelson. **13.21** Digital Image © The Museum of Modern Art/Licensed by SCALA/Art Resource, NY. **13.22** © Erich Lessing/Art Resource, NY. © 2007 The Munch Museum/The Munch-Ellingsen Group/Artists Rights Society (ARS), New York. **13.23** Bridgeman Art Library © 2007 Artists Rights Society (ARS), New York/ DACS, London **13.24** Photo by Tom Van Eynde, Courtesy Chicago Department of Cultural Affairs, Jin Soo Kim. **13.25** Courtesy Ronald Feldman Fine Arts, New York. **13.26** Courtesy Paula Cooper Gallery, New York. **13.27** Photo © 2004 Metropolitan Museum of Art, New York **13.28** Photograph by Dominique Darbois. **13.29** Courtesy of the Estate of Ana Mendieta. and Gallerie Lelong, New York. **13.30** Collection of the artist, courtesy Studio One. **13.31** © 2007 Pollock-Krasner Foundation/Artists Rights Society (ARS), New York. **13.32** © LEFRANC DAVID/Corbis **13.33** © Bettmann/Corbis **13.34** © Museum of Fine Arts, Houston, Texas, USA, Gift of Mrs. Harry C. Hanszen/The Bridgeman Art Library. **13 TN.01** Tokyo National Museum. **13 TN.02 Photo** © Bob Schalkwijk **13 TN.03** Superstock.

14.CO The Rijksmuseum Amsterdam. **14.01** © MOMA/Art Resource, NY/© 2007 Artists Rights Society (ARS), New York/ADAGP, Paris. **14.02** © Donna Mussenden VanDerZee **14.03** Photographed for the UC Berkeley Art museum by Bnjamin Blackwell **14.04** Museum of Man, San Diego. **14.05** Photograph by Tseng Kwong Chi © Muna Tseng Dance Projects Inc, New York **14.06** Museum der Kulturen, Basel Switzerland **14.07** © SCALA/ Art Resource, NY. **14.08** © Réunion des Musées Nationaux/Art Resource, NY. **14.09** © SCALA/Art Resource, NY. **14.10** Courtesy of the Artist **14.11** Courtesy www.guerrillagirls.com **14.12** © Gianni Dagli Orti/Corbis **14.13** Photo by Arthur G. Miller. **14.14** Seattle Art Museum. Gift of Mr. John H. Hauberg. **14.16** Photograph by Tobias Schneebaum. **14.17** Photo by John Pemberton III. **14.18** © The Museum of Modern Art, New York/ Art Resource, NY. Art © Marisol Escobar/Licensed by VAGA, New York, NY. **14.19** Walker Art Center, Minneapolis, Minnesota. **14.20** By permission of General Idea. **14.21** © John P. Stevens/Ronald Sheridan Ancient Art & Architecture Library. **14.22** © RMN/Art Resource, NY. **14.23** Institut Amatller d'Art Hispanic © Museo del Prado. **14.24** Photo Wallace Collection, London. **14.25** Photograph by John Pemberton III, 1971. **14.26** The Palace Museum, Beijing. **14.27** The Rijksmuseum Amsterdam. **14.28** Photo © The Art Institute of Chicago. All Rights Reserved. **14.29** From the Collections of the Library of Congress. **14.30** Tokyo National Museum. **14.31** Tokyo National Museum. **14.32** © Bettmann/Corbis. **14.33** Metropolitan Museum of Art **14.34** © Princeton Museum of Natural History, New Jersey, USA/The Bridgeman Art Library. **14 TN.01** Photograph courtesy of Gwendolyn Knight Lawrence/Art Resource, NY © 2007 Gwendolyn Knight Lawrence/Artists Rights Society (ARS), New

York **14 TN.02 Photo** © Bob Schalkwijk **14 TN.03** Canali Photobank **14 TN.04** Photograph by Bob Hashimoto. Reproduction: The Art Institute of Chicago **14 TN.05** Dayi, Sichual, China, 1965.

15.CO Photo Pam Taylor **15.01** The Metropolitan Museum of Art, NY. **15.02** The Metropolitan Museum of Art, New York, Cloister Collection **15.03** Indiana University Art Museum, Bloomington, Indiana. Raymond and Laura Wielgus Collection (RW 60-197) Photo by Michael Cavanagh/Kevin Montague **15.04** Photo Pam Taylor **15.05** Courtesy Chris Ofili-Afroco and Victoria Miro Gallery. **15.06** The British Museum, London. © Bridgeman Art Library **15.07** Alamy Images **15.08** Indiana University Art Museum, Bloomington, Indiana. Raymond and Laura Wielgus Collection. IUAM 100.7.4.75 (RW 62-233). Photo by Michael Cavanagh/Kevin Montague. **15.09** Photo; The Metropolitan Museum of Art, New York **15.10** National Gallery, London **15.11** The Art Institute of Chicago. © 2007 Artists Rights Society (ARS), New York/ADAGP, Paris. **15.12** Copyright © 1993 by the Trustees of the Ansel Adams Publishing Rights Trust/Corbis. All rights reserved. **15.13** National Palace Museum, Taiwan. **15.14** © Archivo Iconograpfico, S.A./Corbis. **15.15** Victoria and Albert Museum, IM 276-1913. **15.16** © Paul Chesley, Stone/Getty Images. **15.17** © Richard A. Cooke/Corbis **15.18** Courtesy James Cohan Gallery, New York. Art © Estate of Robert Smithson/Licensed by VAGA, New York. **15.19** Photograph by John Cliett. © Dia Center for the Arts.. **15.20 Courtesy Ronald Feldman Fine Arts, New York.** 15.21 no credit neccessary **15.22** North Carolina Museum of Art. **15.23** © Werner Forman/Art Resource, NY. **15.24** © Digital Image The Museum of Modern Art/Licensed by SCALA/Art Resouce, NY. **15.25** © Museum of Modern Art/Licensed by SCALA/Art Resource, NY © 2007 Salvador Dali, Gala-Salvador Dali Foundation/Artists Rights Society (ARS), New York. **15.26** Milwaukee Art Museum. Gift of Mrs. Harry Lynde Bradley, m1977.140. © 2007 Kate Rothko Prizel & Christopher Rothko/Artists Rights Society (ARS), New York **15.27** Baker Memorial Library, Dartmouth College, Hanover, New Hampshire. Commissioned by the Trustees of Dartmouth College, Hanover, New Hampshire. © 2007 Artists Rights Society (ARS), New York/SOMAAP **15.28** The St. Louis Art Museum. Courtesy Sperone Westwater. **15.29** C.C. Wang, New York **15.30** Philadelphia Museum of Art. © 2007 Artists Rights Society (ARS), New York/ADAGP, Paris. **15.31** Image © National Gallery of Art, Washington, D.C. Art © David Smith/Licensed by VAGA, New York, NY. **15.32** © Art Resource, NY. **15.33** © 2004 David Gahr. © 2007 Artists Rights Society (ARS), New York/ADAGP, Paris **15.34** Courtesy Holly Solomon Gallery, New York. **15.35** The Phillips Collection, Washington, D.C. **15.36** National Gallery of Australia, Canberra © 2004 Artists Rights Society (ARS)/New York/VI$COPY, Australia **15 TN.01** Photo Hans Hinz. **15 TN.02** © Jennifer Steele/Art Resource, NY.

16.CO Photo Constantino Reyes. **16.01** Hellenic Ministry of Culture. **16.02** © Roger Ressmeyer/Corbis. **16.03** © Alan Schein/Corbis. © 2007 Frank Lloyd Wright Foundation, Scottsdale, AZ/Artists Rights Society (ARS), NY **16.04** Photo by Al Seib. © Lucy Nicholson/Reuters Newmedia Inc./Corbis. **16.05** Reconstruction in the Museum of Roman Civilization, Rome **16.06** © Michael S. Yamashita/Corbis. **16.07** © Courtesy Japan National Tourist Organization. **16.08** © 2004Photographer: Adam Jones/Getty Images **16.09** © Richard Glover/Corbis. **16.10** Photograph © 1990 The Metropolitan Museum of Art, NY. **16.11** Justin Kerr K2022 **16.12** Photo Constantino Reyes. **16.13** © SCALA/Art Resource, NY. **16.14** Photograph © 1996 The Metropolitan Museum of Art. **16.15** The British Museum, London. **16.16** Nationalmuseum, Stockholm **16.17** © Michael S. Yamashita/Corbis. **16.18** © Robbie Jack/Corbis. **16.19** © Erich Lessing/Art Resource, NY. **16.20** The dancers in the photo are; Viola Farber (standing) and Carolyn Brown. and the photographer is Richard Rutledge. Cunningham Dance Foundation **16.21** © 2007 Allan Kaprow. Used by permission of the J. Paul Getty Museum, Los Angeles. **16.22** University of Pennsylvania Museum. **16.23** Photo by Tobias Schneebaum. **16.24** © 1995 Bruce Wendt Productions/Makoche Recording Company. Photo by Bruce Wendt Courtesy Makoche Recording Company. **16.25** Hutchison Library. **16.26** Tribune Media Services. **16.27** © Sunset Boulevard/Corbis Sygma. **16.28** © Bettmann/Corbis **16.29** Photo by Michael James O'Brien, Courtesy Barbara Gladstone Gallery. **16.30** © TOUHOKU SHINSHA/THE KOBAL COLLECTION **16.31** © Bridgeman Art Library **16.32** © The Philadelphia Museum of Art/Art Resource, NY. **16 TN.01** © Adam Woolfitt/Corbis **16 TN.02** Photo: David Heald, courtesy Solomon R. Guggenheim Museum. © 2007 Jenny Holzer/Artists Rights Society (ARS), New York. **16 TN.03** © Araldo de Luca/Corbis **16 TN.04** © Bettmann/Corbis **16 TN.05** © Smithsonian American Art Museum, Washington, DC/Art Resource, NY. **16 TN.06** International Museum of Photography at George Eastman House, Rochester, New York.

Cover.01 Courtesy: Mary Boone Gallery, New York. Photo © Zindman/Fremont. **Cover.02** © SCALA/Art Resource, NY **Cover.03** © Réunion des Musées Nationaux/Art Resource, NY **Cover.04** © Bildarchiv Preussischer Kulturbesitz/Art Resource, NY **Cover.05** © Gianni Dagli Orti/Corbis **Cover.06** © Erich Lessing/Art Resource, NY **Cover.07** Courtesy of Gallery Koyanagi, Tokyo, and Deitch Projects, New York.

TN 1.01 St. Louis Science Center./Photo © 1985 Dirk Bakker, Detroit Institute of Arts. **TN 1.02** © North Carolina Museum of Art/Corbis **TN 1.03** Pubbli Aer Foto **TN 1.04** Seattle Art Museum. **TN 2.01** © 2004 Allan Kaprow. Used by permission of the J.Paul Getty Museum, Los Angeles. **TN 2.02** © Michael S. Yamashita/Corbis. **TN 2.03** © SCALA/Art Resource, NY. **TN 2.04** © Roger Ressmeyer/Corbis. **TN 2.05** © Comstock **TN 4.01** © Werner Forman/Art Resource, NY **TN 5.01** © E. Strouhal/ Werner Forman/Art Resource, NY. **TN 5.02** North Carolina Museum of Art. **TN 5.04** Museum of Northern Arizona. **TN 5.05** Art Institute of Chicago **TN 6.01** © SCALA/Art Resource, NY **TN 6.02** © SCALA/Art Resource, NY **TN 7.01** © Gianni Dagli Orti/Corbis **TN 7.02** © Art Resource, NY **TN 7.03** © Art Resource, NY **TN 7.04** Phillips Collection, Washington, DC. **TN 7.05** Henri Stierlin **TN 7.06** © Bettmann/Corbis **TN 8.01** Metropolitan Museum of Art, New York, Rogers Fund.# 47.100.1 **TN 8.02** From Whakairo Maori Tribunal Art by David Simmons, 1985, pp. 38-39. Reprinted by permission of Oxford University Press, New York. **TN 8.03** Photograph © 2004 Museum of Fine Arts, Boston **TN 9.01** Photo Petri Museum of Egyptian Archaeology, University College, London UC. 30096, 29022, 30095, 30093, 30091 & 30094. **TN 9.02** Courtesy Just Art Gallery **TN 9.03** Photograph © 1990 The Metropolitan Museum of Art, NY **TN 9.05** © Michael S. Yamashia/Corbis **TN 9.06** © 2003 Charles Walker/TopFoto/Image Works.

Index